Ansel

ELEMENTARY SCHOOL SCIENCE

and
HOW TO TEACH IT

ELEMENTARY SCHOOL SCIENCE
and
HOW TO TEACH IT

EIGHTH EDITION

Glenn O. Blough
Julius Schwartz

HOLT, RINEHART AND WINSTON, INC.

Fort Worth   Chicago   San Francisco   Philadelphia
Montreal   Toronto   London   Syndey   Tokyo

Publisher   Ted Buchholz
Acquisitions Editor   Jo-Anne Weaver
Project Editor   Michele Tomiak
Copy Editor   Anne Lesser
Manager of Art and Design   Guy Jacobs
Production Manager   Annette Dudley Wiggins
Interior Design   Barbara Bert/North 7 Atelier Ltd.
Cover Design   Rhonda Campbell
Cover Photos   HBJ photos by Richard Haynes and John Bateman
Part and chapter opening photograph credits appear following the Index.

Library of Congress Cataloging-in-Publication Data

Blough, Glenn Orlando.
  Elementary school science and how to teach it / Glenn O. Blough,
Julius Schwartz.—8th ed.
    p. cm.
  Bibliography: p.
  Includes index.
  ISBN 0-03-011559-0 : $29.00
  1. Science—Study and teaching (Elementary)—United States.
I. Schwartz, Julius, 1907–   II. Title.
LB1585.3.B55 1990
372.3'5044—dc20   89-15288
                                              CIP

Address editorial correspondence to: 301 Commerce Street, Suite 3700, Fort Worth, Texas 76102

Address orders to: 6277 Sea Harbor Drive, Orlando, Florida 32887 1-800-782-4479, or 1-800-433-0001 (in Florida)

ISBN 0-03-031312-0

Printed in the United States of America

9   0   1   2   000   9   8   7   6   5   4   3   2   1

Holt, Rinehart and Winston, Inc.
The Dryden Press
Saunders College Publishing

PREFACE

This eighth edition of *Elementary School Science and How To Teach It* includes, as did previous editions, both a broad review of science and ways of teaching science to children. It is addressed to the teacher as an inquisitive adult *and* as a professional educator seeking techniques to stimulate children to pursue science as a lifelong adventure.

The first five chapters provide a comprehensive look at the role of science in elementary education. This overview covers objectives and trends; how children's development guides us in planning what to teach and how to teach it; issues in science curricula and teaching methods; processes of science investigation; and the organization of the science program. To meet the challenges of the 1990s, many sections have been expanded or added: the relationship of science to technology and society; a variety of classroom strategies for teaching science; science projects and science fairs; working with handicapped children; computers in science education; science in early childhood education; and the role of the textbook in science education.

Elementary School Science and How to Teach It is intended both for the general teacher who has the responsibility for the entire curriculum, including science, and for the specialist whose major assignment is developing the science program for the school. A need is often expressed by both to have the content of science presented in a concise and readable form. This is our aim in the "A" chapters. The accompanying "B" chapters supply practical approaches to classroom teaching of that content at several levels, from prekindergarten up.

The fifteen parallel A and B chapters present the content and methods of teaching specific areas of science. Each of these paired chapters stands on its own, thereby making for clear, uninterrupted reading, but they are connected with numerous cross-references. Under the three major part titles of The Earth and the Universe, Living Things, and Matter and Energy, the chapters illuminate significant concepts and principles by linking science to everyday observable phenomena, to events and issues reported in the daily newspaper, and to the ideas and activities of scientists. The aim here is to promote a sense of the relatedness of science to people and their problems, and an awareness that science is a way of thinking and investigating.

The A chapters have been updated to cover recent events and discoveries: the new intimate photographs of the planets by space vehicles and the new discoveries about the birth and death of stars; the nature of AIDS and its methods of transmission; the Chernobyl nuclear disaster; environmental problems including the threats of toxic wastes, the greenhouse effect, the ozone hole, and acid rain; new ways of tapping the energy of the sun; space planes, labs, stations, and telescopes. As in the past, the A chapters include fundamental concepts, principles, and illustrations in the broad span of science, from the atom to the universe, from the gene to the human organism.

The B chapters reflect the firm belief that science is for *all* children, that it is an essential and irreplaceable part of their education. Recognition is given to the wide variety of talents, interests, and different levels of understanding of children, and to the different environments in which they live. Emphasis is placed on their active participation in the science program, in engaging their muscles as well as their brains. In structuring the

B chapters we are guided by the words of physicist Niels Bohr: "Our experiments are questions that we put to nature ... the very word 'experiment' refers to a situation where we can tell others what we did and what we learned." For this reason the problems in the B chapters are couched as questions, the kind that children or teachers might ask. The "questions that we put to nature" may arise spontaneously from the lips of children in many circumstances: as they observe changes in the classroom aquarium or in the school playground, in the clouds in the daytime sky and in the moon at night, in neighborhood streets and stores and parks. They are encouraged to "tell what they learned" in many ways: by their manipulation of materials, by inventing theories to explain their findings, by engaging in projects, and by their creative writing.

Of special help to teachers are the end-of-chapter materials. Each of the first five chapters concludes with a section entitled "Discovering for Yourself," which constitutes an invitation to apply the educational principles discussed to concrete teaching situations. The A chapters conclude with a summary of the "Important Generalizations." The section "Discovering for Yourself" helps teachers identify the potential for science fieldwork in their own environments. In the B chapters, the sections "Preparing to Teach" and "Resources to Investigate with Children" provide special activities related to the problems to be studied. In all of the chapters there are many references to current periodicals and books in science and in science education.

The inspiring words of scientists, science writers, philosophers, and educators are quoted directly throughout to impart the meaning and the beauty of science and to assist teachers in conveying the spirit of science to children.

Emphasis has been placed on making this book a guide for teachers in a number of situations—in training, in service, or in workshops or conferences. Although it was not written with the National Teacher Examination Core Battery Tests in mind, it does cover all of the nine major science themes in that test. Above all it should serve the teachers in the classroom as a multipurpose reference that will continue to be useful over many years.

ACKNOWLEDGMENTS

Throughout the preparation of the manuscript we have received much valuable criticism and advice from colleagues and specialists in different subject matter areas. We would like to thank the following specialists who reviewed specific chapters for content: Dr. Richard Brewer, Department of Biology, Western Michigan University, Kalamazoo; Dr. Marvin Druger, Biology Department, Syracuse University; Dr. Harry B. Herzer III, Aerospace Education Specialist, NASA; Dr. Robert F. Kelly; Dr. Harold L. Levin, Department of Earth and Planetary Science, Washington University, St. Louis; Dr. Victor J. Mayer, Center for Science Education, Ohio State University, Columbus; Dr. Frederick E. Trinklein, Department of Astronomy, Nassau Community College, Garden City, N.Y.; and Dr. Don Witten, Public Affairs, National Oceanic and Space Administration.

Our appreciation also goes to the following general reviewers of our text:

Richard H. Blake, Weber State College; Robert W. Brown, NASA Educational Affairs Division, Washington, D.C.; Ralph Cioppa, Jr., Manhattenville College; Edward Donovan, University of South Carolina; Darrel W. Fyffe, Bowling Green State University; Jean Hazelton, Saint Johns University; Evan McFee, Bowling Green State University; Cordell Perkes, Weber State University; Fred Prince, University of South Florida; Betty Quinn, Belhaven College; and Grady Sue Saxon, Samford University.

We extend grateful acknowledgment and thanks for the expert secretarial help of Libby Dunlap in the preparation of this and previous editions, and to Phyllis Marcuccio, director of publications and editor of *Science and Children*, for supplying many of the excellent photographs.

Washington, D.C. G.O.B.
Palm Beach, Florida J.S.

Brief Contents

Contents

PART II
THE EARTH AND THE
UNIVERSE   102

PART III
LIVING THINGS   258

PART IV
MATTER AND ENERGY 450

CHAPTER 14A
MOLECULES AND ATOMS 453

CHAPTER 14B
TEACHING "MOLECULES AND ATOMS" 468

CHAPTER 15A
HEAT AND HOW WE USE IT 479

ELEMENTARY SCHOOL SCIENCE

and
HOW TO TEACH IT

PART ONE

TEACHING
ELEMENTARY
SCHOOL SCIENCE

CHAPTER 1

SCIENCE IN THE
ELEMENTARY SCHOOL

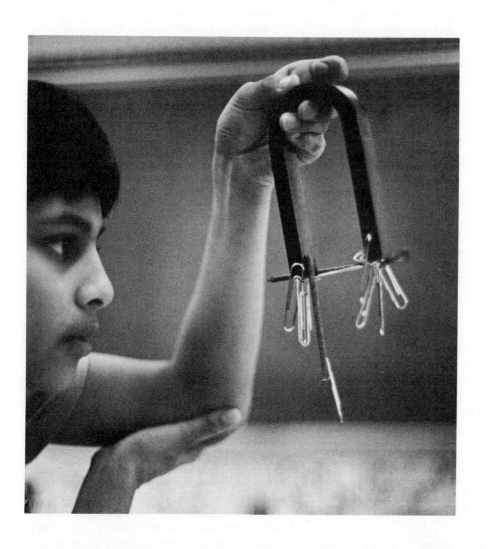

Science is active, is asking and wondering, looking and listening, pushing and pulling, counting and measuring, proposing and testing. Thus science teaching at any level, but especially in the elementary grades, must share in that dynamism.

F. JAMES RUTHERFORD[1]

Throughout the millenia people have wondered about their environment. Explorers have penetrated the natural world to new lands and seas. Scientists have advanced the frontiers of knowledge and formulated the grand ideas—theories, generalizations, and laws—that have changed human lifestyles and our perception of ourselves in the universe. And the wonder goes on; the possibilities of science are endless.

We have long since moved from innocent wonder and from ascribing phenomena such as lightning and thunder to the anger of the gods. We have turned to deliberate investigation into why and how things happen.

The wonder continues for those who open their eyes to what is going on around them. Teachers who retain the wonder and the desire to know will transmit it to the children they teach.

To be effective, teachers need some basic knowledge of science content—from starfish to stars—and of methods of science investigation. They should know how the science content may be structured into teachable units and what good classroom procedures are helpful. Providing teachers with these essentials is the purpose of this book.

But before we go further, let's consider what science means to you. It may be helpful if you write down your ideas and later compare them with what you read. What *does* science mean to you?

The following quotations concern the nature of science as seen through the eyes of scientists, philosophers, educators, and others. As you read and, we hope, enjoy these provocative statements,

ask yourself, "What are the implications for me as a teacher of science and children?"

Unexpected Vistas
Of one thing, however, we may be reasonably sure. If developed and applied in good faith, the methods called scientific are bound to lead to unexpected vistas and unpredictable solutions.

RENÉ DUBOS

Most people probably imagine that science advances like a steam roller, cracking its problems one by one with even and inexorable force.... Science (actually) advances as though by pulling out of a drawer which gives on one side only to jam on the other.

C. D. DARLINGTON

The progress of science from the beginning has been a conflict with old prejudices.

T. H. HUXLEY

New Configurations
Research is to see what everybody has seen and to think what nobody has thought.

ALBERT SZENT-GYÖRGYI

No man of science wants merely to know. He acquires knowledge to appease his passion for discovery.

ALFRED NORTH WHITEHEAD

Thus invention, scientific thinking, and aesthetic creation do have in common a facility for rearranging the previously experienced elements into new configurations. When Sandburg says that "the fog creeps in on little cat feet," and a child calls eraser scraps "mistake dust," and a painter shows the four sides of a barn at once and a writer speaks of something as being as "relentless as a taximeter," and a man converts a runner into a wheel, and a Newton sees the analogy between apples and planets, there is manifest an activity of the mind that

[1]"Elementary School Science," *Science and Children* (January 1987).

seems to be of the same weave despite the differences of coloration.

H. BROUDY

The Great Ocean of Truth

... any particular scientific theory is a provisional tool with which we can carve knowledge of the material world.... The scientific theory is, however, only true as long as it is useful.

E. N. da C. ANDRADE

Science is built up with facts, as a house is with stones. But a collection of facts is no more a science than a heap of stones is a house.

J. H. POINCARÉ

Science is an interconnected series of concepts and conceptual schemes that have developed as a result of experimentation and observation and are fruitful of further experimentation and observations. In this definition the emphasis is on the word "fruitful."

JAMES B. CONANT

The white man drew a small circle in the sand and told the red man, "This is what the Indian knows," and drawing a big circle around the small one, "This is what the white man knows." The Indian took the stick and swept an immense ring around both circles: "This is where the white man and the red man know nothing."

CARL SANDBURG

I do not know what I may appear to the world; but to myself I seem to have been like a boy playing on the seashore, and diverting myself in now and then finding a smoother pebble or a prettier shell than ordinary, whilst the great ocean of truth lay all undiscovered before me.

ISAAC NEWTON

What can be distilled from these quotes? In essence they say that science is more than a collection of facts, it is a structure of linked concepts created by humans. Imagination, even dreaming, form a part of scientific research. Science grows, constantly building on past experience and on the discoveries of many investigators, and often leads to unexpected discoveries. A scientific theory is a provisional tool for discovery; it is retained only as long as it produces new knowledge.

In contrast to these learned quotations consider the following school experiences:

Children in grade 5 connect a dry cell with wires to a light bulb. They find that the bulb does not light. They offer different explanations and test their theories.

Children in grade 4 "adopt" a tree near the school. They visit the tree regularly to watch its changes and to observe the animals that live on or under it. They make sketches and paintings, take photographs, and write stories and poems about "their" tree.

Kindergarten children collect snow. They predict what will happen to the snow when it is brought indoors. The teacher provides each child with a plastic cup which the children fill with snow. They find that a cupful of snow melts into much less than a cupful of water.

A sixth-grade class conducts a survey on "Sun Day" of environmental conditions in the streets surrounding the school. They note evidence of air pollution, litter, noise pollution, and plant and animal life. After collecting and interpreting the data, the class considers ways in which it could participate in corrective measures.

Second-grade children make a simple indoor sundial with a pencil inserted into a spool, and set it up on a piece of cardboard that will serve as a dial. They keep it in a fixed place in the sun and mark off the hours of the day on the dial, based on the shadow cast by the pencil (with the help of a watch the first day).

Kindergarten children roll balls down a ramp that they construct from blocks and planks. They compare the distance the ball rolls from a gentle slope with that of a steep slope.

Fourth-grade children watch the moon at night for several weeks and make sketches of its changing appearance. In the classroom they experiment with a model moon and a light source to find out why the moon appears to change shape.

Second-grade children measure the growth of bean seedlings for a period of three weeks and make a bar graph (actually drawings of the seedlings on a chart) of their observations. They discover unexpectedly that some parts of the plants grow more rapidly than others.

Prekindergarten children play with a pinwheel out-of-doors. They decide to use their toy as a wind "detector." They try to find a place in the schoolyard where the wind is not blowing. They try out their wind detector on subsequent days.

Kindergarten children experiment to find out how to make their wet gloves dry more quickly.

After a heavy rain, second-grade children find puddles remaining in their school grounds. They discuss what will happen to the puddles. The teacher suggests that they make a map of the location of the puddles. They observe the puddles the following day.

A sixth-grade class constructs a questionnaire to discover practices with respect to the use of water in and around the home. They summarize their findings and make a list of recommendations with respect to water conservation.

Do these experiments (which actually are fragments of larger activities) constitute what we might call "science"? How? As you read on in this and in subsequent chapters, return to these experiences and evaluate them again.

WHAT IS SCIENCE EDUCATION?

Science is essential to understanding the world we live in—and of equal importance, it is *learning how to learn* about our world. This involves the use of the processes of science (also known as "problem-solving skills") such as observing, classifying, describing, experimenting, measuring, inferring, and predicting to discover ideas that can be put together to formulate science concepts and principles.

Science covers both *what* is discovered and *how* it is discovered. That is, it includes content (facts and generalizations) and methods of discovery. In actual practice what is discovered (the content) is inseparably linked to the process of investigation. To be consistent with this concept of science the school must provide children with experiences in both of these facets of science. This idea will become more obvious as you proceed with your study. Our classrooms and the out-of-doors are laboratories where children, for example, not only learn that shadows change in a certain way during the day but also *how to find*

out how they change. Children make mistakes; revise their methods; and discover that there may be many answers, only tentative solutions, or no answers at all.

SCIENCE AND CHILDREN

A knowledge of children and how they learn is essential to good teaching. Observation of their experiences in science indicates that they are natural investigators and ask an unending stream of questions: "What makes the moon change shape?" "If the earth is round why don't people in Australia fall off?" "What makes a satellite stay up?" "Why did the fish in our aquarium die?" Good teachers make use of this innate curiosity in children by using such questions as a launching pad for helping children investigate and discover answers through the methods of inquiry—sensing the problem, hypothesizing, gathering data, drawing conclusions or not drawing them, and testing them. In this way they are learning how to learn. They are inquiring. They are using processes to discover. So also is their teacher.

It appears natural for children to take things apart to see how they work, to experiment, to manipulate, to be curious, to ask questions, to seek answers. These tendencies make science a natural part of their education and a necessary subject in their school experiences. It is a basic part of their education.

But science is not a thing apart from the rest of the interests and activities in school life. It is closely interwoven with other interests, and its methods of study are much the same as those used in exploring any interest.

We all live with science, but that doesn't mean that we think scientifically, nor are we all scientifically literate. Throughout this book we will emphasize scientific thinking—observing clearly and objectively, asking questions, evaluating evidence and drawing tentative conclusions, withholding judgment, and avoiding prejudice. These and other elements of scientific thinking are or should be a part of everyday living. It is through their use that we not only learn to solve science problems but also such problems as the following: How shall I vote? What makes acid rain, and what can be done about it? Why is some of our animal life disappearing? How shall I make up my mind about what to believe?

THE TEACHER'S BACKGROUND

It is not surprising that within any classroom the science taught and the way it is taught is dependent primarily on what the individual teacher knows and does.[2] This is obvious when you visit classrooms of your fellow teachers and when you examine your own ways of working with children. One important thing to remember is that science teaching is not significantly different from the teaching of other subjects in the elementary school curriculum. A skillful teacher of any subject area is capable of effectively teaching science in a way that encourages children to want to learn more. In fact, teaching science is easier than teaching some of the other subjects because most children, given the opportunity, are enthusiastic about it. Science provides plenty of opportunity for using materials and for doing things outdoors as well as in the classroom. There are plenty of opportunities for hands-on experiences, that is, learning by participation, by handling objects and being a part of the science experience.

Many teachers already teach more science than they realize.[3] They keep an aquarium or a pet animal in the classroom; they help children keep a weather chart, raise houseplants in their classrooms, and plant gardens, or take students to the zoo and planetarium. These activities are high in science potential, but many teachers need a more scientific approach to help children get more sci-

What is it? The sock contains various unidentified objects. Using the sense of touch, children attempt to describe, compare, and identify. With some leadership from the teacher, this becomes more than a game—it emphasizes using the senses to collect information that leads to discoveries. (*Courtesy of Phyllis Marcuccio, Potomac Elementary School, Potomac, Maryland.*)

ence learning from these activities. For example, teachers and children set up an aquarium but may pay little attention to it. Water evaporates from it, snails lay eggs on the glass, plants reproduce, tadpoles grow legs. Often these happenings pass unnoticed. The aquarium is full of information (or answers) if children are encouraged to notice and ask questions such as, What? Why? How? With planning, happenings such as these can be uti-

[2]Peggy Teters, Dorothy Gobel, and Patrick Geary, "Elementary Teachers' Perspectives on Improving Science Education: What Research Says," *Science and Children* (November/December 1984).

[3]Mary B. Harbeck, "Getting the Most out of Elementary Science," *Science and Children* (October 1985).

lized for the greater enrichment of children's science experiences.

If you are a teacher who says, "My children sometimes seem to know more science than I do," there are several sources you can turn to for help. For example, acquaint yourself with the innovative projects that are described and incorporated in this book. Consult your state, county, or city bulletins on the teaching of science. (Write to the agency producing the appropriate material.) Use the teacher's manuals that are issued with the elementary science textbooks used in school.

Read science material that is written for children, in addition to books (such as this text) written on your own level. Don't be ashamed of approaching a new science area through the use of a children's book. If it helps you, use it.

Join a science association where you can learn more about current practices in science teaching—the Council for Elementary Science International, the School, Science and Mathematics Association, and the National Science Teachers Association (NSTA), for example. Talk to other teachers, observe them as they teach science, listen to their ideas, and weigh them for your own use. Attend workshops or take an extension course designed especially for elementary school teachers.

Work through some of the "Discovering for Yourself" and "Preparing To Teach" sections in this book, and make use of the "Resources To Investigate with Children." These may lead you to creative and useful ideas of your own invention. Do some of the experiments suggested for students. There is no substitute for firsthand experience for teachers as well as for students.

Remember that science is always subject to change, as are the ways of teaching it, so be open-minded. Keep up via newspapers, magazines, and professional journals. Examine some of the learning materials described in this book that are especially designed to promote inquiry. Above all, allow yourself to experience the wonder and excitement of scientific knowledge in everyday life.

What is science teaching like in today's schools? Let's take a look at the following summary.

SOME DIRECTIONS

Over the past several decades, every major report on the status of science education has stressed the importance of the elementary school in generating our interest in science and shaping our attitude toward it.[4]

Science now has a recognized place in elementary schools: It is accepted as important for all students. The following represent some generally desirable trends in elementary science education. Since directions in science teaching are constantly shifting and vary considerably from one school system to another, these trends should be regarded as guidelines to better science instruction rather than a description of current practices.

Methods of Teaching

Hands-on teaching is giving rise to new ideas and techniques and is fostering creativity and problem-solving skills. Hands-on teachers are "guides" rather than "tellers." Emphasis is placed on "discovering for yourself" and on allowing children both to determine what problems are to be solved within the content area under study and to propose methods of solution. There is a more open-ended approach where a variety of solutions are possible, and where solutions can lead to other problems.

Teaching tools—books, television tapes, computer software, and other audiovisual equipment—have improved in a number of ways: The science is more accurate, the format more attractive, and creativity and investigation are promoted.

[4]Phyllis R. Marcuccio, "Forty-Five Years of Elementary School Science: A Guided Tour," *Science and Children* (January 1987).

Hands-on experiences foster creativity. Children try out different widths of rubber bands to produce different tones. They also discover that tightening a band around the box raises its pitch. *Photo by Lloyd Wolf, Concord School, Forestville, Maryland.*

Laboratory materials—thermometers, aquaria, magnets, living forms, and so on—are more available. These materials can be supplemented with homemade or contributed items.

There is considerable emphasis on the interdisciplinary nature of science, particularly with regard to mathematics, reading, writing, and social studies. Conservation of soil, forests, and water, and pollution are examples of problems where some or all of the disciplines may be employed together.

Science must compete for time in the curriculum in many school systems. The curriculum is long and time is short. State and local educational authorities are mandating time to be spent exclusively on science, while recognizing that there are many opportunities to integrate science instruction with other parts of the school program such as reading and language arts.

There is emphasis on the use of the metric system as it becomes a part of our everyday living, although there is still wide variation in the teaching of metrics in our schools. The metric system is used throughout this text in conjunction with the traditional U.S. system. The end papers of the book provide conversion tables for length, area, mass, volume, and temperature.

Classroom teachers are experimenting with a variety of approaches to the teaching of science. Different administrative procedures are being employed to varying degrees, such as team teaching and learning centers. This experimentation varies with the amount of emphasis placed on science in the curriculum and on other local needs.

An important trend in relation to *what* is taught, is an effort to determine *how well* it is taught. Kellogg[5] indicates, "There is wider practice in the use of assessment tools in our schools. There is an increased attempt to determine not only the amount of science being taught but the quality of science education." Although there is considerable variation from state to state, a majority employ a variety of tests that attempt to assess skills as well as progress in knowledge.

[5]Theodore M. Kellogg, "Science and State Assessment Programs," *Science and Children* (April 1987) includes a detailed chart of K–8 programs in various states and a brief description of each.

Teacher Education

Teacher education institutions, often in collaboration with nearby school systems, are providing preservice teachers with direct hands-on contact with the materials elementary students use and with problems and procedures related to the content under study. Science centers and labs at a college and at a nearby school allow students, preservice, and in-service teachers to interact. Preservice teachers practice teaching science in classes with the help of the classroom teacher.

National science teacher organizations (see p. 8), as well as local teacher groups, are reaching out to teachers with their publications, conferences, and field activities. The reporting of up-to-date research in science education is readily available through ERIC[6] (The Education Resources Information Center).

Meeting Needs of Children and Society

There is an increased need (and recognition of that need) to help children learn how to make choices about their personal and social problems, to begin to apply science skills to their everyday problems, and to learn to live with the results of their decisions. This means an increased emphasis on helping children develop a set of values they can live with. All of these emphases are directly related to our total school objectives and to the development of children.

In many school systems there is an increasing use of individualized instruction. Ideally children work in small groups or by themselves, progressing at their own rates with less pressure from the teacher or their classmates. New teaching materials and equipment such as computers and new classroom designs make such instruction possible.

Emphasis is placed on recognizing and dealing with children on the basis of their individual growth and development. Children with special aptitudes and interests are urged to work up to their capacities; children with learning difficulties are given special help. At the same time there is importance placed on providing a challenging and interesting program for *all* children. Science at the preschool and kindergarten levels is receiving more and more attention in school systems where there are good science programs.

There is greater focus on the human applications of science, on its use in solving such problems as the deterioration of the earth's environment, hunger and disease, ignorance and prejudice. Children are learning to grapple with real problems concerning their environment. In this connection there is greater emphasis on helping children make choices and in so doing helping children develop. (See Chapter 13B for specific examples.)

The present trend is to focus on science-based problems which require gathering and processing of information from many sources. The student is engaged with real life problems, such as energy, pesticides, ... pollution, transportation, world food conditions, health delivery systems and many others. These problems involve science, technology, society and people, and cut across many disciplines.[7]

Mainstreaming

Placing handicapped children in regular classrooms is in practice in all schools because it is the law and because it is believed that the best education for these children will result if they are placed in an environment with so-called normal children. Moreover, this is the least restrictive environment possible to meet the needs of these handicapped children. Mainstreaming is being reexamined and modified to fit specific needs in various school systems. (For further discussion, see Chapter 5.)

---

[6]Write to ERIC/SMEAC Information Center, The Ohio State University, 1200 Chambers Road, Columbus, OH 43212-1792 for information.

[7]Paul De Hart Hurd, "Science Technology and Society: New Goals for Interdisciplinary Science Teaching," *The Science Teacher* (February 1975).

Understanding Children's Development

There is an increased interest in understanding how children develop intellectually and how children learn, stimulated in part by the research and theories of developmental psychologists, in particular Jean Piaget, Jerome Bruner, and Robert Gagné. The full implications of these theories for elementary science instruction are yet to be worked out, but modern science programs agree that children learn best by working with concrete materials, by thinking about what they do, and by sharing these experiences. (See Chapter 2 for further discussion of the findings of psychologists.)

Using Resources

Business and industry—concerned about the interrelationships between science, technology, and society—have sought a role in science education. They recognize that the schools serve an important role in providing scientifically literate individuals for their enterprises.

Nonschool settings, such as outdoor education centers and museums, have increased their support, often introducing subject matter that includes issues of social concern, such as pollution, ecology, and energy education.

Community resources are used to bring science to life. Local printed guides have been de-

This boy collecting aquatic specimens will take them to the classroom for further study. He may use local printed guides that have been developed by teachers and students to assist in the identification of these forms. (*Courtesy of U.S. Dept. of Agriculture, Soil Conservation Service.*)

veloped by teachers and students in elementary and high schools to assist in the identification and use of such resources as parks, rivers, rock formations, farms, gardens, museums, zoos, water supply and sewage disposal systems, and industrial plants. (See "Discovering for Yourself" at the end of the A chapters and "Resources to Investigate with Children" at the end of the B chapters.)

Textbooks as a teaching resource have been influenced by the emphasis on the broader goals of elementary science education. Several graded series of such textbooks are available and are in wide use. In fact, in some school systems the textbook is the course of study. Some educators are concerned that such dependence may get in the way of good science instruction. (See Chapters 4 and 5 for further information regarding the use of textbooks as resources.) The textbook selected should stimulate children to make decisions from data available, to practice problem solving, and to learn to relate science to daily living—rather than encourage the mere presenting of information by the teacher and rote learning by the student. There is considerable variation, however, in the way textbooks are used.

A number of science programs were initiated as national projects but are now available from different publishers. (See Chapter 4 for a discussion of these projects.)

The foregoing are some indications of how science programs in the elementary schools are changing. Some may be "wishful thinking"; many are true for relatively few school systems. There is much good science teaching that remains unreported and unrecorded. In some places science in the elementary school is losing ground for various reasons. This book reflects desirable directions in its presentation of both subject matter and methods of teaching.

But we emphasize again that it is the teacher's enthusiasm, preparation, and understanding of the goals and methods that makes or breaks the success of the elementary school effort.

Success in science teaching depends to a large degree on the answer to the basic question, "*What are our goals?*" Cupboards full of equipment, shelves of books, and a first-class curriculum are beneficial only if there is a teacher willing to use them in an enthusiastic and effective way. The greatest asset to successful science teaching is a basic understanding of the goals.

DISCOVERING FOR YOURSELF

1. Which of the following phrases, culled from this chapter, might apply to each of the school experiences on pages 5 and 6?
   a. Science is . . . proposing and testing.
   b. There is considerable emphasis on the interdisciplinary nature of science.
   c. Science provides plenty of opportunities for doing things out-of-doors.
   d. Children learn to apply their scientific methods of learning to their everyday problems.
   e. Science is counting and measuring.
   f. We have turned to deliberate investigation into how and why things happen.
   g. The methods called scientific lead to unexpected vistas.
   h. Children are learning to grapple with real problems concerning their environment.
   i. Teachers make use of the innate curiosity of children as a launching pad for helping children investigate and discover answers.
   j. The processes of science are observing, classifying, describing, experimenting, measuring, interpreting, and predicting.
2. Prepare a statement that explains why you think that science is an essential subject in the curriculum.
3. Observe *one* child in a school situation for part of a day. How might his or her questions and activities serve as a springboard for science investigations?
4. Read the science news reported in a local newspaper and current magazines for a period of one week. What specific areas of science were involved in these reports? What difficulties did you encounter in reading this material? What in your own science background helped you? What additional background would have been helpful?

CHAPTER 2

THE GOALS IN ELEMENTARY
SCHOOL SCIENCE

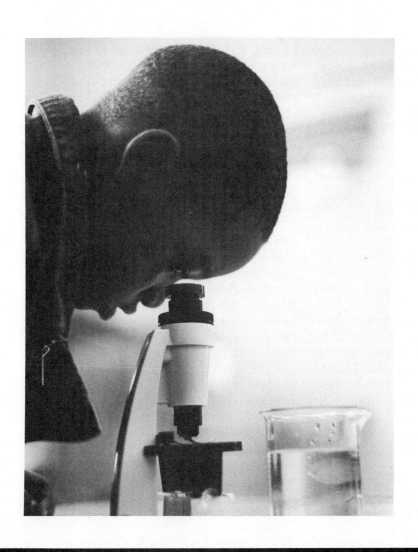

But we submit that our goals are complicated ones, that they were not set for us clearly in advance from some higher source of authority: rather they evolved as we worked, from our knowledge of and love for science, and from what the children teach us. It is too simple to think that we saw a set of specific needs, and proceeded to meet them. What we saw was a magnificent opportunity to explore with children an area that we believe is important to the present world.

PHILIP MORRISON
PROFESSOR OF PHYSICS
MASSACHUSETTS INSTITUTE OF TECHNOLOGY

What goals do we hope to reach through teaching science in the elementary school? Are they evident when we watch what goes on in the classroom, when we talk with children about their experiences in science, when we hear them discuss how they feel about science? In fact it is difficult to find and define our goals at the outset. Yet it is essential that we try—in order to have some general guidelines to shape our teaching as we go along. We should be ready to modify our goals in response to "what the children teach us" as we explore areas important to them and to the present world.

Science is an integral part of the elementary school program. In considering the goals for science teaching it is important to look first at the general objectives of education.

We can agree with the National Science Teachers Association's summary of the general goals of all education as "learning how to learn, how to attack new problems, how to acquire new knowledge—using rational processes—building competence in basic skills—developing intellectual and vocational competence—exploring values in new experiences—understanding concepts and generalizations—learning to live harmoniously within the biosphere."[1]

What is involved in reaching these broad general purposes of education? Certainly we must teach the skills of reading, writing, and arithmetic,

for they are essential equipment for enjoyment, for gaining information, and for communication. Add the skill of seeing things around us and reporting observations correctly. Include the skills of listening and of speaking effectively, so that we can express our ideas coherently and accurately. Add the skill of sensing problems and solving them in a scientific way, so that the results are dependable. This involves being open-minded, fair, careful in arriving at conclusions, accurate, and free of prejudice and superstition.

Without going into details and technicalities at this time, we can sum up the broad objectives this way: to help children gain the ideals, understandings, and skills essential to becoming well-rounded adults who have achieved their fullest potential. It is equally important that science experiences help create in children a sense of wonder and curiosity about their immediate environment.[2]

Classroom experiences should provide many occasions to identify and understand social procedures and problems, to make hypotheses, and to have opportunities to test them through working together from a plan. Children need to check results, to say to each other, "Was our plan good?" "What would have made it better?" "Was it worthwhile?"

While students are working together, they should be developing social sensitivity to the

---

[1]National Science Teachers Association, "Priorities for Improving Science Education," Robert Yager (ed.), *Science and Children* (January 1982).

[2]H. Pratt, "Science Education in the Elementary School," in *What Research Says to the Science Teacher,* Vol. 3, (NSTA, 1981). Describes important goals for science teaching.

needs of one another and of the group. They should be learning cooperation, democratic procedure, and group planning; they can learn these skills only through using them every day and seeing how they operate.

To achieve these goals the school environment should be a place conducive to developing the mental health of children. Among other things, this means that the schoolroom should be a cheerful place, alive with purposeful industry, where children have successful experiences and develop good feelings about themselves. It should be a place of real achievement, where children learn to work diligently and to take pride in accomplishment. It should be a place where children are free to say, "I don't understand." "I think such and such." "I want to ask a question." It should be a place where children feel secure and at home, where they belong, where they can live happily, a place from which students often go home tired at the end of the day, having engaged in hard work that has real purpose.

Furthermore, the elementary school, if it is to achieve our purposes, ought also to be a place where children learn to develop wholesome interests for their leisure time. Because of school there ought to be less of "There's nothing to do" on rainy Saturdays and summer days. There ought to be numerous interesting things children want to do at home because they have experienced pleasure and satisfaction in doing them at school. Although this may indeed be a long-term goal, it is also of direct value in producing in children a sense of wonder and curiosity about their immediate environment.

Finally, the elementary school must be a place where children acquire useful knowledge. In fact, we expect children to learn some meaningful content that is important to them.

Science is important in the total elementary school curriculum because it is intrinsic to the goals of the entire school experience both in content and in basic skills development. Some examples of how science makes a contribution are presented in the remainder of this chapter and in the B chapters that follow.

Our goals should indicate our expectations and describe, as far as possible, how these expectations are to be realized and how we can tell to what extent they are reached. Some goals are chiefly concerned with understanding concepts and generalizations in science—in other words, the knowledge and understandings that we hope children will assimilate. But we also hope that they will develop certain attitudes, interests, appreciations, and values (see later discussion), and that they will develop manipulative and other skills as a result of their science learning experiences. We must, then, formulate goals involving all of these areas. It is quite obvious that some of these goals are easier to state in specific terms than others.

BEHAVIORAL OBJECTIVES[3]

Our general goals or objectives for science teaching present overall intentions. These are indeed general. For example, when we say that the science program will "help children to develop science skills," we are stating a broad objective that underlies our teaching. This kind of goal is used widely, in this book and elsewhere. Such goals, broad in scope, are important because they help us to decide what we want to include in the curriculum, but they are sometimes so broad that they may be difficult to implement and evaluate.

To make goals more specific, easier to check on, and therefore more helpful in the evaluation of student learning and our teaching, we can define goals to include what kinds of *behaviors* we expect from children as a result of their engaging in science activities. For example, we might say that as a result of working with thermometers, "Each child will be able to read a room thermometer within an accuracy of one degree." This specific goal, or so-called *behavioral objective,* can be identified and checked. If we find a large percentage of the class has succeeded with the task, we can feel good about the teaching. Examine the

[3]J. M. Atkins, "Behavioral Objectives in Curriculum Design: A Cautionary Note," *The Science Teacher* (May 1968).

chart for some sample broad objectives and the specific goals related to them.

Broad Goals or Objectives	Specific Related Objectives
The science program will help children to develop science skills.	As a result of working with thermometers, each child will be able to read a room thermometer within an accuracy of one degree.
	After using a magnetic compass and weather vane for several days, the child will be able to demonstrate ability to determine wind directions and record them on a chart in the classroom.
The outdoor education program will help children develop understandings and appreciations about the environment and their place in it.	After investigating the school environment and the surrounding neighborhood, each child will be able to locate at least three habitats where animals live.
	After comparing the appearance of city street trees with those in the park, a child will be able to make three recommendations about city tree locations and choice of the type of tree to be planted.
	After exploring a pond, a child will be able to identify a minimum of five living things in or on the pond.
	After studying air pollution in the neighborhood, a child will be able to identify several different sources of pollution and suggest ways of correcting the problem.

Notice what the foregoing sample objectives have in common:

1. They all make a statement about what the child will be able to do at the end of the lesson or unit; this is sometimes referred to as the *desired behavior*.
2. They describe the *conditions* under which a child is expected to achieve the objective.
3. They indicate how well the child is doing. They state what the acceptable *level of performance* is for the child to reach.
4. They contain an *action verb:* read, use, record, locate, identify, compare. These verbs call for a specific, easily measurable action on the part of the student.

Although there are many formal patterns for writing objectives, the writing should not become an end in itself. Remember that behavioral objectives are intended to be useful tools when you are trying to discover what kinds of measurable changes have taken place in learner behavior as a result of your instruction.

One widely used system of classifying educational objectives is described by Bloom and Krathwohl.[4] They divide all learning into three categories or domains: the cognitive, the affective, and the psychomotor. Writers of behavioral objectives, curriculum planners and designers, and program developers use this classification system as a guide when arranging objectives in order from simple to complex. A brief outline of the various levels in each of the domains follows:

The Cognitive Domain   The first category deals with intellectual skills and abilities, with knowledge and understanding. Most objectives in science teaching fall in this category. Sample action verbs used in behavioral objectives constructed for the levels of learning involved are *name, divide, state, predict, demonstrate, describe, devise, identify, compare, classify, interpret, evaluate,* and *measure.* There are six hierarchical divisions for these objectives.

[4]B. S. Bloom, ed., *Taxonomy of Educational Objectives. Handbook I: Cognitive Domain* (New York: Longmans, 1956); D. R. Krathwohl, ed., *Taxonomy of Educational Objectives. Handbook II: Affective Domain* (New York: McKay, 1964).

Gathering seeds and other plant materials for examination in the classroom. (*Courtesy of NSTA.*)

1. *Knowledge:* the skills of recognition and recall of information. Example: After studying the solar system, the child will be able to name the nine planets and place them in their correct position in space.
2. *Comprehension:* the ability to relate knowledge in your own words and the skill of seeing relationships and trends. Example: When given a model of the sun, moon, and earth, the child will be able to demonstrate how the moon shines by reflecting light from the sun.
3. *Application:* the skill of applying acquired knowledge and comprehension to a specific situation. Example: After a lesson on the expansion of fluids as they are heated, the child will be able to explain how a thermometer works.
4. *Analysis:* the ability to break down an idea into parts and identify the interrelationship of those parts. Example: Given a complete electric circuit (dry cell, bulb, wires, switch) whose bulb will not light, the child will be able to identify the various possible causes.
5. *Synthesis:* the ability to put together elements that form something original. Example: Given seeds that have been grown under various conditions, the child will be able to describe three conditions that appear to be related to optimal growth.
6. *Evaluation:* the skill of making judgments about the values of materials and/or methods used. Example: After using both the U.S. and metric systems for measurement of various objects, the child will be able to state one commonly accepted advantage of using the metric system.[5]

The Affective Domain[6] Educational objectives in the second domain deal with values, attitudes, and interests as well as the development of appreciation. Sample action verbs for these objectives include *participates, performs, tolerates, pre-*

[5]This example and the preceding one come from *How to Use a Behavioral Objective,* J. J. Koran, Jr., E. J. Montague, and G. E. Hall (NSTA, 1969).

[6]H. H. Birnie, "Identifying Affective Goals in Science Education," *The Science Teacher* (December 1978).

fers, creates, acts, assists, chooses, and *asks.* The five divisions are

1. *Receiving:* involves the awareness of events, the willingness to receive these events, and the controlled or selected attention given the events. Example: After a field trip to the zoo, the child voluntarily examines and reacts to a bulletin board display of wild animals.
2. *Responding:* includes a more active quality of response than when receiving. There is a willingness to "go along with," volunteer, or enjoy. Example: When given choices of extracurricular activities, the child selects participation in a science club.
3. *Valuing:* involves preferences, acceptances, and commitments to a value (related to establishing the worth of ideas). Example: When crossing a litter-strewn path, the child picks up the scattered items and encourages his or her classmates to help.
4. *Organization:* includes the ability to group together related values and to formulate a value system. Example: Following a series of encounters with litter around the school grounds and in the neighborhood, the child formulates an anti-litter campaign and elicits the help of classmates, teacher, school, and community.
5. *Characterization:* relates to value or value complex in that the behavior toward others verifies his or her value system and expresses his or her own character. Example: When using materials in a science learning center the child assumes responsibility for replacing material and is willing to share the material.

The Psychomotor Domain   The third domain covers manipulative skills or skills that are dependent upon physical abilities. Sample action verbs include *writes, discusses, walks, explains, pours,* and *draws.* There are three divisions, according to Krathwohl.

1. *Simple Motor Activities:* require simple reflex or voluntary physical perception.
2. *Skills:* involve coordination of muscular movement with sensory perception such as focusing a microscope, pouring liquid from one container to another, and drawing specimens.
3. *Complex Skills:* demand a combination of motor skills and some cognitive skills such as writing reports, discussing events, and explaining ideas.

No matter how objectives are stated, developed, and used, these descriptions of goals are useful as guides. They can be used to evaluate the achievement of children and procedures in teaching.

PROBLEMS AND LIMITATIONS OF BEHAVIORAL OBJECTIVES

Although behavioral objectives have been used as an assessment tool for learning and curriculum designing, there are educators who express concerns and cautions about their use for science education. One reservation suggests that behavioral objectives may limit scientific investigation because of their specificity. Morrison's comment at the beginning of this chapter addresses this problem. There is concern that the pursuit of such objectives may not leave the learners free to identify and pursue a problem as they see it. The critics contend that behavioral objectives are restrictive to such freedom of movement because they are too narrow in defining learning outcomes.

Another concern is that it is often difficult, if not impossible, to state a specific behavioral objective when dealing with the affective domain—values, attitudes, interests, and appreciations. Likewise, it is impossible to write behavioral objectives for all possible learning expectations, for all kinds of activities, and for all kinds of learners with all kinds of talents.

The impact of the writing and use of behavioral objectives on the teaching of science in the elementary school has been of considerable importance; it also has created some questions. Behavioral objectives provide measurable data, and there is a tendency to assume that measurable data implies that what is being measured is worthwhile and what is not is not worthwhile. What is happening is that more data about behavioral objectives are accumulating and less is being learned about other less definable aspects of learning.

In short, teachers should be aware that behavioral objectives have their limitations. They can and should be used with discretion and where appropriate, and in such a way that they do not clash with free investigative science.[7] Behavioral objectives are included in many places in this book as are statements of objectives of a more general nature.

MAJOR GOALS OF SCIENCE EDUCATION

Concepts and Generalizations

The subject matter of science is important. We do need persons in our society who are scientifically literate about the world in which they live. Research indicates that today's children and young people fall short when they are tested for knowledge of everyday science. An informed person is likely to be an interesting one, we would probably agree. But let us not consider people "educated in science" just because they know how many legs a cricket has, that a pair of pliers is an example of a certain kind of lever, what a tufted titmouse looks like, or the definition of chemical change. Such items are important when people learn how to put them together with other facts into meaningful ideas.

We must teach facts in context, in relation to broad concepts. The distance to the moon, for example, is meaningful when it is compared with the diameter of the earth, leading to the understanding that the moon is "30 earths away" from the earth. When we say that children should learn science subject matter we mean that they should be able to formulate concepts and generalizations useful in interpreting the world in which they live. This leads us to a summary statement of one of the general objectives for teaching science: *to help children to understand some generalizations or "big meanings" that they can use to solve problems in their environment.*

The following description of a classroom experience illustrates a strategy for helping children

reach this general objective. Although the experience obviously intends to do more than deal with the aspect of attaining science knowledge, we will concentrate chiefly on that phase of the lesson, leaving the other objectives until later where we discuss them in greater detail.

Children are working with a problem about what heating and cooling does to matter—solids, liquids, and gases. A question has arisen: Why does running hot water over the metal lid of a glass jar make it easier to unscrew? In investigating this problem, some children suggest, "The hot water washes away some sticky food between the cover and the jar." (Incidentally, this may be a factor.) Other children suggest, "The heat does something to the metal cap itself, makes it looser in some way." Children suggest other hypotheses to explain what happens.

They decide to use several clean empty jars (to test the sticky food hypothesis) with the caps screwed on tight. They again find that a cap held in hot water turns more easily. Someone suggests, "Let's hold a lid in cold water." They find that now the lid seems even tighter than before. Why? It is proposed that heating makes the metal lid get larger—expand—and pull away from the glass. (Some children may object, saying that the glass will expand, too! But will it expand as much?) Cooling does the opposite. Is it really true that heating a metal can make it larger? How about other solids? How about liquids and gases? Children propose a series of experiments involving other predictions, hypotheses, tests, and observations, as well as some research reading. The children arrive at some generalizations: *Solids, liquids, and gases expand when they are heated and contract when they are cooled. They do not expand equally.* Such generalizations come as a result of many experiences; they are put together gradually; they are not memorized from printed material; they are not caught by slight exposure as children catch mumps (see Chapter 15B).

Now what can the children do with this information? They examine a thermometer to see that it works by expansion and contraction of a liquid—mercury or alcohol—with changes in tem-

[7]M. C. Weber, "Behavioral Objectives: Another Look," *Science and Children* (January/February 1974).

perature. They observe how sidewalks and pavements and metal bridges are constructed to allow for expansion resulting from an increase in temperature.

Concepts and generalizations are an economical way of organizing vast amounts of information. Scientists use concepts in their research; teachers and children can use them to facilitate learning. To know that the fluid in a thermometer "rises" when the temperature is higher is useful but limited; to know that heating a substance makes it expand is to have the key for the understanding of many phenomena.

At the end of each of the A chapters and at the beginning of the B chapters you will find lists of science concepts that should be helpful to you and the children you teach. They will focus your attention on the "big meanings" we all seek.

For example, some of the concepts covered in Chapter 7B, "Teaching 'The Sun and the Planets,'" are the following: The sun's energy is the source of life on earth. Day and night are caused by the earth's rotation on its axis. Eclipses occur when the earth, sun, and moon are in a straight line in space. The moon and the planets shine by reflected sunlight.

Processes of Discovery: Inquiry

W. W. Welch[8] has defined inquiry "to be a general process by which human beings seek information or understanding. Broadly conceived, inquiry is a way of thought. Scientific inquiry, a subset of general inquiry, is concerned with the natural world and is guided by certain beliefs and assumptions."

Rice and Dunlap[9] indicate that through inquiry "students gain practice with science processes such as the use of tables and graphs, counting, measuring, problem solving, classifying, organizing data and development of understanding of the experimental method."

Goldberg[10] in discussing "learning how to learn" says, "Actively striving to find answers through interesting and significant investigations can engage the whole child, not just part of his or her mind."

With this in mind let us examine the experiences just described with heating and cooling from the standpoint of what we expect in terms of inquiry skills from children.

Our thinking goes along this path: As a result of investigating in different ways (experiences, experiments, environmental observations, discussions, and exploratory reading), the children should be able to *gather data* (information) from the experiences in which they have participated; *describe* what happens when hot and cold water are applied to various solids under different conditions; *demonstrate* these happenings when provided with the essential materials; and *construct* a generalized statement that describes the results of heating and cooling of certain solids under specified conditions. These are examples of the inquiry skills we expect and concentrate on.

This leads us to another major objective for the study of science: *to help students to grow in ability to use scientific processes.* This is a general statement of our objective. As we proceed we shall indicate inquiry aspects that make it more specific.

A science class should be a place to ask questions as well as to answer them. It is probably true, unfortunately, that we as teachers are in the habit of giving greater recognition to the students who know the answers than to those who ask thoughtful questions. The thinking child says, "If that is true, *why*. . . ?" "I understand that, but *why*. . . ?" Science is problem seeking as well as problem solving.

We begin, then, to give more and more attention to helping children formulate problems.

---

[8]W. W. Welch, "Inquiry in School Science," in *What Research Says to the Science Teacher,* Vol. 3 (NSTA, 1981).

[9]For further illustration, see Dale R. Rice and William P. Dunlap, "Introducing the Ways and Means of Scientific Inquiry," *The Science Teacher* (March 1982).

[10]L. Goldberg, "Learning How to Learn," *Science and Children* (April 1982). For further discussion see J. L. Nagalski, "Why 'Inquiry' Must Hold Its Ground," *The Science Teacher* (April 1980).

These problems may arise because of children's experiences: "Miss Brown, last night I saw the moon come up. It was big and the color of oranges. How come?" Problems may result from the children's reading: "Mr. Jacobs, it says here that sunlight is made of all different colors. How can that be?" Problems may arise on trips, as a spillover from the investigations of other problems, from current events, and from many other sources. An important role for the teacher is to plan situations that provoke children to pose problems. See "How Can We Grow in Ability to Ask the 'Right' Questions?" in Chapter 5.

For example, a second grade is studying magnets. Students have played with magnets, found out some things they will attract, and separated objects into magnetic and nonmagnetic materials (steel paper clips from bits of paper). Questions about the relative strengths of magnets have arisen ("My magnet is stronger than yours." "My magnet doesn't pick up anything!") This raises the question of "How can we find out how strong our magnets are?" Different methods are suggested by the children: "See how many paper clips the magnet will pick up and hold." "See how far a clip will jump to the magnet." "See how long a chain of clips you can make with the magnet" (see Chapter 17B).

The children decide on the "chain of clips" method. They use it on their different magnets, record their observations, and summarize their results. They are surprised to discover that the largest magnets are not necessarily the strongest. The children speculate on why a clip attached to a magnet can pick up another clip. They hypothesize that the "pull of the magnet goes through the clip"—that "the clip becomes a magnet" (at this level these are perfectly acceptable answers).

Some children try to find out what happens when the chain is removed from the magnet. They observe that the clips fall off one by one. They speculate, "When the clips are not on the magnet, they lose their magnetism."

Reviewing the magnet–clip story we note that the children are using inquiry processes: observing, hypothesizing, experimenting, recording, generalizing, and communicating. There are many other values implicit in the way this study developed. What do you think they are? Keep in mind that science is an integral part of the total school program.

Observing Observing is a fundamental process that in a sense underlies many of the other processes. It is quite possible to look but not actually to see. Real observation requires thoughtful looking, keen listening, and touching. It is closely linked with being able to describe what is observed.

Play the game "Are you a good detective?" or "Are you a good reporter?" Take a quiet walk with the class around the block. The only instruction given is to observe—to hear, see, smell everything possible. Back in the classroom have the students report on their observations. Summarize them on the chalkboard. Did they report on the color of any objects, any unusual sounds or smells, clouds?, and so on. On a subsequent trip ask the students to focus on one aspect of the environment, for example, "How do you know that the wind is blowing today?"

Ask an upper-grade class to examine a pinch of beach sand on a piece of paper with a magnifying glass. The students observe that it is made of many individual grains. What shape are the grains? What colors are they? How many grains are there in your sample? (Use a toothpick to spread the grains.) (See Chapter 6B, pp. 140–141.)

These are approaches used in stimulating children to use and sharpen their powers of observation. Observations should lead to exactness. How much? How many? How long? Observing may, and often does, involve all of the senses, and children should be encouraged to make use of them.

We sometimes extend the use of our senses by using instruments. A hand lens, for example, helps us see the hooked barbs on cockleburs, which enable them to attach to the fur of an animal and get a free ride. A telescope extends our vision into space, helping us see the craters, the mountains, and the valleys of the moon clearly. See Chapter

3 and the B chapters for further examples and discussion.

Communicating   When we urge children to tell what they observe, we are stimulating the use of a skill that is fundamental to our everyday living. Children and adults are frequently heard to say, "I know what it is, but I can't tell it." Learning to communicate orally, in writing, through the use of diagrams, graphs, and in other ways is an integral part of processes that help discovery and understanding in science. It is here that correlation of science and language-arts skills including reading is important. When children have something to say they have an opportunity to grow in ability to do so.

Children should be encouraged to express their responses *in their own words.* For example, on the street trip described in the preceding section children might say: The lamppost made a long shadow on the sidewalk; the clouds were white and fluffy; the breeze blew Agnes's hair over her face; the tree bark felt rough; I could smell the bakery before I saw it; the sun was on top of the red brick house across the street.

In the examination of sand, children might report: Some grains were white, some black, some brown, some pink, some like glass; the grains looked like tiny rocks; there were about 200 grains in my pinch.

Specific examples for the integration of language arts with science activities are given in Chapter 3.

Hypothesizing   We encourage children to formulate possible explanations of puzzling events. In the illustration of the experiences with heat and cold, children proposed various explanations about why the placing of the metal-capped jar under hot water made it easier to open. Formulating hypotheses is one of the early steps in the process of discovery. An "educated guess" for our purposes is like a hypothesis.

Experimenting   The term *experimenting* has often been used loosely to mean following directions from the text or demonstrating something that is already known, or "playing" with apparatus. However, when it is used as a process to discover something that is not known to the child, to test a hypothesis, or to attempt to solve a real problem, it becomes a scientific endeavor. For example, children may wonder about what made the

Counting the annual rings to determine a tree's age. Why are some rings thinner than others? Children should be encouraged to make hypotheses. Answers may come later. *Photo by Lloyd Wolf, Ann Beers School, Washington, D.C.*

water in the classroom aquarium turn green. They give different reasons and design experiments to test their theories. As in the other processes, there are many degrees of sophistication in experimenting. These and other aspects of experimenting are discussed in the next chapter.

Measuring   Exactness is fundamental to many of the processes of discovering. How much, how many, how often, and so on, are important. Learning to use the tools of measuring, to record the results in some graphic form, and thus to have available some quantitative basis for predictions or generalizations or hypotheses is an integral part of many science experiences and experiments.

For example, children measure the length of the shadow of a flagpole each hour from early morning to three in the afternoon. They record their results on a chart and make a graph of their findings.

Science and mathematics are closely related: Mathematics makes science exact; science makes mathematics meaningful.

Classifying   When children divide a number of objects into two major groups, for example, those attracted to a magnet and those that are not, they are classifying. This simple activity helps them understand the *common properties* of some objects (paper clips and scissors). They also discover that not all materials are attracted to magnets.

Similarly, a separation of objects that float from those that do not, for example, helps them understand that floating depends on more than the material the object is made of: A steel boat of a certain shape can float as well as a wooden one.

Grouping leaves according to their shape, size, edges, and veins, for example, helps in *identification* of the leaves.

In summary, classification reveals characteristics of a group of objects or situations, likenesses and differences, and helps in the identification of objects or organisms.

It is important for young children to be encouraged to devise their own systems of classifi-

Weighing and measuring are two skills that take on importance when children realize the need for accuracy as they experiment to solve problems. (*Courtesy of Phyllis Marcuccio.*)

cation, even if these do not correspond with standard "scientific" criteria. For children to understand classification it should serve a need that they deem important for them. As they grow older the value of more sophisticated systems will become apparent to them.

Generalizing   The generalizations of science give us command over thousands of discrete facts and varied phenomena. The generalization that *the earth rotates on its axis* helps explain the cause of night and day, why shadows change, why the sun, moon, and stars appear to move across the sky, how a sundial works, the meaning of such locations as the North Pole, the South Pole, and the equator.

It is desirable for children to base generalizations on their own experiences, observations, experiments, and readings. Again they should be expressed in their own language. The teacher will be surprised at the unique, colorful, imaginative, and insightful phrases children use—if they know that their words are accepted and cherished.

To quote Philip Morrison again, "The student who uses a symbol system of his own, who . . . often develops novelty . . . needs and demands credit and recognition even if he does not express himself in the words or equations that convention dictates."

Predicting   (See also *Hypothesizing*) To be able to make reasonable predictions on the basis of available data is an important process. In the study of the flagpole's shadow from morning to 3 P.M., children noted how the shadow's length and direction changed. They should be able to predict what will happen from 3 P.M. to sunset.

There is no intended implication in the foregoing that the order in which these processes are presented is the order children must follow, nor that they *all* must be present in any investigation or that the processes of inquiry are limited only to these.

Learning how to use processes of inquiry is one of our important goals. How does this fit into our general elementary school plan for children? Certainly our success in living with one another is increased if we are skillful in solving our daily problems—knowing what is pertinent, reliable information, learning how to apply it, and knowing how to check the validity of results.

Students need help in seeing how the inquiry processes in science are like processes of discovery in other areas. The teacher may frequently say, "You remember how we found some of the answers when we worked on the problems about rain? How can we use what we learned there to help us find the answers to this new problem in our social studies?" The new problem may be, "How can we organize a good water conservation project in our school and neighborhood?" Such problems as this help students to transfer lessons in using processes to their everyday living.

Can a child give a teacher a lift? Many suggestions are offered, and trials are conducted to test the predictions. (*Courtesy of Elementary Science Study of Education Development Center, Inc.*)

Scientific Attitudes

In general terms we say that the *experiences in science should help children develop and use scientific attitudes*. The development of scientific attitudes, like the development of processes of discovery, come about only through conscious effort. First, to achieve this important objective we must understand what it means, and we must think of it in terms of the behaviors and performances we expect from children. Then, we must teach so that children cannot get along without using scientific ways of thinking. Here are some of the characteristics that you as a scientifically minded person would possess.

You are open-minded, willing to change your mind in the face of reliable evidence, and you respect another's point of view.

You look at a matter from many sides before you draw a conclusion. You do not jump to conclusions or decide on the basis of one observation; you deliberate and examine until you are as sure as you can be.

You go to reliable sources for your evidence. You challenge sources to make sure that they are reliable.

You are not superstitious; you realize that nothing happens without some cause.

You are curious. You are careful and accurate in your observations.

Every time children attempt to experiment, whenever they use other inquiry processes, whenever they read, take a field trip, see a motion picture, communicate their findings to the class, or identify a problem to solve, their scientific attitudes ought to be showing. These processes should become a real part of their thinking equipment. There should be much of "Hey, wait a minute!" "Let's try that again." "How do you know that's true?" "I've changed my mind since I read what scientists say." "Where did you find that answer?" "You may be right, but tell me more about where you found your information." "I think our hypothesis should be revised." These remarks and similar ones should often be heard in our science classes as well as in social studies, arithmetic classes, and other places where children are working together and using processes of inquiry.

In a fourth-grade class the children are learning how to use a magnetic compass. This is part of a unit on the voyages of Columbus, during which he experienced serious difficulties in using the ship's compass (see Chapter 17A).

Before this lesson, the children had learned that magnets are "attracted" to iron; that a steel needle can be magnetized by stroking it with a magnet; that unlike poles of a magnet attract each other, that like poles repel; that a freely suspended magnet becomes a compass.

Each child is provided with a standard compass in which the needle's north-pointing end is blue and the south-pointing end is silver-colored. The teacher asks the children to point to the north after their needles have come to rest. One by one the children point to the front of the room—except for Joseph, who points to the rear.

After the uproar of the class subsides, the teacher asks for explanations for the strange behavior of Joseph's compass.

The following hypotheses are offered, listed on the blackboard, and numbered:

1. Joseph is always different.
2. The needle is stuck.
3. The compass is broken.
4. The needle is not magnetized.
5. Joseph has a steel ruler in his desk.
6. The magnetism isn't strong enough.
7. There must be some iron on one side of the compass case.
8. The needle is rusty.

How can we test these explanations? The following are suggested and tried. Joseph exchanges his compass with Louisa's. Now Louisa points in the wrong direction. What does this do to the theories? Evidently theories 1 and 5 are incorrect. Emily at the blackboard crosses them out. The compass is jiggled, and the needle is observed to swing freely. It is not "stuck," so number 2 is eliminated. The needle always comes to rest in the same position as before; evidently it is magnetized and it isn't broken. That takes out theories 3, 4, and 6. There is no visible evidence that the needle is rusty, eliminating number 8. On turning the compass case the needle maintains its same position—blue end pointing south. Emily crosses out number 7, the last of the theories.

What other possible conclusions remain? Either the needle was "painted" the wrong way in the factory, or after it was painted it was magnetized in the "wrong" way—which amounts to the same thing. How can we be sure? One student asks for a bar magnet. She brings the north pole of the magnet near the compass. The blue end of the needle swings around toward this pole. The blue end must be the south-pointing end of the needle, since opposite poles attract each other. Joseph was right in the sense that he used the compass in the way he was expected to use it. The compass was right, too—except that the needle had the wrong "tag" on it!

As teachers, we know that many puzzling phenomena occur during the school year, when no one, including the teacher, knows the answer. Examples:

When an electric circuit set up by the children does not work (see p. 40, item 11).
When children find wide differences when they count the number of peas in a pod (see p. 45).
When an unusual, unidentified rock (or plant or animal) is brought to school.
When there is a newspaper report of a strange "human" ("Bigfoot").
When a student reports seeing an unusual light in the night sky.
When a fish in the aquarium dies.
When the Halloween pumpkin turns moldy.

When young children ask, "Is that really a true story?" there is opportunity for them to get acquainted with the difference between factual material and fiction, and to learn that one is used for the purpose of finding answers or getting information and the other more usually for entertainment and inspiration.

The students' discovery of mistakes (or what appear to be mistakes) in books or other printed material may be a landmark in the development of their scientific attitudes. To realize that a statement's appearance in print is no guarantee of its accuracy may be an eye-opener to a child who is being introduced to reliability as a criterion for selecting material to read for gathering information. One book, for example, may state that the earth has only one satellite; another may say that the earth has only one *natural* satellite, although it has many manufactured ones. Here is an opportunity for communication and discussion. Children come to appreciate the importance of using up-to-date material for reference work. They come to know that such words as "known" and "natural" are extremely important, as are such phrases as "scientists think," "it is generally believed," "it may be true that," "some people say," and "evidence seems to indicate that." This same attitude should permeate our activities in social studies and other areas of learning in the elementary school.

The following letter written by an eight-year-old to an author is an illustration of challenging the accuracy of information:

Dear _____

You wrote a book called the *Pet Show*, didn't you? One of the stories in it is called the "Guinea Pigs at the Show." One sentence says, "They can run about when they are only a few days old."
This is not true.
They can run about the day they are born.

Yours truly
Mary Lou _____

P.S. I raise them.

Here, obviously, is a student who is learning to evaluate some of her reading and to relate it to her own experience. Some adult, either at home or at school, may have urged her to write to the author to find out why her experiences and the book did not seem to agree. Through such an experience the child learns something about how books are written, how limited experience may sometimes be misleading, how scientific observations may differ from a child's observations, and how different statements of fact may only *seem* to be in disagreement.

Interest and Appreciation

Science is supposed to create in children *an interest in and an appreciation for the world in which they live.* The attitudes that we have just discussed are closely related to interest and appreciation. They, too, are difficult to achieve and hard to measure. Let us examine a background situation to clarify the idea.

Just now, as this is being written, the late afternoon sky is flaming with a hundred hues. The clouds five miles away, made of countless droplets of water, are reflecting some of this light through the window. Growing almost into the window, vine leaves glisten green in the light of late afternoon. In leaves such as these the food for the world is being made. The leaf is a wonderful manufacturing plant where water, lately fallen from the sky as rain, comes up from the roots in the ground and meets with carbon dioxide from the air. In the green leaf, in the presence of sunlight, food is manufactured from this water and carbon dioxide. All living things depend on this process. In the world about us there are, indeed, great things to wonder about: How can sunlight be changed to brilliant colors at sunset? How are clouds formed? How do plants manufacture food? How did the world itself come to be, and how has it changed through the ages?

Young children deserve to find in schools a nurturing influence for their natural curiosity about the world. They deserve also to have this curiosity extended to new fields about which they have never wondered because they did not know they exist. They deserve the opportunity to come to appreciate, through understanding, the wonders of the world—to be "at home" in the world. Exactly how this appreciation is to be developed, we still have much to learn. Experience seems to show that most do not gain it through listening to sentimental gushing from an adult. Perhaps it

comes about when adults provide opportunities for children to discover *for themselves*—to observe firsthand, to feel, to see, to use the senses so that satisfying experiences will result. Perhaps through knowledge thus gained, children may develop for themselves an appreciation that fits each person. Certainly there can be great thrills in discovery, through contact with natural objects and phenomena.

As these paragraphs were being written the colors disappeared from the west. Twilight is here and soon night will come. Our side of the earth is turning from the sun; darkness comes. Elsewhere the dark side of the earth is turning toward the sun, and day is coming. In a few weeks the leaves will drop from the vine outside the window, the days will grow colder; autumn will be here, then winter, then spring, and summer. Here is the cycle of the seasons. There is also the cycle that water follows as it disappears from the surface of the earth and appears again, falling from the sky as rain; the cycle of seeds occurs, from tiny cells to adult plant and the production of seeds again. These and similar phenomena are what we have in mind when we think of providing opportunities to increase children's interest and develop their appreciations, which, in turn, will lead to a growing comprehension and insight. As in the case of other objectives discussed, this one is realized only if we intend it to be and plan learning experiences for children accordingly. We hope to bring about changes in behaviors, and think of our results in terms of children showing evidence of a broadening interest through asking more searching questions; bringing to class examples that show increased curiosity; selecting science books of a more diversified content; and expressing their thoughts more vividly and accurately.

Science, Technology and Society

Knowledge of science concepts, understanding of science processes, and the development of attitudes, interests, and appreciation are all to little avail if we produce adults who are unable or unwilling to use these in helping to solve the serious problems that face the world today.

The goal of science education during the 1980s is to develop scientifically literate individuals who understand how science, technology and society influence one another and who are able to use this knowledge in their everyday decision-making. Such individuals both appreciate the value of science and technology in society and understand its limitations.[11]

Paul DeHart Hurd, Professor Emeritus, Stanford University, in a farsighted statement some years ago urged the adoption of a new perspective for the teaching of science, based on the greatly changing conditions of life and world events.[12] The following excerpts from his article define the problem and advance proposals for the role of science education in meeting the challenge.

Science describes the world as it is, technology remakes the world to serve human desires.

Technology serves as a bridge between science and society and unifies the various disciplines. In the curriculum it puts science concepts where the student confronts them, in everyday affairs.

The problem is one of developing a system of values and ethical considerations by which scientific achievements and technological innovations serve the common good.

Science provides knowledge; technology provides ways of using this knowledge; and our value concepts guide what we ought to do with both.

The present trend is to focus on science-based problems which require gathering and processing information from many sources. The student is engaged with real-life problems, such as energy, pesticides, the "green revolution," pollution, transportation, world food conditions, health delivery systems, and

many others. These problems involve science, technology and society, and people, and cut across many disciplines.

Science taught in relation to society, technology and people suggests the need for an interdisciplinary curriculum.

We are only beginning to realize how serious some of our social problems are. The interest in ecology and the state of our environment came with an almost explosive suddenness revealing many urgent problems: general deterioration of the environment (acid rain, for example), the exhaustion of our natural resources, overpopulation, drug addiction, illiteracy, ignorance and prejudice, threat of nuclear war, poverty, urban decay, disease, and the crisis in transportation.

Although the production of responsible, intelligent citizens is a general goal for all education, it is obvious that science education has some very significant concepts and methods to contribute. The science experiences in the elementary school lay the groundwork for these contributions when we involve children in projects in their schools and communities. With these projects children have the satisfaction of knowing that *what they do can make a difference.* Problems such as the following may trigger worthwhile projects (further related material will be found in Chapters 13A and B).

How can our school and community make better use of our energy sources?

What can we do about the lot next door to our school that is filled with papers and rubbish?

Where does the soot on our playground come from? What can be done about this?

How does acid rain affect our community?

Where should trees be planted in our neighborhood?

What rocks are used in the buildings and streets in our neighborhood? (See Chapter 6B, p. 140.)

How would rising temperatures, resulting from the "greenhouse effect" change conditions on earth? (See index for many page references.)

How can we conduct a study of our city environment? (See Chapter 13B, pp. 435–438.)

How can we study a rural environment? (See Chapter 13B, pp. 446–448.)

---

[11]National Science Teachers Association.

[12]Science, Technology and Society: New Goals for Interdisciplinary Science Teaching," *The Science Teacher* (February 1975).

What are some safety rules for the use of electricity? (See Chapters 17B, pp. 564–565.)

How have space techniques helped provide more products for everyday living and given us added information about the earth? (See Chapter 20A, pp. 626–627.)

Although we cannot overestimate the importance of helping children to develop into responsible, intelligent citizens, we accomplish little when we impose adult views on them. As with the other aims we have discussed, the interests, drives, capacities, and the developmental levels of children must be understood and respected. Nor should we be deceived by children's verbal performance in the use of ecological terms. We must continue to search for evidence that the *behaviors of students* have changed, that they have established certain desirable attitudes and *values* as evidenced by their discussions and actions.

What happens in the classroom will be of critical importance in this process. The next chapter concentrates on specifics for improving what happens there.

DISCOVERING FOR YOURSELF

1. Assume that children have completed a unit "Investigating Pollution Around the School" (or any other unit of your choice). Give an example of one specific objective that might be realized in each of the three domains—cognitive, affective, and psychomotor—as stated on pages 16 to 18.

2. As part of a unit on the moon in the late fall, the teacher asked the children to observe the moon for a week. What objectives might be expected from this activity?

3. A concept stated in Chapter 9B with respect to the study of air and the weather states, "We live at the bottom of an ocean of air." How does this concept change or enhance your perception of the earth and its atmosphere? How could you use this statement to open new vistas for your students? How might your students illustrate this statement with a drawing, a painting, or in creative writing?

4. Take a walk after a heavy rainfall. Explain how you might use such a trip to involve your students in some of the processes of inquiry.

5. Select a TV commercial promoting some product. How might a scientific attitude help you in evaluating such an advertisement?

6. Recall and describe any experience (in school or out of school) that created in you a deep interest in and appreciation of some aspect of the world. How is this interest or appreciation evident in your present thinking or activities?

7. How might the setting up and maintaining of a school garden or the preparation of a class science fair contribute to behaviors that promote "responsible, intelligent citizenship?" What precautions should be followed in such group projects to prevent negative, destructive behavior?

8. Compare the opening statement of Philip Morrison about "our goals" with what has been presented in this chapter. Is there any conflict? In what way? Any agreement? How?

9. Plan a visit to one of the following facilities that serve the community, or any other you choose: dairy, power plant, bakery, weather bureau, water purification plant, airport, telephone exchange. How would you prepare students for this trip? What follow-up activities could be used? What are the science implications of this trip? How could it be used to develop understandings of the importance of the particular facility to the welfare of people?

CHAPTER 3

HELPING CHILDREN
LEARN SCIENCE

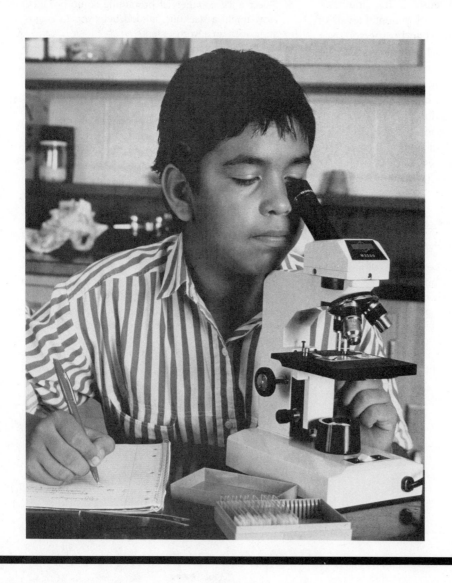

Most teachers try many different ways of teaching a given lesson or unit. They experiment and adapt their teaching style to what the situation seems to call for. They learn to ignore some of their professors' injunctions about teaching and finally to appreciate others. They discover strategies that were never discussed in education classes. As they go through this process of trial and error, teachers realize that they are refining their skills, but few think of their efforts as "research." However, conducting research is just what they are doing. Though the scope is limited and the results may not go outside that classroom, the teacher who experiments with various teaching methods is a practical researcher who is amassing a body of data about what works in the classroom.

DOROTHY GABEL,[1] *PROFESSOR OF SCIENCE EDUCATION AT INDIANA UNIVERSITY,*
BLOOMINGTON

The more we know about children and how they learn, the more successful we can be in helping them learn. In this chapter we consider how a knowledge of children's development can guide us in planning what to teach and how to teach it.

Helping children learn how to learn is the very heart of our science teaching. We shall deal with some of the activities children engage in as they attempt to solve problems. How do they investigate and experiment? How do they use their senses to explore? What place do reading and writing skills have in these investigations? How essential are field trips, visual aids, including computers, and learning centers? What kinds of science experiences are appropriate at different age levels?

STUDYING CHILDREN

Before we explore teaching strategies we would do well to learn as much as possible about the children we teach. This is no easy task. We observe them as much and as thoughtfully as we can both in our classrooms and elsewhere. We observe their growth and development to discover

how they think and how their interests and capacities change as they mature.

The Work of Piaget

We are aided in the study of children by those who have made detailed studies of children and have organized, recorded, and interpreted their findings to provide sound approaches to teaching and learning. The work of the Swiss psychologist Jean Piaget, among others, is important.

For over fifty years, Piaget did research into how the minds of children develop. He explored the nature of children's spontaneous ideas about the physical world and the characteristics of their mental processes. He provided insights into the creative nature of children's thinking and found that children think quite differently from adults— a profound idea for teachers to consider, especially when they believe they are pursuing a logical line of reasoning in a lesson.

In addition, Piaget's and his colleagues' observations have revealed insights into how children's learning actually takes place. We say that children "learn by doing." Piaget suggests that children learn by thinking about what they are doing, and that the kind of thinking each child does is related

[1]"What's Your Choice?," *Science and Children* (January 1986).

to the particular level of cognitive (knowledge and understanding) development he or she has reached. The thought process and language development, furthermore, although related, are actually different systems of development. Piaget described four major stages in every child's intellectual development. Each of these stages will be discussed briefly.

Sensory-Motor (0–2 years) At the beginning of the sensory-motor stage, a child has neither sense of objects as distinct from self nor a sense of self as distinct from objects. In other words, when something disappears from sight—a ball rolls away—it is not only out of sight to the infant, but out of mind. As the child approaches the second year of life, a sense of objects develops, a sense of their permanence, and a limited interaction with them, including memory and labeling.

Preoperational (2–7 years) The self-centered nature of the child's view of the world dominates behavior at the preoperational stage. Language is acquired during this period. The child identifies words and symbols and eventually can distinguish between them. A child also discovers and practices symbolic play and experiences dreams for the first time. This stage is considered preoperational because the child is unable to reverse the order of events in thought. Operational thinking involves the ability to reverse events and return to the beginning point.

Concrete Operational (7–11 years) During the concrete operational period, the child develops an ability to reason in a systematic or logical way, from premise to conclusion. As a result, he or she is able to create and follow rules. The child begins to think about things and to see relationships among classes of things.

Formal Operational (12–15 years) At the formal operational stage, the child moves from a dependence on the perception of objects for intellectual stimulation to independent, abstract thinking. The child begins to think about thinking

and to trace step-by-step procedures in solving a problem. It is important to remember that these stages are not watertight compartments: All children are not alike in their development and will not reach the suggested stages at the same time.

Although Piaget and his followers have tried to trace the course of children's mental development, they have not applied their discoveries to methods of teaching school subjects to children. Nevertheless, their findings have influenced the development and placement of content in the elementary school science curriculum. Planners have tried to arrange and sequence science experiences related to what children are able to do at their level of mental development. For example, at the primary level, teachers stress perception activities. For eight- to nine-year-olds, problems that involve concrete and manipulative materials are most successful. Fifth and sixth graders are challenged to use their concrete base of experiences to build and develop abstract ideas.

Tasks In an effort to identify specific intellectual characteristics in children, Piaget and his followers have designed a series of "tasks" that can be used with a learner to reveal what level of mental development has been reached. Ideally, these tasks, if being handled in Piagetian research style, are presented by an interviewer to individual children.

A few samples of the type of Piagetian tasks used to distinguish between preoperational and concrete operational thinking appear in the following section.[2]

Description of Conservation Tasks

Task 1: Conservation of Number Six black checkers in one row and six red checkers in another row are arranged for the child.

[2]Reproduced by permission from J. W. Renner et al., "Piaget IS Practical," *Science and Children* (October 1971). Copyright 1971 by the National Science Teachers Association. See also R. Bybee and A. McCormack, "Applying Piaget's Theory," *Science and Children* (December 1970).

The child is asked if he or she agrees that there are the same number of red checkers as there are black checkers. After the child agrees to this fact, the red checkers are stacked, one on top of the other, and the black checkers are left as they were; the child is then asked the same question again.

To thoroughly understand the concept of number, as opposed to memorizing the digits, or learning how to count, a child must conserve number. Perhaps this will explain why some children have trouble with mathematics in the primary grades.

Task 2: Conservation of Matter Task 2 and the ones that follow require that a child holds the image of an object in his mind while it is distorted and then be able to recognize that the distorted object still has many of the same properties as the nondistorted one.

Present the child with a ball of clay. Ask the child to observe it. Then roll the clay into a long cylinder—a "snake." Ask, "Does the snake have less, more, or the same amount of clay as the ball?" (If the child is confused, say, "Was the ball bigger, smaller, or the same size as the snake?") *Justification*: Then ask the child, "Why did you think the snake was (bigger, smaller, the same)?"

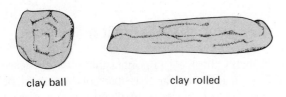

clay ball   clay rolled

Task 3: Conservation of Volume Use two jars (a baby food jar and a tall cylinder) and enough colored water to fill the tall jar. Present the jars,

with the water in the short jar. Ask, "What will happen if I pour the water into the tall jar? Will I have more, less, or the same amount of water?" Pour the water into the second container. "Is there less, more, or the same amount of water?" *Justification*: Then ask the child, "Why did you think the amount of water was (more, less, the same)?"

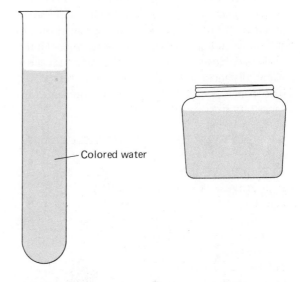

Colored water

Task 4: Ordering Events Say, "For this problem you will think about how a pencil falls. This is what I mean." (Place a pencil in a vertical position on a desk and allow it to fall to a horizontal position on the desk.) "Here are some drawings of the pencil falling. Place them in order showing how the pencil would look as it falls." *Justifica-*

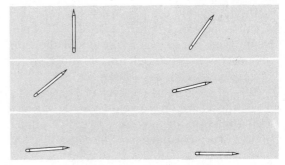

tion: Then ask the child, "Why did you place the pictures in the order you did?"

Task 5: Conservation of Length   Use a complete and a sectional straw. Start with both straws lined up parallel. (See Figure A.) Note with the child that both straws are the same length. Move the straws to the position shown in Figure B. Ask, "Would two ants starting a hike at this end of the straws (point to one end) and walking *at the same speed* both finish the hike at this point (point to the other end of straws) at the same time?" (If the child is confused, ask, "Would they both travel the same distance?") *Justification*: Then repeat the question, "Would they both travel the same distance? Why do you think so?"

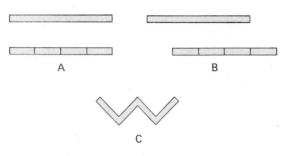

Now move the straws from Figure B into the position shown in Figure C. Repeat the question, "Would the ants both travel the same distance?" *Justification*: "Why do you think so?"

Task 6: Conservation of Area   Present the child with two identical pieces of green construction paper. Tell him or her that these represent fields or pastures. Place one toy animal on each piece of paper.

Ask the child to compare the fields. Note they are the same size. Comment that since the fields are the same size each animal will have the same amount of grass to eat. Tell the child you are going to use blocks to represent barns.

Next, place four barns on each of the two fields. (Leave the animal on the field.) Ask, "Now which animal will have the most grass to eat, or will the amount of grass be the same?" *Justification*: "Why

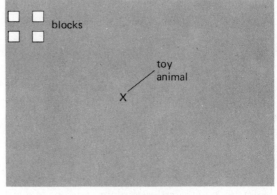

Clustered barns
Field A

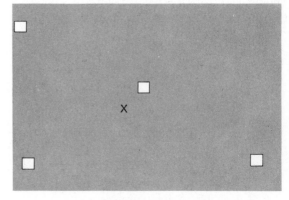

Spread-out barns
Field B

do you think this is true?" Continue adding equal numbers of barns to each field. Each time repeat the question, "Which animal will have the most grass to eat?"

Implications for Teaching Science

Probably the most important thing we can learn from Piaget's research is that children must be allowed to experience firsthand as many objects and events as possible so that they can develop their own creative powers. Further, children must be able to share their experiences with others, to consider other viewpoints, and to evaluate these social interactions thoughtfully. Finally, Piaget's research has reinforced the idea that children need to explore the physical properties of objects especially in their early years.[3]

Teachers will find it interesting and enlightening to try out some of these tasks with children. Perhaps the most important *application* of Piaget's ideas about science teaching is that it makes us pause when we meet failure or difficulty in planning and ask ourselves, "Are we asking a question that is beyond children's present stage of development?" For example, when are children or an individual child able to distinguish between the concept "metal" and a specific metal like "iron"? (See the experience with magnets on pp. 556–557.) When we meet with such a difficulty we might try to set up a Piagetian-type task to check.

We can often avoid difficulties of a developmental nature if we listen carefully to the questions children ask naturally. Even then we must probe a bit because children do not always mean what you think they do (from Piaget). When children ask "Why is it raining?" they do not always want the scientific cloud condensation story; at a certain level what they really want to know is "Who made it rain?" They may not be interested in or able to understand the scientific explanation.

It is also helpful in launching a topic to ask, "What would you like to know about . . . ?" For example, when a question like this was asked about spaceships, a variety of questions was asked that guided the discussion that followed. The teacher was surprised at the great number of questions about the physical conditions of life for the astronauts—food, toilet, and so on—and the few questions about actual rocket propulsion.

Bruner and Gagné

We make reference to the work of Jerome Bruner in Chapters 1 and 4. For the study of science in the elementary school, he urges us to begin with a focus on the manipulation of materials. The child, he says, makes connections between experiences he or she is having in the outside world with models already in mind. In other words, it is not usually something *outside* the learner that is discovered but a reorganization of previously known ideas.[4]

Essentially Bruner organizes the development of children into three stages that correspond somewhat with those of Piaget that we described earlier. An important difference lies in the concept of language and its use. Piaget, you remember, believed that the thought process and language development, although they are related, are actually different systems of development. Bruner assumes that thought arises from within and is essentially internalized language. The learner then transfers these experiences into language useful in thinking.

Bruner has exercised a primary influence on establishing the discovery-learning processes. He describes the learning processes as acquiring knowledge, applying this knowledge to unfamiliar situations, and then evaluating the applications and knowledge. Thus the science program should be centered around the important science ideas (conceptual schemes) and skills. The selection of this subject material and these skills should conform to the child's stages of development.

Further applications of Bruner's ideas lead us to emphasize learning by discovery-inquiry. Children so far as is possible use the skills of inquiry and discover for themselves. As we have emphasized in other discussions the emphasis is on children *learning how to learn*.

---

[3]For further information, see E. A. Crittenden, "Piaget and Elementary Science," *Science and Children* (December 1970); C. S. Lavatelli, *Piaget's Theory Applied to an Early Childhood Education Curriculum* (Boston: A Center for Media Development, 1970); J. Piaget, *The Child's Conception of the World* (New York: Harcourt, Brace, 1929); B. J. Wadsworth, *Piaget for the Classroom Teacher* (New York: Longmans, 1978).

[4]J. S. Bruner, *Toward a Theory of Instruction* (The Belnap Press of Harvard University Press, 1966); H. V. Peckins, *Human Development and Learning* (Wadsworth, 1970).

Robert Gagné begins his approach to learning by an analysis of the instructional objectives. He asks, "*What* is it that you want the learner to know or to be able to do?" and urges that these be stated *specifically* as behaviors—a stress on the ability to perform certain specific tasks under specific conditions. In contrast, Bruner asks, "*How* do you want the child to know?" Both consider knowledge as the major objective, but their concepts of *knowledge* and *knowing* are quite different. With this in mind, we see Gagné's students actively involved in step-by-step procedures. The sequence is from the simple to the complex as a child progresses. With the use of the various skills of inquiry the learner also comes to possess knowledge of scientific principles.[5]

Thus Gagné concentrates on a hierarchy of learning capabilities. Each learning ability depends on having understood a previously learned one. This progression of learning levels continues throughout the school experience. In the early grades of the elementary school, children will have experiences involving observing, use of numbers, simple manipulative skills, describing, and classifying. Later, elementary children will build on these and begin to assemble a background of knowledge in the many areas of science. Building on these skills and knowledge, the student concentrates on methods of inquiry in a more advanced, organized, and sophisticated manner.

Piaget, Bruner, and Gagné—all concerned as they are with child development—are important when we consider curriculum and methods of teaching in elementary school science.

Research and the Teacher

The theories of psychologists and others who do research in learning give us some directions for establishing curriculum and for directing the learning activities of children. The teacher is the important activist in translating these theories into actions. As the teacher observes children learning, the following implications of research must be kept in mind:

1. Begin learning where the children are: Concepts that are too hard are discouraging, and those that are too easy cause children to become disinterested.
2. Readiness to learn a particular concept is important. What related experiences have children had? How can we build on these experiences?
3. Sequence in learning is important. New experiences must develop new ideas not just repeat previous ones. There must be conscious efforts to help students see relationships between old and new. This applies to concepts development, development of skills of inquiry, and other aspects of the learning process.
4. Readiness to learn plus motivation are essential to the learning experience. What interests and what rewards can motivate the learning?
5. Development of the *processes* of learning come along with the *product* of learning; the teacher gives attention to both.
6. Hands-on experiences should be emphasized. They should result in development of the improved skills of careful observation, increased ability to devise experiments, and learning both to draw valid conclusions and to evaluate experiences.
7. *The teacher is a researcher*, working in the classroom environment with the minds and muscles of today's children and making discoveries for herself or himself.

Progress in improving the teaching process depends on the teacher's ability to study and learn about the students. This includes attention to such problems as (1) What activities seem most challenging and interesting to children? (2) What procedures and situations seem to block learning of children? (3) What procedures are needed to help children focus on the objectives involved? (4) How can methods of instruction and material to be learned be adjusted to the various levels of interest and abilities of children? (5) What can be done to stimulate interest of students who appear not to be challenged?

[5]"Theories of Learning and Curriculum Planning," in *Readings in Science Education: A Source Book* (New York: McGraw-Hill, 1974); R. M. Gagné and L. J Briggs, *Principles of Instructional Design*, 2d ed. (New York: Holt, 1979); R. M. Gagné, *The Conditions of Learning* (New York: Holt, 1977).

We direct your attention to the material contained in the publications *What Research Says to the Science Teacher,* Vols. I–V, published by NSTA. Materials from these volumes are footnoted elsewhere.

Knowledge of Children: A Guide to Instruction

We study the nature of children because it guides us in selecting and organizing the material we teach, in determining our methods of instruction, and in learning to adjust these methods and the curriculum to fit the needs, interests, and abilities of children. The following summary indicates how knowledge of children results in better teaching.

1. Knowledge of how children learn indicates that *we help them most when we help them discover, help them see relationships in these discoveries, and organize what they discover into meaningful ideas.* We find that they learn how to learn better through such experience rather than by being told, and that a variety of learning experiences is highly desirable.
2. Observation and experience also indicate that *what the child learns depends in part on what he or she already knows and thus can bring to the new situation.* This idea gives some clues about the importance of a developmental curriculum (see Chapter 4).
3. Anyone who has observed children knows that *they are "natural born" investigators.* This tendency indicates the importance of providing opportunities for them to manipulate, to try out, to see "what will happen if..." and take apart and put back together. It is important to try to keep this desire alive by providing opportunity for it to grow and develop. Without encouragement this sense of inquiry may completely disappear by the time the child has passed through the elementary school. Sometimes our approach is so academic that children with this natural tendency to manipulate have to wait until Saturday when they are free and can express it. Good teachers realize the value of this inclination and apply it to more *purposeful doing* in science teaching.
4. *Children are interested in, and react to, all aspects of their environment.* Interest studies seem to show, as everyone who has worked thoughtfully with children knows, that children's questions concern all kinds of environmental objects and phenomena— astronomy, electricity, jet planes, spaceships, and dinosaurs.
5. *Children like to plan and carry out their plans.* When they have opportunities to plan they become increasingly able to do this as they grow and develop. The examples of classroom procedures described in this book show how children may help to plan ways for solving their problems and to continue planning as they proceed in their experimenting, reading, observing, and other experiences. If more attention is paid to children's desire for participation—the importance of which is difficult to overestimate—we as teachers must make fewer of the planning decisions ourselves and place more and more responsibility on the children. This does not mean that the teacher is unimportant in the plans: The teacher knows many things that should be considered in planning and should not hesitate to use this knowledge when it is advisable.
6. *There is no reason to expect all children to arrive at an understanding of a science concept at the same time.* Even though children may all be exposed to the same experiences, each child may arrive at different concepts as a result of these experiences. Furthermore, these concepts may not be the ones the teacher had in mind; they may be quite different. There is also great variation in the abilities of children to carry on the various aspects of inquiry. These change as children mature. Some of this variation may be due to the differences that exist between the teacher's objectives and those of children. We are often inclined to believe that the two are the same when in reality they may be quite different.
7. These circumstances indicate that *we must evaluate, insofar as possible, on an individual basis and that the evaluations must be continuous.* The fact that many different types of activities (experimenting, observing, reading, and so on) are involved in science investigating makes it possible for students of varying interests and aptitudes to participate.
8. It seems reasonable to assume that *children who have a purpose will work more profitably than those who do not.* The more the child sees the sense of this purpose, the better. We all know that motivation is an extremely important factor to learning success. When children want to learn they usually do. As teachers, the more we learn about how to motivate children the more success we are likely to have.

Keeping these eight points in mind, let's examine some of the ways we use them to help children attain the goals for science teaching.

INVESTIGATING AND EXPERIMENTING

There is something fascinating to children about experimenting. "Great, we're going to experiment today!" may be heard, when science material is brought out. This interest in "trying out" is an important one to capitalize on. We should not take away any of the fun of experimenting, but at the same time we should help children to realize that experimenting is an important aspect of the inquiry method of attempting to discover answers.

Following printed directions and recording the results in blank spaces is not experimenting in its best sense. Following the recipe is generally quite sufficient when baking a cake, but our goals for experimenting are quite different. There is a significant difference between an experiment and some of the experiences we sometimes call experiments: An experiment involves a problem for which students and sometimes the teacher do not know a solution.

There are many examples of very young children experimenting. When children in the kindergarten try to find out how to dry wet mittens quickly, and place one on a hot radiator and one on a pie plate on a table, they may be dealing with hypotheses, variables, and controls. Although they are not expressing it in words, they are *hypothesizing*—"I think my mittens will dry faster on the radiator." They are testing one *variable* (heat); they are using *controls* (comparing the glove on the radiator to its mate on the pie plate). Of course, this is not a perfectly designed experiment in a technical sense. (Were the two mittens equally wet to begin with? How do we know when they are equally dry?) But these and other shortcomings are less important at this stage than they are later. It is important for the teacher to recognize this as a good opportunity for making children aware that they have discovered or tested something by experimenting. It is also significant

that the experiment began and ended in the real world of the children.

When children roll balls down an incline and try to discover how to make them roll farther by proposing to make the incline steeper, and then trying this out, they are also hypothesizing, using variables, measuring, and drawing conclusions.

In connection with experimenting on a somewhat more advanced level, consider this illustration.

Students in a sixth-grade class have learned how to make electromagnets by winding a coil of insulated wire around an iron core (a large nail) and then connecting the ends of the wire to a dry cell (see Chapter 17B, pp. 562–563). They have found that an electromagnet, like the permanent magnet they are familiar with, attracts iron, has poles, and is strongest at its poles. As students compare their electromagnets and discover that some are stronger than others (determined by their ability to pick up paper clips and lift heavy iron or steel objects) a question arises. "How can we make our electromagnets stronger?" This is where the experiment begins!

Various ways are suggested: Wind more turns of wire around the nail, use a larger nail or a number of nails, use more dry cells, and other methods. Committees are formed to test each idea, and a master plan is devised to conduct the tests and record the results. It is agreed that in each case the electromagnet is to be dipped into a pile of steel paper clips and the number pulled up are to be counted and recorded. The students find that all methods work in varying degrees, some better than others. Along the way new problems arise: How many extra turns of wire help? Is there a limit? How many nails in the iron core are best? Should the dry cells be connected in series or in parallel?

What is good about this procedure? The experimenting was done in response to a challenging problem; experimenting seemed the logical way to attempt to find answers. The design for the experiment and the plan for its use was made by students with some help from the teacher. The students made some observations and predictions and did not generalize from too little evidence. The experience contributed something toward accomplishing the overall objectives of science teaching. The children were actively involved in the inquiry activity.

Reexamine the discussion of behavioral objectives in Chapter 2. What behaviors can we expect as the result of many experiences such as the one described here? *After* you have attempted to answer this question read the concluding statements in this section (see item 15, p. 40).

What is also significant is the spirit—*the atmosphere*—of the classroom. The teacher encouraged students to experiment. Opportunity was provided for them to engage in informal activity and free exchange to show each other what they had observed. They felt the classroom was the place to ask and investigate. They were involved in a hands-on activity. The "solutions" opened up new problems. Further open-endedness may be encouraged by questions beginning: "What would happen if . . . ?" "Where could you find . . . ?" "What other ways are there of . . . ?" "How could you show that . . . ?" "How could you make a . . . ?" Other illustrations of such ideas will be found in the B chapters.[6]

A further improvement in experimenting is to make the results more scientific through the use of mathematics. Both science and mathematics are made more meaningful when they are related. This use of mathematical skills runs all the way from counting the number of paper clips that different electromagnets can hold to measuring the lengths of shadows made by a stick at various times of day. It might include such projects as working out the relationships of the amount of effort needed to lift a weight to the length of the part of the lever on which force is being applied. Where feasible, graphs should be used to show changes and relationships.

[6]L. G. Geller, "Conversations in Kindergarten," *Science and Children* (April 1985). A complete lesson that illustrates how a teacher elicited and encouraged free discussion of the meaning of "space," in which answers were sought by the children but not provided by the teacher.

In connection with the use of mathematics we should take into account the certainty that the United States is slowly converting to the metric system. Such a transition will involve much direct teaching in schools. When we measure distance, weight, and so on, in science we have opportunities for practical and meaningful experiences with the metric system. Teachers will need to accept that they will be teaching dual measurement systems for their entire career. (See Chapter 5 for a detailed discussion and suggestions.)

The following are specific suggestions to help make investigating and experimenting more effective.

1. *Keep the experiment simple,* or break a complicated experiment into simple parts. Whenever possible use simple homemade equipment. At times, however, it will be important for children to use more sophisticated apparatus and materials such as weighing scales, microscopes, and thermometers.
2. *Provide opportunities that require children to think.* If you plan to *tell* children the answers or let them read the answers, why bother to experiment? Experimenting to find answers to a genuine problem raised by children is sure to be more thought-provoking than experimenting to demonstrate something that is already known by many of the students.
3. *Let students do as much of the planning as they can.* Then follow the plan. When it is necessary to make changes, students will have some basis for making them, because they themselves helped make the original plan.
4. *Challenge students when they make sweeping generalizations from one experiment.* "Magnets will pick up all nails." After a limited experience with a box of nails the teacher may say, "Do all of you believe that we can say this?" The discussion will result in further experimentation.
5. *Keep experiments simple and safe enough for students to do by themselves.* If classes are large and there is sufficient material available, subjects may work in groups to give many of them the opportunity for experimentation. It is often possible to leave the material available for individual use at a learning center or station (see pp. 46–48), where a child might explore at his or her own pace. The

best situation exists when *every* child has an opportunity to experiment or engage in the activity.

6. *Provide opportunities for children to react to. "Can anyone think of something we can try or some ways of experimenting that may help us solve this problem?"* This procedure gives a chance for real thought, careful planning, organizing, predicting, and interpreting. We reiterate: Do not expect all young students to be proficient with these in-depth skills.

7. *Help students to apply the information gained by experimenting to the world about them.* It is this application to real-life situations that is often missed.

8. *Urge students to keep in mind the purposes of experimenting.* It is often advisable to have on the chalkboard a simple statement of the problem to guide the thinking as the experimenting goes on and as the conclusions are drawn. Individual students with varying backgrounds and interests should be encouraged, as time and space allow, to follow their own paths. The examples of open-endedness throughout this book illustrate the point.

9. *It is not always necessary or desirable for students to make a complete record of the procedures and results of an experiment.* Sometimes it seems sensible to record in a sentence or two the important discoveries of an experiment, either for future reference or to be sure that the ideas are clearly understood. If the experiment is one that takes several days to complete, it may be helpful to record each day's observations by making drawings, writing a short paragraph, or by making a graph or chart of the findings. The guiding idea may well be: "Is there any good reason for writing, or communicating in some other way, anything about this experiment?"

10. *Keep experiments as "scientific" as possible,* stressing the importance of control of the variables. For example, if the importance of light to plants is being investigated, light should be the only variable. A number of plants should be kept in the dark, a number of similar plants in the light. But all other conditions should be the same for both groups.

11. Remember that *when experiments do not follow the predicted path, real problems arise,* and students, in attempting to discover why, think more, plan better, and learn more. In a truly scientific sense every experiment "works" although it may not take the course anticipated.

12. Remember also that *an experiment is an experiment in the true sense only if students do not already know the outcome.* Such experiments will provide opportunity for thoughtful observing, communicating, and interpreting.

13. *Include mathematics* as part of the observations and predictions. Record measurable data, and chart or graph results whenever possible.

14. *Emphasize interdisciplinary aspects* of activities and experiments whenever possible in writing, reading, and other forms of communication.

15. *Keep in mind the behaviors expected* that can result as children participate in science experimenting. For example, after students experiment with an electromagnet, we expect that they will be able to (1) *construct* an electromagnet, (2) manipulate an electromagnet to *test* its strength, (3) *understand* that an electric current has a magnetic effect, (4) *describe* and *compare* different ways of making an electromagnet stronger, (5) *record* the results of the experiments.

This book cannot possibly provide an exhaustive list of experiments in the chapters that follow. However, many are included and suggestions are made for helping students devise others. The 15 points just given are illustrated in the examples you will find throughout the B chapters. Science books are rich sources of experiments.

READING TO FIND OUT

"Reading, writing, and science are—or should be—inseparable because the science activities that introduce children to a particular way of looking at the natural world also help them gain the skills they will need as readers."[7]

Despite our emphasis on firsthand experiences—experimenting, direct observation, and doing—let's not neglect reading as a way to learn science. It is legitimate to read. Children cannot learn everything by experimenting or by firsthand experiences. Neither can anyone else. We learn

[7]R. J. Fisher and R. L. Fisher, "Reading, Writing and Science," *Science and Children* (September 1985).

Reading opens new doors to children. *Photo by William E. Mills, Montgomery County Public Schools, Maryland.*

much from reading textbooks, supplementary books, bulletins, magazines, and newspapers, as well as from written records.[8]

There is presently much emphasis on "the three Rs" in our schools. Probably the R that gets the star for emphasis is reading. It is also the target of much criticism. "Our children can't read" is a common comment. Some of them can't, and there are a variety of reasons. High on the list is the matter of interest. Many children do not connect with many of the words and sentences that are put before them. A well-known reading expert has said, "If you don't have anything to read *onto* a page you are not likely to get much from it." For many children (especially beginners), science ex-

periences have often been the motivating key that unlocks the words and sentences.

To be specific: The children in a first grade have several goldfish in their aquarium. In small groups the children are asked to observe the fish to see what they can discover. After the experience the teacher brings the group together to share their observations. Then they make a record of some of the observations. Several students supply these sentences and the teacher writes them on the chalkboard:

There are five fish in our aquarium.
The fish move their mouths.
The fish move in the water.
The fish move up and down.

The children are urged to read the sentences, first in unison, then individually. They help each

---

[8]D. Norton and D. Janke, "Improving Science Reading Ability," *Science and Children* (January 1983). A practical treatment.

other when necessary. They make a list of unfamiliar words: aquarium, move, mouths. They are urged to copy their own records.

The teacher frequently uses such an experience chart, and the children make their own copies and perhaps collect them as a book. They also add the words to their own vocabulary lists. Experience charts are standard procedures for elementary school teachers. Science experiences are natural subjects for these charts.

Such a chart, entitled "Robert's Rabbit," was made about a rabbit Robert had brought. When Robert's mother visited the room later on Parents' Day, Robert proudly read the account and finished by saying, "That story is about me!"

Although experience charts shouldn't be overdone and are certainly not the cure for all reading ills, they do give children the opportunity to observe, report, listen, discuss, record, read, and use other language-arts skills at the same time that they are learning science. There is no doubt that the present emphasis on reading can reduce the time available for the science program. But it is also true that the study of science and the emphasis on reading skills can go hand in hand to achieve the general goals of the elementary school experience.

Reading is sometimes condemned as a way to learn science because it is often used so much that the science course degenerates into a course of reading about science. This criticism is leveled not against reading as a way to learn but against the way in which we use reading and the amount of reading we do. Let us examine one way to use a science book as a way to learn.

Assume that the area of study has been decided on: Children are going to study sound. One of the big problems is "How are sounds made?" Suppose we begin by suggesting to the class that each student bring something that will make a sound. To heighten interest we may say, "Try to bring something that no one else will think of."

As preparation for attempting to solve this problem, you, the teacher, have read carefully the section in the students' textbook about sound, and have also read Chapters 18A and B in this book; you have explored to see what other reading materials are available; you have located in the school building and in the neighborhood examples of the use of the principles of sound; and you have assembled some material you may need that the children probably cannot find themselves.

The next day, students come in with their sound-makers. You suggest that as each child demonstrates his or her sound-maker, students observe carefully to (1) see what makes the sound, and (2) tell how the sounds are different from each other. This procedure may promote interest, stimulate observations, and raise questions and problems.

The sound making begins. Ned has brought his violin, Charlie his trumpet, and they make sounds with them. Mary and Alice use rubber bands, plucking them when they are stretched; Paul stands up in front of everybody and shouts. "Hey!" There are several other examples of sound. After these demonstrations you suggest that everybody listen quietly to hear any sounds around them. They hear the clock tick. A car starts up outside, and the sound changes as the car gains speed. Across the street someone is hammering—perhaps driving a nail into a board. A bell rings somewhere in the school building. The big problems are "What makes sounds?" and then "How are they made?"

After each sound is made, the students state what they think may be the answers to the two questions. They formulate hypotheses. "It's made if something moves." "You have to hit something." "Some are made in one way, some in another." They are not at all sure what it is that makes the sounds, but they have classified them. Some are loud, some soft, some high, some low. There is discussion about how Paul made sound when he said, "Hey!"

"Let's feel our throats when we talk," the teacher suggests. "Something in there quivers," somebody volunteers. "That's what my violin string does when I draw the bow across it. It vibrates," Ned says. But what is it that makes the sound? The teacher suggests that students observe closely to see if something is vibrating. They set up further experiments to test this idea. But other questions have arisen, for example, "What has this to do with the sound I hear, and how does the sound get to my ears?"

Students are now faced with a problem they cannot solve through the use of experiences and experiments alone. This is a time for reading. The teacher has assembled a number of library books, and the students also find the section on sound in their textbooks if they are available. They find pictures that show students making sounds. The students read to see whether they can discover answers to their questions. They read about vibrations. They find experiences they can have with a tuning fork. The teacher produces tuning forks. "How can we use these to help us?" she asks. The students suggest ways. They feel the vibrations in the tuning forks. Mary and Alice are asked to demonstrate their rubber bands again, because the book mentions vibration in connection with rubber bands of various sizes. After these experiences students return to their books and finish reading about vibrations, how they make sounds, and how sounds travel in waves from place to place.

As the study proceeds, the students read further, study pictures and diagrams in their books, search for supplementary books on the subject of sound, pursue some of the experiences described in the books, follow up some of their own experiments, and do other things to find information. Bibliographies provide an extensive list of books of a supplementary nature. These books often supply the exact material needed, and should be relied on heavily for their contribution to the science program.

Contrast the foregoing procedure with: "Today we are going to study sound. Open your books to page 18. Read the first six pages and then answer the questions on page 24."

There is much to be said in favor of building a classroom library of science books in addition to the basic text or texts: (1) They meet the needs of *individual* children, (2) they provide in-depth information, (3) children develop the habit of using many sources, (4) they permit pupils to work

independently, and (5) they may serve with special effectiveness those students who have reading difficulty.

In one fifth-grade class the teacher obtained the help of the school librarian in assembling all of the resources available for a unit on "An Expedition to Mars." Encyclopedias, trade books, magazines, picture files, and newspaper clippings covering the subject were placed on tables in the library. Children inspected these. Finally each child was allowed to borrow items and report to the class an important idea or experiment that was helpful in planning an expedition. The purpose here was, of course, not only to develop the unit but to help children gain library skills and intrigue them with the fascination, beauty, and range of the books and other materials available.

Reading, then, is one of the important tools to use in learning science. We can step up the effectiveness of reading if we keep in mind the following guidelines:

1. Read with specific purpose—to check conclusions, to answer a question or find information helpful in solving a problem, to find additional information, to learn how to experiment, or for other reasons. Helping children to be selective in recording and reporting only the material that is appropriate to solving problems may be one of the most important skills children learn as they read in science.
2. Reading is more effective if it is done from several supplementary sources that provide more information and different points of view. Communicating the results then becomes a part of the science experience, because not everyone has read the same material.
3. Selecting the material to be read may be done by both the students and teacher. Tables of contents, indexes, and other reference tools are necessary. Students may take notes on their reading. This may be an essential part of the "research reading" done in science. Selecting material on varying levels of difficulty is essential if reading is to function as a tool for learning. In any grade it is unusual for all students to be ready to read the science book written for that grade.
4. Selecting books for use by children should be done with considerable care. For example, they should

be up-to-date and accurate; the illustrations should be attractive and helpful; the writing should be clear and appropriate to the subject matter; the entire work should be directed toward helping children achieve the objectives we have set up for the science program.

5. Science is also an important experience when very young children are getting ready to read. The conversations about science objects and questions, the use of new words, the labeling of science material, and many other more or less incidental activities are all experiences that contribute to helping children connect words and sentences to the reading process.[9]

Let's also remember that reading opens new doors to children, that an interest in science developed in the classroom will stimulate children to read for pleasure—about spaceships, stars, or dinosaurs, for example. The possibilities are endless. "However, like all other skills, reading critically . . . must be taught and practiced."[10] See also the section "The Curriculum and the Textbook" in Chapter 4.

WRITING TO EXPRESS IDEAS

"Competency in writing can only be accomplished through active practice, not simply by learning discrete grammatical skills. Children need motivators to develop their writing abilities. Obviously, science activities are natural vehicles for increasing writing competence."[11] In this quote, "practice," "motivators," and "increasing competence" are key words that suggest the

relationship between science experiences and writing.

No one questions the importance of developing children's ability to express themselves in writing. It clarifies their ideas, helps them organize their thoughts, gives them experience in expression, and can develop their creative ability. There are plenty of opportunities resulting from science experiences for writing sentences, descriptive paragraphs, stories, directions that describe how experiments can be done, and so forth. An important aspect of these experiences is that the opportunities are not manufactured—they are a part of the total science activities. They can also provide an opportunity for creativity and permit self-expression for each child. Summary sentences that tell what has been discovered, descriptions of projects for others to read, letters of appreciation for help on a museum trip, creative letters to imagined characters—all will be encouraged.

Requests for materials are examples of real reasons to write. A word of caution here. Urge children to be specific with their requests. "Send me everything you have about earthquakes" is not practical! Send only one letter, not one from each student, and if possible on school letter paper.

Any science unit can be enriched by allowing and encouraging children to express what happened in their own language, to record their thoughts rather than those of the teacher. Again, let's not overdo the writing idea lest we put ourselves in the position of the child who said during a field trip, "Don't look, or Miss Agnes will make you write!" There will be many examples of the use of writing skills in the activities described in the B chapters that follow.

Eddie Whitfield and Larry Hovey[12] suggest that teachers "consider the advantages of regularly

[9]D. B. Neuman, "Promoting Reading Readiness through Science," *Science and Children* (September 1981).

[10]Gwyn Carl, "The Well-Read Textbook," *The Science Teacher* (March 1987). Good practical suggestions.

[11]M. S. Simon and J. M. Zimmerman, "Science and Writing," *Science and Children* (November/December 1980); S. Koeller, "Expository Writing: A Vital Skill in Science," *Science and Children* (September 1982); Edna D. Main, "Science and Creative Writing. A Dynamic Duo," *Science and Children* (January 1984). Specific suggestions.

[12]"Science in the News," *Science and Children* (January 1980). The following feature topics are suggested: Weather News, Seasonal News, Famous Scientists, Interviews, Sky News, Health News, Animal News, Future Predictions, Field Trip News, Science Economic News, Home Experiments, Science Career News, Plant News, and Letters to the Editor.

publishing a classroom newspaper devoted to science. Such a project can be a valuable way to promote more science in the curriculum and can also reinforce basic skills in reading, writing, spelling, interviewing, researching, reporting, and experimenting."

OBSERVING

When children bring an unfamiliar science "thing" to school, the wise teacher may say, "Let's examine it carefully to see what we can find out." The senses are used to gather information that may be used in making discoveries. This is an important method of inquiry. What can you find out by looking, feeling, listening, and using your other senses? The observations are assembled. Questions are raised, and now there is some information to use as students plan other means of gaining more information. Effective science experiences often begin with thoughtful observation.

We hope children will become more skillful in observing, more accurate in reporting what they see, and more scientific in their interpretations. Observing is not a skill divorced from experimenting, reading, and other ways to learn. It is an essential part of all activities that students engage in. As we shall see in the following examples, observing is prerequisite to predicting and inferring, to comparing and contrasting, and to interpreting. Children should grow in ability to differentiate between the process of observation and the inferring that they may do as a result of the observations. Students can learn to become more accurate observers as they progress in their study of science, and see that observing and using the results of their observations are two different processes.[13]

[13]Margaret McIntyre, "Learning to Observe Animals," *Science and Children* (May 1981). Gives excellent guides helpful in observation of animals. C. C. Cleare, "Scallops, Whelks and the Process Skills," *Science and Children* (April 1985). A practical lesson with the use of a shell collection, or a good reason for making one.

As children report what they see, the teacher and students will often discover variations in what individual children report even though they have all been observing the same objects or processes. It is often worthwhile to investigate the reasons for such differences. For example, each first grader was given a pea pod and asked to report the number of peas in his or her pod. The variation reported ranged from three to nine peas. Investigation of the reports showed the following: (1) The number of peas in the pod does vary; (2) Joe and Joan ate some of their peas; (3) Rosa lost some of hers when she popped open the pod; (4) Since there were some undeveloped peas in some of the pods, some asked if these should be counted or not.

We often characterize a good observer as one who has learned to use his or her senses—to feel, see, hear, smell, and taste—purposefully. In a study of sound, children *feel* vibrations of a piano, *see* the vibrating strings, and *hear* the sound. Careful use of the senses makes learning more vivid. Students observe to see changes in seeds as they sprout and to see changes in frog eggs as they hatch.

As we have said, we must help children to distinguish between an observation and interpretation. For example, a jar of water is exposed for a number of weeks. The level of water is marked on the jar. Children *observe* that the level is 6 inches deep (about 15 centimeters) at the beginning, $5\frac{1}{2}$ inches deep (about 14 centimeters) one week later, $4\frac{1}{2}$ inches (about 11 centimeters) two weeks later, and so on. An *interpretation* of the data is that the water level in the container dropped consistently over a two-week period. Moreover, the interpretation placed on the data provides a basis for *prediction*: "What do you think will happen in the weeks to come?" This may lead to hypothesizing: What really happened to the water? They may say, "It went into the air." Their hypothesis may then lead to *experimenting*. Although we are not suggesting that the steps always take place in this order, they are the processes used in learning, and these steps often begin with observation.

In summary, the following criteria are helpful in evaluating observational skills:

1. Do children use all of their senses in describing objects or events? *Example:* Ask children to recall what they observed during a thunderstorm. Ask them to recall different odors they sense in a walk around the school building (an odor hunt).
2. Can the children distinguish between what they expect to happen and what really happens? *Example:* Ask children to predict which of the following objects will, if dropped, strike the floor first: a penny or a half dollar. They will usually predict that the heavier object will hit the floor first. Is this what they report after the trial is conducted?
3. Are they aware of changes? *Example:* Has the water level in the aquarium changed since Friday?
4. Can they compare? *Example:* How are these leaves (or rocks, bones, etc.) similar? How are they different?

USING LEARNING CENTERS[14]

Learning in science, as well as in other areas of the curriculum, is an individual matter. Many different learning situations have been devised to make this possible. Among them is the learning station or learning center. A typical example is pictured and described here. Let's examine the picture and description and then discuss in some detail the varieties, purposes, and some practical aspects of learning centers.

In this example there are four related learning units on the table. This may be ideal for a small schoolroom or where teachers and students are just beginning to experiment with the idea of learning situations. Materials to develop concepts about magnets and magnetism may be placed in each station. The children progress from station 1 to station 2, and so on.

[14]P. C. Manning, "Creating Science Inquiry Centers," *Science and Children* (April 1980); D. C. Orlie, R. Grebhardt, R. Harms, and G. Ward, "Science Learning Centers—An Aid to Instruction," *Science and Children* (September 1982); K. A. O'Sullivan, "Creating a Learning Center," *Science and Children* (March 1984). Specific suggestions.

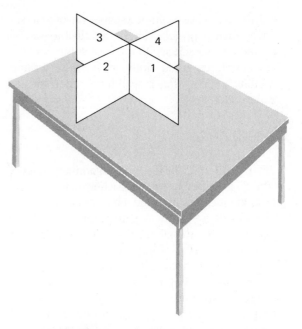

Station 1:   May contain a magnet and a variety of materials to see which ones a magnet will attract. This may be accompanied by duplicated record sheets for the children to use to indicate results. Each child or small group of children will fill in the record. The problem in this station may be *which of these materials will a magnet attract?*

Station 2:   May contain several shapes and sizes of magnets (bar magnet, horseshoe magnet, etc.) along with a box of thumbtacks or paper clips. The problem here may be *which of these magnets do you think is strongest?* The record sheet may contain an outline drawing of each magnet. Opposite each, a space may be provided for children to record results.

Station 3:   May consist of several magnets and a box of paper clips. The problem is *where do you think these magnets are strongest?* The record sheets may contain drawings of the magnets with the directions to place an X at the strongest points on the magnets.

Station 4:   May contain the material for finding out *which of these materials will magnetism travel through?* Use a magnet and some thumbtacks, a piece of cardboard, a glass of water (to test water and glass), a thin piece of wood, a flat piece of copper, and one of iron. Use small drawings to show how to use the apparatus and a mimeographed list of the materials with space to check "yes" and "don't know."

Other questions for a higher grade using this same station setup may be for electrical experiments. For example:

1. *Can you make this nail into a magnet?* Needed: magnet, iron nail, insulated copper wire, a knife switch, a dry cell, and some thumbtacks. Children may make a record by finishing a partly completed diagram. See Chapter 17A.
2. *Can you make a circuit that will make this light go on?* Needed: dry cell, insulated wire, light in socket. A simple record-keeping page may be mimeographed for each problem. See Chapter 17B for further suggestions of possible problems.

To develop observational skills[15] some of the following activities may be set up in stations, each of which is equipped with a magnifying glass and a choice of the following materials:

1. A pinch of beach sand on a piece of paper and a toothpick to separate the grains. *What are the colors of the sand grains? What are their shapes? How many grains are there in your sample?*
2. A fresh flower, tweezers, and a labeled diagram of the flower. You are permitted to take the flower apart. *What parts can you find? What color are they?* Draw one part of the flower and label it. *Can you see pollen grains?*
3. Crystals of table salt and Epsom salt: *What shapes do the crystals have?*

Note: Ideally table salt (sodium chloride) crystals are cube-shaped, but when commercially prepared may have altered shapes.

4. Germinating radish seeds (see p. 295). Find root hairs on a root. *Can you guess how many are on a single root?*
5. Seeds used as spices: banana-shaped caraway seeds, bean-shaped poppy seeds, basketball-shaped whole black pepper seeds, and others. Draw each kind of seed.
6. A flashlight bulb. *Can you see the filament of the bulb? What is its shape?* Draw it.

After the children have completed their tasks at the stations they may discuss their findings individually with the teacher or may do so as a group. This discussion will raise problems and disagreements for further experimentation.

Ukins[16] has classified science learning stations into three categories: (1) "Direct Discovery Learning Stations" (of which the magnet and electricity stations just described are examples); (2) "Skill Development Learning Stations," in which a specific skill such as observing is an example (as in the magnifying glass stations just described); (3) "Open Learning Stations,"[17] in which children are asked to invent something from the materials provided. This type provides students with opportunities to make their own decisions about problems, methods, records, and results.

Learning stations are designed to accomplish certain goals that should be kept in mind as they become a part of teaching. They can provide opportunities for hands-on experiences that may further develop skills such as connecting dry cells in a circuit and using magnifying glasses, as illustrated in our examples. They can extend interests and provide enrichment experiences as children work through the assignments; they can individualize instructions for exceptional children such as slow or fast learners and handicapped children, depending on how the stations are designed; they

---

[15]J. Schwartz, *Through the Magnifying Glass; Little Things That Make a Big Difference,* 1954 and *Magnify and Find Out Why* 1972, McGraw-Hill.

[16]L. L. Ukins, "Learning Stations and Science Teaching," *Science and Children* (November 1972); M. McIntyre, "The Science Learning Center for Preschool"; G. R. Sherfey and P. Huff, "Designing the Learning Center," *Science and Children* (November/December 1976).

[17]R. C. Voight, *Invitation to Learning 1: The Learning Center Handbook* (Washington, D.C.: Acropolis, 1974).

Observational skills are developed as children examine, compare, and draw different kinds of seeds in a learning station. *Photo by Lloyd Wolf, Concord School, Forestville, Maryland.*

can also provide review experiences for those who need it; and they can supply opportunities for creative experiences as students work by themselves or in small groups.

How elaborate and extensive a learning center is depends on several circumstances: the amount of space available, the time available for devising and setting up the center, the materials available, and the nature of the children who will use it. All materials should be safe for children to use by themselves.

The center is probably most effective if it is connected to the ongoing science program. It may be used either to begin a science unit or as an outgrowth of a unit or to summarize and extend it. Ideas for subjects will come from many sources. For example, the B chapters provide many suggestions, as do textbooks and courses of study.

The success of learning stations depends on several factors. Are the materials of interest to the learners? Are the directions for experimenting and recording clear? Is there provision for creativity on the part of the learner? Is the setup inviting and attractive? Are the children aware of the objectives for the center? Is there time for as much teacher supervision as necessary?

FIELD TRIPS USEFUL IN PROBLEM SOLVING[18]

Trips to the zoo, the museum, a greenhouse, the water purification plant, a new building under construction, the park, and similar places are important in making science more meaningful. In taking a field trip the following points should be observed:

1. There should be a real reason for making the trip, and it should be obvious to all. The trip should be a part of an ongoing study and have the support and endorsement of the principal.
2. There should be planning for safety, transportation, possible parent aides, a suitable guide, time schedule, note taking, and other details before the trip.
3. The teacher, with a committee of students, might well make a preliminary trip to determine the suitability of the place, brief the institution about the nature and needs of the group, and make other nec-

[18]M. Jenness, "Schoolyard Hikes," *Science and Children* (March 1987). Gives details for various short trips. S. K. Shugrue, "Studying Science Out-of-Doors," *Science and Children* (March 1982); B. Shapiro, "A Planning Checklist," *Science and Children* (May 1980). An important checklist for all phases of field trips.

A learning center is most efficient if it is connected to the ongoing science program. Here children enrich their field trip experiences with new insights provided by the pictures and text in this center. (*Courtesy of Phyllis Marcuccio, Lynbrook School, Bethesda, Maryland.*)

essary arrangements. Certainly the teacher should, if possible, make such a preliminary trip.

4. There should be group discussion about conduct and courtesy on the trip. Public relations are at stake every time children leave the school to make a visit. The adults who help children on the trip are quite reasonable in expecting interested attention from them. Groups not accustomed to making trips need standards to ensure a profitable visit. This does not mean that the discipline has to be so rigid as to spoil the fun. It means reasonable conduct, often determined by the students themselves, taken seriously. Parent participation has been very effective in helping to ensure a good field trip.

5. Individuals and small groups may be designated to watch or listen for certain things and report them to the class. Specific responsibility of this kind often produces very good results.

6. Do not hurry children too much or plan for them to see more than they are able to take in at one exposure. Sometimes in our zeal to keep the group together we forget that children are individuals and cannot all react with the same speed or be interested at the same time in the same things. A hurried trip to see too many things may be as unsatisfactory as not going at all.

7. The follow-up conversations and recording of information are important. Accurate reporting of what was seen and observed is essential, but the child who said to his friend on the field trip, "Don't look, or you'll have to write!" had a point: Do not overdo the writing. Application of information to the specific problems and questions is best done in the classroom on return.

Potentially, "going to see" is one of the most enjoyable and instructive ways to learn. When teachers, students, and the adults in the place to be visited work together in planning and carrying out the excursion, the results are most likely to be those we hope for. Specific suggestions for field trips for special purposes are described in the B chapters. (See also "Resources to Investigate with Children" in the B chapters for suggestions.)

AUDIOVISUAL AIDS

Instructional media should be used as an integral part of the science curriculum. Equipped with a quality film/video, science teachers can provide students with access to content and processes that would not be possible through other instructional means. All students, regardless of reading ability, can, through visual media, participate in the meaningful learning of science and become equipped to be citizens—and the scientists—of tomorrow.[19]

Children cannot learn everything through firsthand or direct experiences. The reasons for this are obvious. There are many approaches to learning, and audiovisual aids have some unique contributions to make to the process. In the past few years many new and excellent audiovisual materials have been produced. It is quite possible that there have been greater strides made in producing them than we have made in improving how we use them.[20]

Films

Each year more films are produced for use in science classes in the elementary schools. They vary in quality, and some are expensive for what they offer. With curtailed budgets it is even more important to preview before purchase and to pay close attention to the criteria we suggest.

Films are widely used but are not always as effective as they might be, perhaps because we

---

[19]K. Edwards, "Teaching Science With A.V.," *Science Books and Films* (March/April 1987).

[20]R. Culyer, "Making the Most of Audiovisual Aids," *Science and Children* (March 1982).

expect them to teach by themselves. In the hands of skilled teachers a film has unique contributions to make toward achieving our objectives for science teaching. Take, for example, the time-lapse sequence of seeds sprouting or buds opening. Here, as in many similar instances, *motion* is important. The film provides something that even firsthand experiences do not. Films take children on vicarious field trips to places not otherwise available. By animation they show processes and phenomena (the circulation of air, water vapor, and so on) that produce more complete understanding or raise further questions. Their comprehensive scope makes them ideal for use in summarizing and extending the knowledge gained through firsthand experiences.

The following suggestions will help improve the use of films in the teaching of science:

1. Select the film as carefully as you would a book. Children cannot comprehend a film that is too difficult for them any better than they can a book. The explanation should be clear, the vocabulary appropriate, and the content well organized. The film should be accompanied by a useful teacher's guide. Using the teacher's guide may make the difference between an effective use of the film and a near waste of time. Any film indicated as appropriate for both high school and elementary school is almost certain to be useless at one level or the other, unless it is on some relatively nontechnical subject like life in a beaver colony, for example.
2. The film selected should bear directly on the problem or problems under consideration if it is to give the best service.
3. Films should be previewed before they are used. This is done by the teacher, sometimes with the assistance of a committee of students, to plan for its wise use. Film guides often provide excellent suggestions for the use of the movie.
4. Students should be prepared for seeing the film by arranging problems and questions in sequence as they are dealt with in the film; acquainting children with any unfamiliar vocabulary used; calling attention to difficult spots that need advance discussion and to new material in the film that the class has never considered; and in other ways paving the way for good listening and looking.

5. There should always be a real reason for using a film. Just because there is a film in the school building about the Great Wall of China, the teacher is probably not justified in calling off work on "How we can make our community a better place to live in" in order to see the film.

6. It may be important to show a film more than once. If it is especially long or difficult it may be shown in parts, with discussion at the stopping places. The attention span of children may be a clue to how much of a film may be shown at any one time.

7. The follow-up discussion of a film, like the follow-up of a field trip, is often the most important part of its use. It will be based on the preceding "things to look for" discussion or other preparations made before the showing.

8. There are many commercially prepared films and videotapes available, and many schools keep a classified list of these along with descriptions that help teachers decide about their usefulness. Films shown on television shouldn't be overlooked. Advance notice of the times for showing them are often available and some schools provide such information. Local educational television programs have improved significantly in recent years. They can be especially valuable when they are prepared and used to enrich ongoing science programs in the schools.

Slides and Filmstrips[21]

A filmstrip is a series of pictures on a length of film. The pictures usually make a continuous sequence. Using a filmstrip has certain advantages: The projector is easy to operate, and filmstrips are relatively inexpensive. The filmstrip presents the pictures in a fixed sequence; this may be a disadvantage if that sequence is not suitable. As in the case of films, many filmstrips are now accompanied by teacher's guides that provide objectives, a list of problems to guide students, some follow-up activities, and sometimes the text used by the narrator. The guides are usually very practical and are helpful to teachers in getting the most from the use of the filmstrips.

An increasing number of excellent filmstrips is now available. Many are with an accompanying sound track that make them more useful. Additional learning may take place when children produce their own commentary after they have viewed the filmstrip.

Many of the suggestions made for the use of films apply to the use of slides and filmstrips, which can easily be projected and studied by individuals or small groups. In addition, children can sometimes produce their own slides.

COMPUTERS IN THE CLASSROOM

It is generally agreed that there is hardly an area in our lives that is not affected in some way by computers. Our concern here is with the use of computers as a tool for learning in the elementary school, particularly in the field of science. Certain facts about the use of computers appear evident as indicated by the many comments of teachers and other educators: "Their use is increasing throughout the country." "An immense amount of money is being budgeted for their purchase." "Many teachers and supervisors are not trained in their effective use." "Children are generally enthusiastic about using them." "They are only as good as the material that is put into them." "There is a lack of effective program material for use in science instruction as well as personnel schooled in producing such appropriate material (software)." "The use of computers has improved education for many youngsters." "Computers are great motivators." "Children are already into computers in a big way, and computers are arriving at schools by the truck loads."

In summary, certain questions[22] should be resolved when introducing computers into a classroom or school.

1. Is there a provision for in-service teacher training in advance of student use?

---

[21]J. C. Wahla, "Using the Overhead to Stargaze," *Science and Children* (May 1982).

[22]Adapted in part from "Computers in the Classroom" by Francis Roberts in *Parents Magazine* (February 1983).

With proper software, computers can provide opportunities for every child to be active in the learning process. *Photo by Lloyd Wolf, Concord School, Forestville, Maryland.*

2. Does such instruction center on classroom application, not just on the mechanics of computer operation?
3. Before installing (or accepting donations of computers), is the cost of maintenance and repair known and planned for?
4. What kinds of educational programs for the computer are available?
5. Are the computers to be used by all students or just the gifted and talented?
6. Does the machine accept all or almost all suitable software?
7. Is there planning for the evaluation of the computer and the software by teachers and supervisors?

Software[23]

During the past few years much software for elementary school science has been produced. (See

[23]K. K. Lind, "Which Computer Magazine?" *Science and Children* (January 1984) lists computer magazines and describes their contents. K. E. Reynolds, E. Walton, and T. Logue, "Software Evaluation," *Science and Children* (September 1985); L. E. Klopfer, "The Coming Generation of Tutoring Software," *The Science Teacher* (November 1986). Includes criteria for evaluating science software.

"Computer Software in Science Education" in the appendix on p. 638.) Several magazines, including the publication *Science and Children*, now include reviews of software. Teachers and supervisors are now beginning to share in the important task of evaluating computer programs. The following are some helpful guidelines.

With respect to the computer program (software)

1. Does it provide opportunities for every student to be active in the learning process?
2. Does it provide for individualization? Are there multiple tracks that can be varied, depending on the students' needs?
3. Does it open minds and expand the imagination, or does it reduce children's schooling to narrower goals, measured only by short answer tests?
4. Does it take into account our knowledge of the learning process?
5. Does it make appropriate use of the color, sound, and graphics capabilities of the computer?
6. Does it help develop the science skills of observing, communicating, hypothesizing, experimenting, measuring, recording, generalizing, and predicting?
7. Does it propel children into science activities out-

side the computer such as investigating their environment, taking field trips, or engaging in community projects?

8. Is the science content accurate?
9. Can children easily and independently operate it after a modest period of orientation?
10. Does it do something that cannot be done as effectively by other instructional methods?

Important Considerations

Two overriding problems exist: (1) What can we expect to result from the use of computers in schools, and closely allied, (2) How does the use of computers relate to the overall objectives for teaching science? The answers to these questions should be uppermost in the minds of those responsible for the use of computers in schools.

One common use of computers as reported by teachers is as basic review in science subject matter to reinforce classroom instruction. This use often takes the form of games or similar activities that repeat ideas and draw attention to responses when they are incorrect. Another perhaps more important use is in promoting problem-solving ability. These problems relate to ongoing class work and require student responses that indicate seeing relationships and on this basis selecting appropriate solutions. Such material is often presented by drawings, graphs, and other visuals. The problem-solving situations may be designed for use by individual students working alone or in groups. Opportunities are provided to correct errors and to adjust responses as the problem solving proceeds.[24]

DISCOVERING FOR YOURSELF

1. Try one of the Piagetian tasks, individually, with

[24]The authors are indebted to Professor Darrel W. Fyffe of Bowling Green State University, Bowling Green, Ohio, for suggestions in the preparation of the section on computers.

each of two children of different ages. Describe the results from such tasks.

2. Design an experiment to solve a problem whose answer *you* do not know. Write an account of your procedures and indicate your results. Indicate any limitations involved in your experiment.

3. How can a situation when an experiment "doesn't work" be used to engage children in real experimentation? Describe such a situation.

4. Select any topic that you might wish to teach in elementary science. Find and annotate three children's trade books (not textbooks) that might be helpful in developing this topic. Describe how you would use the books.

5. Describe how you might help children improve their writing and reading skills in developing the topic from number 4.

6. Take a walk around the block. Focus on engaging all of your senses in making discoveries on such an excursion. Describe what you have sensed. (Did you feel the bark of a tree? Did you sniff the air near a restaurant? Did you sense differences in the pavement underfoot?). How would you use this experience with children?

7. Deliberate lying excluded, why do witnesses at a trial sometimes give contradictory "observations" of what they saw, heard, and so on? What has this to do with what you have learned in this chapter?

8. Take a field trip to investigate some aspect of your local environment. (Examples: changes after a snowstorm or rainstorm, excavations, stones in buildings, plants in backyards, lights at night). How would you use such a field trip with children?

9. Design a learning center with four stations on any topic you choose. Include the instructions, the materials, and any required constructions and descriptions. What skills do you think your learning center will help students develop?

10. If possible, observe a child using a computer to view a science program. Evaluate the program, using the criteria on pages 6–7. Question the child to help you in your evaluation.

11. Reread the introductory quotation to this chapter on page 31. What specific kinds of skills or strategies that you have used or observed could be the subject of research problems?

CHAPTER 4

ORGANIZING
THE SCIENCE PROGRAM

We shape our programs, and then afterwards our programs shape us and our children!

RENÉ DUBOS SO HUMAN AN ANIMAL SCRIBNERS, 1968

Jerome Bruner in his book *The Process of Education* includes a statement that has produced much discussion and controversy: "We begin with the hypothesis that any subject can be taught effectively in some intellectually honest form to any child at any stage of development."[1] We do not have the space here to trace Dr. Bruner's development of this idea; we must refer you to his book. But we do wish to call your attention to a significant and sometimes overlooked statement made later in the same chapter: "We might ask, as a criterion for any subject taught in primary school, whether, when fully developed, it is worth an adult's knowing, and whether having known it as a child makes a person a better adult." In other words, we must not only ask whether a subject or part of a subject can be taught, we must also ask whether it is *worthwhile* to teach it.

We also draw your attention to a later book by Bruner[2] in which he stresses the importance of the personal dimension of education. This leads us to consider how to produce a program that takes into account all the individual differences in background, status, and so on of those we try to teach.

Since it is impossible to teach or even expose a child to all available information about anything, teachers are forced to be selective. Even elaborate syllabi, course guides, program manuals, and so on, won't be enough. We know that matching the curriculum to the needs of the child is a continuous process. No one scheme or approach works every time or everywhere. *The process of education thus makes innovators of teachers.* Therefore, in science education, elementary school teachers need to make some basic decisions about their own regard for the nature of science and the role it should play in the lives of their children.

BEGINNING TO TEACH

The Teacher's Attitude

No matter how the science program is organized, its success depends largely on the teacher and the teaching. The teacher's attitude toward science influences the attitudes of children. Enthusiasm, interest, background, willingness to learn, and an understanding of the goals are important ingredients of the teacher's potential. The teacher is the main source from which children attain these characteristics.

At the conclusion of an extensive study[3] of science education in the United States, in *What Research Says to the Science Teacher,* the author states:

> For science education of any sort to prosper at the elementary level, teachers must value science outcomes and consider them worth pursuing. An understanding of the contributions science can make to general cognitive development is one possible aspect of such value system. Another important attribute for teachers at the elementary level is the perception that the study of science is much more than an exercise in reading comprehension. Rather, it is a vehicle for learning about the natural world.

> Teachers who view science in this way will naturally use a variety of techniques including direct observation, experimentation, individual and group projects, questioning, and reading. They will do this

---

[1] J. S. Bruner, *The Process of Education* (New York: Random House, 1960).

[2] J. S. Bruner, *The Relevance of Education* (New York: Norton, 1973).

[3] N. Harms, "Project Synthesis: Summary and Implications for Teachers," in *What Research Says to the Science Teacher,* Vol. 3 (NSTA, 1981).

not only to help students learn about the natural world, but also to develop those processes of inquiry they can continue to use to gather and process information. Although it is unrealistic to expect elementary teachers to have command of a large body of knowledge in science, confidence in the teaching of science is a necessary teacher characteristic. For confidence to exist in the absence of a broad command of scientific knowledge, it is necessary for elementary teachers to see science as a way of investigating simple and common phenomena, especially those in the immediate environment. Conversely it is important that elementary teachers not feel it is their responsibility to convey a large body of facts, theories or "scientific" terms to their students.

A teacher who answers a student's question by saying, "I don't know, but let's see if we can find out," serves as a role model in inquiry.

But the teacher is not alone in efforts to guide children in their science experiences: He or she has the help of locally developed or state curricula, science textbooks, and other publications directed to elementary school teachers' programs — or indeed a combination of all of these and other printed materials. Many teachers have the assistance of science specialists or other supervisory personnel, who may help to make decisions about what to teach and how to teach it, and know sources of materials, apparatus, and other help.

Even though the teacher has the most important leadership role, this does not mean that the teacher makes all the decisions. Teachers guide, plan beforehand, outline general directions, and know the possibilities. In this picture there are still opportunities for children to make decisions — of the kind they are capable of making — and to improvise within the framework of the overall plan.

MAKING UNIT AND LESSON PLANS

There are many ways to make lesson and unit plans, just as there are many ways to teach. Sometimes a class period is spent in group work, individualized instruction, laboratory work, independent study, use of multimedia instructional aids by children, and so on. A unit of work may require only a few days or extend over many weeks. This being the case, there must also be many forms for developing and recording plans. Some plans are formal and include details; some are very sketchy. No matter what the style of teaching, there are legitimate reasons for planning. Good teachers feel that they need some sort of guide to follow. Certainly we are not likely to teach well without some preliminary planning: We need to think out possible ways to teach, to make some provision for materials that we may need, and to formulate carefully what we hope students will be able to do as a result of their experiences. The teacher's outline should allow plenty of opportunity for children to plan together or make whatever decisions they can and should make. Remember, too: *When you begin to work with students, your plan may change entirely; it is almost certain to be modified.*

Finding Important Science Ideas

There are certain first steps that the teacher will make in planning. Let us suppose that the teacher wants to teach some concepts about evaporation and condensation of water in the third or fourth grade. (This might be a part of a larger unit about weather.) There are several things that may be done in preparation. If needed, the teacher should read subject matter on the grade level, as well as material on a more advanced level. If the teacher is inexperienced, he or she may do some of the simple experiments suggested in the books and investigate some of the local resources available. In short, the teacher should do some of the things suggested in Chapter 9B, pages 250–252, and investigate other possible sources of information.

Remembering that one of the overall goals is to emphasize science principles rather than to accumulate isolated, unimportant facts, let us think through what such subject matter might include. The general scope of the unit may come from the readings the teacher has done or the curriculum guide, if there is one. The available textbooks may provide a general outline of the possible scope of the unit. The teacher may make a list of important science ideas gained from readings or find such a basic list in teacher's guides to textbooks. In the study of evaporation and condensation the following are examples of the subject matter ideas:

When water evaporates, it changes to water vapor.
Wind and heat make water evaporate more rapidly.
Water evaporates into the air from many places.
When water vapor changes back into water we say it condenses.
Water vapor often condenses on cold things.
Water vapor may condense to make dew.
Dew evaporates.
Water vapor may come out of the air as frost on freezing cold surfaces.
Frost melts into water when warmed.
Rain comes from clouds.
Some clouds are made of tiny drops of water; some are made of tiny crystals of ice.
Some of the rainwater evaporates; some of it goes into the ground.
There are many kinds of clouds.
Snowflakes are made of ice crystals.
Snow melts into water when warmed.

Structuring the Unit

At this stage the teacher is ready to outline the unit. The title is to be "Water Appears and Disappears." Three main topics selected are

1. How can we speed evaporation?
2. What makes water condense?
3. What is the water cycle?

(See Chapter 9A, pp. 222–226, for a development of these topics.) The following is one way of outlining the unit. (See p. 58.) There are others.

Stating Goals and Objectives

Now the teacher may be ready to focus on the goals and specific objectives that this experience with the phenomena of evaporation and condensation might achieve. Some of the following may be anticipated in the teacher's planning; others may become apparent as the teacher explores with the children. In terms of behaviors expected, the teacher may note that as a result of participating in the discussions, readings, experiments, observations, and other activities, students should be able to

Infer that the moisture that collects on a cold surface comes from the air.
Ask questions and *describe occurrences* involving evaporation and condensation in their environment.
Use a thermometer as a tool of investigation, and *read* it accurately.
Explain the need for a control in an experiment.
Demonstrate the use of materials and apparatus related to evaporation and condensation.
Devise original experiments to test their hypotheses.
State some of the important generalizations about evaporation and condensation.
Write a summary of the water cycle.
Draw a diagram showing the water cycle.
Apply generalizations about evaporation and condensation to everyday phenomena.
Define, in their own words, the terms *evaporation* and *condensation* and use these terms correctly.

Launching the Unit

Up to now the teacher is building background so that he or she will have more confidence and have a clearer idea of the direction the study may take. *This does not mean that the teacher does all the planning in advance,* but that he or she is simply getting ready to do a more intelligent job of guiding the students as they work.

The following description of classroom procedure may give the impression of teacher domination. This is because we intend to indicate the

Topic	Sample Activities	Science Concepts and Ideas
1. How can we speed evaporation?		
a. heating	Compare two trays of water, one in the sun, one in the shade. Or heat one slowly over a hot plate; allow the other to remain at room temperature. Measure the temperature of each from time to time. At the end of several hours pour the water from each into a measuring cup and compare.	Heating makes water evaporate more quickly.
b. wind	Make two wet spots on a chalkboard. Fan one of them. Note the time needed for each to dry.	Wind makes water evaporate more quickly.
c. amount of exposed surface	1. Add equal amounts of water to a tall narrow jar and a wide mouth jar. Compare levels at intervals. At the end pour water from each into a measuring cup, and compare. 2. Wet two handkerchiefs and wring them out. Spread one flat and crumple the other into a ball. Place each on a tray. Compare rate of drying (perhaps by weighing each handkerchief on a scale).	Exposing more surface of a wet object to the air makes it dry more quickly. When water evaporates it changes into water vapor.
2. What makes water condense?		
a. temperature	Place ice and water in a metal cup. Take the temperature. Compare with warm water in another cup. Collect any water that may drip off into a plate. Ask where the water came from. Some students may say that it leaked out of the cup. How can we check this? Add vegetable color to the water in the cup. Are the drops that form outside colored?	When water vapor changes back into water we say it condenses. When air is chilled the water vapor in it may change into water. Water vapor often condenses on cold things.
b. humidity	Compare results of same experiments as in 2.a on a dry day with those on a humid day.	
3. What is the water cycle?	1. Place warm water in a clean, dry glass jar up to the 1-inch level. Do not wet sides of jar when introducing water. Cover the jar. Later, observe condensation on sides and top of jar and dripping of water from top. Discuss the meaning of the word *cycle*.	Water evaporates from lakes, rivers, and oceans and condenses into clouds.
	2. Hold a cold plate or pie tin over spout of heated tea kettle of water.	Clouds are made of tiny drops of water or crystals of ice. Rain comes from clouds.
	3. Draw a diagram of water cycle in nature.	
	4. Write a story or poem about the water cycle: Suggested titles: "I was a raindrop"; "I was a snowflake."	Water moves in a constant cycle from oceans to air to clouds to rain and snow to land, rivers, lakes to oceans.

various kinds of activities the teacher may engage in, rather than to describe children's responses. In actual practice, children will be considerably involved both in planning and carrying out the plans.

Our subject matter has already been selected, and the teacher needs to think of ideas for launching the study—for making it interesting, real, concrete, vital, relevant, and enjoyable—and of raising some perplexities that will result in problems and questions. Where to begin?

Well, the water level in the uncovered schoolroom aquarium keeps getting lower, so that every now and then the water needs to be replenished. Watercolors in paint boxes dry up as they are being used and more water must be added. Why? Wet clothes are hung near heat to help them dry. It rains; puddles form in the schoolyard; the sun comes out; the puddles dry—students can then go out to play. These are everyday happenings involving evaporation. Children see them and are curious. If they have not noticed them, the teacher draws their attention to some and suggests that they look for others. These are all possible starters, and they are all observations that lead to inquiry.

Suppose we use the aquarium as a starting point. Since students have noticed that the water is disappearing, the question arises, "Where do you suppose the water goes?" Students offer hypotheses: "The aquarium leaks." Or, "The water goes into the air." Or, "The fish drink it." These are some of the possible responses. They may be explored briefly but the actual testing of the hypotheses comes after further discussion.

"Have you seen other places where water disappears like this?" the teacher asks. Students list a number of places. "Where do you think the water is going?" Students suggest places. "Sometimes water disappears quickly. Why do you suppose this happens?" Students offer examples and possible explanations: "When my mother uses her hair dryer"; "when I dry my hands at the restroom blower." Through such preliminary discussions, students raise problems, interest is aroused, and a readiness for inquiry is developing.

Such preliminary experiences are essential if we are to establish problems of any consequence that represent children's concerns and are typical of their environment. All questions are listed, even those that may seem trivial. Some of them may be: "What happens to the water when it disappears?" "Why can't we see it then?" "Why does it disappear?" "Could we keep it from disappearing?" "Can we get it back again?" How can we make it disappear faster?" The teacher may add some other questions if the children's questions omit some of the important ideas. In case no mention has been made of heat and wind, questions are added concerning them. Other questions and problems will be added as the study goes on.

"Now how can we find answers?" the teacher asks. Suggestions from the students are important here. We want them to suggest ways to investigate, and then to use some of these ways so that they will arrive at possible conclusions. The students suggest reading, experimenting, asking further questions, observing, and other methods of inquiry. These suggestions will vary. If the children have had previous science experiences their suggestions will be more sophisticated than otherwise.

"What shall we do first?" Students make suggestions. The questions may be arranged by the teacher and children in some order that seems logical for answering. They select a question and decide which way of inquiry will be appropriate. The whole class may work on the same problem, or if it seems best (depending on the age of the children, their experience at group work, materials available, etc.) students may work in groups, each group concentrating on a different problem. Learning stations may be set up. Everyone assumes some responsibility for finding printed materials, finding or devising experiments, or locating necessary apparatus and other learning materials. A special library committee working with the teacher and librarian may search for books. These sources will suggest various experiments and activities. Suggestions have already been made for the use of reading material, for experimenting, and for observing (see Chapter 3).

These suggestions will be kept in mind as the study proceeds.

In the experimenting, as in all other activities, it is essential to keep experiments geared to the purpose of teaching. For example, we want to help students grow in the use of scientific attitudes. We have already stated, "Don't let students jump to conclusions, and be sure to use a *control* whenever possible as children are experimenting." As we have previously indicated, the use of experimenting involves varying degrees of sophistication. Not all children will comprehend the importance of the use of a control. It is essential, however, that children be exposed to the idea, and begin to experience the meaning involved. Let us illustrate.

In this unit one of the problems may be, "Do things really dry faster on a windy day?" Students will suggest hypotheses; to test these ideas, they experiment by putting a wet spot on the chalkboard and fanning it vigorously with a piece of cardboard. The spot will soon disappear.

Students may be inclined to conclude immediately that the wind made by fanning caused the water to evaporate faster. But they shouldn't. As an alert student once said under such circumstances, "I don't know how fast a spot dries without fanning." So the question arises, "How can we arrange our experiment so that we can be sure that it is only the *wind* that is helping the water evaporate faster?" "Put two spots on the chalkboard, fan one, and don't fan the other," someone says. So two spots are made near each other, and only one is fanned. Someone says, "Some of the fanning is getting on both spots." "What shall we do?" "Put the spots farther apart," a student suggests. This is done, but one of the spots is small, the other large. "There's still something wrong with the experiment." "What is it?" "The spots must be just alike or we can't decide that the wind is helping." The experiment is tried again, this time with two spots as nearly alike as possible put on at the same time and sufficiently far apart. The students are willing to decide that the experiment may help them to solve their problem. They make some observations and some predictions. But before they can make reliable inferences they

should repeat the experiment, try out variations of it, and make additional observations.

When we work with high school and college students, we urge them to use a *control* in performing an experiment to make the results more valid. In the case of the wet spots on the chalkboard, the spot that was not fanned was the control. With some groups we may decide not to use the word control; instead we urge students to try to answer the question, "How can we be sure that fanning makes a difference?" In general, questions about control must be designed to have children see the need (1) to exclude influences *except* the one being tested, and (2) to be able to make fair comparisons.

Children will be urged to repeat experiments. Children will caution each other about nonscientific procedures in experimenting if they get in the habit of making accurate observations and of drawing reasonable inferences from the results obtained.

Experiments help us to solve problems, and the application of the conclusions help us to interpret situations in our environment. Consequently, after the experience with wind on the wet spots the teacher may say, "Now, have you ever seen other places where wind helps evaporation?" The students suggest such examples as hanging clothes on a line, use of hair dryers, and so forth; they compare these with what happened in the experiment.

As the study proceeds, textbook and other informational sources will be used as they are needed. Children may see a film or filmstrip that explains the causes of evaporation and condensation.

It is essential that the teacher keep in mind the generalizations originally assembled if the children's experiences are to lead toward an understanding of them. The students will not immediately connect the disappearance and reappearance of water with the concept of what causes rain, snow, and other weather forms. This connection will come to them as their study progresses. As we pointed out earlier, the teacher sees these processes of evaporation and condensation as part of a larger conceptual framework

Two wet spots on the chalkboard. Does fanning one speed up its drying? Is this a properly "controlled" experiment? *Photo by Lloyd Wolf, Anne Beers School, Washington, D.C.*

and, wherever possible, provides opportunities for children to see connections with other weather concepts. The teacher is guided in this by the maturity of the children as well as by other factors.

If there is sufficient interest in the study, students may want to plan a culminating activity. This may be done in many ways. Again, it is important for students to plan—with the guidance of the teacher. They may wish to show the results of their work to another grade, to their parents, or at a school assembly. For this purpose they can plan, perform, and explain a series of easy demonstrations; plan and draw a series of large pictures that show the important ideas they have learned; or write stories to illustrate the generalizations they have discovered. Here is an example of communicating—writing, speaking, and listening—as necessary activities in science.

We could summarize all that we have said by suggesting that in planning a unit of study a teacher should:

1. Review his or her background in the subject matter.
2. Locate and try out possible activities, experiments, and other methods of inquiry to be done in class.
3. List the important science principles involved.
4. Write a tentative unit plan.
5. List specific objectives to be attained.

6. Attempt to relate the topic of study to the children's interests and environment.
7. Involve, when possible, the children in the implementation of the unit through the use of hands-on activities, questions, and discussion.
8. Aid children in controlling experiments by helping them to make fair comparisons and by varying only one factor (independent variable).
9. Help the children to see the need to repeat experiments.
10. Keep in mind the original objectives while teaching.
11. Provide for culminating activities.[4]

PLANNING A LESSON

What is the thinking that goes into planning a lesson? Let's examine the following illustration. Suppose that we are studying the magnetic compass in grade 4 or 5. Let us assume that students have thus far learned the kinds of materials magnets will attract; the substances magnetism will travel through; how to make a magnet by rubbing a needle on a magnet; and the laws of magnets (opposite poles of a magnet attract each other; like poles repel). The children have discovered these

[4]We are grateful to Professor John H. Thoman of the University of Wisconsin, Madison, for suggesting this summary.

ideas through various informal kinds of inquiry, and they have done some reading. Now they are interested in making a compass, which they have learned has something to do with magnetism. You suggest that before the next lesson students try to find out as much as they can about how to make one. This is not a formal assignment. It provides an opportunity for those who are interested to do some research (see Chapters 17A and B).

Assuming that the lesson will be one in which students will more or less work together in attempting to solve a problem, you may think something like this: I want to build on what the students already know, use any investigating they may have done outside of class, help them to formulate some hypotheses and test them, solve the problem of how to make a compass (help them to use their ideas in making compasses), and raise some new problems about compasses and their uses. (See the more organized statement of some of the behavioral objectives in the lesson plan that follows.)

You will probably begin your lesson by letting students tell or show what they discovered about compasses. Naturally, you will not know in advance what ideas they will have. You are prepared with materials that can be used by the students to make compasses: needles, dishes of water, magnets, and flat corks.

It is possible that someone will bring a small compass from home. You may have suggested this to the students in a previous discussion. If so, let the student show it to the class and tell about it. Some of this information may be correct; some wrong. You assume that students will challenge the accuracy of some of the statements, and part of your plan will be to help students find out whether the statements are true or not.

Show the items that you have assembled, and ask, "Can anyone use these materials to try to make a compass?" Students will discuss their ideas and then organize into groups to try them out. Now students have some background for their theories and suggestions from their research.

They attempt to make several compasses in order to compare them and give more students the opportunity to learn by doing. When the compasses are made (the needle is magnetized by rubbing it—one way only—on the magnet and resting it on a cork on a dish of water), you expect someone to ask, "What makes the needle point north and south?" This problem and others will undoubtedly be left for further inquiry in your next lesson. (See the plan that follows and also see Chapter 17B.)

This, in general, is some of the thinking you may do *before* you sit down to plan. Remember: This is just one of the many ways of thinking about a plan; your way may be different, depending on your background and other factors. Look back at your intentions. Is your thinking pointed toward achieving them? Have you provided opportunities for children to plan and to think? Will they use ways of inquiry and of finding devised by themselves? Will this kind of plan keep their interest alive? Is it a flexible plan? How much of a plan you write down depends on you and your situation. You may need only a brief outline of how you hope to go ahead, but you should think out ways of proceeding—especially if you have not done much science teaching (see the accompanying lesson plan).

Several descriptions of teaching procedures in this section of the book are really examples of lesson-planning procedures—see Chapter 2 (Heat, pp. 19 and 20) and Chapter 3 (Electromagnets, pp. 38 and 39; Sound, pp. 42 and 43; Variation in pea pods, p. 45). Many of the B chapters contain materials easily developed into plans.

Lesson Plan for Intermediate Grades—Subject: Compass

Problem
How can we make a compass?

Objectives As a result of the activities and discussions the children will be able to

demonstrate a method or methods of making a compass

describe the behavior of a free-floating magnetized needle

compare the behavior of different compasses and *hypothesize* to explain the differences

identify further problems resulting from making a compass

Note: Depending on the length of the lesson and the maturity of the children, these objectives will need adjustment. These may be a large order for some children and some teachers. They are examples to be modified by individual teachers.

Materials Flat corks, needles, glass or plastic dishes, magnets, large sheet of paper.

Strategy/Procedure (This part of the plan covers motivation, questions to be asked by the teacher or anticipated from students, activities, and science processes to be stressed.) Ask students how they think a compass can be made from the materials you have prepared. Students offer hypotheses and perhaps make some predictions about what will happen when they try out their ideas. After suggestions are made, children formalize their plans and try (working in groups) to use the materials to make compasses. Children tell and show their results and compare the various compasses. If there are differences, students propose hypotheses to account for them, and proceed to check them and attempt to predict what will happen when their plans are carried out.[5]

[5]In a class where there were considerable differences in the behavior of the compasses and a certain amount of confusion and frustration, the teacher, instead of ducking the problem, wisely asked the children to try to account for the differences. The following hypotheses were offered by the children: "Mary's needle was rusty." "There were some iron things (scissors) near Carl's compass." "The magnet was not strong enough." "The cork stuck to the side of the dish." "The needle was not rubbed enough."

The children investigated these possibilities and came to the conclusion that in most cases where there was divergence from the expected results a nearby iron object had influenced the compass. After making corrections for this and retesting, the results were more uniform.

A magnetized steel needle on a floating cork becomes a compass. Children compare their compasses. Do all point in the same direction? If not, why not? *Photo by Lloyd Wolf, Anne Beers School, Washington, D.C.*

Outcomes Outcomes are directly related to your objectives. Some refer to science information and concepts, some to processes of inquiry. There may also be unplanned outcomes based on the actual responses of children to the material and activities, on their "messing around," or their creativity.

Concepts

1. A steel needle can be made magnetic by stroking it in one direction on a magnet.
2. A free-floating magnetized needle points in a north–south direction. It is a compass.
3. Magnets attract other magnets.

Processes

1. *Observing and describing:* How do the magnetized needles behave? What happens under various circumstances?
2. *Predicting:* What do you think will happen to a steel needle if it is rubbed on a magnet? What do you think will happen if you float the needle on a cork?
3. *Experimenting:* Find out if an unmagnetized needle behaves in the same way as a magnetized one. Use both kinds when comparing results.
4. *Comparing or describing:* How do magnetized needles compare with each other? With commercial compass needles? With unmagnetized needles?
5. *Generalizing:* The magnetized needles pointed in a north–south direction.
6. *Communicating:* Describe what happens and discuss the possible causes and results.

New Problems What makes a compass point in a north–south direction? How can we tell which of the ends of the needles are pointing north? How can we use the magnetized needle to find north, east, south, and west? Can we magnetize just one end of the needle? Is the pointed end of the needle always the north end? Are there other ways to make a compass?

The teacher may suggest that students think of ways to solve these problems. They will be the essence of further lessons.

ORGANIZING FOR INSTRUCTION

Now that we have examined some of the teacher's strategies in planning units and lessons, let us consider how to organize science as a body of subject matter for study. There are several factors to be considered, and again we examine the goals. If we are to bring about comprehension of broad conceptual schemes of science, to help students grow in ability to use the processes of inquiry, and to accomplish our other objectives, we must make definite provision in the program to include sufficiently challenging and appropriate material. If we are to satisfy children's curiosity and broaden their interests and strengthen their attitudes, they themselves should have some voice in the how, when, and where of science experiences, depending, of course, on their age, experience, and maturity and on the skill of the teacher in helping children use their talents. Let us now consider some of the possibilities for organizing for instruction.

Incidental or Structured Experience?

Can the curriculum be built and organized entirely around the questions children ask, the things they bring in, or other incidental happenings? Although some of our best teaching may result when incidental problems are raised, a well-rounded program cannot be achieved only through such incidental teaching. Nor can a good program be built if we ignore these incidental learning situations. How, then, can we allow for them and still have an organized program?

Many schools have solved the problem of organization, in part at least, by providing for two types of experiences—incidental and planned—in their programs and through operating within a flexible general framework. Incidental learning may, for example, include a brief consideration of a severe thunderstorm, or it may center around a new construction near the school, or around a recent or anticipated eclipse of the moon. Sometimes, after the short initial discussion, an "investigation committee" studies the problem further and brings a report to the class, finds reading material for interested students, or arranges an exhibit of pictures on the bulletin board. If, on the other hand, the incidental experience turns out to be of more than passing interest, the schedule should be flexible enough to permit a shift in plans. In many instances, with careful planning this experience may result in attaining many of the same objectives as a pre-planned experience. Frequently the incidental experience can be meshed into the planned experience.

Scope and Sequence

Now let us be more specific about organizing an area of subject matter such as astronomy, which is commonly included in the science programs of the elementary school. We need to provide continuity on both subject matter and process throughout the elementary grades.

In the early grades (prekindergarten, kindergarten, and grades 1, 2, and 3) students will have many and varied experiences with astronomy, such as measuring lengths of shadows, watching the changes of seasons and their effects on living things, observing the moon or the Big Dipper and reporting what they have seen, and taking note of the varying length of days and nights. An appropriate problem for prekindergarten to grade 2 might be "How is the sun important to us?" In this connection, students may come to know the following: The sun is very hot. The sun is very large. It looks small because it is so far away. The sun keeps us warm. It helps plants to grow. It helps to make us healthy. The earth travels around the sun.[6]

In grade 3, children relate night and day to the turning of the earth, and the year to the orbiting of the earth around the sun. They learn that the earth's steady turning makes it a kind of clock—

that time has something to do with the turning of the earth.

In grade 4, children study earth's natural satellite, the moon. They observe its changing appearance, learn about its size, its landscape, motions, distance from the earth, eclipses of the sun and moon. They plan a trip to the moon.

In grade 5, they study the sun's family—the solar system—and learn about some of the discoveries made by the space probes.

In grade 6, they study the stars and the Milky Way galaxy.

In the more advanced grades, perhaps in the middle school (depending on the school organization), the picture enlarges: Students study the relationship between the solar system and the universe; learn the cause of seasons and tides; study stars and their distances, size, and composition; study the Milky Way and other galaxies; learn about novae and nebulae; and discuss the possibility of whether or not there are other solar systems.[7] They study in more detail how astronomers make discoveries.

It is apparent that each time an area of science (in this case, astronomy) is encountered, the new work builds on that previously experienced, adds to it, and increases in difficulty. The generalizations become more complex as the students progress; the processes of inquiry become more involved. There is only enough repetition to make a connection, not enough to cause students to lose interest. The same overall objectives hold for all levels. The specific objectives will vary with the maturity of the students. Many textbook series are organized around a scope and sequence in which each grade builds on the previous one, and all experiences are organized around the development of major understandings. On each level students should be left with the idea that there is still more interesting material to learn—indeed, that there are still many things that scientists themselves have not discovered. *And we hope that*

---

[6]G. O. Blough and I. DePencier, *How the Sun Helps Us* (New York: Harper & Row, 1976).

[7]B. M. Parker, *Beyond the Solar System* (New York: Harper & Row, 1970).

teaching proceeds in such a way that students will want to learn more.

We have indicated briefly a possible organization of subject matter (astronomy) to bring out an understanding of principles and generalizations. We have said little about organization to achieve the other objectives of science teaching. We assume, however, that if the teaching is good, no matter what organization of subject matter is followed, there will be continuous emphasis on the processes, on the development of attitudes, and on interest and appreciation. We can assume this, however, only if *we intend* to provide experiences that will attain these objectives.

There is general agreement that science is an essential part of any effective elementary program, and time must be allocated for it. Science often seems to fuse naturally with other learnings; often, however, it stands more or less by itself. Let us examine briefly the implications involved in this statement.

Articulation

If you review our original statement of goals in Chapter 2, you will recall that we discussed the relationship of science to the total school program and indicated that it contributes in many ways to the achievement of our overall goals. For this reason it is sometimes considered in relation to the other curriculum subjects, for example, social studies. As we indicated earlier, sometimes these subject matter areas need each other. Sometimes they do not. How can we tell? One clue appears when we examine our overall objectives. If in order to achieve them we need subject matter from both social studies and science, we put them together. Otherwise we do not. To do anything else might well distort the aims, pull inappropriate subject matter from both areas, and result in a hodgepodge.

Science and social science deal with many similar processes and problem-solving models. When knowledge and skills are connected to the social consequences of science and technology, a powerful decision-making tool is available for use by citizens. The end result should provide citizens with the power to make social policy decisions related to science and technology.[8]

Twelve science/technology problems were ranked by science educators in the following order of importance: population growth; water resources; world hunger and food resources; air quality and the atmosphere; war technology; energy shortages; land use; human health and disease; hazardous substances; extinction of plants and animals; nuclear reactors; mineral resources.[9]

An example of sensible fusion of science with social studies occurs when students work on a problem like, "What are the important ecological problems in our state and how can they be solved?" This overall problem may break down into others such as, "Why did the rains last spring do so much damage in our community?" "Why must we conserve our water supply and how can we do it?" In attempting to solve these and related inquiries we consider soil, water, wildlife, and mineral and human resources. We need a considerable amount of science information in order to understand the formation and composition of soils, the action of wind and water on soil and other materials, the interdependence of animal and plant life, and so on. But these cannot be fully comprehended without a study of our relationship and responsibility in the world. Each learner must see the problem within his or her own frame of reference, and see how his or her action relates to those of others.

Astronomy, on the other hand, needs little or no social studies to achieve its objectives. This science subject matter stands on its own, although a discussion of former beliefs and superstitions of people with respect to the sun, moon, and stars may be of value in enhancing our present understandings. Another possible link is the need to win public support for space stations, manned flights to Mars, and other exploits in space.

One important aspect of the fusion of science and social studies lies in the total objectives for

[8]T. Switzer and B. Voss, "Integrating the Teaching of Science and Social Studies," *School, Science and Mathematics* (October 1982).

[9]*School, Science and Mathematics* (April 1987).

both of them. In both areas we are concerned with learning how to use processes of discovery, and how to foster social and scientific attitudes. We are concerned with producing responsible, intelligent citizens. Here there is a real relationship: Our processes of discovery in both areas are similar and they reinforce each other.

In Chapter 2, in considering the goals in elementary school science, we emphasized the importance of developing scientifically literate individuals who understood how science, technology, and society (often referred to as S/T/S) influence one another and who were able to use this knowledge in their everyday decision making. Such problems as the world oil supply, nuclear testing, acid rain in the environment, disposing of toxic wastes, exhaustion of soil, overpopulation, and the spread of infectious diseases, require a multidisciplinary approach. Considering such broad real-world problems involves basic science subject matter, technical knowledge as well as the attitudes and objectives of society. The extent to which integration can take place in the classroom depends on several factors: the maturity of the learners, the attitude and experience of the teacher, the availability of teaching materials, and the cooperation of supervisors, administrators and the parent body. We have yet to design appropriate S/T/S teaching projects for the elementary schools. Chapter 2 suggests some; some national organizations are researching this area. (See following sections.)

Although as adults we are impressed with the importance of S/T/S, we must not allow the area to become a lecture/listen experience for children; rather it must be, as with other science learnings, a hands-on investigative activity. *The articulation must be in children's bones as well as in their brains.*[10]

---

[10]R. E. Yager, "Problem Solving: the STS Advantage," *Curriculum Review* (January/February, 1987); D. A. Wiley, "STS Curricular Additions," *Science Scope* (February/March, 1987); A. Hofstein and R. E. Yager, "Societal Issues as Organizers for Science Education in the 80's," *School, Science and Mathematics* (November 1982); R. Kromhout and R. Good, "Beware of Social Issues as Organizers for Science Education," *School, Science and Mathematics* (December 1983).

Health education and science may sometimes profit by being fused. For example, in health education, when the problem of diet and foods are being considered, the wisdom of eating certain foods in proper amounts will be more obvious if we treat some of the aspects of diet as more or less pure science. When students learn that their growing bones contain the chemical elements of calcium and phosphorus, they understand more readily the importance of drinking milk, which also has both elements.

Science provides the biological basis for teaching sex education. It is in cases such as these that science and other areas, if they are considered together, benefit each other and increase the contributions to children's learning (see also Chapter 11A).

In the processes of discovery in science it is often essential that students use the skills of the language arts in communication. There is a definite opportunity for fusion. If it seems necessary and desirable to read, we read. If writing and speaking are useful, we use them. If it becomes necessary to use art skills we employ them, but we do not use any area merely to be able to say that we have "integration."

An easy way to kill interest in science is to require students to do unnecessary writing. The idea of writing up in detail each experiment performed is guaranteed to dampen enthusiasm. So, too, is adding technical science vocabulary to the spelling list. Some common science words may be learned through use and reading context, but at age eight or nine it is hardly important that children learn to spell photosynthesis. (Some of the activities in the B chapters will give specific examples of integrating other study areas with science.)

As a further discussion of organizing for instruction let us now examine the role of the science textbook.

THE CURRICULUM AND THE TEXTBOOK

We recognize that for many teachers, especially beginning teachers, the textbook is *the* place where the science program is organized and described. Elsewhere we have discussed the elementary science textbook in relation to reading skills and as a souce of science information. Here we want to examine its general usefulness in science instruction.

During the past several decades elementary science textbooks have incorporated many of the objectives that we have discussed thus far. No longer are they simply readers; they are a source of activities and experiences that propel the reader out of the book and into the real world; they serve as a guide to explorations, demonstrations, and experiments with concrete materials; they ask questions that engage the student in the processes and methods of inquiry. They provide many suggestions for a hands-on science experience.

Like any other teaching tool, textbooks are as good as the ways teachers use them. Here are some guidelines teachers have found useful in getting the most out of textbooks.[11]

1. Examine the books and the accompanying teacher's guides to determine the general scope and sequence of its units. In other words, get acquainted with them—not only for the grade level the teacher will use but with those that precede it and those that follow. How can the illustrations be helpful? Are there study questions that can be used to motivate, to summarize, and to encourage further study? What motivating suggestions are provided? What provisions are made for individual differences? Is there provision for self-checking by the students?

2. Study the teacher's guides in considerable detail. Authors generally spend considerable time and effort in the production of these guides to provide practical suggestions for getting the most from the use of the text. The guides are often a course in how to teach science by using the particular text. The best teachers select from the many suggestions those that seem important and useful in their particular situations.

3. It is not necessary to teach the contents from page 1 to the index. Teachers select those units and experiences that are related to the seasons of the year, to ongoing projects, to the course of study, or to current interests the children are exploring.

4. Determine what resources of the school (library, playground, audiovisual aids, garden) and the community (parks, museums, bodies of water, rock formations, stores) can be used in relation to the selected units. See Chapter 5 for suggestions for use of school and community resources.

5. Make a list of needed concrete materials that are available and those that must be acquired. Children can often help to select and assemble such material. Have them organized and available.

6. Make note of any safety measures that should be followed.

7. Examine the reading level of the material to see what adjustments are necessary for individual students. Using the books can help to develop vocabulary, concept comprehension, organization of material, and other language-arts skills. Some children will need considerable help with this, others will not. Poor readers will be aided by the motivation provided by the concrete materials, experiments, and investigations.

8. Plan the lessons to help the students learn how to use the textbook effectively. Indicate when you need the textbook and for what purposes.

9. Discuss with other teachers of grades above and below your grade which science units they are teaching. Plan with them to avoid repetition and to promote useful sequences.

10. In *selecting* a textbook, teachers and textbook committees should determine, in addition to its accuracy, whether the *writing* is good: Are topics just mentioned or outlined but not developed? Are there too many topics in too little space? Does it provide inspiration as well as information? Can the text be not only a resource but an independent source of learning?

As time goes on, the teacher may find that the role of the textbook in teaching may change. The teacher may lean on it less or use it more depending on the nature of the material being studied. Sometimes it may be the chief resource, sometimes only a reference.

[11]See also P. C. Gega, "The Textbook Plus: Building a Better Science Program," *The National Elementary Principal* (January 1980); P. C. Gega, "Convert Your Text Series into a District Science Program," *Science and Children* (November/December 1982); and E. W. Eisner, "Why the Textbook Influences Curriculum," *Curriculum Review* (January/February 1987).

The teacher may expand some of the units and curtail or drop others. The curriculum may slowly evolve as it is based more closely on the individual needs, capabilities, and interests of the students. The curriculum should be realistically related to the resources and limitations in the school and community, and also allow time and place for unanticipated "teachable moments."

CURRICULUM DEVELOPMENT CRITERIA[12]

It is apparent, as Philip Morrison of the Massachusetts Institute of Technology has stated, "Method is meaningless in the absence of subject matter, stuff to work on," and that "subject matter is sterile if it is not permeated with questions about how, and why we bother to find out." What then are the criteria to take into account when designing or selecting the contents and methods of an elementary science program? Consider the following:

Content and Structure

1. *Is there consideration given to the complete scope of the science program, nursery school through grade 12?* The elementary school curriculum should, in fact must, be decided partially on the basis of a nursery school through high school sequence. The most successful science programs are planned or selected by groups representing all grade levels.
2. *Are the purposes and content of other subject matter areas considered?* The subject matter content of the other elementary school subjects, notably social studies, language arts, and mathematics, also influence the selection of the content of science.
3. *Is the program flexible enough to permit "science excursions" into the unplanned, the unexpected, the unusual, the unknown (to the teacher and children alike)—in unanticipated "teachable moments"?* Experienced teachers know that unplanned-for times are often the most productive, and the curriculum should permit time for exploring such avenues.
4. *Are there built-in procedures of evaluation to permit needed changes?* Constant attempts to determine our successes (and failures) are essential, and we must continue to make changes in light of our discoveries. Programs should always be considered tentative and thus subject to revision.
5. *Are the environmental surroundings of children— supermarkets and factories, roadways and automobiles, earthworms and robins, lawns and sidewalks—used as a laboratory for learning science?* The immediate environment is important. What are the local problems that must be solved in making the home, school, and community safe, healthy places in which to live? Are there problems of soil erosion, weather forecasting, air, water, and other pollution?
6. *Does the curriculum include material from the many areas of science subject matter?* Development in science may include problems from various areas of science—biology, chemistry, physics, earth or space science—and the integrating ideas among them.
7. *Are there themes and threads of subject matter areas evident in the curriculum?* Pervasive themes, such as space, time, change, adaptation, variety, interrelationships, and interaction of forces have been widely used as the bases for selecting material for the elementary science curriculum.

Children's Interests and Needs

8. *Is there individualization of instruction? Are there opportunities for children to work on their own, with adequate materials, and to proceed at their own pace without pressure?* Especially in science, there is ample opportunity for working on individual investigations if we use these opportunities more wisely. Increased emphasis on hands-on experience is a step in this direction.

---

[12]F. Finley, "Selecting a New Science Program?" *Science and Children* (October 1979). Gives evaluation criteria; an important article. R. E. Yager, "Successful Science Programs," *Science and Children* (April 1982); R. E. Yager, "The Search for Excellence in Science Education Begins," *Science and Children* (February 1982). Report of NSTA and the Council of State Supervisors' search for outstanding programs; "A Guide to Curriculum Planning in Science," 1987, *State Superintendent,* 125 S. Webster St., P.O. Box 7481, Madison, WI 53707.

9. *Are there opportunities for children to use science in the investigation of problems that are of real concern to them?* The nearer we come to identifying problems the answers to which make a difference to children, the more nearly we come to achieving our objectives. Relevance is indeed something to be taken into account. See also discussion of science/technology/society on pages 27–29.

10. *Does the organization and selection of content and processes take into account what we know about how children learn?* If we apply our knowledge of how children grow and develop, we are much less likely to select irrelevant material and employ inappropriate methods of instruction.

11. *Are there varied kinds of experience to provide for individual needs, interests, and capacities of children?* It makes sense to consider interests, needs, and capacities of children if we are planning a curriculum for them. If science subject matter is interesting and challenging to children they will want to learn it.

   Interest is a tremendous motivating factor. School experiences should broaden and deepen these interests. It is often caught from others, especially from teachers who have curiosity. Interests differ widely among children in kind, quality, intensity, and longevity. It cannot, therefore, be our only criterion for subject matter selection.

12. *Is provision made for the poor reader or non-reader, as well as for the good reader?* Reading still must constitute a significant part of children's experiences, and reading material must be supplied that fits the many and varied needs of children. The desire to improve reading skills often stems from the desire to know more about the science world.

The School and Its Resources

13. *Does the program provide for the utilization of the talents and interests of the teachers who are involved? Is in-service training provided?* None of the programs can be successful if we do not consider those who are to teach it. The best teachers continue to grow in interest in their scientific environment and expand their knowledge of it.

14. *Does the science program take into account the school organization?* An open school, a team-teaching situation, a school program designed around individualized instruction, a middle school, a departmentalized instruction program, a school dedicated to the self-contained classroom concept—each of these, and there are others—influences the selection of content. Methods of instruction and teaching cannot be effective if these factors are not considered.

15. *Is the apparatus and material required for teaching the program reasonable?* Materials should be appropriate to the level of the learners. They should be safe to use and easily obtainable.

Summary

These criteria indicate that science programs should be based on

1. A combination of factors such as needs of children, their growth and development, their environments, the content of science, and the total school program.
2. The development of skills and processes essential to scientifically literate adults.
3. The broad themes of science.

Each of these represents an emphasis that influences curriculum makers, textbook writers, and most certainly classroom teachers.

Let us turn now to an examination of the national programs to see what efforts are made to provide state and local educational bodies with science curricula options.

THE NATIONAL PROGRAMS

In the 1960s, emphasis on more science teaching resulted in the development of government-supported projects with carefully structured curricula. The funding for these programs has since dried up. However, the results of their efforts continue to exist in several forms.[13] Materials from the programs continue to be used in school sys-

[13]A. Shymansky, W. C. Kyle, Jr., and J. M. Alport, "How Effective Were the Hands-on Science Programs of Yesterday?" *Science and Children* (November/December 1982).

tems and by individual teachers who have been trained to use them. Some have been incorporated in commercial textbook series or work sheets or modules of material.

In the following section, we describe briefly three of the programs initiated in the 1960s and summarize their common features. Later we look at two new programs launched in the 1980s.

The real flavor of any program comes through when teaching it and observing the behaviors of children, discussing their feelings, and evaluating their reactions and accomplishments. It is then that we see the significance of a program that is described as "individualized," "action-centered," "process-oriented," and so forth.

Some school systems use parts of many of the national programs, adapt them to the local situa-

The life cycle of mealworms is observed. By the use of such materials, children acquire basic knowledge, investigative skills, and a positive attitude toward science. (*Courtesy of Science Curriculum Study, University of California.*)

tions, and include them with locally planned program material. Indeed, there are many locally developed programs that bear little resemblance to any other program. They have been developed by teachers, supervisors, and administrators to try to fit the needs of the children involved. Since many of the so-called national projects have been taken over by various commercial sources, they may no longer be designated as national projects but will be named for their publishers. Many science textbooks currently in use reflect the philosophy and findings of these projects.

The following brief summary serves to describe essential characteristics of three of the major projects.

Science Curriculum Improvement Study (SCIS II)

SCIS capsulizes its purpose as the development of scientific literacy in children, meaning a combination of basic knowledge, investigative experience, and attitude. A further concern is the development of a free and inquisitive frame of mind, the use of rational procedures for decision making, and the development in children of a positive attitude toward science and scientists.

Educators frequently distinguish among content, process, and attitude when they describe an educational program or evaluate its outcomes. The SCIS program combines these factors. Children are introduced to knowledge of scientific content through their experiences with diverse physical and biological materials. In the course of their investigations, they engage in observation, measurement, interpretation, prediction, and other processes, and they learn to cope confidently with new and unexpected findings by sifting evidence and forming conclusions.

Elementary Science Study (ESS)

ESS hopes to enrich each child's understanding, rather than to create scientific prodigies or direct all children toward scientific careers. Instead of beginning with a discussion of basic concepts of science, ESS puts physical materials into children's hands from the start and helps each child investigate the nature of the world around him or her through these materials. It incorporates both the spirit and the substance of science in such a way that the child's own rich world of exploration becomes more disciplined, more manageable, and more satisfying. All equipment is carefully selected to resemble materials that are normally accessible to children in their own environment and not imposingly "scientific."

There is little or no emphasis on specific objectives and less attempt at formal evaluation than in many of the other programs. The stress is not on the teaching of a series of science concepts but rather on providing children with experiences such as tadpole development, habits of mealworms, ways of lighting bulbs with batteries, and so on.

Science: A Process Approach II (SAPA II)

SAPA II is a revision of the original project, designed to present instruction that is intellectually stimulating and scientifically authentic. The program for elementary students through grade 6 is based on a belief that the scientific approach to gaining knowledge of the world has a fundamental importance in the general education of every child. It focuses on the processes of science (see pp. 20–24) instead of on science subject matter.

An important concept is that what is taught to children should resemble what scientists do—the "processes" that they carry out in their own scientific activities. Scientists do observe, classify, measure, infer, make hypotheses, and perform experiments. How have they come to be able to do these things? Presumably, they have learned to do them over a period of many years by practicing doing them. If scientists have learned to gain information in these ways, surely the elementary forms of what they do can begin to be learned in the early grades. This does not imply the purpose

of making everyone a scientist. Instead, it advances the idea that understanding science depends on being able to look on and deal with the world in the ways that the scientist does.

Common Features of the Projects[14]

Although each of the projects has distinctive characteristics, there are certain common features. These may be useful guides when we are considering using programs or part of programs and methods of instruction.

1. The role of the teacher becomes that of a guide to learning rather than that of a fountain of knowledge for children.
2. Scientists and classroom teachers have been actively involved in most of the projects in determining content, methods of instruction, and general development.
3. There is emphasis on involvement and hands-on manipulation on the part of the learner. Children are involved in much of the planning. The emphasis is on direct experiences.
4. Some new subject matter not previously included in the elementary school curriculum has been introduced.
5. In many cases there are specifically designed laboratory materials and equipment.
6. Many textbook series and other printed materials are being patterned after the project philosophy and are being used in the schools.
7. In many of the projects, concepts of a more abstract nature are introduced earlier in the learning experience of children.
8. There is less emphasis on subject matter as such and more emphasis on processes—on learning how to learn—on emphasizing discovery and creative and critical thinking.
9. The experiences are characterized as being open-ended: There may be several solutions and an-

[14]Delta Education, P.O. Box M, Nashua, NH 03061 will supply apparatus and materials for teaching these and other programs. Write for their illustrated catalogue. See also B. L. Lockard and G. Dunkelberger, "Beyond the Grocery Store," *Science and Children* (May 1987) for a description of important sources of materials that are custom-made and assembled for teaching various kinds of elementary science programs.

swers, and the activities may lead into other related activities.

10. There is emphasis on exactness. Many projects stress a quantitative approach and emphasize the development of mathematics skills.

THE NEW NATIONAL PROJECTS: A NEW BEGINNING

Despite the efforts of launching the projects just described, and many others in the last decades that involved the testing of K–12 curricula in thousands of schools, the retraining of teachers, and the expenditure of many millions of dollars, there is grave concern that "the deterioration of science and mathematics in American schools over the past 15 years has created a threat to the nation's future and the ability of our citizens to function in a high-technology society."[15]

To meet this challenge two major projects have been launched, one by the National Science Foundation and the other by the National Academy of Sciences.

National Science Foundation: Upgrading Science Education

The National Science Foundation program began with three grants to "foster the development and adoption of science curricula in grades K–6." The goal is "to make high quality science curricula options available to state and local educational agencies with a view to improving the science knowledge of young students." The NSF-funded curriculum development will emphasize hands-on learning and will reinforce lessons on other subjects such as language arts and mathematics. Each of the four-year grants is matched by financial commitments by publishers who will work with the grantees to develop and test materials in participating classrooms and to train teachers to use the materials. Initially three four-year grants have been awarded.

[15]National Academy of Sciences, July 13, 1987.

NSF awarded a grant to the Technical Education Research Center (TERC) of Cambridge, Massachusetts, which will work with the National Geographic Society in developing 10 science units for grades 4 through 6, as well as a classroom-linking telecommunications system. The National Geographic Society will publish the course material, which will be designed to either supplement or replace existing science curricula.

The Biological Science Curriculum Study (BSCS) of Colorado Springs will develop a new science health curriculum for students, K–6. The materials will include 42 hands-on modules, teacher's guides, computer software, and supplementary activities integrating science lessons with reading, language arts, and mathematics. The Kendall Hunt Publishing Company of Dubuque, Iowa, will publish the resulting materials.

The Education Development Center (EDC) of Newton, Massachusetts, will develop a life, physical, and earth science curriculum geared specifically to the needs of urban elementary students and teachers. Twenty-four to 36 hands-on modules and supplementary teaching materials will be tested in six large cities. Delta Education of Nashua, New Hampshire, will publish the resulting material.

The National Science Foundation will continue an expansion of these grants with the same general objectives.

National Science Resources Center: Science and Technology for Children

The National Science Resources Center[16] is mounting a major project to improve the teaching of science in the nation's elementary schools. This project, *Science and Technology for Children* (STC), will produce 24 modular hands-on resource units to support the teaching of science in

[16]The National Science Resources Center is a new institution established by the National Academy of Science and the Smithsonian Institution to improve the teaching of science and mathematics in the nation's elementary and secondary schools. The description of their project is taken from material prepared by NSRC.

grades 1–6. The units, which will address important topics in life science, physical science, earth science, and technology, will actively involve elementary school children in scientific investigations. The investigations will be designed to develop children's problem-solving and critical thinking skills, while broadening their understanding of basic science concepts. The units will be developed, field-tested, and disseminated in cooperation with a network of school systems, state departments of education, science museums, and university science teaching centers that are working with the NSRC to improve the teaching of elementary school science.

Each of the STC units will include a teacher's guide, a student activity booklet, and specifications for the science materials and apparatus needed to carry out the science investigations in the unit. The teacher's guides will include an annotated list of the supplementary resources that can be used with the science unit, such as videotapes and films, computer software, and science tradebooks.

The elementary science materials produced by the STC project will be disseminated in several ways, in addition to the marketing strategies traditionally used by commercial publishers. The STC project will be publicized through special presentations at meetings of organizations such as the National Council of PTAs, the National Association of Elementary School Principals, the National Science Teachers Association, the National School Boards Association, and the Council of Chief State School Officers. The center will also ask the school systems, universities, and science museums participating in the STC project to serve as dissemination centers, to provide teachers, principals, science supervisors, and superintendents of schools throughout the nation with information about the program.

In addition to developing and disseminating high-quality elementary science teaching materials, the STC project will help school systems establish the delivery systems needed to get hands-on science into elementary school classrooms, placing special emphasis on the design of effective in-service training programs and science materials support systems. The project will analyze the lessons learned by school systems that have instituted and maintained exemplary elementary science programs, in order to assist other school systems planning elementary science program improvement efforts. After the completion of the project, the NSRC will continue to disseminate the materials produced by the STC project and will continue to help school systems that would like to improve the teaching of science in their elementary schools.

DISCOVERING FOR YOURSELF

1. Select one of the following topics that you might want to teach. (If you prefer, select any other science topic that interests you.) List the science ideas or concepts that children might learn as a result of a study of

   a classroom pet animal
   the school lunch program
   a bird feeder station
   changes in the moon's appearance
   all kinds of thermometers
   musical instruments
   a snowstorm or rainstorm
   rocks in the neighborhood

2. For the topic you have selected state some behaviors that students might achieve. Be as specific as possible.
3. What specific materials—apparatus, books—will be needed for this topic?
4. Plan a single lesson on any science topic. Include in your plan a statement of the problem, the objectives, materials, strategy/procedure, outcomes (concepts, processes, and possible new problems).
5. Examine an elementary science textbook for any grade.
   a. What are the major units for that grade?
   b. Select one of the units. What are the main ideas suggested in the unit?
   c. What suggestions are given to introduce the unit to the children? Can you add to these suggestions?
   d. Select one lesson in one of the chapters.

(1) How is the lesson introduced?

(2) What activities are the children engaged in?

(3) What questions are used? (See section on questions in Chapter 5.)

(4) What main ideas or concepts are developed? Make a list of them and add others.

(5) What science processes or skills are involved?

(6) What student changes of behaviors might be expected?

(7) What reading and writing skills are used, or could be used?

(8) What optional activities are suggested?

(9) What additional characteristics contribute to the usefulness of the text?

(10) What kind of aids are provided for the teacher?

6. Make a list of characteristics of a good elementary science teacher. Use the list to evaluate yourself.

7. Select a curriculum guide or course of study. Examine it carefully. Then use the criteria listed in this chapter to evaluate your selection. What changes would you suggest in its content and structure?

CHAPTER 5

PROBLEMS AND QUESTIONS ABOUT TEACHING

We hope to imbue students with an experimental, critical, ardent approach to their work and to the social problems of the world. If we can do this, we are ready to leave the future to them.

LUCY SPRAGUE MITCHELL, FOUNDER AND FIRST PRESIDENT
BANK STREET COLLEGE OF EDUCATION

In this chapter we discuss a variety of problems: evaluation as part of the teaching process; helping the gifted and mainstreaming the handicapped; science in early childhood; strategies of classroom management; how to ask the "right" questions; finding resources in the school and the community; and conducting science fairs and teaching the metric system.

ARE WE ACCOMPLISHING OUR INTENTIONS?

If we base a total evaluation on whether or not a student makes a satisfactory grade on a test that covers the subject matter studied, evaluation is simple. But our objectives for science teaching in the elementary school are much broader. The importance of testing only for the recall of facts is questionable. We are really concerned with the understanding of concepts, with how much the children have learned about how to use the methods of inquiry, and with the attitudes, interests, and appreciations that have developed.

Evaluation is an integral part of the learning process. It starts when teaching starts, and goes on long after a lesson or unit is completed. "Success" is revealed to the teacher by many signs. It may simply be the gleam in the children's eyes or the smiles on their faces. In early childhood, it may be the imaginative painting and block building that children engage in following a science experience. It may be the children's capacity to put a science principle to work in a new situation. It may be the number and kinds of questions that children ask. It may be their answers to such questions as "How can we find out?" or "What would happen if . . .?" It may be their skill in manipulating materials, their involvement in long-term projects; their participation in school fairs. It may be what children do after they leave the school building; the hobbies they pursue, the games they play, books they read, television programs they observe.[1]

Evaluation Instruments[2]

As long as we give grades for accomplishment in science and as long as we conduct educational experiments to discover more about teaching and learning, we shall need some kinds of measuring tests. Tests have their limitations, but their effectiveness is improved by observing the following suggestions.

Tests must be designed to measure, insofar as possible, the attainment of all the goals and not merely the children's mastery of subject matter. Test scores should be only one of the criteria for evaluating progress, and results should not be used to interpret or predict more than intended in the original design. Tests should be used as a teaching device, as well as an evaluation instrument of the success of the teacher and the learner.

---

[1]From "Science: K–6," Board of Education, New York City.

[2]C. H. Nelson, *Improving Objective Tests in Science* (Washington, D.C.: NSTA); "More Than a Letter Grade," *Science and Children* (September 1976). E. Victor and M. Lerner, *Readings in Science Education for the Elementary School* (New York: Macmillan, 1975). H. J. Funk, "An Examination of the Levels of the Questions on Standardized Tests for Elementary Science," *Science and Children* (January 1977). Includes a list of tests. S. J. Rakow and T. C. Gee, "Test Science Not Reading," *The Science Teacher* (February 1987). Practical suggestions for test construction. R. D. Anderson, "Has the Objective Been Attained?" *Science and Children* (October 1970).

Tests should be so constructed that students will have to do the following kinds of things: recall information and apply it to new situations, see relationships between facts, analyze data and draw appropriate conclusions from them, make decisions on the basis of material read, demonstrate predetermined behaviors appropriate to their levels of growth and development, and demonstrate the ability to use specific process skills. It is important that the tests are easily read so that success or failure is not based on ability to read but on the objectives to be tested.

The testing program must be designed and administered in such a way that children do not feel threatened; so that they do not get the idea that the whole learning experience was for the purpose of "passing the test"; so that their own self-image is not undermined; and so that the genuine satisfactions and delights and learnings that came with the original experiences are not debased.

A good test may require a child to attempt to *design* an experiment in order to solve some specific problem. It may present an experiment poorly set up and ask the child to *react* to it. It may present a paragraph, a picture, a chart, or some other material and ask the child to attempt to *draw conclusions* from it. The material may be selected to emphasize attitudes or methods of investigation or some other elements of science objectives. The student may be asked to *recognize* relationships to show that he or she sees how facts can be added together to make generalizations. The student may be asked to *identify objects* in order to discuss them or to show what he or she knows about them. He or she may be asked to *classify* objects, to *estimate*, to *predict, measure, infer, demonstrate*.

Achievement of students on standardized multiple choice tests may not measure the attainment of all of the goals just discussed. Such tests do not test creativity or the ability to develop original solutions to problems. There is also a danger that the test items become the totality of what is taught and learned. Although they are tempting, because they are easy to conduct and grade, they certainly should not be used as the sole measure of educational excellence. Their most pernicious use is when they are employed to grade teachers' competence.

It is not always essential that tests be in written form. Laboratory tests, in which children are asked to solve certain problems with materials, are often effective. (Given: wire, bulb, socket, switch, and dry cell, hook them up to make the bulb light.) Oral response to a situation can be more effective for some children.

Above all, remember that all students cannot be expected to progress at the same rate toward any specific goals. Try to consider growth as an individual matter, and remember that children's goals may differ from those of the teacher, that they both change, and that evaluation is long range and continuous.

Evaluating Our Teaching[3]

We wrap ourselves in curriculum construction, theories of teaching, selecting and judging materials, and similar educational matters, and forget that *everything depends on what happens when we work with children*.

There are many ways of setting up criteria for judging our accomplishments. Here are general criteria to use as a nucleus. (Individual teachers may add to and modify them to fit their class situations.) Teachers may ask themselves such questions as the following:

Was there student interest? Did it grow? When children are interested and enthusiastic they are likely to show improvement in all other objectives.

Was there sufficient student participation? Participation is of many different kinds—asking or answering questions, making thoughtful suggestions, giving careful attention, pursuing individual or group activities, and so on.

Did I give attention to the individual needs of

[3]"Evaluating Elementary Science Curricula," *Science and Children* (December 1972). Contains a list of 16 evaluative criteria.

students? Those who need special opportunities, those who need recognition of their special talents and interests, those who need encouragement, and those who for many other reasons need individual attention should receive it when conditions make this possible.

Did students think, and did I give them time to think? If students are challenged and have time and an opportunity to think, we are well on the way to the development of better thought processes.

Did the situation promote good attitudes and appreciations, interests, and fun? Satisfying experiences promote learning.

Was there opportunity for student planning? There are many opportunities for planning, and students grow in ability to plan effectively when they have a chance to do so.

Was there a good student-teacher relationship? This has little to do with always letting students do what they want. When decisions are made cooperatively students can contribute according to their varying abilities and experiences, and there is more likelihood that there will be mutual respect. The good teacher is able to identify situations in which children have the background for making decisions.

Was the material adapted to the ability of the group? Material that is too difficult is discouraging; material that does not challenge causes students to lose interest.

Were the physical needs important to the teaching handled adequately? If the activities call for specific numbers and types of equipment and materials, or if location and time of day are special, they should be planned for. Not enough thermometers, no afternoon sun, no extension cord for the projector are distracting if they are needed but not at hand. Good teachers are well organized and orderly—this enhances a learning environment.

This is obviously not an exhaustive set of criteria. It serves to illustrate the kind of questions useful in evaluating the results of day-to-day teaching. A comparison of these suggestions with the items in "Criteria for Curriculum Development" (Chapter 4) will be helpful in seeing the relationship of these suggestions with those made for the science program.

HOW CAN I HELP CREATIVE AND GIFTED CHILDREN?[4]

Although we are not trying primarily to make scientists of elementary students, we *are* trying to identify students with special interests, aptitudes, and gifts, and to encourage them in their talents. Many famous scientists have shown evidence of their aptitudes in childhood. The most successful elementary school teachers provide opportunities for especially talented students by showing interest in their accomplishments, providing resources (people, places, printed material, and so on) for them, using them as special science assistants, and encouraging them in other ways.

There are many criteria for identifying especially talented and creative children. Such a student shows personal traits such as the following: exhibits continued interest in science problems, is able to do abstract reasoning, has a good scientific vocabulary, persists in attempting to solve problems, is skillful in manipulating apparatus and materials, and chooses to read scientific material generally above the level of his or her fellow students.

[4]Margaret McIntyre, "Checklist for Recognizing a Child's Talent in Science," *Science and Children* (April 1982). Thirty items helpful in identifying talent. S. Cohn, "Searching for Scientifically Talented Youth," *Science and Children* (October 1979). *Science and Children* (March 1979). Contains several articles dealing with identification and treatment of gifted children. B. F. Consuegra, "Identifying the Gifted in Science and Mathematics," *School Science and Mathematics* (March 1982); H. D. Foley and G. H. Krockover, "Selected Activities in Science and Mathematics for Gifted Young Children," *School Science and Mathematics* (January 1982); D. J. Kuhn, "Giving the Gifted Their Due," *The Science Teacher* (February 1979). Contains an excellent bibliography. W. C. George, S. J. Cohn, and J. C. Stanley, eds., *Educating the Gifted: Acceleration and Enrichment* (Baltimore: John Hopkins University Press, 1980), 242 pp.; R. S. Coburn "Schooling the Precocious," *Science 83* (September 1983).

Having identified students that appear to be gifted and creative in science, it is important to remember that they have many of the same needs as all other children have, and these should be provided for. Although their talent should be encouraged, it should not be exploited to the point where overall development suffers.

A good science program is designed so that children with science aptitudes will naturally make themselves known because opportunities for individual expression are provided. Science talent expresses itself in different ways: One student may be gifted in designing apparatus, another in dealing with the mathematical aspects of science, a third in raising especially thoughtful problems. A teacher may encourage talent by allowing time for creative ventures, by giving approval for progress in independent learning, and by having books, science kits, science magazines, and other aids available that will permit individual students to work on their own.

Some schools have special classes for gifted children. This practice has been challenged. Writer and child psychologist Bruno Bettelheim has pointed out, "If you separate the gifted, the best teachers and resources go to those who are gifted. Those who are already disadvantaged get the short end of everything." Science clubs, science projects, and science fairs are ways of inviting creativity without discriminating against anyone.

HOW CAN I HELP SLOW LEARNERS?

Children who may generally be considered as "slow learners" often respond well to science activities because there can be much learning through doing, through observing with the senses, through experimenting and constructing. Coupled with this, evaluation in science can depend less on paper-and-pencil tests and more on the observation of behaviors. Underlying all these factors is our approach to the slow learner. What are the possible reasons for the slowness? Are we

making every conceivable effort to overcome the obstacles? Are we using motivating forces to the fullest? Are we taking potential accomplishments into account? How well have we analyzed the individual's difficulties? How reasonable are we in our expectations? Is too much emphasis placed on reading when this skill is the child's weakness? These are some of the questions we ask ourselves in any area of the curriculum where slow learning is a factor; the answers are the same for any area.

HOW CAN I HELP HANDICAPPED CHILDREN IN MY CLASSROOM? WHAT ABOUT MAINSTREAMING?[5]

"Myths about the capacity of the handicapped to perform in science and the classroom need debunking," states Ben Thompson.[6]

The following are some of the long perpetuated myths he considers unfair and untrue:

Handicapped students are more likely than other students to be injured in a science class.

Most handicapped students need to learn the basics; therefore science is not important to them.

---

[5]M. E. Corrick, Jr., ed., *Teaching Handicapped Students Science* (National Education Association Publication, 1981). A comprehensive treatment including a section entitled "Teaching Mainstream Strategies." C. Blankenship and N. S. Lilly, *Mainstreaming Students with Learning and Behavior Problems* (New York: Holt, 1981), 353 pp.; Rodger W. Bybee, "Helping the Special Student Fit In," *The Science Teacher* (October 1979); G. M. Stanbury, "A Principal's Perspective," *Science and Children* (January 1981); "Position Statement: Science for the Handicapped," *Science and Children* (November/December 1982). From NSTA Board of Directors, J. S. Wielert and P. Retish, "Mainstreaming and the Science Teacher," *School, Science and Mathematics* (November 1983). A comprehensive treatment with specific suggestions.

[6]B. Thompson, "Myth and Science For the Handicapped," *Science and Children* (November/December 1979).

This is one of the stops on a "touch and see" nature trail. Blind and partially sighted children follow a roped-off path to discover and enjoy nature. (*Courtesy of U.S. Dept. of Agriculture.*)

Handicapped students can't learn science. If they are slow learners, science is too hard. If they have a physical handicap, they lack an essential sense or skill.

Having a handicapped pupil in my class will hold the others back.

All handicapped pupils will be mainstreamed. I'll have students who just can't learn.

Thompson explains why he believes that each of these myths are false.

More and more handicapped children—partially sighted, blind, hard of hearing, those with verbal disabilities as well as nonverbal handicapped, emotionally disadvantaged, severely retarded, and others—are being assigned for all or part of the day to the regular classroom.[7] A section of the public law dealing with the education of the handicapped states that "to the maximum extent appropriate handicapped children should be educated with children who are not handicapped and that special classes, separate schooling, and other means of removal of handicapped children from the regular environment occur only when the nature or severity of the handicap is such that education in regular class with the use of supplementary aids and services cannot be achieved satisfactorily." This places a new responsibility on teachers, many of whom are apprehensive about assuming responsibilities for dealing with handicapped children in the classroom. Teachers cite the following concerns: lack of available materials, not trained to work with handicapped, few meaningful supplementary materials, and students cannot work independently.

The process of "mainstreaming" children (placing children in the regular classroom for selected experiences) is being urged because many educators and parents believe that the best education for many handicapped children will result if they are placed in an environment with so-called normal children.

Our discussion of this problem cannot be a course on how to teach science to handicapped children in a regular classroom. We can deal only with general ideas and present some guidelines. Teachers who have had experience with this problem indicate the following reasons why science is ideally suited for inclusion in a mainstreaming situation.

Handicapped children can often experience much needed success in science activities because many of these are hands-on experiences where they can see the results of their efforts.

Science experiences are appealing to most children; exceptional children respond positively to learning

[7]C. R. Cobel, F. E. Mattheis, and C.T. Vizzini, "A Project to Promote Science for the Handicapped," *School, Science and Mathematics* (December 1982).

about pets, using magnets, growing plants, examining rocks, and similar activities.

Although many of the activities are group-oriented, emotionally disturbed children can often work independently with science materials when this seems advisable, as it sometimes does, since these children frequently prefer working alone.

For many children, science experiences are helpful as a therapeutic activity, making them more comfortable as they become involved in experimenting, observing, and using their senses.

Science experiences are helpful in teaching most children to read. This has been found true with many types of exceptional children especially when they read about what they have done, read the directions for doing something, or read to find answers. This is also true of language-arts experiences such as listening, discussing, and vocabulary development. For further discussion see the "Reading to Find Out" section in Chapter 3.

Handicapped children have generally had very limited experience with science, thus it is a new field and sparks their interest.

Science experiences are important in meeting the social and psychological needs of exceptional children. They provide opportunities for all children in the class to work together as they investigate and experiment.

Perhaps not enough has been said about the effects on so-called normal children of having handicapped children in their classroom. Experience indicates that there are many positive results including an appreciation and positive reaction toward handicapped children—a feeling of helpfulness as children work together. Experienced personnel who work with handicapped and "normal" children indicate that handicapped children do not want to be treated differently. Normal children need to learn how to live with the handicapped. The key is empathy, not sympathy.

Teachers in discussing their experiences with including exceptional children in their classrooms contribute the following advice:

1. Read as much as you can about the needs and how to deal with the special handicaps of the child in your room.[8] If possible observe how other classroom teachers as well as specially trained teachers work with such a child. Make as much use as possible of the specially trained personnel. If possible avail yourself of in-service or college courses designed to help.

2. Try not to be impatient. Progress may be slow.

3. Don't confuse the handicap with lack of intelligence. Remember that your good teaching techniques are as appropriate to a handicapped child as they are to any other child and will go a long way toward providing a successful experience.

4. Make all educational opportunities as equal as possible under the circumstances.

5. Observe the handicapped and try to discover how you can adapt the science experiences to their particular limitations and needs.

6. No progress is made without effort and study. Having a handicapped child in your classroom will consume much time, effort, and patience but will also be a very rewarding experience.

7. Generally, handicapped children are more like other children than they are different from them. The differences seem to become less when you get acquainted with these children.

8. Use your techniques for individualized instruction. They are often very successful with handicapped children.

The science teaching objectives are the same for handicapped children as for any other children. The degree of achievement will, of course, vary with the degree and kind of handicap.

Many handicapped children have become accomplished scientists.[9]

---

[8]*Science and Children* (March 1976). Entire issue is devoted to science for the handicapped; contains bibliography. B. Thompson, "Myth and Science for the Handicapped," and D. R. Brown, "Helping Handicapped Youngsters Learn Science by Doing," in *What Research Says to the Science Teacher*, Vol. 2 (NSTA, 1979). Contains practical suggestions for teaching children with various handicaps. R. W. Bybee, "Helping the Special Student Fit In," *Science Teacher* (October 1979). Lists of special guidelines. H. H. Hofman and K. S. Ricker, *Science Education and the Physically Handicapped*, (Washington, D.C.: NSTA, 1980). A source book.

[9]"A Challenge to Teachers from Handicapped Scientists," *Science and Children* (March 1976).

You are not alone in your efforts to educate a handicapped child placed in your classroom. There are almost always trained personnel available to help. The amount and kind of assistance varies under different circumstances. National and local organizations can also supply assistance.[10]

WHAT SCIENCE CAN BE TAUGHT IN PREKINDERGARTEN AND KINDERGARTEN PROGRAMS?[11]

The science program for young children is based on their total school program. It is an integral part of that program and utilizes the daily experiences and routines, the centers of interest in the room, and the changing seasons as resources for science. It is based on the theory that young children are intensely interested in themselves and in their immediate environment. This interest is communicated in various ways: through dramatization, verbalization, block building, art, music, and other forms of creative expression.[12]

At an early age children demonstrate a tendency to explore by using their senses: to participate actively, to inquire, to use techniques of

learning as befits their stages of development. A child's curiosity grows and develops through first-hand experiences. Young children must have many concrete experiences before they can begin to work with abstract ideas. For, as Piaget says, "To know an object, to know an event, is not simply to look at it and make a mental copy or image of it. To know an object is to act on it.... An operation is thus the essence of knowledge."

The following passage summarizes the school's concern:

> The role of the school is to meet the needs of each child through a well-planned, dynamic program which prepares for successful participation in the world. The school gives children the opportunity to inquire, discover, participate, and achieve in the company of their peers. The school helps the children find order and purpose in their environment by providing them with techniques for learning how to cope with the expanding horizons of their world. Meeting the children's needs at an early stage of development provides the basis for a purposeful and satisfying life. There is no doubt, too, that meeting children's needs at an early age will also help to shape their future.[13]

The suggestions that follow are organized around the major goals for teaching science.

Learning and Using Inquiry Skills

1. Try to make as much use of natural curiosity as possible by following and expanding it. Inquisitive children will ask many science questions and not always at convenient times. No one can—or should—answer all of them. Let's guide children in exploring their curiosity as far as they want to go, and give as much recognition to asking as we do to answering. See pages 85 and 86 for discussion about asking the "right" questions.
2. Help children grow in ability to use process skills: asking, listening, observing with *all* their senses, in-

---

[10]Science for the Handicapped Association, Department of Elementary Education, University of Wisconsin, Eau Claire, WI 54701; Council for Exceptional Children, 1920 Association Drive, Reston, VA 22091.

[11]A regular feature, "Early Childhood," appears in *Science and Children* and contains many practical teaching suggestions as well as accompanying philosophy and objectives. M. J. Bricka, "Teaching Science to Preschoolers," *Science and Children* (October 1981). Describes many appropriate science experiences. M. McIntyre, "Learning to Observe Animals," *Science and Children* (May 1981). An excellent survey of classroom suggestions.

[12]For further discussion, see *Piaget's Theory Applied to an Early Childhood Curriculum*, with an introduction by C. S. Lavatelli (Boston: A Center for Media Development, 1970), 163 pp.; B. J. Wadsworth, *Piaget for the Classroom Teacher* (New York: Longmans, 1978); R. L. Roche, "The Child and Science," *Association for Childhood Education International*, Washington, D.C. 1980, 42 pp.

[13]Reprinted from *Prekindergarten and Kindergarten Curriculum Guide*, 1969–1970, Series No. 5, by permission of the Board of Education of the City of New York.

vestigating to see what happens, reporting by showing and telling, manipulating, and measuring. They should be better at using such skills and senses in June than they were in September.

3. Keep tying experiences together: "Remember what we did the other day to find out about our pinwheels? Could we try it again? What else could we do?"

4. Label these experiences *science*: Both children and their parents should know that they are having an early brush with science experiences.

5. Encourage both boys and girls to participate. If you believe that attitudes are established early, then help each child to be successful in science.

6. Remember that the processes involved in discovery are as important as what is discovered.

7. Keep in mind that there are many instances at this level where problems are left unsolved or only partly solved. This is as it should be. We come back to such problems as the children mature.

8. Guide inquiry by helping children to identify new processes to use. The kinds of processes children can handle with success change as children grow and develop, just as the kind of subject matter that they can deal with changes.

9. Remember that you cannot hurry inquiry.

Developing Scientific Attitudes

What can we do to help the very young take the beginning steps in the direction of developing attitudes and expanding their interests and appreciations? These are a part of every experience, every lesson every day, and it is important to keep them in mind. Here are suggestions:

1. We can provide many opportunities for using *all* of the senses to discover.[14]

2. We can help to provide an environment full of interesting experiences, opportunities for exploring, for making things, for expressing ideas.

3. We can use books, and when children ask, "Was that a *true* story?" we can make use of this circumstance to begin the evaluating of materials. Some children

as they listen to reading may at a very early age begin to differentiate between entertaining stories and books that are sources of information. In such a discussion the teacher does not *always* provide answers or try to close the problem. He or she encourages children to express their thoughts and feelings. Remember that a story may be true *emotionally* for a child, although it is in the *form* of fantasy. Young children grow slowly in understanding the distinction between reality and fantasy, and they do not all grow in this respect at the same rate.

4. We can make greater use of trying out things to discover. "Shall we try it again and see what happens?" Repeating experiences under different circumstances intended to show the same idea is important if we want to help children withhold judgment and develop related scientific attitudes.

5. We can make more effective use of observation experiences to develop questioning attitudes. "Could we look in *more* places?" "Shall we each take a turn at looking to check if we all see the same thing?" (Observe carefully and often.) "What can we find out by looking?" "How else can we find out?" "What can we do to be sure?"

6. We can urge children to show and discuss, to listen and to think, to manipulate and wonder. These skills develop slowly at first. They grow as the children do, but they will not develop unless we expect them to.

7. We can provide materials and problems that will develop interests children have not thought about. It is with a variety of materials that children learn to create, broaden their horizons, and work out ideas. Children will not be curious about things and ideas they do not know exist.

8. We must remember that we cannot help another develop interest in, or have some appreciation for science unless we ourselves have some of each.

Learning Subject Matter

The science content in the earliest grades is part of the total science program: It opens up such areas as magnetism, the earth, space, living things, the nature of materials, sound and light, weather phenomena, and motion and force, by providing many experiences in these areas. These form the basis for later science interests and knowledge.

[14]J. M. Schulz and B. Burchett, "Sensory Boxes," *Science and Children* (January 1975).

The early childhood science program is intended to help children gain new perceptions of matter, of space, of time, and of number.

The following suggestions will overlap some of those made earlier when we discussed inquiry skills:

1. Adapt the learning of information to the children's level, but *do not underestimate* children's abilities and interests. Experiences indicate that many are able to go much further and faster in the pursuit of information than we have sometimes thought. Remember, however, it is not only *can* they, but *should* they?
2. Help children put ideas together. Recall related information and help children go as far as they can in seeing relationships.
3. Construct a record of some of the science ideas children have learned. Many children cannot read. They do not need to. They can listen, and they can reach and touch. (See Chapter 3 for description of experience charts.)
4. Provide simple experiences with common materials to open up such science areas as space, living things, sound, light, weather, motion and force, and the nature of materials. The method of organization of the material is based on natural themes that constitute an invitation to explore: "Getting Wet and Drying"; "Discovering with Our Senses"; "Seesaws and Balances"; "Seeds and Fruits"; "Uphill and Downhill"; "Blowing Soap Bubbles"; "Science in a Pan of Water"; "Science in a Sandbox"; "All Kinds of Pets"; "Science in Wheels"; and "Science in Block Building."[15] These are not necessarily developed in one neat, consecutive sequence; they may be picked up and dropped at various intervals.

Let us consider, for example, a science table or science corner as an opportunity for "Discovering with Our Senses." Some typical items are a magnet (with objects to use with it), some seed pods, some stones and seashells, a green plant, a small bell, a deserted bird's nest, a toy, a piece of driftwood. Give children time to examine the objects an ask, "What can you discover about these things?" "How will you find out?" (Feel them, look

[15]See *Science: Grades K–2 and Prekindergarten Curriculum* (Board of Education of the City of New York, 1970).

at them, smell them, lift them, etc.) After there has been time to explore, urge the children to tell each other what they found out. The discussion will raise questions, and children may plan how they might answer them. If the children are able, they may dictate sentences for an experience chart containing some of their findings. It is easy to see how this experience with "Discovering with Our Senses" can become ongoing, can involve language arts, and can contribute to attaining our overall science teaching objectives.

Each of the B chapters describes experiences that are appropriate for use with young children. Each suggests materials to use and procedures to follow in guiding the learning experiences.

HOW CAN WE GROW IN ABILITY TO ASK THE "RIGHT" QUESTIONS?

During open school week, parents visited a fourth-grade classroom where a science lesson was in progress. The teacher had on her desk an aquarium properly set up, with gravel, small rocks, water, plants, snails, and fish, and with air space on top under the cover. Her purpose was to help children classify the objects and living things in the aquarium, first into living and non-living and then to further subdivide these into smaller categories. Perhaps the teacher was overanxious in the presence of visitors; at one point in the development of the lesson (a very good one), when the answer to one of her questions was not immediately forthcoming, she blurted out, "Tell me what I have in mind."

Perhaps too many of our questions expect students to recall facts or to follow our exact line of reasoning. Perhaps we don't always take enough time to find out what students have in *their* minds.

Good questions are the keys to good teaching in all curriculum areas. In science, questions have a special role since they are the starting point for children's investigations. In spirit, this is essentially the way in which scientists initiate research. Questions give purpose and direction to activity. Therefore the science program outlined in the B chapters is developed through problems that are posed as questions.

Children ask questions naturally. An important goal in science teaching is to encourage and cultivate this questioning attitude. Children should feel that school is the place to ask questions, that their questions are important, and that questions often trigger exciting explorations. The teacher helps set the stage by arranging for situations that provoke questions. By the kinds of questions asked, the teacher also serves as a model for the children as they develop and improve their skill in questioning.

Here are some suggestions adapted in part from an article "Asking the Right Questions."[16] (Although some of these items apply particularly to the discussion and development lesson led principally by the teacher, they also may be useful in other kinds of learning activities.)

1. There is value in silence—*your* silence. After asking a question, *wait* in order to provide students with the opportunity to consider your question and formulate their responses. After a student gives an answer *wait again* before giving your reaction. The second "wait" provides students with the opportunity to add to, modify, or elaborate the initial response.

2. Don't allow your students to suffer from "question shock." Picture what would happen to you if you sat all day long being bombarded with questions at the rate of two or three per minute and were given less than a second to answer. Reduce the number of questions. (This will happen automatically if you follow suggestion 1.)

3. Avoid repeating student responses. This takes up class time and also encourages students to listen to you rather than each other. If a student's response is not heard, encourage that student by saying something like, "That's an interesting idea. I don't think that the whole class heard it, though. Would you say it again so everyone can hear?"

4. Ask the questions first before indicating the student who is to answer. In that way, all the students will be challenged.

5. Don't ride along on the wave of raised hands. Call on students who don't raise their hands.

6. Try to get students to listen to and interact with each other. Use such questions as, "What do you think about that?" (There will be more opportunity for student-initiated interactions when they work in small groups.)

7. Ask more "open questions" and fewer "closed questions." *Open questions* anticipate a wide range of acceptable responses rather than one or two "right answers." They draw on students' past experiences, but they also cause students to give opinions and their reasons for these opinions, to infer and to identify implications, to formulate hypotheses or to make judgments based on their own values. Examples of open questions are

> If you were to make a display of space travel for the school bulletin board, what would you include?
> What do you suppose life on earth might be like with weaker gravity?

Some useful open question starters are

> What would happen if . . .?
> How can we find out . . .?
> How can we be sure that . . .?
> Where could you find . . .?

Closed questions are those for which there is a limited number of acceptable responses or "right answers." Examples of closed questions are

> What are the names of the planets?
> What is the difference between a bar magnet and a horseshoe magnet?
> What is sand made of?

Typical closed questions start with who, what, how many, name, how far.

8. Make certain that your questioning techniques and evaluation techniques do not conflict. If you asked open questions in class discussion and then used closed questions for purposes of testing, you have defeated your objectives. If you do this you are telling your students what you really value is their ability to produce "right answers." (See also pp. 77–79 on evaluation.)

Let us not forget to ask children, "What questions do you have?" and to counter children's

[16]P. E. Blosser, "Asking the Right Questions," *Science and Children* (NSTA, March 1975).

questions frequently by asking, "What do you think?"

Children should come to understand that there are many questions for which there are still no answers. For example, we are not sure what caused the extinction of dinosaurs or how to best dispose of nuclear wastes. As children go on with their science studies they will understand that *all* answers in science are man-made, hence subject to error and subject to change. There is no final and absolute authority in science. This does not, however, deny the importance of the principles and theories that scientists have constructed to explain phenomena. But those principles and theories that are most significant in science are those that lead to further discovery of new principles and theories.

The importance for the teacher of this approach to science "answers" is that children's ideas and proposals should be considered, and that the teacher need not become *the* authority or spokesman for *the* authority. Rather, science in the classroom should be an adventure in which children and the teacher participate. Children should come to regard science as an endless quest rather than a finite body of information.

WHAT STRATEGIES WILL IMPROVE SCIENCE LESSONS?

Science lessons come in many shapes and sizes, and so do the teaching strategies for conducting them. They may last for only a short time or over an extended period, and make take place in the classroom, the school grounds, the local park or museum. The experienced teacher may not need many of the suggestions that follow but the new teacher should find that they ease the way to classroom order and achievement.

Elsewhere in the first four chapters of this book and in the B chapters are many ideas for classroom management that are appropriate for the specific content under consideration. Here we focus on techniques but assume that the teacher has already assembled the materials, has determined

the goals, and has motivated the children for the experience that follows.[17]

1. The Laboratory Lesson

   After a brief discussion of the purpose of the problem to be solved, the teacher shows the children the materials they will work with, and what they are expected to do. Several children are asked to distribute the items that the teacher has already divided into the appropriate number of boxes, trays, or whatever other receptacle is suitable. If the children are to work in groups of two, four, and so on, there should be advanced planning about the makeup of the group and the accepted procedures.

   Example: The problem is to find out which of the substances carry electricity and which do not. In the trays there is an assortment of items: paper, eraser, plastic, wood pencil, button, cloth, wire, metal ruler, metal ballpoint pen, and others that the children may have suggested and brought to class to be tested. (Not all trays will necessarily have identical items.) Each tray is provided with a battery, wires, bulb and socket, which are connected to an open switch (see p. 560). The object to be tested is to be placed across the terminals of the open switch to see if it completes the circuit and makes the bulb light. As the children work, move among them; caution a noisy group quietly, not from across the room. The findings are noted on paper by the investigators. After the tests are completed the circuits are disassembled and the items collected in the box that was provided.

   The teacher asks each individual or committee to report their findings and these are summarized on the chalkboard under the headings "conductor" and "nonconductor."

   See also lessons on Learning Centers, pages 46–48, for ways of arranging science materials.

2. The Library Lesson

   The purpose is to introduce individual children to the variety and beauty of books, to motivate them to read, and to help them obtain and use information.

   Example: Children are to report on the topic "Animals Live in Different Kinds of Places." The teacher

---

[17]L. J. Betheland and K. D. George, "Classroom Control," *Science and Children* (February 1979).

assembles enough books so that there will be one in each place. The school librarian, the class library, the local public library, other class libraries, and possibly the home libraries of the children are resources. With the help of a few selected students one book is placed at random on each desk.

The children are allowed to browse through the books, either by moving around the room, or by some prearranged system of moving the books. The children are told that at the end of the library period they should be prepared to tell something about any one of the books, including its title, author, illustrations, and one statement about the kind of a place that a particular animal lives. This may be followed by permitting children to borrow any book they desire.

This lesson may be conducted in the school library, but the purpose in this lesson is not to teach library use techniques. Rather it is to excite children about the world of books by providing them with the freedom to browse.

3. The Overview Lesson

The purpose here is to set the stage for a new problem by having the children reveal their understandings (and misunderstandings), feelings, interests, and past experiences. After a very brief statement by the teacher, the class is asked, "What would you like to know about 'X' (the topic)?" As each question is asked the teacher writes it on the chalkboard, rejecting none, no matter how offbeat. The teacher will often be surprised at how much the children already know and how much of importance the teacher has not thought of. If, on the other hand, the response of the children is meager, it may be necessary to arouse their curiosity and tap their background by some demonstration or by relating some anecdote.

Here are possible overview questions: What would you like to know about space travel; the moon; earthquakes; the ocean; how your body works; earthworms; thunderstorms; raising plants; trip to Mars; sounds in the night; and so on. It is not expected that the study that follows will answer all of the questions, but they will serve as a guide. The teacher, with the help of the children, may group the questions, add to the list, and plan with the help of the children how to find the answers. This overview may take a whole class science period, but it is worth it!

4. The Field Trip

Elsewhere we have discussed (see pp. 48–50) the management of trips to parks, museums, and so on and have suggested possible trips to the school grounds, school neighborhood, factories, and community and city facilities. As indicated, the children should know the purpose of the trip, what behavior is expected, and what they are supposed to do. The follow-up is an important part of the trip experience.

5. The Demonstration

There are occasions when the teacher, a child, or a number of children under supervision will conduct a science demonstration for the whole class to view. This may be necessary when safety is a factor, when the supply of materials is limited, or when the

A stream can be an invaluable source of learning. Where did the stream come from? Why are many of the stones rounded? What living creatures are found when children turn over stones in a creek bed? (*Courtesy of NSTA.*)

teacher wants the entire class to react to what is presented.

Example: To demonstrate the condensation of water, a kettle of water is heated over a hot plate and the steam issuing from the spout strikes a cool pie plate with ice cubes in it.

Some tips on demonstrations:

Make it simple. Do not try to show too much at any time.

Make it large, so that all the children can view it easily from their seats.

Ask questions during the demonstration and encourage the children to ask questions.

Ask children to tell what they actually *see*, distinguished from what they *infer*. (They can *see* a cloud issuing from the kettle and drops of water on the bottom of the pie plate. They may *infer* that cold causes the water in the "steam" to condense.)

6. The Mystery Lesson and the Discrepant Event Lesson
   a. The Mystery Lesson is used to encourage children to discover, using their senses, their knowledge, and their reasoning, to identify and describe some unknown objects, and to explain unusual or puzzling events.
      (1) Place a number of common objects in a dark sock. Children try to identify by feeling, squeezing, lifting, shaking, listening, smelling (see p. 7).
      (2) Place one kind of substance or one kind of object in a closed box. Children try to identify and describe what is in the box in any way they choose except by opening the box. (Suggestions: Ping-Pong balls, pencils, steel ball bearings, marbles, sand, dry cereal, pennies.)

This lesson may be used to introduce the idea of atoms: Although not visible by ordinary means, scientists have been able to describe atoms by their activity, by smashing them, by their impact on other substances, by radiations released by them. Similarly, scientists have been able to describe "black holes," which do not allow light and other radiations to escape from their interiors, by their influence on nearby stars and galaxies.

b. Discrepant Events: Here the children are challenged by occurrences that seem to contradict common sense, which seem to deny what they have learned.

Example: Two ice cubes are used; one is placed in a jar of clear liquid (actually water) and it floats. The other is placed in a jar containing the same amount of a clear liquid (actually alcohol) and it sinks. Why the difference? Children are urged to inspect and to ask questions. Different theories are offered, accepted by the teacher, and written on the blackboard.

"One ice cube is heavier than the other." (This can be checked by lifting the ice cube that sank and placing it in the other jar.)

"It is an optical illusion—a trick." (Children are invited to take a close look.)

"One ice cube is not frozen water; it is frozen something else." (This is a possibility, but the teacher assures them that both are frozen water.)

"One ice cube has a lot of air bubbles in it so it is lighter than the other." (Again this is a possibility, but one that can be checked by observation.)

"One jar has hot water in it; the other cold." (This might have some influence, but children feel both jars and decide that they seem to be equally cool.)

Eventually one child will smell the jars to decide that there is alcohol in one of them. What does this have to do with the ice cube sinking in it? The children may guess that alcohol is lighter (less dense) than water, that the ice cube is heavier (denser) than alcohol, so it sinks. (Somewhere before or during this lesson the meaning of density and the idea that ice is less dense than water, and the "why," may have to be explained.)

Other discrepant events:
(1) A rock that floats (pumice).
(2) A carefully designed circuit battery, switch, wires, bulb—which does not light the bulb.
(3) A paper clip that is tied to a thread attached to the bottom of an open box: The clip seems to float in the air at the end of the thread. (A strong magnet is concealed in a false top to the box.)

In each case the solution to the problem is not important: The kind of thinking evoked is.[18]

7. The Interview Lesson

An "expert"—construction worker, florist, zoo attendant, airplane attendant, nurse, train engineer—is invited to talk to the class on a topic related to the current science work. Before the speaker comes the children prepare questions they would like answered. These are sent in advance to the speaker. The teacher encourages the speaker to use visual materials in the talk, to be brief, and to allow time for questions. After the speaker leaves, the children write a letter to the invited speaker, thanking him or her and indicating what especially interested them (see pp. 93 and 94.)

8. The Poetry Lesson

After a moving experience—a trip to a museum, viewing a film, a visit by a pet, the death of a goldfish, a trip to the park, a look at the night sky—the children are encouraged to write a poem. One possible way to start them is to read several short poems to them, for example:

                If You Want To See Him

        You can't find a dinosaur
            outdoors any more!
        If you want to see him . . .
            try a museum![19]

Each child starts writing during the poetry time but may need more time and then presents the poem the next day, when the teacher will read all the submitted poems to the class. It may be desirable to have all the collected poems typed and included in a photocopied poetry bulletin for distribution to the parents and to other classes. As a result of such lessons, students will grow in their ability to listen and to use new words, and they will perhaps search elsewhere for poems that please them. A similar approach may be used for a science-based art lesson.[20]

Art, poetry or prose gives children an opportunity to express and develop their feelings and to "shine" in unexpected ways.

9. Other Lessons

   a. The News Lesson: class discussion of a science/technology-related article appearing in a newspaper or magazine. Should help children grow in their ability to select appropriate and interesting articles and organize their presentations effectively.

   b. The Textbook Lesson: how to use a science textbook (see pp. 67–69) to gather information: using the table of contents and index; studying photographs and drawings; understanding graphs and charts.

   c. The Show and Tell Lesson: occasionally useful if directed so that students improve their skills at selecting and organizing the material they present.

   d. Bring Your Pet Lesson: the pet may be a rock, animal, plant, or science toy. Provides opportunity for children to ask questions and discuss interesting features. May lead some students to adopt a new hobby or form a club.

   e. The Audio-visual Lesson (see pp. 50–53).

WHAT SAFETY PROCEDURES SHOULD BE FOLLOWED IN TEACHING SCIENCE?

We have indicated elsewhere that there are many good reasons for hands-on procedures in teaching science. It follows that when children are active in handling apparatus, tools, and other learning materials, certain precautions become necessary.

Elementary school teachers should become aware of potential dangers in the teaching of science and know their responsibilities in maintaining classroom safety.[21]

---

[18]R. L. Shrigley, "Discrepant Events: Whey They Fascinate Students," *Science and Children* (May 1987).

[19]J. D. Gozzi, "Spring Poems," *Science and Children* (May 1987).

[20]Jack Wheatley, "Ecology and Art," *Science and Children* (February 1979).

[21]G. E. Downs and J. A. Gerlovich, *Science Safety For Elementary Teachers* (Ames: Iowa State University Press, 1983). Contains checklist and other practical aids for safety in the elementary school. R. A. Dean and N. N. Dean, "Safety in the Elementary Classroom," Washington, D.C.: NSTA: "Some Safety Suggestions," in Elementary Science Syllabus, New York State Education Department, Albany, N.Y.

At the elementary level safety rules and precautions will be more meaningful to the children if the reasons for these rules are explained. Moreover, a well-managed classroom, as described in the preceding section, where attention is directed at the work at hand is likely to be a safe environment. At the elementary level certain general precautions should be kept in mind.

1. Wherever possible the heat supply should come from electric hot plates rather than alcohol burners and candles. Bunsen burners, if necessary, should be used only by the teacher or under the teacher's direct supervision.
2. Prevent loose clothing and hair from coming into direct contact with any science supplies, chemicals, equipment, or sources of heat or flame.
3. Do not allow science materials or audiovisual aids to be transported through hallways by unsupervised students or during a time when students are moving in the hallways.
4. Instruct students in the proper handling of sharp instruments such as pins, knives, and scissors, and of hand tools, generally, before they use them.
5. Instruct students not to touch, taste, or inhale unknown chemicals or materials directly—and known substances only under the direction of the teacher.
6. Do not rub eyes when conducting any investigation. (Iron filings are sometimes used with upper grades in the study of magnetism; these require special precautions.)
7. Instruct students in the proper use of eye-protection devices such as goggles before they engage in activities in which there is a potential risk to eye safety. Eyewash facilities should be identified and readily available.
8. It is quite possible to carry out an excellent science program in grades K–6 without the use of potentially dangerous chemicals. For example, lemon juice and vinegar may demonstrate the properties of acid as well as stronger acid solutions.
9. As far as practicable use plastic containers, tubes, and so on, instead of glass.
10. Batteries and dry cells should always be used in electricity projects, not standard house current.
11. Living things in the classroom present some special problems (see pp. 296–297). When students bring their pets to the classroom, their owners should be largely responsible for them; the teacher together with the owner should set up standards for the pet's housing, feeding, watering, and cleanliness. Only a short stay is recommended.
12. Wild animals, such as frogs, toads, and snakes should be housed properly and released into their natural environment after they have been observed and studied.
13. Teachers should become familiar with the legal liabilities that are in effect locally regarding safety in the classroom.
14. Outdoor activities, such as visits on the school grounds and more extensive field trips (see pp. 48–50) present special safety problems. If the teacher explores the area for the proposed trip, some of the possible hazards can be anticipated. Extended trips to zoos, museums, factories, and parks will need extra supervision (e.g., teacher aides, parents, or other adults) to ensure the general safety.

WHERE CAN I OBTAIN SCIENCE MATERIALS?[22]

There is much useful material in the immediate surroundings. But where is it? How can it be obtained? What is appropriate? It is amazing how many magnets, magnifying glasses, garden seeds, insect specimens, musical instruments, and similar materials children can contribute or lend if they are urged to do so. There are countless places to visit, people to enlist, and other resources to use if we begin to look for them and if we challenge students to help provide them.

Children sometimes get the impression that what they are studying happens only in faraway places. A great many of the things children study in science can be observed within a mile or two

[22]National Science Teachers Association Supplement of *Science Education Suppliers*, compiled by NSTA editorial staff, 1989. Chart of information from over 200 science education suppliers to assist teachers and others in locating and purchasing science teaching materials. Delta Education, Science Catalogue (annual), Nashua, N.H. Elementary science kits and a wide variety of apparatus and equipment for various kinds of science programs.

of where they are. For example, our concern with environmental ecological problems directs us to study our surroundings in a very practical and useful way. Almost everything described in the B chapters can be seen if you look around the room where you are sitting, go outside, walk a mile or so, and keep watching. In addition to the suggestions given here, there are many others in the "Discovering for Yourself" sections at the end of each A chapter and in the "Resources to Investigate" sections at the end of each B chapter. There are often special elementary science teachers, science supervisors, and team teachers who can act as resource personnel in locating materials for teachers in self-contained classrooms. Let us examine some of these resources.

The School

In addition to the material purchased, there is a wealth of useful scientific material in the school. Note the following examples.

Students are learning how heat travels and how heating systems function. Heat is traveling into the schoolroom from somewhere—from a furnace in another building, from one in the basement of the building where the students are studying, or perhaps even from a stove in the classroom itself. The school custodian can help children take a trip to the furnace room or a solar heating element, look into the furnace, trace the water or steam pipes to the room, and discover how and where air currents travel into the room. These and similar activities bring reality to science (see Chapters 15A and B).

Students are studying electricity. They learn about fuses, circuit breakers, lights, conductors, insulators, switches, and meters. If the school uses electricity, examples of all of these may be found in many places. Again, the school custodian knows where the fuse box or circuit breaker is, can change a fuse, knows where the meter is, how the switches operate, and many other things. These experiences help to get the phenomenon of elec-

tricity out of the book and into the realm of the child's experience (see Chapters 17A and B).

Sixth-grade pupils are studying what things are made of. They observe rusting and burning (furnace); note the various products of chemical change in the classroom (window glass, moldy fruit, tarnished spoon, bread, photographs, paper, and so on); and observe how undesirable chemical changes are controlled (metal surfaces are painted to prevent rusting, for example).

Do not overlook thermostats, electric bells, the pulley and other simple machines, light fixtures, pianos and other musical instruments, plants, pressure cookers in the school cafeteria, school radios, telephones, aquariums. The list of materials is nearly endless.

Around the School

Look out of the schoolroom window. The schoolyard is teeming with potential science material, much of it very useful. For example, the class is studying the effects of erosion on land forms. A heavy rain falls. A trip to the edge of the schoolyard reveals a temporary stream, brown as coffee, carrying away the soil of the playground. A tumblerful of this water held to the light reveals the cause of the color. Letting the glass stand for an hour will settle the soil at the bottom. The sidewalk next to the yard is covered with soil washed from the playground. Here is a real example of erosion. A small gully is beginning to form, and the experience of having observed it and of trying to stop the erosion by using appropriate means is a beginning to understanding conservation practices. If the schoolyard is blacktopped, nearby parks or similar areas will do as substitutes (see Chapters 6A and B).

Children are studying problems related to environmental pollution. Unfortunately the schoolyard is usually rampant with examples. Starting with the near-at-hand cannot help but make the problems real and help to provide solutions. Examples are trash of many kinds, air pollution, excessive street noises, and visual eyesores (see Chapters 13A and B).

The class is studying animals and how they live together. In the ground just outside the window ants are busy taking care of their young, guarding the queen, feeding her, getting food, and doing the many other things students have read about. Watching ants under a magnifying glass as their "scouts" search for food sources and seeing them make a tunnel illustrate the science the children are studying.

Many other things wait to be discovered in the schoolyard: birds, insects, and other animals; trees and other plants going through the annual cycle of growth and dormancy; swings and seesaws, which illustrate gravity and leverage; plants with special adaptations; flowers, rocks, and seedpods; dew and other forms of precipitation; fungus growths; nodules on clover roots; and examples of different kinds of soils. Exploration of these helps to bring science ideas to life and to create appreciation of them. They are the sources of questions that children may pose and try to answer.

At Home

The homes of children contain many examples of science objects and phenomena. For children studying machines and how they help to do work, the modern home contains many of the things commonly used to illustrate the principles of doing work. In the kitchen there are egg beaters, can openers, knives, corkscrews, and many other tools. In the shop tool box or tool chest there are hammers, saws, and chisels; in the basement there are washing machines and other appliances. Perhaps there are pumps, farm machinery, a windmill, pulleys for loading hay, inclined planes for loading livestock, balances for weighing, pulleys for hanging out clothes or transporting hay. In a city environment, there are street-cleaning apparatus, trucks that grind up garbage and leaves, and

others. These are all illustrations of the use of science at work.

Suppose children are learning how we use plants in daily living. They keep an account of the different kinds of plants that are growing in their home gardens or farms or in pots on windowsills. They search the kitchen cupboard for examples of spices and herbs. While learning how plants are adapted to the environment they dig up dandelions to examine the long root system, bring various kinds of leaves to school for examination, and bring plants to school that show special adaptations.

Other science resources of the home include heating, cooling and lighting systems and their fuels, refrigeration, pets, farm animals, sources of pollution, methods of insect control, and waste disposal.

In the Community[23]

Every community is rich in resources that are indispensable to good science teaching. They include not only places to visit but persons to consult: members of the sanitary commission, museum directors, firemen, and many others. The use of an individual as a resource carries with it certain responsibilities for both students and teachers. Extending an invitation, planning for active audience participation, introducing the visitor to the group, and conducting questioning periods must all be arranged by the teacher and students. Careful planning is essential if children are to receive maximum benefits from resource persons. A list of questions may be prepared in advance to help give proper focus. There is no reason to assume that Mr. Jones, one of the parents, who built his own telescope and knows more about Mars than anybody in town, can talk helpfully to a fifth

---

[23]Cherie Anna Dawson, "The Community as a Science Resource," *Science and Children* (February 1982).

grade. He may not have seen so many children in one room since his own school days, and he may have little idea of their interests and capacities. The list of questions prepared by the class and teacher and a conference between the teacher and guest prior to the meeting with the children will be very helpful to the guest as well as to the students.

You could make a long list of places to visit in your community that would be fruitful in terms of science experience. Your list would probably include the water purification plant, the airport, industrial plants and laboratories, museums, weather bureaus, parks, radio stations, city departments, greenhouses, and bird sanctuaries. Closer to home are butcher shops, bakeries, grocery stores and supermarkets, dairies and drugstores, music stores, pet shops and candy stores, computer centers and camera stores.

These examples of places to visit in the community are more likely to be accessible to schools in towns and cities. There are, however, many other places to visit in rural areas or in villages. Some of them are a gravel pit or stone quarry, where rocks and fossils may be gathered and where different layers of soil and rock may be observed; woods, where plants and their relationship to the environment may be studied and where the study of ecology can become a very real experience; a burned-over area, where the destructive effects of fire can be seen; a field, where plants can be examined, insects collected, and erosion effects noted; a new building under construction, where machines are at work and insulation, heating equipment, electrical equipment, and other installations can be observed; a sawmill, where tools and trees can be studied and conservation practices or lack of them noted; a farm, where there are problems of raising animals and plants and where many scientific processes go on; a garden, where scientific principles of plant growth and insect control are at work; an apiary, where the social life of insects is easily seen; and a school camp, which is an ideal setting for the study of living things.

SHALL WE HAVE A SCIENCE FAIR?

A science fair may add a new dimension to your science teaching. It provides an unusual opportunity for individual interests and talents of students to be displayed; for presenting the outcome of original investigations; and for exhibiting students' skills in model building, in art, and in language arts.

It encourages students to use the techniques of research: the use of materials from the library and laboratory, the gathering of data, and drawing of conclusions.

A science fair also provides experiences in cooperative planning for the students and the teacher.

When limited to the classroom, it may be used as a culminating activity of a large unit, reinforcing and extending knowledge and its application to everyday living.

On a school and district level, a science fair serves to present the school's efforts and achievements to parents, to business and industry, and to the community at large.

It develops useful relationships with high school and college science departments and with governmental agencies.

A Class Fair

A third-grade class had been studying a unit entitled "The Moon. Our Nearest Neighbor in Space." Their exhibits included original drawings made by some students of the changing appearance of the moon, based on observations made over a period of several weeks; photos of the same taken with the help of a parent; a model comparing the size of the moon with that of the earth, using an apple or Styrofoam ball to represent the moon and a classroom globe for the earth; an imagined lunar station, designed to protect lunarnauts from the rigors of lunar living; a model of man's first moon landing; a painting of the earth as seen from the moon, showing the lunar landscape; a demonstration of the eclipse of the sun and the moon; a model of the moon's surface, showing a crater and a mountain, and other details. One child played a recording she had made on a cassette of Debussy's "Clair de Lune," which provided a pleasant background for the fair.

A School Fair

The following projects were included in an elementary school science fair:

A terrarium with woodland plants and animals collected by two students from a nearby forest. Identifying labels were provided. An explanatory card indicated that permission had been secured to remove the forms and that they would be returned to the forest at the end of the school year. (See "How can we make a terrarium?" p. 306.)

A working demonstration of a solar heating plant, with water running slowly through coiled tubes. A strong light source, instead of the sun, was focused on the tubes. Thermometers measured temperature of incoming and outgoing water. Older students prepared this exhibit.

Grant has stated his purpose and procedure and reported on the data obtained when beans are soaked in water. The diagram illustrates how the gas evolved from the beans in one flask is conducted to a flask containing clear limewater. (The limewater turns milky indicating the presence of carbon dioxide produced by the respiring beans.) *Photo by James Scherwood, Maryland Public Schools.*

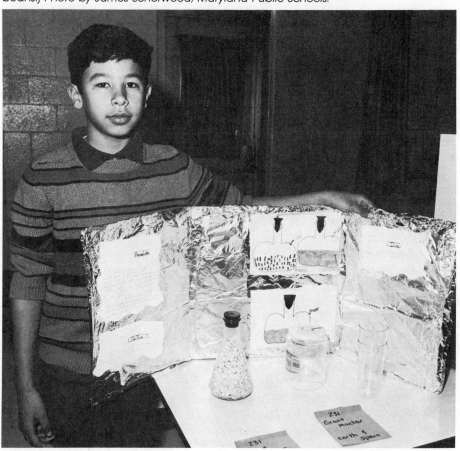

A class exhibit of life in a nearby pond, with a number of jars with different forms of life. Magnifying glasses were provided for examining the plants and animals in the jars. One student demonstrated algae and protozoa with a microscope.

One student exhibited photographs that she had taken of the night sky showing star tracks and meteor trails. Her report indicated that she had seen eight meteors in one hour.

An exhibit of eight plants, grown from slips, four of which had been given plant "food," four of which had not; all were grown in the same kind of soil under similar conditions.

Data and a graph reporting the amount of water lost from an observed leaking faucet in one day and a projection of the loss for a month and a year.

A display of fossils found in a nearby quarry, together with a chart placing these in their proper geological formation, including the name and date. Help from a local college's geology department was acknowledged.

A study of the development of frog's eggs from a local pond, divided into three batches and raised at different temperatures.

Guidelines for Judging Exhibits

Note that in the two fairs just described there are many kinds of projects, ranging from making a model of the moon's surface to investigating the influence of temperature on the development of frog's eggs. Are both of these examples of science? Yes, since in each there is the potential for creativity, questioning, wondering. In each there can be what scientist and writer Jacob Bronowski called "the irresistible need to explore."

It is important that criteria such as the following be used by all evaluators and that students know in advance what these measuring items are. If judges outside of the school are to be used, they should be carefully briefed with respect to these criteria. Each project should be judged by criteria specific to itself. Models, for example, should not be judged by criteria used to judge experiments.

1. Does the project indicate originality on the part of the student?
2. In experimental projects particularly (but not exclusively) is there evidence of the use of the investigative tools of science: asking a question, making an hypothesis, designing procedures, collecting data, using measurement, drawing conclusions?
3. Was the work displayed effectively; was there visual appeal?
4. Is the student able to explain orally the nature of the project?

Some Questions for You to Answer

Because school administrations, schedules, and facilities vary, the holding of a fair must depend on local conditions. Relations with parents and the parents association are important. And not least, the readiness of the teacher to accept the added responsibility must be taken into account.

1. Should we hold a fair?
2. Should participation be required of all students?
3. Should exhibits be displayed and judged by grade levels such as K–2, 3–4, and 5–6?
4. If parents are to assist their children, how should the nature and degree of assistance be limited?
5. Should graded individual awards be given, such as first-, second-, and third-place ribbons or certificates, or should all students who participate be given the same award: a certificate that honors the student for his or her effort? Such an award can be meaningful if the certificate indicates excellence, without a grade, in any or all of the criteria described earlier: originality, use of tools of science, visual appeal, oral explanation, and any other appropriate characteristic.

Bibliography

Smith, Norman F. "Why Science Fairs Don't Exhibit the Goals of Science Teaching." *The Science Teacher*, January 1980.

Cramer, Nancy. "Preparing for the Science Fair." *Science and Children*, November/December 1981.

Chiapetta, Eugene L., and Foots, Barbara K. "Does Your Science Fair Do What it Should?" *The Science Teacher*, November 1984.

VanDeman, Barry A., and Parfitt, Philip C. "The Nuts and Bolts of Science Fairs." *Science and Children*, October 1985.

McNay, Margaret. "The Need to Explore: Nonexperimental Science Fair Projects." *Science and Childen*, October 1985.

Fort, Deborah C. "Getting a Jump on Science Fairs." *Science and Children*, October 1985.

McBride, John W., and Silverman, Frederick L. "Judging Fairs Fairly." *Science and Children*, March 1988.

See also science fair references to articles and books listed on page 16 of *Science and Children*, October 1985.

National Science Teacher's Association. "New Science Fairs and Projects," 1985, 64 pp. $6.00. Send order to Special Publications, NSTA, 1742 Connecticut Ave. NW, Washington, D.C. 20009.

HOW CAN WE TEACH THE METRIC SYSTEM?[24]

The so-called conversion to the metric system continues to have its ups and downs. Currently the big push toward the use of the metric system in elementary schools has, in many locations, cooled off. In others, there appears to be a steady attempt toward including instruction and use of the system beginning in the early grades. Part of the progress, or lack of it, appears to depend on the attitude of parents, teachers, and other adults.

The natural reaction of some teachers is, "I don't understand metrics and I don't have time to teach it. Give metrics to somebody else." However, consider that one of our main responsibilities as teachers is to help students understand their world, which more and more speaks the language of metric. Metric *is* a better system of measurement; it is more logically constructed and simpler to use. We need to help our students use this better way.

At first, learning to be at home with the metric system seems a difficult task, but the more we use it the easier it becomes. Traditionally the metric system has been included in science courses in the secondary school and beyond because the system is universal in the science community. However, if the skill of using metric measurements is to be part of the education of everyone, the elementary school is the place to begin. Here the science program offers many opportunities for using metric: (1) Many of the science activities involve measurements; (2) children have many opportunities to use tools of measurements (scales, thermometers, etc.); and (3) children have many opportunities to use metric measures *without conversion* because of the experimental nature of the science program: They use a 1-liter measure to pour water into an empty aquarium, which they then discover has a capacity of 10 liters. They balance weights on a seesaw scale and find that a certain rock weighs (balances) 3 kilograms. They measure the weekly growth of their pea plant and find that it gains 10 centimeters in one week. In fact, children are soon comfortable with these units and like to use them.

The metric system is used as an international language of trade and technology throughout the world. Only the United States and a few small nations have not converted fully to its use. The metrication of the United States has been described as the longest-running debate in our congressional history. Historically, George Wash-

---

[24]D. Smith and L. J. Bellipanni, "An Elementary Teacher's View of the Metric System," *Science and Children* (September 1979); J. Anton, "Feeling Metrics," *Science Scope* (April/May 1987). Teaching metric before conversions. C. J. Rusink, "Metric Munchies," *Science and Children* (April 1984). Practical advice for using metric. L. Hovey and K. Hovey, "The Metric System—An Overview," *School, Science and Mathematics* (February 1983). S. G. Hanson, "Evolution of Metric in Textbooks," *School, Science and Mathematics* (November 1981); J. F. Newport, "Let's Go on a Metric Scavenger Hunt," *Science and Children* (February 1981); H. C. Clark and A. Richmond, "Seven Years Since the Metric Conversion Act," *School, Science and Mathematics* (November 1983).

How long is your reach—in centimeters? As children use metric for measuring everyday objects and changes, they become comfortable with these units. *Photo by Lloyd Wolf, Concord School, Forestville, Maryland.*

ington asked for some kind of change in our weights and measures in his first address to Congress. By 1866, Congress made it lawful throughout the country to employ the metric system in all contracts, dealings, or court proceedings. In December 1975, President Gerald Ford signed the Metric Conversion Act (Public Law 94-168) declaring a national policy toward increased usage of the metric system. Transition, conversion, and use are taking place throughout the nation, especially in education.

Why is transition to the metric system important? One reason is international trade. The rest of the world is building, trading, and buying goods engineered in metric units because metric units are simple and based upon the decimal sys-

tem. For example, in the U.S. system, there are several units of length (inch, foot, yard, mile); the metric has only one base unit of length (meter). The customary system measures weight (mass) in ounces, pounds, barrels, and tons, whereas the metric system uses the simpler kilogram.

Can you explain the relationship of a 16-ounce pint of milk to a 16-ounce pound of potatoes? Such measures are easily confused or misunderstood because in the customary system, ounces are being used to describe both volume and weight (mass). In the metric system the milk would be measured in liters and the potatoes in kilograms.

What do we lose in the transition to the metric system? Only old habits, familiar quantities that we can picture in our minds when needed, and an endless list of antiquated terms you probably never knew anyway; for example, nautical mile, chain, link, chest, clove, cask, firkin, fodder, bolt, stone, fathom, pole. Actually, we have been using the metric system in science, photography, munitions, medicine, automobiles, and sports for many years. Just try to imagine your camera's film size in inches or aspirin in ounces.

What is the metric system? Several versions of the metric system have existed since its inception in 1670 by a Frenchman, Gabriel Mouton. The modernized metric system of today is known as Le Système International d'Unités (SI), or the International System of Units, and was adopted in 1960 by the General Conference of Weights and Measures, a group of international representatives that meets periodically to refine the system.

The SI version of the metric system is specific; the units of measure and their corresponding symbols (L for liter, m for meter, kg for kilogram) are used throughout the world. The symbols never change no matter what the language, even though the spellings of their units may differ. A kg is a kilogram in Helsinki, Lima, Hong Kong, Tahiti, or anywhere else on earth. In the United States, style guides for proper usage are available from the National Bureau of Standards of the U.S. Department of Commerce, the American National Metric Council, and the U.S. Metric Association, Inc.

The important metric system measures to know for everyday living and for most elementary school activities are shown in the accompanying chart.

Classroom practices and teaching strategies for introducing the metric system vary from school to school.[25]

[25]K. Stuart, "Metric Made Fun: An Individualized Approach," *Science and Children* (February 1977). Describes excellent activities easily incorporated in a classroom. Also, T. E. Thompson, "Ten Commonly Asked Questions by Teachers about Metric Education," *Science and Children* (February 1977).

Mass

1 g	= 1 gram	
1 kg	= 1 kilogram	= 1,000 grams
1 mg	= 1 milligram	= 0.0001 gram

Length

1 m	= 1 meter	
1 km	= 1 kilometer	= 1,000 meters
1 cm	= 1 centimeter	= 0.01 meter
1 mm	= 1 millimeter	= 0.001 meter

Volume

1 L	= 1 liter	
1 mL	= 1 milliliter	= 0.001 liter

Temperature

C	= Celsius
10°C	= 10 degrees Celsius

Several suggestions for successful metric education are:

1. Avoid conversion activities between customary and metric measurement systems.
2. Avoid dual system training, which slows transition and encourages conversions.
3. Avoid extensive conversion activities within the metric measures.
4. Avoid too much emphasis on *all* prefixes used with *all* metric units. Milli-, centi-, kilo-, and deci- are most frequently used and must be reinforced in learning.
5. Be certain to include many hands-on experiences.
6. Do not look to the teaching of the metric system to end the need for the teaching of fractions.
7. Do not overlook the importance of decimals and annexing zeros.
8. Give the learner some personal "feel" for the metric system through an acquaintance with the historic development of the system.
9. Encourage understanding of the interrelationships of metric measurements.

10. Use scales (divisions between whole numbers) that correspond to the decimal system, that is, 0.5 centimeters and not $\frac{1}{2}$.[26]

The secret to learning the metric system is to "think metric." As we've mentioned, try not to spend time doing lengthy conversion calculations from customary measure to metric measure and vice versa. Instead try to think of the size estimates based on a few simple relationships such as those given with the illustrations that follow.

Note: The following are not intended to be used as conversion activities; rather they aim at the direct use of metric for everyday objects or phenomena whose measurements in customary units are given principally for identification purposes.

For Distance

Small Distances (change from inches to millimeters): A $\frac{1}{4}$-inch pencil is about 6 millimeters across; one millimeter is about the thickness of a paper match.

Large Distances (change from feet and yards to meters): A 9 × 12 foot rug is a little smaller than a 3 × 4 meter rug; a meter is a little longer than a yard.

Great Distances (change from a mile to a kilometer): A kilometer is $\frac{5}{8}$ of a mile or a little longer than half a mile.

For Weight (Mass)

Small Weights (change of ounces to grams): A nickel weighs about 5 grams; a quarter-pound (4 ounces) of butter is a little more than 100 grams.

Larger Weights (change of pounds to kilograms): A $4\frac{1}{2}$-pound roast is about 2 kilograms; a kilogram is a little more than 2 pounds of butter.

[26]P. Marcuccio, "Metric Education: Trends and Recommendations," *Science and Children* (February 1977).

For Volume

Small Volumes (change from ounces or pints to milliliters): A 12-ounce can of soda is about 350 milliliters; a teaspoon is about 5 milliliters.

Larger Volumes (change from gallons to liters): A liter is a little larger than a quart; a gallon of gasoline is a little less than 4 liters; a 16-gallon tank holds 60 liters.

For Temperature

Water freezes at 0°C and boils at 100°C. Body temperature (98.6°F) is 37°C. A comfortable spring day (72°F) is about 22°C.

A moderate oven (350°F) is about 175°C.

Note: We include a standard table of comparisons and illustrations from the Bureau of Standards material on the end papers of the book.

DISCOVERING FOR YOURSELF

1. Design a method of evaluating student outcomes for any topic you choose. Include facts, concepts, methods of inquiry and attitudes.

2. After reading the section on mainstreaming, have any of your preconceptions or attitudes changed? How?

3. Design a week's work on a specific science topic for a specific grade. What adaptations would you make for disadvantaged children? How would you know that your plan is working? What unique features of your science program do you think make it a valuable source in meeting the needs of the disadvantaged, of children for whom English is a second language?

4. Prepare several closed and open questions for any science topic or lesson. Evaluate them on the basis of what you have learned about formulating and using questions.

5. Following the guidelines on The Laboratory Lesson (p. 87) how would you manage a lesson in which children are to make and test a compass (see pp. 61–64)? Steel sewing needles, corks, water, dishes, and magnets are to be used.

6. In the preceding "make a compass" lesson, what safety precautions might be necessary?

7. Make a survey of resources for science teaching available in the immediate vicinity of a school or your home, and tell briefly how each of these might be useful in teaching science.

8. Using a metric ruler measure (a) length, width, the thickness of this book; size of your TV screen; the length of a room. What metric units did you find it useful to use? (b) Use the metric ruler found on the end covers of this book to measure the diameter of a quarter of a dollar and the thickness of a pencil.

9. Make a list of similarities and differences you have discovered between teaching science and any other area of learning in the elementary school.

PART TWO

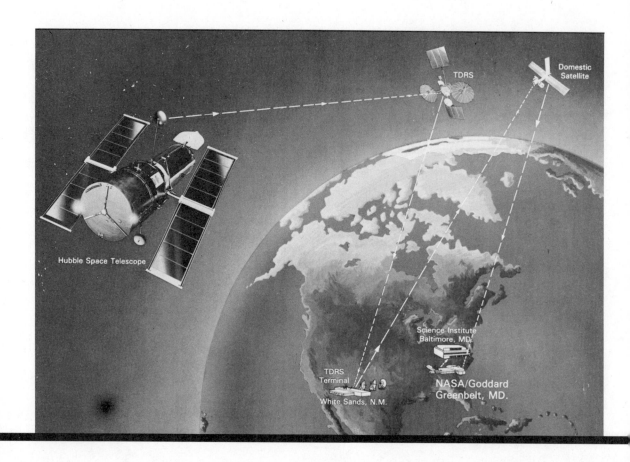

TDRS

Domestic
Satellite

Hubble Space Telescope

Science Institute
Baltimore, MD.

TDRS
Terminal

NASA/Goddard
Greenbelt, MD.

White Sands, N.M.

THE EARTH AND THE UNIVERSE

THE EARTH AND
ITS SURFACE

That the continents move—that huge chunks of crust are split apart and driven thousands of miles and others are swallowed whole, that the very bedrock of earth's surface is a series of rafts floating hither and yon at the mercy of unseen currents—is a staggering idea, perhaps the most important insight since the discovery that the earth is round.

ROGER BINGHAM, EXPLORERS OF THE EARTH WITHIN IN *SCIENCE 80.*

Civilization exists by geological consent, subject to change without notice.

WILL DURANT

AT THE EDGE OF THE SEA

An ocean wave, born of a far-off wind, travels thousands of miles across the open sea and breaks near a sandy shore. Impelled by the tumbling wave, a rush of water carries a load of sand particles up the face of the beach. Here the water spends the last bit of its wind-borne energy, dropping the sand as it slows down and stops. Now gravity takes over and pulls the sheet of water back into the ocean.

Meanwhile, a brisk onshore wind lifts up some dry sand particles that were left on the upper beach by an earlier wave. After the wind hurdles the dune that slopes up from the beach, it is slowed down; gravity snatches part of the sand from it. And so the dune grows.

In this single instant on the beach the forces of wind and of gravity, working on water and sand, have altered a tiny portion of the earth's face. On the sea's edge we are constantly reminded that the earth and its surface are changing today, and that these changes are part of the processes that began in the past and will extend into the future.

FROM THE DEPTHS OF THE EARTH

Some earth changes manifest themselves suddenly and violently. In the early morning of May 18, 1980, two geologists, Dorothy Stoffel and Keith Stoffel, set off on a reconnaissance flight over Mount St. Helens in Washington. Their investigation followed some eight weeks of activity of this ancient volcanic mountain: small earthquakes, explosions of steam and ash, cracks in the snow-and-ice covering of the mountain, the opening of new craters, the release of blue flames visible from the air at night, the emission of gases such as carbon dioxide, water, and hydrochloric acid, and the appearance of new bulges on the flank of the mountain. After several passes around Mount St. Helens the Stoffels were close witnesses to the onset of a huge volcanic eruption. As Dorothy Stoffel recalled, "The whole north side of the crater began to move instantaneously as one gigantic mass." Seconds later there was a stupendous explosion. The Stoffels hurried to escape the mushrooming cloud of ash, lit up by lightning bolts thousands of feet long.

Time magazine later reported[1]

a stupendous explosion of trapped gases, generating about 500 times the force of the atomic bomb dropped on Hiroshima, blew the entire top off Mount St. Helens. In a single burst Mount St. Helens was transformed from a postcard-symmetrical cone 9,677 ft. high to an ugly flattop 1,300 ft. lower. Clouds of hot ash made up of pulverized rock were belched twelve miles into the sky. Giant mud slides, composed of melted snow mixed with ash and propelled by waves of superheated gas erupted out of the crater, rumbled down the slopes and crashed through

[1]*Time,* June 2, 1980

valleys, leaving millions of trees knocked down in rows, as though a giant had been playing pick-up sticks.

Mount St. Helens is one of 15 majestic volcanic peaks of the Cascade Range, which extends from British Columbia to northern California. All the volcanoes are surface manifestations of processes occurring deep in the earth. We will look at these processes and their causes later in this chapter.

TO THE CENTER OF THE EARTH

A journey to the center of the earth, fancifully described by the novelist Jules Verne, would not be feasible for many reasons. For one thing an explorer would experience rising temperatures with descent. At a depth of only 3 miles (about 5 kilometers) the temperature is literally high enough to make the blood boil.

Actually, we have seen very little of the interior of the earth. Even the deepest oil wells are but pinpricks in the earth, penetrating a mere 5 miles (8 kilometers) into a sphere whose center is nearly 4,000 miles (about 6,400 kilometers) from its surface. For our knowledge of the earth's interior, therefore, we have had to rely mainly on indirect evidence, such as the outpouring of volcanoes and seismograph records of earthquakes. We shall look at this evidence presently.

Studies by scientists have revealed that the earth is composed of a series of concentric shells, each made of different materials. The outermost shell is the *crust,* a relatively rigid zone that averages about 25 miles (40 kilometers) in thickness. Most familiar to us is the material on the surface of this shell: soil, sand, gravel, rock fragments, boulders, and the waters of rivers, lakes, and seas. We know that this unconsolidated material is only "skin" deep. If we dig a few feet, or at most a few hundred feet, we strike the solid bedrock in the earth's crust. In mountainous areas much of the bedrock lies exposed to our view. In other areas, such as the plains, the bedrock is almost com-

pletely covered by soil. It is exposed only occasionally by the cutting action of rivers or the digging of humans, or because an isolated mass of hard rock has not yet been leveled and broken down. The exposed bedrock is called an *outcrop*.

Around the earth the covering of soil and other loose materials is discontinuous, varying in depth from zero to a few hundred feet, but the crust forms a continuous rigid layer, underlying the continents and extending under the beds of the oceans.

Before descending to the interior of the earth, let us spend a few moments more examining its surface. Looking at the planet Earth from the moon, one would be impressed by the fact that most of it is covered with water. The Pacific Ocean alone covers about half of the globe; all the seas together cover about 70 percent of the area of the earth. The floors that underlie the oceans are not flat: Soundings have shown that they are as rugged in profile as the continents. The world record for depth, 36,198 feet (11,033 meters), is in the Mariana Trench of the Pacific Ocean. In comparison, Mt. Everest, highest of all our continental mountains, extends 29,028 feet (8,848 meters) above sea level.

The mountain heights and ocean depths of the earth's crust, enormous as they may appear to us, are insignificant in relation to the size of the earth. On the average classroom globe a true scale representation of the irregularities in the earth's surface would be scarcely visible to the eye.

Continents and oceans lie on the crust of the earth. The crust is not uniform in thickness, as is evident in the illustration on page 108, averaging about 20 miles (32 kilometers) under the continents, but only 4 miles (7 kilometers) under the oceans. Over millions of years great forces under the earth's surface have caused the crust to bend and buckle, pushing up mountains and fracturing the crustal rocks.

The crust is made largely of two kinds of rocks: *basalt* and *granite*. Basalt is found under the oceans; granite on the continents. The crust is solid except for deep pockets of hot, liquid rock

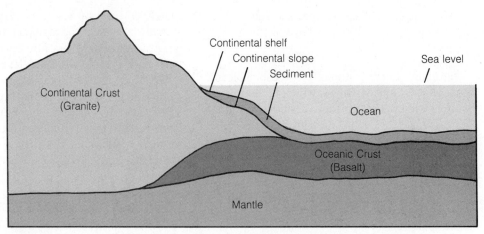

A basic difference between the continents and the ocean basins is that they are made of different crustal materials. The continents are made of granite. The ocean basins are made of basalt. The diagrammatic cross-section shows the difference at the edge of a continent.

called *magma*. These pockets are the reservoirs for volcanoes that occasionally burst through the upper crust.

Beneath the crust lies the *mantle*, a zone about 1,800 miles (2,900 kilometers) thick, composed of rock at red- to white-hot temperatures, possibly as high as 4000°F (2200°C). The rock in the upper region of the mantle is slightly plastic; although not melted, it can move or "creep" slowly. It may seem strange that rock can flow without melting, but this characteristic applies to many materials under constant stress such as steel, glass, and ice. A familiar example of such creep is the behavior of the toy substance known as "Silly Putty," which bounces like hard rubber, but when left overnight collapses and flattens.

Knowledge of the mantle is fundamental to an understanding of the structure and behavior of the earth. There is evidence that the crust and the thin film of ocean and atmosphere have been produced from materials within the mantle. The drifting of the continents on the earth's surface, mountain formation, volcanic eruptions, and earthquakes—all are thought to result from the action of the mantle moving very slowly below the crust (see pp. 122–127).

The rock of the mantle is denser than the crustal rock but less dense than the material in the innermost zone, the *core*. The core is a sphere about 2,150 miles (3,460 kilometers) in radius, just about the size of the planet Mars. The core is hotter than the mantle; its temperature may be as high as 12,000°F (6600°C). The outer part of the core is 1,350 miles (2,170 kilometers) thick, and is probably made of nickel and iron in a hot, plastic condition. The inner core apparently is also made of nickel and iron, but it appears to behave more like a true solid than does the outer core, having a consistency like that of hard rubber.

In summary, the earth may be compared to an apple. At the center is a metallic core. The crust is relatively no thicker than the skin of an apple. Between the crust and the core lies the mantle, which, like the pulp of an apple, is the largest part.

KINDS OF ROCK

We can understand the many rock formations we encounter on the landscape better if we group them according to their methods of origin.

Some rocks have been formed from the cooling and hardening of hot molten material from deep within the earth's crust. Such rock is called *igneous*. An example is basalt, a characteristic rock in the lava that flows from volcanoes.

Some rocks are formed by the cementing together of materials such as sand, clay, mud, and pebbles. These rocks are called *sedimentary*. An example is sandstone, formed by the joining together of sand particles.

Some rocks are formed by the changing of existing rocks into new kinds. These rocks are *metamorphic*. An example is marble, which is derived from limestone.

All rocks, then, may be classified as igneous, sedimentary, or metamorphic, depending on their methods of formation. Let us consider each of these groups more carefully.

Igneous Rock

The millions of tons of molten rock that pour out of volcanoes illustrate the method of origin of igneous rock. Pockets of hot liquid rock—magma—found deep in the earth sometimes erupt to the surface through fissures in the crust and spread over the earth. (When magma reaches the surface, it is called *lava*.) Such rocks as obsidian, pumice, and basalt are formed this way.

Obsidian, sometimes called volcanic glass, results from the rapid cooling of surface lava; it is a dark, glassy rock. In thin slices it transmits light. A mass of this rock makes up Obsidian Cliff in Yellowstone National Park.

Pumice is so full of holes formed by escaping gas at the time of its origin that it is often light enough to float in water. Basalt is the dark-colored, heavy, dull rock common in lava flows such as the series making up the Columbia Plateau in the northwestern United States. This plateau—with its 150,000 square miles (390,000 square kilometers) of hardened lava, in places 1 mile (1.6 kilometers) thick—is one of the earth's greatest volcanic constructions.

Sometimes the liquid magma does not reach the surface of the crust in its upward movement. Instead it forces its way into or beneath masses of rock. Here it solidifies into coarse, granular rocks such as granite, which is the most common of all igneous rocks in the continental crust of the earth. Although granite is formed under the crust, it is often found exposed in some areas because the overlying rocks have been gradually worn away.

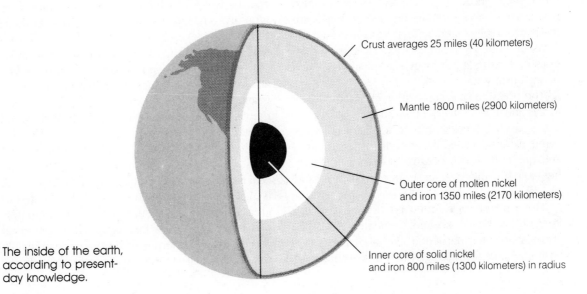

Crust averages 25 miles (40 kilometers)

Mantle 1800 miles (2900 kilometers)

Outer core of molten nickel and iron 1350 miles (2170 kilometers)

Inner core of solid nickel and iron 800 miles (1300 kilometers) in radius

The inside of the earth, according to present-day knowledge.

Granite is a popular building stone in many parts of the world. In the United States, however, its greatest use is for monuments.

Granite is easily recognized because of its speckled appearance. Close examination reveals that the speckling is caused by the different kinds of materials in its makeup. Among these materials, called *minerals,* are quartz, a glasslike substance, and feldspar, which comes in a variety of colors. Mica, a sparkling mineral, is also often present in granite.

Masses of granite rock can be seen in the Rockies, the Adirondacks, the Black Hills of South Dakota, and the White Mountains of New Hampshire.

Sedimentary Rock

Sedimentary rocks are interesting because their method of formation permits them to preserve plant and animal remains in a chronological sequence, as we shall see in Chapter 12A. These rocks are built up under water by the depositing there of materials such as sand, clay, mud, pebbles, and gravel. Such materials, called *sediments,* are brought to the shallow waters of lakes and oceans by the streams or rivers that flow into them. Wind and moving glaciers of ice are also transporting agents. Other sedimentary rocks are made from plant and animal remains, such as ferns and shells. Still others are derived from minerals such as rock salt or gypsum that were once dissolved in water.

The pressure of accumulating materials slowly forces the lower layers of sediment to stick together and to harden into rock. In this process some natural cementing materials such as lime and quartz found in ocean and lake waters may help join together coarser sediments, such as sand or gravel.

The kind of rock produced depends on the kind of materials deposited. Cemented sands become sandstone; hardened clay and mud form shale; pebbles form conglomerate; seashells pro-

vide the material for limestone; plants provide materials for coal.

Sedimentary rocks are very common. Many are easy to identify. Sandstone is obviously made of grains of sand. Sometimes the grains are very loosely joined, and if two pieces are rubbed, grains of sand are dislodged. Shale when wet smells like mud, from which it was originally formed.

Most sedimentary rock formations have a banded, "layer-cake" appearance owing to the different kinds of materials that are deposited, one on top of another, where the rock is forming. For example, if yellow clay is deposited over white clay, different layers of shale will form. If sand is deposited over clay, a layer of sandstone will form over a layer of shale. The kind of layer-cake rock that is made depends on the size, color, and texture of the particles that go into it.

Metamorphic Rock

Soft coal is found in western Pennsylvania, hard coal in eastern Pennsylvania. All this coal was formed in the same geological period. Why, then, are these two coals so different? A study of the coal beds reveals that those in the hard-coal region are buckled into tight folds, whereas those in the soft-coal area are nearly horizontal. We infer from this, and from evidence in other areas, that high pressure and high temperature associated with the crushing and folding of the beds changed the soft coal, which is classified as sedimentary rock, into hard coal, which is classified as metamorphic rock.

The change involved in the transformation of soft or *bituminous* coal into hard or *anthracite* coal is one example of metamorphism. In general, it may be said that when bedrock is subjected to greatly increased pressures or very high temperatures or both, it may be changed in its chemical and physical properties to become metamorphic rock. The pressure may result from large move-

As the Colorado River carved Grand Canyon it opened windows on the past. Some rocks may be 2 billion years old. Layers of sedimentary rock forming the upper two thirds of the canyon provide a record of the evolution of life from about 570 million years ago to 225 million years ago. *(Courtesy of National Park Service, U.S. Dept. of the Interior.)*

ments of the earth's crust that crumple and fold the bedrock. The heat may come from the friction of moving layers, from the proximity of hot magma, or from the depth of burial (geothermal heat).

We list here some of the important metamorphic rocks and the rocks from which they are derived.

Metamorphic Rock	Derivation
Anthracite coal	Bituminous coal
Gneiss	Granite or shale
Marble	Limestone
Quartzite	Sandstone
Slate	Shale

MINERALS IN ROCKS

If a rock is thought of as a kind of fruitcake, the minerals in it may be compared to the cake's flour, nuts, raisins, cherries, citron, and other ingredients. Minerals are natural substances of definite chemical composition. More than 2,000 different minerals have been identified in the rocks of the earth's crust. Some—such as gold, diamond, and ruby—are found in relatively few rocks. Only 10 minerals, including familiar quartz and mica, make up about 90 percent of the rocks.

Rocks, like cakes, vary in their ingredients. Limestone, for example, is commonly made only of the mineral calcite. Granite, as we have seen, always has feldspar, quartz, and at least one other

QUARTZ   *HORNBLENDE*
FELDSPAR   *MICA*

Granite rock is speckled with grains of the different minerals of which it is composed. Four typical minerals found in granite are shown here. *(Courtesy of Dr. Benjamin Shaub.)*

mineral in it. It owes its speckled appearance to the separate crystals of these minerals (see the adjacent figure).

AGE OF ROCKS

Evidence gathered by scientists shows that the earth is very old. Let us see how scientists determine the age of the earth's rocks.

When sediment or volcanic lava is deposited on top of a rock formation by natural processes, later hardening into rock, the layer on top, if undisturbed, must be younger than the one underneath it. This relationship, known to geologists as the principle of *superposition,* may now seem obvious, but the concept was not expressed until the end of the eighteenth century. The law led early geologists to establish the first geologic time scale. This was a rough approximation, but it revealed the enormous extent of geologic time.

A more accurate determination of the absolute age of rocks had to wait, first for the discovery of natural *radioactivity,* the knowledge that some atoms change themselves into other atoms at regular and constant rates, and second for the development of laboratory techniques for measuring the degree of change.

Uranium, for example, which is widely distributed in rocks, undergoes radioactive decay, eventually ending up as lead. With the passage of time the amount of uranium in a rock decreases and the amount of lead increases. We know two things about uranium in rocks, which enables us to use it as a "time clock":

1. Measurement shows that each year 1 ounce of uranium will yield $\dfrac{1}{7,600,000,000}$ ounce of lead.

2. The rate of change of uranium to lead is constant under all conditions of temperature, pressure, and chemical surroundings.

Most radioactive uranium is found in igneous rock. We infer that it was incorporated as a mineral at the time the rock solidified from molten materials. From that point on, the radioactive "clock" began ticking, with uranium breaking down into lead at the rate just given.

It may be helpful in understanding the workings of the atomic clock to think of an old-fashioned hourglass that has just been inverted so that all the sand is at the top. The sand begins sifting through the narrow neck to the bottom. Think of the sand in the upper part as the original uranium and that in the lower part as the lead resulting from its decay. The passage of time is marked by the relative amount of sand in the upper part (uranium) as compared to that in the lower (lead).

In addition to uranium, other elements found in rocks have atoms (isotopes) that are radioactive, breaking down slowly to form other elements. Potassium and rubidium are useful in dating rock for this reason.

Natural radioactivity has provided a more exact measure of the age of rock than any other thus far. The oldest rock measured in this way (found in Greenland in 1971) is about 3.75 billion years old. We infer that the earth itself is 4.6 billion years old.

FORCES THAT CHANGE THE EARTH

People once thought that the mountains, plains, plateaus, and other large features of the earth had always existed. The science of geology reveals that two processes work continuously in sculpturing and altering the face of the earth: the forces of *construction* and those of *destruction*.

The constructive forces, as the geologist defines them, are those that lift up land masses to produce forms such as mountains. Earthquakes and volcanoes exemplify the working of these constructive forces. The destructive forces are those that tend to level down the mountains and hills. The cutting action of running water and scouring by glaciers of ice are among the forces that erase the high places of the earth.

Both of these processes are at work today. Let us consider the constructive process to see how the mountains of the earth are built.

KINDS OF MOUNTAINS

The birth of a mountain in 1943, Parícutin in Mexico, is described on pages 121–122. Parícutin is one of the few *volcanic mountains* that has arisen during historic times. The Aleutian and the Hawaiian Islands are the peaks of volcanic mountains rising from the bottom of the ocean. Mount St. Helens, as we have seen, is one of the peaks of the Cascade chain thrust up by volcanic activity. Volcanic mountains have their origin in deep breaks in the earth's crust that extend to the mantle to supply their building materials.

Volcanic activity may force magma under previously existing layers of rock, as we have seen in our study of igneous rock. This may lift the overlying rocks sufficiently to form *domed mountains,*

Hot liquid rock under pressure from the earth's interior is pushed up to the surface and gradually builds a volcanic mountain.

which are usually oval or circular in shape. The Black Hills of South Dakota, the Henry Mountains of Utah, and the Adirondack Mountains of New York are examples of domed mountains.

Fold mountains are formed when sedimentary or lava rock masses are subjected to tremendous earth pressures that crumple them into long, parallel ridges. Folding of the crust accounts, at least in part, for great mountain ranges such as the Alps, Andes, Appalachians, Himalayas, and Rockies.

Sometimes, however, when the pressuring forces are sufficiently great, the crust may break. The fracturing of rock may be accompanied by slippage along the break; that is, the rocks on one side are pushed up higher than the rocks on the other side of the break, resulting in the elevation of the rock on one side. This sudden slipping, followed sometimes by the tilting of raised rock, results in the formation of *block mountains.* The largest of the block mountains in the United States are the Sierra Nevadas, which are over 400 miles (about 640 kilometers) long and 50 to 80 miles (80 to 130 kilometers) wide, with the elevated side of the broken rock facing eastward to form one side of the Great Basin.

OCEANS

Interest in the oceans has increased markedly in recent years, for a number of reasons. The films of Jacques Cousteau have fascinated millions with the portrayal of the teeming life that abounds in the ocean—from the surface to depths never before seen. We search for many things in the ocean: We drill the seafloor in search of new oil deposits but at the same time are concerned about the damaging effects of oil spills. We seek ways of extracting the untapped mineral wealth dissolved in its waters. We hope to harness the energy of ocean tides and wave movements to generate electricity. We are now conducting large-scale experiments to find more efficient ways of extracting fresh water from the ocean water to relieve shortages and to open up desert areas for cultivation. We study the oceans to understand better the role they play in weather and climate patterns of the earth. From the ocean bottom we bring cores of the sediments that have accumulated for millions of years to find new clues to the earth's history. We try to understand better the origin of the force that is steadily widening the Atlantic Ocean's floor

(Left) When the crust of the earth is subjected to pressure it may buckle up into long parallel ridges to form fold mountains. *(Right)* Block mountains are formed when large blocks of the earth's crust are raised and tilted. Block mountains are usually rectangular in shape.

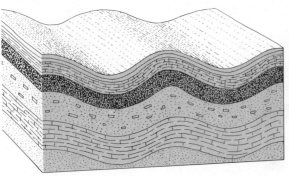 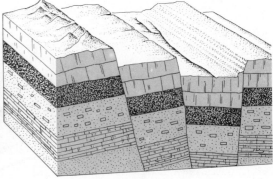

The snow-capped peaks of the Teton Range in Wyoming. Sometimes called the American Alps because of their extreme steepness and glacial carving, the Tetons are the remains of a block mountain formation. *(Courtesy of Union Pacific Railroad Museum Collection.)*

and pushing America away from Europe. We look to the ocean depths as a new challenge for exploration and adventure.

In the past the study of the oceans was limited principally to the search for new trade routes. Today the relatively young science of *oceanography*

uses the principles and techniques of biology, chemistry, geology, and physics for investigating the mysteries of the seas.

Some of the most significant discoveries in oceanography have been made on the floor of the ocean. For hundreds of years navigators have sailed the oceans without knowing the shape of its bottom, except in shallow coastal waters. It was generally assumed that the ocean bottom was shaped like a saucer or soup dish, deepest in the middle and rising smoothly to meet the surrounding continents. It came as quite a surprise, therefore, when it was found that the deepest parts of the ocean were relatively close to land masses.

A simple but effective tool for determining the depth of the ocean was the *sounding lead,* a weight lowered by a hemp line from a ship until it hit bottom. The length of the line gave the depth at any point. After World War I, sound waves were sent from the ship to the bottom. The time needed for the sound to return was a gauge of depth.

With these and other devices, oceanographers found that the ocean bottom is far from being a smooth plain: Its mountains and valleys rival anything found on the continents. Perhaps the most exciting discovery was that of the *ocean ridges,* a system of mountain ranges 40,000 miles (64,000 kilometers) long, which extend through all the ocean basins of the earth like the stitching on a baseball. Part of this system is the Mid-Atlantic Ridge, a crest dividing the Atlantic Ocean from the Arctic nearly to the Antarctic, its path almost exactly midway between the coasts of the Americas and that of Europe and Africa, and running parallel to both (see p. 117). The ocean ridges are regions of frequent earthquakes and volcanic activity. The eruption of Surtsey, a submarine volcano off Iceland in 1963, and the resulting growth of an island there, are evidence of the crustal unrest in the ridge regions of the oceans.

Running along the Mid-Atlantic Ridge and dividing it into an east and west portion is a deep valley or rift, 8 to 30 miles (about 13 to 50 kilometers) in width, extending the full length of the ridge. The significance of the ridge and the rift will be discussed later in this chapter.

Almost as dramatic as the finding of the undersea mountain ranges was the discovery of the deep-sea trenches, which drop precipitously from the ocean floor. Some of the trenches of the Atlantic and Pacific have walls that are steeper than parts of the Grand Canyon.

In summary, the seafloor is characterized by mountain ranges, deep trenches, underwater vol-

canoes, and vast plains. Bordering all continents are shelves and slopes that are submerged parts of the continents. The crust under the oceans is thinner than that of the continents. Both the continents and the ocean basins are fundamental parts of the crust of the earth.

EARTHQUAKES

On February 4, 1976, a devastating earthquake struck Guatemala, killing 23,000 persons. Later in that year, on July 28, two powerful earthquakes hit heavily populated northern China, claiming an estimated 750,000 lives.

The earth scientist, who takes the long-range point of view, describes earthquakes as constructive events because they are part of the process that pushes up and builds rock structures above the surface of the earth. To most of us, however, earthquakes are fearful happenings, resulting in widespread destruction of life and property in the areas where they occur.

Ninety-five percent of all earthquakes occur in two geographic belts, one ringing both sides of the Pacific Ocean and the other crossing the Mediterranean area. These belts also include most of the world's active volcanoes and young mountains. Indeed, earthquakes, volcanoes, and mountain building are all associated with turbulence in the earth, with great crustal pressures and tensions.

The belts of high earthquake activity—sometimes called the Ring of Fire—are believed to coincide with the margins of the great moving plates of the outer shell of the earth, which we will examine in the section on the drifting continents. As the plates collide, pull apart, or slide past neighboring plates, interactions along plate boundaries generate the stress that causes earthquakes.

Not all earthquakes occur on the well-known belts, however: Three of the strongest earthquakes in North American history occurred in 1811 and 1812 in the vicinity of New Madrid (pronounced MAD-rid) on the Mississippi in southern Missouri. The powerful quakes there caused bells to ring in Washington and sent the Mississippi River flooding its banks. Soon after the quakes

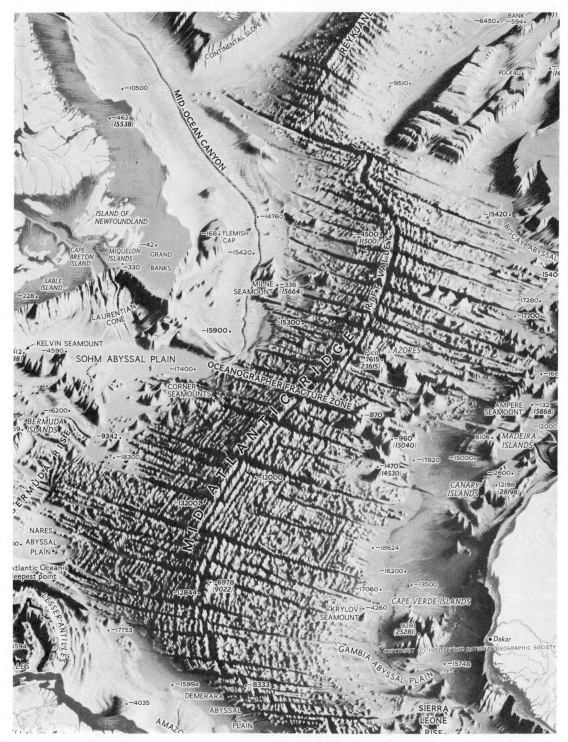

Part of the Atlantic Ocean Floor. The ocean bottoms have a geography that is as varied as that of the continents. They are characterized by high mountains, deep trenches, underwater volcanoes, and broad plains. The text explains why the mid-ocean ridge and the rift valley that lies along it are of particular significance in relation to the theory of drifting continents. *(Courtesy of National Geographic Society.)*

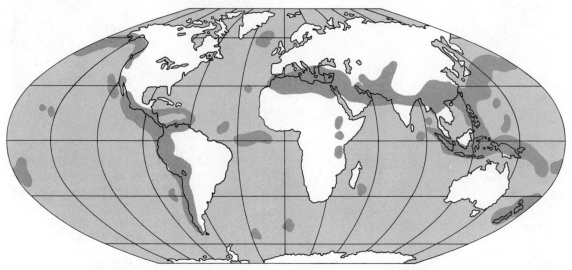

The principal earthquake belts of the earth. These coincide to a large extent with the regions of active volcanoes and growing mountains.

David Crockett visited and named the area "Shakes Country." Even now, this region is shaken by a small quake on the average of every other day.

We have seen, in our study of mountain formation, how the pressures within the crust may cause it to buckle up and fracture. An abrupt movement of large blocks of the earth's crust on each side of the fracture is essentially what happens during an earthquake.

Earthquakes often occur along lines called *fault lines,* which represent an old wound in the earth's crust produced by a previous fracturing of the rock. The San Francisco earthquake of 1906 took place along such a line, called the San Andreas Fault, which extends for several hundred miles from northern to southern California. This line was known to geologists for many years prior to the quake. On both sides of the line, pressures and tensions were built up in the adjoining rocks. The 1906 break released the tensions as rocks snapped, like the springing of a steel trap. Map studies of the location of roads and rivers before and after the break show that this earthquake re-

sulted from a *horizontal* movement along the San Andreas Fault. Roads and fences that crossed the fault were offset as much as 21 feet (6.4 meters), moving northward on the west side of the fault and southward on the east side.

Some earthquakes result from a *vertical* movement of rock, however: In Yakutat Bay, Alaska, a section of seacoast was lifted as much as 47 feet (14 meters) during an earthquake in 1899. In the Alaska earthquake of March 1964 some 35 feet (11 meters) of vertical motion along the Hanning Bay Fault built Fault Cove in Montague Island.

The abrupt release of energy in the snapping and shifting of rocks starts strong destructive waves that can be detected thousands of miles away by delicate instruments called *seismographs.* The principle on which the seismograph operates is shown in the illustration on page 120. In this simplified model a heavy weight is suspended from a spring and a pen is attached to the weight. A drum, driven by a clock mechanism, turns slowly so that the pen writes on it. If an earthquake occurs, the drum shakes, because it is firmly attached to a platform whose base shakes

Looking northerly along the San Andreas Fault, where the Pacific Plate on the west side moves northwest relative to the North American Plate on the east side of the fault. In this photo, the fault is marked by the valley dividing the raised cliffs. *Photo by R. E. Wallace. (Courtesy of U.S. Geological Survey.)*

with the earth. The weight remains stationary because very little of the force of the earth's tremor is transmitted to it through the spring, and because of its own inertia. As a result, a wavy line is inscribed on the turning drum. This is like writing by holding your pen firmly in your right hand and by jiggling a pad with your left hand while moving the pad toward the left.

The *seismogram,* the name given to the lines written on the drum, is a record of earthquake vibrations themselves. From this record the seismologist determines the duration, magnitude, and distance of the earthquake from the seismograph center. The *duration* of the quake is easily read because the minutes and hours are imprinted on the clock-driven cylinder. The *magnitude* of the break is shown by the height of the wavy lines on the seismograph. In comparing the magnitude of different earthquakes, seismologists use the *Rich-*

ter Scale. On this scale, an increase of one unit expresses a tenfold increase in the size of the seismic *wave.* Thus a recording of magnitude 8 on the seismograph represents a disturbance 10 times as large as a reading of 7 and 100 times as great as a reading of 6. A quake of magnitude 2 is the smallest quake normally felt by humans. Earthquakes with a Richter value of 6 or more are considered major in magnitude. The California earthquake of 1906 had a value of 8.3; that of Guatemala in 1976, 7.5. The 1985 earthquake of southwestern Mexico that killed 9,000 people had a magnitude of 8.1.

Magnitude is only an indication of the total energy of an earthquake. An increase of one unit on the Richter Scale represents an increase of 32 times the energy released. Thus an earthquake rated 8.3, such as the one that hit San Francisco in 1906, had a *million* times the energy of

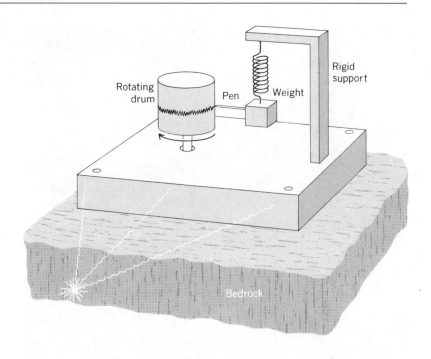

The principle of the seismograph (see pp. 118–120 for
explanation).

those rated 4.2, which are common in California today.

The determination of the *distance* from the earthquake center is based on the fact that several kinds of earthquake waves originate simultaneously at the point of the quake. The exact *location* of the center can be determined by the records of at least three widely separated stations within a few hours after the earthquake has started. Each of three observatories draws a circle using its distance from the earthquake as the radius. The site of the earthquake, its *epicenter,* is the common point where the three circles intersect. This is the place on the earth's surface directly above the earthquake's first movement, its *focus.*

The study of seismograph records has revealed a great deal about the internal structure of the earth. As earthquake waves pass through the body of the earth their *speed* and their *path* are affected by different kinds and states of materials. One kind of earthquake wave, for example, will not pass through liquids at all; from this, scientists hypothesized that the outer part of the earth's core—through which this wave does not pass—

is in a liquid state (see p. 109). Earthquake waves, then, act like X rays, enabling us to "see" through the earth.

Many strong earthquakes originate in the crust under the Pacific Ocean. Here they may start ocean waves that travel as fast as 500 miles (800 kilometers) per hour and may break over coastal areas in waves as high as 60 feet (18 meters). These are mistakenly called tidal waves, although they have nothing to do with tides. The scientific name for these huge waves is *tsunamis* (tsooná-mēz), a word of Japanese origin. In 1946 an earthquake originating off the Alaskan peninsula started great waves that traveled 2,000 miles (3,200 kilometers) to the Hawaiian Islands, causing widespread damage.

Shallow oceanic earthquakes have also been found to occur frequently in the region of the Mid-Atlantic Ridge, particularly in the deep rift valley that separates this long mountain range (see p. 117). This oceanic valley, directly above a belt of crustal unrest, is twice as wide, twice as deep, and, from a scenic standpoint, much more impressive than the Grand Canyon.

The accurate forecasting of earthquakes is obviously of great importance. In recent years scientists have intensified their study of changes in earthquake-prone areas in an attempt to discover any symptoms that would warn of earthquakes. The following are among the phenomena under investigation: The little quakes that precede big ones and certain changes in the speeds of the waves they produce; the uplifting or tilting of the land; increased electrical conductivity of the crust; the accumulation of strains along faults; the growth of cracks in rocks; changes in the geomagnetic field; changes in gravitational strength; the frequency of earthquakes to determine whether they occur according to some time schedule.

Long-term forecasting can only identify areas of earthquake hazards. Short-term prediction—warning of an impending quake a few days or weeks ahead of time—is an elusive goal. But this is the objective of geologists at Parkfield, California. Parkfield is a small town halfway between Los Angeles and San Francisco lying near a segment of the San Andreas Fault, where geologists are trying to monitor the birth of an earthquake in the hours and days before it occurs. Based on the relative regularity of earlier Parkfield quakes—one occurs about every 22 years; the last one struck in 1966—the U.S. Geological Survey made its first-ever earthquake prediction: that an earthquake of magnitude 5.5 to 6.0 would probably occur there in 1988, with a 95 percent certainty of a quake within five years from that date. To determine whether it is possible to predict an earthquake by measurable observations, an elaborate set of instruments are in place in this area. Seismometers will measure upward as well as sideways movement of the earth, and wires strung across the fault near Parkfield will detect movement of the two plates—the Pacific Plate and the North American Plate—past each other. A truck capable of providing small seismic waves, a "thumper," will provide researchers with an opportunity to see if the way rocks respond to these disturbances is symptomatic of earthquakes. Lasers are in place to make precise measurements, accurate to the width of a pencil line, of distances and elevations of the topography.

As we approach the time when scientifically based earthquake prediction becomes a reality, we are confronted with the problem of the effect such predictions may have on the population of an earthquake-prone area. How can a large city be evacuated without enormous social disruption and decline in the local economy? What if the prediction turns out to be wrong, or premature?

Potential dislocations and disruptions need not be too massive if wise action is taken in advance of the prediction. A comprehensive program must include disaster preparedness, a plan designed to reduce vulnerability. Of prime importance are adequate building codes with respect to the kind of construction and the foundation on which buildings are located. Geologists are horrified to see land developers building rows of houses straddling the trace of the 1906 California break.

Such knowledge of the location of earthquake-prone areas is also crucial for the siting and construction of nuclear power plants and for the disposal of nuclear wastes.

VOLCANOES

On February 20, 1943, Dionisio Palido, a farmer in Parícutin, Mexico, went to plow his fields for the upcoming sowing of corn. He noticed with surprise that a small, familiar hole in the ground had opened a little wider to become a crevice. At 4 P.M. he heard thunder and saw nearby trees trembling. In the hole the ground swelled and then raised itself 6 to 7 feet high (about 2 meters). A fine, ashy dust began to issue from part of the crack. Smoke arose with a loud continuous hissing, and there was a smell of sulfur. Dionisio fled back to the village.

Later, red-hot stones, ashes, and sparks were thrown into the air from the opening. By midnight, incandescent rocks were being hurled into the sky from this roaring hole in the earth.

Thus was a volcano born in a Mexican cornfield in our own century. In all written human history we have records of the beginnings of no more than 11 volcanoes, and information about all before Parícutin is meager. Parícutin provided scientists with a case study they could investigate firsthand. From the third day of its birth, skilled observers with many instruments at their disposal recorded all the significant events in the birth and growth of this volcano.

And grow it did. On February 21, the second day of its life, the volcano grew from 30 to 150 feet (9 to 46 meters) in height. Lava, molten rock, began to pour out, advancing slowly over the cornfield at the rate of 15 feet (4.6 meters) per hour.

Seven weeks after its birth, this lusty infant was almost 500 feet (150 meters) high. Heavy ash flying out of the volcano covered the countryside for miles, raining on the fields and eventually destroying the village of Parícutin.

At the age of seven months the Parícutin volcano had become a mountain 1,500 feet (450 meters) high and about one mile (1.6 kilometers) in diameter. By 1952, at the age of nine years, now 7,451 feet (2,771 meters) high, the volcano had become relatively quiescent.

Parícutin and Mount St. Helens are dramatic reminders that the earth and its surface are changing today and that these changes are a part of a process that began in the past and will extend into the future.

Not all volcanoes are explosive, however; some pour lava out of craters or form breaks in their sides. Mauna Loa and Kilauea on the island of Hawaii are famous volcanoes of this type.

Some volcanoes grow rapidly: Parícutin, as we have seen, was 1,500 feet (450 meters) high at the end of seven months; Monte Nuovo, born in 1538 at the edge of the Bay of Naples, rose to a height of 440 feet (135 meters) in one day.

Some volcanoes continue to erupt for centuries; others cease very quickly. Many are *dormant,* or quiescent, at present; they may become active or they may never erupt again.

We have noted that volcanoes are symptomatic of internal disturbances in the earth. They are concentrated in regions of the world where earthquakes and young mountain belts are located. Just why this is so will be discussed in the next section.

Recently we have developed techniques for forecasting some eruptions. Seismograph records are helpful because volcanic activity is accompanied by earth vibrations. For 20 days before the birth of the Parícutin volcano numerous earth tremors were felt in the nearby countryside. Other clues include the tilting of the ground around volcanoes and local changes in the earth's electrical currents and magnetism. The Hawaiian eruptions have been successfully forecast, but volcanoes over zones of tectonic plate collisions, as in the case of Mount St. Helens, are difficult to predict (see pp. 126–127).

The eruptions of volcanoes are not simply agents of destruction. They are the producers of mountains, plains, and seafloors. Their mineral-rich ash is transformed into fertile soil. They may have been the primal source for most of the earth's air and water.

THE DRIFTING CONTINENTS

How were the earth's continents and ocean basins formed? Have these global features remained fixed in shape and in position since their formation? How did the major mountain belts originate? Why are mountain ranges and areas of volcanic and earthquake activity generally located in distinct and usually narrow zones? Why are they not distributed over the earth's surface? Why do the continents on each side of the Atlantic seem to fit together like a giant jigsaw puzzle?

Questions of this nature have puzzled geologists for many centuries, but it is only since the 1960s that an explanation known as *plate tectonics* has provided an answer supported by a wealth of evidence. According to this theory, the outer shell of the earth is divided into a mosaic of rigid plates that move slowly around the sphere. As the plates move apart, slide past each other, or converge, new crust is created, continents drift, and mountains are formed.

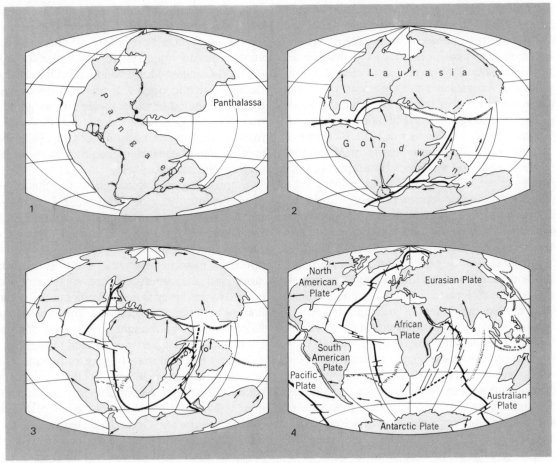

The breakup of the universal land mass of Pangaea into the many continents of today. *(Copyright © 1970 by Scientific American, Inc. All rights reserved.)*

The name *lithosphere* has been given to the rigid shell of the earth; it includes the crust and part of the upper mantle. The lithosphere is divided into seven major plates and a number of smaller ones filling gaps between them (see above). Evidence suggests that the lithosphere plates under the continents are generally between 60 and 90 miles (100 and 150 kilometers) thick; the oceanic lithosphere ranges from less than 6 to 60 miles (10 to 100 kilometers) in thickness. The plates "float" on a white-hot weaker layer of the mantle called the *asthenosphere*, a layer that is capable of slow change in form.

Pangaea

According to the theory of plate tectonics, the continents and ocean basins have been (and continue to be) rafted along by underlying crustal conveyor belts—the moving plates. How has this system changed the earth?

Present evidence indicates that some 300 million years ago all the continents were joined in one land mass, which geologists called *Pangaea* ("all lands"). The remainder of the earth was ocean, or rather the ancestral Pacific Ocean, called *Panthalassa.* Pangaea began to break up about

200 million years ago, and the continents were rafted to their present positions. New ocean basins were formed between the continents as they separated (see figure on p. 123). If this seems incredible, then look at the east coast of North and South America and the west coast of Africa. Can you see how they might have fitted together?

The original concept of drifting continents was proposed by Alfred Wegener in 1912. He puzzled over the matching Atlantic coasts of Africa and South America, and was struck by a report of similarities in certain fossil bones and in living species on these ocean-separated coasts. He postulated that it was not the animals, but the continents that had moved. To add more weight to his theory of drifting continents Wegener studied the world's mountain ranges. He noticed that if he joined the Old and New World, mountain ranges on opposite continents formed a single continuous belt. For example, the Sierras of Argentina linked up perfectly with the Cape Mountains in South Africa. As Wegener said, "It is just as if we were to refit the torn pieces of a newspaper by matching their edges, and then check whether or not the lines of print run smoothly across. If they do, there is nothing left but to conclude that the pieces were in fact joined this way." Moreover, geological dating (see pp. 112–113) showed that the separated ranges were formed at about the same time. Using Wegener's analogy, the newspaper stories on all the torn pieces have the same dateline. In summary, Wegener was asking, How could the same life forms exist on similar rock formations on two coasts separated by thousands of miles of ocean?

Wegener's theory was not accepted for many years. The traditional view at that time was that the earth was still cooling and shrinking from its original molten state. Mountain ranges were thought to have been thrust up in their present locations in the same way as wrinkles form on the skin of a drying, shrinking apple. The earth's crust was considered to be too rigid to permit any horizontal movement of its parts. The occurrence of identical plants and animals on continental borders separated by oceans was explained by the theory that ancient land bridges between the continents had been submerged.

It was not until the early 1950s that Wegener's old ideas were revived. In probing the ocean's depths, as we noted previously, scientists discovered an ocean ridge system some 40,000 miles (64,000 kilometers) long, winding through all the basins of all the oceans. It was also discovered that a depression or valley divided the ridge into two sides. It was conjectured that this valley marked the location of an underlying *rift* in the earth's shell, where new molten rock was pouring up from the asthenosphere.

A spreading rift, according to the theory of plate tectonics, may develop under a continent that is resting on a crustal plate (see p. 125). Molten basalt from the asthenosphere spills out of the rift and hardens into rock, pushing in opposite directions to form new ocean crust. In this way Africa and the Americas were split apart and pushed farther away from each other as the ocean floor of the Atlantic was created. The Mid-Atlantic Ridge with its rift is thought to be the scar or seam left by the splitting and parting land masses.

Iceland is a land mass lying directly across the Atlantic Mid-Ocean Ridge. Continuing activity within the ridge is responsible for the behavior of its volcanoes. Here is one of the few places on earth where the Mid-Ocean Ridge reaches the surface, providing a dry-land view of continental drift in action, where two plates are pulling apart.

If new plate material is constructed, how do the plates fit together around the globe without buckling? Evidently the crustal conveyor belt system connects zones of surface creation to zones of surface destruction. The latter are found near deep oceanic trenches, the kind that ring the Pacific. Here the edge of one advancing plate dives down under the leading edge of another and is consumed in the underlying mantle.

Other Plate Products: Earthquakes, Mountains, and Volcanoes

We have seen how plate tectonics accounts for the drifting of continents and the building of ocean bottoms. The concept of rigid plates moving

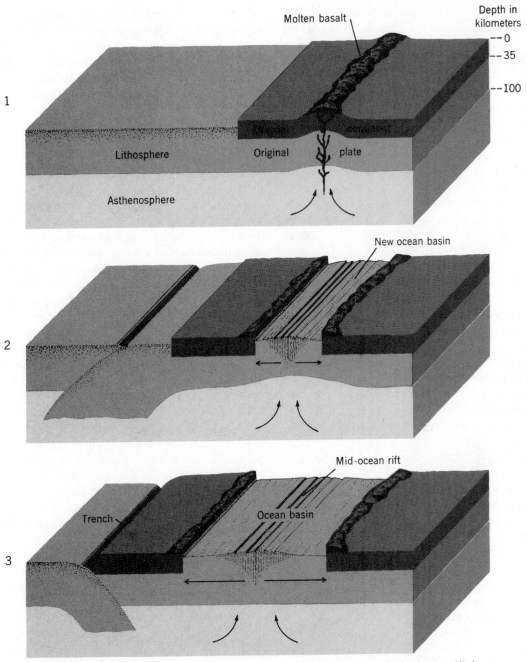

The splitting and drifting of continents according to the theory of plate tectonics: (1) A continent (shown darker) resting on a single crustal plate begins to split as molten basalt from the upper mantle wells up from under the plate. (2) A new ocean basin is created between the two newly separated continents. The spreading crustal plates carry the two continents farther away from each other. (3) The ocean basin widens. A mid-ocean ridge and a rift valley remain. *(Copyright © 1970 by Scientific American, Inc. All rights reserved.)*

around the earth and interacting at their boundaries has been remarkably successful in explaining other phenomena.

Sometimes plates slide past each other in opposite directions, as do the North Pacific and North American plates under California's San Andreas Fault. Here the Pacific plate is slipping northwest in relation to the American plate, at about the rate of 2 inches a year. If the plates become stuck for a while, stresses build up. When the buildup is sufficient, the plates lurch forward and rocks in the earth's crust rupture, causing tremors or earthquakes, such as the one that devastated San Francisco in 1906. It is estimated that the plate motions should bring Los Angeles abreast of the present location of San Francisco in about 20 million years. In another 50 million years the Baja Peninsula and the part of California west of the San Andreas Fault will be an island 250 miles off the coast of British Columbia.

Most earthquakes occur in narrow zones associated with the boundaries of plates. The earthquake network is seen to be associated with a variety of characteristic features such as rift valleys, volcanic chains, and deep ocean trenches. The areas within the plates are largely free of earthquakes, but there are some notable exceptions. In the past 3,000 years over 9,000 quakes have been recorded in mainland China, the most recent in 1976. These are thought to result from forces squeezing Asia from two directions: one from the northeastward drive of the Indian plate, the other from the northwestern movement of the Pacific plate. Interestingly, visible evidence of the effects of these pressures on China has been revealed in part by photographs taken by satellites. Another exception was noted on pages 116 and 118: the continuing earthquake activity in the region near New Madrid, Missouri, which is well within the North American plate. Although it lies on the oldest and strongest rock in the continental crust, it is located over an ancient rift.

A collision of continents may occur when a plate carrying one continent smashes against an opposing plate carrying another: They fold up like an accordian, forming mountain ranges. Evidently the Himalayas were formed when a plate carrying India collided with the ancient Asian plate some 40 million years ago. The devastating Indian–Nepal earthquake of 1988 resulted from the continuing movement of the Indian Plate against the Asian Plate. Later the same year the convergence of the African Plate with the Eurasian Plate caused an earthquake in Armenia that left at least 25,000 dead, 15,000 injured, and 500,000 homeless.

Another kind of collision may occur when a plate that has only an ocean above it descends into a trench. This may occur at the margin of a continent or of a major arc of islands. As the oceanic plate descends, it initiates pressure and heat changes, which result in the thrusting up of a mountain belt. A good example of this is the west coast of South America, where a huge oceanic plate is plunging into a deep trench off the South American plate. As the ocean plate dives beneath the continental plate it pushes up the Andes Mountains and initiates deep earthquakes. On September 19, 1985, as the Cocos plate on the west coast of Central America drove under the lighter American plate, a powerful seismic wave was released, rocking Mexico City 220 miles (350 kilometers) to the west. The resulting earthquake collapsed tall buildings and killed more than 9,000 people. The western North American mountains—the Sierra Nevada and the Coast Range—also resulted from similar interactions of oceanic and continental plates.

Some mountains, such as the Appalachians, have a history that predates the breakup of Pangaea. Some 300 million years ago, huge protocontinents, borne on great tectonic plates, converged to form the original Pangaea, like the joining of pieces of a jigsaw puzzle. The collision of two of these protocontinents raised a mountain belt, remains of which are the Appalachians along North America's eastern coast and the highlands of Central Europe. Later, beginning 200 million years ago, great splits in Pangaea resulted in the present oceans and continents. The jigsaw puzzle came apart, but the pieces were different.

The collision of plates can also produce volcanoes. The Antillian chain of islands is situated along the line where the Atlantic plate of the sea-floor descends under the Caribbean plate. As the Atlantic plate is forced downward its rocks melt under pressure and seek a way out. Molten rocks escaping build up mountains on the surface. As the pressure and melting continue, volcanic eruptions occur. The most disastrous explosion in the Antilles in this century, the eruption of Mount Pelée on Martinique, destroyed the town of St. Pierre and killed 30,000 people in 1902.

The molten material generated when the tiny Gorda plate off California plunges under the North American plate gives rise to the volcanic eruptions of the type that formed the Cascade Range where Mount St. Helens lies. In summary, volcanic activity may take place in one of three places: Volcanic mountain ranges are generally formed at the edge of continents where tectonic plates collide; volcanoes may occur in the middle of a plate over a "hot spot" where pockets of magma break through the earth's crust; or volcanic activity may occur where plates are splitting and are pulled apart, forming new ocean basins.

Certainly no modern theory about the earth was more surprising both to laypersons and scientists alike than that the continents are not fixed in position; that the Atlantic basin is widening and the Pacific is closing; that Asia and America are moving closer together. "The theory of plate tectonics is a concept that unifies the main features of the earth's surface and their history better than any other concept in the geological sciences."[2]

[2]M. Nafi Toksöz, "The Subduction of the Lithosphere," *Scientific American* (November 1975).

This eerie, moonlike wasteland was once a picture-postcard wilderness of lush forests, green meadows, and sparkling lakes. That was before May 18, 1980, when Mount St. Helens (seen in the background) blasted away its near-perfect summit cone, leaving a gaping arena in its stead. The eruption buried an area of 232 square miles with mud, ash, and pulverized rock and took a human death toll of 57. *Photo by Lyn Topinka. (Courtesy of U.S. Geological Survey, David A. Johnston, Cascades Volcano Observatory, Vancouver, Washington.)*

WEARING DOWN OF THE LAND

We have seen how forces working from the interior of the earth have thrust up the large features of our planet. Let us turn our attention now to the forces that have modeled these features into the present face of the earth. First, we shall consider *weathering,* the process by which rocks crumble and disintegrate. Then we shall look at *erosion,* the process that not only breaks rock but also carries the fragments away.

Weathering

Frost Action   Water, entering the pores of crevices of rocks, may contribute to their disintegration. If the temperature drops sufficiently the water changes into ice. In freezing, water increases about 9 percent in volume. The ice in the crevice acts as a wedge, forcing the rock apart and splitting off chunks from it.

Chemical Action   The chemicals found in nature act on rocks, changing them into new materials and breaking them down. The oxygen of the atmosphere unites with the iron that is present in many rocks, making it rust and decay. Water com-

bines with some of the substances in rocks—mica, for example—to form new materials that eventually crumble. The carbon dioxide of the air dissolves in rainwater to form a weak acid known as carbonic acid. This acid works on various minerals. Feldspar, a mineral found in granite, is decomposed by carbonic acid into clay.

Living Things   Plants affect rocks mechanically and chemically. The roots of trees and shrubs sometimes grow into the crevices of rocks and may exert enough pressure to split them apart. Some kinds of lichens (see p. 270) live on rocks and produce acids that attack and dissolve the surface of the rock, thus making it possible for these plants to absorb necessary minerals.

When plants and animals die and decay, acids are formed that react chemically with rock and help to weather it away.

Erosion

Weathering *breaks* rocks into fragments of various shapes and sizes: boulders, pebbles, all the way down to the molecules of the minerals of which they are composed. Erosion breaks rocks and also *moves* broken rock, including that formed by

The rock-dissolving acids produced by lichens make tiny pits in the rock's surface. *(Courtesy of Monkmeyer Press Photo Service.)*

weathering. The agents of erosion are running water, ocean waves, moving ice, wind, and gravity (see pp. 139, 141–144).

Running Water The Grand Canyon of the Colorado River is the work of running water. Long ago the Colorado River flowed on high-level land over the layers of sedimentary rock that had been laid down in previous eras. As time went on the running water, aided by fragments of rock that it carried, cut deeper and deeper into the rock. Weathering, discussed earlier, gravity, and rain helped the river attack the walls of the valley and widen the narrow cut into its present V shape.

A river, then, carves a valley as it flows downhill on its way to the sea. At first the valley is narrow and V-shaped. The young river, using rock fragments as tools, rushes rapidly through the valley—filing, scraping, and sanding out a deeper and deeper bed. As the river's bed deepens, its banks cave in and the valley is widened. The river begins to slow down. Its ability to rush over large boulders and other obstructions is lost. The river is more easily deflected sideways into a meandering course.

Running water is the most important tool of nature in wearing down the surface of the earth. Not only does it cut and dislodge, it transports the materials that it and other forces have pried loose. The rivers of the United States carry about 1 billion tons of materials to the oceans each year. This represents an average leveling down of the entire surface at the rate of 1 foot (.3 meters) every 8,000 years. What is most significant to us now is that much of this transported material is the valuable topsoil that is essential to our existence. This is a conservation problem created in part by humans, and one that can and must be solved by humans. (We shall discuss this more fully in Chapter 13A.)

Running water is also responsible, at least in part, for many land forms that we do not have space to discuss here: gullies, badlands, potholes, rapids, waterfalls, flood plains, oxbow lakes, and deltas.

Ocean Waves Ocean waters also affect the surface of the earth. Ocean waves smash our rocky seacoast with a force that may rise to thousands of pounds in each square foot, splitting and moving rocks and scouring away bedrock by the grinding action of sand and pebbles. Boulders dislodged from rock cliffs are slowly pounded into pebbles and sands.

Ice In the last million years great ice sheets have moved down from the Arctic regions, covering Canada, the northern United States, and northern Europe. During the Great Ice Age the sheets of ice advanced and retreated many times, the last advance reaching its maximum about 20,000 years ago and the last retreat ending as recently as 6,000 years ago. At one time almost a third of the world's present land surface was covered with glaciers: Today only a tenth is under glacial ice. Four fifths of this is on the Antarctic continent. Glacial ice contains close to 90 percent of the world's fresh water above ground.

What is now New York City was once under a solid mass of ice half a mile high. A trip to Central Park in Manhattan will reveal many evidences of this glacial visit. The outcrops, or exposed bedrock, in this city oasis are scratched, grooved, and polished in a way that is characteristic of rock over which a glacier of ice has passed. Here and there, perched on the outcrop, are large boulders made of rock entirely different from the underlying bedrock, which in Central Park is mica schist. Evidently these boulders were plucked out of some mass of rock by the glacier some miles to the north of New York City and then dropped in their present position when the ice melted.

New York City and Long Island mark the southernmost advance of the Atlantic end of the last glacier. This front is revealed to us by a mass of loose earth—including sand, gravel, and boulders—that was deposited when the tip of the glacier melted. This material, forming what is known as *terminal moraine,* extends 140 miles (225 kilometers) from Brooklyn across the northern half of Long Island to its eastern tip.

We are able to study glaciers firsthand because some exist today. Glaciers begin as great snowfields that are slowly compacted into ice by the accumulation of more snow on top. Glaciers form

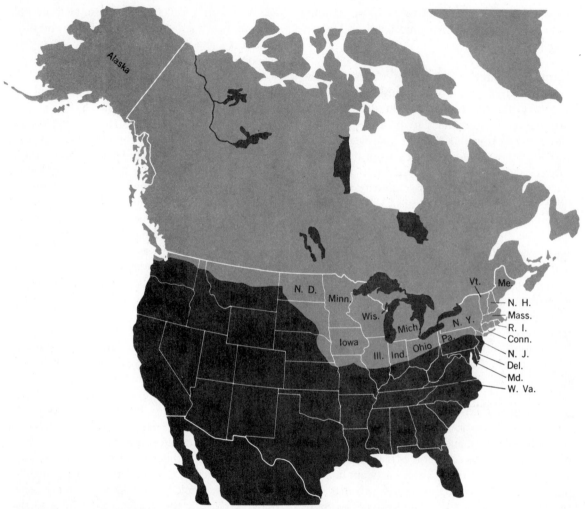

The southernmost advance of the glaciers in the last ice age. There are many evidences of the glacier's visit—rock deposits, lakes, grooves and scratches in rock, moraines, outwash plains, and others—in the regions formerly covered by ice.

in those regions where snow accumulates more rapidly than it melts. This happens in two places: near the tops of high mountains and in the frigid zones of the earth (see p. 131).

Valley glaciers originate in mountains and, as they grow, fill the valleys leading down, as a river might. The western United States has valley glaciers in the Sierra Nevadas, the Rockies, and the Cascade Mountains. The glaciers in Glacier National Park in Montana and Mount Rainier National Park in Washington attract thousands of tourists every year.

Continental glaciers originate over large, cold land masses in the frigid zones, where they cover the land with ice sheets thousands of feet thick. When the ice becomes thick enough it moves out in all directions toward the seacoasts. Greenland and the Antarctic are almost entirely covered by glaciers of this type.

Glaciers, like rivers, move downhill in response to gravity from the upper snowfields where they are formed. Glaciers in the Alps move at average speeds of 1 to 3 feet (.3 to .9 meters) per day; those in Alaska and Greenland may move

A valley glacier, such as the Columbia Glacier in Alaska, is a river of ice. Its origin is in high mountain snowfields, where snow is compressed into ice. As the glacier moves down the valley it grinds away at its walls, slowly transforming the original V-shape into a U-shape. Note the cracks, called *crevasses*, in the surface of the glacier. *(Courtesy of U.S. Geological Survey.)*

as much as 40 feet (12 meters) or more a day. These masses of ice always move forward, but their fronts may advance, remain stationary, or retreat. The front advances over the land as long as the mass of ice moves faster than it melts. When the rates of moving and melting are equal, the front is stationary. In Greenland the glaciers advance faster than they melt, even at sea level. In Greenland and in other places where glaciers reach the seacoast, they break off to become *icebergs*.

In addition to direct on-the-site studies, glaciers are now monitored by remote sensing devices carried by the Landsat Satellites. Such sensors have been useful for mapping the glaciers, for measuring their movement, and for describing the details of their surface structure.

Valley glaciers are great movers of materials on the earth's surface. They gouge out huge depressions and carry the materials along to be deposited elsewhere as the glacier melts. Continental glaciers also carry along huge boulders and soil and deposit them elsewhere. The soil of much of the northern part of the United States has been materially changed by continental glaciers that visited this area during the last million years.

Lakes and ponds are also often the result of the process of *glaciation*. Valleys become blocked with the soil and rocks of moraine deposits, which act as dams to hold back water. In some cases glaciers have gouged out or deepened basins that now hold water. The Great Lakes occupy ancient river valleys that were deepened and dammed by glaciers.

The glacial periods, or Ice Ages, of the past were presumably caused by fluctuation in the earth's temperature, when a drop of several degrees in average temperature allowed a vast accumulation of ice to occur. It is thought that in the glacial periods the sea level may have been as

Sand dunes, such as these in Fremont County, Idaho, are formed whenever there are strong winds blowing from one direction and a sufficient quantity of loose sand. Note the contrast between the gently rising slope on the windward side (on the left), and the shorter, steeper leeward side. The sand ripples duplicate in miniature the windward and leeward slopes of the larger dune. *(Courtesy of U.S. Dept. of Agriculture, Soil Conservation Service.)*

much as 300 feet lower than it is now, because much of the oceans' water was locked up in glaciers.

It is conjectured by scientists that we are now in a warm, or *interglacial,* period. Measurements taken in recent years suggest that the sea is now rising at the rate of $2\frac{1}{2}$ inches (6.4 centimeters) per 100 years. Perhaps this rise is due to the rapid melting of the world's glaciers. It is estimated that if the existing glaciers melted completely, the sea level might rise by more than 150 feet (46 meters). A warming trend may be the result of the increase of the carbon dioxide in the atmosphere during the past century, which has been attributed to the burning of fossil fuels, coal, oil, and gas. Page references to this problem will be found under "greenhouse effect" in the Index.

Wind We have seen how running water and moving glaciers carry soil and other materials across the earth's surface. Wind also is a carrier of soil. This has been dramatically and tragically demonstrated in the dust storms that have plagued some areas of the United States.

There are other results of wind erosion that we see occasionally when the wind piles up sand into dunes (see p. 132). There are huge hills of sand in many parts of the United States. They are alike in appearance, and they are all created in essentially the same way.

We all know that a strong wind can carry sand. Some of the sand carried by the wind is dropped when the wind slows down because of an obstacle or for some other reason. The pile of sand thus deposited gradually forms a hill called a *dune.* The windward slope of a dune is gentle; the lee side drops more sharply. The transfer of sand from the windward to the lee side results in the slow movement of the entire dune in the direction of the wind. Dunes may march as much as 100 feet (30 meters) in one year.

The formation of sand dunes requires a great deal of dry sand to be moved and stretches of flat surfaces over which the wind can sweep. The migration of dunes sometimes buries towns, farms, and forests. On the eastern shore of Lake Michigan westerly winds have built dunes that are migrating inland over Indiana, gradually burying the trees of a forest area known as Dune Park. Such migration of dunes can sometimes be halted, however, by the planting of grasses and shrubs in the sand.

Gravity When weathering separates a rock fragment from a large mass, gravity eventually takes it down to the lowest part of the surrounding area. An accumulation of broken rocks at the foot of a cliff, called *talus,* is a product of gravity.

Gravity is also responsible for the less obvious *soil creep,* causing the soil covering to move very slowly downhill over a period of time. A more dramatic and often disastrous movement of soil results in a landslide. Landslides are sometimes set off by earthquakes, sometimes by heavy rains.

Gravity is also the force responsible for the movement of running waters in rivers and waterfalls and of valley glaciers which, as we have seen, are prime agents of erosion.

Soil Formation

Pour a handful of ordinary garden soil into a jar of water and shake it vigorously. When it settles, skim off some of the material floating on top. Much of this will be bits of leaves, stems, and roots of plants, partially decomposed. Examine the material that has settled to the bottom carefully to find grains of sand and small pebbles, both of which are broken rock (see p. 144).

Soil has its origin in the decay of plants and animals and the weathering of rock. Soil is a final product in the destruction of rock. It is our greatest natural resource.

THE EARTH'S CHANGING SURFACE

Until the 1960s we knew little about the way our planet really works—why volcanoes arise, how mountains and oceans form, and how continents are rafted on crustal plates that ride on hot fluid rock below. Scientists and explorers have uncovered a new portrait of our planet.

Two chapters in this book are related to this study and may profitably be read in connection with it: Chapters 12A, "The History of Life," and 13A, "Ecology, Energy, and the Environment."

Generalizations such as the following will be found at the end of each of the A chapters; their purpose is to emphasize the essential meanings of the subject matter of the chapter.

IMPORTANT GENERALIZATIONS

The earth is very old and has undergone great changes in its lifetime.

Scientists study rocks to learn about the history of the earth.

The earth is believed to be composed of concentric parts of different materials: The outermost is a hard, rocky crust; next is a zone of denser, red-hot rock; the outer part of the core is composed largely of molten metal, the inner core largely of solid metal.

Seventy percent of the surface of the earth is covered by seas.

The study of the oceans has taken on increased importance.

The landscape of the ocean floor is as varied as that of the continents.

An ocean mountain range or ridge 40,000 miles (64,000 kilometers) long runs along the ocean bottoms of the earth.

Rocks originate in three ways: from the cooling of molten materials, the cementing of small fragments, and the changing of existing rocks into new forms.

Rocks are made of one or more kinds of minerals.

Minerals are natural inorganic substances of definite chemical composition.

The co-architects of the earth's surface are the forces of construction and destruction—the forces that build mountains and those that level them.

Mountains are formed from volcanic activities or from the buckling of the earth's crust.

According to the theory of plate tectonics, the earth's outer shell is divided into a mosaic of rigid plates that move slowly around the sphere.

As the plates move apart, slide past each other, or converge, new crust is created, continents drift, and mountains are formed.

The boundaries of the plates are marked by chains of volcanoes, mountain building processes, and earthquake activity.

General acceptance is accorded the theory that a single landmass split and separated, forming the present continents of the earth.

Temperature changes, chemical action, and living things are important in the splitting and breaking down of rocks.

The large forces responsible for the leveling down of the land are running water, ocean waves, moving glaciers, wind, and gravity.

Soil, our greatest natural resource, is a product of the destruction of rocks.

DISCOVERING FOR YOURSELF[3]

1. Make, or obtain if available, a rough map of the county in which you live. Indicate location of streams and bodies of water, unusual land forms, and other geological features. Your state geological survey offers a wealth of information about your area.[4] Many state survey offices conduct field trips, supply speakers, and offer media presentations and publications.

2. Make a tour of the surrounding counties to observe erosion effects, land changes made by rivers, and other landscape changes.

3. Follow a stream to see (a) how the stream has changed the earth around it, (b) the load of sand and soil being carried, (c) the swiftness of the stream, and (d) the deposits of the stream. Examine a sample of water.

4. Observe a local area after a heavy rainstorm to determine (a) where erosion is taking place, (b) why it is taking place, (c) the materials that are being carried away, (d) where materials are being deposited, (e) the effects of deposits, and (f) the effects on the area covered by the rain.

[3]Here, as in each subsequent A chapter, will be found activities designed to help you learn more about the science subject matter, as well as how to teach it more effectively. They are for use by preservice as well as in-service teachers. How many of them will be useful for a specific locality and school system will depend on local conditions. They have all been found helpful in many situations.

[4]J. W. McLure, "Free Tips for Geology Trips," *The Science Teacher* (October 1985). Includes the telephone numbers of state geological surveys.

5. Make a rock collection, using as many sources as you can for identification, and write an informative label for each specimen telling its origin, use, and composition.

6. Find out what the most pressing problems of soil erosion are in your community and what is being done about them.

7. Keep newspaper clippings dealing with earth-quakes, floods, volcano eruptions, and other major "earth-changing" events for a period of two months. How did each of these events alter the surface of the earth?

8. Plan an imaginary summer vacation trip in North America to see important and dramatic geological formations. What is your itinerary? What would you look for in each place? What important principles of geology would be illustrated?

9. Investigate, through printed sources, the San Andreas Fault in California. What is a fault? Can earthquakes be predicted? Should new houses be constructed on the fault site? What is the use of a seismograph?

10. Try to find out about the work of oceanographers. What tools, materials, and apparatus do they use? What are some of the important discoveries they have made during recent years, and how may their findings affect us in the future?

11. What evidence from geography and paleontology support the theory of drifting continents? What additional evidence for seafloor spreading is found in the magnetic properties of rock on the ocean floor? (Consult a geology text listed in the bibliography.)

TEACHING "THE EARTH AND ITS SURFACE"

A Note for All B Chapters: The learning activities in the B chapters are planned to give suggestions for teaching the subject matter in the preceding A chapters, as well as to illustrate the philosophy and methods developed in Part I. Different kinds of lessons are described. Some activities help children relate the subject matter to their environment. They consist of making observations, collecting and classifying materials, making exhibits, constructing learning models, making charts and graphs, and reading printed materials. Others involve investigations using various methods of inquiry. They begin with a problem, plan investigative procedures, carry out the plan, analyze the results, and attempt to draw some conclusions.

The sections "Other Problems for Younger Children" and "Other Problems for Older Children" suggest additional class activities, or topics for individual science projects.

To facilitate the locating of appropriate information in other sections or chapters, cross-references to the A chapters have been added in these B chapters.

To help children find out about the earth and its surface, encourage them to observe changes in their immediate surroundings and to discuss their observations. Some of the changes in the earth's surface are easy to see in any environment, city or country. The hills, valleys, rocks, excavations, and soil in the neighborhood are sources to investigate. The schoolyard, "empty" lot, and park—exposed as they are to the sun, wind, and rain—are excellent places to observe the forces of nature at work. The street becomes a "watershed" area and the gutter a "riverbed" whenever it rains. The bricks or rocks in the school building, the macadam playground, the concrete sidewalks, the steel jungle gym—all are made of materials extracted from the earth's surface.

When investigating the surface of the land, children can compare natural and artificial changes. A river requires millions of years to cut a valley through rock, whereas a machine-made roadcut takes only days. In connection with man-made changes children may attempt to make value judgments: "Should this road be built?" "Should this swamp be filled in?" "Should this mountain be strip-mined?"

Related to the content of this chapter, and helpful to the teacher in planning broad units, are Chapters 13A and B and 14A and B.

SOME BROAD CONCEPTS

The earth is covered with rocks, soil, and water.
There are many different kinds of rocks.
The earth's surface is constantly changing.
Water and wind help change the earth's surface.
Rocks are made in different ways.
Soil is made from the breaking down of rocks and plant and animal remains.
We depend on soil, water, air, and rocks for our existence.
The continents of the earth were once one large mass that later split and drifted apart.

FOR YOUNGER CHILDREN

Although the following activities may be used at any grade level, depending on circumstances, they have been found especially appropriate for younger children from early childhood on. They will need to be adapted to fit specific situations to meet the interests and maturity of children, materials available, and other factors. Some of the problems may require only one or two lessons for their development; some may lead to longer units of study. In many cases the science processes and expected behaviors have been identified.

What Can We Do With Sand?

Sand, a product of the earth's activity, is also a source of endless activity for children because they can dig into it, mold it, pour it, and build with it. Sand is also fascinating because it changes in color, in consistency, and in the way it can be handled when wet.

Encourage children to play freely with sand in a tray or sandbox and to comment on how it feels and what it does. Ask them, "What can you build with sand?" Depending on their earlier experiences with sand they may build hills, castles, roads and tunnels, and other constructions, or they may use sand freely as a medium for working out concepts. When a pail is added they discover that a full pail of sand is heavier than an empty pail. They experiment to find out how high a hill they can build with dry sand and then with wet sand. They examine sand through a magnifying glass to see its grains of different colors. In cleaning up their sandbox, they pour sand through a sifter and note how small objects are separated from the sand, and how the sand "slips," "slides," or "runs" through the holes.

From the suggested activities, children learn that sand can be poured, can be built up into a hill, and is made of many tiny grains; that wet sand holds imprints, can be patted into different shapes and molded into different forms; that dry sand pours more easily than wet sand and that wet sand sticks together better than dry sand.[1]

What Kind of Rocks Can We Find in Our Neighborhood?[2]

Collect different kinds of rocks on a class field trip to a nearby park, vacant lot, excavation, or building under construction, and add specimens brought by individual children. The teacher may also add specimens. Undoubtedly the collection will include some artificial rocks (don't reject them) such as fragments of brick and concrete. Where did the rocks come from? Examine them:

[1]Adapted from "Prekindergarten and Kindergarten Curriculum Guide," Bureau of Curriculum Development, Board of Education, New York City, 1970.

[2]M. McIntyre, "Many Children Are Budding Geologists," *Science and Children* (May 1976). Many suggestions for activities found appropriate for young children. J. R. Blueford and L. C. Gordon, "The Not-So-Rocky Road to Earth Science. Some Geologists Show the Way," *Science and Children* (April 1984). Helpful suggestions about rock collecting.

Feel them, lift them, look at them carefully (use a magnifying glass), smell them, scratch them with a metal nail, scratch a smooth stone with them. Describe what you observe. How are the rocks alike? How are they different from each other? What is their color, shape, size, and what other characteristics do they have? After rocks have been examined carefully put some of them in a bag and break them with a hammer. Look closely at the broken rocks. Compare the inside surface with the outside. Describe how they are alike and how different. Wet the rock samples. What changes in appearance, color, and texture do you see?

A magnifying glass helps to identify the minerals in these rocks, collected on a class field trip. *Photo by Lloyd Wolf, Anne Beers School, Washington, D.C.*

Ask the children to suggest ways of arranging their rock collection to make an interesting display. At this level identifying and naming many of the rocks will be difficult. Some children may wish to classify their rocks according to size, some according to color, some according to weight, shape, hardness, some according to the place where they were found, and other ways. Have them carry out some of their proposals to make a rock display. They may include written information to accompany their exhibit or present an oral report.

What Did the Rain Do?

Walk in the schoolyard or nearby street immediately after a rain. Ask the children to tell what they think is happening to the water that fell. Dig into the soil if possible. How deeply has the water soaked into the soil? Look for tiny streams. Look at the water that is running in the streams. Look at the water along the curb on the street. Where is the water going? Does the water carry away any of the soil? How can we tell? Catch a glassful of water and let it settle. Is there any soil (mud) at the bottom? What has the water done to the soil around trees, on lawns, on grassy hillsides? As a result of these firsthand experiences children may discover that rain water either flows along on the surface of the ground, forms puddles, or sinks into the soil. Depending on the nature of their experiences, other conclusions are possible and desirable.

Other Problems for Younger Children

1. What do ice and snow do to the earth's surface near us?
2. What useful things do we get from the earth?
3. How does water in streams and rivers get muddy?
4. How can we clean muddy water?
5. How can we separate sand from pebbles?
6. What hills can we find in our neighborhood?

FOR OLDER CHILDREN

How Can We Make a Rock Collection?[3]

Making a collection of rocks and conducting related activities can result in children being able to classify the rock specimens either by doing single-stage classifying using one characteristic and then another—that is, color, hardness, method of formation, and so on—or, for some children, by using more than one characteristic. *Arrange* rocks according to their characteristics; *invent* methods of classification; *observe* characteristics through the use of the senses; *identify* some of the common rocks and describe what has been learned by making an exhibit or record. The most valuable rock collection is one that children participate in making on class trips or on trips with their families or friends.

A strong magnifying glass will be of great help to children as they study rocks. Begin with "What can you find out by looking? How are the rocks alike? How are they different from each other? How does the magnifying glass help you?"

Break rocks apart with a hammer to look inside. The inside of a rounded rock looks different from the outside. Children may first *observe* and *describe* the rocks before they are broken and try to account for the appearance (shape, size, texture). After the rocks have been broken, children again examine and describe and attempt to *predict* what would happen if the pieces were put into a swift-moving stream and left there for years.

Many kinds of rocks are difficult to identify. The following resources will be helpful: the local museum's rock and mineral collection, a small rock or mineral collection purchased from a supply house, pictures from books, a local high school science teacher.

Children, even with your help, may not be able to identify all the rocks they collect. Perhaps you

[3]See R. Bartholomew, "What's the Difference between a Rock and a Mineral?" *Science and Children* (October 1979); K. Hill, *Exploring the World with Young Children* (New York: Harcourt, Brace, Jovanovich, 1981).

can put those together in a box with a sign: "We do not know what kinds of rocks these are." An important thing for children to learn is that there will be problems that they cannot solve immediately. There are problems, many of them, for which even scientists do not know the answers.

Students will discover that rocks are made of a variety of minerals. These differ in luster, size, shape, hardness, and so on. Many minerals— quartz, mica, agate, flint, and graphite (the "lead" of lead pencils)—are already known to children. They can test rocks to see which are hardest, and put them in groups. The softest rocks can be scratched with a fingernail. The hardest will scratch glass. Some especially interested and talented students may be able to classify rocks according to their origins—igneous, sedimentary, and metamorphic.

Encourage students to devise their own methods of classifying the collections using such titles as "Rocks Used in Our Community," "Hardest Rocks," "Softest Rocks," "Unusual Rocks," "Rocks Formed under Water," or "Rocks from Volcanoes." They may use other classifying ideas.

Students can use their reading resources to discover how the rocks were formed and how they came to be in their present shape. A written account of the discoveries placed with the collection in the school corridor will create interest (see Chapter 6A, pp. 108–112).

Children may expand their knowledge of rocks in different areas of the United States by arranging to exchange rocks with other schools. This has been a successful activity in many schools and includes some study of geography; it also involves letter writing and other language-arts skills.[4]

How Are Rocks Used in Our Neighborhood?

An interesting rock-hunting trip may be organized to help children observe the uses of rocks.[5] Stu-

dents and teachers, as a result of study and observation, can prepare a guide with "stops" in sequential order. The first trip may be in and around the school itself. A later trip may include places and buildings in the neighborhood. Examples of the stops: (1) the classroom: chalkboards (slate, although in some schools it is made of artificial materials); (2) the corridor: wall behind drinking fountain (marble); (3) basement: drinking fountain (soapstone); (5) main lobby: steps (marble, terrazzo); (6) entrance (limestone); (7) front steps (granite); (8) sidewalk (concrete); and (9) curbstone (concrete, bluestone, or granite). In writing the guide, students tell the origin, color, use, and other special information about each of the rocks.

Note: Some of the building materials may be artificial.

Urge students to observe churches, banks, libraries, and other buildings to see examples of different kinds of rocks. Suggest that they try to find out where these rocks came from. If some of the rocks came from a quarry in the community, perhaps visits may be made there to observe the layers of rocks and to learn how rock is cut and transported. If there is a monument works nearby, students may be able to obtain samples of granite and marble for examination.

Fossils or fossil prints are often found in nearby rock formations. Fossils are frequently exposed on the surface of rocks used in buildings. Soft modeling clay, or a pencil rubbing on paper, may be used to carry away a print of the fossil. See Chapters 12A and B.

What Is Sandstone Made Of?

Suggest to the children that they examine some pieces of sandstone with a magnifying glass. What can be observed? Grind two pieces of sandstone together over a piece of paper. Examine the resulting grains of sand through the magnifying glass. What do you see? Where did the grains come from? What is the sandstone made of?

On a piece of white paper give each child some sand from a beach. Describe what you see. What

[4]M. McIntyre, *Early Childhood Science* (Washington, D.C.: NSTA, 1984).

[5]Adapted from *Science: Grades 3–4* (Brooklyn: Board of Education of the City of New York, 1966).

shape are the grains? What colors are they? Are they all the same size? Touch a magnet to the grains.

The lighter-colored or colorless grains are probably quartz. Reddish-brown or pinkish ones are often garnet. Black ones may possibly be magnetite, an iron compound, which children can identify by using a magnet. These are but a few of the approximately 2,000 minerals found in rocks.

Compare the sand from the sandstone with the sand from the beach. Are the grains alike? In what ways are they different from each other?

From this experience children may infer that sand may be formed by the grinding together of rocks and, conversely, that rocks may be formed if grains become pressed together and cemented. (If sandstone is not available, most of this study can be conducted with sand.)

How Are Mountains Formed?

Sometimes making a small model serves to clarify ideas. For example, a model may illustrate the effects of pressure on layers of rocks that cause them to become curved and tilted in the formation of mountains.

Place layers of different-colored plasticene or other similar material in a cardboard box. Sprinkle talcum powder between the layers so that they will not stick together. After the layers are packed, cut out the ends of the cardboard box, but leave the layers in place; then slowly push the ends toward the middle. This forces the layers into a position resembling folded mountains. With a sharp knife cut down through the middle of the layers and lift the two parts away from each other to expose the layers that were folded into mountains. A baking pan may be used to hold the model. What does the model show? Why were different colors of plasticene used? What caused the curves and the tilting? Have you ever seen a place where something like this has really happened on the earth's surface? Where?

Note: Folding is only *one* way in which mountains are formed. (See Chapter 6A, pp. 113–114.)

How Is the Earth Near Us Changing?

Field trips to some nearby locations reveal some of the changes in the earth's surface caused by various forces. Some of these changes may be observed on school grounds, others on longer field trips. The trips should be taken to gather information for solving such problems as "What forces are changing the earth's surface? How are they changing it?"

The children might go to observe a river or creek to see how it is wearing away its banks, observe the speed of the flow (drop a Ping-Pong ball in a stream and time how long it takes to travel a measured distance), examine stones from the creek bed, and note that sometimes the bed is covered with stones (the lighter material has been carried away by water). They can observe trees and other plants growing out of rock formations, observe how the rocks have split, and examine small plants growing in rocky surfaces. If they try to lift one of the plants from its growing place, they will see how the tiny roots are growing into crevices in the rock itself.

Children may observe movements of a sidewalk by locating a portion of the sidewalk that has been subject to a deforming stress. Children may attempt to connect the direction and extent of cracks with some specified cause. Was the section moved up or down? Could the expansion of sections because of summer heating have been responsible for its buckling? Could the washing away of underlying soil and gravel have caused sinking? Might the growing roots of a large nearby tree have dislodged the sidewalk? How long do you think it took for these changes to take place? Some of these observations may be made by children as they go to and from school, and then reported to the class. (See "Field Trips Useful in Problem Solving," Chapter 3.)

A trip to a so-called empty lot may help students to see the results of forces that change the earth. They try to answer, through careful observation, such questions as (1) How have people changed the surface of the lot? (For example, people make shortcut paths across the lot producing a bare area.) What effect does this have on the surface? (2) What signs of erosion can be seen (soil that has been moved, gullies, exposed rocks and roots of trees and other plants, effects of wind and rain)? (3) What are the rocks like? How do you think they have changed through the years? How do you think they got there?

A trip to an excavation near your school is a good place to see what the earth is like under the surface. Students may note the darker topsoil and compare it with the subsoil. They may also note different rock and soil layers. They may bring samples of soil to their classroom for more careful examination.

If possible, visit an ocean or lakeshore to observe firsthand how part of the earth's surface is constantly changing. How is the size, shape, and surface of the beach changed by waves, tides, rain, gravity, rooted plants, seaweed, marine animals, birds, and humans? Make notes and sketches and take photographs. Return at intervals to note changes.[6] If a field trip is not possible, ask children to report on their experiences at the seashore, or as seen on TV.

An extended trip to look for different land and rock forms will provide information. Observe *land forms* such as hills, bluffs, plains, and beaches; *rock forms* such as outcrops, boulders, layered rocks, and faults; and *effects of glaciers* such as lakes, terminal moraines, and so on. What students are able to observe depends on the location.

The same forces that change the land in a country environment are also at work in the city. Survey of a city block reveals trees disturbing sidewalks, plants growing in cracks in the pavement, water washing surfaces, crumbling buildings, stones with smooth and sharp edges, and so forth.[7] What happens when a water hydrant is

open and the water flows out? How are the bricks in buildings changed by the weather? What changes lawns, pavements, and sidewalks?

Photographs may have to be substituted for some of the experiences just described. Magazines, travel folders, geography books, and other sources supply pictures of topographic features that may be arranged to illustrate the story of earth changes. Pictures taken by the children themselves are preferable, for obvious reasons. Pictures taken in a city environment and compared to rural photographs yield interesting ideas. See discussion of field trips in Chapter 3.

In summary, children learn that sun, water, wind, and plants and animals change the surface of the earth, and that these changes are constantly occurring.

How Can Water Break Rocks?

The experiences and experiments described here are focused on understanding how water changes the earth's surface. It is often difficult for children to observe the effects of freezing water in their environment. They can, however, plan an experiment that will demonstrate the effects of water's expansion when it freezes. Ask them to try to devise a plan for this. If the students need assistance, help them by filling a glass jar with water to the top and screwing the cover on. Now what can we do? Freeze the water. What do you think will happen? Place the jar in a clear plastic bag so that the results can be examined more easily and set it in the freezing compartment of a refrigerator to let it freeze. What happens? Would an *empty* jar with a screwed-on lid also break if it were placed in a similar situation? Try it. What caused the jar full of water to crack? Would it crack if it had not been filled to the top? Try it.

The jar cracks because the water expands when it changes to ice. Where else have you ever seen this happen? Plumbers or garage mechanics sometimes can supply metal pipes or parts that have been cracked by freezing water. Seeing these

[6]*Science and Children* (October 1980). Entire issue is devoted to marine education.

[7]*Operation New York: Using the Natural Environment of the City as a Curriculum Resource* (Brooklyn: Board of Education of the City of New York, 1960); S. K. Shugrue et al., "No Space for Soil," *Science and Children* (January/February, 1972); *Helping Children Learn Earth–Space Science,* a selection of articles reprinted from *Science and Children* (Washington, D.C.: NSTA, 1971).

A field trip is often more effective when the class is accompanied by a specialist, who, in this case, explains what forces change the earth. *(Courtesy of U.S. Dept. of Agriculture, Soil Conservation Service.)*

will help students realize that as water freezes, it exerts a great force that can break things. If there are rock formations nearby, pouring water on them may help students to see how it sinks down into the cracks.

Children are impressed with the "push" that freezing water can give. They may be interested in attempting to find out how much "bigger" water gets (increases in volume) when it freezes.

Ask children to *estimate* how much by filling a clean, empty metal or plastic food can about three fourths of the way with water. Mark or scratch a line to show the height of the water. Then ask children to try to estimate how much the water will expand when it freezes. Mark some of their estimates on the can. Place in the freezer and note the height after freezing. Repeat the experiment with different shapes and sizes of containers. A

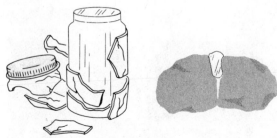

Freezing water has broken the jar in the refrigerator, just as water breaks rocks when it seeps into cracks and expands as it freezes.

rigid *plastic* (not glass) container, such as a toothbrush case, can also be used by individual children at home to report their findings to the class. Ask "How much did it expand? Was the expansion the same with different containers?" Here is an opportunity to use careful measurements both in inches and millimeters. Keep records of the measurements made under various circumstances and help children describe what the data seem to show. (The expansion will be about 9 or 10 percent.) (See Chapter 3, "Investigating and Experimenting to Find Out.")

How Can We Separate Different Parts of the Soil?[8]

Obtain a bucket of soil from a forest, field, park, or other natural site (after permission has been obtained). Spread the soil out on a large sheet of paper and sort out the pebbles, decaying or skeletonized bits of plant and animal matter, humus, and so on, into separate piles. Use a screen or a coarse strainer to separate the larger particles from the smaller ones. The teacher may suggest placing some of the soil in a large jar, adding about an equal volume of water, shaking vigorously, and then allowing the mixture to settle for some time, perhaps a day or so. Before it settles, ask children to predict what will happen. Char-

acteristically, the pebbles will settle to the bottom, then sand, silt, clay, and humus above them in that order. Bits of plant and animal material may float on top of the water.

Ask students to suggest uses for this "jar-shake" technique. Some may suggest using it to compare the contents of different kinds of soil.

Other Problems for Older Children

1. What expeditions have scientists conducted to study the earth?
2. What does the force of gravity have to do with changing the surface of the earth?
3. How do people change the surface of the earth?
4. How deep is the soil in different places around your school?
5. How do the earth satellites help us learn more about the earth's surface?
6. On a world map mark the locations of the earth's active volcanoes.

RESOURCES TO INVESTIGATE WITH CHILDREN[9]

1. Local public buildings, to see the uses of rocks and minerals in construction.
2. Local landscape, to observe land forms and changes in them: rivers, streambeds, banks, pits, shores of bodies of water, valleys, and other forms. In the city: streets and sidewalks, vacant lots, excavations, and similar places.
3. A well driller, to furnish samples of different soils and rock formations from underground and for information about local conditions under the earth's surface.
4. Samples of different kinds of soil, to discover how they are alike and how different, as well as what they are made of.
5. State roads commission, for information about land formations where roads are being constructed.

[8] D. E. Banks, "Investigating Soil," *Science and Children* (November 1971). Prepared with the assistance of personnel from the Agriculture Research Center. D. J. Nelson, "Dirt Cheap and All Around Us." *Science and Children* (March 1985). Practical suggestions for studying soil.

[9] Here, and in each of the subsequent B chapters, will be found a list of people, places, things, and special kinds of resources helpful in teaching chapter material and developing the goals indicated for the various experiences. Whenever the suggestions to write for information are made, the teacher should assume the communicating responsibility with such help from children as seems appropriate.

6. Soil conservation departments and geologists, for information on erosion problems of local area and on conservation practices in action.

7. Pictures from books and magazines that show the earth's surface in various places on the earth, to compare and contrast and discover what changes may have occurred in these places.

8. National Parks Service, Washington, D.C. 20242, for information about park geology.

9. Accounts of earth changes in newspapers and magazines: volcanoes, floods, mud and rock slides, earthquakes, and erosion. What were the causes and the results of these changes?

10. The U.S. Geological Survey publishes topographical maps of various U.S. regions. Write to Denver Distribution Center, Denver, Colorado 80225.

11. Reports on recent history of Mount St. Helens.[10]

12. Demonstration by children of how the continents may have once been connected and then moved through the ages. Use a world map, trace the continents from the map, cut them out, and try fitting them together like a jigsaw puzzle to show how they may have moved.

PREPARING TO TEACH[11]

1. Write the objectives you think may be attained as a result of the study of one of the problems in this chapter. Be as specific as possible and relate the objectives to the material at hand. For example, children should be able to explain how water can break rocks, or state one example of how the earth nearby is changing. Remember that you are trying to determine the changes in values, beliefs, and understanding of scientific procedures. Try to devise some ways of determining the extent to which these objectives have been attained (see discussion of objectives in Chapter 2).

2. Make a list of the materials and apparatus you would try to obtain if you were teaching a unit based on the material in this chapter.

3. Assemble an exhibit of teaching materials you would use in helping children learn about changes in the earth's surface, and describe briefly how you would use the materials.

4. List the experiences, experiments, and demonstrations you would try to provide for children of a particular grade as they study this material.

5. See *Geoscience Resources,* 2990 Anthony Road, Burlington, NC 27215 for catalogue of resources including rock collections and other materials including space science.

6. Prepare a list of out-of-school experiences that will give children an opportunity to use inquiry skills and to make discoveries. Suggest ways children might report their findings.

7. Prepare a pencil-and-paper examination that you think will help to evaluate what students in grades 4, 5, or 6 should learn about the subject matter of one problem in this chapter. (See "Evaluation Instruments," Chapter 5.)

---

[10]"Volcanoes: Coming Up From Under," *Science and Children* (September 1980). With poster in color.

[11]A section called "Preparing to Teach" is also included at the end of each B chapter. As the name indicates, these are practical suggestions to help teachers and prospective teachers get ready to teach the subject matter under consideration more effectively. Teachers may wish to read these sections early in order to order materials suggested and have them on hand when needed.

THE SUN AND
THE PLANETS

> *A space encounter is more than a mark on a mission time line. It is the culmination of incremental approach to a distant world. . . . an accelerating magnification in the final few weeks . . . and then a torrent of incredible new data in just a few days' time. An encounter is also a human event, a celebration, as space junkies from around the world converge on Pasadena to experience the joyous rush of never-before-seen images tickling their brains.*
>
> CLARK R. CHAPMAN
> *ENCOUNTER!: VOYAGER 2 EXPLORES THE URANIUM SYSTEM*
> THE PLANETARY REPORT, MARCH/APRIL 1986

CLOSE ENCOUNTERS OF THE REAL KIND

In the almost three decades of space exploration of the solar system, begun in 1962, we have made many exciting discoveries: giant canyons and ancient, dry riverbeds on Mars; belching sulfurous volcanoes on Jupiter's satellite Io; an ensemble of thousands of ringlets in Saturn's rings; ten new moons on Uranus. We have penetrated the dense veil of Venus's atmosphere and photographed its rocks, mountains, and sky. We have made detailed surface maps of more than a dozen satellites circling the giant planets. Most thrilling to most of us was that moment in 1969 of the "one great leap for mankind," when astronauts first walked on the moon.

In addition to the rocks brought back from the moon and the spectacular portraits of the planets, the space tours have provided significant clues to the origin and future of the planets, including that of our own planet Earth.

THE SUN'S FAMILY

The sun is the center of a family of celestial bodies known as the *solar system*. The head of the family is the sun, and the principal members are the nine known planets that revolve around it. In order of increasing distance from the sun, the planets are Mercury, Venus, Earth, Mars, Jupiter, Saturn, Uranus, Neptune, and Pluto. (Part of the orbit of Pluto is closer to the sun than the orbit of Neptune. Right now Pluto is closer than Neptune and will be for the rest of the century.) They all move in the same direction around the sun; their orbits lie in nearly the same plane, with Pluto the exception. Somewhat less familiar are the thousands of small asteroids that revolve around the sun, most of them in the space between the orbits of Mars and Jupiter.

Six of the planets have close "relatives"—the satellites that revolve around them. More than 60 satellites, or "moons," in all have been observed, one for Earth, two for Mars, 16+ for Jupiter, 17+ for Saturn, 15 for Uranus, 8 for Neptune, and 1 for Pluto. Neither Mercury nor Venus is known to have a satellite.

Also included in the sun's family are the numerous comets, with eccentric orbits that bring some of them close to the sun and then out into the far reaches of the solar system. Billions of meteoroids, varying in size from a grain of sand to a huge boulder, also move around the sun and are counted as members of its family.

The solar system is a vast racetrack with planets and their attendant satellites, comets, asteroids, and meteoroids streaking around the celestial center—the sun.

GRAVITY AND THE SOLAR SYSTEM

Why do members of the solar system not fly away from the sun as they hurtle through space at thousands of miles an hour? What keeps them in their orbits? Sir Isaac Newton provided an answer in the seventeenth century with his *law of gravitation*. In its simplest form the law states: *All bodies, from the largest star in the universe to the smallest particle of matter, attract each other with what is called a gravitational force.*

The strength of the gravitational force between two bodies depends on (1) *their masses* (the amount of material in them)[1] and (2) *the distance between them*. The greater the distance, the weaker the force. (More exactly, the attraction varies inversely as the square of the distance between the centers of the two bodies. If the distance between two bodies is doubled, the gravitational attraction is only one quarter as great. If the distance is halved, the attraction is four times as great.)

The planets and other bodies in the solar system do not streak off into space because of mutual gravitational attraction between these bodies and the sun.

But if all bodies attract each other, why don't they rush toward each other and smash? For example, why don't the earth and sun move together and merge?

Newton helps us again at this point with one of his laws of motion, which states that a body in motion will move forever in a straight line with unchanging speed unless a force changes its motion. The body in motion in this instance is the earth. The *tendency* of the earth to maintain its motion at the same speed of about $18\frac{1}{2}$ miles (about 30 kilometers) per second and in a straight line prevents it from falling into the sun. But, as we have seen, there is also a force that acts to change the earth's motion: the gravitational force between the earth and the sun. The net result— the compromise—of both motion *and* gravity is the almost circular orbit of the earth around the sun.

[1]This is a good place to distinguish between *mass* and *weight*. The weight of an object depends on the pull of gravity on it. It can change. An object weighs less at the top of a mountain than at sea level. On the moon it would weigh $\frac{1}{6}$ as much as on Earth; on Jupiter $2\frac{1}{2}$ times as much. But its mass—the quantity of material in it—is constant anywhere in the universe.

The laws of motion and of gravitation also account for the paths of other planets around the sun and the orbits of the moons around the planets. These laws have enabled scientists to plan for the many artificial satellites that now orbit the earth and the space vehicles that travel to the outer limits of the solar system.

THE SUN

Space travelers journeying to the outer edges of the solar system, to Pluto and beyond, would find the sun appearing smaller and smaller in the sky until it looked just like a star, which is exactly what it is. Our sun is but one of the billions of stars in the universe, and only a moderate-sized one at that. It looks larger and brighter than the other stars because it is so much closer to us. The sun is about 93 million miles (150 million kilometers) from the earth. This figure means more if we translate it into other terms: Assume that a spaceship travels at an *average* rate of 17,500 miles (about 28,000 kilometers) per hour, fast enough to circle the earth in $1\frac{1}{2}$ hours. At this speed it would require about seven months to reach the sun.

Structure of the Sun

The familiar bright disk of the sun has a diameter of 864,000 miles (roughly 1,400,000 kilometers), about 109 times that of the earth. All that we can observe directly of the sun is in its outer layers known as its atmosphere. The brightest of these is the *photosphere*, seen as the white-hot, luminous disk of the sun. Outward from the photosphere are the *chromosphere* and the *corona*. Most of the sun's mass is in its hidden interior.

Ordinarily we see only the photosphere, a layer that is only a few hundred miles deep. Its name, which means "light sphere," indicates that it is the layer from which light escapes from the interior. The brightness of the photosphere prevents us from seeing the outer layers of the sun's atmosphere. During a total eclipse of the sun, however, when the photosphere is hidden by the moon, these outer layers are prominently displayed. At non-eclipse times the chromosphere and the inner brighter part of the corona can also be observed with a *coronograph*, a telescope in which a black disk produces an artificial eclipse.

Just outside the bright photosphere, the chromosphere (color sphere) is a transparent, gaseous layer about 1,500 miles (2,400 kilometers) thick, colored red with glowing hydrogen. From time to time eruptions hundreds of thousands of miles high stream out of the photosphere to form colorful *prominences*.

Enveloping the sun is the transparent corona, which reaches out many millions of miles. Indeed, astronomers now believe that the corona may extend as far as the outer regions of the solar system. This means that the earth and the other planets are *within* the sun's atmosphere.

Photographs taken through a telescope show that the sun's disk (photosphere) is not uniform; here and there are darker areas called *sunspots*. Sunspots have been studied carefully by scientists. They are believed to be associated with magnetic disturbances in the sun. Sunspots grow large and then disappear, but it may take several weeks or months for this to happen. Sunspots appear dark because the temperature in these areas is somewhat less than elsewhere on the surface of the sun.

Sunspots range from about 500 miles (800 kilometers) in diameter, barely detectable through a telescope, to 50,000 miles (80,000 kilometers) or more. If a particular sunspot is watched day after day it appears to move from west to east. This apparent movement is due to the turning of the sun on its axis. As the sun rotates, it carries the sunspots around with it. However, the sun is gaseous; it does not rotate as a solid. As a conse-

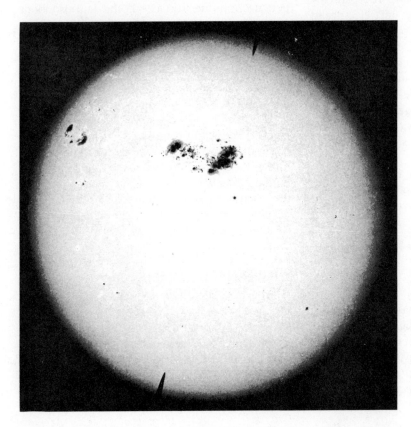

These sunspots were observed on April 7, 1947. The number rises to a maximum roughly every 11 years; 1947 was a peak year. The last visible maximum was in 1979; the next is expected in 1991. *(Courtesy of Mount Wilson Observatory.)*

quence all parts of the sun do not move together: Its equator takes 25 days and the region at the poles takes about 35 days for a complete rotation.

Solar Wind

In addition to light, heat, and other radiations, the sun emits electrically charged *atomic particles*, mostly protons and electrons, from the sunspot regions. Moving at a velocity of millions of miles an hour these particles escape from the sun's corona and sweep through the solar system, constituting what has been called the "solar wind." Orbiting earth satellites and spaceships have detected these particles.

The earth is constantly in the solar wind, but we are more aware of it when there is a *solar flare*, that is, when there is a sudden intensification of the particle bombardment. The particles strike the earth's *ionosphere*, an electrically charged layer of the earth's upper atmosphere (see Chapter 9A). Ordinarily, the ionosphere bounces short-wave radio waves back to earth, making long-range radio communication between distant stations on earth possible. When the ionosphere layers are disturbed by a solar flare, however, the reflection of radio waves back to the ground is disrupted; this results in radio distortion and fade-outs.

Another effect of this barrage from the sun on our atmosphere is an increase in brilliance of the beautiful displays called *auroras*, the northern and southern lights.

The Sun's Energy

For billions of years the sun has been radiating energy into space. The visible light rays that illuminate the earth are one form of this energy. Also emanating from the sun are invisible X rays, ultraviolet rays, infrared rays, and radio waves. Altogether they are known as *electromagnetic radiations*.

What is the source of the sun's energy? The sun is now thought of as a gargantuan nuclear reactor, deriving its energy from a process resembling that of the hydrogen bomb, in which lightweight atomic nuclei join to form heavier ones; this is called *atomic fusion*. In the sun, hydrogen atoms join to form helium atoms. Recently, however, emphasis has been placed on gravitation as a source of energy. If the particles of the sun, like those of other stars, fall closer together because of their mutual attraction, that is, if the sun contracts, some of its potential (stored) energy is converted into heat.

The sun's energy is *not* produced by burning. It has been calculated that if the sun were made of coal there would be a sufficient supply for burning to last only 80,000 years.

By means of instruments that measure the temperatures of distant objects through an analysis of their light, scientists have calculated that the temperature on the surface of the sun is about 10,000°F (about 5500°C). This fiercely hot temperature, however, would not be sufficient to sustain the hydrogen-bomb type of activity going on inside the sun. Scientists calculate that the temperature there is somewhere near 25,000,000°F (about 14,000,000°C).

The small part of the sun's radiant energy that reaches the earth warms its surface, supplies green plants with light essential for the manufacture of food, and thereby makes plant and animal life possible. Ways of using solar energy to meet the energy crisis are discussed in Chapter 13A, "Ecology, Energy, and the Environment" and Chapter 15A, "Heat and How We Use It."

THE PLANETS, COMETS, AND METEOROIDS

Planet means "wandering star," a word used by the ancients to describe those heavenly bodies that changed their position in relation to the "fixed stars" of the constellations. It was found, for example, that the individual stars making up the Big Dipper were always in the same spot in this group of stars, whereas the planets Venus and Mars were seen in different places at different times, appearing to wander among the stars.

Today we know that the planets are not stars. Planets shine by light reflected from the sun, whereas stars (like our sun) shine by virtue of their own internal nuclear activities. (We may have to modify this sharp distinction somewhat: The planets Jupiter and Saturn radiate about twice as much energy as they receive from the sun.) The nine planets are much smaller than most of the stars we see in the sky. Their apparent brilliance and size is caused by their closeness to the earth.

The "wandering" of planets is related to their movement in a solar "racetrack" in which the earth is also moving. If we think for a moment of a real racetrack with nine horses galloping around it at different speeds, a jockey on a horse named Earth would see the other horses and their riders in different *relationships* as lap after lap was completed—both with respect to each other and when viewed against fixed objects in the distant landscape, such as buildings and trees.

Let us look at the planets from another vantage point, that of an observer on the North Star (which is seen overhead from the earth's North Pole). He would see that all the planets move in the same counterclockwise direction, and that their paths, or orbits, except for those of Mercury and Pluto, are almost circular. If he used Earth time as his standard he would find that Mercury on the inside track completes its circuit in 88 days, Earth in $365\frac{1}{4}$ days, outermost Pluto in almost 250 *years*.

A space observer would note that while the planets are moving around the sun they are also spinning like tops. The word *revolution* is used to designate the circuit around the sun; the word *rotation* designates the spinning. Revolution relates to a planet's orbit, to its "year." Rotation relates to its spinning, to its night and day.

It is difficult to visualize the vast distances, the empty voids in the solar system, without recourse to everyday models. Picture the sun reduced to the size of a 50-foot balloon. On this scale Mercury would be a handball $2\frac{1}{4}$ inches in diameter, about 2,000 feet away from the balloon. Venus would

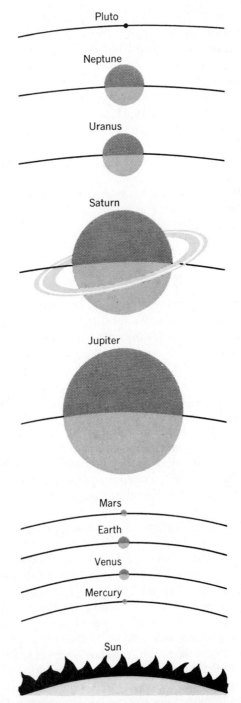

The planets are drawn to scale in this diagram, but not the distance between their orbits. The table on p. 164 gives additional data on the planets.

be a small melon, $5\frac{1}{2}$ inches in diameter, about $\frac{3}{4}$ mile from the sun. Earth, slightly larger than Venus, would be located 1 mile from the sun. Mars, the size of a ball 3 inches in diameter, would take its place $1\frac{1}{2}$ miles from the sun.

Now we come to the "big four" in the planet world. In our scale they have the following sizes and distances from the sun: Jupiter, 5 feet and 2 inches, $5\frac{1}{4}$ miles; Saturn, 4 feet and 5 inches, $9\frac{1}{2}$ miles; Uranus, 22 inches, 19 miles; and Neptune, 21 inches, 30 miles.

Pluto, a small planet, would be a ball about $1\frac{1}{2}$ inches in diameter at an average distance from the sun of 39 miles.

Mercury

Mercury is so close to the sun that most people have never seen it. We must look for this planet near the western horizon just after sunset or near the eastern horizon just before sunrise. Even at these times the brightness of the earth's twilight sky makes it hard to see Mercury.

A new portrait of this planet emerged when the unmanned spacecraft Mariner 10 flew by Mercury in 1974 and 1975. Television cameras carried on this mission sent thousands of pictures back to Earth that revealed a planet strongly resembling the moon, heavily cratered, with some long and steep cliffs, great smooth plains, and no apparent atmosphere.

Mercury is a planet of extremes. Appropriately named for the fleet-footed, winged messenger god, Mercury has the shortest period of revolution about the sun, 88 of our days, and the highest average orbital speed—30 miles or 42 kilometers per second. It is the second smallest of the planets, with a diameter less than half that of the earth. It shares with Pluto the distinction of having a very eccentric orbit, traveling in an elongated ellipse that brings it as close as $28\frac{1}{2}$ million miles (46 million kilometers) to the sun, and as far away as 43 million miles (69 million kilometers). The noontime temperature on the side facing the sun soars to 800°F (427°C), hot enough to melt lead,

while the dark hemisphere chills to -279°F (-173°C). This temperature range is greater than that of any other planet.

For other facts about Mercury, and the other planets as well, see the table on page 164.

Venus

Until comparatively recently Venus was commonly regarded as "Earth's sister." It is approximately the same size as the earth and is our nearest neighbor planet. Its atmosphere seemed similar to ours, and it was thought that its clouds were made of water. Many observers believed that its surface conditions were similar to ours. Science fiction writers even pictured it as a tropical paradise with steamy jungles and lush vegetation.

The studies by planetary scientists over the past 40 years, however, have altered this conception of Venus markedly. Radio waves beamed from Earth have penetrated the Venusian clouds; large features of the planet's surface have been mapped by radar. American and Soviet spacecraft have passed close to Venus or penetrated to its surface, lifting the veil of this mysterious planet. The first color photo of Venus's surface was taken from a Soviet Lander in 1982.

In summary, data from these studies indicate the following:

1. The surface temperature of Venus is very high, apparently approaching 900°F (480°C).
2. The pressure of the atmosphere on the surface of Venus is about 90 times that of the surface pressure on Earth. (This is equal roughly to the crushing pressure of water one would encounter almost a half mile under the surface of the sea.)
3. The atmosphere of Venus is composed of almost pure carbon dioxide (96 percent) with the remainder nitrogen and a small amount of water vapor. This may account for the high temperature within the Venus atmosphere, since the carbon dioxide acts like the glass in a greenhouse roof. Sunlight may pass through, building up heat beneath the carbon dioxide "roof." But, like the glass in the greenhouse, it does not permit the reradiated heat to escape back

into space. (See the Index for references to a discussion of the "greenhouse effect.")

The clouds of Venus form continuous layers at altitudes of 27 to 36 miles (45 to 60 kilometers). They are driven by winds that attain speeds of 200 miles (345 kilometers) per hour. The upper layer of the clouds consists mainly of drops of sulfuric acid.

4. Venus's surface is remarkably flat, with few features more than a mile high. It has craters and large smooth areas like the moon's *maria*. In October of 1975, Venera 9 and 10, unmanned Soviet spacecraft, landed on Venus's surface. The spacecraft's instruments functioned for only one hour in the lead-melting temperature and crushing pressure of Venus's surface, but they were able to transmit two photographs that revealed a rock-strewn landscape. Later radar studies in 1976 indicated that Venus had been a dynamic planet, geologically speaking, with great crustal activity, troughlike cracks, mountain ranges, and a huge peak—apparently a volcanic mountain, 6½ miles (11 kilometers) high, and therefore taller than Mt. Everest. The surface material of Venus is believed to resemble the lava terrain of volcanoes. Recent studies indicate that Venus's volcanoes are active today and that this cloud-covered planet is still evolving geologically.

On May 4, 1989, the spacecraft Magellan was launched from an American space shuttle. It was expected to reach Venus and orbit that planet 15 months later. Equipped with improved cloud-piercing radar, it should map finer details of Venus's surface and reveal more of its history.

Venus moves in an orbit between that of Mercury and Earth, taking about 225 days for a trip around the sun. Named for the goddess of love and beauty, Venus is, with the exception of the sun and the moon, the brightest object in the sky.

The problem of how long the day is on Venus has long been a mystery to scientists. Recent observations indicate that it takes Venus 243 Earth days to turn just *once* on its axis. We have noted that it takes Venus only 225 Earth days to make one revolution around the sun. This means that a full day on Venus is longer than its year. Note also that Venus rotates from east to west—the reverse direction from that of its revolution. Venus and Uranus are the only two planets to rotate backward.

Seen through a telescope Venus and Mercury appear to change in shape over a period of time. These are *phases*, similar to the moon's phases that we discuss later in this chapter.

Look at Venus tonight, if it is visible, with a pair of binoculars or a small telescope, to see what shape this sky goddess is in.

Earth

It is interesting to compare the answers that children of different generations have given to the question: "How do we know the earth is round?" A half century ago the stock answer would have been based on the story of Columbus watching ships sail over the horizon with the mast disappearing from view last. In the last few decades a typical and more spontaneous answer has been, "Because we can fly around it." Today's children can say with accuracy, "Because we have taken pictures of the earth from rocket ships that show its roundness," or "Because astronauts orbited around it and saw that it was round." Perhaps for tomorrow's space-traveling children the question will be an academic one: They will be able to see the earth as a planet in space.

If we measure the planet Earth we find that it is not quite a perfect sphere; its diameter of 7,900 miles (12,700 kilometers) from pole to pole is 27 miles (43 kilometers) less than its equatorial diameter.

Earth, the third planet from the sun, hurtles along in its orbit at the rate of about 66,000 miles (roughly 100,000 kilometers) per hour to complete its yearly tour of approximately 600 million miles (roughly 1 billion kilometers). This path is not a perfect circle; it is slightly elliptical, with the sun not quite in the center. As a result the earth is closest to the sun on about January 3, when it is 91.5 million miles (roughly 147 million kilometers) away and farthest on July 3, when it is 94.5 million miles (roughly 152 million kilometers) away. On about April 1 and October 1 the distance is between these extremes, about 93 million miles (roughly 149.5 million kilometers).

These statistics may be surprising to those who have assumed that the seasons are determined by the distance of the earth from the sun. We shall consider the cause of the seasons presently.

While the earth is executing its yearly orbit, or revolution, around the sun it is spinning on its axis, performing this rotation almost exactly 365.25 times in this period. Places at the equator turn with the spinning planet at the rate of about 1,000 miles (roughly 1,600 kilometers) per hour; Salt Lake City, which is about halfway between the equator and the North Pole, turns at the rate of about 800 miles (roughly 1,300 kilometers) per hour. Spin a classroom globe of the earth on its axis and you will see why this difference occurs.

Day and Night Because the earth is an opaque ball and receives light from one principal source, only one side of it can be lighted at one time. The half receiving light is in daylight while the other half is having night. Because the earth rotates on its axis, day and night alternate in regular fashion (see pp. 181–182).

The apparent daily motion of the sun across the sky from east to west is due to the actual turning of the earth from west to east.

The Seasons The different seasons in the place where you live are determined by the differences in the amount of heat received from the sun at different times of the year. Consider for a moment just one square foot of any open field in your locality. Disregarding local weather conditions, the amount of heat received daily by the designated square will depend on two factors: (1) the number of hours of sunlight and (2) the intensity of the sunlight.

Point 1 is illustrated by the fact that in summer there are more hours of sunlight to heat soil, rocks, and water.

Point 2 refers to the fact that in our summer, when the sun rides high in the sky, the intensity of the sunlight received is greater because its rays strike our part of the earth almost vertically. In winter, when the sun is lower in the sky, the rays of sunlight come to us at more of a slant. These

The causes of the seasons. For a detailed description see pp. 154–155. (Distances and sizes are not drawn to scale. Also, the Sun is not at the exact center of Earth's orbit—the two bodies are closest to each other in January.)

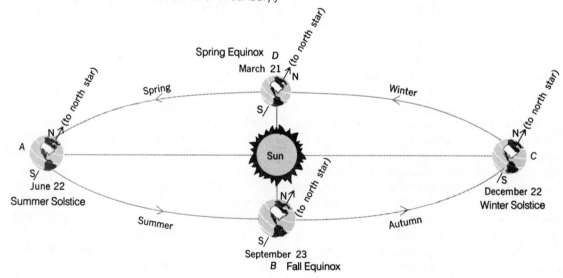

slanting rays are spread over more of the earth's surface than are rays that strike vertically; therefore they give less heat. Furthermore, slanting rays travel a greater distance through our atmosphere than those that strike vertically. The more air they go through, the more their energy is absorbed along the way and the less is left to heat the surface of the earth.

But we have not yet explained why the number of daylight hours varies, nor why the sun's rays are more nearly vertical at some times than at others. To understand this we must leave the little square foot in the field and adjust our vision for a space view of the earth in relation to the sun.

Let us be guided by the following three important space facts:

1. The earth moves, as we have found, in an orbit around the sun.
2. The earth's axis is not upright with reference to the plane of this orbit; it leans over, like the Tower of Pisa.
3. The earth's axis always points in the same direction in space—toward the North Star.[2]

> To imitate this motion, hold your pen firmly at an angle to a sheet of paper and describe a circle on it by moving your arm, not your fingers or wrist, with the top of the pen pointing constantly at one wall of your room.

Because of these three factors the Northern and Southern Hemispheres are alternately slanted toward the sun and away from it.

For simplicity, we shall refer mainly to the Northern Hemisphere in discussing the following sequence of seasons.

At position A in the diagram (June 22) the Northern Hemisphere is tipped toward the sun.

The part around the North Pole has continuous daylight, despite the daily rotation of the earth. There is no night in the "land of the midnight sun" at this time of the year. As we go farther south, the number of daylight hours varies from 24 at the North Pole to 12 at the equator. The Southern Hemisphere is having winter at this time, and the South Pole region is in the midst of its six months of night (see pp. 182–184).

Thus, the tilted position of the earth makes for longer daylight in the Northern Hemisphere at this time. It also exposes the earth there to the intense, more vertical rays of the sun, which contribute to the heating up of that part of the earth. To sum up, long days and intense rays make summer.

Let us bypass position B for a moment and go to C (December 22). Compared to A, conditions are reversed. The Northern Hemisphere is tilted away from the sun. The North Pole is in continuous night. Generally, the Northern Hemisphere has short daylight and long nights. The rays of the sun strike at a greater slant. Short days and slanting rays make winter.

At B (September 23) and D (March 21) the beginning of the fall and spring seasons, respectively, the axis of the earth points neither toward nor away from the sun. Days and nights are equal in length all over the earth. Neither the Northern nor Southern Hemisphere receives more intense rays of sunlight.

Mars

For many years novelists and scientists alike speculated about the possibility of life on the Red Planet. They reasoned that Mars is similar to Earth in many ways: A Martian day is 24 hours and 37 minutes, almost identical with ours; its axis is tilted at about the same angle as that of the earth, producing similar seasonal changes; the Martian atmosphere has clouds; the white polar caps wax and wane, suggesting a possible source of water; the surface of the planet shows seasonal changes in color, which might be attributed to change in

---

[2]Over a long period of time, however, the direction of the earth's axis changes. This phenomenon is known as *precession*. To imitate this motion, hold your pen near the middle of its length and rotate it by moving your wrist so that it makes a small circle. For the earth, this would take about 26,000 years per cycle. In about 12,000 years the celestial pole of the earth will not be Polaris, but near the bright star Vega, which will then be the earth's "North Star." See star maps on pages 196–197.

plant life. The temperature, although much lower than that of the earth, does not exclude the possibility of life.

On July 20, 1976, the Viking 1 Lander set down on Mars, its principal mission to detect signs of life on the Red Planet. Its cameras showed no "little green men" nor any large animal or plant forms on the landscape; none were expected. What was sought was evidence of microscopic life, active or dormant, present or past, in the Martian soil.

The Lander carried sophisticated apparatus for conducting three life-detecting experiments. However, no conclusive evidence for life on Mars was detected by either the Viking 1 Lander or the Viking 2 Lander, which set down a few weeks later. However this does not exclude the possibility of life, present or past, on Mars.

But it must not be thought that the investigation of Mars by the 1976 Viking project and by the various Mariner missions in the previous decade were failures. Far from it. They may not have found life on Mars, but they did uncover evidence of a very lively planet. The following sections summarize some of the findings:

Wind, Air, and Water Mars is a world of winds. Huge dust storms of more than hurricane strength appear suddenly and sweep across the planet. As on earth, the source of energy for such storms is the sun's heat; however, unlike the earth, there are no oceans to absorb the heat, to release it

slowly, and thereby to moderate the planet's climate. On Mars the heat energy is rapidly transferred from the surface to the atmosphere; the resulting winds of 65 to 135 miles (105 to 220 kilometers) an hour pick up the loose Martian dust and sand, raising vast yellow dust clouds.

The Martian atmosphere is very thin. You may recall that on Venus the pressure of its dense atmosphere on the surface was about 100 times that of Earth's. On Mars the surface pressure is only one hundredth that of Earth's. To make some Martian air, you would have to take a bottle of Earth air and then pump about 99 percent of it out of the bottle, leaving a near vacuum. You would then replace only the 1 percent left with a mixture of carbon dioxide (95 percent) and small amounts of nitrogen and argon. To approximate the temperature of Martian air at the surface you would then place the bottle in a deep freeze reaching a low of $-10°F$ ($-23°C$). Clouds in the Martian atmosphere seem to be composed of water vapor and ice crystals of carbon dioxide ("dry ice").

The seasons of Mars are marked by the growing and receding of the polar ice caps occurring alternately at each of its poles. The permanent ice cap, the one that remains after the midsummer thaw, appears to be made entirely of water and is about one-half mile thick. With the onset of winter, water vapor in the air condenses and freezes, causing the polar ice cap to expand. At the same time some carbon dioxide in the air also freezes and lays down a frosting on the cap. In winter the

This spectacular picture of the Martian landscape taken by the Viking I Lander shows a dune field with features remarkably similar to many seen in the deserts of Earth. (The boom that supports Viking's miniature weather station cuts through the picture's center.) *(Courtesy of NASA.)*

cap extends halfway down to the equator; on Earth a corresponding change in North America during our northern winter would produce an ice sheet extending from the North Pole to a line extending from the state of Washington to Maine. (Such a change did occur in the Earth's ice ages of the past; see pp. 129–133.)

The confirmation of the presence of water in the Martian ice caps suggests that the planet has much more water than expected; perhaps there is also an underground reservoir of water frozen in the rocks and dust that extends all over the planet in the form of *permafrost*, similar to that found in the subsoil of arctic regions of the earth. Perhaps in the past on a warmer Mars, the water was released from its frozen bondage and played a great role in sculpting the face of the Red Planet.

Mountains, Canyons, and Water-Sculptured Landscapes The first explorers to walk and ride on Mars will see a much more varied and dramatic landscape than that experienced by the lunar astronauts. They will see the largest volcanic mountain known in the solar system, Olympus Mons, with a summit 18 miles (29 kilometers) above the surrounding plains, almost three times the height of Mt. Everest above sea level. Olympus Mons is but one of many enormous volcanoes found principally in the planet's northern hemisphere. Craters and other surface features associated with volcanoes are also found, indicating volcanic activity over most of the entire span of the planet's history from 4 billion to 200 million years ago. Mars also has many craters formed by the bombardment of meteorites on the surface early in its history.

Another remarkable feature of Mars is an enormous canyon (named Valles Marineris after the Mariner craft that discovered it) that stretches nearly one third of the way around the planet; it would reach from New York City to San Francisco if it were on earth.

There is evidence everywhere that Mars is a planet whose surface has been sculptured by water (see pp. 128–129). Photographs show thousands of meandering channels branching out from smaller and smaller tributaries suggesting

dried-up river systems, carved out at an earlier time when the Martian climate was warmer and wetter. Also seen are vast ancient floodplains, islands, sedimentary deposits, and glacial terraces.

Other findings of the space missions to Mars included vast areas of sweeping sands and dunes; rock-strewn mountain plains; soils rich in iron with near carbon-copy amounts of elements found on Earth such as calcium, silicon, and potassium; and a brick-red ground and salmon-hued sky.

A Martian explorer would observe two small lumpy moons, Phobos and Deimos, pitted with a profusion of craters. Phobos, the inner moon, orbits Mars every 7.7 hours. Deimos, the outer moon, takes 30 hours for a complete circuit. Both moons are close to Mars and move in the plane of the equator, so that neither can be seen from the poles.

In Greek, Phobos means "fear" and Deimos "panic"—appropriate companions of the god of war, Mars. Both of these satellites were discovered in 1877 by the American astronomer Asaph Hall.

Today scientists are concerned that the earth's climate is not as stable as was once thought. Even very small changes in the earth's climate can have far-reaching consequences for the peoples of our planet and for our water supply and agriculture. Thus, knowing what is happening and has happened on other worlds assumes increasing importance in understanding, controlling, and safeguarding our own world.

For this and other reasons, momentum has been building for a return to Mars, the planet most like Earth. Proponents hope to explore Mars first with robots and later with astronauts who could be the first humans to visit another planet.

Asteroids

In a broad zone between the orbits of Mars and Jupiter is a swarm of smaller bodies, the *asteroids*, sometimes called *minor planets*. Twenty-three hundred of these, ranging in size from 1 to 500 miles (1.6 to 800 kilometers) have been registered and named by astronomers. Asteroids were so named because they appear telescopically like stars—as small points of light. The first and largest to be discovered was Ceres, which is 593 miles (954 kilometers) in diameter. Although most of the asteroids move in an orbit between the orbits of Mars and Jupiter, some occasionally come quite close to Earth: Icarus, Hermes, Eros, and Geographos, for example.

It is thought that the minor planets were formed from the same material—dust particles and gases in space—that formed the nine planets of the solar system, and at about the same time. Some of these small bodies remained scattered and separate, much as they are today. Others began to clump together to form a few small planetlike bodies, which later were chipped away by catastrophic collisions into their present sizes.

On March 23, 1989, an asteroid missed hitting Earth by half a million miles, about twice the distance of our moon—a close scrape on the astronomical scale.

Have asteroids ever collided with the earth? Recent observations indicate that possibility: Our study of the fossil record (see Chapter 12A) suggests that beginning about 65 million years ago, many species of plant and animal life, notably the dinosaurs, perished suddenly. Why? Scientists found that at various sites around the earth, rock layers 65 million years old are much richer in the element iridium than in the layers below and above them, which represent older and younger formations. Iridium is fairly uncommon in the earth's crust, but is abundant in meteorites. It is hypothesized that about 65 million years ago the earth was struck by a meteorite of asteroid size. The resulting explosion would have sent dust into the atmosphere, where it would have circulated around the earth and blocked much of the sunlight for a year or two, long enough to interfere with the life-sustaining process of photosynthesis in green plants. The world's food supply would have dropped, and many species would have perished. Eventually iridium-laden dust would have fallen out and settled to be buried in the sedimentary rocks forming at that time, and thus have left a record of this disaster.

Other scientists have questioned the catastrophe theory of sudden extinction following the impact of an asteroid. Fossils found in some areas suggest that the dinosaurs died off *before* the presumed asteroid impact; the last dinosaur bones lay 10 to 20 feet below the iridium layer. Also many paleontologists argue that the decline and extinction of dinosaurs took place over much too long a time to have been caused by a single catastrophe.

The Jovian Planets and Pluto

The next four planets from the sun—Jupiter, Saturn, Uranus, and Neptune—are the giants of the solar system and together are named *Jovian planets*. (Jove was another name for Jupiter in ancient mythology.) The inner planets, which are closer to the sun, are Mercury, Venus, Earth, and Mars: the *terrestrial planets*. The Jovian planets differ from the terrestrial planets not only in size: The Jovian planets have a low density, with an abundance of light elements, hydrogen and helium, whereas the terrestrial planets are dense and composed mostly of rocky and metallic material. The Jovian planets have such deep atmospheres that we have difficulty in determining where the solid part of each planet begins. All of them have more than one moon; around Jupiter we have found at least 16 moons.

Jupiter　The leader among the giants, Jupiter, with a diameter 11 times that of Earth, was named after the supreme god of the ancient Romans (sometimes called Jove). Jupiter has more mass and volume than all of the other planets combined. To the naked eye Jupiter is often the brightest object in the night sky except for the moon, and may be confused with Venus. But through the telescope, Jupiter, unlike Venus, is encircled by yellow, red, sometimes blue bands, called *zones*, alternating with darker stripes, or *belts*. The zones and belts are nearly perfectly aligned along par-

The Great Red Spot on Jupiter, a gigantic oval large enough to swallow several earths, has puzzled astronomers for centuries. Similar whirlpool-like phenomena, such as hurricanes on Earth, have a brief life. Why does the spot on Jupiter persist? Recently scientists have created a model "Red Spot" by rotating a tank of water four times a second. Like its cosmic counterpart the laboratory spot seems to last indefinitely.

Ganymede, Jupiter's largest satellite, can be seen to the lower left of the planet. *(Courtesy of NASA.)*

allels of Jovian latitude; these features are believed to be limited to the outer part of the deep atmosphere of this planet.

In the southern hemisphere of Jupiter is a feature that has been observed for more than three centuries: the Great Red Spot, 30,000 miles (about 50,000 kilometers) long and 8,000 miles (about 13,000 kilometers) wide—an area large enough to hold four Earths at the same time.

With the help of the spectacular photographs taken by the Pioneer spacecraft as they flew by Jupiter in 1973 and 1974 and the Voyagers in 1979, we can better understand the zones and belts and the Great Red Spot. These features are now considered to be products of Jupiter's weather, with wind flows along the zones and a permanent tornado spiraling around the Red Spot.

Despite the dramatic winds of this titanic cloud-banded world, the atmospheric features have an extremely long lifetime and an organized structure that is unknown on Earth. A Jovian weather map shown on a nightly telecast would be remarkably unchanged, day after day, year after year. When Voyager 1 visited Jupiter, it was discovered that the giant planet has a thin but distinct ring like that of Saturn circling around it in the plane of its equator.

The gaseous part of Jupiter's atmosphere, composed mostly of hydrogen, also includes helium, ammonia, methane, and water vapor. It is thought to extend down about 600 miles (1,000 kilometers) from the top of its clouds, only about one seventieth of the way to the planet's center. Below that level the pressure is so great that the hydrogen exists only in liquid form, even though the temperature ranges from 3600°F (2000°C) to 54,000°F (30,000°C). Jupiter probably contains a relatively "small" core of rock and ice that is 10 to 20 times the mass of Earth.

Jupiter's size has led some astronomers to wonder whether this giant body is a true planet or a "failed star." The following observations support the idea that Jupiter is indeed a body that didn't quite make it to stardom:

1. Jupiter's chemical composition is more starlike than Earthlike, consisting mainly of hydrogen, helium, and other light substances.
2. Jupiter radiates about twice as much energy as it receives from the sun, indicating that it has its own internal source of energy, a characteristic of stars. (However, it is probable that the internal heat represents the gravitational potential energy that became available as the planet contracted from its first gaseous state some 4.6 billion years ago—not from nuclear fusion.)
3. Jupiter with its collection of 16+ orbiting moons looks very much like a miniature solar system.

The four largest moons of Jupiter were first observed by Galileo in 1610 and described in his epoch-making book, *The Starry Messenger*. The discovery of this miniature "solar system" did much to establish the similar Copernican picture in a sun-centered planetary system. The Galilean satellites are known by the names of Jupiter's lovers in Greco-Roman mythology. Proceeding outward from the planet, they are Io, Europa, Ganymede, and Callisto. The thirteenth moon of Jupiter was discovered as recently as 1974, the fourteenth in 1975, and two more in 1979.

One of the most important scientific discoveries made by the Voyagers in their space tours to the planets was that volcanic eruptions were in progress on Io, which is now an active, changing moon, with the youngest and most dynamic surface yet observed in the solar system. The first active volcano on Io was discovered by Linda A. Morabito of the Jet Propulsion Laboratory on March 8, 1979, when she detected a faint cloud on the image made by Voyager 1 during its en-

counter with Jupiter. Evidently it was the plume of a volcano, arching 170 miles (270 kilometers) above the surface of Io. Since then no fewer than eight active volcanoes and many associated volcanic features have been found on the surface on this satellite.

Stunning Io, bedecked with red and gold, is different from the other Galilean satellites, which are wrapped in thick blankets of ice. Europa, the next moon outward from Io, appears to be a relatively smooth, ice-clad ball of rock nearly as large as the earth's moon, criss-crossed by stripes and bands that may represent fractures in its icy crust that are filled with dark material from below. Ganymede, which is larger than the planet Mercury, is the largest of Jupiter's moons and the largest moon in the solar system. Its fractured crust is grooved and twisted, and has numerous craters probably formed when the satellite was bombarded by bodies of considerable size. Callisto, about the size of Ganymede, has the most cratered surface found in the solar system—possibly made when this satellite was bombarded billions of years ago.

The comparison of these four of the largest of Jupiter's satellites may help astronomers gain an understanding of how they and the inner planets of the solar system evolved since their formation 4.6 billion years ago.

Saturn (See frontispiece, p. 146). The encounters of the U.S. spacecraft Pioneer 11 and Voyagers 1 and 2 with Saturn in 1979 and 1980 have given us a new portrait of this beautiful planet, in full color and magnificent detail. The seven broad concentric rings in the plane of the planet's equator were revealed as an ensemble of hundreds of thousands of ringlets, resembling the grooves in a phonograph record. Radial "spokes" going across the rings and some twisted and braided ringlets were some of the surprises seen by the electronic eyes of Voyager 1.

The Voyagers also uncovered the surfaces of Saturn's moons, known hitherto only as indistinct, fuzzy balls. In order of their distance from Saturn, beginning with the closest, the seven largest sat-

Two volcanic plumes of Io photographed by Voyager 2 in 1979 are evidence of an active changing moon. The material erupted is not lava or steam or carbon dioxide, all of which are vented by terrestrial volcanoes, but sulfur and sulfur dioxide. *(Courtesy of NASA.)*

ellites of Saturn are Mimas, called the "Eye of the Saturnian System" because of a giant impact crater covering one quarter of its diameter; smooth Enceladus, the most reflective moon of Saturn, with its terrain devoid of craters, possibly because they were covered with water, which then froze; deeply scarred Tethys, with huge, troughlike valleys; icy Dione, which looks like Earth's moon, but is much smaller; pockmarked Rhea, the most heavily cratered body in the Saturnian system; giant Titan, the largest of Saturn's moons, second in the solar system only to Jupiter's Ganymede, the only satellite in the solar system with a per-

manent, appreciable atmosphere; and two-faced Iapetus, a puzzle to astronomers because of the difference in brightness of its two hemispheres, a ratio of 10 to 1. In addition to the 7 large moons, Saturn has 10 or 11 smaller ones.

Saturn has a mass 95 times that of the earth. It is composed largely of hydrogen and helium, resembling Jupiter and the sun. Its surface markings consist of broad colored bands parallel to the equator, much like the dramatic stripes of Jupiter. Its most distinguishing feature, the ring system, is made of trillions of tiny water-ice particles that orbit the planet like tiny moons.

Uranus All the planets described thus far are bright, naked-eye objects, and were known to the ancients. The next three—Uranus, Neptune, and Pluto—revolving in the outer regions of the solar system, were discovered and identified as planets by later astronomers equipped with telescopes. Uranus is 20 times as far from the sun as Earth is, Neptune 30 times, and Pluto 40 times.

Uranus was discovered in 1781 by the astronomer William Herschel, who, while making a systematic survey of the stars, noticed one that didn't stay in place. Barely visible to the unaided eye, through powerful telescopes Uranus appears as a tiny green object with faint parallel bands. Unlike all the other planets that spin like tops on the imaginary platforms of their orbits, Uranus spins like a top that is extremely tilted, so that its axis lies almost in the plane of its orbit. Uranus's satellites and rings revolve in the plane of the planet's equator.

After a journey of nearly $8\frac{1}{2}$ years, traveling more than 3 billion miles, Voyager 2 had a rendezvous with Uranus for less than one day. Yet in that brief period on January 24, 1986, the spacecraft sent back 7,000 images of this blue-green ball, answering many questions about this distant seventh planet, its length of day, its weather, its rings, and its moons.

Most exciting of all Voyager's discoveries were the clear, detailed photographs of each of its five major moons. Named for sprites and spirits from English literature, these satellites, in order of in-

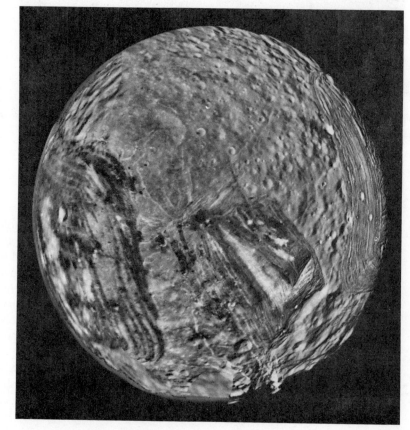

One of the exciting achievements of the space vehicles has been their close encounter with the moons of the planets and the unveiling of incredible minute details of their landscapes. Uranus's moon Miranda is shown here in a mosaic of images obtained by the Voyager 2 spacecraft on January 24, 1986. Miranda, the smallest and innermost of the five major satellites of Uranus, is also its most geologically diverse and mysterious. Miranda's surface consists of two strikingly different types of terrain. One is an old heavily cratered, rolling surface; the other is a young complex terrain characterized by sets of bright and dark bands and ridges, seen in the ovoid regions at right and left and in the distinctive "chevron" feature below and right of center. (Courtesy of NASA.)

creasing distance from their mother planet, are Miranda, Ariel, Umbriel, Titania, and Oberon. Of all the five, Miranda, the smallest and closest to Uranus, was the most enigmatic. Barely 300 miles (about 500 kilometers) across, scientists wonder how such a tiny object could have enough gravity to hold itself together in a ball.

Voyager 2's treasure trove of 12 pictures of Miranda provided clear evidence of its exciting past. Much of its surface is an ancient cratered landscape. Three huge patches are bordered by families of parallel ridges and grooves, nested one outside the other like the lanes of a gigantic racetrack. The oval patches and plains are cut by huge fracture zones that circle Miranda, creating fault valleys whose steep, terraced cliffs are as much as 6 to 12 miles (10 to 20 kilometers) high. Scientists think that Miranda was broken apart and reassembled with chunks of primordial matter that smashed into it. As Bradford Smith, the leader of the Voyager imaging team, put it, "It looks like a satellite designed by a committee."

Each of the major moons had distinctly different characteristics. In addition, Voyager discovered 10 new moons, bringing the total number from 5 to 15.

Uranus has a featureless 5,000-mile-thick (8,000-kilometer-thick) gaseous atmosphere, below which is a 7,000-mile (11,000-kilometer) layer of superheated water at 8,000°F (about 4400°C). At the very center is a rocky core. Based on radio signals emitted from its newly discovered magnetic field, the length of the Uranian day was estimated to be 17.24 hours. It is theorized that Uranus probably once rotated upright as do the other planets, but monstrous collisions between Uranus and one or more earth-sized bodies that existed in the early solar system knocked the planet on its side. It continued to spin, but with one of its polar regions, not its equator, pointed toward the sun.

In addition to confirming the nine principal rings circling Uranus (previously known from earth-based observations), Voyager 2 discovered two more, and in addition many ringlets interspersed within the main rings.

Neptune   Voyager 2's encounter with Neptune on August 24, 1989, after a 12-year, 4.4 billion mile journey from Earth, marked the climax of its tour of the solar system. The spacecraft visited all the giant planets: Jupiter, Saturn, Uranus, and Neptune. The moons of these planets, once not much more than points of light to Earth-bound observers, were seen as sparkling, varied worlds.

Among Voyager 2's discoveries during its rendezvous with beautiful blue Neptune were 6 new moons (before Voyager's visit, Neptune was known to have only 2 moons, Triton and the much smaller Nereid); 3 rings and possibly 5 circling the planet; a magnetic field tilted at an angle of 50 degrees from the planet's spin axis; a surprisingly dynamic atmosphere of hydrogen, helium, and methane, with 400-mile-per-hour winds; and the Great Dark Spot, a storm system in Neptune's southern hemisphere as large as the entire Earth.

Most exciting to astronomers were images of Triton, its pink-colored surface marked by circular depressions and rugged ridges and grooves, suggesting volcanic activity. Triton's diameter is about three-fourths that of Earth's moon; unlike our airless moon, it possesses an atmosphere.

After leaving Neptune, Voyager 2 headed for the edge of the solar system and then to interstellar space, carrying with it a phonograph record of sounds from Earth, from Bach to Chuck Berry.

Pluto   Pluto is the outermost, smallest, and coldest of the known planets. It has an atmosphere of methane gas and ice. The methane icecaps at its poles can extend halfway to the planet's equator. For 20 of its 250-year circuit of the sun, it is inside the orbit of Neptune. From 1979 to 1999 it will be closer to the sun than Neptune.

Named for the god of the underworld, Pluto has one satellite, appropriately named Charon for the mythological boatman on the river Styx who transports passengers to Pluto's domain.

Pluto was discovered in 1930 by Clyde Tombaugh. How can a distant planet be found among billions of stars? Astronomers make use of the fact that planets move in relation to the stars in the sky. Many photographs are taken by aiming the telescope at a portion of the sky that calculation has shown is a place where such a planet may be detected. These are compared with photographs of corresponding portions at a later or earlier date. If comparison shows that an object has changed position with respect to the stars, that object may be a planet.

In June 1988 astronomers in a number of observatories found evidence of the existence of an atmosphere on Pluto by aiming their telescopes at the planet as it passed between the earth and a distant star. Such an event is known as an *occultation*. As the planet moved in front of the star, its light became dimmer and dimmer before it blinked out. When the light from the star reappeared, it was at first dim and then became stronger and stronger as the planet moved on.

Beyond Pluto, are there other planets in our solar system? A search of the skies by Tombaugh and other astronomers, reaching out into space five times the distance of Pluto, has found no other planets. But every now and then there are suggestions that our solar system might have a tenth planet.

Are there planets outside our solar system? Scientists speculate that because stars are suns, it is possible that many of them, too, may have families of planets around them. Our present instruments would be inadequate, however, to see planets as large as Jupiter, even around the nearest star.

Beyond the solar system 3 of the first 12 stars nearest the sun have unseen companions, found by the observation of gravitation-induced "wobbles" in the motions of these stars. Whether or not these are planets is still unknown, but we know of no other explanation for them at present.

Barnard's Star is a case in point. It moves slowly with respect to the background of more distant stars, but shows a wave in its motion. The wave suggests that it and two unseen companions, too small to be detected from Earth, revolve around a common center. Calculations indicate that one of the unseen bodies has a mass about 80 percent that of the planet Jupiter, the other about 40 percent. Both, then, qualify as planets.

The first *direct* evidence of the possible existence of a planetary system outside our own was the discovery in 1983 by the Infrared Astronomy Satellite that the bright star Vega is surrounded by an immense swarm of particles at least as large as pebbles and some possibly as large as planets. It is possible that we are looking at an early solar system growing from debris in the same manner as the sun and the planets of our system. (Vega

THE PLANETS

Name of Planet	Diameter in Terms of Earth's Diameter	Distance from Sun in Terms of Earth's Distance	Length of Day (time for one rotation)	Length of Year (revolution around Sun)	Surface Gravity (Earth = 1)	Moons
Mercury	2/5	2/5	59 days	88 days	.38	0
Venus	1	3/4	243 days (retrograde*)	225 days	.91	0
Earth	1	1	24 hours	365.26 days	1.00	1
Mars	½	1½	24½ hours	687.0 days	.38	2
Jupiter	11	5	10 hours	11.9 years	2.53	16+
Saturn	9	10	11 hours	29 years	1.07	17+
Uranus	4	20	17 hours (retrograde*)	84 years	0.869	15
Neptune	4	30	16 hours	165 years	1.18	8
Pluto	1/5	40	6 days	249 years	0.03	1

*In the *reverse* direction from the rotation of most other planets: rotation from east to west.

forms a triangle of stars with Deneb and Altair, and can be seen prominently in the summer. See the sky map on p. 196.)

Comets

Halley's comet, named after the English astronomer Edmund Halley, is the most famous of all the comets. Halley was the first to show that comets are true members of the solar system, not interlopers from outer space.

Comets differ from planets in a number of important respects. They generally have extremely elongated, elliptical orbits, which may bring them close to the sun at one end of their swing in space. It is when comets come near the sun that we can observe them. Unlike planets, comets may circle the sun in any direction and in any plane.

Experts estimate that a typical comet may have only one trillionth the mass of Earth. Thus, despite the large sizes of comets, they are mostly "empty space." A comet's tail has been described as the nearest thing to nothing that anything can be and still be something.

The comets that attract the most attention are those consisting of a head and a long tail. The astronomer Fred Whipple has described a comet as "a celestial fountain spouting from a large dirty snowball floating through space. The fountain is activated and illuminated by the sun. ... We see the fountain as the comet's head and tail. The tail can extend for tens of millions of miles, but we never see the snowball, whose diameter is only a few miles."

The "snowball" is the *nucleus* of a comet. It is the more permanent part of a comet and spends most of its time away from the sun, its materials frozen into a "dirty snowball." When the nucleus nears the sun it is warmed and begins to evaporate to produce a surrounding *coma* of gas and dust. The nucleus and coma together constitute the *head* of the comet.

When a comet is far from the sun it shines, like planets, by reflecting sunlight. When it is close to the sun it shines almost entirely by the process of *fluorescence*, as its gases are set aglow by ultraviolet radiation from the sun. The solar winds (see p. 150) and solar radiation (photons) exert increasing pressure on the minute particles in the

This photograph of Halley's comet was taken through a telescope on May 29, 1910. (The white streaks are the tracks of stars produced on the film by the turning of the earth in this time-exposure photograph.) *(Courtesy of American Museum of Natural History.)*

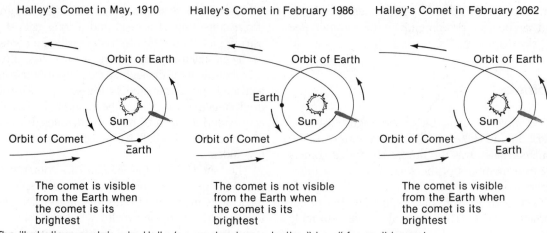

Halley's Comet in May, 1910   Halley's Comet in February 1986   Halley's Comet in February 2062

The comet is visible
from the Earth when
the comet is its
brightest

The comet is not visible
from the Earth when
the comet is its
brightest

The comet is visible
from the Earth when
the comet is its
brightest

The illustrations explain why Halley's comet put on a better "show" for earthbound
viewers in 1910 than it did in 1986. *(Based on figures drawn by Yasu Osawa for
"Orbiting with Halley's," an article in* Science and Children, *November/December 1985
by Dennis Schatz, Associate Director, Pacific Science Center, Seattle, Washington.)*

head as the comet approaches the sun. Some of
the particles are thus pushed away from the head,
forming a glowing tail that may become truly
spectacular as the comet nears the sun. The tail
points generally away from the sun; as the comet
approaches the sun the tail is behind the head; as
it speeds away from the sun the tail precedes it.

Comets, like all orbiting bodies in the solar
system, travel at varying speeds, faster nearer the
sun, slower farther from the sun. Nevertheless,
they do not streak across the sky like a rocket, as
some people think. They may be watched for days,
weeks, or even months in their paths around the
sun. Most comets are small, faint objects in the
sky and require a telescope to distinguish them
from stars.

If comets are only dirty snowballs, why is it
important to study them? It is thought that comets
originate from a huge cloud of ice and dust that
surrounds our solar system, several thousand
times farther from the sun than the outermost
planet Pluto. It is believed that comets are the
most primitive objects in the solar system, possibly frozen since the time that the solar system was
formed 4½ billion years ago. Thus, the composi-

tion and structure of comets carry many clues to
the way in which the earth and the other planets
were formed. Perhaps they also contain a variety
of organic compounds that may have provided a
good start toward the formation of living organisms. It was hoped that the space probes planned
for 1986 to study Halley's comet would throw light
on these theories, and they did.

Comet Halley has been visiting the Earth every
three quarters of a century for thousands of years.
In its 1985–1986 appearance it was met by an
international committee of spacecraft from Europe, Japan, and the Soviet Union, sent up to photograph the comet close up and sample its dust
and gases. Special attention was focused on the
comet's nucleus, which was found to have an irregular, double-lobed shape, and was spewing jet-
like bursts of water, dust, and gas. Most of the dust
particles were rich in carbon, hydrogen, nitrogen,
and oxygen, suggesting the validity of the theory
that cometary dust contains materials for the construction of organic compounds essential for life
(see pp. 364–365). Another finding of the comet-
hunting spacecraft was that the true color of the
nucleus was black as coal, possibly because the

outer layers of exposed ice had vaporized, revealing the more uniform blackness of the dust inside.

Many observers on Earth were disappointed when they compared their viewing of Comet Halley with what they had read and heard about the 1910 apparition. Actually this *was* one of the weakest appearances in the last 2,000 years, for at the time when the comet was closest to the sun—and its brightest—Earth was on the opposite side. Think of trying to see a Ping-Pong ball almost directly behind a bright, bare electric bulb. This was the 1985–1986 situation. Now move the ball one quarter of a circle to the side of the bulb, and you have approximated the 1910 position.

Comet Halley will visit Earth next in July 2061. Tell your children and grandchildren about it! The comet will return periodically for another quarter of a million years, at which time all of its ice will have been boiled away by the sun.[3]

Meteoroids

If there are any visitors from outer space, they are the meteoroids that fly into the atmosphere of the earth. On a clear night, especially at certain times of the year, these "visitors" streak across the sky, causing people to exclaim, "Look at the shooting star!" These streaks are not from stars but from meteoroids, fragments of material varying in size from a grain of sand to a boulder of many tons. The glowing streak we see is not far off in starry space but just 60 miles (96 kilometers) or so up in our own atmosphere.

As the meteoroids are heated by friction with the air, their surfaces boil off to form brilliantly glowing gases; this gaseous envelope may be anywhere from a few feet to several hundred yards in diameter. The heat is sufficient to cause most of the millions of meteoroids that enter the earth's atmosphere each day to vaporize or burn so that

[3]Dennis Shatz, "Orbiting with Halley's," *Science and Children* (November/December 1985). Excellent for learning about comets, including cutouts for making a flip-book to show the orbit of Comet Halley around the sun.

only their fine dust ever reaches the earth's surface. Those that do land in a solid chunk are called *meteorites.* The largest meteorite found so far is called Hoba West and lies where it fell near Grootfontein, Namibia. It has an estimated mass of about 60 tons. The largest meteorite on display is in New York City's American Museum of Natural History and weighs about 34 tons.

Larger meteorites were probably responsible for the well-known Barringer Meteorite Crater in Arizona, which is .75 mile (1.2 kilometers) in diameter and about 600 feet (about 200 meters) deep, and for the New Quebec Crater in Canada, about 2 miles (3.2 kilometers) across.

On June 30, 1908, a brilliant fireball—probably a very bright meteor—was seen in the sky over Tunguska, Siberia, in broad daylight. The impact produced shock waves that felled trees over an area 36 miles (60 kilometers) in diameter, and killed 1,500 reindeer. No pieces of the original fireball have ever been recovered; evidently it exploded in the air. This incident was forgotten until a few years ago when investigators studied the event.

There are three kinds of meteorites: *irons,* about 90 percent iron and the rest nickel; *stony irons,* part iron and part stone; and *stones,* made entirely of stone materials.

This is a good place to summarize the difference between meteoroids, meteors, and meteorites. When the particle is in *space* it is called a meteoroid; when it enters the earth's *atmosphere* and glows it is called a meteor; if it survives and lands on the *ground,* it is called a meteorite.

Billions of meteoroids are scattered throughout the solar system. Some travel alone; others travel in meteoroid swarms. Those that travel alone are known as *sporadic meteoroids;* they approach the earth from all directions and account for the vast majority of meteoroids. Most meteorites recovered on earth are from sporadic meteoroids. A study of sporadic meteoroids indicates that they are 4.6 billion years old, the age of the earth itself. The minerals found in one kind of meteoroid are thought to represent samples of the solid grains which condensed directly out of

Barringer Meteorite Crater, a ¾-of-a-mile scar in the arid plains of northern Arizona, was pounded out some 50,000 years ago by the impact of a million-ton meteorite. *(Courtesy of U.S. Geological Survey.)*

the cloud of dust and gas that gave birth to the sun and the planets.

The meteoroids traveling in a swarm give rise to a *meteor shower* when the earth passes through its path; it occurs at predictable times. The orbits of meteoroid swarms are similar to those of the orbits of known comets. It is thought that these meteoroids are debris spread out along the comet's orbit. For example, twice each year the earth passes through a swarm of particles in the orbit of Halley's comet, giving us the Eta Aquarids in May and the Orionids in October.

Records made during meteor showers show that the streaks or trails made by the meteors appear to radiate from a point in the sky called the *radiant*. Swarms are named for the constellation or groups of stars where the radiant *appears* to be located. Thus, the Leonids are named after the constellation Leo.

No telescope is needed for watching a meteor shower. The best show at present is the Perseid shower, radiating from the constellation Perseus from August 10 to 14, with best viewing about August 11. As many as 40 to 60 meteors per hour may be observed then, preferably after midnight and in the absence of bright moonlight. The Orionids appear around October 18 to 23. The Leonid shower occurs between November 14 to 18, and is best seen after midnight (as are all meteors). The Germinid radiant passes directly overhead on December 14 for locations in the southern United States, and almost overhead for other U.S. locations.

THE MOON

When astronaut David Scott dropped a hammer and a feather together on the moon in 1971, both reached the ground at the same time. This is exactly what almost any high school student knew would happen, but it was instructive for a large TV audience to see this occurring on the moon, where the absence of an atmosphere made this demonstration possible and where the low gravitation force made the fall slower and the landing easier to observe.

The lunar probes and landings similarly confirmed much that we knew, but they also returned an immense treasure of new knowledge about our nearest large celestial companion, providing us with data and materials that can help answer the questions that were unsolved during centuries of speculation and scientific study.

Atmosphere

The kind of atmosphere a celestial body has depends in part on its ability to hold various gases. The molecules of gases are in constant motion; unless gravity can hold them they will be lost to space. Even if the moon ever possessed an atmosphere, with its gravity only one sixth that of the earth, it could not hold it. No liquid water could be retained on the surface of the moon; it would immediately boil off and scatter into space.

The absence of an atmosphere means that there is no weather on the moon: no clouds, winds, rain, or snow. The surface, unprotected by a blanket of air, has temperatures of 243°F (118°C) during the day—higher than the boiling point of water—and −279°F (−173°C) at night. In the vacuum surrounding the moon the barometric pressure is always zero. The sky is always black because there is no appreciable atmosphere to scatter the sunlight; the stars are always visible, but the direct glare of the sun is a problem. The absence of an atmosphere can also mean that communication by sound can only be effected by radio, since there is no air to carry sound waves.

Surface

The absence of air and running water means that these substances could not have been factors in eroding the surface of the moon, in wearing down mountains, or in reshaping its landscape as it does on Earth. Formations on the moon that are billions of years old are still standing, along with those formed in the recent past. Examination of the moon's rocks by studying its radioactive elements (see pp. 112–113) confirmed that they were from 3.1 to 4.3 billion years old. Some tiny, green rock fragments collected by the Apollo 11 astronauts were apparently formed 4.6 billion years ago, the time scientists think that the moon and the solar system originated.

Because of the Apollo explorations we have now learned that the lunar landscape is covered by a layer of fine powder and rubble from 3 to 60 feet (1 to 20 meters) deep. This layer is usually called the "lunar soil," although it contains no water or organic material, or any living organisms. The lunar soil was probably formed by the continuous bombardment of the unprotected moon by large and small meteorites over billions of years.

Galileo's telescope revealed that the moon's surface is characterized by mountains, valleys, craters, and smooth surfaces that appeared to be seas. The *maria* (Latin for seas) are the largest of the moon's features. They are, of course, not seas but great plains with relatively flat surfaces, darker than the surrounding regions. They form the eyes and the mouth of the "man in the moon" that some people imagine they see. The far side of the moon was found by spaceships to be much more rugged than the earth-facing side and without large maria.

Craters are generally found in regions not covered by the maria. Most are found in the rugged, mountainous regions of the moon. The most impressive crater, Copernicus, is surrounded by a ring wall 12,000 feet (3,700 meters) high at its highest point, with a diameter of 56 miles (90 kilometers). Most craters have large central peaks.

The extensive cratering of the moon probably began billions of years ago when the young moon was bombarded by fragments left in the primeval cloud in the slowly forming solar system. Cratering was reduced as time went on but the evidence remained. Craters were made on the earth, too, but these were eroded away.

Most of the moon's mountains are rugged and steep-walled. Because of the absence of running water to alter their appearance they lack the drainage features common to earth's mountains. The highest peaks are about 26,000 feet (8,000 meters) tall, not quite as high as Mt. Everest.

Rays, brilliant white streaks on the surface of the moon up to 2,000 miles (3,200 kilometers) long, radiate from some of the craters, probably representing material splashed outward from the crater at the time of impact of a large meteorite.

Rills are cracks or crevices in the moon's surface, caused probably by a turbulent flow of lava or by *faulting*, in which adjacent rock masses slipped past one another in response to tension, compression, or shearing stress.

Origin

Three hypotheses have been advanced to account for the origin of the moon: The first stipulates that the moon *accreted* (gradually formed a mass from colliding particles) alongside of the earth. The second suggests that both bodies accreted independently and that the moon was captured by the earth later. The third proposes that the moon broke off from the young earth before it had solidified. The preferred hypothesis at present is the first one: The moon accreted from particles at the same time as the earth.

The Moon and the Tides

Two factors are responsible for the rhythm of the tides: the gravitational pull of the moon (and, to a lesser extent, the sun) and the rotation of the earth. (There are also small but measurable tides on the land surface of the earth.)

The U.S. government provides tables and charts for mariners, showing times when high and low tides occur at many places along coasts. There are signs on many beaches for the benefit of swimmers, indicating the day-to-day schedule of tides. Ships' arrivals and departures are timed according to the tides, to make certain that the channels are deep enough for incoming ships and to prevent ships from having to push their way out to sea against an incoming tide.

The everlasting succession of low and high tide makes the edge of the sea a constantly changing boundary. The range of tides varies widely in different localities, depending on the nature of the shoreline and the ocean floor. Thus, in the open ocean the tidal range may be 3 feet (about 1 meter). In Cape Cod Bay the range may be as much as 10 feet (about 3 meters), and in the narrowing Bay of Fundy of Nova Scotia the range may be as much as 60 feet (about 18 meters).

For about 6 hours the incoming *flood tide* rises higher and higher, covering more and more sloping beaches and climbing up on rocky shores. Then for six hours the falling *ebb tide* recedes.

Phases of the Moon

Everyone who has ever watched the moon from night to night knows that it seems to change shape. If the moon is observed for a month it may be seen *waning* from the full moon to a quarter to a thin crescent then to the new moon ("no" moon) and then *waxing* to crescent, quarter, and full. These changes are known as the *phases* of the moon (see pp. 184–186).

To understand the causes of the moon's phases it is essential to keep in mind the role played by the sun, earth, and moon in this celestial spectacle.

1. The sun illuminates the moon.
2. The earth provides a vantage point from which we view the show.
3. The moon, the performer, circles the earth once a month. Half of the moon is always illuminated, but we are not in a position to see the lighted half all the time.

When we do see the whole lighted half of the moon we call it a full moon. When only half of the lighted part is visible we see a quarter moon. When all of the lighted part faces away from the earth we have "no" moon, or a new moon. The suggested demonstration on pages 184–186 will help in an understanding of the phases of the moon.

To correct a common error it must be emphasized that the phases of the moon are *not* caused by "a shadow thrown on the moon by the earth." The dark portion of the moon is dark because it is turned away from the sun.

Why is it that we see approximately the same face of the moon—the same "man in the moon" to the naked eye and the same craters, maria, and mountains with the help of the telescope? One more space fact must be added to the three just given to understand this.

4. As the moon circles the earth it turns on its axis in such a way that it presents approximately the same face to the earth. The moon rotates once as it revolves once. The demonstration described on page 186 will be helpful in clarifying this motion

ECLIPSES

Eclipses occur when the sun, earth, and moon are on a straight line in space. There are two kinds of eclipses: solar and lunar.

Solar eclipses occur when the moon passes directly in front of the sun, obscuring it from our vision. If you shut one eye and look at an electric bulb across the room, you can hide its light with a penny held at the right distance from you. The penny (the moon) has eclipsed the bulb (the sun). Note that although the penny is smaller it can eclipse the larger bulb because it is closer to you (see pp. 186–187).

A friend observing you at this time would see the shadow of the penny on your open eye. Similarly, an astronaut in space would observe that the shadow of the moon falls on the earth during a solar eclipse. The moon is smaller than the earth and close to it, so its shadow falls on only a small portion of the earth's surface, and is seldom more than about 200 miles (320 kilometers) wide. However, the moon is moving around the earth, so the path of its eastward-moving shadow may form a band thousands of miles long. (To return to the penny–bulb demonstration: If you moved the penny to the left its shadow would sweep across your head.) This narrow track is called the *path of totality*. (Also the rotation of the earth in the same direction as the moon's orbital motion slows down the shadow path on the earth and makes an eclipse of the sun last as long as 7½ minutes at a maximum. How would you demonstrate this effect to your friends?)

During a total eclipse of the sun, a small dark nick is first seen in its edge. The dark area grows larger and larger. Just before totality, the sky is darkened considerably, the temperature drops, and there is a strange hush of nature's sounds. When the sun disappears completely a pearly halo—the corona—appears around the blackened disk of the sun. A few stars appear. Astronomers,

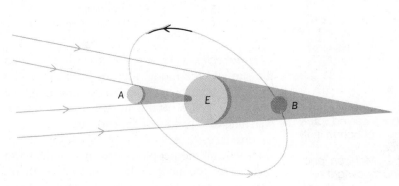

When the moon is at position B it is in the shadow of the earth. We then have an eclipse of the moon. When it is in position A the moon casts a shadow on part of the earth and hides the sun from view there. We then have an eclipse of the sun. (The arrows on the left show the direction of the sun's rays.) Distances and sizes are not drawn to scale.

and amateur eclipse chasers as well, many of whom have traveled halfway around the world to see the eclipse, are in a frenzy of activity at this time—observing, photographing, and recording the event in their effort to learn more about the corona and the prominences of the sun. Then the moon slips off, and the edge of the sun appears again and grows. The eclipse is over.

Note: Do not look at a total or partial solar eclipse directly. None of the so-called protective devices, such as sunglasses, stained or smoked glass, or old film negatives can give absolute protection against the solar rays that burn the retina of the eye. A safe way to view the eclipse is indirectly, for example, by *projecting* the sun's image through a pinhole in a piece of cardboard or through binoculars *onto a white surface*.

The progress of an eclipse can be observed safely by holding a card with a small hole punched in it several feet above a white surface. *(From Exploration of the Universe by Abell, Morrison, and Wolff, Saunders College Publishing, copyright 1987.)*

In any year two to five eclipses of the sun will occur, but no more than three of these can be total. More than half the time the moon does not appear large enough in the sky to cover the sun completely. In that case we may have an *annular eclipse*, in which the moon is seen silhouetted against the sun's disk, with a ring of sunlight showing around the moon. To simulate an annular eclipse, return to the penny–bulb demonstration, but move the penny just a little bit farther from your eye so that you can see a halo of light around it. Sometimes the moon appears to skim over the northern or southern part of the sun, producing a *partial eclipse*. (Of course, a partial *phase* precedes and follows a total eclipse as the moon appears to "slip" on and off the sun.) To simulate a partial eclipse move the penny slightly up or down.

Since solar eclipses follow narrow paths across the earth they are rare for a particular locality. In New York City, for example, a total eclipse of the sun occurred on January 24, 1925. This was the first eclipse of this kind there since the fifteenth century. The next total eclipse will occur there on October 26, 2144. The following are the dates and places of the total eclipses of the sun visible in several locations during the rest of the twentieth century:

1990 July 22	Finland, Arctic regions
1991 July 11	Hawaii, Central America, Brazil
1992 June 30	South Atlantic
1994 Nov. 3	South America
1995 Oct. 24	South Asia
1997 March 9	Siberia, Arctic
1998 Feb. 26	Central America
1999 Aug. 11	Central Europe, Central Asia

Lunar eclipses occur when the earth is between the sun and the moon, thereby blocking off the moon's source of light and darkening it. As we observe an eclipse of the moon, therefore, we are watching the shadow of the earth pass across the moon's face. An eclipse of the moon can be observed by all the people on that half of the earth that can see the moon at the time. All of us, therefore, have many opportunities to observe lunar eclipses in our lifetime. Lunar eclipses can occur two or three times a year. There may also be a year without any lunar eclipses.

Eclipses of the sun occur only during the period of the new moon, for it is only then that a sun–moon–earth lineup, in that order, is possible. Eclipses of the moon occur only during the full moon, when a sun–earth–moon lineup may occur. Then why is there not an eclipse of the sun and an eclipse of the moon every month? The answer lies in the particular track that the moon follows around the earth. Picture the earth and the sun sitting on an imaginary table in space. As the earth moves around the sun its orbit remains on this table, similar to toy railroad tracks.

The moon's tracks around the earth, however, cut through the table at an angle. Sometimes the moon is above the table and sometimes below it. It is only when there is a coincidence of the moon being on or near the table (the plane of the earth's orbit) at the time of a new or full moon that an eclipse occurs.

It is interesting to note that Earth is the only planet with a moon that is just the right size and can be at the right distance to cover the disk of the sun—but not too large to block its corona during a solar eclipse. All the other planets with satellites have either moons that are so large that they would cover both the sun and its corona or so small that they would appear as tiny dots on the solar disk. (Demonstrate this with your penny–moon and light–bulb sun.)[4]

HOW THE SOLAR SYSTEM WAS FORMED

The question of the origin of our solar system has intrigued astronomers for the past 300 years and has resulted in a number of theories. Today there is general agreement that the solar system formed out of a slowly rotating cloud of dust and gas some 4.6 billion years ago, far out along one of the

[4]Stephen Berr, "Solar Spectacular," *The Science Teacher* (April 1984). Many excellent suggestions for learning and teaching about eclipses.

curved arms of our spiral galaxy of stars. This cloud extended beyond the limits of the known planets. Because of the gravitational attraction among its particles, the cloud contracted and, as it did, spun faster and formed a disk. You can demonstrate such an increase in speed by spinning yourself on an old-fashioned piano stool with your arms outstretched and holding some books and then suddenly pulling your arms and books to your side. You will find that this "contraction" of yourself makes you go faster. Similarly, the pirouetting ice skater can increase his or her spin by pulling in the arms.

At some stage, a body collected at the center of the disk that was so massive, dense, and hot that nuclear reactions occurred, and it became a star—the sun. The remainder of the dust particles and gases surrounding the central body came together to form the planets and their satellites.

In the past three decades a vast amount of new knowledge relating to the origin of the solar system has accumulated from the following three sources:

The study of meteorites, many of which are thought to be samples of primitive, unchanged solar system material.

Spacecraft, which have refined our knowledge of the size, surface, composition, and other characteristics of the members of the solar system.

Astrophysics, the study of the galaxy of stars of which our sun is one, where we find evidence of the birth, development, and death of stars.

Even with the new sources of information (or perhaps because of these) there is still considerable uncertainty and controversy about the details of the origin and evolution of the solar system. Any theory proposed must be tested against three criteria.

1. Is it in accordance with known physical principles, with our knowledge of gravitation, heat, light, behavior of atoms?
2. Is it within the realm of probability?
3. Does it account for our present solar system—its size, motions, members?

IMPORTANT GENERALIZATIONS

The sun is the center of a huge system of heavenly bodies that revolve around it. Included in the sun's family are planets, asteroids, satellites, comets, and meteoroids.

The mutual gravitational attraction between the planets and the sun prevents the planets from flying out of their orbits.

The sun is a nearby star; stars are distant suns.

The sun shines by virtue of its own nuclear reactions.

Life on earth would be impossible if it were not for the sun.

Physical conditions on the different members of the solar system vary. Thus far we have no conclusive evidence of life on any planet other than Earth.

The planets move in the same direction in nearly circular orbits around the sun.

Earth is the third planet from the sun. It is one of the smaller planets in the solar system.

Day and night are caused by the rotation of the earth on its axis.

The earth's rotation causes the apparent motion of the sun, moon, and stars across the sky.

It takes the earth one year to complete one revolution around the sun.

Seasons are caused by the tilt in the earth's axis and the revolution of the earth around the sun.

The moon's changing appearance, its phases, results from its revolution around the earth.

Two factors are responsible for the rhythm of the tides: the gravitational pull of the moon (and to a lesser extent, the sun) and the rotation of the earth.

Eclipses occur when the earth, sun, and moon are on a straight line in space.

Scientists believe that the solar system formed from a cloud of dust and gas about 4.6 billion years ago.

Note: See "Discovering for Yourself" section at the end of Chapter 8A.

TEACHING "THE SUN AND THE PLANETS"

Astronomy fascinates us all. Observations of myriad stars and the changing moon in the night sky, the setting sun as day ends make us question and wonder. We follow with great interest the exploits of voyaging spacecraft—the TV showings of landings on the moon and Mars and the close-ups of other planets.

The concepts of distance, direction, length, weight, and motion, essential to an understanding of space, can be developed by experiences in the immediate environment. In early childhood, such concepts may be initiated in the classroom with such questions as, What is in front of you? Behind you? What is high in the room? What is low? Where is your table in the room? How can you go from here to there with the fewest footsteps? What do you see when you turn around slowly? Which is farther away from you—the door or the window? Outdoors in the street, compare the length of a city block to a footstep, or the distance of a smokestack to clouds and other objects in the daytime sky. Observing a cloud moving in front of the sun provides an opportunity for discovering that clouds are closer to us than the sun. Students may *estimate* distances and, when possible, *measure* to see if they are accurate. They can make *inferences* from their observations. There are many opportunities for *interpreting data*.

Arithmetic skills can be used to help a child realize the concept of distance and size in the solar system. For example, if students read that the earth is about four times as far across as the moon, it is important that we attempt to bring meaning to this concept. Here models are helpful: a ball to represent the moon, and a globe four times the diameter of the ball to represent the earth. Space distances are better understood if they are compared to some distance with which students are familiar—for example, distances between nearby places, cities, or landmarks. The concept of years of time may also be developed if students associate their own ages, or some other time span in their experience, with the unfamiliar and much longer time figures associated with outer-space concepts.

The use of models is natural for the material in this chapter to clarify concepts of size, distance, time, motion, and relative position in space. In using models it is important to have children participate, physically and mentally, in their construction and use. Models will be helpful in the transition from an earth viewpoint ("the sun moves across the sky") to a space viewpoint ("the earth turns") and to help children develop the ability to imagine things from different perspectives.[1]

SOME BROAD CONCEPTS

The solar system is made up of the sun and the bodies that revolve around it.

The sun's energy is necessary to life on the earth.

The sun is our chief source of light in the sky.

The sun is farther away than birds, airplanes, and clouds.

Day and night are caused by the sun shining on the earth as it rotates on its axis.

Shadows are caused by objects blocking light.

The length and direction of a shadow in sunlight depends on the position of the sun in the sky.

The tilt of the earth's axis and its revolution around the sun cause the seasons.

The moon's phases result from its revolution around the earth.

Eclipses result when the earth, moon, and sun are in a straight line in space.

The moon and the planets shine by reflected sunlight.

The turning of the earth makes the sun, moon, and stars appear to move across the sky.

Gravitational attraction between the planets and the sun prevents the planets from flying out of their orbits.

The entire solar system moves through space.

FOR YOUNGER CHILDREN

Following are examples of experiences that have been used with younger children to develop an understanding of some of the concepts in this

[1]K. E. Hill, *Exploring the Natural World with Young Children* (New York: Harcourt Brace Jovanovich, 1976). Includes shadow activities. G. F. Consuegra, "Science with Shadows," *Science and Children* (February 1982); D. Levy, "Astronomy Program for Young Children," *Science and Children* (September 1979).

chapter. In cases where elementary school students have had little experience with science these may be used with older children as well.

What Makes a Shadow? How Do Shadows Change?

On a sunny morning take the children for a walk to observe shadows (see Chapter 19B). A playground where silhouettes of children can be marked in chalk or washable paint on the macadam or cement is very good for shadow activities. What shadows can be seen? What things make shadows? How are the shadows like the things that make them? How can we measure the length of a shadow? Choose a child to stand at one end of a long piece of paper so that his or her shadow falls on the paper. Draw an outline of the shadow. Measure the length with a yard or meter stick. Record the length and the time of day. Look for the sun. Where is it in the sky? Low? High? Keep the record. At noon, outline and measure the same child's shadow. Record the length and the time of day. Look for the sun in the sky. Is it high or low? If possible take another measurement near the close of school. Record the data. Again look for the sun's location in the sky. Use the three records and ask children to compare them. Help them to try to account for the differences in appearance of the three shadows. Urge them to observe shadows at home at different times of the day and report their observations. Some children will be able to *infer* a relationship between the height of the sun and the length of shadows. Provide further experiences for them at future times during the year.

Some children will need further experiences with shadow observations before they can demonstrate the idea that objects make shadows when light cannot pass through them. Use a gooseneck lamp and try to make a shadow with a book, a toy, or a clear piece of glass. Turn off the light. Can you see a shadow when the room is dark? Go outdoors on a cloudy day. Can you find shadows? Why?

Observe specific places where sunlight comes into the classroom or other parts of the school building at different times of the day. Ask children to try to account for the change.

How do shadows help us tell time? Sundials range from student-made devices to the more elaborate one shown here. *Photo by Lloyd Wolf, Concord School, Forestville, Maryland.*

As the children record the sun's shadows on paper each half hour, comparisons are made of the length and direction of the shadows cast by a pencil set in a spool. How are the observed changes related to the position of the sun in the sky? (Courtesy of Margaret Harrison, Porter-Gaud School, Charlestown, South Carolina.)

In case of very young children the two problems "What makes a shadow?" and "How do shadows change?" being considered here should be dealt with separately.

What Makes the Earth Warm?

At noon on a sunny day take the children outside and ask them to describe the day (sunny, warm, and so on). Ask them to try to find warm things in the sun by feeling them (grass, the sidewalk, soil, rocks, the pavement, windowsills). Ask them to feel some of these same things in the shade. How do they feel? Why?

Stand a thermometer in a quart milk carton that has one side partly removed so that the thermometer may be read. Place it in a sunny window with the thermometer shielded from the sun by the carton. Do the same with a second thermometer, but place the carton in the shade. Watch the thermometer. What is happening? Why? Inspect at 3-minute intervals for 15 minutes and record the temperatures.

Use two saucers with two ice cubes on each. Set one in a sunny window and keep the other

out of the sun. Why is there a difference? On a partly cloudy day take the children outside to experience the effect when clouds cover the sun, and then when the sky is clear. Help children plan other experiences to note the effects of the sun.

How Does the Moon Change?

Even very young children are aware of the moon. They know about moon flights and have observed the moon at night. Some calendars show moon phases on different days of the month. Ask children to observe the moon on different days of the month to match the moon's actual appearance with these phases. With help at home and drawings from school, some children are able to make observations and infer that (1) the moon does not always have the same appearance, (2) sometimes more of it can be seen than at others, and (3) it is not always in the same place in the sky at the same time every evening. Do they think it's possible for the moon to be seen during the day? Challenge the children to look for it.

At this level it is probably not wise to go into

why the moon seems to change shape but only to observe that it does.

How Much Does Temperature Change in a Day?

Discuss with children their experiences with temperature changes out-of-doors during a day. When is it warmest? Coolest? How much do you think the temperature changes? How can we find out the answers to these questions?

The questions about temperature can be a way to introduce children to using a measuring instrument to provide accurate data from which to draw conclusions. Help the children develop the skill of reading a thermometer. If possible use a large easy-to-read thermometer. It is desirable for all children to have a chance to hold and observe thermometers. Ask children to report on their readings, and place their observations on the chalkboard. Use either the Fahrenheit or Celsius scale, not both, on any one occasion. If children's reports vary, ask "Why?" Possible answers: Elizabeth's thermometer is broken; Andrew maybe held the bulb of the thermometer in his fist; the temperature is different in different parts of the room; Joyce hasn't learned yet how to read the thermometer; Ben read Celsius degrees while the others read the Fahrenheit degrees.

Suggest that children take the room temperature at different times of the day. Help them note the time and the readings on the chalkboard. Take the thermometer outside and find the temperature in sunlit areas (with the thermometer shielded from the sun's rays) and in the shade. Help children by checking their readings. Keep a record on the chalkboard.

Other Problems for Younger Children

1. How do living things change as the seasons change?
2. Which way is it to the center of the earth?
3. What kinds of things do not make shadows?
4. How can you make your shadow change?

5. How can shadows help us tell time?
6. What do mirrors do to sunlight?
7. What can we see in the sky at night?
8. How can you dry some fruits (apples, peaches, apricots, grapes) in the sun?[2]

FOR OLDER CHILDREN

What Are the Planets Like?

One good look at the stars, planets, or the moon with binoculars is more valuable than looking at dozens of diagrams or star charts. If students studying planets can actually see one in the night sky, their enthusiasm will repay any effort a teacher makes to bring about such an experience. In the community, amateur astronomers with telescopes are often more than willing to let children look through their telescopes and, if properly briefed beforehand, will be very helpful to students. Some magazines indicate periodically which planets are visible at any given time and where to locate them.[3] It is helpful to go outdoors with children during the day at school and point to the section of the sky where they may expect to see the planets at night. It may help them to learn where the planet will be on a particular night in relation to the moon (if it is visible in the early evening) or to some easily identified star groups (see Chapter 7A).

Have children investigate the problem "Does a planet move?" by observing one planet for a number of weeks. They will observe that during one evening the planet appears to move across the sky from east to west. Venus, for example, may be seen to disappear over the western horizon an hour or two after sundown. Ask the children to try to interpret this motion. Some may suggest that

[2]L. K. Froschauer and B. B. Boudrot, "Sun: Friend and Foe," *Science and Children* (May 1986).

[3]D. David Batch, "Evening Skies," *Science and Children*. Monthly star maps. Also write to Superintendent of Documents, U.S. Government Printing Office, Washington, D.C. 20402, for a list of astronomy materials.

the turning of the earth causes the apparent motion in the same way as it does for the sun. Ask the children, during this period of observation, to locate the observed planet in relation to nearby stars and to make a sketch of what they see. Continue this for a number of weeks. Children will discover that the planet changes position in relation to the stars and constellations. What causes this? The answer may be deferred (while children speculate and offer ideas) until the next project, a model of the solar system.

How Can We Make Models of the Solar System?

If possible, the model-building project may be initiated by a visit to a planetarium where there is a model of the solar system.[4] Ask children, or a

[4] J. E. Bishop, "Planetarium Methods Based on the Research of Jean Piaget," *Science and Children* (May 1976); P. Ankney, "Classroom Planetarium," *Science and Children* (October 1981). Directions for constructing.

committee of children, to become experts for one particular planet and report findings to the class. During the school year, if new information becomes available, the children may supplement their reports.

Making a clay or Styrofoam ball model of the solar system is particularly useful in the fifth and sixth grades, when students know enough arithmetic to get approximately correct proportions of the sizes of various planets as well as their relative distances from one another and from the sun. From various sources students will get figures that tell distances and diameters of the various planets. Then they will have to decide on a scale that they can use in order to get all the members of the solar system into the classroom and to have the sun (the largest body) as well as Mercury (the smallest body) included. They may, in fact, need to use a larger area than the classroom, depending on the scale they select. Such a project might be started by asking students, "What figures will we have to know to make the model solar system? How can we adjust the figures to a scale?" Students should be urged to make their own plan

Making a chalkboard planetarium affords an excellent opportunity for the meaningful use of mathematics. Concepts of the vastness of space, relationships between the planets, and the place of the earth in the solar system can result when students solve the problems related to making this graphic representation.

and then to carry it out. Here is an excellent opportunity to let them try out their ideas and remedy any mistakes they make. It is important to note that distances in space are so great that it is practically impossible to use the same scales for the size of the planets and the distances between them. An outdoors model where there is more space is an interesting possibility.[5] A "chalkboard planetarium" using the facts on the chart on this page can give students a better concept of space relationships in the solar system.[6]

How Is the Sun Important to Us?

An experiment in growing plants in light and without light is an important experience for children. They can work out the details as they proceed.

It is one thing to read or hear that the sun is necessary for plant growth; it is quite another to experiment and see the results. As far as possible there should be only one difference in the envi-

[5]M. Swan, "Outdoor Model of the Solar System," *Science and Children* (September 1970). Gives data to use in constructing model using only one scale for size and distance. M. Zimmerman, "Time To Build Sundials," *Science and Children* (November/December 1971). Gives directions.
[6]Adapted from *Science: Grade 5* (Brooklyn: Board of Education of the City of New York, 1968).

ronment of the plants: the presence of sunlight. Select two similar plants. Place one in sunlight, the other in a dark closet. Otherwise treat them alike. After two weeks the plants should be compared. Remember that students cannot generalize about *all* plants from their experience here. Moreover, some students may say, and rightly so, that the plants in a dark place probably did not have exactly the same temperature, humidity, air circulation, and so on as did the sunlit plants. Consequently, only tentative conclusions can be drawn from the experiment. Ask children to report on places, such as greenhouses, where artificial illumination is used to supply additional light.

In addition to plants' dependence on the sun, other relationships are important. The sun heats the earth and affects our weather, it gives us light, it affects our ocean tides, and it keeps the earth in the solar system.

What Causes Day and Night?

Before proceeding with the demonstration we describe here, urge students to try to devise their own methods of using a light and a globe to demonstrate the cause of day and night. This may help them to recall the information they need in order to illustrate the causes.

Facts for a "Chalkboard Planetarium"

Number and Name of Planet	Approximate Distance from Sun		Distance to Be Measured from Left Side of Chalkboard (Scale: 1 inch = 20 million miles 1 centimeter = 10 million kilometers)*	
	Millions of Miles	Millions of Kilometers		
1. Mercury	36	58	1 $\frac{3}{4}$ inches	5.8 cm
2. Venus	67	108	3 $\frac{1}{4}$ inches	10.8 cm
3. Earth	93	150	4 $\frac{3}{4}$ inches	15.0 cm
4. Mars	140	225	7 inches	22.5 cm
5. Jupiter	480	770	2 feet	77.0 cm
6. Saturn	890	1430	3 feet 8 inches	1 meter 43 cm
7. Uranus	1,800	2900	7 feet 6 inches	2 meters 90 cm
8. Neptune	2,800	4500	11 feet 8 inches	4 meters 50 cm
9. Pluto	3,700	6000	15 feet 5 inches	6 meters

*Note that these two scales are not equivalent: A ratio of 1 inch to 20 million miles is not equal to a ratio of 1 centimeter to 10 million kilometers. For this reason the indicated distance to be measured in metric and the customary units are not equal. In making this chalkboard planetarium use one system only.

Because many science and geography books suggest how to demonstrate the cause of day and night our description is brief. As a source of light use either a flashlight (use a cardboard tube around the flashlight to concentrate the light beam), floor lamp with a shade, or any lamp with a good reflector. Use a globe as a model of the earth. Remind students to imagine that they are living on the globe. A chalk mark on the spot on the globe where they live will help. Darken the room, shine the light on the globe, watch the chalk mark, and begin to turn the globe from west to east (counterclockwise) slowly. Turn the globe around once on its axis so that students can observe what happens during one complete rotation. Then begin with the position of the chalk mark at sunrise, and let a student tell what he or she would be doing at different stages of the rotation, for example, "Now I am having breakfast." "Now I am on my way to school." If the class is large, let small groups take turns standing close so they can observe easily. Students should remember the following in order to understand the causes of day and night:

The earth is round, like a ball; consequently, only half of it can be lighted at once.
The earth gets its light from the sun. The lighted half has day; the unlit half has night.
The earth makes one rotation every 24 hours. Nighttime follows daytime.

Students may make a chart indicating the number of hours of daylight and darkness during each of the months of the year, making 12 rows across the chart, 1 row for each month. From this chart students can answer such questions as, "When do we have the most hours of daylight?" "When do we have the fewest hours of daylight?" "Is there much or little daylight on your birthday?" "When are the hours of daylight and darkness about the same?" "How do you think this chart would look if you lived at the North Pole?" The data for such a chart may be obtained from an almanac or from daily newspapers and calendars.

What Causes the Seasons?[7]

Help students understand that for any particular part of the earth, such as the United States, (1) In summer there are more hours of sunlight and, therefore, more heating of the earth than in winter, when there are fewer hours of sunlight; and (2) in summer the sun is more directly overhead; it heats the earth more than it does in the winter, when it is lower in the sky and its rays strike the earth more obliquely. Both these phenomena are observable (see Chapter 7A, pp. 154–155).

Children can understand these phenomena much better by actual experience with the sun's heat.[8] To demonstrate the influence of the direction of the sun's rays, use two pieces of black paper placed on pieces of corrugated cardboard (because of its insulating properties). Place one to receive the sun's rays directly (90° angle), the other flat on the surface. On a sunny day place each in sunlight in the schoolroom. Let children feel and compare the warmth on both pieces after 2, 4, 6, 8, and 10 minutes, and record their findings. There may be some disagreement among children about feeling the difference. How can we be more accurate and certain of the results? Place thermometers under each piece of black paper and read them after the same intervals. Record the observations.

The difference in length of days may be emphasized by asking students to recall the differ-

[7]See J. Schwartz, *Earthwatch: Space-Time Investigations with a Globe* (New York: McGraw-Hill, 1977) for a method of placing a geographic globe in a position that corresponds to the real position of the earth in space. If such a globe is observed in sunlight it will reveal where sunrise and sunset are occurring on the real earth at the moment; the earth's present position in its annual orbit around the sun; the changes of the earth during the seasons; the "land of the midnight sun"; the place on earth where the sun is directly overhead; the time of day (thereby making the globe into a sundial); the number of hours of sunlight for any place on earth; and many other space happenings.

[8]Adapted from *Science: Grades 3–4* (Brooklyn: Board of Education of the City of New York, 1966). See also P. H. Joslin: "As Smart as a Fencepost," *Science and Children* (February 1985). Observing and measuring shadows to tell time. Includes time belts and seasons.

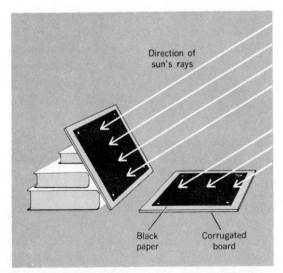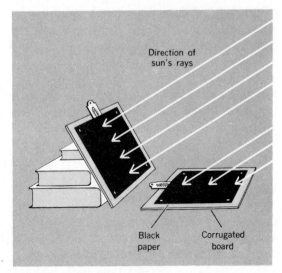

The angle makes a difference in the amount of heat received from the sun's rays. Experimenting without and then with a thermometer helps pupils see the importance of accurate measurements.

ence in light when they get up at 7 A.M. in September as compared with the same time in December. A chart or graph of daylight and darkness hours will also help students to understand seasons. Here again, arithmetic serves as a tool for science, and the activity is another example of helping children to see the importance of collecting data over a long period of time before drawing conclusions.

Both of these experiences, one with the changes in length of day, the other with changes in the angle of the sun's rays, help children understand the cause of seasons. Along with these experiences a model planetarium may help students gain a space view of the cause of the seasons. Let them work individually or in small groups to manipulate the model and to come up with hypotheses about the cause of the seasons. Two questions may help: "Does the model show how the length of daylight might change as the earth travels around the sun?" "Does the model show how the angle at which the sun strikes the earth might change during the yearly orbit?" Use the questions only as a last resort; let the children grope for solutions until you discover what as-

sistance they need (see Chapter 7A, pp. 154–155).

These demonstrations should be supplemented by several outdoor trips to observe the position of the sun during different times of the day and at different times of the year.

The details and construction of a planetarium. In using this apparatus it is important to remember to keep the earth's axis always pointing to the north. Commercially made models use a chain arrangement to rotate the earth and to keep it tipped in the proper direction.

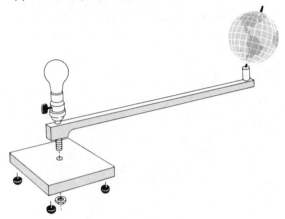

This illustrates the point we have made before: *Demonstrations are done to help students understand the problem or phenomenon that is under investigation.*

Note: Demonstrations should not be confused with experiments. They are done for different reasons. (See "Investigating and Experimenting," Chapter 3.)

What Is the Moon Like?[9]

In this era of actual lunar travel, children will be able to supply much information about the moon's surface, about gravity on the moon, moon rocks, and so on. Inventory their ideas first and then proceed as follows.

What can you discover by looking at the moon using a pair of binoculars? What changes in appearance can you see from night to night? What kind of path does the moon seem to make across the sky? When does it rise and set? Is its path like the sun's path?

Begin by urging children to *observe* for themselves, *record* their observations, *predict* what will happen from night to night, and try to *demonstrate* their observations.

If possible, arrange for children to look at the moon through a telescope and *describe* their observations. There is no substitute for this experience (see Chapter 7A, pp. 168–170).

Many calendars indicate the dates of the new moon and the other phases. Urge students to observe these phases and draw pictures of the shape of the moon on different dates. Have them indi-

cate under their drawings the date, time, and the part of the sky the moon was in (east, west, and so on). They may also note in newspapers, calendars, or almanacs the time of moonrise and moonset.

Why Does the Moon Seem to Change Shape?[10]

Use the results of observations made in the previous problem. Suggest that children draw on the chalkboard the various shapes of the moon they have observed. Suggest also that they try to arrange them in the order that they would occur during the month. Then let them attempt to *construct hypotheses* that might explain these apparent changes. As the demonstration goes on (see the following description), and they begin to develop some ideas, urge them to distinguish between ideas that support their hypotheses and those that do not. They may be able to revise their ideas as they attempt to test their hypotheses.

Many students in the elementary school find it difficult to understand what makes the moon seem to change its shape as it travels around the earth. Even the following commonly used demonstration is not always effective with all students. It is difficult for them to transpose what they see in the demonstration (really a space viewpoint) to what they observe in the sky (an earth viewpoint).

To represent the moon, use a basketball or a ball of similar size. To represent the sun use a lamp such as was suggested for the demonstration of the cause of day and night. Darken the room and turn on the lamp. Stand in the light of the lamp and hold the ball at arm's length, a little higher than the lamp (teacher demonstrates). Your head represents the position of the earth. Remind students that to understand how the shape of the moon seems to change, we must

[9]*Steps to the Moon* (Superintendent of Documents, U.S. Government Printing Office, Washington, DC 20402). See also M. Zimmerman, "The Inconstant Moon," *Science and Children* (April 1970). A detailed account of a moon study in a sixth grade. Also see *Helping Children Learn Earth–Space Science* (Washington, DC: NSTA, 1971). Contains many articles on moon study with activities and diagrams. S. C. Reed, "Observing the Earth's Phasing Moon," *Science and Children* (February 1981); "Astronomy on a Shoestring" (Washington, D.C.: NSTA, 1984). General background for older children and the teacher.

[10]M. B. Leyden, "For It's Only a Paper Moon," *Science and Children* (April 1984). Why the moon seems to change shape with diagrams and suggested activities and observations.

remember the following three things: (1) The moon's light comes from the sun, (2) the moon is ball-shaped and can be lighted on only one side, and (3) the moon revolves around the earth once every month (approximately once every 27½ days). Students should be reminded also that they can see the moon only from the position of the earth. (In this demonstration it is especially important that each student be given an opportunity to participate, because only the demonstrator is in a position to actually see the changes.)

Begin by holding the ball in a position between the sun and the earth, a little higher than the head. This represents the position at the new moon, when scarcely any of it is visible to us on the earth, because the light from the sun cannot strike the side of the moon we see. As you turn slowly toward the left, still holding the ball a little over your head, more of the moon will gradually become lighted. Stop a quarter of the way around, and you are in the position of first quarter. Draw a chalk mark on the ball to outline the lighted part so that the shape becomes apparent. Keep turning in the same direction another quarter of the way around. Now you are in the position of full moon (remember to keep the ball a little higher than your head). Approximately two weeks have passed since new moon. Keep turning and observe the lighted part of the ball. It is now growing smaller. Turn another quarter of the way around and you are in the position of third quarter. Approximately three weeks of the month

The girl is demonstrating the phases of the moon. The ball represents the moon. The light from the window represents the sun in the proper direction. She is a viewer on Earth, standing in one spot and turning in order to move the "moon" in its orbit around the earth. The illustrations shows what she sees.

have gone. Keep turning in the same direction to the original position. A month has passed. The moon has changed from new moon to first quarter, to full moon, to third quarter, and back again to new moon.

Using a lamp to light up a basketball is a way of helping students understand what happens in the night sky, but students' correct answers to the questions we ask about the ball and light do not necessarily mean that they fully understand the cause of the moon's phases. It is quite a mental jump from the schoolroom demonstration out into space where the phenomenon is taking place.

There has been much emphasis on the fact that we see only one side of the moon, and children are curious to know why. Let children suggest their hypotheses. List them on the chalkboard. Suggest that students attempt to demonstrate their ideas. Then do the following: Use a chair or other object for the earth. Your head represents the moon. Now slide to the right and execute a revolution around the object, always keeping your face toward it. Ask the children to describe what has happened. Allow a number of them to repeat the circling around the chair. Children will see that the moon rotates once as it revolves once, and thus the same side of the moon is always toward the earth. Children may recall that some

recent space probes have photographed the side of the moon we cannot see from the earth.

Plan a class trip to the moon, with a simulated space vehicle, assigned responsibilities, and methods of communication. Write farewell notes to parents and descriptions of moon experiences.[11]

What Makes an Eclipse[12]

Ideally the best time to study an eclipse is when it is occurring. Naturally this is difficult to arrange (see Chapter 7A for timetable of future eclipses of the sun). The entire school can be involved in the observations, since an eclipse, like any other of nature's spectacles, has meaning at every level.

Note: See the caution against looking directly at the sun in Chapter 7A.

[11]G. E. Loud, "Off to the Moon," *Science and Children* (March 1986).

[12]*Helping Children Learn Earth–Space Science* (Washington, D.C.: NSTA, 1971). Information, diagrams, and experiences about eclipses. Includes M. M. Milkent and J. H. Dale, "The Moon Box," *Science and Children*. Directions for making a device to study moon phases and eclipses. R. C. Victor, "The Return of the Dragon," *Science and Children* (May 1984). Useful information.

Pupils need help in connecting what they see in a demonstration with what actually happens in space. *(Left)* A pupil demonstrates an eclipse of the moon; *(Right)* An eclipse of the sun.

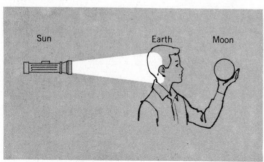
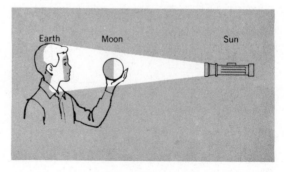

Before using the demonstration that is described here, urge children to try to illustrate their ideas on the chalkboard or by using the materials employed in the previous problem in various ways. Give them help only when they run out of steam themselves.

The demonstration used to show moon phases may also be used to show eclipses. Use an electric lamp, a ball, and the same positions that were used to show moon phases. The question may arise, "Why don't we have an eclipse every month as the moon travels around the earth?" It should be made clear that the earth, sun, and moon are not often in line and in the same plane. A child will see that when his or her head (the earth) is between the light (the sun) and the ball (moon), and all three are in line, the shadow of the head falls on the ball and eclipses it (an eclipse of the moon). If the ball is now moved to a position between the head and light, the children will see that the ball has cut off the light of the lamp (the sun). The shadow of the ball now falls on the child's face (an eclipse of the sun), but this cannot occur unless these heavenly bodies are in the same plane. (See p. 172 for information on the frequency of eclipses.)

What Does Gravity Do?

Students have had many experiences with gravity, but may not have thought much about them. Three problems related to gravity and the solar system are (1) What is meant by weight? (2) why doesn't the earth fly out of the solar system? (3) why doesn't the sun's gravity pull the earth into it? Suggest that students do the following, observe what happens, and then put their ideas together.

1. How much would you weigh on the moon? The purpose of this question is to start students thinking about gravity. Ask the children to write their weights on pieces of paper. (This represents the pull of the earth's gravity on them.) Then have them calculate their weights on the moon by dividing by six. Why is there such a difference? (The moon, a smaller and

lighter body, has a smaller pull than the earth.) What would happen if you weighed yourself on a spring scale on top of a very high mountain on the earth? (You would weigh less because you are farther from the center of the earth.) If the earth is turning why don't we all fly off? (Because gravity pulls us toward the center of the earth.) Suggest that students think of other ways to show that the earth's gravity pulls things toward it.

2. Why doesn't the earth fly out of the solar system? Attach a weight, such as a ball or chalkboard eraser, to a string, and swing it in a vertical plane. (Arrange for many children to have this experience but take precautions against a weight striking anyone.) Ask them to observe what happens and describe it. How is this like the earth's path around the sun? How is it different? Why doesn't the weight fly away? What does the string do? What would happen if it were cut? (In part, the string *represents* the pull of gravity that the sun exerts on the earth.)

3. Why doesn't the sun's gravity pull the earth to it? Again swing the weight on the string. What happens when you stop swinging? (The weight falls.) The earth and all the planets move just at the right speed so that they do not fly off into space or fall into the sun.

Other Problems for Older Children

1. Why is it very cold at the North and South Poles?
2. Why do the seasons in the Southern Hemisphere happen at different times from those in the Northern Hemisphere?
3. How would conditions on earth be different if its axis were not tilted?
4. How do we know that the sun turns?
5. What are comets like?
6. How can we locate planets at different times of the year?
7. How can we make and use a sundial? How did people tell time long ago?
8. How does the sun change its position in the sky during the year?[13]

[13]M. B. Leyten, "Shadows and Changes," *Science and Children* (May 1978). V. E. Neie, "The Multi-Purpose Astrolobe," *Science and Children* (October 1979). Directions for making and using.

9. What happens to a comet when it comes close to the sun?
10. What are sunspots?
11. How does the earth appear from space?
12. How can we plan a space trip?
13. What are the possibilities of life on other planets?
14. How do we know that the earth is round?
15. How much would you weigh on other planets?
16. What have spacecraft discovered as they passed close to the planets?
17. Select one planet and tell what it is like on its surface.
18. What kind of path do planets follow as they orbit the sun?
19. Are there other planets around other suns?
20. Watch a meteor shower. How many meteors did you see in one hour?

Note: See "Resources to Investigate with Children" and "Preparing to Teach" at the end of Chapter 8B.

THE STARS AND
THE UNIVERSE

The serenity of the night sky . . . belies the universe's violent nature. . . . Stars are observed in various stages of life and explosive death. Some massive stars may collapse in death to create black holes. . . . Some . . . stars collapse into rapidly spinning dense objects called neutron stars, or pulsars, whose reflective flashes blink at us like beacons on some celestial shoal. From the explosions of stars, we discover, come the material for new stars. And radiation from all this activity pervades the cosmos, some of it the residual energy from the violent fireball that was the big bang.

JOHN NOBLE WILFORD
NEW YORK TIMES MAGAZINE, SEPTEMBER 15, 1985

TO MEASURE THE STARS

Look at the stars some clear night. They are suns outside our solar system, so far away that they appear as points of light in the blackness of space.

How distant are the stars? What kind of a measuring stick can we use for the immense spaces between the stars? Our imagination, staggered by the millions and billions of miles within the solar system, searches for a new unit to apply to the vast reaches of the space beyond—for some measure that speaks in small, familiar numbers.

We might try to use *time* to measure distance. The American Indians did that when they said that a certain place was two moons away. That meant that the distance was such that it would require two months of journeying to reach it with their limited means of travel. We can use time to make distances in the solar system comprehensible. We can figure how much time a spaceship, moving at an average rate of 17,500 miles (28,000 kilometers) per hour (fast enough to circle the earth in $1\frac{1}{2}$ hours) would take to reach the various points of interest in our planetary system. These figures have had meaning to us ever since February 20, 1962, when John H. Glenn, Jr., made three orbits around the earth, covering each orbit in about $1\frac{1}{2}$ hours, traveling at the speed of 17,500 miles (28,000 kilometers) per hour. From that day on we could think, at that (average) speed a spaceship could reach the moon in 14 hours, the sun

in 7 months and Pluto, 3.6 billion miles from earth, in 23 years.

These statistics are based on manageable units for measuring distances within the solar system. But as we leave the solar system for deeper space we get into difficulties if we use "spaceship time" to measure distances. The numbers get big again. Consequently we look for something that can zip through space at a faster rate, and we find it in a ray of light. Light takes time to travel from one point to another; we are not aware of this because it moves at the incredible speed of about 186,000 miles (300,000 kilometers) per *second*. Such a rate would send it seven times around our earth in one second.

Apply this speed-of-light scale to the distances of the moon and the sun from the earth. Light from the moon reaches the earth after a brief journey of $1\frac{1}{3}$ *seconds;* from the sun about 8 *minutes* are needed. From distant Pluto, near the outermost bounds of our known solar system, $5\frac{1}{3}$ *hours* are required. With this new scale we may now say that the moon is $1\frac{1}{3}$ seconds away from earth, the sun 8 minutes, Pluto $5\frac{1}{3}$ hours.

Now leave the solar system and travel to the stars. The nearest star and the brightest (except for our sun) that can be seen with the naked eye in the Northern Hemisphere is Sirius in the constellation Canis Major (Big Dog). Light from Sirius takes about 8 *years* to reach our eyes.

Astronomers use the speed of light as a convenient method for measuring the universe, with the *light year* as the basic unit. A light year is a measure of *distance,* not of time; it is the distance that light traveling at the speed of about 186,000 miles (300,000 kilometers) per second, traverses in one year (approximately 6 trillion miles, or 10 trillion kilometers). The star Sirius, then, is 8 light years away from us. Arcturus, another bright star, is 36 light years distant. Polaris, the North Star, is about 650 light years away.

This use of time as a cosmic yardstick suggests a fascinating idea. When you look at the North Star you are seeing the light that left it approximately 650 years ago. By now, Polaris may have moved to another place (even the so-called fixed stars of the ancients are not really stationary), or it may have exploded and become cold and dark. Our descendants 650 years hence will know the whereabouts and the condition of the present Polaris.

So, when you look at the sky tonight, you are peering not only into the vastness of space but also into events of the past. You are looking not only far into distance but also far back into time.

THE STARS

Distance, Size, and Color

Ask a young child how many stars he or she sees on a clear night and you will probably hear "thousands" or "millions." Actually, only about 2,500 to 3,000 stars can be seen with the unaided eye from any spot on earth at any time; some 6,000 stars can be seen throughout the year from the whole earth.[1] With the use of telescopes and cameras millions of stars can be detected.

Another assumption of viewers is that the ob-

[1]But this is only possible on a clear night away from the lights and smog of urban areas. In fact, astronomers are finding that even far from cities, smog diminishes the number of stars they see; this is a very clear and sensitive check on what we are doing to our atmosphere here on earth. The number of visible stars is also limited by interstellar (between the stars) dust.

served brightness of stars is indicative of their real brilliance. This illusion occurs because we have no perspective into the depth of space; all the stars appear to be at the same distance. Actually, Sirius appears bright because it is so close; Rigel in the constellation of Orion appears dimmer than Sirius because it is about 100 times as far away. However, if all the stars were moved to the same distance from the earth, Rigel would shine 700 times as brightly as Sirius.

The *apparent* brightness of a star depends on three factors: its distance from the earth, its size, and its temperature. The nearest star (except the sun) to the earth is Alpha Centauri, $4\frac{1}{3}$ light years distant. The most distant single star visible to our unaided eyes is about 3,500 light years away. The most distant star that the powerful 200-inch Hale telescope (see pp. 202–203) can isolate as an individual body is many millions of light years away. The most distant astronomical objects picked out by this telescope, called *quasars,* are estimated to be billions of light years away.

Stars vary considerably in size. Small ones, known as *white dwarfs,* may be only 10,000 miles (16,000 kilometers) or less in diameter, about the size of the earth. A *giant,* such as Antares, has a diameter 450 times that of our sun. In the range of stars from dwarf to giant, our sun is considered an average-size star.

If you look carefully at the stars in the sky, you will see that they are not all the same color. Some are reddish, some yellowish, some white, some bluish-white. The difference in the color is due to differences in the temperature of the stars. If a piece of metal is heated, it first turns red, then orange, then yellow, then white. Blacksmiths used to get a rough idea of the temperature of the iron that they were heating by watching its color. This holds true for stars also. The coolest ones are reddish, hotter ones yellowish, still hotter ones white, hottest ones blue-white. Betelgeuse (pronounced "beetle juice"), in the constellation of Orion, with a temperature of about 4000°F (2200°C), is a red star. Our sun, with a temperature of about 10,000°F (5500°C), and Capella are yellow stars. Rigel, a blue star, has a temperature of about 45,000°F (25,000°C). All these are measurable *surface* temperatures; the interiors of stars are much hotter, running into millions of degrees.

The high temperature of the sun, as we found in Chapter 7A, is not the result of burning but of nuclear reactions in which hydrogen atoms combine to form helium atoms, as in a hydrogen bomb. This is also true of the other stars of the universe.

Magnitude

We have seen how the apparent brightness of a star is determined by distance, size, and temperature. For convenience in viewing and identifying stars, astronomers classify them according to their *magnitude.* In speaking of stars, magnitude does not mean size, but brightness. The smaller the number given, the brighter the star. Thus the *first-magnitude* stars are the brightest. These are $2\frac{1}{2}$ times as bright as second-magnitude stars. A second-magnitude star is $2\frac{1}{2}$ times as bright as a third-magnitude star, and so on. The faintest star that we can ordinarily see with the unaided eye is of the sixth magnitude, but on a very dark night we can see even fainter stars. Stars a good deal fainter than the sixth magnitude can be seen only with the telescope.

There are 16 stars of the first magnitude or brighter, not counting the sun. Some of the more commonly known are Sirius, Vega, Capella, Arcturus, Rigel, Procyon, Altair, Betelgeuse, Aldebaran, Pollux, Spica, Antares, Fomalhaut, Deneb, and Regulus. Sirius, brightest of the first-magnitude stars, is not as bright as three planets in our solar system—Venus, Mars, and Jupiter.

The original brightness scale was devised about 250 B.C. by Hipparchus, a Greek astronomer. Using a scale from 1 to 6, he catalogued about 1,000 stars, using 1 for the brightest and 6 for the faintest stars. Later astronomers refined the scale and extended it to higher numbers (7, 8, and so on) to accommodate the fainter stars dis-

covered with telescopes. In order to include objects *brighter* than magnitude 1, astronomers assigned negative values to them: -1, -2, and so on (zero is also used, between 1 and -1). Thus, very bright Sirius has a magnitude of -1.5. The moon when full has a magnitude of -12.5, and the sun -26.5. There is really nothing "negative" about such brilliant objects. We have been forced to assign negative values to them because we have adhered to the method instituted by Hipparchus.

The brightness in this section refers to *apparent magnitude* as observed on earth. Such measurement does not provide a basis for comparing the amount of light emitted into space by each star. The *absolute magnitude* tells us how bright the stars would appear if all were at the same distance from the earth. Astronomers arbitrarily fix that distance at about 33 light years. Using a scale based on this distance, our sun has an absolute magnitude of $+5$. Most stars would fall between 0 and $+15$; the extreme magnitude of normal stars is between -10 to $+19$. The absolute magnitudes, then, are measures of how bright stars really are, and they represent a way of comparing the actual amount of light they emit.

Double Stars and Star Clusters

In 1650 the Italian astronomer Riccioli observed through his telescope that a star in the middle of the handle of the Big Dipper, named Mizar, was actually two stars. Mizar was the first double star to be discovered. Since then it has been found that such double stars, called *binary stars,* are very common; more than half of the stars in the starry neighborhood of the sun are members of binary or multiple-star systems.

In a binary group one star appears to revolve around the other. More accurately both revolve around their common *center of gravity,* which is a point between the centers of the two bodies. Most binary stars cannot be observed as two stars except with the aid of a telescope or spectroscope, a special instrument that combines a simple prism

Three photographs of Kruger 60, a binary star—a system of two stars that revolve around each other under the influence of their mutual gravitational attraction. The discovery of the motion of double stars was the first observational evidence that gravitation existed outside the solar system. Double stars are not exceptional; they may be the rule for the stars we see in the sky. (Courtesy of Yerkes Observatory.)

with a viewing lens (see pp. 203–205). Bright Sirius is a double star; it circles around its invisible (to the eye) partner once every 50 years.

There are also larger groups of stars, *star clusters,* held together by gravitational attraction, which move together through space. The Pleiades is such a group. You can see 6 of its members with the naked eye; with a telescope we find some 250 members. Star clusters should not be confused with *constellations,* which are configurations of stars named by the ancients for a particular object, person, or animal, or the section of the sky assigned to a particular configuration.

Variable Stars

Some individual stars change in brightness and hence are called *variable stars.* Some vary in brightness at regular intervals. The cycle from bright to dim to bright again may take from a few hours to hundreds of days or longer, depending on the star. Some binary stars, just discussed, only *appear* to vary in brightness. As the stars circle around they periodically eclipse each other with respect to our line of sight like two electric bulbs swinging around each other. Some or all of the light from the eclipsed star is prevented from reaching the earth, and the combined light is diminished. Such stars are known as *eclipsing variables.*

The type of stars known as *Cepheids* are truly variable. The star Delta Cephei, for example, takes five days and seven hours to pass from its brightest phase down to its faintest and then back again to its brightest. The light variation in a Cepheid is due to changes in the temperature of its surface. Evidence reveals also that the temperature fluctuations are accompanied by pulsations in the size of the stars. The Cepheids are part of a larger classification of variable stars known as *pulsating variables.* Polaris, the North Star, is a pulsating variable with a period of about four days.

Eruptive variables are stars that show sudden,

usually unpredictable outbursts of light. They include the *novae* and the *supernovae.*

"New" stars or novae are actually existing stars that have previously been inconspicuous and then suddenly flare up and become as much as 70,000 or 80,000 times as bright. The rise to maximum brilliance is very rapid, often taking less than one day. The subsequent decline to normal, however, may require years or decades.

An extraordinarily bright nova, a *supernova,* burst into the heavens over the southern hemisphere on February 24, 1987. Named Supernova 1987A, it appeared in the Greater Magellanic Cloud (a galaxy nearest to our Milky Way galaxy), some 160,000 light years from Earth. It was by far the closest and most easily studied since 1604.

Scientists are interested in supernovae because they are the final cataclysmic stage in the life cycle of some stars. We know more about supernovae than novae, even though they are rarer, because they leave traces that we can study. For example, Chinese records mention a blazing star that appeared in the year 1054. We have reason to believe that the explosion of this star produced a cloud of starry material observable today as the Crab Nebula, so named because of its crablike appearance. The American Indians also may have seen the 1054 supernova. Several petroglyphs found in Arizona and New Mexico show a bright star next to a crescent moon in the correct position for the time in 1054 when it was most spectacular.

In blowing away most of its "star-stuff," a supernova explosion ejects material that may go into later generations of stars and planets. This is recycling on a celestial scale. Indeed the remnants of such explosions are among the most unusual objects studied by astronomers today: pulsars, black holes, high-energy cosmic rays, high-velocity "runaway" stars hurtling through space at speeds approaching a million miles an hour, and many other products.

Pulsars are stars detected only by radio telescopes (see pp. 205–207) that "blink," giving sharp, intense radio pulses as the star rotates, one "beep" per revolution, like a lighthouse beacon.

The signal is initiated by the magnetic field of the star. Pulsars are thought to be ultradense bodies composed of the neutrons of atoms (see pp. 461–465).

Black holes are bodies so compact that their intense gravitational pull prevents light or any other kind of radiation from escaping. Obviously a black hole cannot be observed; its existence is inferred by its effect on nearby matter. A black hole is thought to be the end stage in the life of a heavy star. When its fuel runs out, the star can no longer maintain itself against its own gravity and it collapses upon itself. Nothing can escape. All that is inside is hidden from us; the star appears to disappear from the universe, but it leaves behind its gravitational field, its pull on nearby stars, and dust—like the Cheshire Cat in *Alice in Wonderland* that vanished leaving only its smile.

A Star Is Born

It is apparent, then, that we live in a dynamic universe, in which stars are born, mature, and die. According to the current theory of stellar evolution, a star comes into being through the contraction of a mass of gas and dust, a *protostar.* This stage, which may be thought of as the star's childhood, is comparatively short. Then, for most of its life, the star is fully grown (adulthood) and more or less stable. Most of the stars we see are in this state. These mature stars range from blue-white (very hot) to red (coolest) in color. The usual fate of stars as they expend their nuclear fuel is to cool and expand to become *red giants.* (If this happens to our sun it will expand until it reaches nearly to the orbit of Mars.) When most of the nuclear fuel is exhausted, red giants contract and become enormously dense *white dwarfs,* tiny stars about the size of the earth. When all energy is exhausted, these bodies are presumed to "die out" as *black dwarfs.*

The route from active, sunlike stars to dead black dwarfs probably represents the fate of most stars. But another pathway in stellar evolution is that of the supernovae, for, as we have seen, their violent explosions produce, among other effects, the material for the formation of new stars and possibly their accompanying planetary systems. Only a few stars in millions are expected to end their lives in this way. But these are giant stars, many times as massive as our sun. Betelgeuse, Antares, and Spica are possible candidates for such an end.

Motion

Even the "fixed" stars of the ancients (in contrast to the planets that were once regarded as wandering stars) are not fixed but are moving rapidly through space in various directions, although the motion is not apparent to the unaided eye during a single lifetime. Some are moving toward and some away from our solar system, most of them at speeds of many miles per second. Despite this speed, the chances that stars might collide are very small because space is so vast and the distances between stars so great. If the sun were the size of an orange, the earth would be a grain of sand 30 feet (9 meters) away and the nearest star would be another orange 1,500 miles (2,400 kilometers) away.

The speeds and directions of hundreds of stars are known to astronomers. This drifting over periods of thousands of years causes even the shape of the star patterns—the *constellations*—to change. The Big Dipper will look very different 50,000 years from now from the way it looks today.

THE CONSTELLATIONS

When night falls, the glittering sky beckons to us to join in the ancient hobby of stargazing. Primitive people long ago traced pictures of familiar objects, animals, and humans in the pattern of stars. The American Indians painted them on buffalo skins. The ancient Greeks and Romans filled the heavens with their gods and heroes.

The resemblance of groups of stars, or constellations, to these imaginary figures may be difficult for us to follow. (Indeed, the consensus of astronomers is that the constellations were not named after objects they resemble but rather in order to honor certain deities or other entities.) We may prefer to think of the stars that make up Pegasus, the Winged Horse, for example, as a baseball diamond with stars at home plate, first, second, and third base and along the right- and left-field foul lines, rather than as a horse. Whether we group stars on the basis of their mythology or in a more modern way, knowing the constellations is fun and also serves as a convenient guide for locating individual stars and other heavenly bodies.

The part of the heavens that we can see on any night is limited by the fact that we live in the Northern Hemisphere of an opaque globe. People living in the Southern Hemisphere look out on a different portion of the sky.

Our view of the heavens is also influenced by the seasons, because the earth is in different positions in its orbit around the sun in the course of a year. Some constellations can be seen only in summer and some only in winter. (Compare the star charts of June and December as shown on pp. 196 and 197.) Fortunately, there are some star groups that are always visible: the constellations around the Pole Star (North Star). Among these are the Big Bear, the Little Bear, Draco, Cassiopeia (kās-ē-ō-pē′-ya), Perseus, and Cepheus. A good way to begin your acquaintance with the stars is to find the Big Dipper, which is part of the constellation of the Big Bear, in the northern sky. (Consult the star charts for the description of the constellations in this section.) Two stars that form the part of the dipper opposite the handle are known as the "pointers." A line drawn through these pointers and extending about five times the distance between them will lead you to the Pole Star, known also as Polaris.

Polaris is also at the tip end of the handle of the Little Dipper, which is part of the constellation of the Little Bear. Polaris, although not very bright, is the brightest in the Little Dipper. The two dippers are so placed that when one is upright the

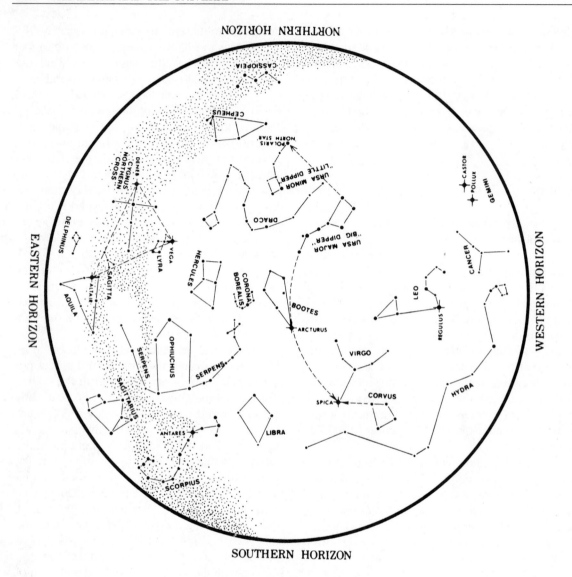

THE NIGHT SKY IN JUNE

Latitude of chart is 34°N, but it is practical throughout the continental United States.

To use: Hold chart vertically and turn it so the direction you are facing shows at the bottom.

Chart time (Local Standard):

10 p.m. First of month
9 p.m. Middle of month
8 p.m. Last of month

Star chart from Griffith Observer *monthly magazine.*

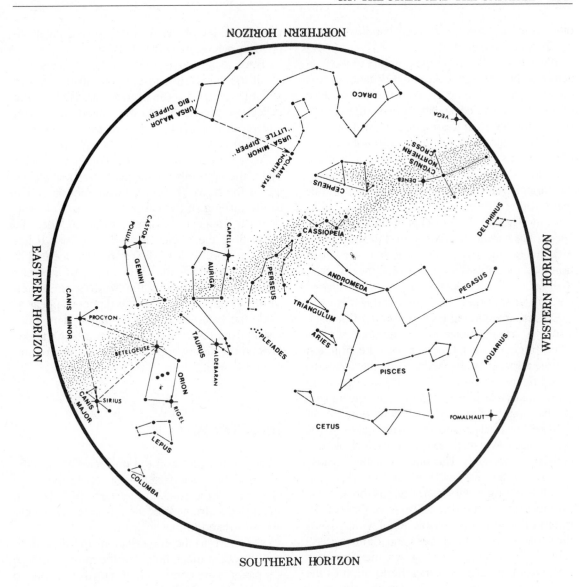

THE NIGHT SKY IN DECEMBER

Latitude of chart is 34°N, but it is practical throughout the continental United States.

To use: Hold chart vertically and turn it so the direction you are facing shows at the bottom.

Chart time (Local Standard):
10 p.m. First of month
9 p.m. Middle of month
8 p.m. Last of month

Star chart from Griffith Observer *monthly magazine.*

other is upside down, with their handles extending in opposite directions.

If you trace a line from the pointers to the Pole Star and then extend it an equal distance across the sky, you will come close to Cassiopeia. Five of the stars in this constellation make up a big W or M in the sky. Near Cassiopeia, the mythological Queen of Ethiopia, is her husband Cepheus. Cepheus forms a pattern not unlike a triangle mounted on a square. One of the most famous of the variable stars, Delta Cephei, is located in this constellation.

Come back to the Big Dipper and follow the curve of its *handle* this time to find the bright star Arcturus (ark-tū´-rus), one of the few stars mentioned in the Bible. Arcturus, which means "Bear Keeper," is located in the tail of a kite-shaped constellation, Bootes (Bō-ō´-tēz), the Herdsman.

Pegasus, mentioned earlier, is one of the outstanding constellations in the autumn sky. Its three brightest stars, together with the brightest star in adjacent Andromeda, form the four-cornered figure known as the Square of Pegasus. In Andromeda, which extends away from the Square, is a hazy patch of light. This filmy wisp in the sky is in reality a galaxy and is actually made of 100 billion stars. We shall have more to say of such collections presently. This one is notable because it is one of the very few visible to the naked eye.

A line of bright stars from Pegasus through Andromeda points the way to Perseus. One of the stars in this group is variable Algol, which has a three-day cycle of brightness and dimness. Perseus is also distinguished, as we mentioned in Chapter 7A, because it marks the location of the brilliant Perseid meteor showers that occur in August.

One of the brightest constellations and the most spectacular of the winter season is Orion, the Mighty Hunter, also named in the Bible. The three stars that make up the belt of this figure, equally spaced in a straight row, are seen even by city dwellers who glance up at the sky. The belt is in the center of a nearly rectangular figure, which makes up the body of Orion. The giant star Betelgeuse marks one corner of the rectangle, the

right shoulder of the warrior. Blazing Rigel, diagonally across, marks his left leg.

Trace along Orion's belt to the brightest star in all the sky, Sirius, in the constellation of the Great Dog. Sirius is the nearest star visible to the naked eye for viewers in the United States. You will recall that light reaches us from the sun in eight *minutes* and from Sirius in eight *years.*

As we watch the sky on a pleasant summer night, the constellations appear to wheel slowly across the heavens. This apparent motion is due to the turning of the earth on its axis. One star, however, appears virtually fixed in the sky throughout the night. This is Polaris, which lies over the North Pole of the earth, over one end of the axis on which the earth turns. All the stars seem to revolve around the North Star. Constellations close to it, such as the dippers, appear to circle the Pole Star during the night. Stars more distant from Polaris trace bigger circles in the sky; those most distant appear to rise in the east and set in the west.

THE MILKY WAY

What is our address in the universe? What is the place of our solar system—the earth, the other planets, and the sun—in the starry sky? What, in short, is the structure of the universe, and where are we located in that structure?

If we turn to the constellations for an answer, we do not get much help. For the most part these sky patterns are composed of stars that happen to lie approximately in the same direction from the earth. When we look outward, our eyes cannot discern the *depth* of space. No wonder the ancients thought that the sky was a round dome studded with twinkling lights. They thought of it as a *celestial sphere* with the North Star, Polaris, as one of the pivot points about which the celestial sphere rotates. Of course, we know that it is the earth that turns, but we use the celestial sphere as an imaginary surface for locating all objects in the sky. Careful observations and calculations by astronomers have revealed that although all the stars *seem* to be equally far away, some of them are great distances beyond others.

The constellations in themselves do not reveal the three-dimensional structure of space. Then how are the stars arranged? If we look up at the heavens on a clear night, away from city lights, we see stretching across the sky a broad luminous band—the Milky Way. Examination even with a pair of binoculars or a small telescope reveals that the Milky Way consists of billions of stars, so concentrated in depth in the direction in which we are looking that they make a "milky" band in the sky. The sky on either side of the milky band has many fewer stars; the farther from the Milky Way, the fewer the stars. What does all of this reveal about the organization of stars?

Astronomers puzzling over this have concluded that we are in the midst of a huge disk, or pinwheel-shaped collection of stars. They call this Milky Way system the *galaxy* (a word derived from the Greek *gala,* which means milk). Because we are within this disk of stars our vision is somewhat obscured. It might help in our understanding if we could view our galaxy from the outside. We would then see it as a giant pinwheel made of billions of stars, one of these our sun, rotating slowly around a compact, brilliant center. Now adopt the viewpoint of an observer inside the pinwheel. Look toward the edge of the wheel: A thick conglomeration of stars in the form of a band is seen. If you look toward the sides of the wheel, however, fewer stars are observed.

Our Milky Way, then, is a view from inside the great galaxy of stars in which we are situated. All the stars that can be seen with the naked eye and most of those observed with telescopes are a part of the Milky Way system, which contains about 100 billion stars. However, there is ample space within our galaxy—enough to hold billions of times as many stars as it does.

How big is our galaxy? To measure it, we again use the speed of light as our yardstick. We calculated previously that, if we traveled at the speed of light, it would take us a little over 1 second to reach the moon, 8 minutes to reach the sun, and

$4\frac{1}{3}$ years to reach the nearest star. Traveling at this speed, about 186,000 miles (300,000 kilometers) per second, it would take us about 100,000 years to go from one edge of the galaxy to the other and about 10,000 years to go across its great thickness. Our galaxy, then, is a wheel about 100,000 light years across and 10,000 light years thick.

Just where is the solar system in this wheel? Astronomers say that we are roughly 30,000 light years away from the center out toward the rim of the wheel and in the central *plane* of the wheel (see illustration on p. 200).

The whole galaxy is turning like a pinwheel. All the stars are revolving in the same direction around the center, but at different speeds. Despite the fact that our sun and its solar system are moving at 155 miles (250 kilometers) per second in a roughly circular orbit, it takes more than 200 million years to complete a revolution around the center.

Perhaps a better understanding of our galaxy can be gotten by looking at another one, at a galaxy outside our Milky Way system. The best known of these is the Great Spiral in Andromeda, which is revealed by telescopes as a collection of 100 billion stars with spiral arms like those of a Fourth of July pinwheel. Pictured at the opening of this chapter is the famous Whirlpool Spiral Galaxy in the constellation Canes Venatici (Hunting Dogs), with distinct spiral arms. This galaxy, like the Andromeda Galaxy, has been likened to our galaxy in shape and in its starry population. Other types of galaxies include the *barred spirals,* the *ellipticals,* and the *irregulars.*

Our Milky Way is one of a cluster of 19 known local galaxies, called the *local group,* which cover a region about 3 million light years in diameter. The three largest members are all spiral galaxies: our Milky Way galaxy, the Andromeda galaxy, and the Spiral galaxy in Triangulum. Beyond the local group we find other groups of galaxies. As far as we can see in all directions we find galaxies and clusters of galaxies. Recent large-scale surveys of the population of stars indicate the existence of *superclusters:* Each is composed of many clusters of galaxies. Our galaxy and its local group lie in

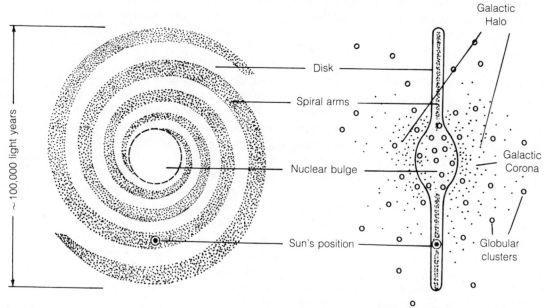

Schematic representation of our galaxy and the sun's place in it as seen (on the left) from the south side of the galactic plane. Compare with the photograph of the Whirlpool Galaxy (which resembles ours) at the beginning of the chapter. On the right is a section through our galaxy. *(From* Exploration of the Universe *by Abell, Morrison, and Wolff, copyright 1987 by Saunders College Publishing.)*

the so-called Local Supercluster. Two other well-defined superclusters are named Hercules and Perseus.

It has been estimated that there are at least 10 billion galaxies in the universe.

BETWEEN THE STARS

How empty is "empty space"? By earthly standards, *interstellar space* (space between stars) is empty, because we have not been able to obtain a vacuum in our laboratories that is as devoid of matter as is the space between the stars. Astronomers have found, however, that there are vast clouds of dust and gas in the almost complete vacuum of space. The term *nebula* (plural *nebulae*) refers to such clouds, some of which are located in our Milky Way and some outside in other galaxies. The universe is probably half stardust.

Relatively dense opaque clouds of dust and gas produce the *dark nebulae*. These clouds are either thick enough to obscure a considerable portion of the starlight passing through them or too far from a star that is bright enough to illuminate the nebulae. They appear as dark curtains, dimming or hiding the stars behind them. The head of the "horse" in the Horsehead Nebula in Orion is part of a dark nebula.

In other nebulae, starlight is scattered or reflected by the interstellar dust so that the dust itself becomes illuminated by the starlight. These are called *reflection nebulae,* an example of which is to be found around each of the brightest stars in the Pleiades cluster.

In some nebulae, known as *emission nebulae,* the gas near the hot stars glows by a process of fluorescence, in which light of one wavelength is absorbed and readmitted at another wavelength. (An example of fluoresence is the conversion of invisible ultraviolet into visible light in a household fluorescent lamp.) Easily seen with binoculars is such a nebula in the middle of the Hunter's sword in the constellation of Orion.

The gas of interstellar space is mostly hydrogen, but it also includes helium, oxygen, and other elements. Hydrogen also makes up most of the gas that is found in stars. It is theorized that all the chemical elements of the stars were manufactured out of hydrogen by nuclear processes (see p. 150), and that this process is still going on.

The clouds of dust and gas in space are of special interest to astronomers, for it is thought that it is out of a compression of such stuff that stars are born. As stars age, cool, and die, by nova and supernova explosions, they return to space a great deal of the gas and dust of which they were originally formed. Then new stars are made again from these clouds.

Thus, as older stars come to the end of their cycle, they provide the material for the birth of new stars. It is thought that our sun is a second-generation star, having been formed about 5 billion years ago from material part or most of which was ejected from older stars.

THE UNIVERSE

Just as a child becomes aware of larger and larger units of space—home, neighborhood, city, and so on—so have astronomers discovered a hierarchy in the heavens. Our galaxy, 100,000 light years in diameter, is only one of the billions of galaxies that make up the universe.

To come back to the original question about our address in the universe, the best answer that can be given at this time is as follows:

Planet: Earth
    Star: Our Sun
        Galaxy: Milky Way
            Clusters of Galaxies: Local Group
                Supercluster: Local Supercluster
                    Universe

One more thought about our address in space. If you were to return to your hometown after an absence of several years, you would be astonished if you found that the distances between all the houses had increased so that your next-door neighbor was now a mile away, and the whole town was spread out over an area 10,000 times its original size. If for each house you substitute a galaxy, you are now prepared to understand what astronomers call an expanding universe. The nature of the expansion can be understood by likening the universe to a loaf of raisin bread, and each galaxy to a raisin in it. Too much yeast has been put into the dough and the bread doubles in size in one hour. What will happen to the raisins? Select one raisin, and imagine that you are an observer on it. What will happen to the other raisins seen from your viewpoint during the one hour that the bread is growing?

1. All the raisins move away from you.
2. Since each raisin doubles its distance from you, those that are farther away appear to move faster than those that are closer.
3. The same observations as the two preceding ones would be made by an observer on any of the raisins. (Of course in the universe there is no pervading medium to carry the galaxies apart.)

The study of distant galaxies with the instrument called a *spectroscope* (see pp. 203–205) indicates that the galaxies are fleeing from each other at a terrific rate, some at a speed of 75,000 miles (120,000 kilometers) per second, or about two fifths the speed of light. Astronomers have also found that the farther away galaxies are from us, the faster they are moving. It should be made clear that the expansion in the "expanding universe" refers to the increase in the space between galaxies and not to the size of the galaxies themselves. Thus, our lonely address in the vastness of space becomes lonelier as our neighbors become more and more distant.

If the universe is expanding, it follows that all the matter of the universe must have once been close together. This suggests that some original "explosion" may have started the universe expanding, from a single, compact mass to its present size. Astronomers calculate that the "big bang" that began the universe occurred some 18 billion years ago.

HOW THE STARS ARE STUDIED

The basic equipment that humans possess for the exploration of the heavens are their eyes, intelligence, and imaginations. To aid the senses humans have invented devices such as the telescope, camera, spectroscope, and radio telescope. With these and other instruments, we have measured the distances and sizes of stars, estimated their temperatures, analyzed their composition, charted their motions, and described their evolution. Let us take a brief look at some astronomical instruments.

Telescope

In 1928 George Ellery Hale, an American astronomer, made a plea for the construction of a large new telescope. Hale based his plea on three unsolved problems of astronomy: the evolution of stars, the structure of the universe, and the composition of matter. A grant made possible the construction of a 200-inch (500-centimeter) telescope and led to the establishment of an observatory on Palomar Mountain, California. The telescope went into operation in 1948 (see pp. 212–214).

The Hale telescope, like all others, gives us a bigger "eye" because it can gather more light than the human eye and because it can magnify the view. The Hale telescope is an example of a *reflecting* telescope, using a large circular mirror 200 inches across (almost 17 feet or 5 meters) to collect and focus the light of stars. The *refracting* telescope, on the other hand, uses a lens to gather and focus light. Galileo used a refracting telescope when he explored the heavens and discovered the plains, mountains, and craters of our moon, and the satellites revolving around the planet Jupiter.

In both kinds of telescopes, reflector and refractor, the image is magnified by a lens in the eyepiece through which one looks. Both are referred to as *optical* telescopes.

The Yerkes refracting telescope, the largest of its kind in the world, has a light-gathering lens 40 inches (100 centimeters) in diameter. The telescope is 60 feet (18 meters) long and is located at Williams Bay, Lake Geneva, Wisconsin. The second largest refractor is the 36-inch (90-centimeter) telescope at the Lick Observatory of the University of California on Mount Hamilton, California.

The reflecting Hale telescope, with the light-gathering power of a million eyes, has taken thousands of photographs of distant stars and galaxies. With it astronomers have detected objects billions of light years away. A major discovery made with this huge light-gathering instrument was that of *quasars*, believed to be the most brilliant, energy-laden heavenly objects known. Other contributions include studies relating to galaxies, pulsars, and the evolution of stars.

Projects for new astronomical equipment have been initiated, first to make it possible to gather more light to see fainter objects and second, to see more detail in these objects. Recently developed techniques for making larger mirrors and for combining a number of mirrors are intended to satisfy the first need. Responding to the second are new methods of combining signals from widely spaced telescopes, thereby increasing the resolution of detail through an optical process known as *interferometry*.

Telescopes are usually placed near mountaintops because the air there is generally freer of dust and haze, and the location is usually distant from the lights of cities. A site on Antarctica is contemplated because of the dryness of air there. Telescopes are protected from the weather by domes that open to the sky. Motors turn the telescope so that it moves westward to compensate for the eastward rotation of the earth. Thus, heavenly bodies "stand still" for prolonged observation.

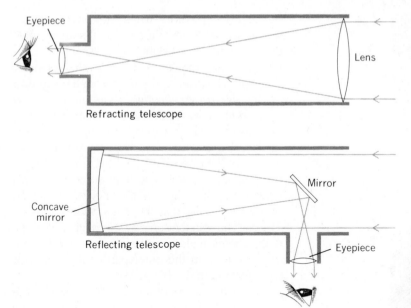

Eyepiece

Lens

Refracting telescope

Concave mirror

Mirror

Reflecting telescope

Eyepiece

In a refracting telescope, light from distant objects is gathered and focused by a lens. In a reflecting telescope, light is gathered and focused by a concave mirror.

Camera

No longer does the astronomer spend much time looking through a telescope. Instead, the eyepiece is replaced with a photographic plate or film, and the astronomer concentrates on keeping the "picture" in view. Thus, the telescope becomes a camera. The human eye, even when aided by a telescope, has limitations; it tires after a while. It is not sensitive to color in dim light. It cannot retain images very long, hence it cannot build up weak images into strong ones. The camera overcomes these limitations: It does not tire. Film can be made that is very sensitive to light and to different colors. Film can retain and build up weak images into strong ones, even if it takes several nights of exposure for the same picture. As a consequence we can photograph through a telescope and detect stars that are too faint to be seen with the eye through the same telescope.

A recently invented device, the *electronic camera*, does its work by intensifying starlight by electronic means. The new and brighter image is then photographed by conventional methods.

Other devices include infrared, X-ray, and gamma-ray detectors, which go beyond the range of visible light.

All large astronomical telescopes are used almost exclusively as cameras, equipped with electronic gear, rather than as instruments for direct viewing. It is through the use of photography that scientists all over the world are working together, charting each section of the heavens to obtain a more detailed picture of the universe and a better understanding of its evolution.

Spectroscope

How can we know the chemical composition of the stars? The answer lies in the fact that the light emitted by heavenly bodies, when analyzed, furnishes scientists with evidence of the types of atoms that are present there. Let us see how scientists analyze starlight.

When sunlight passes through one side of a glass prism a rainbow of colors, called a *spectrum,* emerges from the other side. The white light of

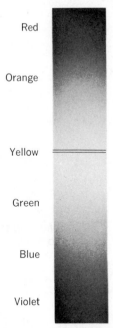

Red

Orange

Yellow

Green

Blue

Violet

The spectroscope, when used with a telescope, provides information about the chemical composition of stars. Each chemical element has its own "fingerprint." In the illustration two dark lines in the yellow part of the spectrum indicate the presence of sodium in the outer gaseous region of the star under observation.

the sun is a mixture of different colors. The prism bends each of these colors at a slightly different angle and fans out the white light into its component colors.

A special instrument called a *spectroscope* combines the simple prism with a viewing lens. If sunlight is examined with a spectroscope the colors separated out by the prism are segregated further into a long band ranging in color from red through orange, yellow, green, and blue, to violet. With a good spectroscope and keen eyes it can be seen that the sun's spectrum is not really continuous, but that it is crossed by narrow, vertical dark lines.

Scientists have found that each of the known chemical elements, if heated to glowing in the laboratory, produces a different and characteristic

"keyboard" of colors when viewed through a spectroscope. Thus, the element sodium produces two separate bright yellow "keys" in a definite place on the keyboard. No other element does this. However, if the light from the sun or a distant star passes *through* a gas on its way to Earth, *dark lines* appear, as the elements in that gas absorb certain wavelengths of light. Each particular element can absorb only certain wavelengths of light peculiar to it. Thus, in the case of sodium, dark lines appear. If an astronomer finds evidence of these lines in the spectrum of a star, he or she knows that the star contains sodium. The dark lines in the sun's spectrum give evidence of the chemical elements between us and the sun, most of them in the outer part of the sun itself (see illustration on this page).

In practice, astronomers combine the spectroscope and the telescope so that light gathered by the telescope from distant bodies is passed through a spectroscope for analysis. A photographic plate is combined with the spectroscope to make a permanent record of the spectrum. When used in this way the instrument is called a *spectrograph*.

Astronomers knowing the color "chord" of each element are able to determine the chemical makeup of a particular star by examining its light with the spectrograph. Some of the astronomical findings that have resulted from this technique are as follows:

1. The sun's atmosphere is composed of many chemical elements; its main constituent is hydrogen.
2. Most stars have a chemical composition similar to that of the sun.
3. The chemical elements glowing in the sun and the stars are the same as those found on Earth. Incidentally, the element helium was first discovered in a spectroscopic view of the sun and later found on Earth.

In addition to determining the chemical makeup of celestial bodies, the spectrograph tells us whether a star or galaxy is approaching us or receding from us. To understand how this is possible it is necessary to understand the *Doppler effect*. Perhaps you have noticed that when a train that is sounding its whistle passes you and speeds away its pitch drops. The apparent change of pitch in *sound* has its parallel in the world of *light*. Motion (with respect to the listener) can change the frequency and, therefore, the pitch of a sound wave. Motion (with respect to an observer) can also change the frequency and, therefore, the color of a light wave. As a source of light moves away from you its color spectrum shifts toward the red end as viewed in the spectroscope. The amount the spectrum lines shift from their normal position gives us a measure of the speed of recession. It was this technique that enabled Edwin Hubble in 1929 to discover that all galaxies are rushing away from each other.

The spectrograph is a valuable astronomical instrument for other reasons.

1. The spectrograph reveals the temperature of individual stars.
2. It may tell whether the body emitting the light rays is solid or gaseous.
3. It reveals the presence of invisible gases between the visible source and us.
4. It may tell whether a body is rotating.
5. It may tell us about the magnetic field of a star.
6. It tells us about the ingredients of the atmospheres of other planets.

Radio Telescope

All of us have had the experience of picking up static on our radios. Static is caused by a jumble of radio waves of different wavelengths. Your radio converts this jumble into "noise," or static, just as it converts regular broadcasts that are beamed over a single wavelength into the sound of music or speech. Static may originate from human-made electrical disturbance, such as that caused by a nearby power line. Static is also nature-made, occurring during lightning storms and, as we found in Chapter 7A, during periods of great solar activity.

In 1931 Karl G. Jansky, an electrical engineer at the Bell Telephone Laboratories, was experimenting with large antennas for long-range radio communication when he encountered interference in the form of radio "static" coming from an unknown source. He concluded from his investigations that the radio disturbance was coming from outer space.

This theory was tested and confirmed by Grote Reber, a radio engineer who, in 1938, built an aerial shaped like an upside-down umbrella, 30 feet in diameter, to scan the skies for radio waves. With this aerial and a sensitive radio Reber plotted the first radio map of the sky. Reber's maps showed that the signals were strongest in the Milky Way region.

Using improvised *radio telescopes,* as these sensitive radios were called, astronomers were able to focus on particular points in space where the signals were strong. These points were called "radio sources." At first, strangely enough, only a small fraction of the radio sources that were located corresponded to objects seen with conventional telescopes. Hundreds of these sources were noted and plotted on new radio maps of the skies.

The radio telescope enables us to detect heavenly objects and celestial events that optical devices had failed to reveal. This new instrument for penetrating space operates day and night. Radio telescopes are not affected by atmospheric conditions, except for human-made radio interference. As interest mounted, new posts were set up all over the world to tune in on these radio waves and to discover more of these radio sources.

Radio astronomy has made it possible to explore certain dark areas in the sky where interstellar dust and gas have blocked the light from our conventional telescopes. With the radio telescope we have found that galaxies are larger than we thought they were. The arms of our own spiral Milky Way have thus been traced out into what seemed to be "empty" space. We have also found that what we have called empty space between the stars is not really empty; it contains hydrogen and other gases. Radio telescopes found faint ra-

The 1,000-foot (300-meter) dish of the Arecebo Observatory in Puerto Rico makes it the largest single radio telescope in the world. The enormous dish lies immobile in the earth, but the receiving and transmitting equipment in the triangular platform hangs 50 stories in the air and can be steered and pointed by remote control equipment on the ground. In this way it can record objects over a wide area of the sky. The dish not only records feeble radio signals from the remote universe but can also be used to study the surface of the planets and the earth's atmosphere. *(Courtesy of Cornell University National Astronomy and Ionosphere Center, under contract with the National Science Foundation.)*

diations from every direction in the skies, possibly the radiations left over from the explosive moments of the big bang at the creation of the universe.

Radio telescopes are extremely important tools in astronomy. They are penetrating deeper into space than optical telescopes and are providing us with significant clues about the structure of the universe and about its past and future.

Space Probes and Space Telescopes

Hundreds of space probes have been launched since 1957. Chapter 7A told some of the remarkable findings resulting from the space flights to Mercury, Venus, Mars, the moon, Jupiter, Saturn, Uranus, and Neptune. (See also Chapter 20A for a discussion of space vehicles.) In addition, credit

The world's most impressive radio telescope is the *Very Large Array* near Socorro, New Mexico. It consists of 27 individual radio antennas arranged along 3 arms, forming a Y-shaped array. The multiple antennas' observations are combined to give a more accurate image of the source (a star or galaxy) than a single one could. *(Courtesy of National Radio Astronomy Observatory operated by Associated Universities, Inc. under contract with the National Science Foundation.)*

is given to the space probes for the discovery of the Van Allen radiation belts, the mapping of the earth's magnetic field, and other significant findings. Mounted on orbiting satellites controlled from the earth, but high above the dust and turbulence of the atmosphere, telescopes and other instruments are revealing hitherto unavailable information about stars and galaxies and about the nature of interstellar space.

Much hope is placed on the space telescope, shown on page 102, the largest astronomical telescope ever orbited, scheduled to be launched by the Space Shuttle sometime in the early 1990s. It is a conventional reflecting telescope, but it is expected to obtain much sharper images than earth-based telescopes, enabling astronomers to see seven times farther into space. The space telescope will be equipped with two spectrographs that can measure the spectra of very distant quasars, and thereby reveal the properties of the universe 10 billion years ago, more than halfway back to the "big bang": the beginning of time. There is the intriguing prospect that it may be able to observe galaxies in the process of formation and help explain how our own galaxy came into being billions of years ago.

Perhaps some day our space instruments may announce the existence of other solar systems in space and of other planets that resemble earth.

IMPORTANT GENERALIZATIONS

Distance in the universe is so great that astronomers measure it in light years.

Constellations are patterns of stars that lie in the same area of the sky.

The apparent nightly motion of the stars is due to the turning of the earth.

The apparent brightness of a star depends on its distance from the earth, its size, and its temperature.

When we view the stars and galaxies we are not only looking far out into distance but also far back into time.

The Milky Way is our inside view of the great wheel-shaped galaxy of stars in which our solar system is located.

Our sun is one of 100 billion stars in our Milky Way galaxy. It seems so bright because we happen to live near it.

The stars we observe are of many different ages.

The stars in the Milky Way are revolving around its center.

Other galaxies resembling ours exist.

In the nearly perfect vacuum in the space between the stars there are vast clouds of dust and gas.

These clouds may be the raw material for the formation of new stars and planets.

Stars are born, they mature, grow old, and "die," some by violent explosions.

The astronomical hierarchy in which we live, according to the most recent knowledge, is planet, star, galaxy, local group of galaxies, supercluster, universe.

Everything in the universe is in motion.

We live in an expanding universe, with galaxies racing from each other at great speeds.

According to the "big bang" theory the universe started from a compact mass some 18 billion years ago.

The most important instruments for exploring the universe have been the telescope, camera, spectrograph, and radio telescope.

In recent years such instruments as photometers, image intensifiers, infrared, X-ray, and gamma-ray detectors, and many others have been added to the tools of the astronomer.

Space probes, space stations, and space shuttles carry astronomical instruments to positions where more information may be gathered.

DISCOVERING FOR YOURSELF[2]

1. Read several issues of *Science News, Sky and Telescope, Astronomy, Planetary Report,* or *Mercury* (see the bibliography) to learn about new astronomical discoveries. How do these discoveries modify or add to the knowledge reported in Chapters 7A and 8A?

2. Observe a planet. Tell at what hour and in what sky location you saw it.[3]

3. Observe the moon through a pair of binoculars. Record your observations.

4. Do further reading about sunspots. Be prepared to discuss your findings from the standpoint of importance to humans.

5. Find out when the next partial or total eclipse of the moon and sun will take place. Consult the magazines listed in item 1, or write to the U.S. Naval Observatory in Washington, D.C. for their advance bulletins of eclipses.

6. Obtain and discuss the latest information about current space probes of the planets.

7. Try to observe meteorites in a local museum and find out their histories. Watch a meteor shower on one of the dates given in Chapter 7A. From what directions do the meteors appear to come? How many meteors do you see in an hour?

8. Observe the moon for a two-week period. Record the time of observation and location in the sky. Keep a record (by making a line drawing) of its appearance.

9. Look at Venus through a pair of strong binoculars or a telescope. Does this planet show phases like those of the moon? Why?

[2]This section gives suggestions for both of the astronomy chapters, 7A and 8A.

[3]Consult the current issues of *Science and Children* (published by NSTA, 1742 Connecticut Avenue, N.W. Washington, D.C. 20009) for information about the planets and stars for each month.

10. For information about asteroids, write Joseph and Diane Flowers, Route 4, Box 446, Wilson, NC 27893, for "Tonight's Asteroids"—free if you enclose a self-addressed, stamped envelope.

11. Find the North Star and make a drawing of the constellations near it that you can see on a clear night.

12. Locate as many first-magnitude stars as you can.

13. Make four observations of the Big Dipper at intervals on the same night. Make a drawing of your observations.

14. Look at the stars, planets, and the moon through a telescope and describe your experience.

15. With a pair of binoculars or a telescope try to observe the following: the double star Mizar in the Big Dipper (middle star in the handle), and the bright nebula in Orion, a cloud of dust and gas out of which stars are forming (look for it just below the easternmost of the three belt stars in Orion).

16. Are galaxies streaming toward a "Great Attractor?" See *Scientific American,* September 1987.

17. Read on page 164 in Chapter 7A how the existence of an atmosphere on Pluto was confirmed by the occultation of a distant star. What would you expect to observe if there were *no* atmosphere on this planet?

TEACHING "THE STARS AND THE UNIVERSE"

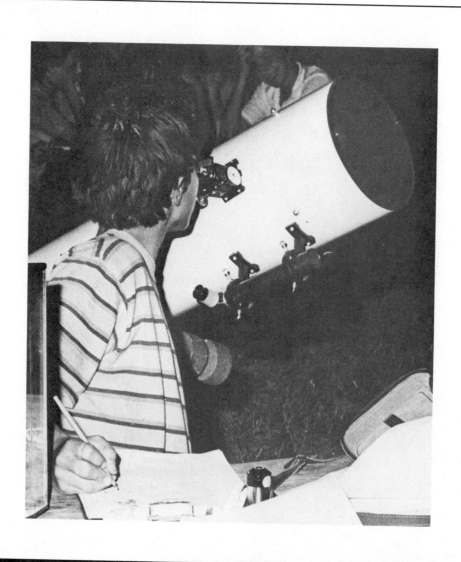

With each new space conquest, children themselves are projected into space—in thought, in imagination, in feeling.

Although the vastness of space is indeed difficult to comprehend, some knowledge of the distances and some observations of stars and star groups will increase the interest and appreciation of children for the vast universe in which our solar system and the earth are but tiny specks.

There is no adequate substitute for actual observation of the night sky. We can help children know the stars and star groups by suggesting that they look for the easy-to-find ones first. Suggest that they look for just one star or one constellation on any evening. In this way they can begin to recognize some of the prominent features of the night sky. Give them specific instructions about the hours, direction, and how far up in the sky to look for each observation. Following this activity the children can describe what they have seen and make additional notes from charts and books. Many of the general suggestions given in Chapter 7B are also appropriate to use here.

SOME BROAD CONCEPTS

The apparent motion of stars each night is due to the turning of the earth.

The apparent brightness of a star depends on its distance from the earth, its size, and its temperature.

The Milky Way is one of thousands of galaxies that form the universe.

The use of instruments has been very important in the study of astronomy.

Our solar system is a tiny speck in the vast Milky Way.

Distances in the universe are measured in light years.

Everything in the universe is in motion.

Our sun is a star.

Constellations are patterns of stars.

FOR YOUNGER CHILDREN

Obviously the investigations of many of the following problems must be done at night, and in many situations a night meeting with younger children is impractical. A knowledgeable adult can help younger children make some easy observations of the night sky. Under most circumstances we must rely on parents or other adults to help children at home with night observation. In a city environment, sky observations are difficult to make because of the lights and buildings. Still, children like to talk about their experiences in looking at the night sky.

What Can We Discover by Looking at the Night Sky?[1]

Urge students to report their night sky observations. Suggest that they try to watch a particular part of the sky after sunset to see what happens as it gets dark. Many will report as follows: Stars do not all look the same. Some are brighter than others. They are not all the same color. Some twinkle. Some stars are in groups. They do not appear at the same time in the evening.

Help students by making sketches of the most easily found star groups, such as the Big and Little Dippers, Orion, Cassiopeia, and so on. Use this opportunity to help children tell the directions by suggesting in which areas certain star groups can be found. Urge children to take the drawings of star groups home to use in their observations. Let them try to make their own drawings and show them to the class. Suggest that they attempt to count the stars to give them an idea of the vast number.

If possible, suggest that they observe the Big Dipper at different times of the evening to see how it changes.

Use star maps to supplement or substitute for the observations. For city children who cannot easily make night observations a visit to a planetarium is especially helpful, as are photographs and diagrams of the night sky.

[1]K.E. Hill, *Exploring the Natural World with Young Children* (New York: Harcourt Brace Jovanovich, 1976). Exploring the sky with young children.

Why Does the Sun Look Smaller Than the Earth Even Though It Is Larger?

Show pictures or models of the sun and the earth that illustrate their relative sizes. There are many experiences that children may have to help them understand the relationship of distance and size— an airplane on the ground and the same airplane high in the sky, for instance. Why does the plane look smaller in the sky? Other illustrations include the following: Two children the same size and height are standing together. One walks to the far end of the playground. Why do they now appear to be different sizes? Two flashlights that are about equal in brightness are observed. One is carried some distance away from observers; the other is near at hand. Now are they the same brightness? Why? This may lead to an understanding that stars look small because they are far away although many of them are much larger than the sun.

Other Problems for Younger Children

1. How do telescopes help astronomers?
2. How is the light from the moon different from the light from the sun?
3. How are stars different from each other?
4. Why are some stars brighter than others?
5. Why can't we see stars during the day?

FOR OLDER CHILDREN

How Can We Find the Constellations?[2]

A first look at the sky on a clear night is a thrilling and awesome sight. It's also confusing if you are

[2]G. L. Mallon, "An Introduction to Constellation Study," *Science and Children* (November 1976); *Helping Children Learn Earth–Space Science* (Washington, D.C.: NSTA, 1971). Many articles, with diagrams, on constellations and stars. G. L. Mallon, "Star Gazing Nights for the Community," *Science and Children* (May 1980). Very helpful sky maps and sky calendar are available each month in *Science and Children*.

trying for the first time to learn your way around. Use some of the suggestions for observing the sky for use with younger children. Discuss the observations children make. Suggest that students try to locate some of the most easily identified star groups, one or a few at a time. Start with the Big Dipper, part of the constellation Ursa Major. If the teacher draws the constellation on the board, relating its position to some prominent landmark, students can find it more easily.

The North Star (Polaris) is easy to locate from the Big Dipper (see the star map, p. 196, and the diagram on p. 213). The two stars opposite the handle are the pointers. A line drawn through these stars away from the Dipper's bottom for a length of about five times the distance between the pointers will locate the North Star. A simple map that the children have sketched will help them to locate the North Star at night. Students can be urged to use a compass in determining the section of the sky where the North Star is located. If they find north, then look up to the sky about halfway from the horizon to straight overhead, they will see the star. There are several constellations in the area of the sky surrounding the North Star (see star map, p. 196).

The constellation Orion is another interesting group and is easily found in the southern sky in the winter months. Three bright stars mark Orion's belt. With the use of the star map the rest of the constellation can be located.

A device for showing star groups can be made from a cardboard box. Leave the cover on, and remove one end of the box. Cut several pieces of paper the size of the end of the box, and on each piece make one constellation by punching holes to represent the stars. Use a flashlight to illuminate the inside of the box. When the constellation cards are held over the open end of the box, the light shines through the holes and the constellation shows up very well, especially if the room is darkened. The details about the kind of paper to use, the brightness of the light, the shape of the box, and so forth, can be worked out by students and the teacher. Another easily made device is constructed from a cylindrical cereal box, as

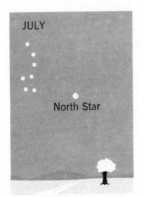   

The Big Dipper is one of the easiest star groups to identify. Since it may be used to locate the North Star, it is one of the most important in orienting a stargazer. Observing it at different times of the night helps pupils understand the effect of the earth's rotation on what we see in the night sky. Observing it at the same time of night during different seasons, as shown in the illustration, leads to an understanding of our changing view of the stars as the earth orbits the sun.

shown on this page. The constellations are made by punching holes in the bottom. Students will think of ways to remove the circular bottom piece and insert similar pieces, each with a different constellation.

Constellations may also be represented on pieces of large paper placed against a bright window, with holes to represent individual stars. Remember that one successful identification night trip outdoors is worth more than any number of these paper representations.

Other Problems for Older Children

1. How do stars differ from each other?
2. How are stars different from planets?
3. Why do stars appear to twinkle?

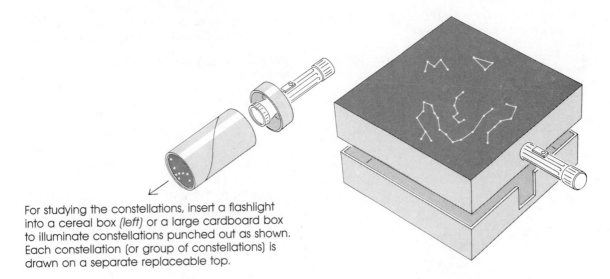

For studying the constellations, insert a flashlight into a cereal box *(left)* or a large cardboard box to illuminate constellations punched out as shown. Each constellation (or group of constellations) is drawn on a separate replaceable top.

4. Do stars appear to move during the night? Why?
5. Do stars appear to move during the year? Why?
6. How do stars get their light?
7. Why are stars different colors?
8. Why do we see a "milky way"?
9. What constellations near Ursa Major can you locate?
10. What is a light year? How can it be used to measure distances?
11. What is a galaxy? Are there other galaxies in space?
12. What is a nova?
13. What is a black hole?
14. What is meant by the "big bang" theory about the universe?

RESOURCES TO INVESTIGATE WITH CHILDREN[3]

1. A telescope in a local observatory, or a smaller telescope owned by an amateur astronomer, for viewing the moon and other objects in the night sky.
2. The evening sky, to observe visible planets and to see the moon through binoculars.
3. The daytime and night sky, to observe the moon and its shape and location in relation to the sun.
4. Meteorites in a local museum collection.
5. Magazine and newspaper accounts of current astronomical discoveries.
6. A local amateur astronomer, to answer questions about astronomy.
7. Leaders of Scouts and 4-H Clubs, to conduct evening trips to study the heavens.

[3]This section suggests resources to investigate for both astronomy chapters.

8. Aeronautic and marine personnel in the community, for information about the uses of the heavenly bodies in navigating and about constellations seen in other parts of the world.
9. Various persons in the community, for binoculars to use in observing the moon.
10. Local planetarium, if there is one in your vicinity.
11. A solar energy collector, if one is available in the community.

PREPARING TO TEACH[4]

1. Plan ways to make a model of the solar system that could be used in the classroom or outdoors (see Chapter 7B). Describe how you would help children make such a model, and develop some of the objectives you would expect to achieve as a result.
2. Assemble up-to-date bulletin board material and plan how it may be displayed and used to help children learn some of the concepts in the astronomy chapters. (Magazines, newspapers, science organizations, and so on, are good sources.)
3. Find out how to make a sundial, and prepare a plan that you can utilize in teaching children how to make and use it.
4. Prepare a large-sized star map showing how to locate a dozen of the easiest-to-locate constellations. Work out plans for using the map with children to help them plan and draw one for their own use.
5. Devise a demonstration that will help students understand how, during an eclipse, a much smaller body, the moon, can blot out a much larger body, the sun. Plan how you would use the demonstration.

[4]This section suggests ideas for preparing to teach for both astronomy chapters.

THE AIR AND
THE WEATHER

> *The atmosphere is the working fluid of the earth's heat engine. Most of the radiant energy arriving from the sun is converted into atmospheric heat energy before it is reradiated into space.... Both the short-term fluctuations of the atmospheric system (the weather) and the long-term fluctuations of the average weather (the climate) are an important part of earth history.*
>
> ANDREW P. INGERSOL, SCIENTIFIC AMERICAN, SEPTEMBER 1983

THE OCEAN OF AIR

In the Space Age we have risen from the bottom of the ocean of air to gain a new viewpoint of the earth and its enveloping atmosphere. With the television eyes of satellites permanently circling in space around the earth we now look *down* at the weather map that nature draws in the sky with clouds. Observations made by the satellites provide warnings of hurricanes and other catastrophic weather, enabling people to strengthen levees, take shelter, and make other provisions to minimize loss. Data gathered in many ways not only help us forecast the weather more accurately, but also provide standards for judging the quality of the air we breathe and for gauging the extent to which factory smokestacks and auto exhaust pollute it.

THE ATMOSPHERE

Hurricanes, thunderstorms, snowstorms, balmy breezes, hot spells, cold snaps, dense fogs, and rainbows are symptomatic of the ever-changing conditions within the earth's atmosphere. To understand weather it is essential to gather information about the air—its composition, temperature, humidity, pressure, movements, and other characteristics—and to combine this information into a comprehensive picture. Meteorologists gather measurements in many places around the earth and at many altitudes, from the surface of the earth up to the top of the atmosphere. They make observations hour after hour, day after day,

and thus are able to write a continuous story about the weather.

We shall see later just what kind of instruments are used for making measurements. First, let us take a look at the atmosphere. Covering the entire earth and extending upward for hundreds of miles, the atmosphere acts as a protective blanket, moderating the temperature and shielding us from the harmful rays and particles from outer space that bombard our planet.

Distribution of Air

The air in our atmospheric ocean is not uniform in density; it becomes thinner and thinner at higher levels. Mountain climbers are painfully aware of this thinner air at high altitudes. At 18,000 feet (about 5,500 meters), or 3.4 miles (5.5 kilometers), there is only half as much oxygen (and other air constituents) in each lungful of air as at sea level. Half of the total mass of air in the atmosphere lies below this mark and half above it. Ninety-nine percent of the air is under the 20-mile (32-kilometer) level, leaving only 1 percent thinly scattered in the hundreds of miles above.

Scientists have divided the atmosphere into a series of layers, one on top of the other, to portray differences in temperature, chemical composition, pressure, and other properties at varying altitudes. We present a simplified profile in which the atmosphere is divided into five layers: the troposphere, stratosphere, mesosphere, thermosphere, and exosphere (see illustration on p. 217).

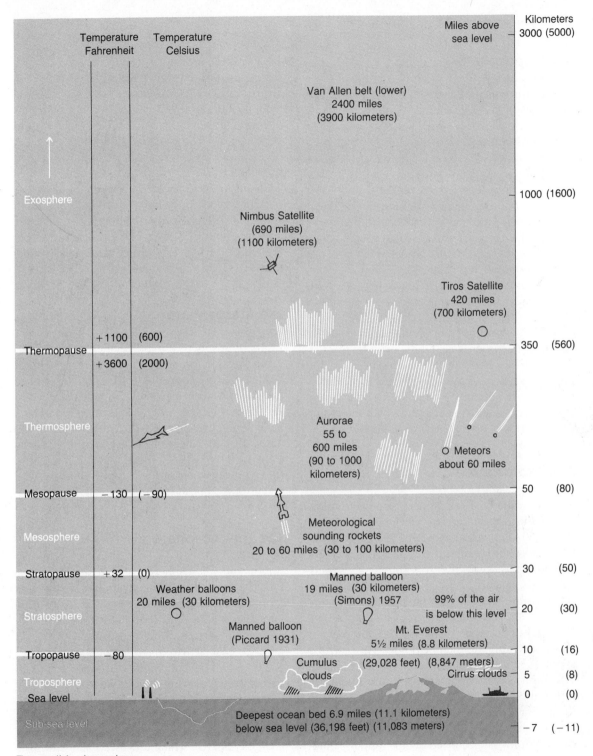

The earth's atmosphere.

The Troposphere

The layer in which we live is the troposphere. The word means "turbulent sphere," and is appropriate, because all storms, great and small, all cloud formations and, indeed, almost all weather phenomena appear to occur in this layer. Another characteristic of the troposphere is the steady drop in temperature with increased altitude. The temperature drops about 3.5°F for each 1,000 feet (2°C for each 300 meters) of ascent. In the upper part of the troposphere are high-speed winds known as the *jet stream*. These winds are discussed more fully on page 235.

The troposphere varies in height from 10 miles (16 kilometers) at the equator to about 5 miles (8 kilometers) at the poles. It is about 7 miles (11 kilometers) high in the middle latitudes. The height of this layer is also influenced by the seasons and by general weather conditions. At the upper boundary of the troposphere the temperature, which is about −80°F (−60°C) below zero, is first constant and then increases with increasing altitude. This is where the stratosphere begins.

The Stratosphere

The layer called the stratosphere extends from the top of the troposphere to a height of 30 miles (about 50 kilometers) above sea level. The air in the stratosphere is almost moistureless and cloudless. Compared with the troposphere, the stratosphere is characteristically free of storms and other visible weather phenomena. The temperature of the stratosphere remains at −80°F (−60°C) until about 14 miles (22.5 kilometers) above the earth and then begins to rise, reaching about +32°F (0°C) at 30 miles (50 kilometers). This surface of maximum temperature marks the top of the stratosphere. We have penetrated the lower stratosphere in balloons and planes.

A concentration of a special form of oxygen called *ozone* is produced in the upper stratosphere and in the layer above it. (The oxygen in the air we breathe is composed of two atoms of oxygen, O_2, whereas ozone has three atoms, O_3,

in each of its molecules. (See Chapter 14A for a discussion of atoms and molecules.) Ozone absorbs most of the powerful ultraviolet radiation from the sun. In this way it protects living things on earth from rays that in full strength would prove deadly. The remaining ultraviolet rays that do penetrate to the earth's surface, however, tan our skins, prevent rickets, and kill bacteria.

In recent years, evidence has accumulated indicating that the fluorocarbon propellants used in spray cans diffuse upward into the ozone layer and cause the breakdown of the protective ozone. (See Chapter 13A for further discussion of this potential environmental hazard.)

The Mesosphere

In the mesosphere ("middle sphere"), which extends from the top of the stratosphere to 50 miles (80 kilometers) above the earth, the temperature falls steadily with increasing altitude, reaching a very cold −130°F (−90°C) at its upper boundary.

In 1961 pilots flying X-15 rocket planes penetrated deep into the mesosphere, reaching heights over 40 miles (64 kilometers) above the earth. Later flights penetrated its "roof," climbing to a height of 67 miles (108 kilometers).

The Thermosphere

Above the mesosphere is the thermosphere ("heat sphere"). In it the temperature increases rapidly with heights up to about 125 miles (200 kilometers) above sea level. Above this level the temperature varies widely according to the degree of solar activity from about 1100°F (about 600°C), when the sun is quiet, to possibly 3600°F (about 2000°C) during periods when solar activity is at its maximum (see pp. 149–150).

The thermosphere contains part of an atmospheric layer known as the *ionosphere* (electrically charged sphere), which moves up and down because of the influence of the sun. In the ionosphere, X rays and ultraviolet rays from the sun are absorbed by the scattered atoms and molecules of the extremely thin air. As a result many of these are electrically charged, and become *ions,* from which the name ionosphere is derived.

The fascinating auroral displays, the northern and southern lights, originate in the ionosphere. Electrically charged particles streak down from the sun, and, guided by the earth's magnetic field, strike atoms and molecules in the ionosphere and cause them to glow, thus producing the display of lights.

In the thermosphere, which extends from 50 to 350 miles (80 to 560 kilometers) above the earth, the air is incredibly thin, being 10 million times rarer than the air at sea level. Thin as it is, the air in the thermosphere offers enough frictional resistance to most of the meteoroids that flash through it to cause them to become white-hot and to be reduced to dust. The thermosphere (and to some extent the mesosphere) serve, therefore, as a screen protecting the earth from the millions of meteoroids that bombard it daily.

The Exosphere

The exosphere ("outer sphere") begins at the upper limit of the thermosphere and extends outward thousands of miles. In the exosphere, the air is so thin that molecules of it can travel vast distances without hitting each other.

One of the major achievements of the exploration of the atmosphere by satellite was the discovery of the existence of two belts of high radiation, known as the Van Allen belts after their discoverer. These doughnut-shaped belts, one inside the other, consist of fast-moving electrons and protons that spiral in the lines of force in the earth's magnetic field (see pp. 217, 461–465, and 534–536).

THE COMPOSITION OF THE AIR

The air that enters your lungs with each breath is not one but many substances. The two most abundant parts of air are nitrogen, which accounts for nearly four fifths of the air, and oxygen, which makes up about one fifth.

Nitrogen, the chief constituent of air (78 percent) is also an essential element in proteins, which are basic in the makeup of all living things. As we shall see in Chapter 13A, some atmospheric nitrogen is made available to plants by the action of certain bacteria in the soil.

Oxygen, a chemically active component of the air (21 percent), is essential for respiration in plants and animals and for the combustion of fuels.

Carbon dioxide, making up only 3/100 of 1 percent of the air, is extremely important to life. Green plants absorb carbon dioxide from the air and combine it with hydrogen from water molecules to produce the food essential for their life and eventually for that of all animals as well. This important process will be discussed in Chapter 10A.

Water vapor, found in amounts varying from 0 percent to 3 or 4 percent of the air near sea level, exerts a profound influence on the distribution of life on this planet because a region's capacity for supporting life is determined principally by the amount of water, in the form of rain or snow, that is available. Most of the water vapor is found in the lower 4 miles (about 6 kilometers) of the atmosphere. As we shall see, water vapor plays an important part in the changing weather picture.

We have thus far accounted for about 99 percent of the air (excluding the variable water vapor content). The remaining 1 percent consists primarily of the gases argon, neon, helium, and xenon. Also sprinkled in the air is a varying amount of dust.

SUN, AIR, AND WATER

The drama of weather is better understood if we follow closely the roles played by the sun, air, and water. The sun is the leading figure in the spectacle, providing the heat energy that keeps the whole show moving. The air is the vehicle that circulates and transports all kinds and conditions of weather around the earth. Water makes an appearance in many forms: dew, sleet, fog, clouds, rain, and snow, and it disappears from view as water vapor.

Sun

From a distance of about 93 million miles (150 million kilometers) the sun warms the earth. If all parts of the earth were heated equally, there would not be much weather to talk about. But the sun's heat is not distributed equally. Let us see why.

1. For one thing, the sun's rays reach only half of the earth at any one time, the side in daylight. We live on a turning earth, so there is a daily cycle of heating and cooling accompanying day and night.
2. Sunshine is not equally strong all over the earth. The fact that the earth is round means that different parts of its surface receive sunlight at different angles. Thus, areas near the equator face the sun directly and receive more radiation than the belts farther away from the equator, which receive more slanting rays. As a result the equatorial regions receive more heat than the temperate, and the temperate more than the polar (see Chapter 7B for a demonstration of the principle involved).
3. We saw in Chapter 7A how the tilted axis of the earth and the yearly revolution of the earth around the sun causes variations in the amount of heat at different times of the year, thereby causing seasons.
4. The amount of heat absorbed by any area of the earth depends in part on the kind of surface that is being heated. Water heats up much more slowly than land. Hence the air temperatures influenced by these underlying surfaces are different: It is cooler in summer at the seacoast than inland at the same latitude.
5. Even without the first four factors operating, the atmosphere of the earth, considered vertically, would exhibit variation in temperature. As we mentioned, temperatures drop off in the troposphere at the average rate of 3.5°F for every 1,000 feet (2°C for every 300 meters) of elevation. It may seem strange that temperatures should drop as one gets nearer the sun until one considers that the few thousand feet involved are a very tiny percentage of the 93 million miles (150 million kilometers) to the sun.

Far overshadowing relative distance from the sun are two other factors.

a. The atmosphere is transparent to most of the sun's incoming radiation. It is heated mainly from below by the earth itself. The sun's radiant energy is first absorbed by the rocks, soil, and water of the earth and changed into heat. These warmed substances, in turn, heat the layer of air closest to the surface of the earth through infrared radiation (radiant heat).
b. The air at the bottom of the atmosphere, being denser, dustier, and more moist, is able to absorb more of the sun's radiation than air in the upper layers (as well as more of the important infrared radiation from the earth). This absorbed radiation is converted into heat, thus warming the air. As a result of these imbalances, temperatures in the troposphere generally decrease from low altitudes to high altitudes.

It is apparent, then, that the amount of solar energy received and absorbed varies considerably from place to place and from time to time. This results in an uneven heating of the earth and has a profound effect on the weather.

Air

Weather, as we indicated at the beginning of this chapter, is a condition of the atmosphere and consequently of the air that makes up the atmosphere. In Chapter 7A we saw how the peculiar "weather" of the moon, or rather the absence of weather, is due to the fact that the moon has no atmosphere. The earth's air acts as a huge insulating blanket, holding in the heat absorbed from the sun's rays by the earth's surface. As an insulator it moderates the temperature of the earth so that we do not freeze at night or broil by day.

The uneven heating of the earth results in an uneven heating of the air above it, so that all around the earth there are parcels of air, big and small, with different temperatures. *Because cold air is heavier than an equal volume of warm air, cold air sinks and pushes up the lighter warm air.* On a small scale this happens in a room heated by a radiator. If the circulation of the air in a room is traced by means of smoke or streamers of tissue paper, it will be noted that the warm air above the radiator rises to the ceiling and then moves away, while the colder air near the floor moves toward the radiator to be heated in turn.

Thus, in a radiator-heated room we see that the difference in temperature in the air causes up-and-down movements, or air currents, and lateral movements across the room, a kind of homemade "breeze."

The same principle that explains the movement of air in a heated room applies, on a larger scale, to a summer seacoast. The sun beating down on the coastal land heats it, and consequently the air over it, more than it heats the ocean and its overlaying air. Because of this the land behaves like the room radiator, and a cir-

culation is started in which a "sea breeze" of cool air sweeps in from the ocean, pushing up the air warmed by the land, which then rises and streams out aloft toward the ocean. At night, however, the land loses its heat more rapidly than the water. The air above it is chilled, while the ocean air is relatively warm. The colder air now sweeps from the land to the water, producing the "land breeze," as shown on this page.

On a global scale the hot equatorial regions may be thought of as the earth's "radiator." Air heated in the tropics accumulates and forms a warm mass of air. In the polar regions the air is chilled to form a cold mass. Circulation is set up in the troposphere, in which warm air rises over the equator and streams toward the poles, while cold air from the poles slips down toward the

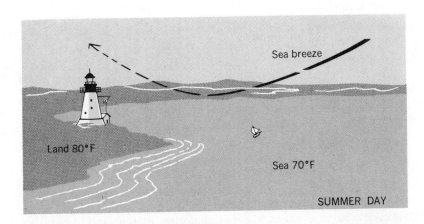

Land 80°F

Sea breeze

Sea 70°F

SUMMER DAY

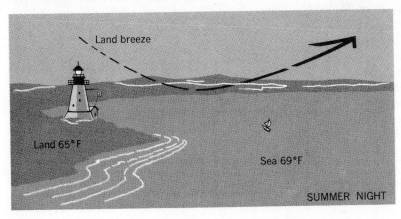

Land breeze

Land 65°F

Sea 69°F

SUMMER NIGHT

During the daytime the air over the sea is cooler than the air over land. A cool sea breeze blows. At night, when conditions are reversed, a land breeze blows.

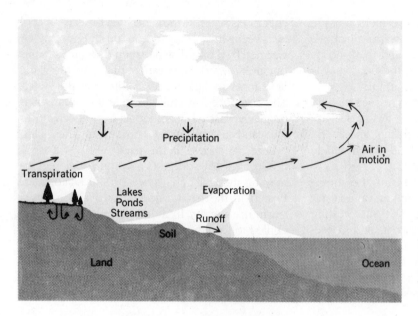

The endless cycle of evaporation and condensation keeps the water of the earth in constant circulation.

equator. The circulation is complicated by many factors, but it is clear that it provides a mechanism whereby the heat of the earth can be distributed, a mechanism that brings to us in the temperate zones air that has been chilled at the poles and air that has been heated at the equator.

Water

The endless cycle of evaporation and condensation, shown in the diagram on this page, keeps the water of the earth in constant circulation. Water evaporates from the soil, from leaves of plants, from the lungs and skin of animals, and from puddles, ponds, lakes, and seas. In the process of evaporation, molecules of water bounce out of their liquid surroundings to mix with other components of the air. This highly scattered, invisible form of water is known as *water vapor.* The heat provided by the sun and the fanning by the winds hasten evaporation, as anyone knows who has hung wet clothes on a line to dry (see pp. 250–251).

Aloft, a chilling of air containing water vapor causes the water molecules to come together in tiny droplets to form a cloud. We see cloud formation on a small scale when we breathe out on a cold day and "see" our breath. The droplets in a cloud may merge to form larger, heavier drops that fall as rain and return to the soil, streams, lakes, and oceans. (See pp. 231–232 for a fuller explanation of cloud droplet formation and precipitation.) Water vapor may also return in other forms—as snow, dew, and frost. We shall consider these and other forms of precipitation presently.

The water cycle, also known as the *hydrologic cycle,* provides a means of circulating water from oceans, lakes, and seas to the land areas. The water cycle also serves as nature's water purification system, because minerals, mud, and debris are left behind when water evaporates into the air. The water that comes down is relatively pure and clean.

MEASURING THE WEATHER

To describe present weather conditions accurately and to forecast weather successfully, it is necessary to use weather instruments. Measurements of rainfall and snowfall, of wind direction and wind velocity, of the temperature, humidity, and pressure of the air must be recorded. The meteorologist collects such information from many points on the earth and as high into the atmosphere as possible. Records are kept and charts are made day after day as a basis for forecasting the weather.

Measuring Rain and Snow

Probably the oldest weather instrument was a rain gauge. Any straight-walled vessel, such as a jar, served as a measure of the amount of rain in any rainfall. A standard rain gauge catches the rain in a funnel whose mouth area is exactly 10 times as big as the opening of the cylinder into which it empties. Thus the amount of rainfall is "magnified" 10 times. If 4 inches (10 centimeters) of rain accumulate in the collecting cylinder, the actual rainfall is 4/10 inch (1 centimeter) (see pp. 249–250).

Snowfall is measured directly by plunging a stick into the snow at an average open location. Snow varies in its yield of water. The rainwater equivalent of the snowfall is determined by melting a given portion of snow. Light, fluffy snow with a good deal of air in it may give only 1 inch (2.5 centimeters) of water for 15 inches (38 centimeters) of snow; a dense, packed snowfall may yield 1 inch (2.5 centimeters) of water from only 6 inches (15 centimeters) of snow. The average is about 1 inch (2.5 centimeters) of water for 10 inches (25 centimeters) of snow.

Measuring Wind

Wind, as defined by the meteorologist, refers to *horizontal* air motion, as distinct from vertical motion. To measure the wind is to determine its direction and speed. The wind vane measures direction. (It is more popularly called the weather vane, because people have known for a long time that wind direction has an important bearing on the weather.) A wind vane points into the wind,

that is, toward the direction from which the wind is blowing. For example, if a wind is blowing from the west, the arrowhead points to the west. Winds are named by the direction from which they come. A wind blowing from west to east is designated a west wind.

The speed of the wind is measured by an instrument called an *anemometer*. A common type is the 3-cup anemometer. Each cup is a hollow hemisphere. The 3 cups are attached by spokes to a central pivot. The wind spins the cups around, as it would a pinwheel, at a speed that is proportional to the wind speed. The speed is transmitted electrically to an indicator.

The *aerovane* is a combined anemometer and wind vane. This instrument, which is now standard at most weather stations, looks like an airplane without wings. A three-bladed propeller is turned by the wind at a rate that is proportional to the wind's speed. The streamlined vane not only indicates the wind direction, but also acts as a rudder to keep the propeller facing the wind. Both speed and direction are conveyed to recording instruments in the station.

The direction and speed of winds at different levels of the atmosphere are determined with the aid of balloons, inflated with hydrogen or helium, that are released into the air. The balloons are equipped with radio transmitters that are tracked by equipment on the ground.

Measuring Temperature

The weather forecaster uses the thermometer to tell the temperature of the air. All significant readings are made in an enclosure open to the air, *but shaded from the sun.* (Reading a thermometer with the sun beating on it will merely show how effectively the thermometer is absorbing the sun's rays. It will not give any significant figure, nor will it agree with another thermometer of different size or shape held in the same location. It is not intended to be used in sunlight. See Chapter 15A for a full discussion of the thermometer.)

It is extremely important for the meteorologist

The aerovane transmitter *(above)* provides accurate and rapid response to wind speed and direction. Wind speed is measured by a three-bladed rotor; wind direction by the position of the vane. Electrical impulses are transmitted indoors to the aerovane indicator *(below)*, where the wind characteristics may be read directly on the dials. *(Courtesy of Bendix Environmental Science Division.)*

to know the temperature at different elevations above the earth. We shall see shortly how the temperature of the air aloft can be measured.

Measuring Humidity

As we have seen, water vapor is the most variable of the gases of the atmosphere, ranging from 0 percent to about 4 percent. The *hygrometer* is an instrument for measuring the water vapor content of the atmosphere. One kind of hygrometer is the *wet-* and *dry-bulb thermometer,* also called a *psychrometer.* You can understand the principle of a

psychrometer if you recall two common experiences: First, you may have noticed how slowly wet clothing dries on a humid day, how rapidly on a dry day. Second, you may recall the coolness you feel on the skin on your hands and face as water evaporates from them.

The wet-bulb thermometer shown on page 225 is one that has a moist cloth wrapped around its bulb. As water evaporates from the cloth into the air, the thermometer fluid drops markedly if the air is dry. If the air is humid, evaporation is slow and the temperature falls little.

In short, we calculate the moisture content of the air from the rate of evaporation of a moist

Some of the instruments housed in a weather instrument shelter. The two thermometers *(left)* show the maximum and minimum temperatures, respectively, for the recording period. The other pair *(right)*, wet- and dry-bulb thermometers, provide data for determining the relative humidity. The instruments are shielded from the sun, but not from the air, which circulates freely through the shelter. *(Courtesy of NOAA—National Oceanic and Atmospheric Administration.)*

cloth. By comparing the temperature of the wet-bulb thermometer with that of an ordinary dry-bulb one, and by using the chart on page 226, the humidity of the air can be determined. The humidity referred to is *relative humidity* and is expressed as a percentage.

Just what is meant by relative humidity? If, for example, we say that the relative humidity is 100 percent, we mean that the air is as full of water vapor as it can be; if more water vapor was added, it would fall out of the air as mist or rain. Fifty percent relative humidity means that the air is holding only half the amount of water vapor that it could.

A glance at the chart shows that the percentages given are true for a particular temperature. In other words, the capacity of the air to hold water varies with its temperature. Warm air can hold more water vapor than cold air. This fact is important in weather phenomena, for it means that if a given portion of the air is chilled, its water-holding capacity decreases. Without any change in its actual water *content* the relative humidity of such a portion of air increases, and, if it exceeds 100 percent, water will be condensed out of it. This is just what happens on a warm summer day when warm, moist air rises in the morning and is cooled aloft to form the thunderclouds of the afternoon.

At this point we wish to correct a very common misconception. Most people assume that the air, in rising, cools to its *dew point* (the temperature below which water vapor will condense out of the air) because the surrounding air is colder. Actually, cooling is due almost entirely to the expansion of the rising air parcel as its pressure decreases, that is, to *adiabatic cooling*. Common examples of adiabatic cooling may be observed (1) in removing the top from a bottle of soda (the decrease in pressure allows the air in the bottle above the liquid to expand, and in so doing it cools to its dew point and condenses into a fog; (2) in the stream of cool air released from an inflated bicycle tire or from a basketball; or (3) simply by blowing air from one's mouth under pressure, that is with the lips compressed tightly leaving only a small aperture. Sinking air, conversely, warms as it comes into regions of higher pressure at lower elevations in the atmosphere.

How to Calculate Relative Humidity   Look at the relative humidity chart. If the air temperature given by the dry-bulb thermometer is 70° F and the wet-bulb thermometer falls to 64°F, the difference is 6°. Look along the 70° line until you come under the number 6. The relative humidity is 72 percent.

Another instrument for measuring relative humidity is the *hair hygrometer,* which makes use of the fact that human hair shortens when the atmosphere is dry and lengthens when it is moist.

A few strands of hair are fastened into a device in such a way that they move a pointer over a scale of humidity percentages. Readings are made directly, without having to consult a chart, but this instrument is not quite as accurate as the wet- and dry-bulb thermometers.

Measuring Air Pressure

It is most important for the meteorologist to know the air pressure, because it is a symptom of existing conditions in the atmosphere and consequently is essential in making a prognosis of weather conditions to come. For example, a difference in air pressure between one region and another serves as a force to move air masses and the weather that attends them.

When we say that air has pressure, we mean very simply that air pushes or presses against things. We are not referring to breezes or hurricane winds but to quiet, untroubled air. We are not aware of this pressure because we live in it and because it pushes in on us equally from all directions. Moreover, the air in our body cavities and the blood in our veins and arteries push our body structures outward with equal pressure. Let

RELATIVE HUMIDITY IN PERCENTAGES

Readings of Dry-Bulb Thermometer	Differences in Degrees Fahrenheit Between Wet- and Dry-Bulb Thermometers															
	0	**1**	**2**	**3**	**4**	**5**	**6**	**7**	**8**	**9**	**10**	**11**	**12**	**13**	**14**	**15**
65°	100	95	90	85	80	75	70	66	62	57	53	48	44	40	36	32
66°	100	95	90	85	80	76	71	66	62	58	53	49	45	41	37	33
67°	100	95	90	85	80	76	71	67	62	58	54	50	46	42	38	34
68°	100	95	90	85	81	76	72	67	63	59	55	51	47	43	39	35
69°	100	95	90	86	81	77	72	68	64	59	55	51	47	44	40	36
70°	100	95	90	86	81	77	72	68	64	60	56	52	48	44	40	37
71°	100	95	90	86	82	77	73	69	64	60	56	53	49	45	41	38
72°	100	95	91	86	82	78	73	69	65	61	57	53	49	46	42	39
73°	100	95	91	86	82	78	73	69	65	61	58	54	50	46	43	40
74°	100	95	91	86	82	78	74	70	66	62	58	54	51	47	44	40

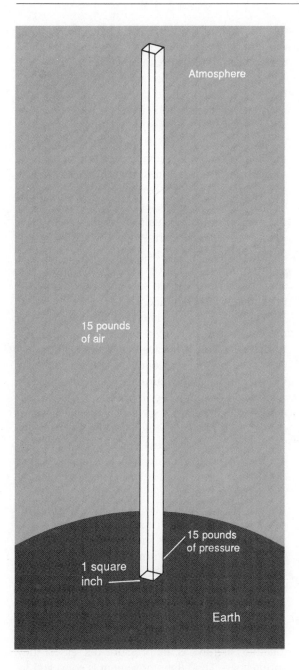

us change our elevation, however—as we do when we descend or rise rapidly in an elevator or in an automobile on a mountain—and our eardrums tell us quickly of the changing pressure.

What gives air its push, its pressure? To answer in one word, it is *weight*. We live at the bottom of an air ocean that rests its weight on the earth. Let us think of just a small portion of the earth's surface, just 1 square inch (about 6.5 square centimeters) of it. Let us assume that we were able to ascend slowly in a balloon from the surface of the earth to the top of the atmosphere, collecting all the air in the column *directly over this square* into an empty (empty even of air) steel cylinder. On returning to earth we would find that the cylinder weighs 15 pounds (6.8 kilograms) more than it did at the outset. There are approximately 15 pounds (6.8 kilograms) of air weighing down on every square inch of the surface of the earth (at sea level). Or, to put it in other words, the *pressure* of the air at sea level is about 15 pounds (6.8 kilograms) per square inch, as shown on this page.

Air pressure, then, is due to the weight of air above us. Obviously, it should be less on a mountaintop, and it is; it is greater in a mine below sea level.

In 1643, Torricelli invented an instrument for measuring air pressure, the *mercury barometer*. To make a mercury barometer, a glass tube about 36 inches (91 centimeters) long, closed at one end, is filled with mercury. It is then inverted into an open jar containing more mercury. If this experiment is performed at sea level, the mercury will fall a few inches, but it will then stop. Approximately 30 inches (76 centimeters) will remain in the tube, as shown in the diagram. The space above the mercury is empty; it is a vacuum (see p. 228).

Why does the mercury not flow out of the tube? Torricelli's first thought was that this might be an example of Aristotle's theory that "nature abhors a vacuum." According to this line of reasoning, if all the mercury flowed out it would leave a long vacuum in the tube, giving nature a great deal to

A column of air over 1 square inch of the earth's surface, extending to the top of the atmosphere, weighs 15 pounds. Another way of saying this: The atmosphere exerts a pressure of 15 pounds on every square inch of the surface of the earth.

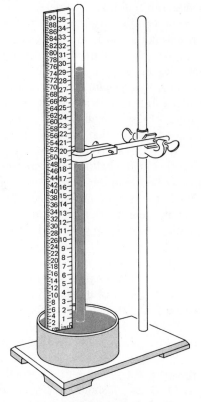

1,000 mbars

A simple mercury barometer. Air pressure on the mercury in the dish supports the column of mercury in the tube. Increasing atmospheric pressure causes the mercury to rise; decreasing pressure allows it to fall.

abhor. But Torricelli noticed something that was to be of great significance in meteorology: *The height of the mercury column varied from day to day.* He reasoned from this that "nature would not ... have a different horror of a vacuum on different days," and he looked elsewhere for an explanation. This brought him to the conclusion that we hold currently: The mercury in the tube is supported by the pressure of the air on the surface of the mercury in the jar. You might think of the mercury barometer as a kind of balance, in which the weight of the atmosphere on the mercury is counterbalanced exactly by the weight of the mercury in the tube. The higher the column of mercury the greater the air pressure; the lower the column the less pressure.

Mercury is used in barometers because it is the heaviest common fluid available. If water was used, the barometer tube would have to be about 40 feet (about 12 meters) high! In meteorology, the pressure of the air is expressed in inches of mercury, which may seem to be a curious way of measuring pressure unless you think of the construction of a mercury barometer. The 30 inches (76 centimeters) represent the equivalent of a pressure of approximately 15 pounds (6.8 kilograms) per square inch. Professional meteorologists prefer to express pressure with a unit known as the *millibar,* based on the metric system. The atmospheric pressure at sea level is equal to approximately 1,000 millibars.

Within a few years after the discovery of the mercury barometer, it was found that a rising barometer (so-called because the level of the mercury was higher) was often associated with fair weather and a falling barometer with unsettled or rainy weather. Much later it was found that air will tend to flow from a region of high pressure to one of low pressure. Knowing the behavior of these high and low areas enables the meteorologist to forecast the circulation of air. We shall discuss the relationship of air pressure to the general weather pattern in more detail presently.

Mercury barometers are awkward to carry from place to place. A much more convenient type is the *aneroid barometer* shown on page 229. The word *aneroid* means "not wet." Instead of containing a liquid, the aneroid barometer contains a flexible disk-shaped metal box from which much of the air has been removed (see partial vacuum in lower diagram). As air pressure increases, it squeezes the top and bottom of the box together slightly; as air pressure decreases, they spring apart. This slight movement is conveyed by levers to a pointer that sweeps over a scale calibrated to correspond with the mercury barometer. Aneroid barometers are used in homes, on ships, and in airplanes.

The dark pointer on the aneroid barometer indicates air pressure. The other pointer is set by hand so that a change for any period of time can be noted easily. The numerals correspond to inches of mercury. Evidently, the barometer shown here fell a bit more than half an inch since it was last set. The delicate mechanism inside the aneroid barometer (see diagram below) consists essentially of a disc-like box from which much of the air has been exhausted, and a connecting system of levers that operates the pointer to indicate the change in pressure. *(Courtesy of Taylor Instruments, Consumer Products Division, Sybron Corp.)*

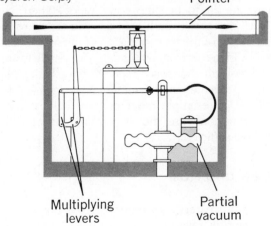

Pointer

Multiplying levers

Partial vacuum

Weather Aloft

As long as the measurement of wind, moisture, temperature, and pressure was confined to the surface of the earth, our knowledge of weather was severely restricted. We had to know the characteristics of the air at various levels above us if we were to have the full picture of the weather at work. In addition to surface weather instruments, however, we now have important new tools for weather forecasting: the *rawinsonde* (a package of instruments yielding wind velocity measurement in addition to the temperature, humidity, and pressure of the upper air); *radar* (a device permitting observation and tracking of small- and medium-scale phenomena, such as heavy rainstorms, tornadoes, thunderstorms, and hurricanes); *satellites* (orbiting spacecraft yielding cloud patterns and supplementary temperature and pressure data at different levels of the atmosphere); and the *computer* (which processes all these observations and supplies predictions of the weather possibilities). Basic to the entire system is the rapid communication of vast amounts of data.

The rawinsonde is a balloon-borne package of instruments that measures the atmospheric characteristics we have described at regular intervals as the gas-filled unmanned balloon ascends to heights of approximately 20 miles (32 kilometers). The measurements are converted into radio signals broadcast back to earth. Eventually the balloon bursts in the rarefied air of the upper atmosphere, and the instruments are parachuted back to earth.

The rawinsonde has extended the "vision" of meteorologists over a greater area of the earth's surface and up into different levels of the earth's atmosphere. Such coverage is essential because *the whole atmosphere is a single closely interacting mass of air.* Disturbances arising in one part may affect distant regions. Worldwide data are needed for long-range forecasts, however, even for a local region. But the majority of the conventional weather stations, even those employing these balloon-borne instruments, are located in the temperate zone land areas of North America, Europe, and eastern Asia. Meteorological, or weather satellites, on the other hand, fly in orbits that provide coverage of the entire globe.

Radar observations of local weather conditions, shown nightly on many TV stations, are described on page 240.

On April 1, 1960, Tiros I, a meteorological satellite bearing two television cameras, was launched into orbit. By June of the same year its cameras had taken and broadcast to stations on earth about 20,000 pictures of entire cloud systems in great detail. Tiros II and Tiros III, which followed, had notable careers. One of the historic achievements of Tiros III was the spotting of Hurricane Esther on September 10, 1961, before it was detected by any other means. A second generation of weather satellites, named Nimbus, with more sensitive instruments, was added to the array of weather stations in the sky.

The National Weather Service, now a division of the National Oceanic and Atmospheric Administration (NOAA), has developed its own series of weather satellites. ESSA 1, launched on February 2, 1966, was the first of this series. ESSA (Environmental Survey Satellite) travels in an orbit that passes over both the north and south polar regions. As the satellite moves along in its orbit the earth rotates below it; in one day, ESSA photographs the entire earth and sends its pictures to stations on its surface.

In 1974, the Synchronous Meteorological Satellite program (SMS) was initiated. A number of satellites were placed in an equatorial orbit around the earth. After being maneuvered into a position 22,600 miles (36,400 kilometers) from the earth in a position "over" the equator, each of these satellites has the same rotational speed as the earth itself (see pp. 615–617). In this way it maintains a "fixed stare" at a particular geographic area of the earth. It is able also to serve as a clearinghouse for data from balloons, ships, and as many as 10,000 ground stations. This weather bureau in the sky is equipped to scan the earth's cloud cover at night as well as in daylight;

to watch the sun for eruptions that might affect space vehicles; to relay signs of earthquakes or tidal waves; to pass along mid-ocean observations of sea conditions; and to transmit weather data to ground stations.

The recent series of Geostationary Operational Environmental Satellites (GOES) are spaced at roughly equal distance from each other in orbit above the equator. They provide overlapping views of the complete cloud cover of the earth—except the polar regions—every 30 minutes. Instruments on the GOES spacecraft also investigate particle emissions from the sun and assist in studying the effects of solar activity on Earth's telecommunications system.

In addition to normal weather reporting, the GOES satellites serve as full-time monitors for dangerous storms. Cloud masses associated with typhoons, hurricanes, heavy rainstorms, snow, and blizzards can be tracked by the hour, providing immediate information on their location and path of travel. The clouds of ash from the eruptions of Mt. St. Helens in 1980 were tracked by GOES, enabling warnings to be sent to aircraft and airports.

WATER IN MANY FORMS

Fog, clouds, dew, rain, frost, snow, sleet, and hail are the visible forms that water assumes. Water disappears from view when its molecules scatter into the air to become water vapor. When we "see" our breath on a cold day, we are viewing the result of the transformation of invisible water vapor in the air from our lungs into a visible form; the molecules of water vapor in the exhaled air cluster together and condense into a small visible cloud. This example also reminds us that for water vapor to condense, the air containing it must be cooled sufficiently.

Dew and Frost

Eyeglass wearers sometimes have the experience of entering a warm room after being outside on a cool day and having a film of moisture form on their lenses. This occurs because the chilled surface of the glasses cools the surrounding air below its dew point (see pp. 224–226). Dew forms in a similar way outdoors, when objects at or near the earth's surface become cooler than the surrounding air. Grass, leaves, automobiles, and outdoor furniture, for example, lose their heat more rapidly at night than does the air around them. If the air contains considerable moisture, these objects may cool the air to its dew point, causing the water vapor to condense on them. A clear night favors dew formation because then the earth rapidly radiates its day-stored heat into the atmosphere. (Clouds act as blankets at night to prevent the loss of heat.) A night with little or no wind also helps dew formation because winds stir up the atmosphere so that no one part of it is cooled sufficiently to permit condensation of water vapor by cold surfaces.

Frost is formed in the same manner as dew except that the temperature of the objects upon which the deposition of water vapor occurs is below the freezing point, that is, below 32°F (0°C). The water vapor changes directly into feathery ice crystals. Frost is *not* frozen dew.

Fog

Almost everyone has walked in a fog. Fogs are clouds touching the ground. They are composed of small droplets of water, about 1/1000 inch (0.0254 millimeters) in diameter, which have condensed from water vapor, but which because of their small size remain suspended in the air. (See the section on clouds, which discusses the method of droplet formation.)

Ground fogs are caused by rapid cooling of the air near the earth's surface at night when the sun goes down. The conditions essential for this kind of fog are similar to those for dew formation, except that light winds, instead of a dead calm, help in mixing the cold air near the ground with air a short distance above. Ground fogs are often found in valleys, where cold, heavy air accumulates at

night and in the early morning. When the sun warms the air the fog disappears. This occurs because warm air can hold more moisture, and the fog droplets evaporate into it. Fogs lift from the bottom upward because the air is heated from the bottom by the warmed earth.

Advection fogs result when the warm, moist air from one region moves horizontally over a cool surface. Such fogs are formed off Newfoundland, where the warm, moist air over the Gulf Stream blows over the cold Labrador Current. Summer fogs occur off California, when warm ocean air flows over cold coastal waters.

There are other kinds of fog that we will not consider here, including frontal, orographic, and evaporation fogs.

Clouds

The clouds aloft, like the fog near the ground, are formed by condensation. We have to add only that each of the tiny droplets in a cloud forms around a very small particle (so, too, do fog droplets). Such particles must be *hygroscopic,* that is, able to absorb moisture. Salt spray from the ocean is one source of these particles, known as *condensation nuclei.* Microscopic particles from the smoke of fires, from explosive volcanoes, and from meteoroids also supply large numbers of condensation nuclei to the atmosphere.

Since ancient times many systems have been devised for identifying cloud types. Today, in accordance with an international meteorological agreement, all clouds are classified according to two factors: form and height. Let us consider form first. Three basic cloud forms are recognized: cirrus, cumulus, and stratus. These are shown in the photographs on page 232.

Cirrus, meaning "curl," are the most delicate. These clouds, sometimes called "mares' tails," are white, feathery, and filmy. They do not obscure the sun very much. The highest of all clouds, they average 6 miles (about 10 kilometers) in altitude. They are composed of ice crystals.

Cumulus, meaning "heap," are dense clouds

Cirrus clouds are high clouds, usually more than 5 miles (8 kilometers) above the earth. They are composed of ice crystals. *(Courtesy of NOAA.)*

Cumulus clouds of this kind usually come with fair weather. *(Courtesy of NOAA.)*

Stratus clouds are generally thin uniform clouds that give the whole sky a gray tone. *(Courtesy of Standard Oil of New Jersey.)*

that build up to huge heaps. They have flat bases, are white and billowy above, and cast shadows on the earth. Cumulus clouds are formed in rising currents of air and are the characteristic clouds seen on fair days.

Stratus, meaning "layer," refers to clouds that cover the whole sky, obscuring the sun. They give us smooth gray skies, and are composed of water droplets in summer and supercooled water droplets (water in a liquid state at a temperature below 32°F) and ice crystals in winter. A fog is a stratus cloud on the ground.

The word *nimbus,* when attached to a cloud name, refers to precipitation. Thus nimbostratus clouds are usually accompanied by rain or snow; cumulonimbus are towering cumulus clouds, called thunderhead clouds, which frequently are associated with thunderstorms.

The basic cloud *forms* are further subdivided by a classification system that takes *altitude* into account. This system includes high, middle, and low clouds, and those with vertical development.

Rain

The droplets of moisture that make up most clouds are so small (only a few hundredths of an inch in diameter) that they remain suspended in the air, kept up by updrafts within the cloud. They are also prevented from falling because of the resistance that the millions of air molecules offer them. (Note how slowly feathers fall.) Moreover, even if these small cloud drops did fall, they would evaporate into invisible water vapor before reaching the ground.

Then how do raindrops form? Meteorologists believe that two processes account for the growth of cloud droplets to raindrop size: *coalescence* and an *ice crystal process.* First consider coalescence. Some of the larger droplets in cloud bump into smaller ones as they fall through a cloud. The larger drops are called *collectors,* because as they fall they capture smaller ones. The collectors may become so large that they break up. Some of the broken drops fall as rain, and others act as collectors, which again grow and produce more raindrops.

But how do the original large droplets form? Some scientists believe that the collector droplets are formed by the condensation of water vapor on *large* condensation nuclei—on large salt particles, for example. When cloud droplets grow in size and become heavy enough, they fall through the atmosphere as rain.

The second process occurs when ice crystals appear in a cloud composed of supercooled water. In this case, the water vapor in the cloud is deposited on the ice, and the ice crystals grow into snowflakes. If the snowflakes fall through the air that is above the freezing point they may melt into raindrops.

Snow, Sleet, Glaze, and Hail

It is often possible for the lower portion of a single cloud to consist of water droplets and the upper portion to consist of snowflakes. In the snowflake portion the temperature is below freezing, so that the water vapor there is changed directly into ice crystals. As more water vapor is deposited on the ice crystals they grow sufficiently large to fall as snow. (Snow is *not* frozen rain.) When snow falls, its beautiful six-sided crystals may come down separately as flakes or they may coalesce into large fleecy clots.

Sleet is rain that freezes as it falls. If raindrops that were formed in a relatively warm layer of air pass through a layer with freezing temperatures, they freeze into small hard ice pellets.

Glaze is formed when the rain falls on trees, streets, and other objects that are below freezing temperatures. The rain freezes into a coating of ice that sometimes becomes so heavy on tree branches and telephone and telegraph wires that it causes them to break.

Hail sometimes occurs during thunderstorms and can be produced only if there are strong currents of rising air. Hail begins as a kernel of ice or packed snow that is carried aloft by vertical air currents. As it falls from great heights it passes through alternate layers of ice crystals and supercooled water. A series of corresponding concentric layers of ice builds up around the kernel. By

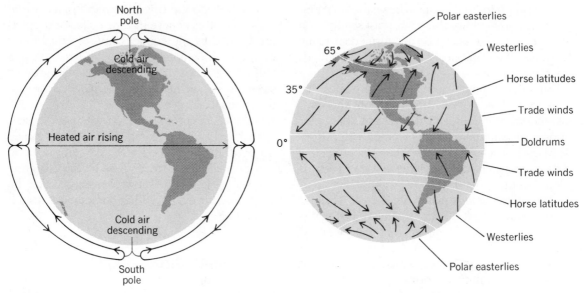

The diagram *(left)* shows how air would circulate over the surface of the earth if the earth did not spin on its axis. The earth's rotation deflects winds to produce the wind systems shown in the diagram *(right)*. The added influence of land and water masses is not shown.

the time the hailstone reaches the ground it may be as large as a hen's egg.

WIND

The basic cause of winds, as we have seen, is the unequal heating of the earth by the sun. Differences in heat create differences in pressure; it is these pressure differences that make winds blow.

Because the earth is hottest at the equator and coolest at the poles, a global wind circulation is set up, with cold air moving on the surface toward the equator and warm air moving aloft toward the poles, as shown on the left diagram on this page.

Wind Belts

But the wind picture is not quite as simple as we have described so far. If it were, in the Northern

Hemisphere we would have surface winds sweeping from the north to the south and winds aloft moving in the opposite direction. In the Southern Hemisphere the reverse would be true. Thus all winds would be either north or south winds. The large scale sun-powered wind system just described is steered in different directions by the rotation of the earth. Without describing the complex mechanism involved, we can say that the result of the earth's rotation is to deflect winds to the east and the west and to produce the wind belts shown in the right diagram on this page.

Land, Water, and Wind

Thus far we have seen that global or planetary winds arise from the unequal heating of the earth and are then steered into belts. This wind picture could apply to any planet that is heated at the equator, rotates like the earth, and has a similar atmosphere. Earth's complete wind picture is determined by its special geography—by its land masses and bodies of water. Land and water affect wind because they do not heat up or cool off at the same rate. On page 221 we saw how land and sea breezes are produced by the differences in heating and cooling of day and night. Winds are also generated by seasonal variations: In winter the continents are colder than nearby oceans. Cold, heavy air sweeps from the continents over the ocean. In the summer the reverse is true, with ocean-cooled air blowing over the continent. Such seasonal tendencies change the prevailing winds to produce what is termed a *monsoon* circulation.

The Jet Streams

For many years we knew of belts of high-speed winds in the upper troposphere, but they have been studied extensively only since World War II. U.S. Air Force pilots flying above 20,000 feet (6,100 meters) encountered unbelievably strong west headwinds, sometimes over 200 miles (300 kilometers) per hour. As commercial airplane flight reached these altitudes and wind observations at higher levels were improved, the existence of these high-speed winds became more and more apparent. These winds became known as the *jet stream.*

The jet stream has been likened to a narrow current flowing around the earth. Actually, the jet stream is not an isolated phenomenon but simply the core of the maximum wind speed within the belts of planetary winds. Two jet streams, traveling from west to east, have been found in the Northern Hemisphere, one near the pole and one over the middle latitudes; apparently there are two similar ones below the equator. The jet streams change their shape to form *waves* that encircle the earth. It seems that the kind of weather predominating in an area over a period of time is associated with the prevailing position and orientation of the jet stream—possibly accounting for

prolonged heat waves and cold spells. However, the exact relation of jet streams and their waves to world weather patterns and to long-range forecasting is still under investigation.

AIR MASSES

If you have ever gone into a cool, dark cellar on a hot day you were probably impressed by the contrast in temperature and humidity between the cellar and the outdoor air. In entering the cellar you moved from one weather to another, from one kind of air to another.

The air in the cellar had acquired its odor, dampness, and temperature because it had stagnated there and taken on the qualities imposed by its surroundings. Something like this happens on a global scale.

When a large portion of the atmosphere comes to rest or moves slowly over land or sea areas, the air will tend to become similar in temperature and moisture to the underlying surface. If the surface is warm, the air above it will be warmed. If the surface is cold, the air above it will be cooled. If the surface is moist, the air above it will become moist; if the surface is dry, the air will lose moisture. A large body of air that takes its character from the surface beneath it is called an *air mass.* An air mass may cover hundreds of thousands of square miles and be miles high, but the temperature and humidity at any particular level are fairly uniform.

The place where an air mass originates is called a *source region.* There are two general source regions—the tropics and the snow- or ice-covered polar areas—for it is in these regions that huge masses of air stagnate long enough to acquire their identifying characteristics. After remaining for some time over the area where they form, air masses eventually begin to move, the cold ones drifting toward the equator and the warm ones toward the poles.

Air masses retain their identity and characteristics even when they move far from their source regions. Only slowly and gradually are air masses modified by the new surface conditions that they encounter.

The analysis of air masses has been made possible by the extensive use of rawinsondes, by the establishment of weather observation stations over wide areas of the earth, and by weather satellites. Thus the meteorologist's view has expanded vertically and horizontally.

Fronts

If the air masses are regarded as armies, then their battleground is the United States and other areas located in the temperate zones of the world. For it is in these zones that there is a meeting of warm and cold air masses; it is here that one air mass advances over the earth, pushing the other back; it is here that the *fronts,* a word borrowed by the meteorologists from the military, extend for hundreds and sometimes thousands of miles and mark the violent clashes of opposing air masses. Almost anywhere in the United States you are in territory occupied by a warm or cool mass of air. The chances are that the present temperature will

not last very long. Soon the advancing opposing army of air will make itself known by clouds, thunder, lightning, and other special effects. When the front passes, you are again in occupied territory—occupied by the new, "victorious" air mass. In the heat of the "battle," some mixing of opposing masses does occur: The front lines that originally may have been straight may be thrown into waves, reflecting local advances of warm air here and cold air elsewhere. But what is most remarkable during the clash is that each air mass, by and large, retains its own identity, its own distinguishing banners of temperature and humidity.

Let us examine the warm front first. Warm air is on the march, pushing against the cold air. Because it is lighter, it rides up the cold air mass. You might think of the boundary as a kind of hill, not as steep as depicted in the picture on this page, but one up which the warm air is traveling. As the warm air moves upward it is cooled; the moisture in it condenses, resulting in cloud formation and the precipitation of rain. The first part of the diagram will be better understood if one keeps *two* kinds of motion in mind: (1) *Warm air is moving up the slope* and (2) *the whole picture is sliding eastward over the map.*

(Left) This is a vertical section through a warm front and the air masses associated with it, which are described in the text. A viewer in Pittsburgh would first be made aware of the approaching warm front by high cirrus clouds, followed by lower and lower clouds as the weather "picture" moves eastward.

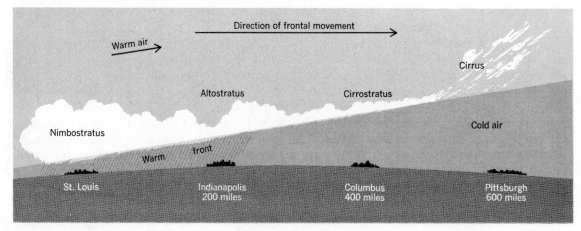

Consider a viewer in Pittsburgh. Within the next 24 to 48 hours he or she may expect the weather picture to slide directly overhead, because St. Louis's weather today is Pittsburgh's tomorrow. At present, the Pittsburgh resident sees high, wispy cirrus clouds, and being weatherwise, knows that this often is the harbinger of a warm front with its attendant weather. As the hours go by the eastward-moving clouds are replaced by lower and lower clouds of the stratus type. When the heavy, low nimbostratus clouds pass overhead, rain falls steadily. Finally, the front that was originally near St. Louis passes Pittsburgh. A new mass of air is now over the city, with higher temperature and higher humidity. The sky clears slowly; the army of warm air is "occupying" the city.

Part of the diagram on this page shows the same area as before, but with a cold front in evidence. This time it is the cold air that is advancing toward Pittsburgh. The cold front differs in several respects from a warm front. The slope of the hill or front is steeper. The front moves more rapidly. The weather phenomena over a cold front are more dramatic, more sudden, more violent. The warm air is lifted above the advancing cold air to form towering *cumulonimbus* clouds, or thunderclouds (see pp. 240–241). Thunderstorms occur along the front.

A weather observer in Pittsburgh would not be given as much advance notice by the clouds as in the case of a warm front. High cumulus clouds appear on the horizon in the direction of Columbus, Ohio. As the front nears, rain falls with increasing intensity. As the front passes, there is often a fairly rapid clearing with a falling of temperature and humidity. A cold air mass now occupies Pittsburgh.

It is apparent that air mass and air front analysis, developed after World War I, are essential to an understanding of weather. *Highs* and *lows,* however, have been well known for many years as an important ingredient of the weather picture.

HIGHS AND LOWS

In the daily weather report on radio and television, and in weather maps printed in newspapers, prominence is given to the highs and lows across the country. Just what is their significance?

Finally the front passes, and Pittsburgh is in a warm air mass. *(Right)* Cold fronts are steeper than warm fronts and move faster. The characteristic towering cumulonimbus clouds arrive rather suddenly. The weather changes abruptly when the cold front arrives.

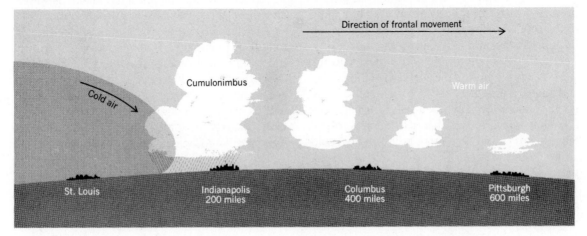

Direction of frontal movement

Cumulonimbus

Cold air

Warm air

St. Louis

Indianapolis
200 miles

Columbus
400 miles

Pittsburgh
600 miles

A *high* refers to an area of high air pressure, and a *low* to an area of low air pressure. In general, a high-pressure area is characterized by clear, dry weather, whereas a low brings with it a host of weather changes, mostly bad.

Low-pressure areas or lows are also called *cyclones* by meteorologists. Cyclones should not be confused with tornadoes, which will be described later in this chapter. A low may cover an area hundreds or thousands of miles in diameter. In a low, the lowest pressure is in the center, with pressure increasing away from the center. Winds blow in a counterclockwise motion around a low in the Northern Hemisphere and veer toward the center.

In high-pressure areas, called *anticyclones,* the opposite conditions exist: Highest pressures are at the center, and winds blow clockwise and outward from the center in the Northern Hemisphere. (In the Southern Hemisphere the winds blow in the opposite direction: clockwise around lows, counterclockwise around highs.)

Cyclones, or lows, generally move southeastward and northeastward across the country with the rest of the weather picture. They usually end their visit in the United States somewhere in New England, and then blow out to sea. Lows move at the rate of about 500 miles (800 kilometers) per day in summer and 700 miles (1,100 kilometers) per day in winter.

The origin of many cyclones in temperate zones is related to the shape of the wind pattern in waves formed by the jet stream. The beginning of the low is indicated by a curve or kink in the front between warm and cold air masses.

Lows, being notorious for their stormy weather, attract most of the attention of the public, and highs are neglected. Highs generally bring good weather because their air is usually descending, which means that it is being warmed. Since warm air can hold more moisture than cold air (without showing it), this is a factor in making the air in highs both dry and clear. Highs are often associated with heavy, cold continental air masses. Such highs bring intense cold waves to the United States. Bad weather may occur at the cold fronts preceding these high-pressure areas, but good weather is soon to follow as the cold high-pressure air mass takes hold. Anticyclones, like cyclones, move eastward across the country.

HURRICANES

A cyclone arising in the tropics may develop into a full-fledged *hurricane,* the most dangerous and destructive of all storms. Like its less harmful cousin, the cyclone or low, a hurricane is a low-pressure area, but its pressure is much lower. In the Northern Hemisphere hurricane winds spiral counterclockwise toward the center at furious velocities often exceeding 100 miles (160 kilometers) per hour. Rain falls at a heavy rate. The area covered by a hurricane averages only 200 to 400 miles (300 to 600 kilometers) in diameter, as contrasted with the 1,000-mile (1600-kilometer) diameter of a typical cyclone low. In addition, hurricanes have a special feature of their own: a calm, clear central "eye" about 15 miles (24 kilometers) in diameter.

The principal danger from a hurricane is its storm surge, a dome of water topped with pounding waves that is driven ashore ahead of the storm. Hurricanes are most dangerous when they sweep ashore at high tide. Nine out of 10 deaths from hurricanes result from drowning. Ships at sea are in danger from a hurricane's mountainous waves and wind, which can sink or ground them.

The strength of the winds must be at least 74 miles (120 kilometers) per hour for a storm to qualify as a hurricane. Maximum wind speeds of 75 to 150 miles (120 to 240 kilometers) per hour are common in hurricanes striking a coast, and speeds up to 200 miles (320 kilometers) per hour have occurred in some hurricanes, according to estimates based on damage to structures.

The area of the most destructive winds along the path of a hurricane may be from 30 to 100 miles (50 to 160 kilometers) wide. As the storm develops and moves forward, it may traverse a

Hurricane David on September 4, 1979. *(Courtesy of NOAA.)*

path several thousand miles long from its birth-place in the Caribbean, or in the Atlantic Ocean just west of the coast of Africa, or off the west coast of Mexico, until it blows itself out over the continent or in the North Atlantic. (In the western Pacific, where they are more frequent and often larger and more violent, these intense tropical storms are called *typhoons.*)

While the winds of the hurricane are blowing at giant speeds around the center, the entire storm system may move forward very slowly, and some-times even remain stationary for a short time. In the tropics the forward speed of the entire hur-ricane is about 15 miles (24 kilometers) per hour; as it moves away from the tropics the speed may reach 50 miles (80 kilometers) per hour.

Hurricane Power

The power of a hurricane has been estimated to be the equivalent of several thousand atomic bombs per second! How does it develop this power? The answer lies in the three fundamental weather factors that we stressed earlier in the chapter: heat, water, and air.

Heat poured down by the sun, day after day, warming tropical waters and the air above them, is the basic source of the power. The resulting evaporation of water from the oceans into the at-mosphere is a process that traps and stores much of this heat. It takes a great deal of heat to change water into water vapor. This energy is not lost but is carried off by the water vapor in a latent or hidden form. The energy is released as heat again when the water vapor condenses into clouds. The enormous heat liberated stirs up the characteristic fierce winds of hurricanes.

A hurricane, then, may be thought of as a gigantic heat engine. Its power stems from the heat released by condensation of the water vapor, and it unleashes its energy in the form of powerful winds. Conditions in the tropics, where the strong sun beats over the ocean, promote the growth of hurricanes. The whole story of how a hurricane forms under these conditions is not known; meteorologists offer a number of different theories to explain this violent phenomenon.

Warning Service

One of the important functions of the National Weather Service is the Hurricane Warning Service, which was set up in 1935. In recent years notable improvements in the tracking and forecasting of hurricane movement have resulted from the use of radar observations at coastal stations; from the receipt of additional weather reports from reconnaissance aircraft; from the more complete data obtained by rawinsonde from heights up to 20 miles (32 kilometers) above the earth's surface; and from the "eyes" of weather satellites in space (see photo on p. 239).

In 1956 the National Weather Service set up a radar network that will eventually blanket the United States, detecting and tracking not only hurricanes but also tornadoes and other severe storms. Radio signals sent out by radar bounce off raindrops and are reflected back to the sets, where they are electronically converted to the picture seen on the radar screen.

THUNDERSTORMS

Thunderstorms are weather "factories." Pilots flying into them can expect to see a great many weather "products," including lightning and thunder, updrafts and downdrafts, heavy rain, snow,

and hail, as well as ice formation on the wings of the plane. It is obvious that thunderstorms, for pilots, represent a severe and dangerous form of atmospheric activity.

Thunderstorms have their beginning in the rising of a large mass of warm, moist air to higher levels, where it becomes cooler due to its expansion under reduced pressure (see pp. 224–226). As it cools, the water vapor in the air mass condenses to form towering thunderclouds. This hoisting up of air may occur, as we have seen on pages 235–237, when an advancing cold front wedges itself under a warm, moist mass of air.

Squall lines are lines or bands of thunderstorms, often forming at an average distance of 150 miles in advance of a cold front.

A second cause of thunderstorm formation arises from the topography of the land. Moist air blowing up the slopes of hills and mountains helps form cumulus and cumulonimbus clouds as it is chilled at higher levels.

Third, the local heating of the ground and the moist air above it on a warm, sunny day give rise to the typical summer thunderstorm.

Lightning and Thunder

When Benjamin Franklin sent a kite sailing in a thunderstorm, he demonstrated for the first time that lightning was electricity. The spark that flashed between Franklin's knuckle and the key he had attached to the kite string in this dangerous experiment behaved like man-made electricity. We shall consider this particular type of electricity, called *static electricity,* in Chapter 17A. For the moment it will do to recall some of our common experiences with static electricity. When we scuff our feet on a carpet and touch a metallic object, such as a doorknob, a spark may jump from our finger to the object. This is an electric spark, small but effective enough for us to feel it. When we comb our hair we may hear a crackling sound as electric sparks jump. When we tear a piece of adhesive tape apart in the dark we can see sparks. In each case a charge of electricity has been built up on a surface by rubbing or tearing; the electricity is then discharged in the form of a spark that jumps through the air.

The production of high electric charges in thunderstorms is a complex process in which water droplets in a cloud become electrically charged. Eventually, the thundercloud builds up enough electricity to cause a discharge. We see this as a flash of lightning. This discharge may take place within the cloud, between one cloud and another, or between the cloud and the earth.

As the lightning leaps through the air, the bolt heats it and causes it to expand suddenly. This starts a tremendous sound wave, which reaches our ears as thunder. Why do we hear thunder after we see lightning? Light travels so rapidly, about 186,000 miles (300,000 kilometers) per second, that we see the flash practically as it occurs. Sound, on the other hand, travels relatively slowly, moving about 1 mile in 5 seconds. It is possible to estimate the distance between yourself and a lightning bolt by counting the number of seconds between the flash and the thunder. Dividing this by 5 gives the answer in miles. For example, if you count 10 seconds between the flash and the rumble of thunder, the distance of that particular bolt is 2 miles.

A building of steel and concrete is practically lightning-proof, because the electricity follows the steel down into the ground. The Empire State Building in New York City has been struck hundreds of times without harm to anyone.

The danger of being struck by lightning is minimized if one observes the following:

Inside a house stay away from the chimney, because it is the tallest part of a house and the most likely to be struck. Stay clear of attics, doors, and windows. Keep out of a bathtub or shower. If adequate precautions are taken, there is little chance of being hurt by lightning in large buildings or modern homes.

When you go outdoors, avoid high ground. If caught in an open field during a thunderstorm, crouch with your feet flat on the ground. Stay away from trees, poles, and other tall objects. If you must stand under a tree choose a short one that is in a group of trees rather than a high or isolated tree. Caves and holes are relatively safe. Stay away from metal fences, pipes, and wires.

Keep off golf courses and open beaches. Avoid, if possible, being in or on the water. If you are inside a car, bus, or train, stay there.

So-called sheet lightning, or heat lightning, consists simply of flashes from distant thunderclouds. Sheet lightning occurs when the electrical discharge is from cloud to cloud. The flashes are hidden, and only a large lighted area is seen. Heat lightning is the flash of ordinary lightning so far away that thunder is not heard.

TORNADOES

A *tornado* is a violent local storm with upward spiraling winds of tremendous speed. Tornadoes are often mistakenly called cyclones; the word *cyclone,* however refers to any center of low pressure, whereas a tornado is the most violent storm known to man. Tornadoes are much smaller in area than hurricanes, averaging only about $\frac{1}{8}$ mile (.2 kilometers) in diameter. The largest of these storms may exceed a mile or more in width. The average distance traveled by a tornado is about 2 miles (3.2 kilometers), with a range from a few yards to more than 200 miles.

A tornado is the product of a thunderstorm, specifically of the interaction of a strong thunderstorm with winds in the troposphere. It is recognized by its rotating, funnel-shaped cloud, extending toward the earth from the base of a thundercloud and taking its color of gray to black from the dust and debris that have been "sucked" into it. All tornadoes have a common characteristic: the rapidly rotating winds that cause them to spin like a top. When it is near, a tornado usually sounds like the roaring of hundreds of airplanes.

The destructiveness of tornadoes is due mainly to the combined action of their strong rotary winds, which have been estimated to exceed 250 miles (400 kilometers) per hour, and the impact of wind-borne debris. The maximum speeds of the internal winds of a tornado have never been

A tornado near Planview, Texas, on May 27, 1978. *(Courtesy of NOAA.)*

measured directly, because no anemometer has yet survived the test. In 1931, a tornado in Minnesota carried an 83-ton railroad coach and its 117 passengers 80 feet through the air and dropped them in a ditch. The most damaging tornado on record was the tri-state tornado of March 18, 1925, which caused 689 deaths along a 211-mile (352-kilometer) path extending from Missouri through Illinois to Indiana.

The devastation caused by a tornado is also due to the extremely low pressure of the whirling column of air, which makes it behave like a giant vacuum cleaner suspended from the sky, "sucking" in trees, houses, cars, animals, and people! Pressure as low as 25.5 inches (65 centimeters) has been recorded (about 30 inches, or 76 centimeters, is normal).

Tornadoes move in erratic paths at speeds averaging 25 to 40 miles (40 to 65 kilometers) per hour. Most move from the southwest to the north-

east. Tornadoes, however, have been known to come from any direction, even stopping their forward movements and looping their paths.

We are not sure exactly how tornadoes develop, but we do know some of the accompanying circumstances. Ordinarily, cold air, being relatively heavy, moves under warm air, as we saw in the description of fronts. Under special conditions, however, a layer of dry, cold air may be thrust over a mass of moist, warm air. Warm air forces its way up through the cold cap in corkscrew fashion. Cold and warm air mix, aided by strong winds aloft. A vortex is formed around a low-pressure center and thus becomes a tornado.

When a tornado passes over a body of water, a dangerous tornadic *waterspout* may result. (This is different from the kind of waterspout that begins at water level in fair weather and is observed mostly in tropical waters.) The lower portion of the tornado's funnel cloud is made of spray, instead of the dust and debris found in a tornado over land. Actually there is very little water in a typical spout: The major element is fine mist or spray, with perhaps a few feet of water at its base.

In 1989, a Next Generation Weather Radar (NEXRAD) program, replacing the national radar network, incorporated technology that is expected to advance tornado warnings from 1 or 2 minutes to more than 20 minutes.

FORECASTING WEATHER

The National Weather Service issues local weather forecasts covering periods for 36 to 48 hours from the present. Updated every 6 hours, these forecasts predict sky conditions, high and low temperatures, visibility limitations, such as fog, and precipitation. Wind speed and direction are given for the first 24 hours of the forecast.

In addition to routine forecasts, the National Weather Service makes special forecasts to alert people of hazardous weather. Forecasting services also extend into the areas of aviation, agriculture, maritime activities, fire weather, traveling, and recreation.

Observational weather data of surface readings are collected hourly by the National Weather Service at 300 offices throughout the United States. Eight times a day these data are used to prepare weather maps, like the kind seen in newspapers or on TV. In addition, observations of the upper atmosphere are made as described on pages 229–230.

WEATHER AND CLIMATE

The difference between weather and climate is chiefly one of time. *Weather* is the state of the atmosphere—its temperature, humidity, wind, pressure, cloudiness, and so on—at any particular hour or day. *Climate* is the history of these characteristics over a long period of time.

Climate may be defined briefly as "average weather." But an average may be misleading. For example, St. Louis, Missouri, has an average yearly rainfall of about 40 inches, and Bombay, India, has 74 inches. In St. Louis, however, the rainfall is usually evenly distributed, so that no one month has less than 3 inches of rain. In Bombay, on the other hand, the rain falls in torrential cloudbursts during four summer months; the rest of the year is almost rainless.

The climate of a region is customarily described in terms of its year-round temperature and rainfall. Climate in any region is controlled by a number of factors.

1. Latitude, the distance from the equator.
2. Altitude, the height above sea level.
3. The presence of land and sea masses.
4. The prevailing winds, which blow steadily across an area.
5. The topography, such as mountains and plains.
6. Ocean currents, such as the Gulf Stream.

At one time, about 18,000 years ago, one third of the land surface of the earth was covered with ice (see pp. 129–133). As might be expected, the earth was much colder at that time. Scientists believe that this ice age, and about 10 other ice ages in the past million years, were caused by small changes in the tilt of the earth's axis (see p. 155) and in the shape of the earth's orbit around the sun. These changes altered the amount of solar energy the earth received and therefore changed its climate.

In recent years there has been increasing concern about long-range changes in the world's climate. Is the earth now in a cooling or a warming period, or are we entering an erratic era, with extremes of all kinds—prolonged droughts, freezes, floods, heat waves, and other unusual climatic patterns? Have the activities of humankind affected the climate? For example, atmospheric carbon dioxide has risen 10 to 15 percent since 1850 because of the combustion of fossil fuels (coal, gas, and oil) and the destruction of forests. The increase continues at the present time. How has the marked rise affected climate? Should we restrict the burning of coal and oil (the chief producers of carbon dioxide) and the clearing of forests?

Although experts differ on the direction and the extent of climatic changes, there is agreement that more intensive study is needed to keep in step with the new global realities of population growth and food and energy resources, and the economic and political disruptions that would ensue from major weather changes.

IMPORTANT GENERALIZATIONS

We live at the bottom of an ocean of air.

Scientists divide the atmosphere into five layers: the troposphere, stratosphere, mesosphere, thermosphere (which includes most of the ionosphere), and exosphere.

Weather happens in the troposphere.

Air is a mixture of nitrogen and oxygen, water vapor, carbon dioxide, other gases, and dust.

Air is essential for life.

Changes in the atmosphere determine the weather.

The sun, air, and water play leading roles in weather.

The sun is the prime source of energy for the weather "machine."

The unequal distribution of the sun's heat on the earth has a profound effect on the weather.

Air serves to distribute heat and water around the earth.

The water cycle involves the circulation of water from oceans and lakes to the air, thence to the land, and then back to oceans and lakes again.

Because weather is a three-dimensional phenomenon, knowledge of the characteristics of the air at various levels is essential.

Wind movements are initiated by the unequal heating of the earth by the sun.

The earth's rotation deflects winds to the east and the west to produce the wind belts.

Large masses of cold and warm air influence the weather of the world.

Weather in the United States and in other temperate zones of the earth is influenced by the interaction of cold and warm air masses.

Climate is average weather.

There is increasing concern about the trend of long-range climate changes.

DISCOVERING FOR YOURSELF

1. Find out about the use of weather satellites.
2. Clip weather maps and reports from a daily paper. Interpret them by telling (a) the different data about the air that are provided, (b) how the forecast is made from the data given, and (c) how conditions on the map have changed since the previous day.
3. Observe cloud formations on several successive days to discover how the clouds change from time to time. Determine what relationship they have to weather.
4. Look out of a window and see what you can tell about the temperature and movement of air by observing birds, smoke, trees, people, and any other things that will provide clues.
5. Explain what makes the various air currents in your house—in the kitchen, near open windows, near air ducts, and elsewhere.
6. Try to find a toy or gadget that operates by the use of air pressure or air currents, and explain its operation.
7. Look for places in your indoor environment where water evaporates and condenses. Explain the conditions that are responsible. Explain how these conditions are similar to those outdoors that cause precipitation. How could you use this activity with children?
8. Observe the different kinds of thermometers that are in use in your home environment. Tell how they differ from each other and how they are similar.
9. Keep a record of the accuracy of local weather forecasts for a two-week period. Observe the elements of the scientific attitude described in Part I. Write a paragraph setting forth your conclusions.
10. Visit a weather station to observe the instruments used and the records kept, and find out as much as you can about how the data are utilized to forecast weather. Find out how computers help to make such forecasts.
11. Select some weather "sayings" and try to test their accuracy by observation. Write a paragraph setting forth your conclusions.
12. Learn to read a hygrometer, a barometer, and other weather instruments.
13. Consult a world almanac to note the record of the average monthly temperature and precipitation in

the city where you live—or the city nearest you—for the past 12 months.

14. What is happening to the quality of the air in the area where you live?

15. Write to your nearest National Weather Service office for a copy of the *LCD Annual Summary*, a source of information about your local climate. For weather safety information ask for the following leaflets published by the U.S. Department of Commerce, NOAA, National Weather Service: *Floods, Flash Floods, and Warnings; Storm Surge and Hurricane Safety; Thunderstorms and Lightning; Tornado Safety; Heat Wave; Winter Storms.*

TEACHING "THE AIR AND THE WEATHER"

Weather phenomena relate to many other areas in science. The role of the sun and the cause of the seasons (Chapter 7); the water cycle (Chapter 13); air (Chapter 14); light and shadow (Chapter 19); how air supports flight (Chapter 20)—all relate to an understanding of the content of this chapter.

Many examples of the processes of inquiry in science are important in the study of weather and are included in the activities described: *observing, using numbers, measuring, predicting,* and *inferring.* Students should understand that weather is the condition of the atmosphere, and that various weather phenomena which they experience are caused by changes in the air around them. Weather should be studied *when* and *where* it is happening—right now outside the classroom.

SOME BROAD CONCEPTS

We live at the bottom of an ocean of air.

Weather refers to the condition of the air: temperature, air pressure, amount of moisture, and wind.

Changes in the condition of the air determine the weather.

Wind is air in motion; it is caused by unequal heating of the earth by the sun.

Air is a mixture of different gases, chiefly nitrogen, oxygen, and carbon dioxide.

There is a constant cycle of water from oceans to air to oceans.

The water cycle involves evaporation of water to form water vapor and the condensation of the water vapor into water.

Weather is influenced by the actions of cold and warm air masses.

The sun, the air, and water play an important role in weather.

Climate is the average weather for a place over a long period of time.

FOR YOUNGER CHILDREN[1]

What Kind of Weather Are We Having Today?

Prekindergarten children respond to weather as they feel, see, touch, hear, and occasionally taste it. On a windy day, ask, How do we know that it is windy today? Can you hear the wind? Can you feel the wind? What does the wind do to our outdoor toys (kites, balloons on strings, crepe paper streamers on sticks, soap bubbles, and pinwheels)?

On a snowy day, ask, What can you do with snow outdoors? Can you make a print in snow? How deep is the snow? Can you catch a snowflake? What happens to snow when you bring a cupful indoors?

On a rainy day, ask, What happens on a rainy day? How can we collect some rain? What happens after the rain?

In later childhood, children are able to describe weather phenomena in more vivid detail; to measure and make records of changes in the temperature, wind, rainfall, and snowfall; and to relate the changes to the activities of animals and people.

How Can We Make and Use a Weather Clock?

Urge children to observe weather conditions—at school and on the way to and from school. Help

[1]M. A. Carroll, "Kindergarten Explorations with Snow, Ice and Water," *Science and Children* (January 1978). A description of an excellent series of experiences with melting and freezing, expansion, and evaporation; gives details of methods and approaches. J. Stephans and C. Kuehn, "Children's Conceptions of Weather," *Science and Children* (September 1985). What research says about children's ideas of weather.

them find words that tell about weather and use them as they observe and describe the weather. Suggest that they listen to the daily weather reports on radio and TV and tell about their experiences.

Make a weather clock by cutting a large circular disk from stiff cardboard. Divide the clock face into sections, and let children select words from their list to place in the various sections. Fashion two clock hands and attach them with brass fasteners. Urge children to suggest how the weather clock might be used. If we set our clock in the morning when we come to school, will it be correct all day? Why do we need two clock hands? Some children may wish to make their own small weather clocks using paper plates, and change them as the weather changes.

Suggest that children find pictures of different kinds of weather and describe the weather shown. What can you tell about the weather by looking at the picture? Is the wind blowing? Can you tell if it is hot or cold? What else can you discover?

How do people and animals change their activities when the weather changes? Suggest that children find pictures that show how living things change with the weather. Some children may draw pictures to show this. For learning how temperature changes during the day see the suggestions on page 179.

How Does the Wind Change?

Begin the study of wind by suggesting that children *observe* things around them that show what wind does (smoke, flags, leaves on trees, papers, and leaves on the ground). Let them *report* what they see and tell how they think the wind changes from day to day. Help them *record* their findings. Let them try to draw some conclusions from their observations. What can we do to learn more about the changes in speed and direction of the wind? Construct something that can show when and to what extent these changes occur. Suggest that children make pinwheels and take them outside. Let them try to *predict* what they think will happen when the wheels are held up in the wind at dif-

ferent times in a day on several days. What can children *infer* from their experiences? Suggest that children continue to *observe* other things that are moved by the wind.

Some children may wish to observe changes in wind direction on their own and report their findings to the class. Children can witness the changes as they see flags moved by the wind. They may make a simple wind vane (see p. 255). Some young children may need help with learning directions, and the use of this instrument will motivate them. Remember that winds are named for the direction from which they come and that arrows in weather vanes point in the direction from which wind comes. Urge children to keep a record of wind direction for several days, examine the record, and make a statement of their discoveries.

How Do Clouds Change?

Children like to watch clouds and think about the cloud shapes they see. On several cloudy days take the children outside and urge them to observe the clouds. What do they look like? What can they discover about them? How are clouds alike, and how do they differ from each other (size, shape, color, movement)? What is happening to them? What makes them move? Are they higher than the flagpole, a high building, birds, airplanes? Are they as far away as the sun? Can you tell what kind of weather is coming by watching the clouds? What difference do clouds make? Draw pictures of the clouds you see and tell about your pictures (see Chapter 9A, pp. 231–232).

What Happens to Puddles of Water?[2]

Ask the children for their ideas. One child may say, "The cat drinks it." She may be right. Another may volunteer, "It sinks into the ground." He may

[2]For further information, see G. O. Blough, *Water Appears and Disappears* (New York: Harper & Row, 1972); M. McIntyre, "Rainy Day Activities," *Science and Children* (November/December 1978).

be right. How can we find out? Investigate the puddle. Observe and measure it for a few days. Leave an open dish of water in the classroom. What happens to it? Adapt the material about evaporation and condensation (see pp. 250–252) for younger children. Apply what they have learned from the dish of water to what they can see outdoors.

What Do Storms Do?[3]

After a heavy rain or strong wind, take the children outside to observe the effects of the storm. Look at the plants. Observe the ground to see what changes the water has made. What is happening to the water? Children can make a list of effects of the storm.

How Can We Measure Rainfall?

A straight-sided coffee can, when placed in the open, serves to measure the amount of rainfall. After the rain has stopped, bring the can inside and measure the depth of the water with a ruler that measures in centimeters as well as in inches. Let the children help measure. Do this on several occasions, and keep a record of the results. After you measure, let the water stay in the can and have children predict what they think will happen to it. How long will it take for all of the water to evaporate? Urge children to repeat this experience at home and to report the results to the class. Can we measure the amount of snowfall? How?

What Happens When Snow and Ice Melt?

What are snow and ice made of? If the weather is cold, collect snow and ice in a container and urge

[3]H. M. Mogil, "Sharpening Your Weather Eye," *Science and Children* (February 1984). Shows weather map with storms and discusses their paths and effects. H. M. Mogil, "Winter Storm Watch," *Science and Children* (March 1984). Weather maps showing progress of a storm and a discussion of the formations of storms.

children to observe what happens when it is brought indoors; otherwise, use ice from a refrigerator and observe the change. What made the ice melt? How can we make it melt faster? How can we change the water into ice? Children may use a thermometer to try to find out how cold the snow and ice are. Suggest that they observe outdoors after a snowfall. What happens? How long does it take for the snow to melt?

Other Problems for Younger Children

1. How do weather reports help us?
2. What makes rain and snow?
3. What are snowflakes like?
4. How should we dress for different kinds of weather?
5. What weather signs show that weather changes are coming?
6. How does wind help and harm us?
7. What happens to clouds?
8. How can we find out what the weather will be?
9. What do animals do as the weather changes?

FOR OLDER CHILDREN

How Can the Amount of Rainfall Be Measured?

How much rain fell last night in the downpour? An inch (2.5 centimeters)? Two inches (5 centimeters)? Students may estimate and then, for future use, make a simple rain gauge to measure the rainfall. The illustration on page 250 shows the completed gauge, which can be made from an ordinary coffee can set in plaster of Paris. Because of evaporation, amounts of rainfall should be measured immediately after the rain (see Chapter 9A, p. 223).

Another type of rain gauge (see page 250) is made by inserting a cork and a funnel into the top of an olive jar. Making such a gauge is an excellent opportunity for children to plan and design their own instrument to solve a particular problem. Discuss the problem of reading the results of small rainfalls with the coffee can instrument, and ask the children how they might make

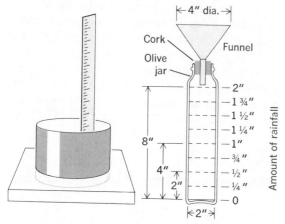

A rain gauge may be made of a metal or plastic container set in plaster of Paris. A more elaborate gauge consists of an olive jar with a funnel, using the dimensions and markings shown here.

an instrument to measure small amounts of rain. The use of a funnel, as shown in the illustration, increases the area for catching rain. This increase in area must be compensated for in the making of a scale. Thus, 4 inches (10 centimeters) of water in the collecting bottle represents 1 inch (2.5 centimeters) of rainfall.

Note: In this instance, the *diameter* of the wide end of the funnel is 4 inches (10 centimeters), whereas that of the reservoir, the olive jar, is only 2 inches (5 centimeters). The *area* of the funnel opening, however, is four times that of the jar. Consequently, the height of the rain collecting in the jar must be divided by 4 to give the correct reading.

Children may use the rain gauge to compare readings at the school with those of the National Weather Service. A discrepancy does not mean that either one is necessarily incorrect, because rainfall is not always exactly the same in the various localities covered by the weather report. Normally, National Weather Service records are more accurate because of the equipment used.

Older children can find out what the average rainfall is for each month of the year in their lo-

cality (obtained from National Weather Service records). They can summarize the information in a chart or graph, and compare averages for their locality with others in the state or in the country as a whole. In this way, they begin to understand that climate is "average weather" for a locality.

When measuring snowfall (or rainfall), try using centimeters. Actually meteorologists first melt the snow, then measure the water and multiply that amount by a factor of 10, since the ratio of snow to water is about 10:1. Thus 1 centimeter of snow corresponds to 1 millimeter of water.

What Makes Water Evaporate?[4]

Evaporation and condensation are related parts of the great cycle of water in nature. How water changes to vapor, how it gets into the air, and how it gets out of the air are important concepts. The effects of temperature, wind, and amount of surface exposed on the rate of evaporation can be determined by experimenting (see the following examples).

About Temperature   Build on the experiences that children can recall about evaporation and temperature. What ideas do they have? Urge them to plan experiences and experiments to test their ideas.

Put the same amounts of water into two identical containers. Heat one over a hot plate or a hot radiator and leave the other at room temperature. Use a thermometer to compare the temperature in each. (Be sure to use a thermometer that reads well above 212° Fahrenheit or 100° Celsius or it may burst.) Or put the same amount of water in similar trays and set one in the sun and the other in the shade. Ask the children to try to predict the outcome. Compare the results by pouring the contents of both into measuring cups. Students should be encouraged to summarize their observations and attempt to make some inferences from these observations. The use of

[4]See also full development of a unit on condensation and evaporation in Part I, pages 56–61.

mathematics is important here. The children may observe the following: After six hours the water in the tray in the sun has gone down from 10 ounces (300 milliliters) to 8 ounces (240 milliliters), while the water in the shade has gone down from 10 ounces (300 milliliters) to 9 ounces (270 milliliters). They may infer that in the sun 2 ounces (60 milliliters) of water evaporated, while in the shade 1 ounce (30 milliliters) of water evaporated. That is, water evaporated twice as quickly in the sun as in the shade. (See "Investigating and Experimenting," Chapter 3.)

Wet two identical pieces of cloth with the same amount of water. Place one in a warm location and leave the other at room temperature. What do the students predict will happen? They will think of situations in which they have seen the higher temperatures speed the process of evaporation: Clothes dry faster if placed in a warm place; the water on the sidewalks in the sun evaporates faster than it does from sidewalks in the shade. We stress the importance of using a control. The only difference between the two situations must be that one is kept warmer than the other. The warm place should be no windier than the other, and the cloths should be hung or placed in similar positions so that equal amounts of surface are exposed. Comparison of the evaporation from the two wet cloths can be made by feeling the cloths or, more accurately, by weighing them at intervals. The latter is a good example of how *measurement* is a useful process of science. (Students must understand that the cloth weighs less as water evaporates from it.) (See Chapter 4, pp. 58–59.)

About Wind   Observing what happens to a fanned wet spot on the chalkboard is a useful experience (see pp. 58–59). From this, children will get ideas for experiments with other materials that show the effects of wind on wet surfaces. Examples are blowing or fanning their art work to dry it, the wind drying wet pavements, and so on.

About Amount of Surface Exposed   Wet two similar handkerchiefs. Leave one crumpled up and one spread out. Ask children to predict from which cloth the water will evaporate first. Urge them to suggest other experiences that will show the effects of surface exposure.

Put the same amounts of water in a tall, narrow olive bottle and in a saucer. Students may predict what the results will be. Compare the results mathematically as described in the experiments on temperature. Make graphs to show the amounts of water remaining in each container after equal intervals of time. Possible applications are wet bathing suits and towels spread out to dry, water spilled on the floor evaporating faster if spread out, and so on.

What Makes Water Condense?

Students may observe condensation (the change from gas to liquid) taking place on cold water pipes and faucets, on pitchers of cold liquid, on a cold window or a cold mirror, and in the air on a cold day when they can "see" their own breath. Discuss these questions: Where does moisture come from? What causes it to form?

Place some ice in a metal cup. Stir for a few moments, and note the result. Let students formulate predictions about where the moisture outside the cup comes from. If they think that the droplets "leaked" through from the inside, help them to devise some way to test their idea. They might add coloring to the ice water and see if the droplets are also colored. Suggest putting hot water in another tin cup to observe the results. What does this show? After they have inferred that the air is the only possible place from which the drops could have come, they must answer the question, "What was done to make the water come out of the air?" Students may suggest that the cup cooled the air in contact with it. They experiment on different days to see if there are differences. If necessary, suggest that they keep records of the relative humidity as shown by a hygrometer or the weather report to see what relationship exists between the humidity in the air and the condensation on the chilled cup. They may record their findings and try to interpret them.

After students have experimented with evaporation and condensation, suggest that they go to the window and tell how many different kinds of places they can see from which water is evaporating. Do the same for condensation. Then name places in the school building where these two processes take place. Ask children to suggest a way of showing that plants give off water into the air.

Ordinarily students at the elementary school level do not concern themselves about how relative humidity is calculated. Children can, however, read a hair hygrometer, which gives a direct reading of the relative humidity, and understand the meaning of the term relative humidity even though they do not go into *how* the percentage is determined.

As these experiments and observations go on, it may be advisable to keep a record of the important science concepts that students have learned so that they can later be put together and used to understand weather phenomena. The breadth of these concepts will depend on the experience, interest, and intellectual maturity of the students.

Here are examples of important ideas students should have encountered from the experiments and observations in evaporation and condensation.

Water evaporates into the air from many places.
Heat makes water evaporate more quickly.
Wind makes water evaporate more quickly.
Cooling of the air may cause water to condense out of the air.
Water condenses on many cool surfaces.
Water evaporates more quickly when it is spread out.

How Is Water Recycled?[5]

Now students can begin to put together what they have learned about evaporation and condensation

[5]K. U. S. Labor, "Possible Pathways Along the Water Cycle," *Science Scope* (April/May 1987). A complete description of the water cycle with diagrams. Also write to U.S. Department of Agriculture for resource guides for study of water and soil conservation.

in order to understand some of the causes of rain and other forms of precipitation.

The covered terrarium in the schoolroom is an excellent place to observe the water cycle (see Chapter 10A). Suggest that children watch the glass surface of a terrarium for several days, report their observations, and try to interpret them. The water evaporates from all of the wet things in the terrarium. When moist air cools, the water vapor condenses on the glass. Discuss, "Where does the water come from?" "Why did it form on the glass?" "Why does it then sometimes disappear?" Show the same idea by using a clean, dry glass jar with a lid. Place an inch or so of water in the bottom. Screw the lid on. Set the jar so that part of it is in sunlight. In a short time the vapor that evaporates will condense in droplets on the cool part of the glass.

The children can easily demonstrate "rain" by holding a cold plate or pie tin over the spout of a tea kettle of boiling water. They can observe the condensation. If the drops of water are collected as they fall and left standing the children can observe that the water soon evaporates.

In using the materials described in the previous paragraphs, it is important that students see the relationship between what happens to these materials and what happens outdoors. Thus, in the kettle demonstration the heating device represents the sun; the white cloud that comes from the kettle symbolizes the clouds in the sky; the cold plate represents cold temperatures aloft; and the drops are rain. In the terrarium (see Chapter 10B) the cooler sides of the terrarium stand for the cold temperatures experienced aloft. Urge children to look for and report examples of water cycles. Suggest that children draw a diagram of the water cycle on the chalkboard to show that they understand the idea.

What Makes the Wind?[6]

Refer to the drawings on pages 253 and 477. The surrounding cooler, heavier air pushes into one

[6]C. Burns, "Tails and Strings and Bright Flying Things," *Science and Children* (March 1987). Causes and effects of wind currents.

This convection box, which may be made at school or purchased from a supply house, is used to show how wind is caused by the unequal heating of air.

chimney and forces the warmed, lighter air up the other chimney. The flow of cool air across the box is a small-scale wind. You cannot see the wind, but if you hold a smoking splinter of wood or piece of burning damp paper near the top of the chimney you will see the direction it is moving the smoke in the chimney. (The word *tracer* is useful to describe the role of the smoke in this demonstration.) Caution should be exercised in the use of this apparatus because it involves lighting matches. Students should not strike matches unless an adult is present. Also, water should be nearby to douse the splinter or damp paper if necessary.

To carry over the principle of this demonstration to the cause of winds on the earth, develop the idea that the air around the burning candle represents our equatorial regions. The large winds start blowing as the heated air in this region is pushed up and starts flowing toward the poles. Cold air from the poles flows toward the equatorial regions (see Chapter 9A, pp. 234–235).

After children have observed the currents in the chimney, they are ready to apply what they have seen to the schoolroom. Why is the ceiling the hottest place in the room? With the door closed, open a window at the top and bottom and

hold a stick with tissue paper streamers tied to it at each of these openings. Why is the wind coming in at the bottom and going out at the top?

Demonstrate the difference in the heating and cooling of land and water (which causes land and sea breezes) with these materials: two baking dishes, two thermometers, soil, and water. Put soil in one dish and an equal volume of water in the other. Place a thermometer in each. Let both stand until the temperatures are the same. Place both in the sunlight for about 15 minutes in such a way that the bulbs of the thermometers are shielded from the direct rays. Note the temperatures. Place both in the shade for about 15 minutes. Note the temperatures again.

After these experiences the children are ready to try to explain what is making the wind blow today. They can answer such questions as, "What heats the earth?" "Is it heated to the same temperature everywhere?" "If not, why not?" "Would the wind blow toward the warmer place or toward the cooler?"

At this point, students may add to the lists of concepts about air such statements as the following:

Wind is moving air.
Winds blow because of unequal heating of the air.
Warm air is pushed up by colder air.

WHAT DO WEATHER MAPS SHOW?

Many newspapers carry weather maps, which may be posted on the bulletin board along with forecasts. As students study the maps they will discover how the measurements of temperature, air pressure, wind direction, wind speed, and precipitation are indicated, and become familiar with the symbols used. Children also see weather maps on television and are accustomed to hearing the descriptions and the weather forecasts.

Ask all the children to bring in the weather map from a local newspaper on a particular day. Guide them to study it to extract information about the weather picture across the United States on a particular day. The following may be helpful:

1. What is the time and date of the weather map?
2. What is the temperature of six large cities?
3. What is the temperature where you are?
4. Where is it raining or snowing?
5. Where is there a warm front?
6. Where is there a cold front?
7. Where is there a high pressure area?
8. Where is there a low pressure area?

Students may try to determine how forecasts were made from the maps. Excellent aids in learning about weather maps, as well as other weather materials, are available from the Government Printing Office.[7]

Keeping track of the accuracy of local weather reports over a period of time is interesting for children. Reports may be taken from the radio, newspapers, or by telephone. A committee may be appointed to obtain the report each day and decide whether or not it has been accurate. Stress the importance of making accurate observations, withholding judgment, and other elements of scientific attitudes discussed in Part I. For example, if the forecast is for rain in the vicinity of the school and it does not rain at the school itself, additional investigation is necessary before a decision on the accuracy of the forecast can be reached.

What Does a Barometer Measure?

Aneroid barometers are now often found as standard equipment in an elementary school or as home weather instruments. Students should learn to read the barometer scale to the first decimal place. The printed words on the dial—RAIN, CHANGE, FAIR—have only limited significance. (Some students might keep records to judge the reliability of these designations.) The barometer measures only one thing: air pressure. A movement toward high pressure *usually* indicates the approach of clear, dry weather. A movement to-

ward low pressure *usually* indicates the approach of unsettled weather (see Chapter 9A, pp. 226–229).

To learn more about how the barometer works, children might observe to see if a difference in reading can be detected if the barometer is carried to the top floor of the school or to a nearby hill; keep a daily record of the reading over a period of a month and compare it with general weather conditions; make a graph to show observations; for example, what connection there is between barometric pressure and weather conditions; and observe to see if there is a difference in the reading indoors and outdoors. As they progress with their study of air and weather students may want to keep track of barometer readings given in the newspaper and on the radio.

Students might also keep records and compare their readings with those of the National Weather Service. They should learn that a barometer is a delicate scientific instrument and not a toy, and that it is for the purpose of supplying information and must be handled carefully.

How Do Anemometers Measure Wind Speed?

The wind gauge illustrated on this page is made from two hollow rubber balls cut in half and nailed to the ends of crossed sticks. The anemometer may be fastened to a post or a part of a

A 4-cup wind-speed wind gauge may be used to compare wind speeds on different days.

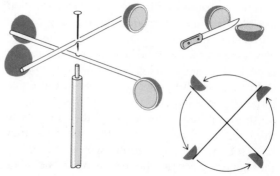

---

[7]Write to Superintendent of Documents, U.S. Government Printing Office, Washington, D.C. 20402, and ask for the latest list of pamphlets and other materials on many aspects of weather.

building where the wind is unobstructed. An electric fan can be used to test ease of operation before it is installed outside.

Again, we have an instrument with which students make use of mathematics. If one of the half balls is painted red it will be easier to count the number of turns per minute. Knowing this, students will be able to see the comparative wind speeds on different days in a relative sense. Thus, 90 turns per minute on one day compared with 45 turns on the next means that the wind speed on the first day was twice that of the second.

How can we tell the wind speed without an instrument? Look up the Beaufort Scale in an encyclopedia for a method of determining wind speed based on the movement of smoke, leaves, twigs, dust, branches, trees, and other objects.

How Do Wind Vanes Show Wind Direction?

The wind vane illustrated consists of an arrow placed on a pivot. It is important that the arrow be carefully balanced and that the pivot hole be large enough to permit the arrow to swing freely

but not large enough to permit the arrow to tilt. A washer between the wooden arrow and its support will allow the arrow to move more freely. A compass should be used to determine wind direction.

Other Problems for Older Children

1. What is the difference between a tornado and a hurricane?
2. How does air pressure affect weather?
3. What information do weather satellites supply?
4. What causes lightning and thunder?
5. What is the difference between weather and climate?
6. What makes climate different in different places?
7. Why is the weather different at different times of the year?
8. What causes the temperature to change from time to time?
9. What is the relationship of the jet stream to weather forecasting?
10. How does radar help meteorologists?
11. What is a temperature inversion? How does it keep smog hanging over a city for days? (see pp. 440–441).
12. How do we change Fahrenheit degrees into Celsius (Centigrade) and vice versa?
13. What records are kept by the National Weather Service?
14. How are computers used by the National Weather Service?
15. What is meant by ozone pollution of the atmosphere? What can be done about it?
16. Is the world getting warmer? How do we know? Why is it occurring?

A wind vane. Wire wrapped around the arrow will help to balance the instrument so that it can swing freely. Used with a compass, it will indicate wind direction.

RESOURCES TO INVESTIGATE WITH CHILDREN

1. Local newspapers, for weather maps and weather forecasts.
2. Local or nearby weather station, to observe weather instruments and to learn how data are used in forecasting.
3. Local farmers, nursery people, and fruit growers, to learn how the National Weather Service helps them,

and how they protect their crops in extreme or unusual weather.

4. Truck drivers and sailors, for information on how they learn about sudden weather changes and what the National Weather Service does for them.

5. Airports, to observe weather instruments and to learn how information is gathered and disseminated.

6. Newspaper accounts of unusual weather conditions such as tornadoes, hurricanes, and heavy frosts, for explanations of causes and results and other information.

7. National Weather Service and its branches, for samples of available information.

8. Local small-craft owners, for information about how they use the barometer and other weather instruments, and for accounts of how they get weather warnings and other weather information.

9. Newspaper accounts of recent advances in meteorology, such as the use of satellites.

PREPARING TO TEACH[8]

1. Plan an introductory activity for the study of weather that you can use to create interest and provoke thoughtful questions from children.

2. Select from various reference books a series of experiments that will help students learn about air pressure, evaporation, condensation, temperature, and weather instruments.

3. Construct some of the weather instruments described in the text or elsewhere. Make a weather clock that can be used with young children.

4. Plan a lesson that can be used in the third grade to introduce the thermometer and its uses.

5. Assemble pictures that can be used to acquaint young children with different kinds of weather. Plan questions to go with the pictures.

6. Construct an examination that will help to check understandings developed about weather in one specific grade. Try to expand the test to include methods of gathering data, evaluating, and using it.

[8]An excellent survey of weather is contained in *The Science Teacher* (December 1971).

PART THREE

LIVING THINGS

THE NATURE AND VARIETY OF LIFE

Viewed from the distance of the moon, the astonishing thing about the earth, catching the breath, is that it is alive. The photographs show the dry, pounded surface of the moon in the foreground, dead as an old bone. Aloft, floating free beneath the moist, gleaming membrane of bright blue sky, is the rising earth, the only exuberant thing in this part of the cosmos.

LEWIS THOMAS, THE LIVES OF A CELL, *VIKING PRESS*, 1974

LIFE EVERYWHERE

Three scientists aboard the submarine *Alvin* made a remarkable discovery while exploring an area of volcanic geysers $1\frac{1}{2}$ miles down on the Pacific Ocean floor near the Galápagos Islands. To their great surprise they found giant clams, white crabs, and 5-foot-long worms clustered around the deep ocean vents associated with cracks in the earth's crust. These forms of life (and others discovered later) were able to survive and thrive at pressures 250 times that on the surface of the sea, in the total absence of sunlight, at temperatures varying from near freezing to several hundred degrees Fahrenheit, and in water charged with poisonous hydrogen sulfide.

Life is found almost everywhere on earth—on frozen tundras, on dry deserts, and in hot springs. Life exists on wave-battered shores, in sunless caves, on windswept mountain peaks, and high in the earth's atmosphere.

But one doesn't have to be a world explorer to discover the richness of life. A pond near home is populated with an astonishing variety and number of plants and animals. A floating water-lily leaf is a natural landing field for insects. Its underwater surface is home to many tiny animal forms. A frog with turreted eyes sees above water while most of its body is submerged. Whirligig beetles gyrate in crowds on the surface, capturing small insects there. A female dragonfly skims over the water, laying her eggs as she dips the tip of her abdomen beneath the surface. Any drop of the pond's water is a little world teeming with microscopic plants and animals, many kinds of green algae, and a host of active one-celled protozoans.

Flatworms, water fleas, leeches, snails, crayfish, turtles, salamanders, water snakes—the directory of pond residents becomes longer and longer as we search more and more.

WHAT IT MEANS TO BE ALIVE

The forms of life are many and varied. What makes these different forms alike—and alive? All are adapted to the environment they inhabit; all respond to stimuli; all secure food and obtain energy from it or transform it into living material for growth; all reproduce their kind. Let us consider these characteristics of living things.

Adaptation

The kangaroo rat is well adapted to life in the desert. Its sole supply of water is in the food that it eats and the water produced by its own cellular respiration. Cacti have fleshy, succulent stems in which large quantities of water may be stored. Such plants are able to survive for long periods without an external source of water. The beaver is adapted for life in the water, possessing webbed hind feet for swimming and sharp teeth for cutting trees in its dam-building activities.

The term *adaptation* includes all the characteristics, structural and functional, which enable an organism to survive and reproduce in a particular environment. Adaptation is the result of evolutionary processes operating over millions of years.

A crab feeds on tubeworms that are clustered near a hot volcanic vent in the inky darkness of the seafloor. At a depth of 7,300 feet (about 2,200 meters), this unique oasis was found at the ridge between the Pacific and the Juan de Fuca crustal plates, some 300 miles (500 kilometers) from the coasts of Oregon and Washington. Since the original discovery of living forms associated with deep sea vents near the Galápagos Islands (see text), many similar seafloor habitats have been found along the plate ridges of the Pacific and Atlantic Oceans, harboring, in addition to crabs and tubeworms, limpets, snails, shrimp, and mats of bacteria. *Photo by William R. Normark. (Courtesy of U.S. Geological Survey.)*

Sensitivity

A living thing is sensitive. It responds to outside forces, or *stimuli*, generally in a way that improves its chances of survival. The leaves of the geranium plant growing in its pot on the windowsill respond to the rays of the sun by turning toward the light. The chilling of a pond to temperatures close to freezing is the stimulus for a series of responses in a frog: It dives down to the bottom, covers its eyes with the transparent "third" eyelids, expels air from its lungs, digs into the mud, and hibernates.

In responding to changes in the external en-

vironment, living things have the ability to maintain a relatively constant internal environment. This important property is known as *homeostasis,* which means "staying the same." In mammals, for example, homeostasis involves monitoring and regulating body temperature and the concentration of oxygen and carbon dioxide in the blood. When the external temperature rises above the body temperature, an increase in perspiration and the subsequent evaporation from the skin removes heat, thus keeping the body temperature constant. When the external temperature decreases, blood vessels under the skin constrict, reducing heat loss through the skin. Similar mechanisms exist to regulate blood chemistry and the water balance of the body.

Securing Energy

Living things have the capacity to take in energy from the environment and to transform and use it. Green plants, for example, absorb light energy from the sun and store it in the food molecules that they manufacture during *photosynthesis*. The energy stored in these molecules is used by the plant to power its life processes and to build its structures. Animals secure the energy they require by eating plants, or by eating animals that eat plants.

The energy-capturing reaction, photosynthesis, takes place in the chlorophyll-containing cells of plants (see pp. 277–278.) The energy-releasing process, the burning of fuel, occurs in all cells—plant or animal—and is known as *cell respiration*.

What is the source of energy for the creatures living near the deep sea vents, $1\frac{1}{2}$ miles down from the surface of the ocean, where there is no sunlight? Investigation by scientists reveals that hydrogen sulfide is formed from minerals released in these ocean-bottom geysers. Certain bacteria thrive on this chemical. In turn, the bacteria become the primary food source for the worms and other creatures living in this environment. Thus the energy locked in hydrogen sulfide molecules plays the same role as the sun does on the earth's surface.

Growth

One of the characteristics of living things is growth. A human baby that weighs about 7 pounds (3 kilograms) at birth matures into an adult weighing 140 pounds (63 kilograms) or more. Where does this increase come from? Part of the food taken in is converted into the complex chemical materials of life. Within a plant or animal the living materials are characteristically found in

separate building blocks, or *cells*. As a living thing grows and builds more living substance out of the food it consumes, it also increases the number of cells of which it is composed.

Reproduction

The bread mold scatters its spores so successfully that a piece of bread exposed to the air almost anywhere on earth will be invaded by these reproductive bodies, which, if conditions are favorable, will develop into new cottony molds. Bacteria multiply so rapidly that within a day one becomes millions. An oak tree produces thousands of acorns, each capable of becoming a new tree. The female oyster produces as many as 60 million eggs each season. The female housefly lays up to 600 eggs at a time. One female fly in April could have $5\frac{1}{2}$ trillion descendants by September if all survived. Mammals, such as deer, elephants, and squirrels, have smaller numbers of offspring. What they lack in numbers, however, they make up for in parental care, in intelligence, and in other characteristics that ensure their survival.

Living things pass a store of information to the next generation through the mechanism of heredity. Thus, they are able to reproduce themselves with remarkable fidelity.

The cell is the building block of life. The typical cell contains a nucleus surrounded by streaming cytoplasm, and is covered by a thin cell membrane. Plant cells, in addition, have a protective cell wall outside the membrane. Cells multiply by splitting in two. Each then grows to the size of the original cell by converting food into all kinds of molecules essential for its structure and functions.

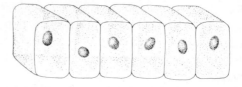

CELLS

Cells are the basic units of life. Like the bricks in a building, their arrangement influences the structure of a living thing. More importantly, the molecules and the chemical happenings within individual cells account for the functioning of the total organism.

One essential feature of all cells is the outer *cell membrane,* which separates cells from their external surroundings and which regulates the flow of materials in and out of the cells. Filling the cell is *cytoplasm,* where complex structures carry out chemical changes such as the building of proteins and the releasing of energy from food. Typically, *chromatin* is found in the *nucleus,* a large, often spherical body, usually the most prominent structure within the cell. Chromatin is the genetic material that directs the cell's activities and enables the cell to pass on its characteristics to the new cells derived from it. In addition to the cell membrane, cytoplasm, and nucleus, plant cells usually have a nonliving *cell wall,* which is manufactured by the cell. Green plant cells also have chlorophyll bodies, called *chloroplasts,* in their cytoplasm.

The great magnifying power of the electron microscope opened up a new world inside the cell. The diagram on this page shows that it is crowded with a variety of complex structures.

During the process of cell division the fine threads of chromatin form into *chromosomes,* with characteristic shapes and numbers for each species. Within the chromosomes are *genes,* the controllers of specific cell activities. The genes serve also as the bearers of heredity.

In the last few decades, great progress has been made in understanding the inner workings of the cell machinery. Fundamental to this knowledge was the unraveling of the chemical structure of the genes by James Watson, an American biologist, and Francis Crick, an English physicist. In 1953, they constructed a model of the genetic material DNA (deoxyribonucleic acid). Their model of the DNA molecule explained its biological role in di-

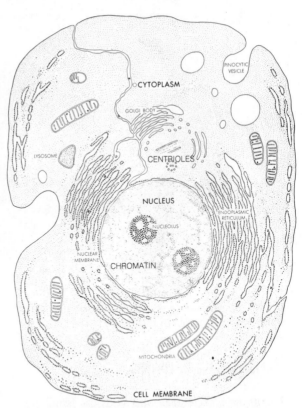

This modern diagram of a generalized animal cell is based on what is seen through the electron microscope, which magnifies 100,000 times and more. Aided by such magnification and by the revelations of chemistry, the biologist now envisions the cell as a highly organized molecule factory.

recting the activities of the cell (for example, the manufacture of proteins) and in transmitting genetic "information" so that faithful copies could be passed on from cell to cell in the process of cell division and from parent to offspring generation after generation.

The new science of molecular biology has made it possible to describe the role of specific molecules in controlling the functioning of cells and has led to the manipulation of these molecules by scientists to change the characteristics of living forms.

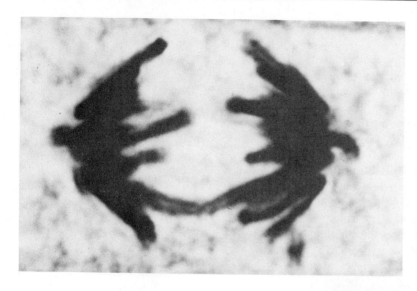

A cell in the root tip of an onion in the process of dividing into two cells. Each new cell obtains an exact replica of the hereditary information of the parent cell, incorporated in the chromosomes seen in this photograph. *(Courtesy of Carolina Biological Supply Co.)*

More discussion of cells and their role in living things will be found in the next chapter.

CENSUS OF THE LIVING

Taxonomists (scientists who study the family tree of living things) have thus far described some $1\frac{1}{2}$ million *species,* or kinds of living organisms. Most of these are small organisms seldom noticed by the average person. The insect group includes by far the major number of species, over 700,000 having been described and named to date. New kinds of insects continue to be discovered at the rate of nearly 2,000 each year.

If we include the yet unnamed organisms, there are probably 4 to 5 million species existing today, possibly as many as 30 or 40 million unnamed species. To complete the roll call we should add the more than 500 million species that have lived and died out since life began on earth (see p. 309).

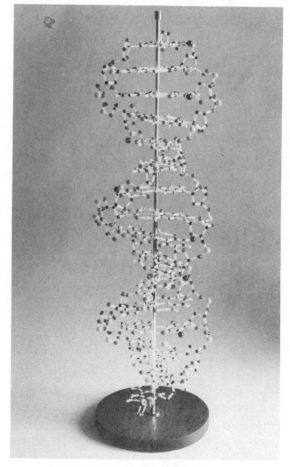

The model of the DNA molecule is used to explain how it is able to carry genetic information and how it can transmit this information to new cells. *(Courtesy of Kemtee Educational Corp., Kensington, Maryland.)*

A drop of pond water examined under the microscope reveals a world of tiny plants and animals. These have been skillfully depicted in this exhibit of glass models at the Museum of Natural History in New York City. *(Courtesy of American Museum of Natural History.)*

For many years biologists have classified all living things as either animals or plants. Generally, animals move and eat food. With some exceptions, plants do not move and they manufacture their own food. This rough division into an animal kingdom and a plant kingdom worked nicely if you wished to distinguish between a rabbit and an oak tree. But how about a form such as Euglena, a single-celled organism that swims freely like a "typical" animal but can manufacture its own food by photosynthesis with its green chlorophyll bodies like a "typical" plant? For clarification of problems such as this one and for a number of other reasons, a variety of classification schemes has been in use during the past few years, replacing the two kingdoms with three, four, or five.

Classification schemes are devised by humans to make order out of the jungle of living things. Kingdoms, and their subdivisions down to species, are based on relationships—for example, on evidence that birds evolved from a reptilian ancestor. Criteria such as structural characteristics, method of nutrition, details of chemistry, patterns of reproduction, and development of organisms help determine such relationships. The following represents an adaptation of the five-kingdom classification with these divisions: Monera, Protista, Fungi, Plantae, and Animalia.

The *Monera* are the simplest known organisms, the single-celled bacteria and the cyanobacteria, formerly known as the blue-green algae. These forms lack a well-defined nucleus.

The *Protista* include both plantlike and animallike organisms with a single well-defined nucleus. Included here are several groups of one-celled algae that commonly manufacture their own food by photosynthesis, and the protozoans, or one-celled animals.

The *Fungi*—the molds, yeasts, and mushrooms—lack the pigments essential for photosynthesis and consequently must absorb nutriment from their surroundings.

The *Plantae* include the many-celled mosses, ferns, and seed plants familiar to everyone, all of which carry on photosynthesis.

The *Animalia* are the familiar many-celled organisms that ingest food and are able to move around.

It would be helpful to read Chapter 12A, which deals with the evolution of various forms of life, in connection with the following brief survey of living things.

MONERA

Bacteria are the tiny one-celled organisms that reproduce typically by splitting in two. Most bacteria do not have chlorophyll and consequently cannot manufacture their own food. They obtain food from other living things or from dead plants and animals. Some bacteria, for example, live parasitically on plants or animals, causing disease. Bacteria, however, are also of great benefit to living things. Every plant and animal is a storehouse of valuable chemicals. If these chemicals remained locked up within the organism after death, there would soon be a scarcity of them for the living. Bacteria cause the rotting or decay of

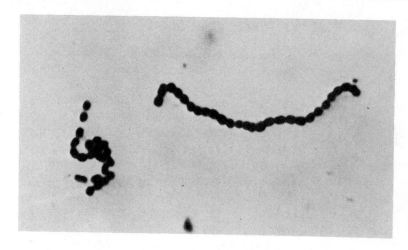

Photomicrograph of strepto-coccus bacteria taken with an electron microscope. *(Courtesy of Charles Pfizer and Company, Inc.)*

dead plants and animals, thus restoring their essential chemicals to the soils or to the waters in lakes and oceans. These chemicals—nitrates, for example—then become available again for use by green plants and eventually by animals. It is probably true that without bacteria, most life on planet Earth would disappear.

Cyanobacteria are universally distributed in soil, fresh water, and the oceans. These are one-celled organisms with nuclear material scattered throughout the cell, rather than contained within a single body. With the help of pigments, they are able to conduct photosynthesis (see pp. 277–278). It is believed that cyanobacteria changed the nature of the early atmosphere of the earth by enriching it with free oxygen, a by-product of

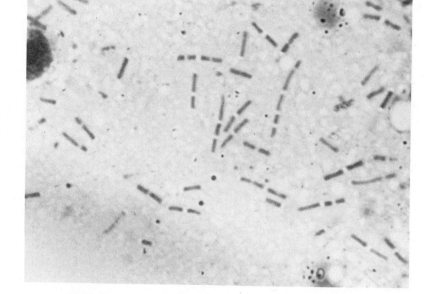

Three principal shapes of bacteria exist: spherical (coccus), rod-shaped (bacillus), and twisted-rod (spirillum). Shown above is a chain of spherical bacteria, and below, filaments of rod-shaped bacteria. *(Courtesy of Fisher Scientific Co.)*

photosynthesis, and thus made possible the flourishing of the many kinds of life we know today.

VIRUSES

Viruses do not fit easily into any of the kingdoms of living things, but are included here because of their simplicity. Like many chemical compounds of the nonliving world, viruses can be crystallized into regular geometric forms. In this state they have none of the characteristics discussed earlier in the section about what it means to be alive. Viruses are usually not regarded as living organisms but rather as parts of cells with a partially independent existence. One biologist has described them as "bits of heredity looking for a chromosome." Made only of nucleic acid (the substance of RNA or DNA) surrounded by a protein coat, viruses lack the other structures usually found in cells. Able to multiply only within a living cell, the virus uses the cell's genetic machinery to make more of itself. When the infected cell breaks up, hundreds of thousands of viral particles are released, causing the symptoms associated with the viral infection. Viruses are specialized and selective: Flu virus attacks only cells of the human respiratory tract; tobacco mosaic virus attacks only tobacco leaves.

The study of viruses is of obvious importance because of its linkage to many infectious diseases such as measles, hepatitis, and AIDS, and the finding that some kinds cause cancer in laboratory animals. In addition, viruses have played an important part in the discovery of DNA, the basic material of heredity. Lastly, viruses may be a possible link between prelife and the first life on earth.

PROTISTA

The Protista kingdom includes a variety of simple plantlike and animal-like forms. *Algae* play an im-

portant part in ocean life. Certain algae, particularly *diatoms,* are the principal food-makers in the assortment of tiny plants and animals called *plankton.* In turn, plankton, which is found at or near the surface of the sea, serves directly or indirectly as the basic food supply for all marine life, from the smallest fish to the great whales. It is for this reason that the plankton layer has been called "the pastures of the sea," and the diatoms "the grasses of the sea."

Other kinds of algae include the green algae, red algae, and brown algae. Algae play a major role as the primary food and oxygen producers of the oceans and lakes of the earth; it is estimated that they produce five times as much living material as do all land plants together.

Algae are generally simple aquatic plants that lack true stems, leaves, and flowers. All algae contain chlorophyll, and may vary in size from microscopic single-celled forms to the many-celled 100-foot- (30-meter-) long giant seaweeds, or *kelp,* which live attached to rocks at the edge of the sea.

Algae for microscopic study may be obtained by scraping the green film that is sometimes seen on the walls of an aquarium. Pond water is a rich source of many algae.

Among the Protista are the puzzling *euglenas,* with their plantlike and animal-like characteristics.

Most of the *protozoans* move about actively, scouring their surroundings for food. They are barely visible to the unaided eye, so it is not surprising that they were not discovered until the microscope was invented. Antony van Leeuwenhoek, a Dutch lens grinder of the seventeenth century using a single-lens microscope of his own making, was the first person to see protozoans. Among the thousands of protozoans that have been described since, there is an amazing diversity. Some, such as the amoeba, widely studied today in biology classes, are without a fixed shape and possess few parts. Others have intricate internal structures. Most live as independent animals, but some are parasites.

Protozoans reproduce characteristically by splitting in two, or, as many biology teachers are

A photograph of a living amoeba taken through a microscope. This one-celled animal changes its shape as it streams along. It feeds by wrapping itself around its food, which in this case includes several paramecia. (*Courtesy of Carolina Biological Supply Co.*)

fond of remarking, they multiply by dividing. Most are one-celled but some species consist of a colony of cells.

FUNGI

The *fungi* include a variety of groups of organisms lacking chlorophyll: yeasts, molds, and mushrooms. Fungi play a similar role to that of bacteria: They are typically organisms that promote the decay of plant and animal materials. Somewhere in the life cycle of fungi, *spores* for reproduction are formed.

Yeasts, like bacteria, are microscopic and one-celled. Some yeasts produce a chemical change in sugar, causing it to break down into alcohol and carbon dioxide gas. Humans have put this to practical advantage: Yeasts ferment the sugar in crushed grapes into alcohol, thereby making wine. In bread making the carbon dioxide pro-

duced by the action of living yeast plants "raises" the dough and so helps make a light, tasty bread.

Molds are commonly seen growing on fruit, bread, and in other places where they are not wanted. Some molds are useful in the aging of cheeses. Molds have taken on added importance because their extracts have been found useful in fighting bacteria harmful to humans. Penicillin, streptomycin, and neomycin are but a few of the growing list of *antibiotics,* as these substances are called.

The *mushroom* is known best by its stalk and cap, which is actually the reproductive part of this fungus. There is no simple rule for telling edible from poisonous mushrooms. The only way to be sure is to know the particular mushroom you pick to eat by all of its characteristics.

A *lichen* is difficult to classify because it is really two organisms growing together: an alga and a fungus. Lichens are found commonly as greenish-gray patches on rocks and soil. They grow in extremes of temperature and moisture and are found in habitats ranging from the Arctic to equatorial jungles. The alga produces food for both partners by photosynthesis, while the fungus protects the alga and provides moisture and mineral salts. Lichens disintegrate rocks to which they adhere and thus help form soil.

PLANTAE

The Mosses

All the members of the moss division of the plant kingdom possess chlorophyll. Mosses have no true roots, stems, or leaves such as are found in the more complex flowering plants. The size of mosses is severely limited because they lack a good conducting system of tubes for the distribution of food, water, and minerals. These tubes, found in the higher plants, are needed to carry vital supplies long distances from the soil. Hence, a moss plant more than a foot high would be a rarity.

The Ferns and Their Relatives

In the gamut of simple to complex plants the *ferns* are the first to be equipped with well-developed roots, stems, leaves, and an efficient conducting system of tubes. This enables them to grow to great size. The heyday of the ferns in the early days of life on earth is described in Chapter 12A. In the carboniferous period, ferns were the most highly developed plants on the earth, comparable in size to our present forest trees. Horsetails and club mosses, small relatives of ferns, also flourished in this period, reaching heights of 75 to 100 feet (23 to 30 meters).

If you turn over a fern leaf you will frequently find brown spots. These contain the *spore cases,* within which are numerous minute spores. When these spores are scattered, they start the growth of new ferns.

The Seed Plants

The *seed plants* are the most complex of all plants. They include all the common herbs, shrubs, and trees. Differences in the method of seed production determine the separation of the seed plants into two major groups: In the first group, there are no flowers, and the seeds are generally produced in cones, as in the pine tree. This group, known as the *gymnosperms* ("naked seeds"), includes the yew, hemlock, spruce, fir, cypress, sequoia, and redwood. It was once thought that the giant redwood qualified for the distinction of being the oldest and largest land plant now on earth. Today we believe that the Big Tree of Tule in Mexico has this honor. It is at least 5,000 years old, and its trunk diameter is 50 feet (15 meters).

The second group of seed plants are the flowering plants, called the *angiosperms* ("case seeds"). These bear their seeds inside closed seed cases. Angiosperms generally have thin, sheetlike leaves, in contrast to the needlelike or scalelike leaves of the gymnosperms.

There are over 250,000 kinds of flowering plants. They are found as small herbaceous plants and as vines, shrubs, and trees. It was from this group of plants that people long ago selected those with useful qualities for cultivation. A large part of our food is derived from seeds, mainly from the grains. From grain comes the flour that makes bread, the "staff of life." Our clothing is woven from such plant fibers as cotton and linen. When we become ill we often heal ourselves with plant products. Although modern chemists can synthesize many drugs, we still depend on plants for such vital extracts as digitalis for regulating heart action, opium and its derivatives for relief of pain, and cocaine and its derivatives for anesthesia. Modern chemical industry uses cellulose, which the plant makes as a covering around its cells, as the raw material for such products as rayon and the cellulose-based plastics.

We should not overlook the aesthetic appeal of flowering plants, which bring a rainbow of colors and many exotic odors to the planet Earth.

ANIMALIA

What in common speech is called an "animal" is usually one of the four-footed fur- or hair-bearing mammals, such as a sheep, dog, horse, or cow. These are simply the most familiar animals. There are many markedly different forms—worms, starfish, birds, for example—equally entitled to be called animals. Animals fall readily into one of two types: Some have a backbone, and some do not. Animals without a backbone are called *invertebrates*; those with a backbone are called *vertebrates*. The vertebrates come first to our minds because they are more familiar and are generally large. Of all the different kinds of animals, however, only 5 percent are vertebrates.

The major divisions of the animal kingdom are called *phyla* (singular *phylum*).

Sponges

The *sponges* are the first phylum of many-celled animals with cellular *specialization*. Certain cells take food out of sea water, digest it, and pass it along to others that specialize in protection, mechanical support, and reproduction. The saclike bodies of sponges are living waterways. Currents of water sweep in through microscopic pores that cover the entire surface. Minute food particles are removed from the water, which is then swept out through a large opening at one end of the animal. The *natural* sponge used occasionally in homes and in industry is the dried and cleaned skeleton of sponge animals.

Corals and Their Relatives

Extending partway around the continent of Australia is the famed Great Barrier Reef. A *reef* is a complex association of plants and animals that are responsible for the massive accumulation of limestone that gives the reef its body. The chief plants are limestone-secreting algae, and the chief animals are the corals, member of the *coelenterate* phylum of animals. The reef is built from thousands of generations of the cemented skeletons of corals and algae, together with the remains of many other animals.

The corals and their relatives—the sea anemones, the jellyfish, the hydras, and the Portuguese man-of-war—are alike in having a body that is essentially a hollow sac, with a single opening surrounded by movable tentacles. The tentacles are used for capturing tiny animals and bringing them into the sac, where they are digested. There is more division of labor in the coelenterates than in the sponges: Muscle cells move the tentacles, or in times of danger contract the entire body into a compact cylinder; elongated nerve cells coordinate the contractions; and specialized sensory cells respond to external stimuli such as gravity, light, or direct contact. The saclike body of the corals and jellyfish, with its hundreds of special-

ized cells, is the forerunner of the more complex body form of higher animals with organs and systems.

Worms

We include here three phyla of animals: flatworms, roundworms, and segmented worms. A free-living, that is, nonparasitic flatworm, *Planaria*, is commonly found in ponds, where it feeds on small organisms. A planarian worm exhibits *bilateral symmetry*: Its right half is approximately the mirror image of its left. Associated with such symmetry is an anterior (head) and a posterior (tail) end, and an upper and under surface. With the head goes a concentration of nerves and sense organs. These characteristics (among others) distinguish the flatworms, and the round and the segmented worms as well, from the corals and jellyfish. Bilateral symmetry is the rule in the animals that are most familiar to you. Free-living flatworms such as the Planaria are exceptional: Most, such as the tapeworms and flukes, live parasitically at the expense of other animals.

The roundworms are widespread over the earth. A spadeful of garden soil teems with millions of them. Some roundworms are parasitic on other animals. The one of chief importance in the United States is the hookworm. The scientific name of this worm is indicative of its role: *Necator americanus*, which means "the American killer." Hookworms were once the scourge of the southern states. They enter the body from the soil by burrowing through the soles of the feet. They make their way to the small intestine where they hook on, feed, and reproduce. The eggs pass out with the feces and develop into worms. Another parasitic roundworm is the *trichina worm*, which is taken into the body by eating insufficiently cooked pork.

The segmented worms are typified by the common *earthworm*. This burrower makes its way through the earth by swallowing soil, digesting the plant and animal matter in it, and discharging the rest. In doing this it performs a useful function in agriculture. Tunneling up, it brings the lower layers of soil with rich mineral content into the upper part, making the minerals available for plant growth. Also, the worm's progress through the soil makes the soil porous, so that water and air, essential to plant life, can percolate through and reach the roots of plants. One of the first scientists to point out the significant contribution of the earthworm was Charles Darwin, who estimated that earthworms brought 18 tons of soil to the surface of one acre each year.

Mollusks

The *mollusks* are the second largest phylum of invertebrates, numbering about 80,000 species. Their tasty, soft, fleshy bodies have made them an important source of food in the human diet. The mollusks with one-piece shells include snails, conches, and whelks. Many people collect the colorful and decorative shells of these animals. Some are used in making jewelry and ornaments. The mollusks with two shells are represented by oysters, clams, and scallops. Oysters are the makers of the treasured pearl. When a foreign particle gets into its body, the irritated mollusk secretes a pearly material around the particle. Humans take advantage of this reaction and induce oysters to make pearls. A particle of sand or other substance is put under the shell, and the oyster proceeds to build a pearl around it. A third group of mollusks includes the nautilus, the squid, and the octopus. The squid is a jet-propelled animal. It usually moves by taking in water and ejecting it forcefully to the back through a narrow tube or funnel. This action pushes it rapidly in the opposite direction from the squirted water. It can steer itself by turning the funnel in different directions.

The giant squid is the largest known living invertebrate; it may grow up to 50 feet (15 meters) in length and weigh as much as 2 tons. It is probably one of the animals responsible for the age-old legends of "sea monsters."

The Joint-legged Invertebrates

Of all the major phyla in the animal kingdom, the *arthropods* contain by far the largest number of described species of animals, numbering 1 million. All the arthropods have an external skeleton made of a tough material, called *chitin,* and jointed legs. The three major classes in this tremendous group are the crustaceans, the arachnids, and the insects.

The *crustaceans* (krŭs-tā-shănz) include crayfish, lobsters, shrimps, and crabs. With a few exceptions these animals breathe with gills, and most of them live in the sea. They range in size from microscopic water fleas, to barnacles an inch wide, to the 50-pound (23 kilogram) American lobster and the Japanese spider crab, with a span of 9 feet (3 meters) between the tips of its first pair of legs. This group is an important source of food for human beings.

Spiders and their relatives have four pairs of walking legs and are generally air breathers. Included in this class, called the *arachnids* (ă-răk-nĭdz), are not only the spiders but also scorpions, ticks, and mites.

The *insects* have three pairs of legs and their bodies are divided into three parts: head, thorax, and abdomen. They are the largest class in the animal kingdom, represented by 700,000 separate species. There are 112,000 known kinds of butterflies and moths alone! The insects have penetrated almost every niche of the earth, adapting themselves to an amazing variety of environmental conditions: Insects live in frigid and in tropical zones, in deserts and in rain forests, on prairies and on mountaintops.

Some insects are harmful to humans. The corn borer destroys our food while it is growing in the fields. The clothes moth destroys our clothing, and the termite our wooden homes. The anopheles mosquito carries the protozoan that causes malaria.

Insects also exist that are helpful to humans. Bees, wasps, and butterflies help in the pollination of flowers of many plants that we depend on for

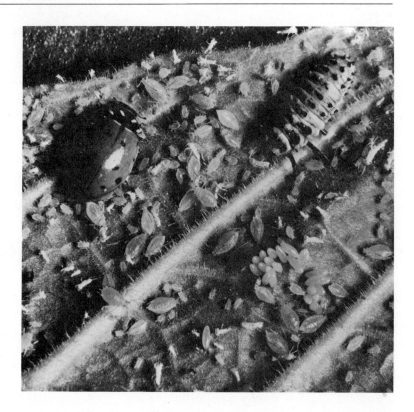

Adult and larva of lady beetle, feeding on aphids. *(Courtesy of U.S. Dept. of Agriculture, from Clemson Agricultural College.)*

food. The products of the honeybee and silkworm are used directly. Some insects help to keep harmful insects under control. An example is the dragonfly, which devours flies and mosquitoes.

Three other classes of arthropods are the *centipedes,* the *millipedes,* and the *horseshoe crabs.*

Spiny-skinned Animals

The *echinoderms,* or spiny-skinned animals, are typified by the starfish. All the starfish and their relatives live in salt water. Despite their name the starfish are no more akin to fish than are the shellfish, such as oysters and crabs. In addition to their spiny skins, starfish are noted for their system of water tubes. Water is drawn into an opening in the body and then forced under pressure into thousands of small cylinders called *tube feet,* which protrude from its arms. These feet have

suckers at their ends. The starfish moves itself from place to place by applying and then releasing its tube feet on the surface on which it is moving. The pull of the tube feet also helps the starfish open the clams, oysters, scallops, and mussels that serve as its food.

In addition to the starfish, the echinoderms include animals with such self-describing names as brittle stars, basket stars, sea urchins, sand dollars, sea cucumbers, and sea lilies.

Animals with Backbones

The most highly developed group of animals is the backboned animals, the *vertebrates,* characterized by an internal bony skeleton. There are five main classes of backboned animals: fish, amphibians, reptiles, birds, and mammals. We shall consider them briefly here because they will be referred to frequently in the latter part of this chapter and in the next chapter.

Fish have scaly skins and two-chambered hearts, breathe by means of gills, lay eggs without a shell, and are cold-blooded.

A cold-blooded animal is one whose body temperature is not regulated by internal body mechanisms as it is in a mammal. Rather, it maintains a favorable body temperature by *behavioral* means: For example, it may migrate, or burrow, or bask in the sun. Fish, amphibians, and reptiles are cold-blooded. Cold-blooded animals become sluggish and frequently hibernate when the temperature drops. Birds and mammals are warm-blooded, maintaining approximately the same temperature at all times. The ability to do this makes these animals relatively independent of outside conditions, so that they can remain active in very cold weather. (Some birds apparently conserve energy by having their body temperature drop sharply at night, when they are unable to feed.)

Amphibians include frogs, toads, newts, and salamanders. They have three-chambered hearts and moist skins, lay eggs, and are cold-blooded. In most cases, the amphibians spend part of their life in water and part of it on land. Some, such as the mud puppies and hellbenders, never leave the water; some, such as frogs and newts, divide their time between water and land; some, such as toads, some frogs, and some salamanders, spend most of their adult life on land.

Almost all amphibians mate in the water and lay their eggs there. The young, or *tadpoles,* breathe through gills, but the adult uses its lungs and moist skin for respiration. (Recent findings suggest that the skin serves as an effective organ of gas exchange of oxygen and carbon dioxide, and can supplement or replace the work of lungs or gills not only in amphibians but also in many vertebrates—fish, reptiles, and in the embryonic stages of birds and mammals.) A few of the amphibians are used by humans for food; many are helpful because they feed on harmful insects.

Reptiles breathe through lungs, have three- or four-chambered hearts and scaly skins, lay eggs

covered by a tough shell, and are cold-blooded. Typical reptiles are snakes, lizards, alligators, crocodiles, and turtles. Some of these are used for food by humans; others are prized for their skin or shell. Some of the reptiles, notably certain snakes, make venom with which to poison their prey. The poisonous snakes in the United States are the coral, copperhead, water moccasin, and rattlesnake. Despite their deadly venom, rattlesnakes kill few people in this country. Given a chance, a rattlesnake will silently glide away rather than join in battle with humans.

Birds have achieved mastery of the air. They have feathers and four-chambered hearts, breathe through lungs, lay eggs covered with a hard shell, and are warm-blooded. If you have ever held a live chick in your hand you are well aware of how warm birds are. They are the warmest of all animals, with average temperatures of 100° to 110°F (38° to 43°C). This need to keep warm makes birds large eaters. Many of the smaller birds, such as the warblers, will eat their own weight of food in a day. Birds are very valuable to human beings in helping to keep insect pests under control. The birds of prey, such as hawks and owls, are now recognized as important aids in helping to keep down the numbers of four-footed vermin, such as mice and rats. Birds are also an important source of food to humans.

The *mammals* are warm-blooded animals that possess hair and nurse their young on milk from mammary glands. They are the only vertebrates possessing a *diaphragm* that separates the abdomen from the chest cavity. They are distinguished by the complexity of their brains, which is greatest in human beings.

Within the mammal group there is wide variety in structure and in ways of living. Some mammals, such as the bat, whose forelimbs are fitted for flight, have taken to the air. Other mammals, such as the whale, live in the ocean but must rise to the top to breathe in air with their lungs. Some mammals, such as the hoofed camel, deer, and horse, are vegetarians. Others, such as the lion, tiger, and wolf, are flesh eaters. The animals with the greatest development of the brain are the monkeys, apes, and humans. Mammals vary widely in size from the tiniest rodents to the sulphur-bottom whale, the largest animal that ever lived, past or present.

In this brief survey of the kingdoms of living things we have stressed the economic importance of the various forms of life to human beings. In so doing we do not wish to leave the impression that the different organisms have evolved for the particular purpose of serving humans or that they should be considered solely in this light. Each is a living thing, from bacteria to human being. Humans are but one of the multitude of living things on this planet.

THE METHOD OF CLASSIFICATION

Biologists classify living things according to the following scheme:

Kingdom
  Phylum
    Class
      Order
        Family
          Genus
            Species

To understand this system, let us see how it is used to classify human beings—literally, to put them in their place:

Kingdom: *Animal.* We are one of 1¼ million species of animals.
Phylum: *Chordates.* Most of the animals in this group are known as vertebrates, animals with backbones, which include fish, amphibia, reptiles, birds, and mammals.
Class: *Mammals.* Humans are one of 6,000 kinds in this hairy, warm-blooded group that feeds milk to its young.
Order: *Primates.* We are a distinguished member of this order, which also includes monkeys, lemurs, and apes.
Family: *Hominidae.* This group includes not only present-day humans, but also ancient prehuman

forms (see pp. 377–378), some of which are believed to have lived 20 million years ago. (The word *family,* when used in classification, has nothing to do with our everyday use of this word.)
Genus: *Homo.* A smaller group that includes Peking man and present-day humans.
Species: *Sapiens.* This group is limited to human beings only. It includes all humans living on earth today, but has recently been expanded by some taxonomists to include Neanderthal and Cro-Magnon man.

An examination of this method of classification reveals that as one proceeds from kingdom to species there are fewer and fewer kinds in each group, and the kinds of living things in each group are more and more alike. This method of classification also provides a scientific way of naming an organism: The name consists of the genus and species designation. Thus, the scientific name of human beings is *Homo sapiens.* This two-name system of naming plants and animals (known as *binomial nomenclature*) was invented by Linnaeus, a Swedish botanist, and described in his book *Systema Naturae,* published in 1735. The method provides a name that is internationally accepted and recognized for every organism. At the same time the name fits the living thing into its natural place in its kingdom. For example, the common house cat has the name *Felis domesticus*; the lion is *Felis leo*; the tiger, *Felis tigris.* The system of naming reveals that these animals belong to the same genus, and are all closely related.

What criteria have been used by taxonomists for determining the place of an organism in the classification scheme? A review of the plant and animal groups just described would indicate that *structure,* both internal and external, is of paramount importance. Having six legs separates the insects from the eight-legged spiders. Within the insect class the kind of mouth parts, number and type of wings, and the nature of the *metamorphosis* (change from egg to adult) determine the *order* of an insect, such as beetle, true bug, butterfly, or moth. More recently taxonomists have also employed such characteristics as chromosome number and shape, and subtle chemical differences and similarities, particularly in the nature of DNA, the molecules that comprise the heredity material of cells.

THE FLOWERING PLANT

The landscapes of the earth are bedecked with over 250,000 varieties of flowering plants. The diversity of form, size, and color of the herbs, shrubs, and trees create the varied fields and forests of our planet. Yet all these plants show basic similarities in their internal structure and in the functioning of their roots, stems, leaves, and flowers.

The Leaf: Food Factory

Climb to the top of a hill and look out over the countryside. The dominant color of the meadows, valleys, and hillsides is green. This is no accident, for green is the color of *chlorophyll,* the stuff that makes life on earth possible. It is this green pigment that enables every plant possessing it to combine atoms from two of the commonest substances on our planet, water and carbon dioxide, to form sugar. In plants we take this process for granted. But if you were looking at a glass of carbonated water (which is nothing but water and bubbles of carbon dioxide gas) and suddenly the water and bubbles disappeared and just as suddenly a lump of sugar appeared in the bottom you would say, "Magic!" Yet green plants perform this chemical "magic" every day (chemical changes are discussed more fully in Chapter 14A).

The main food factory of common plants is located in the leaves. A leaf is well adapted for its job. Leaves are constructed to present a broad surface to the sunlight for energy for the food-making process. Yet because they are so thin no cell is far removed from the surface. Immediately below the upper *epidermis,* as the layer of cells comprising the leaf surface is called, is a closely packed group of cells of the *palisade* layer, which are conspicuous for the large number of green *chloroplasts* within them. Beneath the palisade layer is the *spongy* layer, composed of irregularly shaped cells that have fewer chloroplasts. It is in the palisade and spongy layers that food manufacturing occurs.

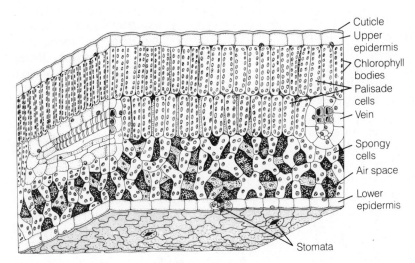

Cuticle
Upper epidermis
Chlorophyll bodies
Palisade cells
Vein
Spongy cells
Air space
Lower epidermis
Stomata

The food factory of the plant—a block diagram of a section of a leaf.

The sun's rays coming through the semitransparent epidermis reach the chloroplasts in the palisade and spongy cells. The raw materials for food making come to these cells from two sources, the air and the soil. On the surface of the leaf are found numbers of microscopic openings, each between two *guard cells*. These openings are the *stomata* of the leaf. Changes in the shape of the guard cells cause the stomata to open or close. Air passes freely through the stomata into air spaces inside the leaf. The gas carbon dioxide is then taken out of the air by the food-making layer of cells. Meanwhile, water is absorbed from the soil by the millions of minute cells, the *root hairs*, projecting from the plant's roots. From the root-hair cells, water moves to tubes inside the roots, which transport it up through the stem into the veins of the leaf. At last the water reaches the food-making cells. Here the green chlorophyll has trapped some of the energy of sunlight. The energy is used (in a series of steps) to make sugar from atoms supplied by molecules of water and carbon dioxide. A valuable by-product, oxygen, also results from the chemical process (see the chemical equation for this process on p. 460). The oxygen is released by the leaf through the stomata to the air. In this way the atmosphere of the earth is freshened with some 400 billion tons of oxygen each year, replacing the oxygen used up by living things.

The knowledge that green plants take in carbon dioxide and release oxygen during sugar manufacture should not make us forget that *in the process of respiration, plants, like animals, take in oxygen and give off carbon dioxide*. It is *untrue* to say that "plants breathe in the opposite way that animals do."

The scientific name for the process of sugar making is constructed of two words that emphasize the key aspect of the action: photo, which means "light," and synthesis, which means "putting together." *Photosynthesis*, "putting together by means of light," is exactly what happens in the process.

Much has been added to our knowledge of photosynthesis in recent years. It is now known that light energy, water, carbon dioxide, nitrates, and sulfates are combined in the chlorophyll bodies of leaves to produce many organic compounds. *Amino acids*, the building blocks of proteins, are synthesized there. These are essential for cell growth. Carbohydrates—sugars and starches—are synthesized to meet the energy requirements of cells.

The remarkable process of photosynthesis not only produces the basic materials essential for the existence of green plants, but eventually supplies all living things on our planet with the chemical compounds needed for the substances of their structures and for the energy to carry on life processes. Moreover, as we have seen, photosynthesis returns to the atmosphere the oxygen that is taken out of it by living organisms.

In recent years scientists have succeeded in duplicating part of this process in test tubes. Perhaps someday they will be able to manufacture food in large quantities from abundant chemicals. Until that day we shall have to continue to depend for our food upon the living cells of plants, using chlorophyll to trap energy from sunlight, and carbon dioxide and water as the basic raw materials.

The Stem: Transporter and Supporter

The stem of a plant supports the leaves and flowers and serves as a passageway for the exchange of materials between the leaves and roots. Two streams of vital materials flow through the living plant: One stream carries water and dissolved minerals from the roots through the stem and into the leaves through a pipelike tissue known as *xylem*. Some of the water is used in photosynthesis, as we have seen. Most of the water evaporates from the air spaces of the leaf through the stomata to the outside air. The loss of water, known as *transpiration*, can be considerable. It has been estimated that a single corn plant, which requires 100 days to grow from seed to maturity, releases 50 gallons of water to the atmosphere in that period.

The second stream in plants transports manufactured food, principally sugar, from the leaf down through the stem and then to other plant structures, such as flowers and roots. The tissue responsible for the distribution of food is known as *phloem.*

In the stems of herbaceous plants, such as the soft stems of low-growing plants, the xylem and phloem tissues are contained within *vascular bundles.* The "strings" in a plant structure, such as a celery stalk, are a familiar example of these bundles. Branches of the vascular bundles run into the leaves, where they become the veins. In a tree the water-carrying xylem tissue makes up the sapwood, generally the outer part of the solid center cylinder of the tree. The sugar-carrying phloem lines the inner bark. Between the xylem and phloem lies the *cambium,* a thin sheet of dividing cells that contributes to the growth of the stem by adding new xylem and phloem cells (see pp. 295–296).

Girdling a tree, that is, removing a complete ring of bark and cambium from it, kills the tree, for it severs the pipelines that carry food and destroys the layer of cells responsible for the continued life of the plant.

The cambium grows new layers each year, adding to the girth of the tree. It grows more actively in the spring, so there is a marked difference between the spring growth and that of the rest of the year. This results in *annual rings,* which can be seen when a tree is cut across. Counting these rings gives an estimate of the age of the tree.

The Root: Anchor and Absorber

The root is both an anchoring and an absorbing device. The outer layer of the root contains cells with long projections called *root hairs.* These microscopic "hairs" reach out into the soil to a surprising degree and absorb water and dissolved minerals. In a single rye plant it was found that there were 14 billion root hairs. If the surfaces of all these hairs were spread out flat, they would cover an area 4,300 square feet (about 400 square meters). This means that these root hairs are in

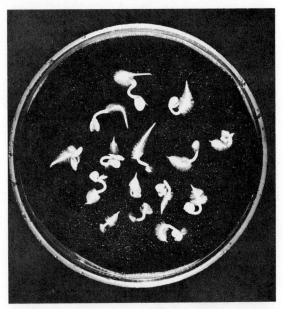

A magnifying glass shows that the fine fuzz of these radish seedlings is made of thousands of delicate root hairs. *(From* Botany *by Carl E. Wilson; © 1952 by Holt, Rinehart and Winston, Inc. Reprinted by permission of Holt, Rinehart and Winston.)*

contact with 4,300 square feet (400 square meters) of soil, from which they can absorb valuable minerals and water. The materials absorbed by the root hairs are passed through other cells into the xylem and thence to the stem and leaves of the plant (see pp. 283–285).

The larger roots have tough fibers that give them the great strength needed to hold the plant in the ground. This, added to the gripping effect of the enormous root system, with each root hair firmly embedded in soil particles, enables even large trees to withstand the buffeting of strong winds.

The Flower: Seed Producer

The flower contains the organs devoted to *reproduction,* the process in which two cell nuclei unite to form a new individual. The flower makes these nuclei—sperm and egg—and also provides for their coming together and uniting.

A typical flower has a number of brightly colored petals that often have a distinctive odor. The color and odor serve to attract insects needed for *cross-pollination,* which is the transfer of pollen from one flower to another of the same kind. Some flowers do not require insects to carry their pollen; the wind serves this purpose. *Wind-pollinated* flowers make huge amounts of pollen, which compensates for the pollen wasted by this hit-or-miss method. Some flowers are *self-pollinated,* the transfer of pollen taking place from the male to the female parts of the same flower (see pp. 302–303).

The part of the flower engaged in pollen making is the *stamen.* The top of the stamen is an enlarged sac, called the *anther,* where the pollen is formed. Supporting the anther is a long thin stalk, the *filament.* The pollen grain is a microscopic structure containing the male reproductive nucleus, the *sperm.* To succeed in its function the pollen must be carried to the *pistil* of a flower of the same kind. The pistil generally consists of three parts: the ovary, the style, and the stigma. The large lower portion of the pistil is the *ovary.* Within it are produced the *ovules;* inside each ovule is an *egg,* the female reproductive cell. Above the ovary is the slender stemlike *style.* The top of the style is the *stigma,* which is equipped with hairs and a sticky secretion to hold any pollen grains that may land on it. The pollen grain grows a tube that extends down through the style and into the ovary. Finally it reaches a special opening in the ovule. The sperm of the pollen grain passes into the ovule through the channel thus made and unites with the egg. This union of the sperm and the egg is called *fertilization.* The fertilized egg resulting from this union will develop into an *embryo,* a baby plant.

After fertilization the flower begins to wither. Parts no longer needed, such as petals, stamens, and parts of the pistil, wither or fall off, but the remaining parts of the flower grow to many times their original size. The fertilized egg develops into

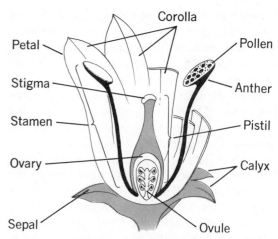

The flower contains the reproductive organs of the plant. Shown here are the characteristic structures found in most flowers.

an embryo. The ovule develops into a seed. The ovary develops into the *fruit.* A fruit, then, is the ripened ovary containing seeds. That is why the tomato is really a fruit, even though people customarily call it a vegetable.

There are many different kinds of fruits. They include edible varieties such as apples, string beans, green peppers, and cucumbers, as well as inedible varieties such as milkweed pods, rose "apples," winged maple keys, and sycamore "button-balls."

A seed is made up of the young plant, a food supply, and a protective coat. The embryo has two parts, one of which becomes the roots and the other the stem and leaves. As the seed dries, its food supply is concentrated or "dehydrated." This makes a seed a prime food for human beings. The most important plant foods are seeds, such as corn, wheat, rice, barley, oats, and beans. In addition to their food value, plant seeds furnish such valuable substances as oil—for example, linseed oil—and drugs, such as opium from the poppy seed.

The Scattering of Seeds

Many seeds and fruits are a colorful part of the autumn scene. Formation of the fruit with its seeds is only the first step in the propagation of plants. To germinate next year, the seeds must reach a suitable place. If the seeds of a plant simply fell beneath it they would have to compete with each other and with the parent for room, soil minerals, water, and light. The conflict is diminished by the scattering of seeds. Examination of the varied devices and agencies of seed dispersal is an excellent study in adaptation. We shall consider how seeds are adapted for dispersal by wind, animals, water, and by mechanical means.

For many seeds, the wind is the distributing agent. Some wind-dispersed seeds and fruits are equipped with fine, feathery plumes or tufts of hair that act much as a parachute does. The seed is sustained in the air long enough for the wind to blow it some distance. Familiar examples of plants whose seeds are so equipped are the cattail, milkweed, aster, dandelion, goldenrod, and the sycamore tree. Children are familiar with the ethereal, gray sphere of dandelion seeds, each equipped with a delicate parachute. They take delight in seeing how few puffs it takes to dislodge all the seeds. Other seeds are adapted for wind journeys by having wings. The familiar "polly nose" of the maple tree is an example of this type.

Nectar-collecting honeybee on alfalfa blossom. The bee also picks up alfalfa pollen, seen here as the white mass packed on the hind leg. *Photo by W.P Nye. (Courtesy of U.S. Dept. of Agriculture.)*

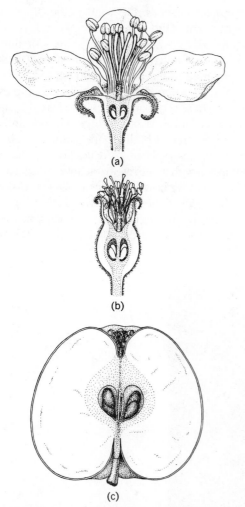

The apple blossom produces the apple. Note how some of the floral parts become less conspicuous or drop off as the ovary ripens to become the core of the seed-carrying fruit. (a) Flower of apples; (b) older flower after petals have fallen off; (c) section of the mature fruit.

drops its seeds. This happens in tumbleweeds, which include amaranth pigweeds, Russian thistle, and some grasses. One pigweed plant may scatter as many as 10 million seeds in this way! (See pp. 302–303.)

Seeds that are adapted for dispersal by animals may have an edible fruit with seeds whose coats are indigestible. In this case, as in the apple, the fleshy, edible part of the fruit is eaten by an animal, such as a deer, together with the seeds. The indigestible seed coat prevents destruction of the seed in the juices of the animal's digestive system. Ultimately, the seeds are eliminated with the other food wastes. By this time the animal will probably be distant from the site where the fruit originally grew, and so the plant is spread. The scattering of edible nuts, such as walnuts, acorns, and hickory nuts, depends on a slight variation of this process. If the animal eats the nut the seed is destroyed. But many animals—squirrels, chipmunks, and field mice—bury such nuts in the ground for future feeding. Those nuts that the animals do not dig up may germinate in the following spring and further colonize their species.

Animals help scatter seeds in another way. Some seeds have hooks that catch on the fur of an animal as it brushes past the plant. Later on, the seed is brushed off, but by this time the animal may have carried the seed a long way from the mother plant. The common cockleburs, burdocks, "sticktights" of the burr marigold, and "beggar's ticks" are examples of seeds that "hitchhike" on the fur of animals or the clothes of humans.

Water is also an agent in the scattering of seeds. Seeds and fruits are often transported over short distances by the washing of rain along the ground, or over long distances by streams. The classic example of a water-dispersed seed is the coconut. As it comes from the tree it is a massive fruit whose outer bark, or husk, is made of a myriad interwoven fibers in which air is trapped. (This outer part is removed before the coconut reaches the market.) The husk is buoyant enough to support the heavy inner nut that contains the embryo. The covering of the coconut is waterproof, an-

Other common winged seeds are those of the ash, elm, tulip, pine, and ailanthus trees. Wind dispersal is sometimes accomplished by the movement of the entire above-ground part of the plant, which, when mature, rolls along the ground and

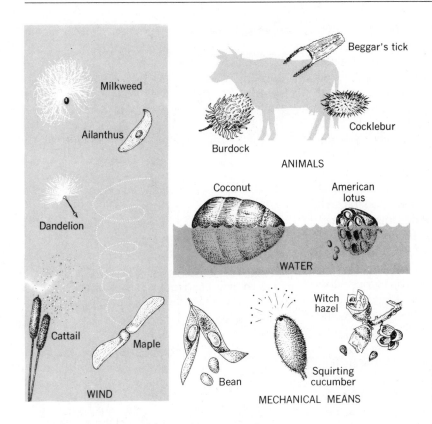

Examples of seeds dispersed by wind, animals, water, and mechanical devices.

other necessity of a water-borne seed. How effective this device is may be seen from the fact that the coconut palm is one of the first plants to appear on newly created coral islands or atolls in the South Pacific. There is no doubt that some of these coconuts float thousands of miles on the ocean surface.

Some seeds are scattered by being propelled from the plant. An example of this is found in the witch hazel tree, which blooms in the fall when the nutlike fruits formed from flowers of the previous fall are also evident. These trees have an interesting seed-scattering device: As the fruit dries, the cover suddenly breaks open and the small black seeds are shot out some distance in a way similar to the shooting of an orange seed from between the fingers.

The Seed: Plant Producer

Germination, the development of a seed into a plant with roots, stems, and leaves, depends on the availability of food, oxygen, suitable temperature, and water. The food supply is contained within the seed. There is enough food there to last until the roots are established in the ground and the first green leaves exposed to the sun are ready to carry on photosynthesis. Oxygen is essential for the oxidation of food and the resulting release of energy. The soil in which plants grow must be porous to allow air to circulate down to the roots. The warmth needed for germination is supplied by the sun, which warms the ground. Water is essential for the germination of the seed. Water softens the hard seed coat and penetrates the seed. The cells take in water, become active, and multiply. All chemical processes in the cells, such as the digestion of stored starch into sugar, require water as a medium. Water is also needed as a vital component of the new living material forming in the cells of the rapidly growing plant.

With the softening and swelling of the seed coat the part of the embryo that will form the roots breaks out. Roots serve to obtain water and to anchor the plant in the soil. In seeds such as the bean the root-making part forms an arch that soon breaks through the soil. Thereupon the arch straightens out and the two food-storage halves of the seed, the *cotyledons,* are thus pulled out of the ground. Protectively sandwiched between the cotyledons are the first leaves and the embryo stem. Once above ground the cotyledons separate. The food stored in the cotyledons is slowly digested and transported to other parts of the seedling. The stem elongates and the leaves grow, turn green, and start making food.

In seeds that have only one cotyledon, such as corn, development is a bit different. The roots develop first, but then a spearlike sheath emerges that encloses the first leaves. Its spear shape permits it to push through the soil readily while protecting the tender leaves within. Soon this spear

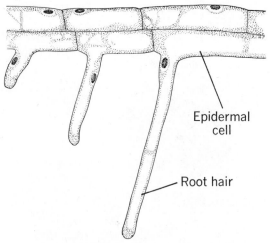

The stages of development of root hairs from a root of timothy. Each root hair is an extension of a cell.

(Left) Stages in the germination of the garden bean. The two cotyledons provide food until the plant is able to make its own. *(Right)* Germination of the corn seed. The single cotyledon of the corn seed remains underground as the seedling grows.

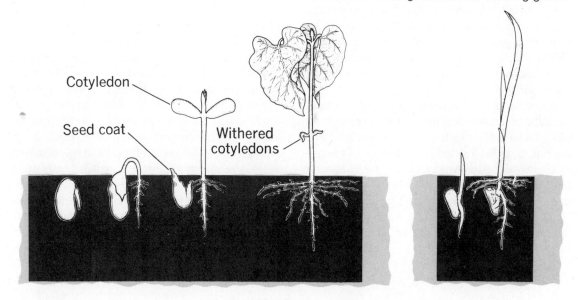

point shows above ground, and the leaves unfold, turn green, and start making food. In these plants the main bulk of the seed, containing the food for the embryo, remains below ground. The food is soon used up, and the seed remnants shrivel as the seedling grows.

The water, minerals, and carbon dioxide that the plant takes in are used in food manufacture and in building living material in its cells. The plant enlarges as millions of the building bricks, cells, are added. The stem reaches higher and higher, and more and more leaves are formed. The plant is now on its own.

LIFE CYCLE OF SOME VERTEBRATES

Samuel Butler once said, "The hen is the egg's way of making more eggs." We may not accept this definition, but we can see in it an emphasis on the continuity of life; egg to adult to egg to adult. . . .

The life of most animals begins when an egg and sperm join. The fertilized egg resulting from the union of these two sex cells begins to divide into many cells and to form an embryo. The embryo continues to develop, ultimately becoming an adult, either male or female. Sperm produced by the male and eggs by the female unite, and the cycle is repeated. Let us examine the life history of some typical vertebrate animals.

Fish

The spawning season for fish in temperate zones is in the spring. The return of the salmon to the Columbia River for spawning is well known. Salmon live in the ocean, but travel far up rivers to breed. The 10,000 or more eggs produced in the ovaries of each female fish are released into the waters of a quiet pool. Millions of sperm, made in the testes of the male, are deposited on the eggs, fertilizing them. After spawning, the exhausted adults usually die. The fertilized eggs develop into young salmon, which eventually swim to the ocean. When mature, these salmon will find their way back to the same stream where

they were spawned and continue the cycle of reproduction.

Some fish, such as many of the tropical fish with which people stock their home aquaria, seem to bear their young alive. This is only an illusion, because the fish actually lay eggs, but these eggs after fertilization are retained within the body of the female to complete their early growth. These "live bearers" are not live bearers in the sense that mammals are, because there is no direct connection of the tissues of the growing embryo with those of the female. Hence neither food nor oxygen can be supplied from the bloodstream of the mother, as is the case in mammals.

Frogs

Frogs mate in the spring, the male typically clasping the female until the eggs are expelled. The male fertilizes the eggs in the water by discharging sperm over them. Mating thus increases the chances of sperm meeting eggs. After mating, the pair separate, having no interest in their offspring. What the eggs lack in safety they make up in number, anywhere from several hundred to several thousand eggs being laid by one female, the number depending on the species of the frog. Moreover, each egg is amply stocked with yolk, which supplies the developing embryo with food until well after hatching has occurred.

Each egg is embedded in a clear jellylike sphere. All the eggs laid by the frog stick together in a mass; this provides some degree of protection against fish and other pond enemies. The development of the egg from its very first stages to adult frog may be watched easily if some of the eggs are placed in a jar or aquarium with some pond water. While still inside the jelly the egg changes into a tiny embryo that wriggles occasionally. After about ten days to two weeks the tadpole wriggles out of the jelly, which by now has started to disintegrate.

The tadpole breathes through gills, which are flaps of tissue with thin outer membranes and a rich supply of blood. As the pond water streams over the gills, oxygen dissolved in the water passes through the thin membrane into the bloodstream. At the same time the excess carbon dioxide waste in the blood is discharged through the gills into the water.

The tadpole grows, eating bits of plant material that are in the pond. Its tail grows into a fin capable of moving the tadpole rapidly through the water. At this stage the developing frog is indeed very much like a fish. This is no accident, for the frog, like all higher vertebrates, reveals in its early development traces of its fishlike ancestry. (More precisely, in their early development higher animals exhibit similarities to the *embryonic stages* of lower forms. The tadpole resembles the *embryo* fish.) After some time, hind legs and then front legs develop; the material of the tail is broken down and absorbed by the frog to build other parts of its body. The gills are replaced by lungs; other internal changes occur. The frog changes its diet, eating only living worms and insects (see pp. 298–299, 303–304).

The common leopard frog completes this change or *metamorphosis*, as it is called, in a few months. The bullfrog, on the other hand, remains a tadpole for two years before changing into an adult frog.

The frog is a cold-blooded animal. In the

The gradual metamorphosis of the frog illustrates how completely some animals change as they develop. The frog's fishlike ancestry is revealed in its early stages of development.

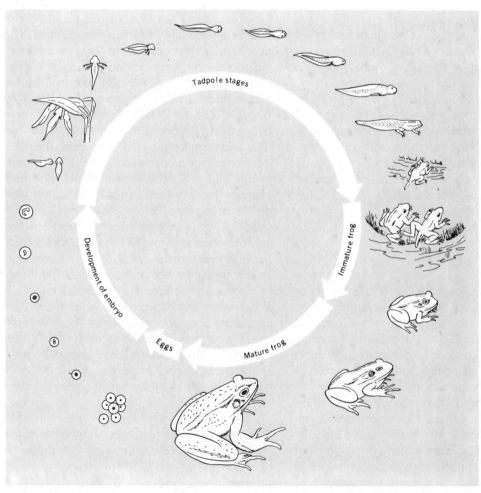

Tadpole stages

Immature frog

Development of embryo

Eggs

Mature frog

colder parts of the country, with the approach of winter, it slows down and hibernates in the mud at the bottom of its pond. In this torpid state all body functions are reduced to a minimum. Living on food stored during the lush days, it is able to survive until warm days arrive again. The moist skin of the frog is thin enough to permit the passage of oxygen from the pond water into its blood and the exit of carbon dioxide.

Reptiles

In land animals fertilization is internal; that is, the sperm reaches the egg while it is inside the body of the female. This is essential, because the sperm and eggs require a moist environment to survive. Consequently, reptiles, birds, and mammals must have internal fertilization.

Most reptiles lay eggs covered with a soft leathery shell. Some, like the turtle, deposit the eggs in sand and then depart, providing no care for the young. The sun warms the sand and incubates the eggs. The newborn turtle is ready to fend for itself and soon starts off in search of food. In some snakes, the eggs after fertilization are retained in the body of the female. The young snakes hatch from the eggs inside the mother and then leave the body.

Birds

Birds reproduce in essentially the same way as reptiles. Fertilization is internal; development, however, is always external. Nest construction follows mating, which takes place at different times for different birds. Owls and hawks mate early. Their offspring can be fed on the young of such animals as rabbits, rats, and field mice, which are abundant in early spring. Birds that feed their young on insects mate later. When the young are hatched, there is a sufficient supply of insects to feed them.

Most birds' eggs hatch after about three weeks of incubation. During the period of incubation the mother bird is confined to the nest to keep the eggs warm; she leaves only for a few moments to get water and to exercise. In many species of birds the mother is fed during incubation by the father, who is kept busy bringing food to the nest. The eggs are carefully drawn up into the feathers of the mother bird for greater warmth. The shell is porous, permitting oxygen to pass through it from the air to the developing embryo. The bulk of the bird's egg furnishes a complete "diet" for the embryo. Many birds hatch out in a helpless state and depend on their parents for food for some time.

Mammals

In mammals the minute egg (barely visible to the unaided eye) is fertilized within the body of the female; it then attaches itself to the mother. Here it remains for the period of development. The mother and the embryo develop a special membrane, the *placenta*, through which food and oxygen are supplied to the developing embryo. The wastes of the embryo pass through this membrane into the bloodstream of the mother. There are, however, two mammals that lay external eggs: the remarkable duck-billed platypus and the spiny anteater. Both, however, exhibit the mammalian characteristic of feeding their young with milk from mammary glands.

Most mammals take care of the young after they are born. They supply food and protect their young. In human beings, this period of care is longer than in any other mammal. A detailed summary of human reproduction will be found in Chapter 11A.

IMPORTANT GENERALIZATIONS

Life exists almost everywhere on earth.

Living things use food for energy and growth, are sensitive and are adapted to their environment, and can make others like themselves.

Living things are built of basic units called cells.

Within the cell there is an architecture of many special structures that carry on the activities of life.

More than $1\frac{1}{2}$ million different kinds of living things have been identified.

Classification systems have been devised by biologists based on their common ancestry. Criteria for classification include similarities and differences in their basic structures and in their chemical makeup.

Organisms are named according to a binomial (two-name) system that designates the genus and species of the organism.

Five kingdoms are recognized in this text: the Monera, Protista, Fungi, Plantae, and Animalia.

Living things need food, water, and oxygen to stay alive and to grow.

The process of photosynthesis not only produces the basic materials essential for the existence of green plants, but eventually supplies all living things on our planet with the chemical compounds needed for the substance of their structures and for the energy to carry on life processes. Moreover, photosynthesis returns to the atmosphere the oxygen that is taken out by living organisms.

Living things reproduce their kind in a variety of ways.

Some living things, such as protozoa and bacteria, reproduce simply by splitting in two.

Most plants and animals reproduce by producing sperm and egg cells that unite to form new organisms.

Living things go through a series of stages in their development from fertilized egg to adult.

DISCOVERING FOR YOURSELF

1. Visit a greenhouse to find out how plants are supplied with what they need for growth, and investigate any experiments with plant growth that are taking place.

2. Collect and examine current seed and nursery catalogues to find new varieties of fruits, vegetables, and flowers. Learn as much as you can about the processes by which these are produced.

3. Collect various kinds of seeds and seed cases. Examine them to determine methods of seed dispersal; observe the arrangement of contents; examine them with a magnifying glass.

4. Examine a flower. Study the arrangement, number, and placement of sepals, petals, stamens, and pistils. What adaptations for pollination can you find? Tease the flower apart with tweezer and needle, and inspect it with a magnifying glass or low-power microscope to find pollen grains and ovules.

5. Sprout different kinds of seeds. Plan an exhibit to show likenesses and differences in the ways in which these seeds change as they germinate and how the seedlings begin to grow.

6. Dig up five different common weeds or other plants. Wash the root systems and examine them. Explain what you have discovered about adaptation to environment and the functions of the various plants' roots. Make an estimate of the total length of all the root structures of one plant.

7. Visit an orchard or a nursery to find out how plants are cared for (pruned, protected against weather changes, kept free from damaging insects, and so forth).

8. Investigate firsthand the plant and animal life associated with any of the following: pond, vacant lot, swamp, lawn, woodland, stream, beach, field. Find out as much as you can about adaptation to environment in each case. Visit the setting at different times to determine changes in plant and animal life associated with changes in the season. Keep a record that includes date, temperature, appearance and disappearance, and changes in habits and structures of specific plants and animals.

9. Study one square foot of lawn, swamp, or forest floor. List all the plants and animals you discover there. Observe over a period of time for changes.

10. In winter dig up a square foot of soil to a depth of 4 or 5 inches. Bring it indoors and place it in a box, empty aquarium, or any other available container that can be covered. Observe the emergence of life—insects, worms, sprouting seeds, and so on.

11. Examine a drop of water from a stagnant pond under the microscope. What kinds of organisms can you identify?

12. Collect frogs' or toads' eggs, place them in a large jar or aquarium with pond water, and watch the young develop.

13. Raise some tropical fish under suitable conditions. Observe their behavior and, if possible, the production of young.

14. Observe birds in your vicinity during spring or fall months to determine how the kinds and numbers seem to vary with the seasons. Try to find out about the migratory habits of birds.

15. Construct a winter feeding station for birds. Keep a list of the birds that are attracted to it. Keep a log of the times various birds appear, and try to determine what kinds of foods attract various birds.

16. Conduct the following "thought experiment": You are given a box containing 3,000 coins of various dates, denominations, and countries. How would you arrange and display your collection in a useful way? Is there just one "right" way? How is this "experiment" related to the classification of living things?

17. If representatives of *all* the species of living things that ever lived were on the earth today, how many kingdoms would there be? None? One? Many more than five?

TEACHING "THE NATURE AND VARIETY OF LIFE"

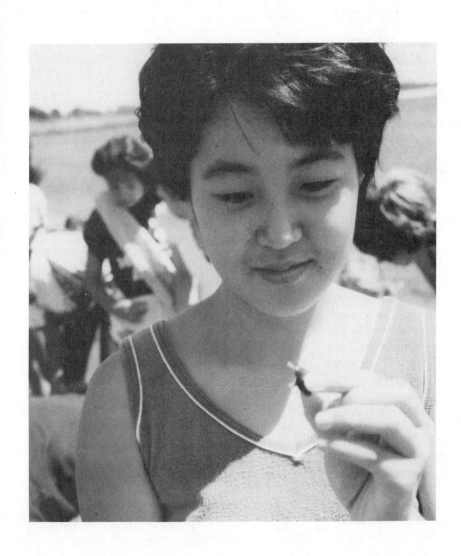

Children are fascinated by living things. They identify with animals and are curious about the varieties of plants. The study of living things offers opportunities for many activities: caring for animals, raising plants, conducting experiments, taking trips to parks, gardens, and zoos, and exploring fields and forests.

A city as well as a rural environment provides settings for meaningful activities. A tree and a strip of grass by the sidewalk, the schoolyard, a window box, a small home garden, classroom plants and animals, pet shops and supermarkets—all supply materials for observations and learning.

The information gained through experiences with living things should be related and organized into important generalizations. We are interested not so much in teaching isolated facts about birds, trees, and butterflies as in understanding these living things in relation to the environment. We are interested in interrelationships: for example, how insect-eating birds affect plant life, how the trees in a particular area play a vital role in providing a home for animals, and how trees and other plants are essential in protecting the soil from erosion. We are concerned with the relationship of humans to other living things and with helping students learn to enjoy the outdoors and develop a desire to explore and especially to protect it.

Each of the chapters in Part III is an essential part of the study of living things: This chapter deals with the nature and variety of plants and animals, 11B is devoted to the human body, 12B to the history of living things, and 13B to the relationships of living things to each other and to the environment.

The unity of the chapters in Part III is found also in their common behavioral objectives. As a result of the activities, students will be able to *observe* properties and characteristics of living things and *construct classification schemes*; *predict* certain events and possibilities on the basis of observations of living things in their environment; *identify* and *control variables* when experimenting with conditions of living things; *de-* *scribe* structures and conditions observed; and *communicate* possible interpretations of these observations.

SOME BROAD CONCEPTS

The Nature and Variety of Life

Life exists almost everywhere on the earth.
Living things need food, air, and water. They can dispose of wastes, grow, and reproduce.
Living things are made of different kinds of cells.
Living things reproduce in different ways.
Green plants manufacture their own food; animals depend on plants.
Living things change as they grow.
Animals may be classified by their structure into two large groups: those with backbones and those without backbones.

FOR YOUNGER CHILDREN

What Can Our Pet Do?[1]

Young children identify themselves with animals in many ways. They like to run, hop, climb, jump, and crawl. They imitate the sounds that different animals make. As each pet comes into the classroom, children become more aware of its uniqueness as well as its similarities to other animals. (See pp. 296–299 for the care of animal pets.)

The following may be classroom pets or occasional animal visitors: fish, turtle (see note about turtles on p. 299), furry animal, and bird. For each animal children find out how it protects itself, moves, breathes, eats, sees, hides, and makes sounds.

Other activities that follow may include a trip to a pet shop, a study of the kinds of babies their

---

[1]Adapted from *Prekindergarten Curriculum Guide* (Brooklyn: Board of Education of the City of New York, 1967–1970).

pets have, and the making of a class picture book of the animals observed.

From the suggested activities children learn

There are many kinds of animal pets.

Animals swim, hop, crawl, run, or fly.

Some baby animals look like their parents. Some look different.

Animals use different parts of their bodies to do different things.

How Can We Prepare Foods?

Children learn how different foods are prepared by whipping, cutting, heating, peeling, popping, and coring and how foods change in size, shape, color, consistency, and texture at different stages of preparation. They help make butter, orange juice, cranberry sauce, vegetable soup, and fruit cup dessert. They eat the product of their work and become acquainted with the taste of new foods. For many children the knowledge that orange juice comes from oranges is a revelation.

What's Alive?

Children observe and compare living and nonliving things in their environment.

What Can We Discover with Our Senses?

Children develop skills in using their senses of smell, touch, taste, sight, and hearing as tools of discovery (see Chapter 11B, pp. 346–347).

What Can We Find Out About Seeds and Fruits?

Children visit a supermarket to find seeds and fruits in the foods we eat. They compare the arrangement and the number of seeds in the fruits.

They find seeds outdoors in the local park or garden, in or near trees, bushes, and small plants. They plant seeds from a Halloween pumpkin and watch them sprout.

What Plants Live in Our Neighborhood?

Explore the immediate environment of the school grounds and the areas near school to learn about living things. With younger children, observations of plants may be made at one time and animals at another.

Our objectives are to help students become aware of their surroundings, to *observe* carefully, *to make comparisons,* to *identify* characteristics, and to *report* what they see. Prepare for the trip by asking, "Where shall we look?" "What do you think we may see?" "What can we bring back to study?" The following three examples provide occasions for making observations: (1) *Trees and leaves.* "What can you discover by looking at it?" (Its parts: trunk and leaves, branches; the characteristics of leaves: green and flat; its bark: rough or smooth; the tree's shape, size, and so on.) Suggest students "hug" a tree to gain a sense of its size, strength and texture. "What do you think the tree needs in order to grow?" "How old do you think it is?" "Trees that are surrounded by pavement and sidewalk often die. Why?" Let each child examine a leaf carefully and report observations. A few leaves may be taken for more careful examination later. Children may "adopt" a tree and make a record of its seasonal changes—special events such as buds forming and then opening to produce flowers and leaves; leaves changing color, falling, and so on. (2) *Grass.* "Where did it come from?" "How is it like the other plants we have seen?" "How different?" "What happens if a path is made over it? Why?" Dig up a few grass plants and take them for further observation. (3) *Small plants* growing in the grass—dandelion, clover, plantain, and others. "How do you think they got there?" "How are they different from each other?" Dig up some different kinds of plants with root systems for further study. (See Chapter 3, "Field Trips Useful in Problem Solving" and "Observing.")

If possible, observe vegetable and flower gardens using a similar procedure. What plant parts can we find (stem, leaf, root, flower, seed)? Pictures from books and other references may be used to supplement children's experiences with information about plants in other environments.

As a follow-up to the trip, examine the leaf specimens with a magnifying glass to see the veins, the edges of the leaves, and the leaf thicknesses. Grow some grass seeds. What can you discover about seeds and the young plants? What do they need to sprout? To grow? Examine a plot of grass and the plants that are growing in it. Report the observations. How are they different from each other? How alike?

The selection of activities will, of course, depend on the kind of environment that surrounds the school, the homes of the children, their backgrounds, experiences, and maturity.

Inner-city children have fewer plants to examine and may need to explore vacant lots, small parks, and plantings along the sidewalk.

What Do Plants Need To Live and Grow?

Use the observations made on the field trip in the neighborhood as a beginning. "What do you think these plants need so they can stay alive and grow?" List the children's suggestions. Then assist them in setting up experiments to test the importance of the things they suggest, such as water, light, soil, temperature, air, and other factors. If possible, each child should plant a few seeds, care for the plants as they grow, observe them, record changes, compare the plants with others, and report the findings. Sometimes this activity may arise if children forget to water their plants or

otherwise neglect them. Children may also select a specific plant outdoors to observe buds, seeds, leaves, flowers, and other parts, and to use the data in a similar way. If possible, plant a garden (see details later in this chapter) so that children can see the results when plants have, or fail to have, the proper conditions for growth. If an outdoor garden is not a feasible activity the garden may be planted in a window box or even in some flowerpots. The objective is to give children an opportunity to plant seeds, watch the plants as they grow, and care for them. (See Chapter 3, "Investigating and Experimenting.")

Here is an opportunity for making a record of the observations. Depending on the maturity of children, they may write their own brief sentences, or they may dictate their ideas to the teacher for recording. They may decide to make simple illustrations to go with the record. Learning to read the record may constitute a reading lesson or lessons. This procedure may be used in conjunction with some of the other problems suggested here. (See Chapter 3, "Writing to Express Ideas.")

What Animals Live in Our Neighborhood?

Again, a trip to the immediate environment is a good beginning. Before the trip discuss where the children may look to find animal life: in trees, in grass, in the ground, in the air, on the ground, and other places. Urge the children to stop, look, and listen. It is desirable to make more than one trip to solve the problems. Urge children to observe animals in their home environments, as well as in their surroundings on the way to and from school. Concentrate on some of the following: identifying the animals; looking for likenesses and differences; observing the methods of moving, the structure, and activities; and comparing the places where the animals live. Children, depending on the location, will probably see bees, ants, and other insects, birds, squirrels, domestic animals, and many others. After the trips, help children to list the animals they saw and discuss some of the observations. This will in all probability raise problems. In a city environment, it is worth exploring a vacant lot, trees along the sidewalk, cracks in the sidewalk, window boxes, and small parks.[2] A comparison of such an environment with a large park presents an interesting problem of why there are more animals living in the park than in some other city environments.

What Do Animals Need To Live and Grow?

Caring for an animal at home or at school is one of the best ways to discover the needs of animals (see pp. 296–299). Keeping caterpillars and other insects, a few fish in an aquarium, a tadpole, or other easily kept animals will be helpful. From this, children may extend their experiences by observing other animals to determine what common needs all animals have.

Observations may also include how animals obtain the things they need and what things different kinds of animals eat. How they eat, where they find food, and how they protect themselves are just a few of the problems to be explored. If animals are caught and brought to the classroom for care and observation, the creatures should be returned to their original habitats after the interest

and study are over. Children should develop the attitude that they are responsible for the animals they are caring for, and that these creatures are not playthings.

How Do We Use Plants and Animals?[3]

Suggest that children observe their home, school, and community environments to find examples of ways plants and animals are used (food, clothing, shelter, beauty, and so on). Under each category list examples. Children may like to work in groups, each group exploring one place (a grocery store, the school, the street, at home, for example). Children may assemble pictures of plant and animal uses from magazines and other sources, and classify them according to the categories they make up. Depending on the group and the interest, students may discuss such problems as, "How can we help to make a better place for the animals and plants to live?" "What kinds of farm crops are raised in our neighborhood?" For other suggestions see Chapter 13B on "Teaching Ecology, Energy, and the Environment."

Other Problems for Younger Children

1. What happens to seeds when we plant them?
2. What do the different parts of a plant do?
3. How do animals build homes?
4. Where are the seeds in some of the different fruits we eat? How many seeds are there in the fruits?
5. How can we make a place to raise earthworms in our classroom?

[2]K. E. Hill, *Exploring the Natural World with Young Children* (New York: Harcourt Brace Jovanovich, 1976). Contains activities about observing plants and animals with young children. M. Jenners, "Schoolyard Hikes," *Science and Children* (March 1987). Gives specific helps for exploring the school environment to observe living things. H. H. Carey and D. R. Hanka, *How To Use Your Community as a Resource* (New York: Watts, 1983); P. Burch, *Exploring as You Walk in the City* (New York: Lippincott, 1983).

[3]See also G. O. Blough, *Useful Plants and Animals* (New York: Harper & Row, 1972); M. E. McKee, "Some Plants We Eat," *Science and Children* (February 1984).

FOR OLDER CHILDREN

What Do Plants Need?[4]

When students are considering the problem of what plants need in order to grow, they may list things they think are needed and then consider the question, "How can we set up experiments to find out if plants need water, sunlight, good soil, and a proper temperature?" Students can plan the experiments themselves, make a summary of the plan on the chalkboard, and then follow the plan, change it if necessary, and note the results. Here is an example of a record of such a procedure as a fifth-grade class planned it. (See Chapter 3, "Investigating and Experimenting.") *Purpose of the Experiment:* to find out whether green plants need sunlight.

Our Plan:

Bring four small geranium plants that are alike. (George will bring them.)

Be sure that all plants are healthy and that they are all growing in the same kind of soil.

Set two plants on the window ledge where they will be in sunlight at least part of the day, and set the others in a dark closet.

Water all plants with the same amount of water. (Perry and Nicole will do this.)

Put a label on the plants so that no one will move them and spoil our experiment. (Alice will make the label, which will say "Please do not touch.")

Every week bring the plants together and compare them for growth, for color, and for anything else that we can see.

This plan evolved only after lengthy discussion and with some help from the teacher, necessary

in order to design the experiment to guarantee valid conclusions. The students understood the reasons for including plants that were not subject to the experimental condition (darkness); they saw that the control served as a basis of comparison. As they put it later, "If we didn't have the plants in the light we wouldn't know whether darkness or something else made the difference in the plants." In drawing conclusions, students were urged not to decide from the one experiment that *all* plants need sunlight. Several students volunteered to perform a similar experiment at home.

After the experiment was finished and students had reported on their home experiments, the class took a trip around the schoolyard to see places where plants did not grow well—*perhaps* because of lack of light. They observed places where plants were growing toward the light. In a shaded place they found plants that had grown much taller and more spindly than the same kinds of plants growing in direct sunlight. It is also important for children to understand that some plants require less direct sunlight than others.

When the students returned from this trip one of them reported on an experiment in a book that was designed to find out whether plants grow toward the light. They planted bean seeds in the soil in two 4-inch flowerpots. After the seeds sprouted, the students cut a round oatmeal box in half to make a cardboard cylinder that fitted over the growing plants in one of the flowerpots and excluded light. They then cut a round hole in one side of the box near the top to create a single source of light. The young plants covered with the box grew toward the hole where the light came in. The other pot was left uncovered. The students frequently compared the two. They observed that the plants in the uncovered pot grew toward the windows. They also noted that the plants growing in their schoolroom turned toward the light.

We have illustrated some methods used in experimenting to see that plants need light. Their need for the other essentials (water, good soil,

[4]R. Mattingly, "From Root to Fruit: Botany for Beginners," *Science and Children* (February 1987). Plant information with interesting activities. M. Schneider, "Setting Up an Outdoor Tub," *Science and Children* (January 1984). Practical suggestions for studying plants and animals in their natural setting. For all levels.

This simple demonstration may be used to show that the stem and leaves of a plant grow toward light. Similar plants should be grown uncovered to indicate the difference in growth.

air, and proper temperature) may be demonstrated in similar ways.

How Does Water Get into the Plants?

Urge children to suggest ways to solve the problem of how water gets into plants. The pathway of water into and through a plant may be studied in the following ways: Sprout some radish seeds on moist blotting paper in a covered plastic container and look at the rootlets through a magnifying glass. The "fuzz" on the rootlets is made up of hair roots through which water enters the plants. Discuss the advantages of a plant's having thousands of root hairs instead of a single root.

Plant about a dozen lima bean seeds in soil. After the shoots have come above the ground and the first leaves have appeared, try the following experiment to see what happens when the root hairs are injured. *Pull* two or three of the plants out of the soil. Replant them in other soil. *Lift* two

or three of the other plants out of the soil with a trowel or spoon, being careful not to disturb the roots. Replant them also. Do not disturb the remaining plants. Suggest that students try to predict what will happen to each group. Children should grow in ability to see the difference between a *prediction* (made on the basis of some knowledge and considerable observation) and a *guess* (made on less background). They may also grow in *ability to evaluate* their predictions in terms of their confidence in them. Which prediction is supported by the best ideas? (See Chapter 3, *"Investigating and Experimenting."*)

Observe all three groups of plants. The plants pulled up by the roots will probably wilt, since many of their root hairs were torn off. New ones must be formed before the plant can take in water. The plants that were lifted gently will probably not wilt. The remaining plants are left as a control so that students can see what happens if plants are not disturbed at all. Now compare the predictions made earlier with the results.

When water once gets inside the plant it must be carried to the leaves, for it is there that the manufacturing of food takes place. By the use of stalks of celery and some red ink, students can observe how water goes to the leaves. Try to have the children propose the use of ink by first showing just the celery stalks and a glass of water and then asking them how they might detect the rise of water in the stalk. Use celery stalks with yellow leaves, if possible. With a sharp knife, cut the bottoms from the stalks of celery. Put just enough red ink in a glass of water to color the water a bright red. Place the celery stems in the water and set them in the light. Observe the leaves from time to time. After two or three hours, cut one of the stalks and look for the tubes that are carrying the colored water to the leaves. Let the children describe what they see and try to interpret their observations. Look closely at the leaves and you will see the red liquid in the veins. The red color makes it easy to see the parts in which water is moving. It is useful to introduce the word *tracer* here: The colored ink makes it possible to trace

Colored water   Clear water

The nature of the transportation system of the plant is revealed by using colored water as a "tracer."

the course of the water. (This is similar in principle to the use of radioactive atoms to trace the flow of materials in living things.) An interesting variation of this experiment is shown in the drawing. The celery stalk has been split partway so that the difference can be noted (see above).

How Can We Keep Animal Pets?[5]

Pet rabbits, guinea pigs, hamsters, or gerbils may be successfully kept in classrooms. Children enjoy observing them; many pet shops stock these animals.

Here are some things to keep in mind, whatever the purpose of keeping a pet animal: (1) It should never be kept in a schoolroom unless it can be made comfortable; (2) unless an animal is accustomed to captive life it should never be kept for a long time; (3) children should plan to consider the needs of the animal and to share responsibility for its care; (4) children should exercise care in handling the animal, and animals should not be handled too much; and (5) arrange-

---

[5]"An Open Letter to Science Teachers on the Uses of Live Animals in Science Teaching," *Science and Children* (October 1970). Questions and answers about the NSTA point of view about keeping animals in the classroom; an important article. NSTA's "Code of Practice on Animals in Schools," a position statement of NSTA. (September 1980). Another important article. F. B. Orlans, "Selecting an Animal for Classroom Use," *The Science Teacher* (February 1980); G. K. Pratt, *Care of Living Things in the Classroom* (Washington, D.C.: NSTA, 1978). J. A. Reed, "Survey of Living Animals Recommended for Elementary School Science," *School Science and Mathematics* (1980). A comprehensive article. D. C. Kramer, "The Classroom Animal," Care and Maintenance Series. See current and back issues of *Science and Children* for the study of living things in the classroom. A. Silverstein and V. Silverstein, *Gerbils: All About Them* (New York: Lippincott, 1976).

ments should be made for the care of the pet over the weekends and during vacations.

Each animal should have

1. Enough space to move around and be comfortable.
2. An environment as nearly like its natural habitat as possible.
3. A place to hide from sight.
4. Proper food, clean water, and good ventilation.
5. A cage that can be kept clean and free of odor.
6. Adequate food, heat, and water over weekends.
7. Its freedom after its purpose has been served.

Taking care of pets should not become a chore and responsibility of the teacher. These duties are real, and it makes a difference if they are not carried out correctly—one of the important prerequisites for helping students learn to assume responsibility. As students observe the animal, they may make a list of things the animal needs in order to grow. "What can you discover by observing the pet?" may be an initial problem when children keep an animal. How does it eat? How does it move about? Protect itself? Clean itself? *A word of caution:* Be sure to check your local, state, or district regulations about keeping animals in the classroom, especially vertebrates, as keeping them may not be permitted.

As children keep a pet animal, there may be an opportunity for purposeful use of mathematics. The children might weigh the pet periodically and, if feasible, measure its dimensions. The making of tables and graphs clarifies and defines more exactly the growth of the animal. The children can express their observations mathematically with such statements as, "Our pet gained 4 ounces (110 grams) last week," or "Our pet gained about 2 pounds (1 kilogram) during the first month in the classroom, but only about 1 pound (½ kilogram) during the second month," or "The graph shows that our pet gained slowly when it was first brought to school, but then its weight shot up rapidly. Now it is slowing down again."

The feeding of animals in the classroom and outdoors sometimes presents problems. Here are specific suggestions for kinds of animal food as well as some advice based on classroom experience in coaxing animals to eat various things.

Ants Dead spiders or insects, bread crumbs, small food scraps, cracked rice, sugar and water, crumbled nut meats, honey or molasses, and water. Place on top of soil where ants live, either on the soil or in a small dish.

Birds, Tame Prepared bird foods, cuttlefish bone, lettuce, watercress or chickweed, carrot, apple, pieces of bread, hard-boiled egg, grit of some sort. Special food is needed during moulting season (consult pet store). Fresh water.

Birds, Wild Birdseed for wild birds, small flower seeds, peanut butter, grains, bread broken into small pieces, suet, apple, unsalted nuts, raisins, grit, cranberries, sunflower seeds, and fresh water, placed on *outdoor* feeding tray.

A very satisfactory food for outdoor birds in winter is known as bird pudding. It is made of suet, birdseed, and other kinds of seeds, raisins, and unsalted nuts. Heat the suet until it liquifies. Let it cool and then stir into it the ingredients listed. As it begins to thicken, pour the pudding mixture into paper cups, pine cones, or other feeding devices. Be sure the mixture is packed under the scales of the cones. The cones may be tied to branches of trees where birds will find them. The cups may be put into feeding trays and fastened so that the wind will not blow them away.

Butterflies Fresh, thick sugar-and-water solution. Will sometimes take nectar from flowers.

Caterpillars The leaves upon which the animals were found feeding. Give fresh leaves daily. Experiment with various kinds of leaves. (See also *Moth Larvae.*)

Chameleons Any small moving insect. When hungry, they will eat bits of hamburger on a thread moved before their eyes. Chameleons do not drink as many animals do. Dewdrops are their source of water. Green branches with their stems in water should be kept in the case and frequently sprinkled with water.

Chickens and Ducks   Commercial chicken feed, vegetables, meat scraps, grit, water.

Crayfish   Chopped meat, water, plants.

Crickets   Pulpy fruit, lettuce, bread, peanut butter, crushed seeds.

Earthworms   Obtain their food from the soil.

Frogs and Toads   Earthworms, mealworms, caterpillars, nearly any living insects, soft grubs. Small bits of ground meat if it is moved in front of the animal suspended on a thread. (See also *Tadpoles*.)

Goldfish   Commercially prepared fish food, ant eggs, ground-up dog biscuit, a small pinch of oatmeal or cornmeal. Do not overfeed. Do not give more food than they will eat immediately.

Grasshoppers   The leaves they were eating when found. Celery, ripe bananas. Experiment with different kinds of foliage.

Guinea Pigs or Cavies   About the same foods as rabbits eat. Do *not* feed potato parings. Clean drinking water. (See *Rabbits*.)

Guppies   Food commercially prepared, same as other tropical fish.

Hamsters   Dog biscuit, plus a small supply of fresh vegetables such as carrots, cabbage, and lettuce; bits of fresh fruit, sometimes a little meat. Nuts, corn, oats, wheat, and other grains. Peas can be used to vary the diet. Water is necessary, but if enough green food is given, use less water. The animals must have dog biscuits, pellets, or grain frequently to keep their teeth sharp.

Horned Toads   Ants, mealworms. (**Note:** Horned toads are not toads—they are lizards.)

Lizards   Flies, crickets, mealworms.

Mongolian Gerbils   Seeds, roots, grass, lettuce, carrots, kibbled dog food.

Moth Larvae   *Cecropia*: leaves of willow, maple, apple, and many other trees. *Polyphemus*: leaves of willow, oak, apple, plum, birch, basswood, and other trees. *Promethia*: leaves of wild cherry, ash, lilac, tulip, and sassafras trees. *Luna*: leaves of hickory, walnut, sweet gum, and several other trees. *Cynthia*: lilac, sycamore, cherry, and others.

Newts   Parts of dead insects, ant eggs, finely ground beef.

Praying Mantis   Living insects.

Rabbits   Commercial pellets. If the pellets cannot be obtained from a pet or feed store, feed wheat or buckwheat mixed with soybeans or peanuts. Rabbits eat various kinds of green vegetables (not wet), a little chopped clover, some greens, and a little dry bread now and then. Wild rabbits get water from dew-covered grass; tame rabbits must be given water. Feed twice a day. Do not overfeed.

Rats (White) and Mice   Small grain, bread crusts, vegetables, egg yolks, meat scraps, breakfast foods, water.

Salamanders   Insects, small bits of ground meat moved before their eyes on a suspended thread, earthworms, mealworms.

Snails, Land   Lettuce, celery tops, spinach or any soft vegetables, grapes, apple.

Snails, Water   Fish food, lettuce, aquarium plants, spinach, shredded shrimp.

Snakes   Earthworms, many kinds of insects, small pieces of meat wriggled in front of their noses, eggs. They need not eat every day. Some will not eat in captivity; some do not eat for weeks at a time. Do not keep them if they will not eat. Let them escape into a suitable environment.

Tadpoles Water plants or green pond scum. Much food is obtained from the water. Cooked oatmeal, cooked spinach, cornmeal, lettuce or spinach leaves, and bits of hamburger put into water in small quantities.

Turtles Commercially prepared foods, nearly all kinds of insects, bits of hard-boiled eggs, lettuce, berries, mealworms, earthworms. Place the food for turtles on the water. Many of them eat only under the surface of the water. Do not overfeed. (**Note:** There are conflicting reports on the advisability of keeping turtles in the classroom because some are contaminated with salmonella bacteria. Check with the Public Health Service.)

What Does a Seed Need in Order to Sprout?

What can we learn about seeds by examining them? Collect many kinds of seeds (beans, pea, birdseed, grains, and others). Compare the seeds. How are they alike? How different? What are their shapes? Find the scar. What is it? Soak the seeds and then examine and compare them. Sprouting seeds can show many things about how plants grow.[6]

Large seeds are best because their germination and the growth of the seedlings may be observed easily. In some communities beans, corn, and other seeds can be brought from home by the children. In others, seeds can be purchased. Some of the experiments with growing seeds can be done as class projects, but it is desirable for children to have seedlings of their own to watch each day and to compare with those of other students. Often students enjoy doing some of the experi-

[6]C. D. Hampton and C. H. Hampton, "Care and Maintenance of Seeds," *Science and Children* (March 1981); P. Richard, "Going to Seed," *Science and Children* (February 1984). Many practical suggestions.

ments at home and bringing the results to school. In one class each student brought a different kind of seed, watched it sprout, and compared results: "How are the seeds and plants alike?" "How are they different from each other?" "Why did some plants grow better than others?" "What do all of the seeds need to sprout?"

Seeds may be sprouted in a number of different ways: on moist blotting paper or cotton in a covered, flat plate or dish; next to the glass in a drinking glass lined with paper toweling or a blotter so that students can watch the roots grow down and the stem grow up; or directly in soil. It is quite easy to make a diary that tells what happens as the seeds sprout. The record may be illustrated by simple drawings to show how growth takes place, or students may find drawings in books and other sources and compare their sprouting seeds with the drawings.

Urge students to examine seeds to see their structure. Lima beans are good because the parts are large and easily seen. Each child should have one or more seeds to examine. Soak the seeds in water overnight, to soften them and hasten germination. Leave them on moist blotting paper for one or two days or until the germinating parts can easily be distinguished. Use toothpicks to take the seeds apart. Look for the three parts of the seed (coat, tiny plant, stored food). After children have identified the parts, they can discuss the function of each part and make predictions about what happens to these parts as the plant grows. As they observe seeds sprouting, they can verify their predictions. They may examine other seeds to find the three parts and try to make some generalizations about seeds and their germination.

Children may experiment to determine the effects of varying one of the external conditions: light, moisture, soil, and air. They may also devise experiments to find out whether a bean seed could grow into a plant if the stored food were taken away from it. (Lift the tiny plant out from between the halves of a soaked bean, plant it, and see what happens.) It will die because the first food for the plant is stored in the seed. The children may try to determine what happens if half of the food material is removed, leaving the tiny plant attached to the other half. They may also set up an experiment to discover which part (the stem or the root) comes out of the seed first as it germinates. This open-ended approach also lends itself to many other experiences with seeds and plants.

Collecting seedpods and fruits that show methods of seed dispersal is a standard activity in autumn. Get more mileage from this by examining the materials to see how the structure ensures dispersal (use a magnifying glass); find the seeds, try to count them, try to sprout them, and open them to see the inside structure.

Students can devise experiments to try to determine the following: What happens when seeds are planted at different depths? What difference does soaking seeds before they are planted make? Will seeds germinate and grow if they are kept *under* water? What difference does temperature make in the germination of seeds?

How Can We Plant A Garden?[7]

The school garden is an outdoor laboratory for science education. Here children can observe plants in the natural environment of soil, sunlight, air, and water. Through the experience of planting and caring for a school garden students can learn much about how plants grow. In order to produce a truly valuable science experience, however, much planning must be done. Weeks before the time for planting there should be discussion of such questions as, "Why shall we have a garden?" (Responses might be for pleasure; to give flowers and vegetables to other people; to learn about growing plants; to grow vegetables to eat; to make

our schoolyard more attractive; and so on.) Students can use these aims to evaluate their progress and results. They also should discuss, "What shall we plant in the garden?" "What must we do to the soil in the garden before it is ready for seeds?" "What kinds of tools do we need and where shall we get them?" "Where and how can we get the seeds for planting?" The school garden should provide a real opportunity for problem solving: Children decide on the problems, make and carry out their plans, and then evaluate their work. Insofar as possible, all children in the school should be involved.

The following resources are helpful in planning and planting a successful school garden:

1. The county agriculture agent, a high school agriculture or biology teacher, or a greenhouse owner can test the soil so that students can decide whether it needs fertilizer and whether the drainage is proper.
2. Seed catalogs can help children decide what to plant by use of the illustrations and the descriptions, which tell how long the plants take to mature, what kinds of soil they need, and so on.
3. Seed packages contain directions for depth and time of seed planting.
4. Interested parents who are experienced gardeners may be willing to give assistance and advice.
5. Inexpensive government publications and other published materials about gardening and insect-pest control will be helpful.[8]
6. Enlist the support of the school principal and custodian. They can both be invaluable in selecting a site, maintaining the garden, and in inviting community cooperation.

In school gardening it is important to remember that (1) there is considerable mathematics involved in gardening: numbers of rows, distances apart, number of plants that will fit into a given space, amount of space for each student, and so on (here again, children should be encouraged

---

[7]A. Ballin, "Gardening at Horizons," *Science and Children* (April 1984). Many suggestions for getting the most out of a gardening experience. M. Brown and J. Sawyer, "A Child's Garden of Radishes," *Science and Children* (April 1984). Concrete suggestions.

[8]Write to Superintendent of Documents, U.S. Government Printing Office, Washington, D.C. 20402, for pamphlets and other low-cost material about insects and gardening.

to concentrate on the use of the metric system); (2) there is opportunity to help children learn cooperation and thoughtfulness in sharing tools, seeds, and plants; and (3) a garden is an ideal place to evaluate a plan. If the rows are straight and even, if the plants are not crowded and so forth, the plan has had some degree of success. Evaluation should be made on the basis of all the reasons for making the garden, not merely in terms of its yield.

The gardening experience provides a practical application of what has been learned through observing, reading, and experimenting. Specifically, it shows what plants need to grow, how they

This experimenter measures and records plant growth. *(Courtesy of Phyllis Marcuccio.)*

change as they grow, how long it takes various plants to mature, how plants grow under different conditions, what happens when plants are too crowded, how plants of different kinds reproduce, and how plants change as the seasons change. Provision must be made for caring for the garden when school is not in session.

How Can We Raise Plants Indoors?

The plants that are commonly grown in schoolrooms are good for plant study. Their possibilities are often overlooked. Geraniums, coleus, ferns, ivy, begonias, bulbs of different kinds, cacti, and other plants may be observed to discover the answers to such questions as, "Where do the new leaves grow?" "Which plants grow fastest?" "How are they all alike in their growth?" "Are seeds formed on any of them?" "Are there spores on the ferns?" "Do all of the plants need the same amount of light and water?"

Since most schoolrooms contain plants the following specific suggestions may be helpful to teachers and students:

Sufficient Water Plants should be watered only when the soil feels dry. However, when adding water be sure to give the soil a thorough soaking, not just a sprinkling.

Good Drainage The pot or box should have holes in the bottom to allow excess water to escape. (The roots of a plant require air. Water that remains may prevent air from entering the soil.)

Suitable Temperature Plants should not be placed on hot radiators or in hot or cold drafts. Protect plants over cold weekends.

Proper Light Conditions Experience is the best teacher here. A geranium, for example, needs a good deal of sunlight. Cactus also thrives in sunlight. Begonias and some ferns, on the other hand, should not be kept in direct sunlight for many hours at a time. Many plants will grow well with only a few hours of sunlight. No green plant will do well in a dark area.

Good Soil Although each plant has its own soil requirements, any good garden or potting soil will usually be satisfactory. The addition of sand will make the soil more porous. If the soil dries too quickly peat moss or humus can be added. Commercial fertilizer may be used according to the directions on the package.

Other Care Leaves should be showered or washed with a sponge from time to time. Insect pests can be removed by washing or by the use of specific insecticides.

How Do Plants Reproduce?

Seeds are but one of the several ways by which plants reproduce. In some plants a part such as a root, stem, or leaf may be separated from the plant to start a new plant. Students can plan experiences to discover some of these ways. Some plants reproduce by bulbs. If a bulb is cut open a series of fleshy layers may be seen, as well as the flattened stem. Narcissus and other plant bulbs can be grown in the schoolroom if the simple directions that accompany them are followed.

New geranium plants can be started from cuttings (*slips*) from older plants. Take off most of the large leaves and put the cutting in moist sand until roots develop. New ivy plants can be started in this way or by putting the cuttings in water until roots appear. Pussy willows brought to school and placed in water often start roots and can be planted to grow into willow trees if there is a suitable place.

Children will be interested in the use of a plant hormone (Rootone) to stimulate rooting. They can try to devise experiments with and without its use to compare them. Directions are included with the product, which may be purchased at hardware stores, nurseries, or garden shops.

Children can watch underground stems of the potato grow into a plant by putting a potato in some good soil. One potato will supply several plants if it is cut up so that each piece contains an "eye." If several potatoes are planted, students may dig them up now and then to see where the roots develop and where the stems come from, and to note that the potato itself is shriveling up, partly because it is supplying food to the growing shoots. If the potatoes are left growing, students can watch the shoots come above ground and see the leaves develop. If a potato is left in a closed container on the table without being planted, students can see the sprouts begin to grow and note how differently the potato develops if it has no soil.

A strawberry plant, either wild or cultivated, growing in rich soil in a large flowerpot will send out runners. New plants grow out from these runners.

Some nongreen plants such as molds reproduce by *spores.*[9]

How Do Flowers Make Seeds?

Children can examine flowers to discover answers to these questions: "Where do seeds come from?" "What must a plant have in order to produce seeds?" "Where in the flower is the seed formed?" "What must happen in a flower in order to produce seeds?" The following suggestions will be helpful in solving some of these problems.

Perhaps the best way for children to discover the seed-making role of flowers is to watch one

[9]M. McIntire, "Growing Mold," *Science and Children* (October 1978); D. N. Schumann, "Spores Disperse Too!" *Science and Children* (October 1981); R. R. Powell, "Going to Seed," *Science and Children* (February 1984). Gathering and sprouting seeds. S. E. Dyche, "Samara (Winged) Science," *Science and Children* (October 1985). Gathering and studying winged seeds.

kind, *alive,* day after day on a small plant, bush, or tree. A magnifying glass is most useful in revealing the minute structures and the beauty within a flower. If they can begin with a flower bud they will see it swell and open. They will observe the flower to see the anthers grow, split open, and expose their load of dustlike pollen. They will observe the sticky top of the pistil ready to receive the pollen. As the flower matures, they will observe the base of the pistil (the ovary) swell with its developing seeds. As other parts of the flower shrivel and drop off, the ovary will grow larger into a full-sized fruit, laden with seeds (see Chapter 10A, pp. 279–280).

Even a cut flower standing in water will reveal some stages in its development toward seed production. *The advantages of beginning with living flowers is that it permits children to make their own discoveries and record changes as they observe them. This is in marked contrast to the method of presenting children with a picture of a flower and having them identify its parts and then trying to have them understand the complexities of its structure and its functions.*

The process of discovery comes as children are able to observe living things engaged in the processes of living. Later they may consult books, charts, and other references to deepen and extend their understanding. They will then have some basis for trying to answer such questions as, "What does the pollen do?" "How do bees help some flowers in seed making?" "Where is the part that becomes the seed?" "How does the pollen get to the seed-forming part?"

Flowers from a garden and from house plants may be examined as soon as they begin to fade. Students should be urged to bring from gardens some examples of flower specimens that show seeds forming. After the seeds have been formed, the seed container can be opened to show the seeds inside. Pumpkins, squash, melons, peas, beans, morning glories, and marigolds are interesting to examine. Vacant lots in the city provide wild seeds as well as the flowers that produce them. On some of these, dead parts of the blos-

som can still be seen hanging from the seed-bearing part.

How Can We Raise Tadpoles?

Wherever frogs and toads croak in the spring there are eggs for the taking. Hatching them in the schoolroom is not difficult and is very helpful in showing children how some animals go through their development from egg to adult.

Frogs' eggs are laid in clumps, toads' eggs in long strings. Both may be scooped up from ponds or quiet waters in the park or elsewhere in spring and brought to school for observation. Bring only a few eggs. Toads and frogs are useful animals, and this is a specific occasion to teach conservation. If the eggs are kept in glass jars (gallon pickle or jelly jars are good) they can be observed easily, or if there are no fish or turtles in the aquarium the eggs and tadpoles can be kept there. Bring some water plants with the water from the pond. The young tadpoles will eat algae or decaying bits of plants and animal material. As they grow, they will eat tiny bits of hard-boiled egg, but the pond water will probably contain the necessary plant food for them.

The length of time for hatching and the rate at which tadpoles develop depends in part on the kind of frog. Some kinds of frogs mature faster than others. The rate of hatching and developing also depends on the temperature. This provides an excellent opportunity for setting up a carefully controlled experiment. Children can make some predictions and after the experiments make some inferences (see Chapter 10A, pp. 285–287).

Divide a batch of eggs into three equal parts. Place one batch in a jar of water in a cool place. Place another batch in a similar jar in a warm place. A third may be kept at room temperature. Except for temperature, all conditions should be the same (controlled variables). Thus, if it is necessary to place the cool batch in a dark cellar, the other two batches should also be in darkness.

Day-by-day records of changes in size and appearance should be kept.

Here is a general plan used by a group of students as they observed eggs and tadpoles:

1. Students observed the eggs to see how they changed as they hatched. They made large drawings to show these changes.
2. They observed the tadpoles to see how they moved, how the legs formed, what happened to the gills, and what happened to the tails. They kept a record of the dates of these changes.
3. They compared their observations with the information they had read, and made an outline of the most obvious and important changes that the animals underwent.
4. A library committee assembled reading material from books and encyclopedias about frogs and toads and their development.
5. At the end of the study the tadpoles were returned to the pond from which they were taken as eggs.

How Do Animals Care for Their Young?

To guide observations, the class may prepare a series of questions such as, "How are the young fed?" "How are they protected?" "How long will they stay with their parents?" "Do both parents help to take care of the young?"

It is surprising how many kinds of animals with young are available for observation. Students can make a list of animals that are known to live in the community and then do as much firsthand observing as possible, reporting their findings.

Students may visit—as a class, in small groups, or individually—the zoo, a pet shop, a kennel where dogs are bred, a city aquarium, a place where canaries are raised, a fur farm, a dairy farm, and the schoolyard or park to see birds, squirrels, and other animals. They can find out how fish, reptiles, insects, and amphibians, as well as the mammals we have suggested, care (or do not care) for their young.

A good beginning in sex education has been made when children observe the birth of puppies and kittens, watch the mother care for them, and frankly discuss with their parents and teachers what they have seen. Intelligently answering the questions children ask helps to satisfy their curiosity in a normal fashion and provides opportunities for parents and teachers to enter naturally into a discussion of sexual matters (see Chapters 11A and 11B).

How Do Animals Eat?

There are also many opportunities for students to observe how animals get their food. Children can list the animals that they might possibly watch, plan for observing them, and report their findings. Here is a list of animals studied by a third grade: snails, earthworms, fish, silkworms, canaries, chickens, dogs, cats, frogs, horses, cows, sheep, and squirrels. Each animal was observed to find out what kind of food it eats, what parts of its body help it to eat, and any other interesting things about the way the animal eats.

At the zoo, students can observe how different kinds of animals eat, and how they are adapted for food gathering. The zoo also provides examples of various ways in which animals protect themselves, and live in various environments.[10]

How Can We Set Up an Aquarium?

An aquarium set up by the teacher before school begins in the autumn is never as much fun for the children or as useful to them as one they plan and make themselves. Children often volunteer to bring fish to school from a pond, and this motivates the making of the aquarium.

[10]G. O. Blough and M. H. Campbell, *When You Go to the Zoo* (New York: McGraw-Hill, 1955). Details of animal adaptation for food gathering. J. L. Milson, "Looking Around the Zoo," *Science and Children* (February 1984). Contains a "Data Sheet For Animal Observations."

The planning may begin by letting the students discuss such questions as, "What kind of place shall we make for the fish?" "What materials shall we need?" "Where can we get them?" "How shall we use them?" There will be opportunity to share, to contribute to the group, to work together, and to assume responsibility.

You will need a container, some sand, some small stones, a few water plants, a few snails, and the fish. The container may be of almost any size or shape, but one that is rectangular and holds 3 gallons (11.4 liters) or so is preferable. It can be purchased locally or ordered from a supply house. Many supply houses furnish detailed directions for stocking and caring for an aquarium. Begin by scrubbing the aquarium thoroughly. The sand may come from a variety of sources: the beach, a sandbar of a river, a builder's supply yard, or a pet shop. Wash it by running water through it until the water is clear. Water plants are usually most satisfactory when purchased from local variety stores, pet shops, or biological supply houses, although it is possible to get them from ponds or lakes or from an outdoor pool.[11] Buying water plants at a pet shop may be an interesting experience for young children or for a committee. While they are there they can also buy some snails. Only a few are needed; there will soon be more.

Having assembled the materials, plan with the children how they are to be put together.[12] If you are using city water pour it back and forth from one container to another to let chlorine from the water escape into the air, or let it stand for a day in a container before placing plants and animals in it. After putting the sand in the bottom of the aquarium, set a saucer or plate on it so that when you pour the water in, it will not stir up the sand. Half fill the aquarium with water, put stones around the base of the water plants to hold them down, and finish filling the aquarium. Put in the fish and snails. Later you may wish to add tadpoles or other suitable water animals. The aquarium may be covered with a piece of glass to prevent the water from evaporating.

Although goldfish are commonly used in aquaria, other kinds of fish are also available. Tropical fish, however, need considerable attention; the water temperature must be kept nearly constant, and for other reasons they are not easily reared in the usual schoolroom aquarium unless the teacher or some student has made a hobby of raising such fish.

After the aquarium is set up, if the proportion of plants and animals is balanced, it needs little attention. The green plants provide cover for shy and young fish, remove some of the nitrogenous wastes released by animals, and absorb carbon dioxide. The role of plants in oxygenating aquarium water has been exaggerated. If there is enough surface area over the water, oxygen will be absorbed from the air, and its concentration in the water will reach the saturation point. Overfeeding is one of the chief causes of the death of fish. It leads to the buildup of organic wastes, cloudy water, lowered oxygen concentration, and in some cases, death. It is better to underfeed than overfeed. Remove any food that remains 30 minutes after feeding.

An aquarium is useful in helping to solve many of the problems that arise in the study of plants and animals. Children may observe animal life to see how the animals are adapted for life in the water, and watch both plants and animals to see how they grow and change. An aquarium is also useful in stimulating children to ask such questions as, "What are the bubbles coming out of the plant?" "Where did all the snails come from?"

[11]C. E. Raun and W. C. Metz, "Exploring Pond Water," *Science and Children* (October 1975). Collecting and studying the organisms in pond water with emphasis on the discovery processes.

[12]G. O. Blough, *An Aquarium* (New York: Harper & Row, 1972). An easily read book to consult in making and using an aquarium in the elementary school. J. Hoke, *Aquariums* (New York: Franklin Watts, 1977). A good guide. C. H. Hampton and C. D. Hampton, "Care and Maintenance: A Freshwater Aquarium," *Science and Children* (February 1979); D. C. Knammer, "Snails," *Science and Children* (September 1985). Raising and studying snails in an aquarium.

"Why does the fish open and close its mouth?" "Why do the fish sometimes come to the top of the water?" When aquaria are utilized as a source of information and for raising problems they are excellent teaching tools.

In connection with a study of oceanography you may wish to try your hand at making a salt-water aquarium. It involves some expense and "know-how."[13]

How Can We Make a Terrarium?[14]

A terrarium is a replica of a land habitat made with suitable soil, water, and plant and animal life characteristic of the kind of environment it represents. It provides a home for plants and animals brought in by children: small toads, frogs, small snakes, turtles, and salamanders. The general procedure suggested for use with children in initiating an aquarium project is also appropriate in making terrarium.

The container may be of almost any general shape or size, from a 1-gallon glass jar to a large aquarium tank. A discarded aquarium tank that leaks may be adequate for use as a terrarium.

A trip to a woodlot to gather material is an opportunity for careful observation of the ecology of an area and for learning conservation practices. Take only a little moss of different kinds, a few varieties of wood plants, some rich soil, and anything else that you think will give the terrarium a "woodsy" touch. Do not collect rare plants. Some pieces of charcoal placed in the bottom of the terrarium will absorb gases and help to keep the soil from becoming sour.

Cover the bottom of the terrarium container with coarse gravel or sand, bury several pieces of charcoal in it, and then add rich soil from the woods. Plant the small plants in this mixture, and cover the remaining soil with the moss. Brightly colored stones placed here and there, where the different pieces of moss meet, add interest. Sink a small dish into the soil to hold water, and cover the terrarium container with a piece of glass, which the school custodian can cut to the size of the container. When you have finished planting the materials, sprinkle the plants with water, put water in the dish, and the habitat is ready for a small animal. It will probably not be necessary to add water for some time.

Suggest that students examine the terrarium independently for a few days and then give them an opportunity to report their observations and try to explain them. Water will evaporate and condense as the temperature changes, so that it seems to "rain" in the terrarium. Observing this is very useful in studying air and weather.

Changes will occur in the plants. If it is too wet, mold may appear. If it is too dry some plants will wither. If there are animals (earthworms, small toads, salamanders, and so on) their behavior will be interesting. They must be fed and cared for (see pp. 309–310). There are many variations of this procedure in making terraria that may be used to reproduce different kinds of habitats in miniature, for example, desert and rain forest.

How Can We Maintain a Bird-Feeding Station?

Which birds stay with us all winter? How can we find out? Maintaining a bird-feeding station may prove a very enjoyable experience if it is done carefully and planned well. On the other hand, if the feeding station is not well placed or is not stocked with proper food the experience may be

[13]W. R. Hobbs, "The Saltwater Aquarium," *Science and Children* (May 1966). Gives directions and references for a saltwater aquarium. D. Crowe, "Learning About Sea Life: A Saltwater Aquarium," *Science and Children* (October 1981). Directions for making and using. "Instant Ocean," a commercial seawater preparation, is available in many pet shops.

[14]J. Hoke, *Terrariums* (New York: Franklin Watts, 1972). An excellent source book.

disappointing. Books that describe bird-feeding stations often mislead children, for they depict cardinals, bluejays, woodpeckers, chickadees, and other winter residents all clamoring for food. Such a rushing business is usually not done by a school bird feeder—certainly not the day after it is installed.

There are many kinds of bird-feeders that students can make.[15] Some are trays fastened to a window; some may be hung from pulleys and pulled away from the window on a line; some can be fastened to trees or posts.

The following are some hints about making and maintaining a feeding station. The school custodian, parents, someone from an upper grade, or in many classes the students themselves can make the feeding station. Be sure that the station is out of the reach of cats and squirrels. Water, especially in dry and freezing weather, helps attract birds. Various grains, birdseed, sunflower seeds, bread crumbs, raisins, suet, apples, and other fruit are satisfactory foods. Be sure that the wind does not blow the food away, keep the station well stocked, and remove any uneaten food if it is spoiled. The feeder should be in a sheltered place, but, if possible, in view of the schoolroom window. It should be placed as near trees as possible. Birds usually will not use the feeder if it is in the midst of playing children. Suet attracts birds, especially woodpeckers.

Discovering what kinds of foods different birds eat is an activity that presents opportunity for the use of scientific attitudes. Students should not generalize from one instance, should not decide without careful observation, and should withhold conclusions until there is sufficient evidence from observation and reading to justify them. For example, the fact that birds have not eaten sunflower seeds on the feeder for several days is no reason for deciding that birds do not like sunflower seeds.

[15]G. O. Blough, *Bird Watchers and Bird Feeders* (New York: McGraw-Hill, 1963).

What Can We See with a Microscope?[16]

Many elementary schools are in possession of one or more shiny new microscopes, and many teachers and supervisors wonder what to do with them.

[16]J. Schwartz, *Magnify and Find Out Why* (1972) and *Through the Magnifying Glass* (New York: McGraw-Hill, 1954); D. A. Karstaedt, "The World of Tiny Living Things," *Science and Children* (January 1984). Observing and experimenting with microorganisms.

A new world of tiny plants and animals is revealed to this investigator as she examines a drop of pond water with a microscope. *Photo by Lloyd Wolf, Concord School, Forestville, Maryland.*

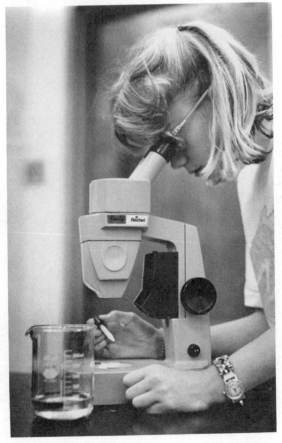

Although it is not good policy to permit apparatus to determine the curriculum, it is worth considering the potential of the microscope in the study of living things. Some general rules follow:

1. The younger the child, the lower the power of the microscope that should be used.
2. Move step by step from the visible world to the microscopic world (naked eye, 5-power magnifying lens, 25-50-100-power microscope).
3. The microscope should serve as a tool in the understanding of some large ideas, and not as an end in itself.

A few suggestions for things to see:

1. A drop of water from a stagnant pond to see tiny plants and animals there.
2. A thin strip of tissue from an onion to see cells.
3. Pollen from a flower to see the thousands of grains in a small bit of pollen.
4. A bit of yeast in water to see thousands of living yeast plants (high-power lens).
5. A thin strip of material taken from the outside of a leaf to see the many openings (stomata) in it.
6. A bird's feather to see the way in which it is "hooked" together.
7. Some snail eggs to see evidence of their development.
8. Green film scraped from the side of an aquarium to see algae (and possibly protozoans).
9. Bread mold to see growing threads, reproductive spore cases, and spores.
10. Tail of tadpole or small goldfish (whose body has been wrapped in moist cotton) to see capillaries, blood cells, and circulation of blood.
11. Water fleas (Daphnia) obtained from pet shops to see their heartbeat, digestive tract, and reproduction.
12. Parts of insects to see the compound eyes, pads at ends of legs (in flies), and so on.

This leaf is compared with other leaves seen on a field trip. The collection of leaves gathered will form the basis for a classification lesson on the trees. At first, students should be encouraged to devise their own classification schemes. *(Courtesy of NSTA)*

How Can We Classify Living Things?[17]

As we have indicated earlier (see pp. 138–139) there are degrees of classification. Younger children often group things in their own systems, often on the basis of one characteristic—color, size, shape, and so on. Older children may develop the skill of using many characteristics. The skill of classification rests on the ability to observe and identify characteristics and to compare and contrast.

To make classification meaningful to children it must serve a useful purpose. For example, in studying the inhabitants in and near a pond children may notice the variety of insects. They begin to observe insects, collect them, and perhaps raise them. They note similarities and differences in their size, parts, habits, and developments. They begin to see, with the aid of references, that insects all have certain common structural characteristics. *All* children will not arrive at this conclusion at the same time, nor will they all recognize which characteristics are significant.

As they continue to observe and have other experiences with insects, they will begin to see that insects have characteristics in common and can therefore be placed in a group by themselves (see pp. 266–267, 276–277).

Children can assemble many different kinds of plants or animals or both and observe them carefully to find classifying characteristics. "How can the living things be put into groups?" is the problem. They may at first separate plants from animals, then separate the vertebrate animals from the invertebrates, then try to classify vertebrate animals into five groups. Encourage children to go as far as they can without consulting books. After they have established the distinguishing characteristics with the live or preserved animals available, they can use pictures that are detailed enough to show structure. They begin by originating their own scheme of classifying them. As they improve in the skill of identifying significant likenesses and differences, they will probably change their original schemes.

How Can We Study Ants and Spiders?

A convenient observation house in which to watch life in an ant colony can be made from a clear glass 1-quart jar that has a screw top and soil to fill the jar. A block of wood placed in the center of the jar will prevent the ants from tunneling too far to be seen.

Wrap black paper around the outside of the glass jar to make it dark inside, and remove the paper when you want to see the ants. On top of the soil scatter bread crumbs, sugar, and various other foods, experimenting to find out what they eat. Give the ants a little water in a small dish on top of the soil, and not too much food. The story of "What We Saw the Ants Do" is an interesting one for children to write and illustrate.

Spiders are fascinating creatures to watch, and web making is an awe-inspiring operation. Students may be encouraged to search for spiderwebs that are in the process of construction to observe the operation, and then to observe how the web functions in the capture of food for the spider.[18]

Can Animals Learn?[19]

The question "Can animals learn?" will provoke a flood of answers from students, who will be only

[17]H. E. Caldwell and S. Patsko, "A Game for Classifying Animals," *Science and Children* (May 1975).

[18]J. Schwartz, *Through the Magnifying Glass* (New York: McGraw-Hill, 1954); R. Mills, "Insects and Others," *Science and Children* (May 1984); P. McClug, "Don't Squash It! Collect It!" *Science and Children* (May 1984). Collecting and classifying insects. K. Jacobson and W. Van Scheik, "Bitten by Biology," *Science and Children* (April 1987). Studying mosquitoes. C. Eubank, *Insect Zoo: How to Collect and Care for Insects* (New York: Walker, 1973).

[19]B. Ford, *Can Invertebrates Learn?* (New York: Julian Messner, 1972).

too happy to relate how their pet dog, cat, turtle, fish, or other animal "learned" how to do something. An experiment that can be easily conducted is to see if fish in an aquarium can learn to respond to tapping by coming to the surface. Each time fish are fed (and this should not be more than once every two days), the feeding is preceded by tapping the aquarium glass with a coin. After some days (or weeks) the fish may respond to the tapping by coming to the top. As a control the fish in a similar aquarium should be fed without the tapping, and then compare with the others to see if they respond to the tapping.

Experiments such as this and observations of animal behavior will open up many other questions. Children will learn to understand that much of animal behavior is unlearned or inherited, whereas other behavior is learned.

Mealworms are easy to raise in the classroom and are interesting to study.[20] Students ask and investigate such questions as, "How do mealworms explore a box?" "How does a mealworm sense the presence of a wall so that it can follow it?" "How does the mealworm find bran?" Students can, through careful observations, formulate some interesting hypotheses and attempt to evaluate them.

How Can We Study Earthworms?

Since earthworms are such important animals, easily obtainable and interesting to observe, children will enjoy making an earthworm farm.[21] Collect several earthworms from a garden or buy a

---

[20]D. C. Kramer, "Mealworms," *Science and Children* (January 1985). Details for raising and studying.

[21]From M. J. Atyea, "Learning about Dirt—An Earthworm Farm," *Science and Children* (September 1972); D. C. McGuire, "Project Warm Bin," *Science and Children* (March 1987). How to raise and study earthworms. M. McLaughlin, *Earthworms, Dirt and Rotten Leaves: An Exploration in Ecology* (New York: Athenaeum, 1986). Investigations and experiments make this a very useful book. D. C. Kramer, "Earthworms—the Classroom Animal," *Science and Children* (March 1984).

supply from a bait shop. An earthworm farm can be constructed by covering the outside of a wide-mouthed jar with dark construction paper. Add gravel to the bottom of the jar and then fill the jar with loosely packed, slightly damp soil that contains an ample amount of humus (decaying plant and animal material). Add the earthworms.

Feed the earthworms cereals or small portions of lettuce, oatmeal, or plants. Each day add enough water so soil continues to be slightly damp. Carefully observe the earthworms building tunnels in the soil. Children may note that the worms literally eat their way through the soil. Develop the idea that the worms are cultivating the soil by keeping it loose.

Carefully take an earthworm out of the farm and place it on a piece of construction paper. Use a magnifying glass to observe the features of the long body. Watch to see how the body moves. Darken the room, then turn on a flashlight near the earthworm. Does the earthworm move toward or away from light? Pour a portion of soil on the paper near the earthworm. Does it try to hide in the soil? Can you find out how it gets food?

Other Problems for Older Children

1. How do animals move from place to place?
2. How do living things depend on green plants?
3. What one-celled plants and animals can you find in pond water or in your aquarium?
4. How do animals reproduce?
5. How do bees live together in a hive?
6. How do seeds travel?
7. How can we grow mold?
8. What insects in your neighborhood are useful? Harmful?

Resources to Investigate with Children

1. Garden clubs, for information and for a person to assist with school gardening.
2. County agriculture agent, for help in answering questions about gardening and as a general resource person.

3. Florists, nursery personnel, and gardeners, for soil and other supplies, and for information about growing things in the classroom and in outdoor gardens.

4. Pet shops and dealers, for information about care of animals and for supplies.

5. Animal hospitals and veterinarians for information about care of animals and for other assistance.

6. Practicing farmers, for information about local crops and how they are planted and cared for.

7. Forester, to learn about how tree seeds are gathered and planted and how the young trees are cared for.

8. State agricultural college and experiment stations, for information about plant-growing experiments and similar information.

9. Museums and botanical gardens, for a better understanding of the orderly classification of plants and animals.

10. Local resources for the study of living plants and animals in their environment: parks, ponds, lakes, streams, swamps, fields, woodlands, vacant lots, lawns, home gardens, trees on streets, seashores, rivers.

11. Local beekeeper for information about habits and care of bees.

12. Exterminators for samples of dead termites and other insects and for information about their habits.

Preparing to Teach

1. Make a terrarium and aquarium as described in this chapter so that you will be better able to assist children in similar activities. List problems that would be appropriate for children to try to solve as they make and observe these teaching tools.

2. Write for some of the material suggested in the footnotes so as to have it on hand when you need it. Include National Wildlife Federation, 1412 16th St. NW, Washington, D.C. 20036 for "Conservation Education Catalog." Much helpful material.

3. Collect teaching pictures of plant and animal life and classify them according to the problems given in the chapter. This will be a nucleus collection, and children can be encouraged to add to it.

4. Try to obtain a soil-testing kit and get acquainted with its use.

5. Try starting house plants from cuttings, seeds, and so on, and raising them.

6. Make a list of other experiments not described here that may be used in solving some of the problems listed in the chapter.

7. Find larvae on different outdoor plants; feed and observe them. Keep track of your difficulties and successes to help you when you use such activities with children.

8. Prepare a list of experiences especially useful for children with special interests and abilities in the area of plant and animal study. Add a bibliography of books especially rewarding to them.

9. Make a unit plan to follow in helping students of a specific grade do one of the following: (1) Make a garden; (2) keep a pet in the classroom; (3) raise plants indoors.

10. List inquiry processes that are an important part of the experiments described in this chapter.

THE HUMAN BODY
AND HOW IT WORKS

Man wonders over the restless sea
The flowing water and the sight of the sky
And forgets that of all wonders
Man himself is the most wonderful

ST. AUGUSTINE, 4TH CENTURY A.D.

In various ways the machines we build are modeled in our own
image to extend our natural capacity. However, even the most
sophisticated man-made machines are primitive compared to the
human body. The body is not a machine, but a machine plus, the
first wonder of the universe.

CHRISTIAN BARNARD, CONSULTING EDITOR, THE BODY MACHINE,
CROWN PUBLISHERS, 1981

HOW WE STUDY OURSELVES

We view the body in many ways. The older view was concerned mainly with the body's gross structures—its systems and organs, its bones, muscles, and blood vessels. Today we study the body alive. We record the fluctuations of the heartbeat electrically on a graph. We observe the rhythmic waves of the food tube through a fluoroscope. We inject a radioactive substance into the bloodstream and follow its progress through the body with a Geiger counter. We use a television camera to view the inside of the human body in color.

We place bits of the body's tissues under the microscope, and the magnified view thus obtained reveals the billions of building blocks of the body—the cells. With the electron microscope, which magnifies up to 200,000 times, biologists have penetrated the innermost parts of the cell and revealed unimagined structures there. We use the most refined techniques of chemistry and physics to detect the molecules of living material inside each cell and to discover how the activities of these molecules in cell "laboratories" make life possible. Thus we have discovered how DNA (deoxyribonucleic acid) acts as the master chemical that makes up the genes in which the messages of heredity are encoded. We have mapped over 400 of the genes in the 46 human chromosomes; we hope that knowing their location, and eventually that of 100,000 or so genes that contain the human complement of hereditary material, will lead to a better understanding of human characteristics and will facilitate genetic engineering to prevent birth defects and to treat inherited diseases.

We have made great progress in the many fields of research that have contributed to our health. In the last 100 years we have detected the microscopic organisms—bacteria, protozoans, and viruses—that are responsible for many diseases. We have found how to combat these diseases with serums, vaccines, drugs, and antibiotics. We have discovered the role of the hormones, important chemicals released into the bloodstream, in regulating the development and functioning of the body. We have discovered the vitamins, essential components in the foods we eat. We have prolonged life for some individuals by replacing diseased hearts, kidneys, and other organs with healthy substitutes. We are increasing our knowledge of the body's internal defense mechanisms and are learning how to prevent such mechanisms from attacking the tissues of organ transplants.

We now employ new techniques for looking inside the living body, known by the acronyms CAT, PET, and MRI. CAT scanning combines X rays with computer technology to give cross-sectional views of body structures, soft parts as well as bones. CAT (computerized axial tomography) can select a picture of a slice of the body in any plane—like reading the middle card of a hundred stacked decks. PET (positron emission tomography) provides views of changes in metabolic activity, revealing the rate at which particular tissues consume biochemicals. PET scanning promises to be valuable in diagnosing disorders of the brain. MRI (magnetic resonance imaging) reveals the distribution of atoms by generating images of internal structure without using X rays. Thus it shows differences in the chemical composition of tissues, which may make it an invaluable tool for detecting cancer and for diagnosing multiple sclerosis, a condition in which the sheath surrounding the nerves deteriorates.

We study the heredity and environment of humans to see how each of these influences human development. We see in heredity, not without some difficulty and uncertainty, the contribution of parents, grandparents, and more distant ancestors. We investigate the impact of the environment, which includes not only climate, food, and shelter but also the social forces in human society. Finally, we see humans as a part of the continuing story of life that started over 3 billion years ago.

CELLS

The human body, like all living things, is built of structural units called cells. The cell, as we saw it in Chapter 10A, typically contains a nucleus surrounded by cytoplasm, and is covered by a thin cell membrane. Cells of the body come in many shapes and sizes. They are fitted to do many jobs: to protect and cover the body's surfaces, to receive and transmit nerve impulses, to contract and relax, to manufacture special chemicals, to store foods, and to perform dozens of other services. A body cell, unlike the one-celled amoeba, is not independent. It is affected by its relation with other cells and by the behavior of the whole cellular community—the body—of which it is a part (see p. 350).

BLUEPRINT OF THE BODY

Let us take a close look at the body to see how it is built and how it works. The body is made up of a number of obvious large parts: the limbs, eyes, ears, and the internal parts, such as the stomach and liver. Such large parts of the body, called organs, have a special job to perform. The legs are used to carry us from place to place. The eyes respond to light, enabling us to see. The arms and hands are used for doing all sorts of jobs, including grasping, lifting, and turning. The heart pumps the blood around the body. The stomach is active in a special phase of digestion. Each organ performs an essential task.

Select a convenient part, such as the forearm, and examine its structure. On the outside is skin. Within the arm you can feel the hard, supporting framework, the bones. If you wiggle your fingers while clasping the forearm with the other hand you can feel the muscles that activate the fingers. When the skin is cut, even by the merest scratch, blood flows out. At some point you have undoubtedly struck your "funny bone" in just the way that produces a tingling sensation, caused by your unwitting stimulation of the nerve near the surface of the elbow. The various parts of the arm—skin, bones, muscles, nerves, blood vessels—are held together by connective bands.

Organs are composed of different kinds of tissues. Thus, in the arm there is blood tissue, epithelial tissue, and supporting tissues of cartilage, bone, and fibrous connective tissue. As in any good organization the tissues must cooperate with each other to perform the work of an organ. Another way of saying this is that an organ is a group of tissues working together to perform a major function in the body.

Tissues, Organs, and Systems

All the tissues are made of cells and their products. We may say that a tissue is a group of similar cells working together for a specific job. Different

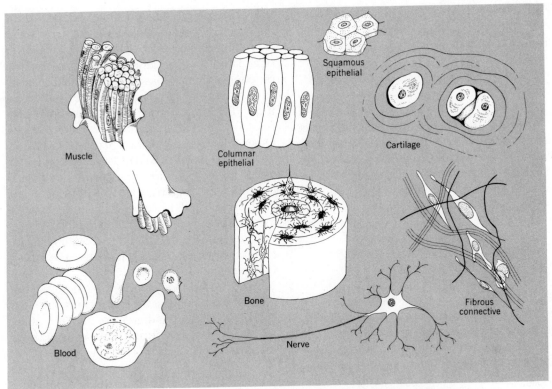

Squamous
epithelial

Muscle

Columnar
epithelial

Cartilage

Bone

Fibrous
connective

Nerve

Blood

Each tissue cell is uniquely fitted for its job: the long thin fibers of muscle cells that can contract quickly; the bricklike cells of epithelium, functioning as a protective wall and as a regulator of the passage of materials, as in the capillary walls which consist of a thin layer of cells; the freely moving cells of blood tissue; the long complex cells of nerve tissue with their specialized receiving and sending parts; and the scattered cells of bone and cartilage, with their tough intercellular material.

kinds of tissues work together for a larger purpose. Thus, as we have seen, the arm contains muscle, nerve, bone, blood, and other tissues working together to make possible the functioning of the arm. The same is true for all the organs of the body, such as the heart, stomach, liver, and kidneys.

Efficient operation of the body requires division of work into different departments just as in a city government or a large industrial plant. The departments of the body are called systems. All the organs concerned with preparing food for the use of the body are part of the digestive system. The circulatory system handles transportation of materials throughout the body. The respiratory system is made up of the organs that supply oxygen and get rid of certain wastes. The excretory system is the sanitation system of the body, ridding the body of its wastes. The nervous system has as its primary job controlling the body. The reproductive system is responsible for the making of sperm cells in the male, and for the making of egg cells and the nurturing of the embryo in the female.

NUTRITION

It's a very odd thing—
As odd as can be—
That whatever Miss T eats
Turns into Miss T.

WALTER DE LA MARE[1]

The body has the remarkable ability to select needed chemical substances from the beans, beef, milk, and lettuce consumed, and to convert them into just the kind of substances needed to make the body's own flesh and bones. When you have ceased growing, food is essential for the repair and replacement of worn-out tissue. Food also fills the energy needs of the body.

Food Essentials

A trip to the supermarket provides convincing evidence of the tremendous number of food products that are available for human consumption. This variety, however, is only on the surface. There are only a few kinds of essential substances in all these foods: carbohydrates, fats, proteins, minerals, vitamins, and water (see pp. 349–350).

The common carbohydrates are sugar and starch. They are similar chemically, and both are changed into the same substance—glucose—by digestion. Carbohydrates constitute the prime fuels of the body. Fats and oils are the other large class of fuel nutrients. Measure for measure, fats produce about twice as much energy when oxidized in the body as do the carbohydrates. In cold climates such as the polar regions, people rely heavily on fat intake to supply the heat needed to maintain normal body temperature. Eskimos, for example, eat large amounts of blubber, the fat of the whale.

[1]From *Poems for Children* by Walter De La Mare. Courtesy of the Literary Trustees of Walter De La Mare, and The Society of Authors as their representative. Copyright 1930 by Henry Holt and Company, Inc.; reprinted by permission of Holt, Rinehart and Winston.

Water, minerals, and proteins are essential for the structure and the workings of the body. Water is taken in directly in the form of drinking water or as part of food, because foods have a great deal of water in them. Minerals are required in small amounts. These are provided by the food we eat if our diet is a good one. Calcium and phosphorus, found in milk, are needed for building bones. Other minerals serve other vital functions. Iron, for instance, is an essential constituent of hemoglobin, the oxygen-carrying pigment in red blood cells. Iodine is required for proper functioning of the thyroid gland. Fluorine has been included in the list of needed minerals (and now is added to drinking water in the compound sodium fluoride in some localities), because it seems to be a factor in preventing tooth decay.

Proteins, the most complex of the food substances, are abundant in meat (muscle), eggs, cheese, and beans, and are essential in building cell structures, enzymes and hormones, and other essential body materials.

Not all proteins are identical in their chemical makeup. The dissimilarity among proteins arises from the nature of the protein molecules: Each is made of an assortment of one or more of about 20 kinds of smaller units called *amino acids*. Proteins might be compared to words, each of which is made of one or more of the 26 letters of the alphabet. In the process of digestion proteins are broken down into their amino acids, which then pass into the bloodstream. The body cells select from this assortment of amino acid "building blocks" those which are needed for their particular structure and their particular function. A variety of proteins from different sources is required in a good diet to provide the essential amino acids. (Of the 20 amino acids, 12 can be synthesized by humans; the other 8, which cannot, are known as essential amino acids.)

As might be expected, those proteins of *animal* origin—for instance, the proteins of milk, eggs, and meat—have the highest nutritional value for humans, because the assortment of amino acids in animal proteins most closely resembles that of the body's proteins. However, it does not matter whether the essential amino acids come from a cow, pig, fish, soybean, or any other source; they always end up in distinctly human protein.

Vitamins are found in foods in minute amounts. Unlike most of the other food essentials, vitamins are not used directly as fuels or growth materials. Instead, they act as regulators of chemical activity and of growth in the body.

Millions of Americans are convinced that vitamin and mineral supplements are essential for vibrant health. They are encouraged in this belief by the drug companies, health food store owners, certain nutritionists, and some scientists. However, it is probably fair to say that science research in nutrition indicates that the best place to obtain the required vitamins and minerals—the micronutrients—is from a diet of mostly fresh foods from the four major food groups (four servings of vegetables and fruits, including one citrus fruit; four servings of breads, cereals, and grains, including some whole grains; two of milk products and two of meat, fish, poultry, or high-quality vegetable protein).

Megadoses of vitamins and minerals containing hundreds of thousand of times the quantity of the U.S. RDA (Recommended Daily Allowance) should be taken only on the advice and under the supervision of a physician who is knowledgeable about nutrition. Self-prescribed megadoses of vitamins and minerals have produced severe side effects; some can be dangerously toxic. Many claims for the health benefits of megadoses of micronutrients have not been substantiated by properly designed studies.

Diet

According to Dr. Mark Hegsted of the Human Nutrition Center, "the diet of the American people has become increasingly rich—rich in meat, sources of fat and cholesterol and in sugar. . . . The risks associated with eating this diet are demonstrably large."

Following are some practical suggestions for improving your diet:

1. Eat three balanced meals each day. Skipping meals makes you overeat at the one or two you take. Confine between-meal snacks to fruit or raw vegetables.
2. Increase your carbohydrate diet from natural sources. Raw fruits and fresh vegetables provide natural sugars and dietary fiber. Whole-grain flours and breads supply essential vitamins, proteins, and minerals.
3. Reduce your diet of meat products, particularly red meats. Substitute more fish and skinned chicken to reduce your consumption of fat.
4. Decrease the amount of cholesterol you eat. A single whole egg contains a day's maximum allowance of cholesterol. Egg white and skim milk are low in cholesterol.
5. Cut down on refined sugars and salt. Do not eat prepared sugar-coated cereals, some of which are more than 50 percent sugar. Eat hot cereals. You can obtain all the salt you need for good health from what is naturally part of the foods you eat. We consume two to three times as much salt as we need.

The word *Calorie,* as used in discussion of diet, is frequently misunderstood. Not a substance in food, it is simply a measure of heat (see p. 484). A Calorie as defined in nutrition is the amount of heat needed to raise the temperature of 1 liter (a bit more than 1 quart) of water 1° Celsius. In other words, to speak of the calories that a portion of food contains is merely to indicate how much heat will be produced when that food is burned. Here are a few examples of the approximate daily calorie requirements of human beings: a worker doing heavy manual labor—4,000 Calories; a homemaker—1,800 to 2,300 Calories; an active teenage schoolgirl or schoolboy—2,500 to 3,800 Calories.

The problem of losing weight engages the attention—and the conversation—of millions of people. A flood of books, pills, injections, and various panaceas distract would-be weight losers from the simple truth that they must consume fewer calories than they burn up. Fad diets don't work because (1) the person loses weight too quickly, and (2) when the diet is over the weight is regained. To lose weight safely one must maintain a balanced diet, cut down the amount of fats and refined sugar, restrict eating to mealtimes, control the size of portions consumed, and engage in brisk exercise daily. Calories *do* count—and you must count them. Having achieved a satisfactory weight one must maintain permanent control over food intake.

DIGESTION: PREPARING FOOD FOR THE USE OF THE BODY

We would starve, despite all the food that we eat, if it were not for the digestion of food. Most of what we eat is not in proper form to pass into the blood or to be used by the cells of the body. The digestive system is composed essentially of a long tube together with digestive glands that secrete chemicals that act on food in the tube. The entire tube is known as the *alimentary canal*. It is surprisingly long—about 30 feet (9 meters) in adults. Most of this length is made up of the coiled small intestine, which is about 22 feet (about 7 meters) long.

Inside the Food Canal

Before we consider the changes in food as it travels through the alimentary canal let us preview what is going to happen. The food mass is going to be chopped, ground, and finally reduced to a liquid mush. At the same time the molecules of the proteins, carbohydrates, and fats in the food are going to be split into smaller molecules. This molecule splitting will be accomplished by the action of enzymes of the various digestive fluids.

Enzymes are proteins that trigger chemical changes at great speed and at relatively low temperatures. A single enzyme molecule may act on thousands of molecules without being perma-

nently altered in the process, and so it can be used over and over again. Over a thousand different enzymes are known, each able to cause a particular chemical change in a particular substance.

The enzymes in the digestive tract serve two purposes. First, they permit the molecules to pass through the membranes of the small intestine into the bloodstream and thus become available to the entire body. Second, they transform the complex molecules into a form in which they can be used by the cells of the body for building new structures or for the production of energy.

The food enters the body via the mouth. Solid food is cut, ground, and mashed by 32 specialized tools, the teeth. Breaking up the food into small particles exposes it to the chemical action of digestive juices. While the food is being chewed, the muscular tongue mixes the food with saliva and kneads it against the mouth's bony roof. Saliva

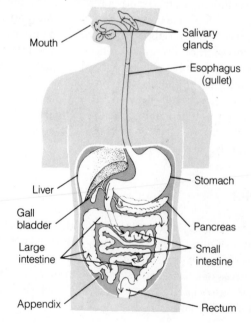

The general appearance and location of the main digestive organs. Various glands secrete chemicals that change food as it moves through the alimentary canal.

is made in three pairs of salivary glands, whose secretion is brought into the mouth by tubes or ducts. Enzymes in saliva start the digestion of cooked starches by splitting the larger molecules into the smaller ones of sugar. After a few moments in the mouth, the food is swallowed and passes through the gullet, or *esophagus,* into the stomach.

Food may remain in the stomach up to four hours, depending upon the kind of food. While there, it is churned about and mixed with gastric juice from the gastric glands. This juice contains, among other substances, an enzyme that helps to digest proteins. Surprisingly, some of the stomach glands manufacture hydrochloric acid. The minute amount of this acid that is made helps the enzymes to work and also helps dissolve minerals in the food. After it leaves the stomach, the food is pushed into the small intestine, which is the main center for digestion in the body. And, as we shall see, it is the place where digested food leaves the food tube and enters the blood. Into the small intestine pour the juices of three digestive glands: intestinal juices given off by the glands in the walls of the small intestine itself, bile from the liver, and pancreatic juice from the pancreas. The enzymes in the juices of the intestinal glands and the pancreas, as well as certain salts in bile, complete the process of breaking down the carbohydrates, proteins, and fats into simpler substances.

Out of the Food Canal

In a process known as *absorption,* digested food is then able to pass through the thin membranes of the small intestine into the blood. The small intestine is admirably fitted for this job: Its 22-foot (7-meter) length, thin walls abundantly supplied with capillaries, and millions of microscopic, fingerlike projections called *villi*—all serve to make it an effective "blotter" for carrying out the function of absorbing digested foods and then transferring them to the circulatory system.

Waste Disposal

The indigestible part of food goes into the large intestine. This is large in diameter as compared to the small intestine, but it is much shorter in length, being only about 5 feet (1.5 meters) long. The material in the large intestine is composed mainly of cellulose from plant foods and of bacteria. Water is removed from this mass as it moves along. The waste products form semisolid feces that are then eliminated from the body through the rectum.

RESPIRATION: HOW THE BODY BREATHES

A person may be able to survive without food for a week or more. Without oxygen, however, the human being cannot live for more than a few minutes. Oxygen is required by every cell for the oxidation of food to produce energy. It is the job of the respiratory system to supply oxygen vital for life and also to rid the body of the carbon dioxide wastes resulting from cellular oxidation.

Mechanics of Breathing

The lungs and structures connected to it form a continuous open system with the air outside. The lungs are enclosed in an airtight chest cavity whose size is increased during breathing. If you place your hand on your chest you will notice that it rises and falls as you breathe. Not so readily noticed is the movement of the diaphragm, an arched muscular partition between the chest and the abdomen. During inhalation the diaphragm contracts and is thus pulled *downward.* At the same time the muscles of the ribs contract and pull them up and out. These movements enlarge the chest cavity and reduce its pressure on the lungs. The outside air, with its greater pressure, is thus pushed into the lungs.

During exhalation the diaphragm moves up, and the ribs move down and in. These movements decrease the size of the chest cavity, increasing its pressure and squeezing the air out of the lungs. When a person is at ease this cycle takes place about 12 to 15 times per minute. During exercise, or other strenuous activity, we breathe more rapidly and more deeply. This supplies added oxygen necessary for the increased energy required by such activity (see p. 347).

Pathway for Air

Inhaled air passes through the nostrils, where small hairs strain out large dust particles. The air then traverses the nasal passages, whose labyrinthine arrangement of bones enormously increases the area of mucous membrane over which the air must pass. This is desirable because the mucous membrane moistens, cleans, and warms the air to body temperature.

The air now enters the throat cavity and then passes the trapdoor guarding the entrance to the windpipe. This trapdoor, the *epiglottis,* closes when we swallow food to prevent food particles from entering the windpipe. The windpipe

The pathway of air from the nostrils to the air sacs.

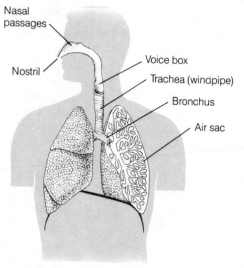

Nasal passages
Nostril
Voice box
Trachea (windpipe)
Bronchus
Air sac

branches into two pipes, the *bronchi.* These lead the air by means of smaller and smaller tubes ultimately into the *alveoli,* or air sacs of the lungs.

Exchanges in the Air Sacs

The air sacs are microscopic chambers in the lung tissue. The lungs have nearly 1 billion of these balloonlike structures, which provide an enormous area for the absorption of oxygen from the air. The air sacs have very thin walls, richly supplied with capillaries. The oxygen passes through the thin walls of the air sacs and capillaries into the bloodstream and eventually is carried to every cell in the body. Moving in the opposite direction, carbon dioxide and water vapor leave the blood capillaries and pass into the air sacs. When we breathe out, these gases pass out of the body as part of the exhaled air.

Cigarette Smoking and the Respiratory System

Cigarette smoking has come to the forefront as a cause of respiratory system damage, notably cancer of the lungs. A 1987 report of the American Cancer Society stated that cigarette smoking was responsible for 85 percent of lung cancer among men, 75 percent among women; that smoking accounts for 30 percent of all cancer deaths; that those who smoke two or more packs a day have lung cancer mortality rates 15 to 25 times greater than nonsmokers.

Cessation of smoking can delay or avert a substantial portion of deaths from lung cancer and early deaths from chronic bronchiopulmonary disease and heart disease. Smoking is restricted in many public places, since it has been established that even nonsmokers may be injured by the exhaled smoke of others. Recent laws have been enacted banning smoking on airplane trips of less than two hours.

It is probably true that if cigarette smoking were not a national habit, the overwhelming evidence of the hazard it presents to health would have resulted in legislation barring the manufacture and sale of cigarettes. At this time the most urgent question for parents and teachers is "How can we prevent this habit from establishing itself in youth?" In this effort nonsmoking advocates must have the backing of legislation that not only regulates cigarette advertising but also makes use of the mass media to promote a desirable image of the nonsmoker in the eyes of young people.

CIRCULATION: HOW MATERIAL IS TRANSPORTED AROUND THE BODY

The Heart

More than 300 years ago William Harvey demonstrated that blood flows in a continuous, closed circuit through the body. This was the first time in history that an accurate concept of circulation was formed. Even now, when knowledge of circulation is widespread, we are awed at the marvels of the heart mechanism. Here is a living pump that pushes blood through 40,000 miles (about 65,000 kilometers) of blood vessels, and beats 100,000 times per day every day of our lives.

The heart is a muscular pump about the size of a fist, weighing less than 1 pound (.45 kilograms). It is made of four compartments: The upper two are known as *atria* (singular *atrium*), the lower as *ventricles*. The left ventricle is the largest chamber, making up three fourths of the whole heart in size. Its muscle wall is three times as thick as that of the right ventricle. This difference is related to the job performed by each of these parts: The left ventricle must push the blood completely around the body, but the right ventricle pushes the blood only to the nearby lungs.

Around the Circulatory System

With the help of the illustration on this page, join the blood entering the right atrium and journey

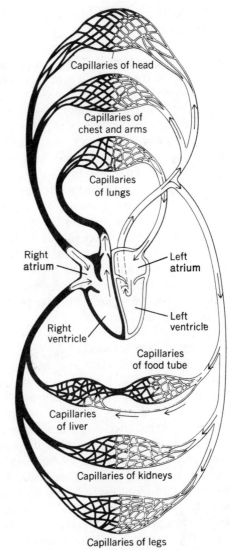

Blood moves around the body in a continuous closed circuit of arteries, veins, and capillaries, with the heart serving as a pump. Note that to make a complete round trip, blood has to flow through the heart twice.

with it throughout the body until it makes a complete circuit.

Blood is brought to the right atrium by two veins, the *venae cavae* (singular *vena cava*). This blood has come from every part of the body except the lungs. When the right atrium is filled with blood the trapdoor, or *valve* as it is called, between it and the right ventricle opens, and the blood flows into the ventricle. The valve closes as the right ventricle contracts and sends the blood through *arteries* (blood vessels that carry blood away from the heart) to the lungs. In the *capillaries* that envelop the air sacs of the lungs, the blood picks up oxygen and gets rid of carbon dioxide and some water. The blood now goes back to the left side of the heart by means of *veins* (blood vessels that return blood to the heart).

The oxygenated blood from the lungs enters the left atrium. When this chamber fills, the valve between it and the ventricle opens and the blood flows into the left ventricle. The valve then closes, which prevents a backflow of the blood as the large muscles of the left ventricle contract. This sends the blood coursing throughout the body by way of the *aorta*, the largest blood vessel in the body. In the adult it is slightly thicker than a man's thumb. The aorta sends branches into the head and arms, and the main line continues down through the chest and abdomen and sends off a number of branches. It finally divides into two arteries that supply the legs.

The blood from the arteries is widely dispersed through a branching network that divides first into *arterioles*, and then into millions of thin-walled *capillaries* to reach all the cells of the body. Here oxygen, food, and other needed substances are transferred from the blood to the cells. In turn, the body tissues give up their waste products to the blood. The capillary network reunites to form the veins, which then return the blood to the heart again by way of the *venae cavae*, the largest veins in the body. The cycle then starts over again. It has been estimated that it takes about 15 seconds for the blood to make one complete circuit of the body.

Of the 4,000 gallons (about 15,000 liters) of blood that are pumped through the heart daily, none is distributed to the walls of its chambers. The muscles of the heart receive blood containing oxygen and food in the same way as all other tissues. For this purpose a special set of arteries branch off from the aorta and go immediately to the heart structure. These are *coronary arteries*. The coronary veins bring the blood back from the heart tissues to rejoin the main circulation. Blockage of the coronary blood vessels leads to heart attacks.

Blood

The bloodstream is the distribution system of the body. This surging fluid carries food and oxygen to all the cells of the body. It receives and delivers many chemical products, such as the hormones. It collects wastes and brings them to the organs that remove them from the body. The blood also contains chemicals and cells that protect the body from disease. In addition, the blood has its own built-in clotting system for plugging leaks in any of its pipes. Blood is composed of *red* and *white blood cells, platelets,* and the liquid in which they are immersed called *plasma.*

The red cells (also known as *red corpuscles*) are the oxygen carriers. These cells contain hemoglobin, an iron compound combined with protein. Hemoglobin, which is responsible for the red color of blood, is the substance that enables the red cells to carry oxygen. In the lungs the hemoglobin combines with oxygen. When the blood reaches the tissues of the body, the oxygen is released. Lack of iron in the diet may lead to one type of *anemia*, a blood condition in which there is an insufficiency of hemoglobin.

The white corpuscles may be regarded as the standing army of the body. One of their primary jobs is to fight off invading bacteria and other harmful microorganisms. This they do by engulfing the harmful organisms, digesting them, and thus destroying them. White corpuscles are able to squeeze through tiny openings in the capillary walls and leave the bloodstream. They move, much like an amoeba, to any part of the body where danger threatens. Another function of certain kinds of white cells, called *lymphocytes*, is the production of antibodies, specific proteins that act against foreign substances.

Platelets play an important part in forming clots, which stem the flow of blood from injured blood vessels.

The plasma is about 90 percent water, in which many substances are dissolved. These include fats, sugars, proteins, antibodies, hormones, enzymes, minerals, and wastes. The adult human has about 5 quarts (5 liters) of blood. The donation of 1 pint ($\frac{1}{2}$ liter) of this precious fluid to local blood banks, for building up their stockpile of plasma for emergencies, will not harm a healthy adult. The body replaces such losses quickly.

The circulatory system is a *closed* system of arteries, veins, and capillaries. The capillaries, however, are thin-walled enough for some of the liquid part of the blood to pass through them and to bathe the tissues of the body. This escaped fluid, together with the white blood cells that have forced their way out of the capillaries, make up the fluid called *lymph*.

Care of the Circulatory System

Care of the circulatory system is attracting increasing attention at the present time. Health statistics show that in the United States heart disease is the number-one cause of death. Part of this is the inevitable result of those measures that have enabled people to live longer. Circulatory ailments are particularly the problem of middle and old age, so in an aging population it is to be expected that these will become prominent health concerns. Although the toll is exacted in later life it is during our younger years that we pave the way for an ailing or a healthy old age. The normal rules of healthy living apply with equal force to the heart and its blood vessels. These include a moderate, balanced diet, exercise, sufficient sleep, freedom from excessive worry, and a periodic medical checkup. The detection and treatment of high blood pressure, a high risk factor in heart disease, is also very important. Cigarette smoking is significantly related to coronary artery disease.

Over the past several decades evidence has shown that a high level of cholesterol in the blood is associated with atherosclerosis—the narrowing of arteries caused by the buildup of fatty plaques in its walls. The fatty plaques inhibit the flow of blood; eventually a clot may form, obstructing the artery and causing a heart attack or a stroke.

The cholesterol of these plaques is derived from low-density lipoproteins (LDL) that circulate in the bloodstream. LDL is a particle composed of cholesterol molecules (a lipid) and a protein. The more LDL there is in the blood the more rapidly atherosclerosis develops. Another lipoprotein, high-density lipoprotein (HDL), does not carry as much cholesterol as LDL.

The typical American diet of eggs, red meat, whole milk, cheese, and other foods high in saturated fats is very high in cholesterol. (In general saturated fats are those that are solid at room temperature, in contrast to polyunsaturated fats such as vegetable oils that are liquid or soft. Two vegetable fats are also saturated, coconut "oil" and palm "oil." They happen to be two of the most popular fats used in processed foods because they are cheap and do not turn rancid readily. Fats from fish are less saturated than other animal fats.)

Recent studies show that HDL carries fats away from body cells and is therefore important in preventing the accumulation of cholesterol along the artery walls. LDL, on the other hand, transports cholesterol *to* the cells. Consequently a high level of HDL in relation to LDL is desirable.

Factors that influence the HDL–LDL ratio include heredity, sex, exercise, diet, and cigarette smoking. Doctors recommend that people with over 200 milligrams of cholesterol per deciliter in their blood attempt to reduce it by diet—by reducing the intake of saturated fats—and by exercise. When these measures do not work, certain drugs may be prescribed.

Extraordinary advances have been made in the surgical treatment of disorders of the heart. In the *bypass* operation a portion of a superficial vein is removed from the leg of the patient and is attached to the aorta, replacing the blocked heart artery in such a way that blood can flow freely. *Artificial pacemakers* have helped to overcome problems arising from irregular heartbeats. A small battery-operated device delivers repeated electrical shocks through wires connected to the heart. In *heart transplants,* pioneered by Dr. Christian Barnard in 1967, all or part of the donor's heart is connected to appropriate cardiac structures of the recipient. The lives of a number of patients have been extended significantly by this procedure. William Van Buren, the longest living survivor of a heart transplant, who received his new heart at the age of 40, has lived thus far (1988) for 18 years.

On December 22, 1982, doctors at the University Medical Center in Salt Lake City successfully implanted an artificial heart in a 61-year-old dentist, Barney B. Clark. The heart itself, made of polyurethane plastic and aluminum, had been developed by Dr. Robert Jarvik. Weakened by lung and kidney problems, Barney Clark died 119 days after the implantation. The world's longest surviving recipient of a permanent artificial heart lived 620 days after the implantation. Research has now focused on using artificial hearts for patients awaiting human donor hearts.

EXCRETION: GETTING RID OF BODY WASTES

During the normal activity of the body, waste products are formed. The chief wastes of the body are carbon dioxide, water, urea, and salts. Water and carbon dioxide are formed in cells as a result of the oxidation of food to produce energy. We have already described how carbon dioxide is eliminated through the lungs. Water is disposed of in three places: the lungs, the skin, and the kidneys. The water exhaled from the lungs can be seen readily on a cold winter day. Sweat coming from the sweat glands of the skin is mostly water together with some salt. This is brought to the sweat glands by the blood circulating in the skin. Evaporation of the sweat not only rids the body of excess water but it is an important way of cooling the body.

Urea is a product resulting from the breakdown of protein foods and of cellular structures.

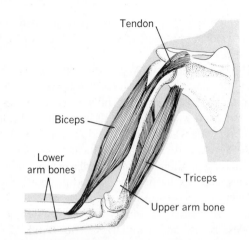

One muscle, the biceps, bends the arm and another muscle, the triceps, straightens it.

It is excreted chiefly by the kidneys. Each of the two kidneys has about 1 million microscopic filters through which the blood flows and the urea, salts, and water are removed. These then pass into the bladder as *urine,* which is eliminated from the body periodically. The kidneys also perform the essential job of controlling the concentration of practically every chemical in the blood. They eliminate excess substances and retain valuable ones. As a result, the fluids that eventually leave the blood capillaries to bathe the cells of the body provide the cells with a uniformly favorable environment.

Urine gives valuable clues to body health. Among the substances for which urine is analyzed are sugar and albumen. Sugar in the urine may be indicative of diabetes. Albumen may signify that the kidneys are not functioning properly.

THE BODY FRAMEWORK AND HOW IT IS MOVED

The human body is built on the same plan as a modern skyscraper. There is a rigid internal arrangement of beams and girders, the skeleton, to which the rest of the structure is attached. The human framework has the added feature of flexibility; its parts can be moved. The long bones are designed as levers that are moved by the muscles attached to the bone framework. All in all, the bones and muscles are a wonderful mechanism of struts, arches, levers, and pulleys for supporting and moving the body.

Muscles move bones by pulling, never by thrusting or twisting. The pulling results from the shortening or contraction of a muscle. Therefore, when you move any part of your body in one direction you are using a different muscle from the one you use to move the same part in the opposite direction. Through cooperating pairs of muscles humans can move all the limbs in almost every useful direction. Complex motions, such as handwriting, may involve many pairs of muscles.

BODY CONTROL

The human body is under the dual control of the nervous system and the endocrine system. The primary control is exerted through the nervous system, whose branching nerves penetrate the entire body. Chemical control is effected by the endocrine system through the hormones that are secreted into the bloodstream. Let us look first at the nervous system.

The Nervous System

The headquarters of the nervous system is the brain. Nerve pathways for most parts of the body enter and leave the brain by way of the main trunk line, the spinal cord. An exception to this are the important cranial nerves, which connect directly from the brain to various organs, principally in the head, without passing through the spinal cord. The exact nature of a nerve message is not known, but a combination of electrical and chemical changes pass along the nerve cells when a nerve impulse is transmitted. The eyes, ears, and sense organs in the skin, tongue, and nose are specialized for receiving sensations (see Chapter 18A for a description of the ears, and Chapter 19A for a

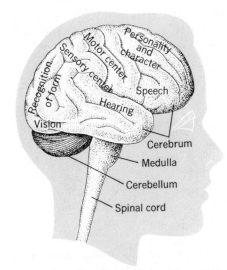

The three parts of the brain control different levels of activity. The cerebrum is the center for voluntary movement, for the reception of sensations, for reasoning and memory. The cerebellum controls balance and coordination of muscles, as in walking. The medulla controls such automatic functions as breathing, digestion, and heartbeat.

description of the eyes). The unit of structure and function of the nervous system is the nerve cell, or neuron.

Three important parts of the brain are shown in the illustration on this page: the cerebrum, the cerebellum, and the medulla. The *cerebrum* is the part of the brain where the centers that control consciousness, intelligence, reasoning, memory, imagination, and learning are located. Also in the cerebrum are centers that receive and interpret sensations, such as sight, hearing, smell, taste, pressure, and others. Here also are the centers for initiating and directing voluntary activities. When you lift your arm, the impulse for this action originates in the cerebrum, speeds from there down a nerve pathway in the spinal cord, and then along a nerve to muscles in your arm, causing them to contract.

The cerebrum is divided into two halves, known as the *cerebral hemispheres,* by a groove running front to back. Recent studies have revealed that each hemisphere has its own specialized talents. The left hemisphere excels in speech, logic, writing, and mathematics. The right side predominates in the recognition of complex visual patterns, in aptitude for music, in nonverbal communication, in general creativity, and in the expression and recognition of emotion.

Lying at the base of the cerebrum, inside the brain, is the *thalamus,* and beneath it, the *hypothalamus.* The thalamus is a giant relay system for sensory nerve impulses to the appropriate centers in the *cortex,* the "gray matter," or outer layer of the cerebrum. The hypothalamus controls eating and body temperature; it is also involved in regulating thirst, pleasure, pain, and sexual and reproductive activity.

The *cerebellum* is a coordinating center for muscular movements. Any action, such as walking, requires the coordinated functioning of many muscles. The precise timing of muscular contraction and relaxation is regulated by the cerebellum. Another job of the cerebellum is the control of balance. In the mastoid bone of the skull, which also contains the inner-ear mechanism, are three canals oriented at right angles to each other in three planes of space (see p. 574). As a fluid moves in the canals the position of the body in space is communicated to the cerebellum by the effect of this fluid on the sensitive nerve tissue lining the canals. The cerebellum automatically interprets these messages and sends impulses to the proper muscles to maintain the body in balance.

The *medulla* controls what might be termed the housekeeping functions of the body. Heart rate and breathing are some of the activities regulated by the medulla. In addition nerve impulses pass through it in both directions between the spinal cord and the rest of the brain.

The *spinal cord* is the main pathway between the brain and the rest of the body. Through the spinal cord go many of the nerves that bring impulses to the brain from the body receptors, the sense organs. In the opposite direction impulses from the brain to many parts of the body pass through nerves in the spinal cord. In addition, the spinal cord is the center for many *reflex actions.*

A reflex action is the simplest type of action in the nervous system. If, unthinkingly, you touch a hot object with your fingers, you pull your hand away before you are aware that it is hot. Awareness comes later. The action starts with stimulation of receptors in the finger by the hot object. The nerve impulse generated in the heat and pain receptors of the skin is carried along by sensory nerve cells to the spinal cord. Connections are made to motor nerve cells, which carry a message out to the muscle. The muscle contracts, pulling the arm away. All of this takes but a few thousandths of a second. Meantime, a second series of connections is made in the spinal cord, and a message starts up to the brain to "advise" the brain

Chemical control of the body is exercised by the endocrine glands, whose secretions are carried by the blood to all parts of the body.

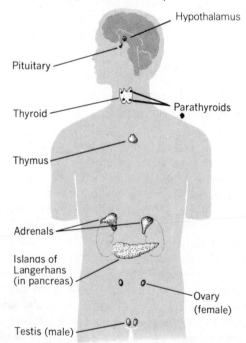

Hypothalamus

Pituitary

Thyroid

Parathyroids

Thymus

Adrenals

Islands of Langerhans (in pancreas)

Ovary (female)

Testis (male)

that the object was hot. This message, however, does not arrive in the brain until some thousandths of a second after the hand has been pulled away. We can appreciate the protective advantage of reflex actions when we realize that hundreds of these inborn, automatic actions are built into the workings of the human body.

Chemical Control

The *endocrine* system constitutes the other controlling mechanism of the body. The action of the endocrine glands was first discovered in the middle of the nineteenth century. Scientists found that certain glands poured chemicals into the bloodstream that affected various parts of the body. Such chemical messengers were named *hormones*, after the Greek word meaning "to excite." Minute amounts of hormones produce large effects. They enter the blood directly from the gland where they are made and are then quickly carried to all parts of the body. This explains the rapid action of some hormones. The main endocrine glands of the body are the pituitary, hypothalamus, thyroid, parathyroid, islets of Langerhans, adrenals, thymus, and gonads, but, as is explained later, hormone production is not limited to these glands.

The *pituitary gland* is attached to the base of the brain. It produces a number of different hormones, one of which regulates bone and body growth. Excessive secretion during childhood may produce a giant. Undersecretion, on the other hand, may make an individual a dwarf. Other hormones of the pituitary gland regulate blood pressure and many phases of the reproductive cycle. The pituitary gland is often called the "master gland," because it produces hormones that control many other endocrine glands.

The pituitary gland lies beneath the *hypothalamus*, an area of the brain that is also regarded as an endocrine gland. The hypothalamus produces two hormones that are stored in and released from the pituitary gland. One stimulates contraction of the uterus in childbirth and the making of milk when the infant begins to suckle. The other regulates the excretion of water from the kidneys. In addition, the hypothalamus regulates the pituitary's secretion of hormones, which, in turn, stimulate the secretion of hormones from the thyroid, adrenal cortex, and the gonads. The hypothalamus, as part of the brain, receives information from other parts of the brain, which allows it to respond to the external and internal environment of the body. Thus it becomes clear that the nervous and endocrine systems are in fact a single regulating system.

The *thyroid gland* is in the neck in front of the voice box. Its secretion, *thyroxin*, regulates the rate at which the body works (body metabolism) and body development.

The four *parathyroid glands* are embedded in the tissue of the thyroid. They regulate calcium metabolism.

The *islets of Langerhans*, located in the pancreas, regulate the body's use of sugar. Two kinds of hormones are secreted here: One stimulates the conversion of stored *glycogen* (animal starch) in the liver to blood glucose; the other, *insulin*, promotes the use of glucose by muscles and other cells and thus decreases blood sugar concentration. Insulin also stimulates the storage of sugar in body tissues. Insulin extract, first used in 1922 for the treatment of diabetes, has prolonged the lives of hundreds of thousands of people.

The *adrenal glands* lie on top of the kidneys. One of their secretions, *adrenalin*, made in the inner tissues of the adrenal, is important in regulating blood pressure. It causes the heart to beat faster and more strongly, and has been used as a lifesaving drug when the heart falters. Other secretions of the adrenal glands from its outer tissues, or *cortex*, are involved in regulating cellular oxidation. One of the hormones, *cortisone*, has been used in treatment of arthritis and other conditions.

The *thymus gland*, located just below the neck and behind the top of the breastbone, stimulates antibody and white cell production, particularly the T cells (described on pp. 338 and 342), and therefore is significant in body defense against bacteria, viruses, and other foreign substances. Various thymic hormones may also be significant in countering cancer, in influencing the functioning of the reproductive system, and possibly in retarding aging.

The *gonads,* the testes and ovaries, not only make the reproductive cells but also manufacture hormones. These influence the so-called *secondary sex characteristics* such as the deep voice and broad shoulders of the male, and the breasts and broad hips of the female. In the female they are also involved in the cycle of egg production and menstruation. Sex hormones also influence the body far beyond sex, affecting the brain, the liver, the salivary glands, and the muscles and skin.

By 1970 only 20 human hormones had been identified. Researchers now think there may be as many as 200. Within the past few years, for example, the heart has been discovered to be more than a pump. It also secretes a powerful hormone that has an important role in the regulation of blood pressure and blood volume, and in the excretion of water, sodium, and potassium. It exerts its influence on the blood vessels, on the kidneys and the adrenal glands, and on a large number of regions of the brain.

A broader definition of hormones is emerging: "anything produced by one cell that can get to another cell by any means and change what it does," according to Wyle Vale at the Salk Institute at La Jolla, California.

The brain itself has been found to be a gland secreting hormones and reacting to others. This breakthrough came with the discovery in the brain of hormones called opiates—pain blockers that some say account for a jogger's "high." Subsequently scientists have identified 45 hormones in the brain, many of which perform special tasks elsewhere in the body.

In summary, the endocrine system enables us to adapt and respond to our environment, both internal and external. It is a system with intricate feedback networks and chemical or nerve signals to keep the various hormones and the body in proper balance.

HEREDITY

The passing of traits from parents to children has engaged human interest for many centuries. But it was not until 1865, when Gregor Mendel, an Austrian monk, reported on his classic experiments on thousands of pea plants, that the science of heredity, *genetics,* was founded. Mendel's work was ignored until 1900 when it was rediscovered by three geneticists working independently. Thus genetics is a twentieth-century science.

Heredity has its base in reproduction. The sperm contributed by the male and the egg by the female contain all the hereditary material that the new individual is going to receive from the parents. This hereditary material is concentrated in the nucleus of each of these cells. There it is organized into structures called *chromosomes,* which are visible under the microscope.

Every cell in the human body, with one exception, contains 23 pairs of chromosomes, or 46 chromosomes. The exception is the egg or sperm cell that the mature individual produces. These contain only 23 chromosomes, one from each of the pairs. When the sperm and egg unite to form the fertilized egg this new cell contains 46 chromosomes, or 23 pairs of chromosomes. Therefore, the new individual arising from the fertilized egg has the same number of chromosomes as each of the parents, having received half from each.

Sex Determination

A careful study of the photos on page 329 of the 23 pairs of chromosomes in a human body cell suggests how sex is determined. (Try to work it out for yourself before reading the following.) Note that the shapes of the chromosomes in fe-

Each human body cell contains 46 chromosomes. The chromosomes shown here are those of human white blood cells, enlarged 1,400 diameters. Those on the left are from a male, those on the right from a female. (The symmetrical appearance of each chromosome is caused by the duplication of each of the 46 in preparation for cell division.) *(Courtesy of Scientific American.)*

male and male are almost identical—with one exception. The female has a pair of chromosomes identified as XX, and the male a corresponding pair XY. These are known as the *sex chromosomes.* When a female produces eggs the chromosome pairs separate; only one from each pair will be included in one egg. Each egg cell will therefore have a single X chromosome. In the male, however, half of the sperm cells will have an X chromosome and the other half a Y chromosome. Sex is determined at the moment of fertilization. If an X sperm enters the egg the combination XX will result in a female. If a Y sperm enters, the resulting XY combination produces a male. Since there is an equal number of X and Y sperm, the chances of either fertilizing the egg are equal. This ex-

plains why approximately half the individuals born are male, half female.

Recently scientists have discovered a single gene on the Y chromosome that is responsible for initiating male sexual development. The gene acts as a biological switch, turning on other genes essential to the production of maleness.

Sex is determined by chance.

Genes and DNA

Within the chromosomes are thousands of the basic determiners of the body's traits, the *genes*. It is beyond the scope of this book to go into the ways in which genes operate or to discuss in detail the principles of heredity. However, we cannot overlook the spectacular discoveries of the last few decades that have led us close to the unraveling of the chemical nature of gene activity. It appears that the gene material is a complex molecule known as DNA, which is a convenient way of referring to deoxyribonucleic acid. The DNA molecule may be considered a kind of code, or form, which sets patterns for the making of the vital substances, particularly proteins, within a cell. From the viewpoint of the entire body, DNA may be compared with the architect whose plans eventually result in the construction of a building from a heap of steel, concrete, and wood. The particular kind of DNA that individuals have determines their characteristics. In reproduction the basic "information" encoded in the parental DNA is meticulously reproduced, *replicated,* and passed on to the offspring via the sperm and egg.

One outcome of gene research has been that of *genetic engineering*—the altering of the genes of living things by separating and recombining DNA. Characteristics of an organism can be altered by splicing in DNA pieces from another organism. Transplants of genetic material from organisms as diverse as mammals and plants have been joined together in host cells of certain bacteria.

Gene splicing, also known as *recombinant DNA technology,* has been used to convert bacteria into factories for the manufacture of antibodies, hormones, and drugs. One of the most important products of this new technology is human insulin. Millions of diabetics depend on a daily injection of this hormone, which is extracted from the pancreatic glands of pigs and cattle slaughtered for food. However, many diabetics are allergic to animal insulin. By splicing appropriate genes extracted from human cells to genes in certain bacteria, these organisms were induced

to manufacture human insulin. As the bacteria reproduced, the new spliced-in trait was replicated. Thus large amounts of human insulin were produced. In 1982 human insulin manufactured by genetically engineered bacteria reached the marketplace for the first time in the United Kingdom, and is now approved for use in the United States.

Human growth hormone and *interferon* have also been produced by gene splicing. Interferon is a group of proteins that the body's cells produce as a defense against virus infections. Tests are now in progress to determine the value of different types of interferon, particularly in combatting some forms of cancer.

Gene splicing has tremendous potential for making rare biochemicals for humans and for agriculture. Biotechnology promises that genes of viruses and bacteria will be placed in plants to enable them to produce their own insecticides and fertilizers. Sperm and egg cells of animals are manipulated to enable breeders to select their sex and characteristics.

Before leaving this discussion of heredity, we should understand that the characteristics of individuals are determined both by the particular packages of genes they have inherited from their parents and by the environment in which they grow up. Heredity and environment work together to produce the individual.

REPRODUCTION

The basic design of sexual reproduction in all animals is a simple one. Life for the individual begins when a sperm meets and unites with an egg. Each egg is a special kind of cell split off from other cells in an organ of the female called the ovary. Each sperm is similarly a special kind of cell made in the *testes* of the male. The union of sperm and egg, *fertilization,* is followed by the rapid dividing of the fertilized cell into the many cells that eventually form the structures of the new individual.

In the animal kingdom there are many variations with respect to the place where fertilization and development of the embryo occur. In some animals, as in frogs and many fish, fertilization occurs outside the body in the waters of ponds, streams, lakes, or seas. In land animals the meeting of egg and sperm, and the protection against the drying up of the sex cells, is ensured by having fertilization occur within the female's body. This is true in insects and birds, for example. In fewer animals the resulting fertilized egg also develops internally. But only in mammals are special structures established for the nourishment of the developing embryo inside the female before birth, and for the production of milk for feeding after birth.

The following description of reproduction in human beings will be understood more clearly by reference to the illustrations on pages 332 and 333.

The Male

Puberty is initiated at age 10 or 11 in boys but manifests itself markedly at ages 13 to 15. Puberty is triggered by the activity of the pituitary gland, which produces hormones that stimulate the testes to engage in their dual roles: producing sperm and secreting hormones. The sex hormone *testosterone,* which is manufactured by the testes, triggers the full development of sexuality in the male: the growth of sex organs, the appearance of pubic and body hair, the deepening of the voice, the growth of the beard and of the Adam's apple, and the broadening of the shoulders. Accompanying these structural changes are also the profound changes in behavior characteristic of puberty.

The male sex structures consist essentially of a pair of testes and a tube from each that leads into . the *penis.* The testes are external and are contained within a sac, the *scrotum,* suspended from the abdomen. Each testis has hundreds of tiny *tubules* in which sperm are formed. (Between the tubules are the tissues that manufacture the male sex hormone.) The sperm-making tubules in each testis lead to a common many-coiled tube, the

epididymis, which half encircles the testis. Sperm then passes into the *sperm duct,* which extends from the scrotum into the abdomen. Near its end the duct flares out into a sperm reservoir (not shown in the diagram). When sperm are discharged they pass from this storage space into the *urethra,* a channel through the penis to the outside. In human males, as well as in other mammals, the urethra is used as a passageway both for sperm and for urine, although not at the same time.

Secretions of other glands—the *seminal vesicles* and the *prostate*—are added to the sperm on their way out of the body. The secretions provide a fluid medium for launching the free-swimming sperm and for protecting them after they are deposited in the female. This combined fluid, sperm plus secretions, is known as *semen.*

The penis is made of three columns of spongy tissue permeated with blood sinuses, or wide blood spaces. During sexual excitement the blood vessels draining these sinuses are constricted by reflex action. The blood coming into the penis piles up in the spongy tissues making the penis hard and erect.

When a climax of sexual excitement is reached, the storage sac of the sperm duct contracts and discharges sperm into the urethra, where it is joined by secretions of the other glands as previously noted. The semen is ejected from the urethra with considerable force as a result of the contraction of a muscle at the base of the penis.

In the life of a typical male the discharge of semen may occur under different circumstances. It may occur involuntarily during sleep, often accompanied by a dream of a sexual nature. Such occurrences, known as *nocturnal emissions,* are perfectly normal. The stimulation of one's sex organs for the purpose of sexual excitement, *masturbation,* is almost universal among males, particularly in youth, and also leads to the discharge of semen. No harm is known to result from this practice. (Masturbation in females is likewise common, but does not lead to a discharge as in males.) From the viewpoint of the biological survival of the species the fruitful type of semen dis-

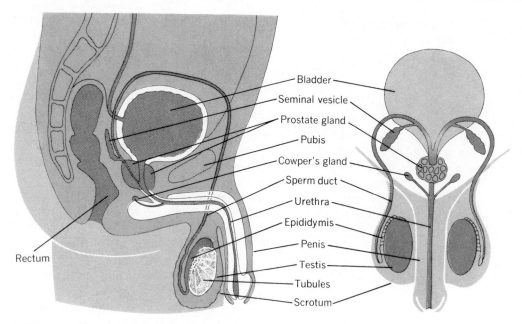

(Left) The male reproductive system, side view. *(Right)* The male reproductive system, front view.

charge occurs during *coitus,* or sexual intercourse, in which semen is propelled into the upper part of the vagina, the female structure adapted for receiving the penis. However, as we shall see shortly, coitus may or may not lead to fertilization, depending on whether or not an egg is available.

The Female

Puberty begins somewhere between the ages of 9 and 12 for most girls, but marked development is initiated betwen the ages 11 and 14. Here again it is hormones from the pituitary glands that awaken sexual development. One pituitary hormone stimulates the ovary to produce eggs. It also stimulates certain structures in the ovary to produce hormones, which in turn influence the development of sexuality: the enlargement of the sex organs, the deposition of fat that rounds the body contours, the development of the breasts, the broadening of the pelvis (making normal childbirth possible), and the growth of pubic hair. Psychological changes also result from the influence of the sex hormones.

The female sex organs consist essentially of a pair of *ovaries,* two *egg tubes* leading from the ovaries to the *uterus,* followed by the *vagina,* which opens to the outside of the body.

The ovaries, located in the lower abdomen, are approximately the size and shape of unshelled almonds. Near the ovaries, but not directly connected to them, are the openings of the egg tubes, also known as the *Fallopian tubes.* These two egg tubes lead into the single uterus, also known as the *womb* in humans, a pear-shaped muscular organ that lies in the middle of the lower part of the body just behind the urinary bladder. The smaller, narrower end of the uterus, the *cervix,* is directed downward, and opens into the upper end of the vagina. The vagina, a narrow, sheathlike

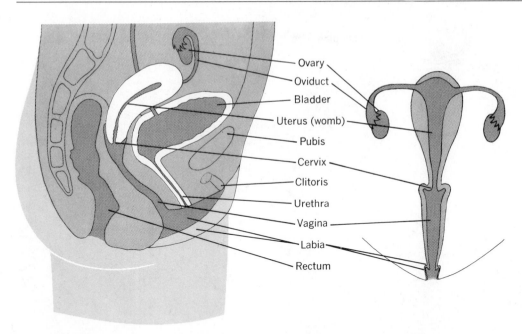

(Left) The female reproductive system, side view. *(Right)* The female reproductive system, front view.

canal of muscle, lined with mucous membrane, has three functions: to permit the discharge of menstrual fluids to the outside, to receive the penis and the seminal fluid during coitus, and to serve as a birth canal for the passage of the emerging infant into the outside world.

In virgin females the external opening of the vagina is partially closed by the *hymen,* a thin membrane. The hymen usually remains intact until the first coitus, but is sometimes broken through vigorous activity before then.

Externally, two double folds of skin (the *labia*) surround the openings of the urethra and the vagina. In contrast to the male, the female has separate passageways for the excretion of urine and for reproductive functions. Also found in this region is the *clitoris,* a small structure located at the anterior (forward) juncture of the inner folds of the skin of the labia. The clitoris is sensitive and possesses erectile tissue similar to that found in the penis, capable of enlargement during sexual excitement. Under the influence of a variety of stimuli, the clitoris, the labia, and other tissues in the pelvic area become engorged and distended with blood, as does the penis of the male. The distention of the tissues is accompanied by the secretion of a fluid into the vagina which lubricates its walls. As sexual arousal increases, the inner two thirds of the vagina expand like a partly inflated balloon. Sexual arousal after a time is followed by *orgasm,* marked by rhythmic contractions, but there is no ejaculation of fluid as there is in the male.

Egg Production

Inside the ovary are thousands of immature egg sacs, or *Graafian follicles.* During the 30 or more years following the beginning of puberty, one of these follicles will enlarge approximately every 28 days. Within each sac one cell will ripen into an

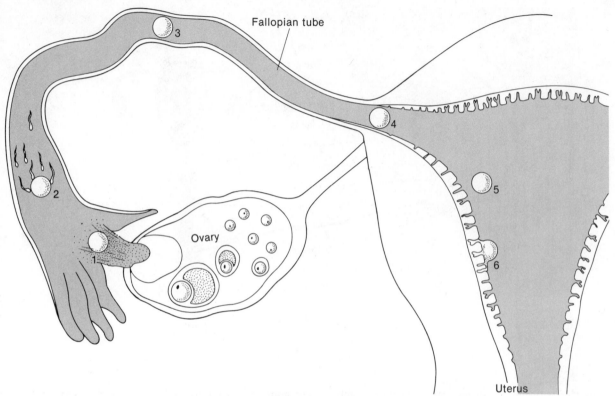

Ovulation, fertilization, early development, and implantation. Ovulation occurs when a Graafian follicle ruptures through the ovary wall and discharges an egg (1). The egg is drawn into the Fallopian tube. If sperm are present one of them may fertilize the egg (2). The egg begins to divide into many cells and travels down the tube (3,4, and 5). The embryo is implanted in the wall of the uterus (6).

egg. As the follicle grows, it fills with fluid. Finally it ruptures right through the ovary wall and the egg is discharged out of the ovary. The discharge of the egg is called *ovulation*. The mature egg is only 0.14 millimeter in diameter, just visible as a speck to the unaided eye. (About 200 eggs could be lined up in 1 inch.)

The opening of the egg tube is lined with cells equipped with threadlike *cilia*. The beating of the cilia creates a current that draws the egg into the tube. For the next three to six days the egg will move down the egg tube on its way to the uterus. The life of an unfertilized egg is only about two days, so it follows that the egg is usually fertilized about halfway down the egg tube.

Fertilization

The sperm cells are deposited in the upper part of the vagina and must travel 7,000 times their own length to reach the egg. (A person 6 feet—2 meters—tall swimming across a body of water would have to traverse about 8 miles—13 kilometers—to cover a comparable distance.) The number of sperm produced in one discharge is between 200 and 500 million. The fertilizing power of sperm in the female's body lasts from about 48 to 72 hours. If we take the higher figure for sperm survival, three days, it follows that coitus can lead to fertilization for only a *maximum* of about five days in each 28-day cycle: the three days before and the two days after ovulation. It is not necessary for the female to experience pleasure or reach a climax (*orgasm*) for fertilization to occur.

The sperm is much smaller than the egg: 75,000 sperm weigh only as much as one egg. The head of the sperm contains the nucleus; its long tail propels it through the liquid medium in which it travels. Although only one sperm will fertilize the egg a large number are required at the outset to ensure the completion by at least one sperm of the long and arduous journey to the egg. Most of the sperm simply do not make it. Once the egg is penetrated by the successful sperm, changes occur that make the fertilized egg entry-proof to all other sperm.

The world's first baby conceived outside the body was born in England in 1978. An egg was taken from a woman's body and fertilized in a plastic dish containing a nutrient solution with

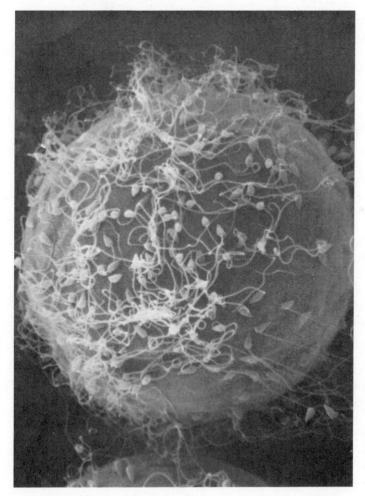

Many hundreds of sperm swarm around the surface of a sea-urchin egg, as shown in this scanning electron micrograph made by Mia Tegner in the laboratory of David Epel at the Scripps Institution of Oceanography. The fusion of a single sperm with an egg triggers a series of changes that prevents the fusion of the remaining sperm with the egg and initiates the development of the embryo. The magnification is 1,900 diameters. *(Courtesy of David Epel.)*

sperm from the husband. The fertilized egg was nurtured in the dish—the so-called test tube—for two-and-a-half days and then implanted in the wall of the mother's uterus, where it developed normally to full term. Other effective fertilizations of human eggs outside the body (called in-vitro fertilizations or IVF) gave hope to couples suffering from several forms of infertility that they might have a child of their own. Since 1981 about 800 IVF babies have been born in the United States.

Development of the Embryo

If the egg is not fertilized it disintegrates. (Other changes associated with nonfertilization will be discussed presently.) If the egg is fertilized, it starts development immediately as it moves down the egg tube to the uterus. For the next 6 to 12 days the egg divides many times to form a hollow ball of cells. In the meantime the uterus wall, stimulated by certain hormones, thickens and becomes enriched with many blood capillaries. The "soil," so to speak, is now ready for the reception, or the *implantation,* of the developing egg. After implantation, which occurs about a week after ovulation, the uterine lining surrounds the embryo, which will live there for the next nine months during the period of *gestation.*

As development proceeds, a new organ, the *placenta,* is formed jointly by the embryo and the uterus of the mother. The placenta, a disk of spongy tissues richly supplied with blood, functions, as we shall see shortly, as a place of exchange between the mother and the embryo. As development continues a membrane, the *amnion,* completely surrounds the embryo and encloses it in fluid. The liquid environment of the embryo cushions it against blows it might sustain from the normal movements of the mother or from accidental injury.

A stalk grows out of the embryo, later becoming the *umbilical cord,* which connects the embryo to the placenta. It has arteries and veins in it that conduct blood pumped by the embryo's heart to the placenta and then back to the embryo.

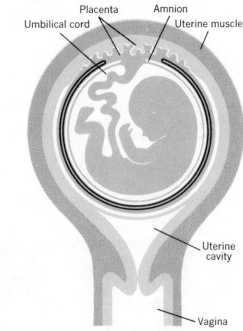

Diagram of advanced fetus in the uterus.

It is important to note that there are no nerve connections between the mother and the embryo. So-called maternal impressions on children have no physical basis in nerve pathways. There is also no direct blood connection between mother and embryo. All exchanges take place by diffusion across the membranes of the placenta. Molecules of digested nutrients and oxygen pass out of the maternal blood across the membrane to the embryo; carbon dioxide and other wastes filter from the bloodstream of the embryo across the same membrane into the maternal blood.

It is important to note that certain damaging substances other than nutrients may also pass across the placenta: addictive drugs, certain hormones taken by the mother during pregnancy, the virus of German measles in nonimmune mothers, and the AIDS virus.

The embryo, which is a microscopic mass of cells on implantation, grows to about $\frac{2}{3}$ inch (1.65 centimeters) in six weeks. By then the embryo is distinctly human in appearance with all major features, such as fingers, toes, lips, ears, and nose. From the eighth week on, it is called a *fetus*. At five months it is 12 inches (30 centimeters) long from head to feet. At this time the mother begins to feel "life"—the stretching and kicking of the fetus in its aquatic gymnasium.

Childbirth is heralded by contractions of the uterine wall causing "labor pains," which last for 12 to 24 hours before birth occurs, but may be of much shorter duration in subsequent childbirths. As the contractions become stronger the membranes around the fetus are broken and the fluid flows out. The contractions push the head of the baby downward against the opening of the uterus. The opening and the vagina itself are greatly enlarged at this time. The connections between the pubic bones become loosened somewhat so that they can spread apart. Finally, powerful uterine contractions force the baby into the vagina and out of the body. In its new environment of air the baby begins to breathe with its lungs, or may be induced to do so.

The *umbilical cord* is still attached to the newborn infant. The doctor or midwife ties it off near the child and then cuts it. The tied region will heal and later form the navel. Further contractions of the uterine wall will force out the rest of the cord and the placenta, the *afterbirth*.

The Menstrual Cycle

The building up of the uterine walls and the ripening of the egg in the Graafian follicle are preparations for pregnancy. If the egg is not fertilized, however, it disintegrates, as we have noted. Sometime later, about two weeks after ovulation, the uterine wall, with its extra supply of blood, also disintegrates. For a period of three to five days menstruation occurs. The sloughed-off uterine lining together with blood passes out of the vagina. Except during pregnancy, menstruation and ovulation occur about every 28 days for a period of 30 or more years from puberty until *menopause,* sometimes called "the change of life." The total menstrual (after *mensis,* Latin for month) cycle consists of menstruation and ovulation, and will be better understood by reference to the diagram. Menstruation occurs from day 1 through day 4. For the next 10 days the egg sac ripens. At about the same time the uterus wall builds up in preparation for pregnancy. At about day 14 after the onset of the previous menstruation, ovulation occurs. About day 28, assuming that the egg is not fertilized, menstruation begins again.

It is important to note that there is considerable variation among females in the length of the menstrual cycle and in the timing of events in that

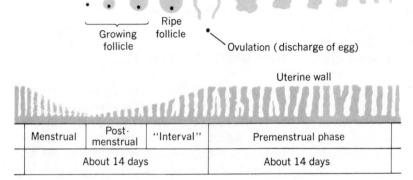

The cycle of menstruation and ovulation.

cycle. Cycles may be as short as 21 or as long as 35 days in different individuals. They may be irregular in the same individual. It follows that contraceptive procedures based on a so-called safe period in the menstrual cycle must be worked out with the help of a specialist in such matters and cannot be considered entirely "safe" even then. Pregnancy is suspected when the menstrual periods cease, but a menstrual period may be skipped for other reasons.

HEALTH AND DISEASE

Many people think of health only when they do not have it. They regard health as the absence of illness. On the contrary, health is a positive phenomenon. It is the normal condition of the body with all of its parts working efficiently together. The old Greek concept of "a sound mind in a sound body" is still a good definition of health.

The body has natural lines of defense that ordinarily keep it safe from infectious diseases. The skin that surrounds the entire body is the first line against invasion. As long as the skin remains intact it serves as a strong wall to ward off harmful disease agents. A second line of defense is the standing army of the body—the white blood cells—which crowd into the site of an invasion to engulf the foreign bodies.

A third line of defense involves the *immune system,* which develops a specific response to a foreign substance entering the blood. Certain kinds of white blood cells called *B cells* multiply rapidly on meeting a foreign substance and become antibody factories. Released into the bloodstream, the antibodies react with and destroy the invading material. In the past decade scientists have come to recognize that the most important factor in the ability of the immune system to react to specific viruses are other kinds of white cells called *T cells.* These cells are also important in the immune response to bacteria. T cells are also involved in the rejection of organs such as the kidney or heart or skin that are transplanted from one individual to another.

Illness may result from various causes. Some diseases develop from nutritional lacks. These are the deficiency diseases, such as scurvy and rickets. Some diseases result from a breakdown of one of the body organs: An example of this is diabetes, a disease caused by a breakdown of cells of the islets of Langerhans in the pancreas. When the cells stop secreting sufficient insulin the body cannot effectively oxydize the sugar taken in with food. Some diseases such as hemophilia are caused by inherited defects.

Diseases Caused by Germs

Probably the most widespread diseases are those caused by other living things invading the body. The chief among these living things are certain disease-causing *microbes*—microscopic organisms often called *germs* that include certain bacteria, protozoans, and viruses. Tuberculosis, diphtheria, scarlet fever, meningitis, typhoid fever, and one type of pneumonia are examples of diseases caused by bacteria. The second group, the protozoans, also contains disease producers. Probably the most widespread disease in the world is malaria, caused by a protozoan. The parasite is injected into the blood by an Anopheles mosquito carrying the organism. Another protozoan disease is amoebic dysentery, common in tropical regions. A third group of microbes is the viruses, which are extremely minute particles having characteristics of both living and nonliving material. AIDS, smallpox, measles, poliomyelitis (infantile paralysis), yellow fever, and influenza are some of the virus-caused diseases.

How Germs Invade

Prevention of diseases caused by germs requires that we know how the microbes are spread. Some enter the body with the air breathed in, usually near an infected person. Measles, diphtheria, scarlet fever, whooping cough, the common cold, and smallpox are examples of diseases spread in this

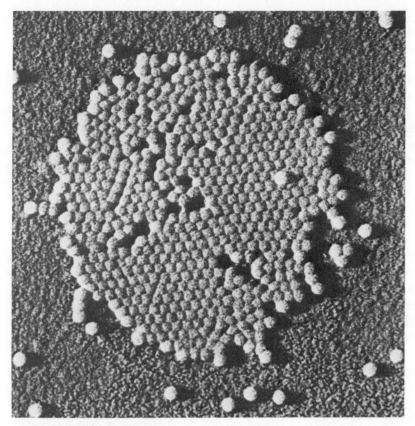

Each tiny sphere is that of the polio virus enlarged approximately 100,000 times. This photograph was taken by an electron microscope, which employs electrons rather than available light to form real images. *(Courtesy of March of Dimes Birth Defects Foundation).*

way. Some microbes, such as those causing typhoid fever and amoebic dysentery, enter the body with food or water. Other microorganisms enter the body through breaks in the skin—boils and skin infections may be caused in this way. In other cases the infective organism must be introduced by the bite of a carrier, as is the case with malaria. Yellow fever is likewise transmitted through the bite of a mosquito carrying the yellow fever virus. Rabies is acquired through the bite of a dog sick with rabies. The saliva of the rabid animal contains the rabies virus.

Vaccines

Protective substances that enable the body to resist disease have been a goal of medicine since earliest times. Only within the last century and a half has this aim been partially realized. In 1790 Edward Jenner, an English country doctor, discovered that individuals infected with cowpox, a mild disease resembling smallpox, acquired immunity against smallpox, a dangerous disease. Today, vaccination is recognized in all civilized communities as a preventive against the dread scourge. After Jenner's work almost a century passed before another immunizing agent for human beings was discovered. This was the *vaccine* against rabies produced by Louis Pasteur.

A vaccine is a preparation of killed or weakened germs. When a vaccine is injected or placed on a scratch in the skin it causes the blood in a human to start chemical warfare against the particular type of germ in that vaccine. The blood produces antibodies to combat the weakened or killed germ in this simulated "invasion." These antibodies remain in the bloodstream for many years, and will be effective against a real invasion by the active, living germs of the specific disease. Vaccines are used against typhoid fever, smallpox, rabies, whooping cough, and yellow fever.

A great victory in medicine were the vaccines developed by Jonas Salk and Albert Sabin against infantile paralysis. The Salk polio vaccine consists of dead viruses, whereas the Sabin oral polio vaccine consists of live but altered viruses. Each vaccine has the ability to stimulate the body to produce antibodies that are active against virulent forms of polio virus. They have markedly reduced the incidence of polio, with its toll of paralysis and death.

Several kinds of measles vaccines are now licensed for use. The U.S. Public Health Service has recommended immunization for all children over nine months old without a history of measles. In state after state measles vaccination has been required for schoolchildren. We look forward to the same victory against measles as was won against polio.

A vaccine may be made from poisonous substances, called *toxins,* produced by some disease-causing microorganisms. The toxins are first changed chemically into *toxoids,* which are used in developing immunity to such diseases as diphtheria, lockjaw (tetanus), and whooping cough. The toxoid causes the body to produce its own antibodies.

Serums

Sometimes we use the antibodies produced in an animal to treat a human disease. We "borrow" the antibodies from an animal, such as a horse, which has been inoculated with weakened germs or toxins of the particular disease that is being combated. Blood extracted from such animals and prepared for injection constitutes a *serum*. Serum injections are used for diphtheria and lockjaw. The type of immunity acquired in this way is temporary and is frequently used as a cure rather than as a preventative measure.

Drugs Against Disease

For thousands of years humans have searched for drugs to fight disease. We are indebted to primitive peoples for quinine from the bark of the cinchona tree, so effective against malaria. Many other valuable drugs have been extracted from plants. It was not until 1932, however, that a drug that would destroy many kinds of bacteria in the body was discovered. This was sulfanilamide. Since then a chemical family of *sulfa drugs* has been synthesized by scientists to fight different bacteria effectively. Between 1936 and 1940 the number of deaths from pneumonia decreased by 50 percent as a result of the use of sulfa drugs.

Antibiotics

In 1927 Alexander Fleming, an English scientist, noted the peculiar behavior of some bacteria cultures that he had left untouched for some time. They had been contaminated with some mold

Growing in this petri dish are four different molds. Scientists grow thousands of cultures in hopes of finding new molds that can serve as the sources of new antibiotics. *(Courtesy of Charles Pfizer & Company, Inc.)*

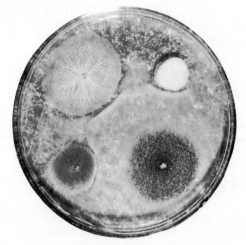

growth and, oddly enough, where the mold was growing the bacterial colonies seemed to dissolve. This was the beginning of the golden age of antibiotics in modern medicine. An *antibiotic* is a substance produced by a living organism that can kill microbes or stop their growth. The bacteria in Fleming's culture had been destroyed by an antibiotic produced by the mold: It was named *penicillin,* after the mold *Penicillium.* The availability of penicillin in World War II probably reduced the number of deaths markedly, and Fleming was awarded the Nobel Prize for his work. Since the finding of penicillin, many other antibiotics, derived from other species of molds, have been used successfully against various diseases.

Cancer

Cancer has been known from ancient times, but it has only become a paramount health problem in this country in this century. It is now the second largest cause of death in the United States. This has come about, in part, because we are living long enough to be stricken by cancer, which is mainly a disease of middle and old age. A cancer is an abnormal growth of cells. For reasons yet obscure, the cells seem to become outlaw: They multiply out of control of the normal body limits. They invade neighboring tissue, crowd it, rob it of its nourishment, and destroy it. The greatest danger occurs when cells break away from the original growth and move through the body to colonize elsewhere. The aim of cancer fighting is to detect and remove the cancerous growth before colonization occurs. Most cancers, if detected early enough, are curable. One method of achieving a cure is to see a doctor if you detect any of the following signs of *possible* cancer, described by the American Cancer Society:

1. A sore that does not heal.
2. A lump or thickening in the breast or elsewhere.
3. Unusual bleeding or discharge.
4. Change in a wart or mole.
5. Persistent indigestion or difficulty in swallowing.
6. Persistent hoarseness or cough.
7. Persistent change in bowel or bladder habits.

In addition, periodic medical examinations are recommended for the detection of early signs of cancer, especially in the case of suspected hereditary predispositions. The New York Health Insurance Plan's study suggests that screening for breast cancer in females produces significant findings; and that about one fourth of the total mortality from breast cancer (that is, one fourth of 35,000 deaths a year) might be prevented if all women in the United States over age 50 were offered and accepted a free examination every one to three years.

How can cancer be fought when it is detected? At present, the best known methods are surgery, radiation, chemotherapy, and hormone treatment. Surgery is still the primary treatment. The entire growth must be removed without leaving one cell behind. The second method involves destruction by means of X rays, radium, and other radioactive substances including radioactive isotopes. It is fortunate that cancerous cells are more easily killed by these radiations than are normal cells.

Chemotherapy, the use of specific chemicals, is a more recent approach to fighting cancer. Leukemias, breast cancers, prostate cancer, and lymphomas have been known to respond to chemotherapy. Cure rates for cancer have improved sharply in the past decade, thanks in good part to chemotherapy. More than 40 percent of the victims of cancer can be saved today, compared with only 25 percent 30 years ago. New drugs and more sophisticated ways of using them are promising to make chemotherapy safer and more effective.

A new approach to cancer therapy involves the use of the body's natural immune system to treat this disease. There is evidence that cancer cells may be rejected and destroyed by the immune response (see p. 338) without an individual or a physician detecting it. Cancers that persist may represent a failure of the immune system.

Immunotherapy uses drugs that help the body's immune system attack cancer just as it would an infection.

Interferon, for example, is a protein produced by body cells to fight off viral infections. In the case of cancer, it is thought that interferon causes the release of enzymes that inhibit or prevent cell growth. As described earlier, bacteria can be programmed genetically to manufacture enough interferon for testing on a large scale.

Science holds out the hope that one day we may find the specific cause or causes of cancer and learn how to prevent this disease. Currently, more stress has been placed on the *prevention* of cancer. Carcinogenic (cancer-producing) agents in food, air, and water are being identified; governmental regulations are being formulated to exclude such agents from our environment.

Does nutrition play a role in cancer? Some researchers think so. Based on evidence from population eating habits and the incidence of cancer, and from animal experiments, they recommend the following: reduction of fat intake, eating more fiber and more fruits and vegetables, consumption of complex carbohydrates (such as the starch in potatoes and in flour), and decreasing the consumption of pickled, salted, or smoked foods and refined sugar. Further studies are needed but these recommendations do form the basis of a diet that is not likely to be harmful and has a good possibility of reducing the risk of diet-induced cancer.

AIDS

AIDS is modern plague, probably the result of a new infection that began in the 1950s. By the end of 1986 about 15,000 Americans died of the disease. By late 1987, almost 50,000 cases of AIDS were reported. By now as many as 2 million Americans may be infected.

AIDS, acquired immune deficiency syndrome, is characterized by a collapse of the body's natural immunity against disease. Thus individuals with AIDS are vulnerable to infections that do not pose a threat to individuals whose immune system is operating normally.

As noted earlier, the immune system constitutes a line of defense against foreign substances. Important in this defense are the T cells, which are one kind of white blood cells that "recognize" foreign molecules and mount a response to them. Under normal conditions the T cells signal to other immune system cells and stimulate them to join in the battle against foreign organisms.

The T cells are the specific target of the invading AIDS virus. In general, viruses consist simply of a core of genetic material, either a DNA or RNA molecule and a protective coat made of proteins. In nature, a virus occupies a place somewhere between the living and nonliving. It lacks the cell structure common to living organisms and cannot reproduce without the help of its host. As one biologist put it, viruses are "bits of heredity looking for a chromosome." Unfortunately for humans, in the case of the AIDS virus that chromosome resides in the T cells.

The AIDS virus consists of an RNA (ribonucleic acid) molecule surrounded by a protein coat. When the virus enters the T cells, a viral enzyme called reverse transcriptase uses the RNA to assemble a corresponding molecule of DNA. The DNA inserts itself into the chromosome of the T cell. Under certain conditions the virus bursts into action, using the host's cell facilities to reproduce itself so rapidly that new virus particles riddle its cell membrane, destroy the T cell, and escape into the bloodstream to infect many new host cells. The depletion of the T cells causes the body's immune system as a whole to unravel and to collapse.

The AIDS virus is present in the blood, semen, and possibly vaginal secretions of infected persons. Minute amounts of the virus have been found also in the saliva of some carriers.

To become infected an individual's bloodstream must be invaded. Infection may occur in a number of ways: sexual contact, homosexual or heterosexual, vaginal, anal, or oral; through the sharing of needles with an infected individual; less commonly through the transfusion of blood before blood supplies were protected. The virus also can be transmitted to babies during pregnancy or during childbirth.

From a study of AIDS patients and their families, there is no evidence of the transmission of the virus by prolonged interaction of the members. AIDS is not spread by casual contact—from a swimming pool, from casually kissing an AIDS patient, from sharing a room or bed with an AIDS patient; or from going to school with an AIDS patient. In summary, one cannot get AIDS from someone with AIDS unless one shares a needle or has sex with that person.

The most promising therapies under investigation involve the use of drugs and the development of vaccines. One drug, AZT, seems to be helpful in blocking the reverse transcriptase enzymes as it assembles the viral DNA. For the long run perhaps the most important therapy would be the development of an effective vaccine—a killed or weakened virus, or a strain that does not cause disease. This is the route taken in successfully combating smallpox, measles, yellow fever, and polio. One problem in developing a vaccine for AIDS is that the virus mutates so that there are many strains, just as in the common cold.

Since no drug has yet been produced to cure AIDS and no vaccine has been developed to prevent the disease, the only way to combat it at present is prevention. Health officials are urging those who do not abstain to limit their sexual activity to the confines of a mutually monogamous relationship and to use condoms and spermicides. Primary focus must now be placed on AIDS education, which is discussed in the next chapter.

Health and Society

Over the years society has found that some health problems can be helped by legal methods. Today every state has laws relating to health. Some of these are compulsory vaccination as a prerequisite to entrance into school, quarantine in cases of certain contagious diseases, medical licensing, sanitary and health codes, and many others. We also rely on education to play an important role in guiding each individual to eat an adequate diet, to engage in suitable physical activities, and to develop habits of cleanliness and personal hygiene.

IMPORTANT GENERALIZATIONS

The unit of structure and work of the body is the cell.

Similar cells are organized into tissues for efficient performance of their job.

Groups of different tissues cooperate in organs that perform the major work of the body.

We require food for energy, for growth and repair, and for proper functioning of our bodies.

Food is prepared for the use of the body by the process of digestion.

A continuous supply of oxygen is needed to obtain energy from food.

The body has a number of automatic mechanisms that maintain a constantly favorable internal environment.

The respiratory system supplies oxygen to the body and gets rid of carbon dioxide.

Materials are transported around the body by the circulatory system.

Blood flows in a closed system of tubes around the body, pumped by the heart.

The skin, the kidneys, and the lungs rid the body of liquid and gaseous wastes.

Growth is the result of cell multiplication.

Movement in the body is powered by the contraction of muscles.

The bony skeleton serves as a framework for the body.

The body is under the dual control of the nervous and the endocrine systems.

The genes in the nucleus of the cell carry the hereditary traits.

The gene material is a complex molecule known as DNA.

The DNA molecule may be regarded as a kind of code that sets patterns for the making of vital cell substances.

Heredity and environment work together to produce the individual.

The life of the new individual starts with fertilization, the joining of egg and sperm into a single cell.

Sex is determined at the moment of fertilization by the kind of sperm that enters the egg.

Development of the embryo follows from the splitting of the fertilized egg cell into billions of cells.

The developing embryo in humans is nourished by the diffusion of nutrients across a membrane shared by mother and embryo.

Wastes are removed by diffusion across the same membrane from embryo to mother.

Sexual maturity is guided and stimulated by hormones of the pituitary and the sex glands.

Reasonable adherence to the rules of hygiene will go far toward keeping the body in good health.

Application of medical discoveries has greatly prolonged life.

We have developed powerful weapons in fighting disease.

Education is of prime importance in keeping our nation in good health.

DISCOVERING FOR YOURSELF

1. Acquaint yourself with the latest research findings concerning the relationship of lung cancer and smoking.

2. Learn how to give artificial respiration, to restore heartbeat, and to attend to simple injuries.

3. Look through a microscope at slides of body tissues, bacteria, or other slide material related to the human body.

4. With the assistance of your local Board of Health, conduct a study of the communicable diseases that have been prevalent in your community during the past two years. Find out how they are spread and what the public health service does about control.

5. Visit a research laboratory where experiments in nutrition or other related areas are being carried out. Learn as much as you can about the methods employed.

6. Take your body temperature and pulse and your rate of breathing. Exercise and note the change in pulse and respiration.

7. Find out more about molecular biology and DNA.

8. Find out how the electron microscope has contributed to new knowledge of cells.

9. Investigate recent advances in genetic engineering.

10. List the ingredients of some packages of prepared dinners, cereals, and so on, that you find on the shelves of a supermarket. How do these rate against the nutrition advice given in this chapter?

11. Investigate findings about AIDS as reported in current magazines and newspapers.

TEACHING "THE HUMAN BODY AND HOW IT WORKS"

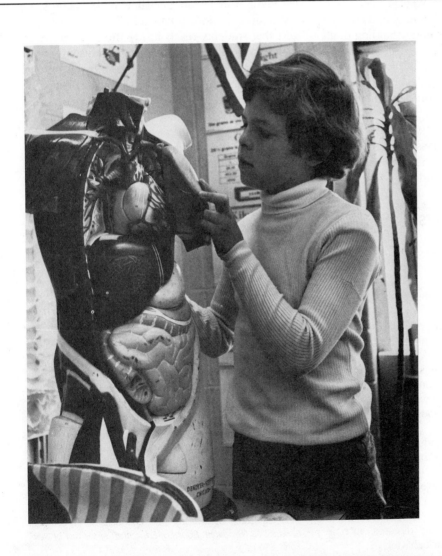

Children come to the study of the body with many questions, and with some misunderstandings and unwarranted fears. It is expected that our study will develop the following attitudes: The human body is a wonderful machine; its development is natural; with reasonable care the body can remain healthy.

Because the body breathes, grows, and responds to stimuli, it should be observed and used as a firsthand source for developing concepts of how it is built, how it works, what it needs, and how it keeps well. Through the study of their own bodies children add to their understanding of all living things. The increased emphasis on sex education in the schools, often under the umbrella of family life education, puts an even greater emphasis on helping children understand the human body.

Later chapters (18A, 18B, 19A, and 19B) give further information, as well as suggestions for teaching about the eye and ear in connection with the material on light and sound.

SOME BROAD CONCEPTS

Life begins with the joining of an egg and a sperm cell.
Traits are passed from parents to children through genes in sperm and egg cells.
The parts of the body work together to carry on body functions.
Our bodies need proper food for energy and growth.
The body is composed of different kinds of cells that perform various functions.
The body is composed of systems of organs that cooperate to carry on its many functions.
The body does some things automatically.
The skeletal system holds the body up, protects parts of it, and gives it shape.
Muscles are fastened to bones and make them move.
The food we eat must be digested before it can be used by the body.
We get information about the objects and happenings in our environment by seeing, hearing, touching, tasting, and smelling.
The prevention of communicable diseases, such as AIDS, depends in part on our behavior.

FOR YOUNGER CHILDREN

How Do Our Senses Help Us?[1]

Using our senses to discover is one of the most important elements in the process of learning. Resourceful teachers will devise different ways of helping children see how important the senses are. One interesting idea is to give each child a closed paper bag containing the following or similar items: a small rubber ball, a marble, a rock, a toy, a piece of cloth, a nail, a bell, an onion. Suggest that students reach inside the bag (but not look) and find out what they can discover by *touching,* then by *smelling,* then by *listening* while shaking the bag and last by *looking* at the items.

Prepare several "smell" jars—onion, orange, cucumber, cheese, and so on. Cover the jars with aluminum foil secured with rubber bands so that children cannot see inside, and perforate the top with small holes. What can you discover by using the sense of smell?

Assemble various objects of different textures—fur, sandpaper, wood, smooth and rough rocks, and such. Put them in a box or bag. What can you discover by using your sense of touch? Tell how the various materials feel.

Behind a screen make various sounds with a bell, crumpling paper, tapping a table, and other things. What can you discover by using your sense of hearing? Similar experiences with tasting can also be used. Children might list discoveries they make with the use of each sense. There are many other suggestions in this book for helping children use their senses to discover (see Chapter 3, "Observing").

The activities described are not just a one-time experience. Especially with young children, the use of the senses to find out is an important activity that leads to discovery. Children should be-

---

[1]Adapted from "Discovering with Our Senses," in *Science, Grades K–2 (Brooklyn: Board of Education of the City of New York, 1966).*

come aware that they are using their senses to find things out.

How Fast Are We Growing?

A favorite activity in many schools is to exhibit pictures of the children when they were babies or were very young. In what ways have you changed since your picture was taken? How much do you change in weight and height over a period of a year? Children might estimate the figures and perhaps compare their record with those of other class members. Again the use of metric measures is suggested.

Where Does Our Food Come From?

First, let students recall their experiences of a visit to the grocery store, to a farm, to the cafeteria, and other places. Or better yet, arrange for a group visit to some of these places, with emphasis on discovering where the foods come from. Individuals or small groups may take such trips if it is not possible for the entire class to go. Children may try to answer some questions such as, "Where does milk come from?" "Where does bread come from?" The children may try to classify the foods. Let them attempt to make their own classifications, such as meat, cereal, fish, apples, potatoes, lettuce. There are many ways to group these foods—"Meats We Eat," "Vegetables We Eat," "Fruits We Eat," "Sources of the Food," and so on. The purpose of the activity is to help children see both the great diversity and the many sources of food. Pictures illustrating some of these ideas are good to use as bulletin board displays with appropriate titles.

Related to this problem children may consider, "How are these foods kept from spoiling?" "What do we do to them before we eat them?" "Where did the foods grow?"

Other Problems for Younger Children

1. Why should you know about your body?
2. How is your body like a machine? How is it different from a machine?
3. How do your fingerprints compare with those of your classmates? Touch a finger to a stamp pad. Roll the finger on a piece of paper. Examine with a magnifying glass.
4. What happens to the food you eat?
5. What are some of the most important parts of the body? What does each of these parts do?
6. How have your senses helped you today to find out about the world you live in?
7. How can you keep your body healthy?

FOR OLDER CHILDREN

How Much Air Do We Breathe?

Before recess or your outdoor activity period, ask the children to count the number of times they breathe in and out in a minute (about 18 to 20 times), while sitting quietly. Make a record of the findings. After the outdoor activity have the children make another count. They will find a significant difference. Discussion should bring out the idea that the body requires air for its activities, and that the more active the body is, the more air it needs.

A simple way of seeing the amount of air breathed out is to breathe into a tube connected to a jug of water, as shown on page 348. As the air goes in, water is pushed out of the jug. Using this device (which is called a *spirometer*), students may compare quiet and rapid breathing by seeing how many exhalations are necessary to empty the jug in each case.

By *dividing* 1 gallon (4 liters) by the number of exhalations needed to empty the jug, students can estimate the amount of air in one breath. By *multiplying* the amount of air in one breath by the number of breaths in one minute, students can estimate the amount of air breathed in one minute.

How much air can you breathe out of your lungs in one exhalation?

How Fast Does Your Heart Beat?[2]

One way of measuring heartbeat is to measure the pulse, which is caused by the surge of blood through an artery. Two fingers (not the thumb) of one hand should be placed on the thumb side of the wrist of the other hand. A pencil or drinking straw balanced carefully over the pulse will also show the pulse beat. Rest the hand on a table or desk to keep it as steady as possible. Suggest that each student determine his or her heartbeat while sitting quietly by counting the number of beats in a minute. Record it. Now suggest that they walk briefly in the schoolyard and again record the heartbeat. Now do the same after running. "What effect does exercise have on the number of heartbeats per minute?" The students should understand that the increased rate of heartbeat brings blood, containing food and oxygen, more rapidly to all parts of the body.

How Does Blood Travel Around the Body?

Ask children for their ideas about how blood circulates.[3] Have them examine models and diagrams of the circulatory system. Ask them to write about an imaginary trip around the blood system, including their experiences as the blood passes through the heart, the arteries, and veins and capillaries (see pp. 321–322). Use a stethoscope to listen to the heartbeat. A working model of a stethoscope can be made with a piece of rubber tubing about 2 feet long with a funnel fitted on to one end of it. The funnel end is pressed on the chest near the region of the heart and the other end is brought to the ear.

Can You See Your Veins?

Ask children if they can see the veins on the back of their hands. Then ask them to hold their hands

---

[2]M. Thompson and J. Strange, "Keep Your Heart Healthy," *Science and Children* (March 1980); D. W. Van Clear and P. A. Hamilton, "Feeling the Pressure," *Science and Children* (January 1985). Study of blood pressure.

[3]M. W. Arnaudin and J. J. Mintzes, "The Cardiovascular System: Children's Conceptions and Misconceptions," *Science and Children* (February 1986). Includes the children's ideas about blood, its path, and the heart.

low. Are the veins more visible? Why? Raise one hand high. Compare it with the other that is low. Is there a difference? Why?

Which Way Does Blood Run in the Veins?

Make the veins prominent by holding a hand or arm down for a few moments. Try to empty a vein by running a finger over it for a short distance and then holding it pressed against the vein. What happens depends on *which way* you ran your finger. If you run it up the arm (toward the heart) it fills up immediately. If you run it down the arm (away from the heart) it remains empty. If you then lift the finger, the vein fills up again. Why the difference?

Valves in the veins prevent the backward flow of blood. When you push blood out of the vein by moving it toward the heart it fills up immediately from blood coming in from lower down. When you push blood away from the heart, the vein remains empty because the valves prevent a backward flow from above.

What Kinds of Foods Should We Eat?

Assemble a list of all the sources useful in finding information about kinds of foods and how they help us. Think of places, books, magazines, newspapers, and names of people. This activity of locating material will not only supply much useful informational material but will give students an opportunity to use their originality and resourcefulness in finding it. The teacher may help to point out to students the importance of seeing whether or not material that is commercially prepared is honest in presentation (see Chapter 11A, pp. 316–318).

A school cafeteria is a practical place to learn about foods. The manager or someone else on the staff can be asked to explain how the menu is planned to provide a balanced diet.

In connection with the study of foods, radio and television advertising may be considered. For example, the fantastic claims that are made about some kinds of bread can be discussed. The fact that you eat a certain kind of bread is no assurance at all that you will be healthy. Bread is only one of the important foods. The fact that your favorite TV personality advertises a certain brand of breakfast food is not sufficient reason for using it to the exclusion of others. It may be interesting for students to copy down some of these advertising claims and try to analyze them. A scientific approach is essential in trying to interpret advertising, and certainly a science class is an appropriate place in which to be introduced to this approach. Obviously young students cannot test these foods scientifically, but once they can see, for example, that every kind of bread cannot be the best, they may become more alert in interpreting advertising. This same attitude holds true for patent-medicine advertising.[4]

A very practical application of the principles learned about foods and a balanced diet can be made if children plan refreshments for a party; plan, prepare, and serve a meal at school; or plan the menu for a picnic. The selection and preparation of foods involve many of the ideas that students have learned. Children can investigate diets in other countries to see how the diets compare with their own. (In connection with the study of food and how it supplies the needs of the body, the practice of selling candy and soft drinks in school should be evaluated and made to conform to what are considered good health practices.)

The sources of foods are sometimes surprising to children, especially those who live in large cities. It may be interesting to list the foods served in the school lunchroom or at home on one typical day and let each student choose one kind of

---

[4]W. Jackson and B. Janes, "The Investigators," *Science and Children* (November/December 1982). Describes how children conducted investigations into food advertisers. R. E. Yager and D. S. Sheldon, "Nutrition made REAL," *Science and Children* (February 1984). Practical suggestions for improving children's eating habits.

food and report as much as he or she can discover about its source. The following are good choices to explore: sugar, cereal, bread, milk, fruit juice, honey, vinegar, spices, butter, and cooking oils. Labels on packages help supply information.

A rewarding experience for children is a trip to a supermarket to read the labels of ingredients on processed-food cans and packages. They will find listings of preservatives, artificial coloring and flavoring, thickening agents, supplemental vitamins and other "nutrients," and even nonfood ingredients (wood fibers—by-products of paper making—are added to some high-fiber breads, for example). Even fresh fruits and vegetables have been subjected to herbicides, pesticides, and fertilizers in their production. We are becoming increasingly aware of the possible effects of some of these chemicals.

What Happens to Food in the Digestive System?

From a study of drawings or models of the human digestive system ask children to write a story about an imagined trip down the food canal (see pp. 318–319). Included in their description should be the chopping and wetting of food in the mouth, the pushing of food along the canal, the squeezing and churning in the stomach and the pouring in of juices along the way; the breaking up of the molecules of food into simpler form by enzymes; the exit of digested food in the small intestine into the bloodstream; the ridding of undigested food from the rectum.

How Can We See Cells?

Cells are the units of life of all living things. There are many kinds, and living things are composed of them. You might begin by asking, "What do you know about cells?" "Have you seen cells?" "How can we get some cells to examine?"

Children will suggest using a microscope to see cells. If they are inexperienced with the use of a microscope this will be a natural opportunity to help them use one. (See also Chapter 10B, "What Can We See with a Microscope?")

The thin skin from an onion has long been the standard source for obtaining cells for examination. Strip a slice of onion to obtain the thinnest layer possible. Place on a glass slide, add a drop of water and a drop of tincture of iodine. Cover with a cover slip and examine under a microscope.

The moist lining of the cheek is another easy source of cells. Use a tongue depressor or a toothpick to rub the inside area *gently*. Put a drop of water on a microscope slide and touch the tongue depressor to the water. You may have to do this several times, and it may be necessary to stain the material as you did the onion skin. You will see groups of cells that are probably dead cells. They are outside the living cells that form the protective lining of the inside of the mouth. Ask the children, "Can you see the nucleus? The cell membrane?" "How do these cells compare with the onion cells with respect to size, shape, and parts?" "What do you think you would find if you looked at other parts of the human body or of the onion plant?" (See Chapter 11A, p. 315.)

Other cell studies can include blood, one-celled animals (protozoans), plant cells from an aquarium plant (elodea), and so on.

How Can We Keep Healthy?[5]

As students learn more about the human body and what is needed to keep it well, they will begin to

---

[5]D. R. Strovick, *Understanding the Healthy Body,* SMEAC Information Center, The Ohio State University, 1200 Chambers Road, Columbus, OH 43212. A source book on health education. A. Klein, *You and Your Body* (New York: Doubleday, 1976); S. E. Seixas, *Alcohol: What It Is, What It Does* (New York: Greenwillow, 1977).

find out what good health practices are and how their own practices and habits can be improved. The following activities may be carried out as children work in groups to make a survey of health practices in their homes, in the school, and in the community.

To begin, the teacher can ask students to make plans for the activity. The groups list questions and the places they want to investigate. For example, *at home* they may find out how food is kept and prepared to avoid the effects of harmful bacteria, how dishes are washed, how milk and water are made safe, how the house is kept clean, and what safety measures are observed. *In the school,* students can investigate how the drinking fountains are kept in a sanitary condition, how the building is kept clean, and what the health authorities do to prevent the spread of diseases in school.

In the community they can study the work of the health department to see what health practices are required in restaurants, food stores, and public buildings, and how garbage and sewage disposal and water purification are carried on. Rat control has become very important in many areas. Children can investigate why it is necessary to rid areas of rats and other harmful animals. This committee can arrange for a member of the health department to come to the school to answer questions and explain the work of the department, a good example of the integration of science, technology and society.

A school nurse may be a helpful source. That students learn about health, develop good health habits, and grow in ability to find and organize information is obviously important. A visit to a dairy or a local food-processing plant or cannery may yield considerable practical information about sanitary practices in preserving and handling foods.

Students should become acquainted with the purpose and methods of inoculation against smallpox, diphtheria, polio, measles, and other diseases—often carried out in school (see Chapter 11A, pp. 338–341).

What Can We Learn about AIDS?[6]

Special attention should be given to helping students learn about AIDS. There is a great deal of material available (see footnote) to help teachers and students become informed about the disease. See also Chapter 11A for a discussion of the nature of AIDS, its modes of transmission, and methods of its prevention. The Surgeon General's Report is especially helpful in providing detailed information and developing useful attitudes toward this disease in working with children. As former U.S. Surgeon General C. E. Koop has indicated, "We need to motivate students to avoid the kinds of behavior that place them at risk. The men and women who work in America's schools make up the only committed, caring, nationally dispersed network of professionals that can reach young people before they engage in behavior that invites disease."

Following are some general guidelines for teaching about AIDS. As we learn more about AIDS and how best to teach the subject these guidelines may change.

To be most effective, a plan for teaching AIDS in a school should be developed cooperatively under the leadership of an advisory council composed of school board members, school personnel, and representatives from the community.

AIDS instruction should be age appropriate and consistent with community values.

AIDS should be taught as part of the study of communicable diseases.

The *climate* in the classroom is as important as the information presented. A good beginning is to ask children to describe everything they have heard

[6]M. O. Hyde and E. H. Forsyth, *AIDS: What Does it Mean to You?* (New York: Walker, 1987); *The Facts About AIDS,* available from the National Education Association, Washington, D.C.; *AIDS: The Surgeon General's Report,* available from the U.S. Dept. of Health and Human Services, Washington, D.C.; J. Hiatt, *Talking with Your Child about AIDS,* Network Publications, P.O. Box 1830, Santa Cruz, CA 95061; *AIDS—Instructional Guide Grades K–12* (1987), The University of the State of New York, The State Education Department, Bureau of Curriculum Development, Albany, NY, 12234.

about AIDS. The teacher can take cues from this discussion for developing a unit that answers their questions, clears up misunderstandings, and relieves anxiety.

Children should come to understand that AIDS is caused by a virus that is transmitted through sexual contact with a person having AIDS or by using needles or syringes of a person infected with AIDS.

AIDS is not spread by common everyday contact but by sexual contact.

To quote former Surgeon General Koop, "Everyday living does not present any risk of infection. You cannot get AIDS by "shaking hands, social kissing, crying, hugging, or sneezing. . . . Nor has AIDS been contracted from swimming in pools or bathing in hot tubs or from eating in restaurants (even if a restaurant worker has AIDS or carries the AIDS virus). AIDS is not contracted from sharing bed linens, towels, cups, straws, dishes, or any other eating utensils. You cannot get AIDS from telephones, office machinery, or household furniture."

A person acquires AIDS during sexual contact with an infected person's blood or semen and possibly vaginal secretions. The virus then may enter a person's bloodstream through their rectum, vagina, or penis.

The best way—the only way at present—to combat AIDS is by the prevention of infection; there is no cure.

Care should be taken that children do not come to think that sex is a disease, and that they do not equate AIDS with sex.

Classes on AIDS for parents are recommended, since education of children in the home constitutes an important defense against AIDS.

What Can We Learn about Sex?

The science program can make certain unique contributions to sex education because it can (1) place reproduction in the setting of all living things, both plant and animal; (2) affirm the natural and necessary character of reproduction; (3) teach some of the vocabulary and describe the structures of reproduction; (4) provide a basis for objective discussion of reproduction; and (5) pro-

vide a wealth of living material for the firsthand study of reproduction in other forms of life.[7]

The practice of teaching sex education in elementary schools ranges all the way from virtually ignoring the subject to including a carefully designed program built around the five points just enumerated. The following guidelines have been helpful to teachers and others interested in the problem: (1) Parents, teachers, school administrators, and community leaders should plan together the content, approach, and methods of the program. (2) There is much to be said for continuing planning sessions in which all concerned can listen to each other, explore the possibilities, and become acquainted with the programs and plans that have been tried and found successful. (3) Much depends on the ability of teachers and others to create a climate in which children can communicate and face up to the problems related to sex education. (4) Although the ultimate success of the program depends on the ability of the teacher to communicate sensibly and openly with children, it is obvious that the continued interaction of parents, school personnel, and community leaders is also essential. Fortunately, there are now several excellent books for children and audiovisual aids that are proving to be very helpful in sex education. One of the responsibilities of parents and administrators may be to assist in reviewing these aids and preparing a list of useful ones (see Chapter 11A, pp. 330–338).

Following are examples of science concepts that are essential in developing an understanding of the biology of sex in elementary school children.

[7]R. Stronck, *Discussing Sex in the Classroom: Readings for Teachers* (Washington, D.C.: NSTA, 1979); J. W. Maben and R. K. Westheimer, "Building a Sex Education Curriculum," *Science and Children* (September 1974); J. J. Aho and J. W. Petras, *Learning about Sex* (New York: Holt, 1978); W. S. Calderone and J. W. Ramey, *Talking with Your Children about Sex* (New York: Ballantine, 1984); O. F. Wattleton and E. Keiffer, *How to Talk with Your Child about Sexuality* (New York: Doubleday, 1986).

Prekindergarten–Grade 2

Living things produce other living things of the same
   kind.

Human beings and most other animals begin their lives
   as eggs.

Before birth, the egg grows and develops in the mother
   into a fully formed baby.

Grade 3–Grade 4

A mother has two ovaries inside her body. Ripe eggs
   are produced in the ovaries.

A father has two testes outside the body. Ripe sperm
   are produced in the testes.

An egg from the mother and a sperm from the father
   unite to produce a fertilized egg that develops into
   a baby.

In humans the egg is fertilized inside the mother's
   body.

Grade 5–Grade 6

The unborn baby (called the fetus) develops and is
   nourished in a specific part of the mother called the
   uterus.

After a period of approximately nine months the baby
   passes out of the uterus into the vagina of the
   mother and then outside the body to be born.

Many changes begin to occur in the preadolescent
   period.

Other Problems for Older Children

1. What happens to your body as it grows?
2. What functions are performed by the various body
   systems?
3. How does your body protect itself from germs?
4. What does blood look like under a microscope?
   What does each part of the blood do?
5. How do the bones in your body support and protect
   you?
6. How do your eyes see?
7. How do your ears hear?

8. How does your tongue taste? Make a map of the
   areas of the tongue sensitive to sweet, sour, salt, and
   bitter.
9. What senses of touch are in your skin? Using a dull
   pencil point, find senses of pain, pressure, heat, and
   cold in the back of your wrist.

RESOURCES TO INVESTIGATE WITH CHILDREN

1. Local doctors, dentists, and nurses, for information
   about the human body and health.
2. Life insurance companies, for bulletins, charts, and
   other information.
3. Meat markets, for bones and other animal body parts
   to examine.
4. Local Red Cross, for printed information about
   health and safety matters.
5. High school biology teacher, to show blood sample
   under microscope and for other aids.
6. Local health and sanitation officers, to discuss health
   practices and rules and to obtain information about
   symptoms of childhood diseases.
7. Local museums, for displays of models of the human
   body.

PREPARING TO TEACH

1. Prepare a list of the most essential problems that
   might be encountered in initiating a sex education
   program and plan how you would try to solve these
   problems.
2. Perform some of the exercises suggested for discovering by the use of the senses, and make a record
   of the results to use in your teaching.
3. Learn as much as you can about drugs and youth.[8]
   Unfortunately the problem is often encountered in
   the elementary school.

[8]Write to Superintendent of Documents, U.S. Government
Printing Office, Washington, DC 20402. State nature of your
needs to ensure proper response.

THE HISTORY OF LIFE

*It is interesting to contemplate a tangled bank, clothed with many
plants of many kinds, with birds singing on the bushes, with various
insects flitting about, and with worms crawling through the damp
earth, and to reflect that these elaborately constructed forms, so
different from each other, and dependent on each other in so
complex a manner, have all been produced by laws acting around
us. . . . There is grandeur in this view of life . . . that whilst this planet
has gone cycling on according to the fixed laws of gravity, from so
simple a beginning endless forms most beautiful and most
wonderful have been, and are being, evolved.*

CHARLES DARWIN, THE ORIGIN OF SPECIES, 1859

Living species are the topmost twigs of a vast phylogenetic (historical)
tree whose larger branches and trunk are no longer visible.

C. G. SIBLEY AND J. E. AHLQUIST
SCIENTIFIC AMERICAN, FEBRUARY 1986

THE CHANGING EARTH

One of the most important achievements of science has been the discovery of *change,* the discovery that everything in the universe, from the
scenery outside the window to the stars in the
sky, has always been changing.

Hills are worn down into plains; rocks crumble
into soil. New mountains rise from the earth; sea
bottoms become dry land; continents break up
and drift apart. The face of the earth changes and
with it the kinds of animals and plants that live
on it.

So slowly do these changes occur that our
memory, even when aided by written records, can
scarcely be expected to encompass them. The few
thousand years of civilization are but a fleeting
moment in the giant calendar of earth events. Indeed, only in the last century have we understood
the meaning of the evidence that lies around us,
evidence that says: The earth is very old; the earth
is ever-changing.

Animals and plants of the past have recorded
their own history in a number of different ways.
Let us consider some of these.

RECORDS OF PAST LIFE

Actual Remains

The remains of the woolly mammoth, an elephant
with long, thick hair that became extinct thousands of years ago, have been found in the ice
and frozen soil of Alaska and Siberia. Arctic explorers reported that the animals were in such an
excellent stage of preservation that their sled dogs
even enjoyed eating the flesh. Ancient humans
must have known living mammoths, for they
made paintings and carvings of these creatures on
the walls of their caves.

In addition to ice, natural asphalt is an excellent preserver of animals. At the La Brea tar pits
in Los Angeles, California, there is an ancient pool
of hardened asphalt from which the bones and
teeth of thousands of animals have been dug.
Among these are the remains of birds, wolves,
horses, and bison that lived about 15,000 years
ago. Many animals were probably trapped while
attempting to prey on creatures struggling in the
sticky mass. The tar sealed the bones and some
soft tissue of these creatures and preserved them

perfectly from decay. Best known of the entombed animals is the extinct sabertooth, a member of the cat family.

The teeth of sharks and the shells of shellfish are other examples of original materials that are sometimes preserved intact. For such already hard materials, preservation is not as difficult as for fleshy substances.

The remains of the woolly mammoth, the sabertooth cat, and ancient shellfish are examples of *fossils,* which may be defined simply as the remains or traces of ancient life. When most organisms die, they are not preserved. They usually decompose into chemicals that enrich the soil and waters of the earth. Only under special conditions do animals and plants leave some kind of permanent fossil record of themselves. Normally these special conditions include rapid burial and the possession of hard parts (bone or shell) by the organism that will become a fossil.

Ice and asphalt—and lava flows and volcanic ash as well—provide unusual means for preserving the remains of living things. A much more common method occurs when plants and animals are submerged in water and covered with sand and mud. Let us see how such buried organisms become fossils.

Altered Remains

In the Petrified Forest in Arizona are found the stony relics of great conifers, the cone-bearing trees, that once grew there. About 220 million years ago, these trees were submerged in water that flooded the ancient forests or were trapped in log jams and covered with sand and silt. How were their trunks changed into stone? The first stage in this transformation was the filling of the cavities inside the empty wood cells with minerals carried in solution in the water. Silica was the common mineral deposited in the cells by the waters percolating through the sand in which the trees were buried. Later the silica hardened to form the hard mineral quartz. During the process

the wood cell walls were replaced almost to their original state by the mineral matter, molecule by molecule.

This method of fossil formation, called *petrification,* is unique in that it preserves the finest details of organisms. Thus we can still see in the stony trees at the Petrified Forest and in Yellowstone Park the annual growth rings, knots, and even the microscopic cellular structure of these ancient plants. The bones of animals, being porous, may also be petrified by the infiltration of minerals such as silica or, in some cases, lime.

Prints in Stone

We have all seen footprints of children or dogs in concrete sidewalks. These, obviously, were made while the concrete was moist and soft. Many plants and animals of the past have made records of themselves in a similar way.

Certain types of rocks, notably the *sedimentary* rocks, were once mud and sand, and therefore, impressionable like unhardened concrete. Most sedimentary rocks are formed by the gradual settling of materials to the bottom of bodies of water. (These rocks are discussed more fully in Chapter 6A.) Plants and animals that happened to be buried in this yielding material, called sediment, left an impression that became permanent when the sediments hardened into stone. The shell of a clam, for instance, may have fallen into the mud and sand at the bottom of a lake. Later the mud and sand slowly hardened into rock. The shell disintegrated and disappeared, but a permanent impression was left in the surrounding rock.

The impression of the shell is called a *mold.* It shows the shape of the original organism and the ridges, grooves, or other features of the shell surface. Sometimes the mold is filled with new mineral material, which then forms a *cast* very much like the original animal or plant. Shellfish commonly produce both molds and casts; ferns and fish leave mold fossils.

In some cases carbonized remains are found within the imprint. Flattened fossils, such as those of leaves in which a thin film of carbon remains, are called *compressions* or *carbonizations.*

The impressions of moving animals may be preserved as fossils in the form of footprints and trails. Dinosaurs wandering in the Connecticut Valley about 220 million years ago left their footprints in the sand of that time. Later the sand hardened into red sandstone rock.

In traveling over sand and mud bottoms of lakes and seas, such forms as worms, shellfish, and arthopods left trails that were preserved. Like footprints these are called *trace fossils,* and can

yield much information about the habits and structure of the animals that made them.

Finding Fossils

Fossils are not as rare as some people think. In many localities in the United States fossil hunts are practicable for amateurs. Local geological societies, museums, and state geological surveys will often be glad to furnish fossil prospectors with essential information. You may not find dinosaurs,

These large holes were recognized as dinosaur footprints by paleontologist Roland T. Bird. Brontosaurus, or Thunder Lizard, left these prints in mud flats in a region now called Texas 135 million years ago. *(Courtesy of American Museum of Natural History.)*

but you may be able to discover fossils of seashells, fish, and leaves. Amateurs should cooperate with organizations just named to avoid indiscriminate collecting and possible destruction of valuable specimens (see pp. 381–383).

Fossils may occur in any region where there are layers of sedimentary rock. Fortunately for fossil hunters these underlie most of the United States. Rocks exposed in cliffs, along the sides of ravines, in streambeds, in quarries, and in excavations along railroads and highways may yield fossils. In many cases good specimens are to be found in loose fragments of rock in these places. Sometimes the fossil must be broken from the rock. For this a hammer and stone chisel or a mason's hammer are useful as well as goggles to protect the eyes from flying chips of rock. Permission of property owners should also be sought before entering private areas and prospecting for fossils.

Importance of Fossils

Fossils tell us many things. Some, like those of the dinosaur and the saber-toothed cat, tell us of strange animals of the past that are now extinct. Some fossils, like those of ferns (plants that usually live in warm places) found in the Arctic regions, suggest that the climate there has changed. Fossil seashells found high in the Catskill Mountains and fossil coral reefs in Chicago indicate that these areas were once covered by seas. They may even provide evidence that whole continents moved from a region having a certain climate to another quite different region. They may furnish evidence for plate tectonics, discussed in Chapter 6A. But most important of all, fossils, when studied in relation to the rock formations in which they are found, reveal the *sequence* of life down through the ages.

Ancient life has left us a monumental library inscribed in stone, in which the rocky books are stacked one on top of the other. The oldest volumes in this picture-book library are on the bottom of the pile and the most recent acquisitions are on top.

The three lobes of the trilobite are clearly visible. The trilobites pictured here were found near Lockport, New York. Over 3,000 species of trilobites have been identified; they were the dominant form of animal life in early Paleozoic times. *(Courtesy of American Museum of Natural History.)*

The library of stacked volumes is made of the layers of sedimentary rocks that have accumulated down through the ages. We recall from our earlier discussion that these rocks and the fossils in them were formed underwater from soft mud and sand that later hardened into stone. Layer upon layer of rock was built in this way. In a later period the whole mass may have been elevated by a great earth movement or the sea may have receded, making the rock a part of our visible landscape.

The Grand Canyon of Arizona furnishes us with such a sample of ancient history. There, layers of rock a mile high have been exposed to our view by the slow but relentless cutting action of the

Bright Angel Point, North Rim, Grand Canyon National Park. A climb up the canyon is a trip through time, for the building of these layers of rock from bottom to top required over a billion years. *(Courtesy of Union Pacific Railroad Museum Collection.)*

Colorado River and by weathering. A climb up the walls of the canyon is a trip through time, for the building of its rock required hundreds of millions of years. At the lowest or oldest rock formations we search in vain for fossils. As we proceed upward we find our first evidence of life—the remains of simple water plants, the algae. Climbing higher, we find fossils of animals without backbones. The trilobites, which we shall describe later, are a notable and characteristic example of these. Seaweeds are also represented here. A few hundred feet higher we detect the first evidence of vertebrate life in the fossilized remains of fish scales, along with relics of the shellfish and corals that lived in the sea with the fish. Much farther up the canyon walls we discover the first evidence of land plants and animals. Primitive "evergreens" and fernlike plants are seen here; insect fossils are in evidence for the first time; tracks of crawling amphibians and reptiles are found along ledges of sandstone. We notice also that some invertebrates, such as the trilobites, are no longer seen. Perhaps, we think, they had become extinct.

The Grand Canyon is but one of the thousands of places where the earth has written its own history. From a study of the Grand Canyon and many other sites around the earth, scientists have come to the following conclusions:

1. The earth has a long history, extending back, by present calculations, for 4.6 billion years. During this time it has experienced major structural and climatic changes.
2. Life has existed on earth for more than 3 billion years.
3. Because life changes through time, the kinds of living things on the earth have been different in different periods.
4. Some types of life have become extinct.
5. Simple forms of life appeared first; more complex forms appeared later.
6. The more complex forms arose originally as modified descendants of simpler forms.

HOW LIFE CHANGES

The conclusion that life has changed over millions of years of earth history is as solid as the rocks that furnish evidence of such change. This firm law of nature, known as *evolution* or the *theory of evolution,* is accepted by almost all scientists. However, it must be understood that when scientists use the word *theory,* they do *not* use it as a synonym for the word *hypothesis* or *notion* or *guess* or *myth* or *legend.* To a scientist, a theory is a framework of ideas, confirmed by preponderant evidence, which explains a body of observations, and so explains some aspect of nature. Evolution is a great central theory of biology; it transforms a collection of facts into systematic science.[1] Still open to investigation are problems of *how* changes occurred and whether the changes were sudden or gradual.

What mechanism changes one species into another? Consider an observable change that occurred in recent times. A certain British moth, *Biston betularia,* commonly known as the peppered moth, rests on tree trunks in the forests where it is found. The trees there were originally covered by light-colored lichens. The speckled moths were camouflaged on this background, making it difficult for birds to detect and eat them. In this population of speckled moths there were relatively few dark gray moths of the same species.

The spread of smoke-producing factories in certain parts of Britain, beginning about 1850, polluted the woods in some areas with soot, killing the lichens and darkening the tree trunks. As the trees darkened, the speckled moths became more conspicuous and apparently were easily detected and eaten by predatory birds. Now the color of the dark gray moths matched that of the tree trunks.

Between 1848 and 1898 the percentage of dark gray moths of this species increased in smoky industrial areas of England from 1 percent to 99 percent of the moth population. The speckled forms became rare. (A similar tendency for dark-colored forms to replace light-colored forms has been observed among 70 other moth species in England and in some 100 species of moths in the Pittsburgh area of Pennsylvania.) Where did the dark gray moths come from?

The British peppered moth story is a case study of *natural selection* in action. The principle of natural selection was originally proposed in the nineteenth century by Charles Darwin, the British

---

[1]L. S. Lerner and W. J. Bennetta, "The Treatment of Theory in Textbooks," *The Science Teacher* (April 1988).

There are light and dark moths in *both* of these photographs. Which can be seen most easily in each? How might camouflage play a role in evolution? Read the text for a discussion of natural selection.

    Biston betularia, the peppered moth, and its black form, *carbonaria,* at rest on a lichened tree trunk in the unpolluted countryside.

Biston betularia, the peppered moth, and its black form, *carbonaria,* at rest on a soot-covered oak trunk near Birmingham, England. *(Courtesy of Dr. H. B. D. Kettlewell, University of Oxford.)*

naturalist, to explain the origin of species. Let us examine this principle, modernized to accommodate findings since Darwin, to see how it would operate in the case of the peppered moths.

Variation Individuals of a species may vary in color, shape, size, structure, and thousands of minute characteristics, many undetectable except under special circumstances. A good example of this is the many breeds of dog with which we are familiar.

    Only those traits resulting from heredity, such as blue eyes in the human or the dark gray color of the moth *Biston betularia,* are of potential sig-

nificance in evolution, for it is only these that can be transmitted to future generations.

    New characteristics constantly appear in individuals in the course of heredity because of *mutations*—sudden changes in the genes that govern traits—or because of recombinations of existing genes during the process of reproduction. In the fruit fly of the genus *Drosophila,* a favorite for the study of genetics since the early part of this century, hundreds of mutations have appeared.

Selection If industrialization had *not* occurred in Britain, if the trees had *not* darkened, the change in the moth population from 1 percent dark gray to 99 percent dark gray probably would not have occurred. The presumption then is that a changing environment, in this case the darkening of the tree trunks, *favored the survival* of the dark gray moths and operated against the survival of speckled moths. This is an example of natural selection at work.

Note that it is the *population* that evolves, not the individual organism. (A population may be defined as a group of individuals of one species that occupy a given area at the same time—genetically, an interbreeding group of organisms.) The new environment did not change any individual moths from speckled to dark gray; the soot did not soil their wings. Rather, the environment had a selective influence, determining which moths would survive and reproduce.

Time, Place, and Moving Continents   It is true that the dark gray moth cannot be regarded as a different species from the speckled moth. (The dark gray moth will mate successfully with the speckled one. This is one test of a species.) But picture what could happen in hundreds, thousands, or millions of years with the two factors just discussed in operation: the tendency for living things to vary and for the environment to be altered. Change could be added to change until a new species was formed.

Place affects evolution. When the members of a species in some area are separated by physical barriers such as a river, mountain range, or ocean, each new population will change in its own way, partly because of the new environment that each population may encounter and partly because of chance. The influence of continental drift and plate tectonics (see Chapter 6A) on the evolution and dispersal of species over the earth must have been great. The drift of continents through different latitudes would have affected the climate that prevailed on that continent and, therefore, the evolution of plants and animals there. Volcanic eruptions and earthquakes associated with the collision of continental plates, the flooding of continental margins and low inland areas as seas spread, and other tectonic events would affect the

rate and direction of evolution, causing some groups to become extinct and others to flourish.

Over long periods of time not only do new species arise but also the major groups, phyla, classes, and so on, of plants and animals. Thus small subtle changes lead not only to new species but also to all evolutionary change.

Postscript to the peppered moth story: Recent studies have shown that as the quality of air improves, the environmental conditions that formerly put light-colored moths at a disadvantage are changing, sometimes at a rapid pace. The proportion of light-colored moths increased from 5 percent to 10 percent in a period of 13 years in one "smokeless" locality in England; similar reversals of the nineteenth-century darkening trend were observed elsewhere.

THE ERAS OF THE EARTH

Current estimates of the age of the earth vary, but all agree in counting it in billions of years. Recent studies indicate that the earth is about 4.6 billion years old. The evidence for this and the methods of dating rock layers were discussed in Chapter 6A.

Geologists, the scientists who study the changing earth, divide the history of our planet into long time intervals called *eras*. Generally each era is separated from the next one by some great disturbance in the crust of the earth and by some marked changes in living things. The chart on page 363 identifies the four time divisions of earth history and gives some of their outstanding characteristics.

In thinking about the vast span of geological time it is helpful to remember that

1. For about one fourth of its long history the earth was apparently barren of life.
2. Humans are newcomers. If all earth time were compressed into one year, human beings would come on the scene on December 31 just a few hours before midnight.

The four divisions, in chronological order, are Precambrian, also called the Cryptozoic ("obscure

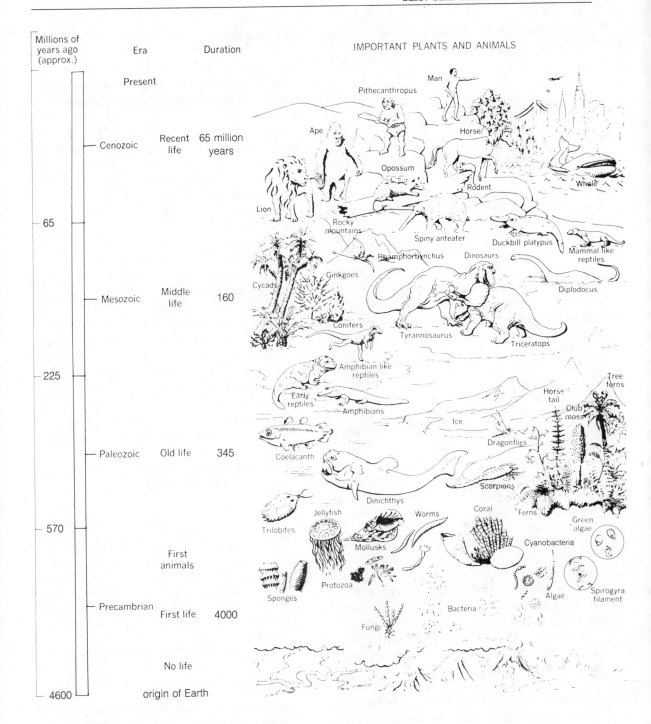

Millions of years ago (approx.)	Era	Duration	IMPORTANT PLANTS AND ANIMALS
		Present	
—65	Cenozoic	Recent life	65 million years
—225	Mesozoic	Middle life	160
	Paleozoic	Old life	345
—570		First animals	
	Precambrian	First life	4000
		No life	
—4600		origin of Earth	

Progress of life through the eras.

life"), Paleozoic ("ancient life"), Mesozoic ("middle life"), and Cenozoic ("recent life").

THE PRECAMBRIAN (CRYPTOZOIC) ERA

The way in which the earth, the other planets in the solar system, and the sun were formed is discussed in Chapter 7A. According to the current popular theory, the earth began as a cloud of cold dust and gas, which in time contracted to form the body of the planet. The primeval earth heated up slowly, taking perhaps 1 billion years to reach a molten or partially molten state. It may be imagined that during the early Cryptozoic era the entire earth was a huge chemical laboratory in which the future materials of this planet were put together. In this partially molten stage the heaviest substances sank to the center of the earth, the lighter floated to the surface, and the others found their place in between. Various gases, including water vapor, erupted from the molten mass to form the first atmosphere.

A thin crust of rock formed on the surface of the earth. As the surface rocks cooled and hardened, more water vapor and other gases escaped from cracks and fissures and rose into the atmosphere. The earth gradually became wrapped in an atmosphere so dense and cloudy that the sun could not penetrate it. After a long period of cooling, water in the upper part of the cloud blanket was able to condense, and rain began to fall, to trickle down the slopes, and to collect in pools.

Then the rains increased. Rivulets became torrents, raging across the rocky land, filling the valleys and the basins of the earth. Thus were the oceans born. As more and more water poured down, the clouds thinned and the sun finally broke through, illuminating a landscape of rocky land masses and shallow seas. But upon the whole earth there were no living things, except possibly emerging unicellular microscopic bacteria and algae.

Life Begins

The origin of life is the mystery of mysteries. Down through the ages philosophers and scientists have sought an answer to the question, How did life begin?

In those early Cryptozoic times when the seas and the atmosphere seethed with chemical turbulence, it is possible that molecules joined together to form specks of living material, the starting points of all life. How did this happen?

In 1953 Stanley L. Miller, then a graduate student at the University of Chicago, performed a now-classic experiment on the origin of life. Miller constructed an airtight apparatus for circulating steam through a mixture of ammonia, methane, and hydrogen, a combination thought at that time to be like that of the earth's early atmosphere. (Ammonia is a gas used in many cleaning fluids; methane is part of the natural gas used in home cooking and heating.) The mixture of steam and gas was subjected to high-energy electric sparks (simulated lightning). After a week of such treatment the condensed water in the apparatus became deep red and turbid, and on analysis it was discovered that it contained a mixture of amino acids.

To appreciate the significance of this experiment, consider the following:

1. Miller's experiment was based on the then held theory that the primitive atmosphere of the earth consisted of ammonia, methane, hydrogen, and water vapor, in contrast to the present atmosphere of nitrogen, oxygen, carbon dioxide, and water vapor. (Methane is found today in the atmosphere of the planets Uranus and Neptune; methane and ammonia gases are found in the atmospheres of Jupiter and Saturn.)

2. Ammonia (NH_3), methane (CH_4), hydrogen (H_2), and water vapor (H_2O) contain four of the essential elements—carbon, oxygen, hydrogen, nitrogen—necessary to make the complex amino acids essential for life. Electrical discharges such as lightning in an early atmosphere of ammonia, methane, and hydrogen, together with radiation from the sun, may

have provided the energy needed to juggle the atoms in these chemicals, causing them to recombine into amino acids. Over millions of years the amino acids may have combined to form larger and more complex molecules—proteins. Other essential compounds that may have been formed in this prebiological period were nucleic acids and carbohydrates.

3. These new compounds may have accumulated in ponds, lakes, and seas, forming what has been called a "thin organic soup." Slowly the earliest forms of life evolved from nonliving chemical systems. Precells formed from clusters of organic compounds, which were able to grow and replenish themselves from materials originally formed by nonbiological reactions. The first organisms were able to obtain energy by a fermentationlike process in which no oxygen was required.

It is now believed that the ammonia–methane–hydrogen–water atmosphere was the *original* one present as a residue of the formation of our planet from a cloud of gas and dust. As the earth heated, the methane and ammonia was largely driven off and replaced by a *second atmosphere* of carbon dioxide, carbon monoxide, nitrogen, and water vapor. It was probably in this second atmosphere that life originated (not in the methane–ammonia atmosphere). A Millerlike experiment yielded amino acids for these gases also.

Since Miller's original experiment, others have been performed using other energy sources, such as ultraviolet radiation and different combinations of gases likely to be present in the primitive atmosphere of the earth. In 1983 Cyril Ponnamperuma, director of the University of Maryland's Laboratory of Chemical Evolution, confirmed and advanced earlier findings about the origin of life by subjecting a mixture of methane, nitrogen, and water to electrical discharges. He found that all five of the chemical bases of DNA, the key molecule of the genes, were produced. He also found these five precursors of life in a meteorite, thereby giving a tremendous boost to the theory that life arose by natural chemical processes and may have arisen by the same processes elsewhere in the universe as well.

Comets also may have been a source of the organic precursors of life on earth. Instruments on the *Vega* and *Giotto* spacecraft found that Halley's comet, which visited here in 1985–1986, was rich in organic material, including formaldehyde, which has a central role in forming certain amino acids and carbohydrates.

Thus the early earth, showered with meteorites and comet dust, may have received enough organic material to start the chemical processes leading to biological compounds. The most difficult task remaining in unraveling the origin of life still lies ahead; how did the precursor chemicals combine to create life?

These ideas concerning the interrelationship of the evolution of the earth's atmosphere and the evolution of life are so new that they have yet to be tested and fully accepted by scientists, but they are the most consistent and plausible proposals yet advanced to explain the origin of life.

Life Develops[2]

According to current theory, life originated about $3\frac{1}{2}$ billion years ago. The earliest forms were bacteriumlike organisms that lacked a well-defined nucleus enclosed in a membrane. As the stock of nutrients in the primordial soup became depleted, natural selection resulted in the evolution of the cyanobacteria (formerly called blue-green algae), organisms that were able to synthesize food from the plentiful carbon dioxide and water in the environment.[3]

[2]In reading the material that follows, it will be helpful to refer to Chapter 10A for a fuller description of the nature and variety of living things.

[3]The bacteria and cyanobacteria are known as *prokaryotes* (pro = before; karyotes = nucleus; prokaryotes = before a nucleus). The prokaryotes are distinguished from the eukaryotes (eu = true; karyotes = nucleus; eukaryotes = true nucleus). The eukaryotes include all other forms of life. In modern classification systems the accepted division is not between plants and animals but between prokaryotes and eukaryotes.

From such beginnings there appeared cells with a definite nucleus. The original organisms in this group, the kingdom Protista, would probably have been hard to classify as either plants or animals. Some possessed whiplike tails for locomotion and were able to ingest food, but also contained chlorophyll for the chemical synthesis of food. As time went on, modified descendants of these first organisms appeared: the higher algae, the protozoans, and the slime molds.

The appearance of algae marked an important step in evolution, for now, with the aid of the green chlorophyll that these simple organisms possessed, it was possible to utilize the energy of sunlight to synthesize foods quickly. At the same time, as a result of photosynthesis, great quantities of free oxygen were added to the atmosphere. Food-ingesting organisms began to use this oxygen for the burning of food. Thus an ample supply of building materials and energy was made available. New forms of life appeared, including the protozoans (represented today by *Paramecium* and *Amoeba*) that were incapable of manufacturing their own food but able to use the free oxygen and food produced by the algae. Thus photosynthesis gave the earth the oxygen-rich atmosphere we enjoy today, and made our planet unique in the solar system.

Perhaps the best way to get a picture of early life is to examine a drop of stagnant pond water under the microscope and to discover there the teeming, lilliputian world of bacteria, algae, protozoans, and other tiny organisms.

During the closing stages of the Cryptozoic a few groups of higher animals without backbones, the invertebrates, made their appearance in the sea. These included the sponges, jellyfish and their relatives, and various types of wormlike animals. The most advanced of the invertebrates, the arthropods—jointed-foot animals that were later to include crustaceans, spiders, and insects—had their beginnings in late Cryptozoic times.

The Cryptozoic era did not leave many fossil remains. After years of search in the rock of this era, we have only a few specimens of algae and fungi, and low forms of marine invertebrates. In

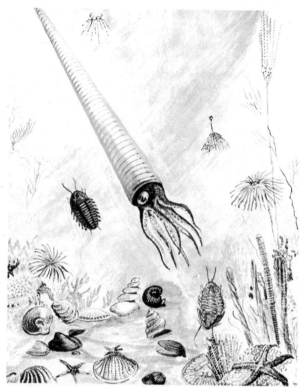

Much of North America was submerged beneath marine waters in Ordovician times (Paleozoic era). Creatures such as these are found as fossils in many parts of the country. *(Courtesy of Buffalo Museum of Science; wall painting by James Doherty.)*

1977, Dr. E. S. Barghoorn pushed life's origin back to 3.4 billion years ago by his discovery in Africa of blue-green algae fossils in rocks of that age. In 1980, Dr. J. W. Schopf announced the discovery of 3.5-million-year-old bacteria in rocks from western Australia. Radioactive dating (see Chapter 6A), chemical analysis, and microscopic examination confirmed his conclusion.

THE PALEOZOIC (ANCIENT LIFE) ERA

The next 370 million years of earth history, which began about 570 million years ago, were filled with important events. Plant and animal forms emerged from the seas and inhabited the land. Invertebrate animals multiplied and became the rulers of the earth, only to be dethroned by the first-evolving vertebrates, the fish and amphibia. Reptiles had their beginnings.

The plant world flourished, clothing the barren land with green. The first forests appeared, including those that gave rise to most of the world's present supply of coal. Many of the major groups of plants were established before the end of the Paleozoic.

The physical events of this era were marked by widespread changes. Seas covered wide areas of the earth—at one time more than three fifths of North America. Huge mountain ranges, the Appalachians and the Urals, were thrust up and folded by gargantuan forces in the crust of the earth.

The Rise and Fall of the Trilobites

Most fossils of early Paleozoic life are those of marine creatures. In the shallow seas covering large parts of the continents and in the surface water of the deeper oceans lived protozoans, sponges, corals, jellyfish, worms, snails, clams, starfish, crabs, and shrimps. Except for fish, which had not yet appeared, these were the types of animals we find in the sea today. But most of these ancient forms would look strange to our eyes because they were quite unlike their modern descendants. And these ancient seas would appear strange also because of the trilobites who lived there. Trilobite means "three-lobed," and the trilobite was so named because it was divided longitudinally into three clearly distinguishable parts. These ancient relatives of lobsters and crabs have since disappeared from the earth, and we know them today only as stony fossils (see p. 358).

The Advent of Fish

The first animals living in the early Paleozoic era did not have backbones. Whatever supporting structures they possessed were external, consisting of shells or plates. The emergence of fish from these lower forms was a most significant event, marking the origin of animals with backbones, the vertebrates, a group that includes the fish, amphibia, reptiles, birds, and mammals, including humans.

Fish, then, were the first animals with backbones. The earliest forms, however, were quite different from the fish we know today. One of these was the 20-foot-long (6-meter-long) Dinichthys, the "terrible fish" of the Paleozoic era. Remains of this animal have been found in black shale rock near Cleveland, Ohio.

Before the close of the Paleozoic era sharks appeared, and then the fish with hard bones, which are the ancestors of today's forms.

Plants Invade the Land

The scorpions and insects apparently were the first *animals* to emerge from the waters of lakes and seas in the late Paleozoic era. However, the invasion of the land was first made by plants. For 2 billion years the plant kingdom had been confined to water, and had not yet advanced beyond unicellular algae and a simple seaweed level of development. Then, in a relatively short period, plants overran the land, carpeting it with green mosses, ferns, and seed plants.

Naturally, the transition from water to land was made at the edges of seas and lakes. On the seashore any of the new water plants that could withstand partial exposure to air might survive on the moist beach when ocean tides retreated. Similarly, lake plants that could withstand seasonal receding of lake waters in dry seasons might survive.

Having established a foothold on the rocky land, plants advanced steadily. Soil formed for the first time from the organic matter furnished by the decay of many generations of the first plant invaders and from the decomposing rock underneath.

The mosses may have been the first land plants to evolve from aquatic plants. However, their con-

Giant ferns, club-moss trees (lycopods), and horsetail rushes are some of the plants shown in the restoration of an ancient landscape. Swamp forests of Pennsylvanian times, such as this one, provided the material for the formation of coal. In the foreground are two kinds of amphibians and a giant dragonfly. *(Courtesy of American Museum of Natural History.)*

quest of the land was limited because they lacked the internal "tubes" needed to carry watery sap any great distance from roots through stems to leaves. As a result the representatives of this group were small and were confined to moist areas.

The ferns, however, did evolve the tubes through which water could be elevated many feet above the ground. Plants were now able to extend their invasion of the ground to the conquest of the air above it. Ferns towered over the Paleozoic landscape.

How would natural selection account for the present appearance of land plants? Marine plants generally have both light and moisture and are supported by the water that is their habitat. Land plants must derive their water from underground, where there is no light, and light above ground, where there is little water; hence the development of extensive roots to extract water from the soil and of stems and trunks to project the plant toward the light. Most important are the tubes running from the roots to the upper plant to convey water and to provide support.

The Coal Forests

Most of the world's present supply of coal had its origin in late Paleozoic forests. For a period of about 50 million years the prevailing moist climate and swampy terrain provided conditions favorable for the luxurious growth of a group of spore-bearing flowerless plants, many of which were destined for conversion into coal. Included in this group were the club mosses, horsetails and scouring rushes, and the true ferns.

Horsetails, which today are small plants characterized by hollow, jointed stems, were then trees 75 feet (23 meters) tall and 3 feet (1 meter) in diameter.

Club mosses, which today include the small, inconspicuous plants used as Christmas decorations, were the real giants of the coal forests. One of these, *Lepidodendron* (lep̓-ĭ-dō-dĕn-drŏn), had large needlelike leaves and a branched, expanded crown. A fossil trunk of this plant found in an English coal mine was 114 feet (34.7 meters) long.

There were also many kinds of true ferns, some of which were 50 feet (15 meters) tall.

The conversion of the wood of these swamp plants into coal is not difficult to understand from a chemical point of view, especially for anyone who has accidentally scorched the wooden handle of a pot. Wood is essentially a chemical compound of carbon, hydrogen, and oxygen. Coal is essentially carbon. To change wood into coal it was only necessary to drive off the hydrogen and oxygen and subject the remaining black carbon to pressure.

Two peculiar conditions in the Paleozoic swamp forests favored the formation of coal. First, as generation after generation of trees died, they were protected against rapid rotting through oxidation by their immersion in the waters of the swamp. Thus bacterial action, instead of decomposing the whole mass of wood, worked slowly on it, removing the hydrogen and oxygen and leaving a substance that had a high percentage of carbon in it.

The second condition responsible for coal formation was the sinking of the land. The resulting floods from nearby seas and rivers dumped thick layers of mud and sand over the accumulated vegetation. The coal forest's existence was thus terminated. In time the pressure of the overlying layers of mud and sand and the heat generated by the great pressure changed the buried vegetation into coal. The mud and sand eventually changed into rock.

The process just described would account for one layer or *seam* of coal. Later, as the floodwaters receded and the land rose again the entire cycle was repeated, on top of the previous formation. Each swamp forest provided another layer of coal. In parts of present-day Illinois, 50 such cycles have resulted in the deposition of 50 seams of coal.

The plant origin of coal is apparent because fossil impressions of fern fronds and other late Paleozoic plants are frequently found in coal beds, as well as whole tree trunks that have been transformed into coal.

Animals Go Ashore

The luxuriant plant cover of Paleozoic times provided a home and a supply of food for the animals that were emerging from the crowded seas. Both air-breathing scorpions and spiders, descendants of the sea scorpions, made their appearance. These eight-legged creatures were followed by the six-legged insects. Notable among insects for a time were 800 different kinds of cockroaches, some of them 4 or 5 inches (10 to 13 centimeters) long. No wonder this period is sometimes called the Age of Cockroaches.

Primitive dragonflies with a wingspread of $2\frac{1}{2}$ feet (.8 meter) flitted around the giant horsetails and club mosses in ancient coal forests. Fossils of these largest insects of all times were discovered in certain fossil sites in Belgium. The richest occurrence of Paleozoic insect fossils yet discovered, however, is in rock a few miles south of Abilene, Kansas, where more than 12,000 specimens have been collected.

The development of the insect group from Paleozoic times on is a fantastic success story, having its climax in the more than 700,000 different kinds of insects inhabiting the world today.

Land Vertebrates

In 1938 an odd-looking fish was dredged up by fishermen working along the coast opposite East London, South Africa. "I would hardly have been more surprised if I met a dinosaur on the street," said J. L. B. Smith, a renowned ichthyologist, when this massive steel-gray fish was brought to his laboratory. The strange fish was well known to scientists, but only as a fossil. In fact, hundreds of fossil specimens of these ancient fish, called coelacanths (seal'-a-canths) had been found during the excavation for a new library at Princeton University, New Jersey. The scientific world bubbled with excitement as this "living fossil" was studied and compared with its fossil counterpart.

In 1987 scientists in a submersible dove 660 feet to observe the coelacanths in their natural habitat. They found that the creatures moved their paired fins in synchrony, a pattern common to horses and other four-legged animals, but rare among fish. Such coordination may have facilitated the transition to locomotion on land.

Coelacanths are of particular interest because they are descendants of the primitive lobe-finned fish, which are believed to have given rise to land vertebrates. We shall find out more about the lobe-fins presently.

The successful emergence of vertebrate animals from their aquatic environment depended on the acquisition of two important organs— lungs and legs. The breathing structures of fish are gills, essentially flaps of tissue, richly supplied with blood vessels. In the water, which must constantly flow over the gills, there is dissolved air containing oxygen. Some of the oxygen passes through the thin gill membranes into the circulating blood. In air-breathing vertebrates, on the other hand, oxygen passes from the *air sacs* of the lungs through moist membranes into the bloodstream.

How did lungs arise? There is evidence that seasonal dryness, with the receding and even drying up of large areas, occurred during some periods of the Paleozoic. Thus the environmental conditions were favorable for the emergence of air-breathing animals.

The lung developed first in primitive fish by the evolution of small saclike bodies on the esophagus (the gullet). These became lined and later enlarged to become lungs. Those fish developing these accessory breathing structures had an enormous advantage over others. It was a crucial step toward the eventual appearance of land vertebrates. In most modern fish the respiratory function of these lungs has been lost, and the lung has become a saclike air bladder, a kind of "float" that helps the fish maintain a stationary position at different depths in the water without muscular effort.

In the curious lungfish that live today in Africa, South America, and Australia the sac takes on another function during the dry seasons. The African lungfish, instead of trying to follow the receding waters into the river, burrows into the mud and forms a hardened mud capsule around itself. The capsule has a tube that permits air from the outside to pass into the mouth of the fish and thence to its air bladders, which function as lungs. The fish lives in the mud capsule for nearly half of the year, breathing with its lungs and living on the fat that it stores up during the wet season.

Legs were also essential for the liberation of the vertebrates from an aquatic existence. In fish, however, the principal locomotive structure used to change direction, stay in one place, or move slowly is the muscular tail, aided by the paired fins. But the ancient lobe-finned fish were different. The paired fins were connected to the body by fleshy lobes that are believed to be the evolutionary forerunners of limbs, with a basic bone pattern remarkably like that of four-legged animals. It is probable that the forerunners of land animals were lobe-finned fish who were able to crawl out of water and move about to some extent on land, possibly to move to another body of water.

Descendants of walking lobe-fins spent more and more time on land. From these were probably evolved the amphibians, which today are represented by frogs, toads, and salamanders.

The life history of modern frogs provides a good parallel to the evolution of life from water to land. Frogs begin life as fishlike tadpoles, propelling themselves through the water with their tails and breathing through gills. Before our eyes they transform themselves into land creatures, growing first hind and then front legs, losing their fishy tails, and developing air-breathing lungs. However, their exodus from the aquatic environment is only partial, because most species must return to the water to mate and to lay their gelatinous masses of eggs.

Complete liberation from the water, however, was achieved by the reptiles, who made their appearance in the late Paleozoic era, probably as descendants of primitive amphibia. These reptiles had developed an egg with a tough covering that protected the embryo from drying up on land and yet was porous enough to permit it to breathe.

It must not be thought that *all* animals became terrestrial, however. Corals, clams, snails, fish, and many other forms continued to live and flourish in the sea.

End of the Paleozoic

The distance between Altoona and Philadelphia, both in Pennsylvania, was once 100 miles greater than it is today. Such is the estimate of the State Geological Survey of Pennsylvania. How is this possible?

Geologists tell us that the closing period of the Paleozoic was marked by revolutionary earth changes. At this time most of the major land masses of the earth were assembled into the super-continent Pangaea (see Chapter 6A). The compressional forces of continental collision raised great mountain ranges along eastern and southern margins of North America.

Terrific pressures on the rocks of the earth's crust caused them to buckle up, just as a rug might if it were pushed together. As a result, mountain ranges, including the Appalachians, were thrust up, reaching majestic heights of 20,000 to 30,000 feet (6,000 to 9,000 meters). Hence a shortening of lateral distances between places occurred.

This period of mountain building also produced a great range of mountains across southern Europe, now mostly eroded. It was followed by the receding of inland waters and the advance of sheets of ice across what are now Brazil, South Africa, and peninsular India. Great extremes of climate marked these later Paleozoic times.

Naturally these revolutionary upheavals caused great destruction of life. Many marine invertebrates were hard hit by the draining of their homes at the edge of the sea. The warmth-loving, swamp-living plants of the coal forest were replaced by hardy seed-bearing plants such as the conifers and cycads.

THE MESOZOIC (MIDDLE LIFE) ERA

The Mesozoic is truly the age of reptiles. During these times reptilian dinosaurs ruled the land, reptilian "sea serpents" invaded and conquered the ocean, and reptilian "flying dragons" dominated the air. For over 100 million years the reptiles—modestly represented today by turtles, crocodiles, alligators, lizards, chameleons, and snakes—were the masters of all the habitats of the earth. Our museums are filled with the massive bones left by this mighty group in their Mesozoic graveyards.

The Mesozoic was also the era in which two new vertebrate classes appeared: birds and mammals. It was the time when the land mass of Pangaea broke up into continents we know today, with profound consequences for the distribution and evolution of plants and animals.

The Dinosaurs

The stars of the ancient reptilian world were the dinosaurs. Traditionally regarded as ruler of them all was *Tyrannosaurus rex* (Tĭ-răń-o-sô′-rŭs), 50 feet (15 meters) long from nose to tail and 18 feet (5 meters) tall when it stood erect on its hind legs (see pp. 381–383). The head of this meat-devouring creature was 4 feet (1.2 meters) long and was armed with sharp teeth projecting 6 inches (15 centimeters) from the jaw. *Tyrannosaurus's* huge mouth provided the animal with a mighty weapon

An even dozen of dinosaur eggs—cracked. Fossil dinosaur eggs were first discovered in the Gobi Desert in Mongolia in 1923. Distinct bones of embryo dinosaurs were found in some of the eggs. *(Courtesy of American Museum of Natural History)*

against less powerful dinosaurs. In 1979 paleontologist J. S. Jenson discovered in Dry Mesa, Colorado, the bones of a dinosaur that he estimated to weigh 80 tons and to be 80 feet long. This new form, named *Ultrasaurus,* may be the new king of the dinosaurs, dethroning *Tyrannosaurus. Ultrasaurus* was a herbivore, however, not a predator like *Tyrannosaurus.*

Stegosaurus (Stĕǵ-o-sò-rŭs), perhaps the queerest-looking of all the dinosaurs, was equipped with a single row of long triangular plates carried erect along its body and extending from its relatively tiny skull along the whole length of its back, almost to the end of its tail. Near the end of its short tail were two pairs of heavy spikes, each 2 feet (.6 meter) long, which must have been an effective weapon against the meat-eating dinosaurs. Despite this, *Stegosaurus* was vulnerable to a flank attack from an enemy.

Triceratops (trī-sĕ́r-a-tŏps), with its curious bony shield extending backward from its 7-foot (2-meter) head, was protected by three formidable horns. *Brontosaurus* (brŏn-tô-số-rŭs), the "thunder lizard," another huge dinosaur, was 60 to 70 feet (18 to 21 meters) long and weighed about 30 tons (27 tonnes). In contrast to *Tyran-*

nosaurus, this creature walked on all fours and had a long slim neck ending in a small head adapted for its vegetarian habits. *Diplodocus* (dĭ-plŏd́-ō-kĭs), a close relative of *Brontosaurus,* was the longest creature ever to walk the earth. The best skeleton of this animal, now in the Carnegie Museum in Pittsburgh, is 87 feet (27 meters) long.

Reptiles Return to the Sea

The reptiles were the first vertebrates to achieve complete liberation from the water; they were also the first to return. The marine reptiles became the largest and most powerful creatures of the Mesozoic seas while their dinosaur cousins ruled the land. The aquatic *Ichthyosaurus* (ĭḱ-thĭ-o-số-rŭs), for example, reached lengths up to 10 feet (3 meters). Instead of legs, it had relatively small paddlelike limbs; a well-developed fishlike tail was its main organ of locomotion. Instead of going back to shore to lay eggs, it gave birth to its young alive. *Ichthyosaurus* retained, however, its reptilian characteristic of breathing with lungs.

Another group of marine reptiles consisted of the *mosasaurs* (mṓ-så-sôrs), slender creatures some 50 feet (15 meters) long, looking very much like the legendary "sea serpents" supposedly "seen" every few years by impressionable mariners.

Reptiles Invade the Air

The insects, as we have seen, were the first creatures to extend their domain to the regions of the air. The first *vertebrates* to leave the ground and the trees were the reptiles, represented by a group called the *pterosaurs* (těŕ-o-sôrs). These pioneer gliders derived their flight power from a wing membrane made of skin that stretched from the greatly elongated joints of the fourth finger of the forelimb to the body as far back as the hip. The first three fingers were of ordinary length, each terminating in a claw that was probably useful for climbing and for clinging to branches of trees.

In 1975 the fossilized skeleton of a large pterosaur was found in the Big Bend National Park in western Texas. With a wing span of over 50 feet (15 meters)—wider than the wing span of most executive jet planes—it is the largest flying creature presently known. On the other hand, some pterosaurs were no larger than sparrows.

The location of the Big Bend pterosaur bones in sedimentary rock formed by deposits of ancient inland streams, far from lakes and seas, and the large size of these creatures suggest that it was a carrion eater; previous discoveries of other pterosaurs elsewhere in marine sediments indicated a fish-catching mode of life. Despite the large wing span, the Big Bend pterosaur, like other pterosaurs, was relatively light in weight because its body was small and its bones were hollow.

Hot or Cold Dinosaurs?

Today's reptiles—snakes, turtles, lizards, alligators, and crocodiles—are cold-blooded (see p. 275). We have assumed that the extinct dinosaurs were also cold-blooded. Recently a number of investigators have challenged that view, arguing that the erect posture, the mode of locomotion, and the spurts of energy required in combat with others were possible for dinosaurs only because they possessed a constant body temperature, relying on heat produced as a by-product of a high metabolism, as is the case in birds and mammals. This viewpoint is not shared by all or even most paleontologists; however, there seems to be agreement that certain dinosaurs were not "typical" reptiles.

The First Birds

Another branch of the reptiles took to the air at the same time as the pterosaurs. From this group evolved a form that for some time was thought to be the first true bird, called *Archaeopteryx* (är-kē-ŏp-ter-ĭks). Based on a study of its bone structures, some paleontologists believe that this creature is a direct descendant of a small carnivorous dinosaur. *Archaeopteryx* was about the size of a domestic pigeon, but was only partially covered with feathers. The short rounded wings were probably not powerful enough for real flight, the animal being more of a glider than a flier.

Archaeopteryx had three fingers at the end of each wing, which were equipped with claws used for grasping and tearing. These early birds had strong jaws without bills; they had teeth—something no modern bird has. Also unique were their long bony tails. Thus the only strictly birdlike characteristic of *Archaeopteryx* was its feathers.

In 1986 a team led by Sankar Chatterjee, a paleontologist at Texas Tech University, announced the discovery of the fossil bones of one of the world's oldest known birds. Seventy-five million years older than *Archaeopteryx,* the creature named *Protoavis* for "ancestral bird," was dug out of 225-million-year-old mudstone in Texas. About the size of a crow, it had teeth, a long bony tail, powerful hind legs and claws—the characteristics of its reptilian heritage. But from the breastbone and wishbone to the skull it had the attributes of a bird—wide eye sockets and a large brain case. Although it was older than *Archaeopteryx* it was

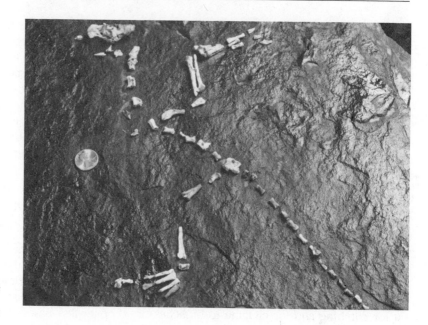

Fossil bones of Protoavis shape the outline of a 225-million-year-old bird. The remains may provide new insights into birds' origins. *Photo by Barbara Laing. © 1986 National Geographic Society*

more birdlike, perhaps because it had advanced further along the mainstream of avian evolution. Although no feathers were found on Protoavis, tiny bumps on the forearm and hand were probably the places of attachment of feathers.

In the next era there developed birds without teeth and claws, similar to the birds we know today. Modern birds, however, still reveal their reptilian ancestry in the scales that cover their legs.

Mammals Get Their Start

During much of Mesozoic time the *mammal-like reptiles* were important land vertebrates. Later in the Mesozoic, the dinosaurs, which we have already described, flourished and became masters of the land. Only recently have paleontologists emphasized the abundance of the mammal-like reptiles that preceded the dinosaurs by 125 million years and inhabited the land for almost as long. One group of these mammal-like reptiles, the *therapsids,* is of particular interest. During most of the Mesozoic the therapsids, some of them no larger than rats, scurried around, surviving largely by their quickness of foot and agility in dodging dinosaurs. Therapsids gave rise to the earliest mammals in the Mesozoic. Then in the next era mammals became the rulers of the earth. Mammals are warm-blooded creatures that are covered with hair and suckle their young by means of mammary glands.

The early mammals, themselves descendants of reptiles, played second fiddle, however, to the dinosaurs and their cousins throughout the Mesozoic.

Other Mesozoic Events

The rise of reptiles, birds, and mammals in the Mesozoic era should not obscure the fact that

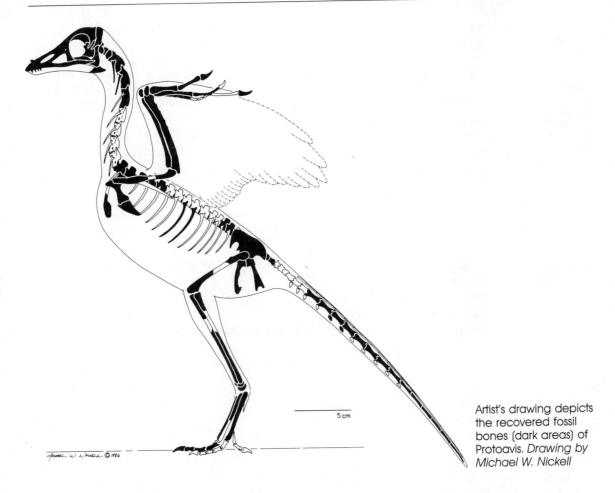

Artist's drawing depicts the recovered fossil bones (dark areas) of Protoavis. *Drawing by Michael W. Nickell*

5 cm

changes were taking place in the other and older groups of animals. In the invertebrate world of protozoans, mollusks, starfishes, lobsters, and insects, and also in the fish world, significant changes were occurring.

Notable advances were also being made in the plant kingdom. The cycads, palmlike seed plants without true flowers, were so abundant that the early Mesozoic is sometimes referred to as the Age of Cycads. Conifers, such as the spruces, pines, junipers, cypresses, and cedars, were abundant. Some of these probably reached a height of 200 feet (60 meters), judging from the logs in the Petrified Forest of Arizona, described earlier. A third group that flourished during the Mesozoic was the ginkgoes, now represented by only one species, the ginkgo tree. This species was probably protected from extinction by cultivation in China and is now common as an imported tree all over the world.

The cycads, conifers, and ginkgoes are part of a group of seed-bearing yet flowerless plants. Another group, the plants with true flowers, also got its start in the Mesozoic, expanding rapidly near the end of this era to become the dominant plant form. The flowering plants include those which are best known and most valuable to man—hardwood trees such as oaks, maples, and elms, and the grasses and grains.

Plant evolution affected animal evolution. We

find that bees and butterflies put in their appearance with the advent of flowering plants. Hardwood trees furnished shelter, and the cereal grains furnished food for many of the evolving mammals.

By the end of the Mesozoic and the beginning of the next era, all the common types of familiar plants had made their appearance. The animal kingdom, on the other hand, was still to expand enormously, admitting many new members to its ranks.

End of the Mesozoic

The fossil record reveals that the end of the Mesozoic, some 65 million years ago, was a time of crisis for living things. It marked the total extinction of the dinosaurs, as well as three fourths of other plant and animal groups. What caused the mass extinction? Many theories have been proposed.

A weakening of the earth's magnetic field may have made its atmosphere and surface more susceptible to damaging radiations from space.

A blast of lethal rays from a nearby exploding star—a supernova.

The collision of the earth with an asteroid (see Chapter 7A, pages 157–158) may have kicked up a cloud of dust in the atmosphere, blocking much of the sunlight for a period of months or years. The consequent interference with photosynthesis would result in a drop in the world's food supply.

The sudden warming of the earth due to the "greenhouse effect" (see Index) resulting from an increase in the carbon dioxide in the atmosphere. The increase in temperature may have affected the reproductive capability of animals.

A spillover of (the supposedly) cold fresh water from the Arctic Ocean, flooding the world's oceans, reducing their salinity and killing susceptible marine species. The cold water would have also altered the world's climate sufficiently to kill plants and animals.

Tectonic plate activity, discussed on pages 122–127, which altered the earth's environment. The restless tectonic plates may have triggered volcanic erup-

tions that released carbon dioxide into the atmosphere resulting in the greenhouse effect already noted; or crustal movement may have sent frigid ocean currents to invade tropical waters, with consequences noted.

A combination of some of the preceding factors.

Thus the closing of the Mesozoic brought the curtain down on the dinosaurs. Of the different kinds of reptiles, only lizards, snakes, crocodiles, turtles, and the rare tuatara of New Zealand survived into the next era—the Cenozoic.

Rulers of the earth for 100 million years, about 50 times as long as the time of humans on earth thus far, the dinosaurs disappeared completely, giving way at the close of the Mesozoic to the mammals.

Mass Extinctions

The disappearance of the dinosaurs led to interest in the periodic extinction of many other forms of life. Recent evidence from the study of fossils in rocks indicates that mass extinctions occur about once every 26 million years. Why? No known earthly phenomena, no Vesuvian eruptions, no ice ages, no tectonic movement of the earth's plates could explain the *regularity* of these periods. The source had to be an extraterrestrial mechanism.

According to one theory, our sun has a sister star, named Nemesis after the Greek goddess of doom. Astronomers have turned their telescopes toward possible locations of this postulated star. It is assumed that in its elliptical orbit around our sun, Nemesis comes close enough to the solar system every 26 million years to nudge billions of comets out of their natural habitat in the "Oort cloud," the swarm of comets that circle the sun far beyond the orbit of Pluto.

The comets rain down on the earth; their impact raises enough debris into the atmosphere to block the sun's rays for months, years, or centuries. Temperatures fall and plant and animal species perish. According to the record in the rocks the next catastrophe will not occur for at least another 13 million years.

Another theory proposes that a yet undiscovered tenth planet of our solar system, "Planet X," follows a sharply inclined elliptical orbit that intersects a disk of comets that lies beyond the orbit of Neptune. As Planet X passes through the disk, it dislodges comets and sends some of them hurtling toward Earth, with the same consequences as presumed in the Nemesis theory.

Other scientists, rejecting both the Nemesis and Planet X theories, favor a volcanic theory of extinction. Volcanic eruptions, as noted earlier, spew carbon dioxide into the air resulting in the greenhouse effect.

Perhaps both the extraterrestrial (Nemesis or Planet X) theory and the volcanic theory are right: The impact of comets may have caused volcanic eruptions.

THE CENOZOIC (RECENT LIFE) ERA

The Cenozoic is the most recent era, the one in which we live. Highlights of its 65 million years would certainly include the birth of the Alpine-Himalayan mountain system; the drift of continents to their present locations; the uplift of mountains around the perimeter of the Pacific; the development of the ice age; and the appearance of *Homo sapiens*. During these years the earth's surface was given the form familiar to us. Rivers in the western United States cut deep channels in rock to form magnificent gorges, such as that of the Grand Canyon. During the last million years of the Cenozoic, glaciers advanced and retreated over the continents, putting their finishing touches to the face of the land.

The Cenozoic is often called the Age of Mammals. Ranging from the surface waters of the seas to the highest mountain peaks, from dense forests to open plains, from the torrid tropics to the freezing Arctic, mammals made the whole earth their home. Showing remarkable adaptations in their teeth, limbs, and their sense organs, mam-

mals found food and safety in an amazing variety of habitats, including even the air, as demonstrated by the bats.

The Parade of Mammals

The diversity of mammalian life is reflected in the many groups that are familiar to us today. These animals had their origin in the primitive mammals of the Mesozoic, mentioned previously, which were on the average no bigger than a rat or mouse. Two lines of evolution developed from these early forms. One led to the *marsupials,* the pouched mammals, of which the American opossum of today is an example. Marsupials are found almost exclusively in Australia, where all the native mammals are pouched.

Another line of evolution led to the *placentals,* those animals that nourish their developing young internally through a common membrane, the placenta. In the placenta food and oxygen are passed from the bloodstream of the mother to the separate but adjacent bloodstream of the embryo. The placentals include the carnivores, the rodents, hoofed mammals, whales, primates, and some other groups.

The *carnivores,* or flesh-eating mammals, have claws and sharp teeth that fit them for their way of life. Included in this group are the popular animals of the zoo: cats (including the lions, tigers, leopards, lynxes, and jaguars), dogs, wolves, foxes, weasels, badgers, minks, ermines, ferrets, skunks, and otters.

One group of mammals returned to the seas. This group includes the whales, porpoises, and dolphins, who became totally adapted to the sea, never having to return to land. Their forelimbs have been modified to become finlike paddles. The hindlimbs are absent, and the tail is fishlike. The young are born alive and are nourished by milk from mammary glands, as are the young of other mammals. Included also in this group of mammals are the seals, sea lions, and walruses that are modified for an aquatic existence, but also must live partly on land.

The *rodents* are gnawing animals with two long chisel-like teeth at the front of each jaw. This group includes mice, rats, chipmunks, squirrels, woodchucks, muskrats, beavers, and porcupines.

The hoofed mammals include pigs, hippopotamuses, camels, sheep, goats, cattle, bison, giraffes, deer, and horses.

Humans Appear

The primates, which include monkeys, apes, and human beings, are distinguished by having large brains. Our knowledge of human evolution is incomplete because relatively few fossils of our immediate forerunners have been unearthed, and most of these are only fragments of skulls and limb bones. However, our knowledge is constantly increasing. This we do know: Modern humans appear to have been present on earth 40,000 years ago, humanlike creatures some 3 to 4 million years ago, and their prehuman ancestors perhaps 20 million years ago; today only one species of humans, *Homo sapiens,* exists.

In the last two decades finds of great significance were made in Africa. Outstanding in making these discoveries were Louis and Mary Leakey and their son Richard, who together uncovered evidence indicating that Africa was a place of major importance for human evolution.

The ancestry of humans has been subject to some misunderstanding. No *living* member of the apes is the ancestor of humans. Apes (as well as other primates) and humans had common ancestors, but the two lines separated 4 to 6 million years ago.

CHANGE GOES ON

From our knowledge of the past there is every reason to believe that change will go on. The geo-logic forces that have been shaping the earth for billions of years will continue to be active. New forms of life will emerge.

With the coming of humans to the earth a new force has been added—intelligence. With this intelligence humans have the power to change the earth in many ways. For the first time a species exists that can deliberately and consciously influence its own future evolution—or its own extinction.

IMPORTANT GENERALIZATIONS

The development of living things upon the earth has progressed from the very simple organisms to complex ones. Modern life developed from ancient life.

In general, the changes have been extremely slow.

Great changes have taken place in the physical appearance and conditions of the earth during its long history.

The physical changes have influenced the evolution of plant and animal forms.

Natural selection provides a mechanism for evolutionary change. It accounts for the adaptation of plants and animals to the environment.

Many plants and animals that once lived on the earth have entirely disappeared.

Fossils tell us many things about ancient animals and plants and about conditions on the earth in past ages. Fossils in rock formations reveal the sequence of life through the ages.

Scientists believe that the earth is about 4.6 billion years old and that the first forms of life appeared about 3.5 billion years ago.

There were living things in the seas long before they existed on the land.

Most biologists now believe that life originated on earth by a process of slow development from chemicals present in the primitive earth's atmosphere and seas, first to nonliving chemical systems, then to simple life forms.

Humans are newcomers; modern humans appeared only about 40,000 years ago.

Intelligence is a new factor in evolution today.

DISCOVERING FOR YOURSELF

1. Make a time line chart and arrange in order the important changes that occurred on the earth and to life on it through the ages.
2. Visit a museum, select one fossil, and try to determine how the organism may have become fossilized, and what present living things it may be related to. The museum description will be helpful.
3. Watch newspapers for accounts of fossil discoveries. Read the articles and apply the principles you have learned in this chapter to understanding the various implications of the newspaper stories.
4. Make a cast of an animal track.
5. Find out what fossil animals and plants have been found in your state. What do these fossils tell you about changes that have taken place in your state through the ages?
6. Investigate the theories that try to explain how evolution is caused.
7. Investigate theories that try to account for the beginning of life on earth.
8. Make a survey of and write a report on recent discoveries about the evolution of primates, including humans.
9. If possible visit an area where fossils are found. A local college or high school may be helpful.
10. Investigate theories that account for mass extinctions.

TEACHING "THE HISTORY OF LIFE"

The story of life on earth is written in its fossils. A museum trip to see fossils will provoke discussion and raise searching questions. Children sometimes bring fossils to school from gravel pits, quarries, and rock ledges; they bring pictures of fossils from magazines, newspapers, and advertisements. Frequently, newspapers tell about fossils that have been discovered in the local area.

Although in the study of ancient life there are not so many opportunities to experiment with materials as, for example, in the study of sound or electricity, there are many occasions to stress the types of problems that scientists tackle. For example, "Why did dinosaurs become extinct?" "How do we know that the climate has changed?" "What do we know about how the oceans were made?" "How can a plant or animal leave a print in hard rock?" "How did life start?"

There are many occasions for research reading, especially since there are countless numbers of good books for children on fossils and ancient life.[1]

There are also many opportunities to promote the use of scientific attitudes. For example, why must scientists use such words or phrases as, "it seems evident that," "many people believe," "evidence seems to show," "it may be," and "it is generally believed" in telling about the earth's past? The puzzling over clues of ancient life is a good place to stress the importance of holding conclusions tentatively and of searching for reliable evidence.

SOME BROAD CONCEPTS

Changes in the kinds of living things on the earth have been from the simple organisms to complex ones. Changes have been very slow.

Physical conditions on the earth have changed greatly through the ages.

Many animals and plants that once lived on the earth have become extinct.

Animals and plants of the past have left their records in rock.

Fossils tell us many things about past life and conditions on the earth.

The earth is very old.

FOR YOUNGER CHILDREN

Since the study of the nature and sequence of ancient life involves interpreting evidence, much of which is beyond the understanding of young children, our emphasis here is on something that children can touch, something that tells its own story—the fossil records of plants and animals. The most spectacular of fossils, the dinosaurs, excites children's imagination and helps them picture the different kinds of life in the past.

What Is a Fossil?

If possible, make available for examination by children some small fossils—leaf prints, shell prints, and so on. Ask them to examine these carefully to see what they can discover by using their senses. Feel them. Lift them. Look carefully at them. Tell what you think they are. "How do you think the prints got there?" "How could a print get into something hard like this?" Children share their ideas. "Could we make prints like this?" (see later suggestions in chapter). "Where do you think these came from?" "Can we find fossils near our school?" "Where should we look?"

What Were the Dinosaurs Like?

The most exciting fossils for children are the dinosaurs. Many museums, even small local ones, have examples or collections of dinosaurs. Give children time to examine the giant fossils and later an opportunity to tell about what they saw

[1]F. M. Branley, *Dinosaurs, Asteroids and Superstars: Why the Dinosaurs Disappeared* (New York: Crowell, 1982); H. R. Sattler, *Baby Dinosaurs* (New York: Lothrop, 1984); C. S. Sunal, "Inferring about Dinosaurs," *Science and Children* (November/December 1984); H. R. Sattler, *The Illustrated Dinosaur Dictionary* (New York: Lothrop, 1983); D. Cohen, *Monster Dinosaurs* (New York: Harper, 1983).

and to ask questions. Help them read the labels and explanations.

If a trip is not possible, or to supplement it, use pictures, books, and models of dinosaurs. Many models of dinosaurs are sold in toy stores. (Why should models of ancient man not be included in a display of dinosaur life?) Children may listen as descriptions of the giant animals are read, and discuss their ideas. Supplement the visit and the examination of pictures and models by a discussion of what "long ago" means. Start with children's ages, adult ages, how old their town is, and other ages that may be a basis on which to build the concept of long ago. This abstraction, like distances in space, is difficult for children (and teachers) to comprehend (see Chapter 12A, p. 363).

Other Problems for Younger Children

1. What can we tell by looking at a dinosaur skeleton?
2. What do fossils tell us?
3. What were the dinosaurs like?
4. How do we know about dinosaurs?
5. What happened to the dinosaurs?
6. What is a mammoth?
7. Do you think you will ever see a living dinosaur? Why?
8. Make up your own story about one of the dinosaurs.

FOR OLDER CHILDREN

What Fossils Can We Find?[2]

Finding fossils may be a first step in developing interest and arousing curiosity in children. Some fossils may be found in a "natural" state in many localities in rock and sand deposits. Many are to be found in large and small museums, and some can be discovered in the limestone of buildings in the community.

[2]C. L. Camp and F. Egan, "Hunting Fossils? Where Do You Look?" *Science and Children* (February 1981).

Children are interested in such questions as, "What kinds of fossils are found in our surroundings?" "How old are they?" "How were they formed?" "Are they like any plants or animals living today?" "What were their surroundings like when these animals lived?" "How do scientists find out answers to questions like these?" (See Chapter 12A, pp. 355–360.)

A nearby stone quarry, gravel pit, or ocean shore may be a good place to find fossils. Try to find a person who knows something about the place, and ask him or her to accompany you and the class if you plan a trip. Let students formulate questions to answer, and list things they might find. If it does not seem advisable for all students to go, certain interested ones may wish to take the trip and report to the class. (For other suggestions for field trips refer to Chapter 3.)

The museum trip also needs preplanning. If possible, obtain the services of a person at the museum to accompany the class as a guide. The guide can probably help you find any published material about fossils and early geology in your state. If students have collected fossils they may take them along to the museum for examination. The resource person can explain how to identify the specimens and will answer other questions. The museum or your local library may have a file of newspaper clippings describing local or state fossil discoveries. Frequently the museum's curator is willing to give the school some common fossils or duplicates of the collection. These gifts may be the beginning of a school fossil collection.

A trip to a museum, even a short one, can be of help to children in learning about the importance of fossils in learning about life in the past, about how bones are assembled and fit together, and about how scientists learn about the habits and "fleshy" appearance of fossil animals.

Limestone is formed under water from materials derived from the shells of marine animals. Sometimes their fossil remains are left in the rock. When it is used in buildings these small fossils can sometimes be observed.

How Are Casts and Molds Made?

Making a cast of a seashell may help students to understand better how fossils are formed. Place a layer of modeling clay in the bottom of a cardboard box. Press a clam shell into the clay to make a deep print. Carefully lift the shell out so that a clear print is left. Make a thick paste of plaster of Paris, add a little salt or vinegar to keep it from hardening too quickly, and pour the mixture into the shell print. When the paste hardens, you have a *cast* of the shell. Children should understand that a real fossil cast is made when the animal or plant makes a print of itself in mud or other soft material and then decays. The space is subsequently filled with material that later hardens, somewhat as the plaster of Paris did. Students can make a cast of the footprint of a pet dog or cat.

Making a print of a seashell will also help to develop the idea of how some fossils were formed. Make a thick paste of plaster of Paris. A milk carton can be used to hold the plaster. Cover some shells with a thin film of petroleum jelly to keep them from sticking, and cover them with the plaster. Let the plaster harden, then break it open to see the prints of the shells. It is important to compare this method of printmaking with the way in which real fossil prints were made. Such prints are called *molds* (see p. 356).

How Can We Make Models of Dinosaurs?

Dinosaurs are wonderful subjects for modeling, and students seem to like to model them in clay or in papier-mâché. If the models are to be successful from a scientific point of view they should be as nearly accurate as possible in structure and proportion details. If dinosaurs are to be placed in the natural habitat in which they were found, further study of text and pictures is necessary to ensure an accurate result. This is a sensible situation in which art and science may well make use of each other.

If various models are made to the same scale (including one of modern man) children will be able to compare their sizes more easily. The dimensions of some ancient animals seem either unbelievable or incomprehensible to children. Many children have no very clear idea of how high, for example, 30 feet is. Try measuring some of these proportions, and attempt to decide whether the animal could fit into the classroom, see over the school building, stretch the length of the corridor, or fit into the principal's office.[3]

In addition to model making, children may enjoy drawing large pictures of ancient birds, amphibians, mammals, and plants, and organizing the pictures to show important ideas.

Other Problems for Older Children

1. How are layers of rocks formed in the earth?
2. How does sedimentary rock provide us with clues to past life on earth?
3. How can we tell the age of a fossil?
4. What were the earliest animals and plants like?
5. How have living things changed through the ages?
6. Why is the work of paleontologists important?
7. Where are some of the large deposits of fossils in North America?
8. What changes would a water-living plant or animal need to make in order to live on land?
9. How did life begin on the earth?
10. Why are so many fossils found in the La Brea tar pits in California?
11. How have horses changed over time?

RESOURCES TO INVESTIGATE WITH CHILDREN

1. The local, state, college, or university museums, to look at fossils collected nearby. Sometimes such institutions lend collections to schools.

[3] G. O. Blough, *Discovering Dinosaurs* (New York: McGraw-Hill, 1960).

2. Newspapers and magazines, for pictures and accounts of recent fossil discoveries.
3. A place where the highway cuts through a hill, to observe layers of soil and various rock formations (see Chapters 6A and 6B).
4. The state geologist and publications from local geological societies, to learn about local land forms, rocks, fossils, and mineral deposits.
5. A local individual who makes a hobby of rock or fossil collecting.
6. Gravel pits, beaches, and other places, to yield fossils of different kinds.
7. Local environment, to find club mosses and horsetails, examples of present-day plants that are now very small but were once of huge proportions.

PREPARING TO TEACH

1. Make a "teaching collection" of pictures that can be used in solving the problems in this chapter, and make brief plans about how to use them.
2. Select one of the "Other Problems" listed for younger or older children in this chapter and make a long-range plan for developing it with children (see Part I for suggestions).
3. Try to make a small collection of fossils that you can use in teaching. Consult *Hunting For Fossils: A Guide to Finding Fossils in All Fifty States* by M. Murray (Macmillan, 1967).

ECOLOGY, ENERGY, AND THE ENVIRONMENT

More than a century ago, an Indian chief named Sealth wrote these words in a letter to President Franklin Pierce: "What is man without the beasts? If all the beasts were gone, men would die from great loneliness of spirit, for whatever happens to the beasts also happens to man. All things are connected. Whatever befalls the earth, befalls the sons of the earth."

That land is a community is the basic concept of ecology, but that land is to be loved and respected is an extension of ethics.

ALDO LEOPOLD

A lily pond, so the French riddle goes, contains a single leaf. Each day the number of leaves doubles—two leaves the second day, four the third, eight the fourth, and so on. Question: If the pond is completely full on the thirtieth day, when is it half full? Answer: On the twenty-ninth day. The global lily pond in which four billion of us live may already be half full.

LESTER R. BROWN, THE TWENTY-NINTH DAY:
ACCOMMODATING HUMAN NEEDS TO THE EARTH'S RESOURCES,
W. W. NORTON, 1978

SPACESHIP EARTH

We travel together, passengers on a little spaceship, dependent on its vulnerable reserves of air and soil; all committed for our safety to its security and peace; preserved from annihilation only by the care, and the work, and, I will say, the love we give our fragile craft.

ADLAI STEVENSON

The concept of Earth as a spaceship is perhaps one of the most significant achievements of the Space Age. From the moon we view our planet whole, a tiny blue-white sphere in space. A closer view reveals that life on this sphere is confined to a very thin layer, only 13 miles thick, of air, water, and soil. We call this sun-bathed zone the *biosphere* or *ecosphere*.

Until comparatively recently we have regarded the earth and its bounties as limitless. The earth-spaceship concept compels us to recognize that the air, water, soil, food, and available energy resources are limited and perishable.

Spaceship Earth is a system with many inter-connected transactions of materials and energy. The wastes of animals are food for soil bacteria; the excretions of bacteria provide minerals for green plants; plants are food for animals. What happens in forests, fields, and lakes eventually affects the environment of the entire earth, its atmosphere, its soil and its waters, and consequently all living things. Our planet is a closed system in which indefinite expansion or exploitation of its resources would be disastrous to all life, including all human beings.

As Norman Cousins has stated so precisely:

The real meaning of the expedition to the moon, if it is written correctly, is that the conditions required to sustain human life are so rare in the universe as to constitute the greatest achievement of creation. Yet the prime beneficiaries of this bounty are now engaged in converting their habitat into a wasteland, not less uncongenial to life than the surface of the moon. The biggest challenge of all, therefore, is to prove that intelligent life can exist on Earth.[1]

[1]"The Search for Intelligent Life," *Saturday Review,* August 9, 1969.

It is the responsibility of all engaged in teaching, at all levels, of all subjects, in school and out of school, to meet this challenge with planned programs of environmental education.

A DEADLY DOWNPOUR

A uniquely modern postindustrial blight, acid rain is as widespread as the winds that disperse it. In the northeast U.S., and in Canada and northern Europe, it is reducing lakes, rivers and ponds to eerily crystalline, lifeless bodies of water, killing off everything from indigenous fish stocks to microscopic vegetation. It is suspected of spiriting away mineral nutrients from the soil in which forests thrive. Its corrosive assault on buildings and water systems costs millions of dollars annually.... In New York's Adirondack Mountains, 212 of the 2,200 lakes and ponds are acidic, dead and fishless. Acid rain has killed aquatic life in at least 10% of New England's 226 largest fresh-water lakes....[2]

Acid rain is but one of a number of the diseases of the biosphere that are shocking us into the realization that a pollutant-producing society can so diminish the quality of its environment that life itself is endangered. In recent years we have been subjected to other environmental shocks: brownouts and blackouts, closed gasoline stations, shortages of oil and gas needed to heat homes and power industry, the finding of cancer-producing chemicals in drinking water, and mass starvation in some areas of the earth.

More and more, concerned people are asking, What is wrong? How did it get that way? What should be done? What can I do? What will it cost? Can we do it in time? These are questions we must ask about all the resources that make Earth the planet with life on it.

THE ENVIRONMENTAL CRISIS

Only within the moment of time represented by the present century has one species—man—acquired

significant power to alter the nature of his world. *During the past quarter century this power has not only increased to one of disturbing magnitude, but it has changed in character. The most alarming of man's assaults upon the environment is the contamination of air, earth, rivers and sea with dangerous and even lethal materials.*

RACHEL CARSON

The crisis that faces us today is deeper than the threatened depletion of a particular resource, the loss of some areas of unspoiled nature, or even the serious question of feeding ourselves adequately. What is the nature of the environmental crisis?

1. The advance of technology, which has brought us high-powered automobiles, chemical fertilizers, plastics, synthetic fibers, and electric power has reached a level where its processes and products threaten the earth's environment. "We are in an environmental crisis because the means by which we use the ecosphere to produce wealth are destructive of the ecosphere itself."[3]

2. The environmental crisis is global in nature. The oceans and atmosphere have no boundaries as they distribute life-destroying pollutants to people everywhere. The whole earth is everybody's environment. We can no longer escape an undesirable environment by packing up and moving on.

3. We are in a crisis because time for taking the necessary corrective measures for survival seems to be running out. How many years or decades do we have to effect a reversal or slowing of the current downhill slide to avert disaster? How much contamination can the oceans accept before they die? And if the oceans die, and with them the oxygen-producing algae, how long can life exist anywhere?

4. We are in a crisis today because economists, legislators, manufacturers, city dwellers, and farmers do not fully understand the nature of the human being's relation to the total environment. Because our schools, in the decades when the crisis has been growing, have not engaged in vital, imaginative programs of environmental education. Because the concept of "exploiting nature" still prevails. Because the ethic that we are the *custodians* rather than the owners of the earth's resources and that each generation

[2]Frederic Golden, *Time,* December 6, 1982.

[3]B. Commoner, *The Closing Circle* (New York: Knopf, 1972).

has the obligation to pass this inheritance on to the future is not part of our code. Because many still believe that unlimited growth is a good thing. Because we have not yet earnestly gotten into the business of planetary planning.

ECOLOGY: KEY TO CONSERVATION

From Nature's chain, whatever link you strike
Tenth, or ten-thousandth, breaks the chain alike.
ALEXANDER POPE

The understanding of *ecology,* the study of the interrelationships of living things with each other and of living things with their physical environment, is the key to sound environmental practices.

Barry Commoner, noted biologist and ecologist, defines ecology in an informal set of "laws":

1. *Everything is connected to everything else.*
2. *Everything must go somewhere.*
3. *Nature knows best.*
4. *There is no such thing as a free lunch.*

As you read the remainder of this chapter, look for illustrations of these laws.

The diet of Eskimos in their natural surroundings consists largely of seal meat, fish, and birds. All these food sources are ultimately dependent on tiny plants that live in the sea. Let us see how: The seals and birds feed on fish. The fish feed on smaller fish. Little fish feed on copepods, tiny relatives of shrimp. Copepods feed on microscopic one-celled plants, called diatoms, which live near the surface of the sea. Diatoms are green plants that are able to make their own food by the process of photosynthesis (see pp. 277–278). Hence the diet of an Eskimo depends on diatoms.

This is a long chain—a chain of "who eats whom." Ecologists call it a *food chain,* and the elimination of any link in it would mean the elimination of the Eskimo. If, for example, an increase in ultraviolet radiation resulting from the depletion of ozone in the atmosphere were to destroy the diatoms, it would inevitably mean the

A food chain: who eats whom.

elimination of the Eskimos in their natural environment.

Consider another food chain, one closer to home. In a field, green plants are eaten by meadow mice, which, in turn, are preyed upon by hawks. The green plants are the *producers*: They manufacture the food. The meadow mouse is a *consumer*; it feeds directly on the plants, so it is a *first-order consumer*. The hawk in this food chain is a *second-order consumer* (see illustration on this page).

Another simple chain also begins with a field of grass—the producer. Cattle feeding on the grass are the first-order consumers, and people eating the cattle are the second-order consumers.

The concept of producer and consumer in the world of nature is a helpful one, because it reminds us that food is not manufactured in canneries or frozen-food factories. When we say that a green plant is a producer, we mean that it takes simple nonliving material—water, carbon dioxide, and minerals—from its environment and rearranges the atoms in these substances to put together the organic molecules of food needed

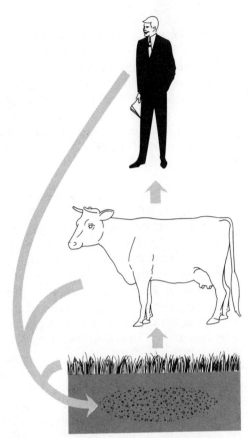

Grass is the producer, cattle the first-order consumer, and man the second-order consumer in this food chain.

for its own nutrition. (It is a mistake to call the minerals we use to enrich soil "plant food"; minerals are essentially raw materials that a plant incorporates in the food it makes.)

The food-making process that sustains the chain of life is dependent on the nonliving environment—the physical environment—of carbon dioxide in the air, and water and minerals in the soil. To these materials must be added *energy*, the energy of the sun that is incorporated into every food molecule that is put together in the green leaf "factory." The sun energy thus drives the chain from producer to consumer.

Other features of the physical environment—

temperature, space, gravity, wind, oxygen, together with those previously named—are important influences in the total living of all the organisms in the chain.

Eventually death overtakes the plants and meadow mice that survive the who-eats-whom process; even the predatory hawk succumbs. The return of the tissues of these organisms to the soil is the work of the microscopic bacteria and fungi of decay. They, too, are consumers, but because of their unique role, it is helpful to call them *decomposers*.

Thus the food chain is continuous, requiring a flow of energy and a recycling of materials from producer back to producer. Food is the medium through which the materials needed for the construction of body tissues and the energy for life processes are passed along the chain.

It is important to note that the sun energy that drives the chain is a one-way flow from the constant solar supply, whereas carbon, water, and minerals are used over and over.

Food Webs

We have elected so far to construct an artificially simple chain. In the field we started with, the green plants are also eaten by rabbits and insects, which join the mice as first-order consumers. The insects may be eaten by toads, the toads by snakes, the snakes by hawks. The rabbit, too, may be preyed upon by hawks. And the field mouse may be eaten by a snake. The simple food chain begins to branch to become a *food web*, which is much closer to the true pattern of nature (see p. 390).

The web becomes more tangled when we include the many interconnected food chains inside the bed of soil that support the plant life above. The activities of such organisms as bacteria, fungi, algae, protozoans, worms, and insects on bits of leaves, bark, and other dead organic matter release the minerals essential for green plants.

Implicit in food chains and webs is a natural system of checks and balances. If for some reason

A simple food web suggests the complex interrelationships of living things.

be consumed by the meadow mice, or all green life there will be destroyed. There must be more mice than will be eaten by hawks; otherwise the hawks will finish the mice in one last meal.

If we express the quantity of living matter in this field in pounds we might find that a half a ton of grass supports 50 pounds (about 25 kilograms) of mice, which in turn supports 10 pounds (about 5 kilograms) of hawks. (In each step we are also assuming that enough individuals survive to reproduce a new generation.) A pyramid of numbers with a broad base of vegetation at the bottom and hawks at the apex summarizes the quantitative interrelationships in this small community. In the sea 100,000 pounds of marine algae must be transferred through the food chain to produce a single pound of codfish.

The reason for a pyramid organization in nature is that only part of the energy is passed along at each step in the chain. The remainder is dissipated as heat by the oxidation requirements of the primary producers (the plants) and the consumers (herbivores and carnivores). Raymond L. Lindeman, ecologist at Yale University, described this as the "10 percent law," which states that only about 10 percent of the energy at any one level can be transferred to the next level in a food chain. Thus it takes 10 energy units of grain to produce only 1 energy unit of chicken or cow.

Obviously the shorter the chain the greater the efficiency from the standpoint of energy flow. It is no accident that people in densely populated countries such as India and China feed primarily on plant foods. This is the shortest food chain; in this way a given area of land can support the largest population of people. The introduction of cattle in the chain between plant and human reduces the efficiency by a factor of 10 to 20.

Ecologists have constructed pyramids for large regions called *biomes,* which are communities of living things associated with a particular kind of vegetation typical of the area. The tundra of the Arctic, the tropical rain forest, and the grassland are examples of biomes. A grassland or prairie pyramid and a pond pyramid are shown in the illustration on page 391.

the field mice multiply rapidly, their numbers will be diminished by the predation of hawks, or by disease, or by crowding effects that reduce reproduction and thus slow down or stop multiplication. Humans, however, can disturb the balance. The killing of hawks by farmers, for example, may result in an increase in meadow mice (and other rodents) harmful to their crops.

Pyramid of Numbers

The food chain tells us who eats whom, but it does not tell us enough. We must also know "how much." Apply this question to the simple plant–meadow mouse–hawk chain but disregard the many other strands of the food web in a field. There must be more plants in the field than will

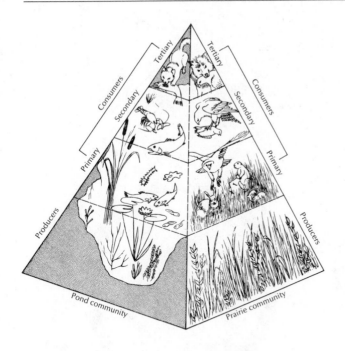

Pyramid of numbers in a pond community and a prairie community. Each level depends on the broader one under it for a supply of food. *(From Biology by Johnson et al; © 1972 by Holt, Rinehart and Winston, Inc. Reprinted by permission of Holt, Rinehart and Winston.)*

NATURAL RECYCLING SYSTEMS

On planet Earth we enjoy the advantages of an automatic self-renewing natural environment of water, air, and soil. Evolving over billions of years of Earth's history, the environment is in tune with the plants and animals that inhabit it. Barring a human-made ecological disaster, the environment can keep itself going indefinitely as long as sun energy continues to flow into the earth (see pp. 441–442).

The Water Cycle

The water cycle is one of our planet's great recycling systems. Water evaporates into the atmosphere from the surface of the ocean and other bodies of water, from soil, and the leaves of plants. In the atmosphere it is held as invisible water vapor, which under certain conditions forms clouds. The water in clouds falls back to the surface of the earth as rain or snow, eventually working its way back to lakes, seas, and oceans and thus completing the cycle. The process continues without end (see p. 222).

Here again, as in the food chain, it is sun energy that drives the cycle (see p. 389) and does the work of lifting water "uphill" through the lower atmosphere so that it can run downhill. When humans tap the downhill flow for their cities' water systems they are using solar energy in its natural form.

The water cycle, then, circulates water from oceans, seas, and lakes to land areas. It also serves as a water purification system because when water evaporates to become water vapor it leaves behind minerals, mud, and debris. The water that falls from the clouds is relatively pure and clean.

The Carbon Dioxide–Oxygen Cycle

The carbon dioxide–oxygen cycle is driven by the complementary life processes of green plants and animals. In the process of food making, green

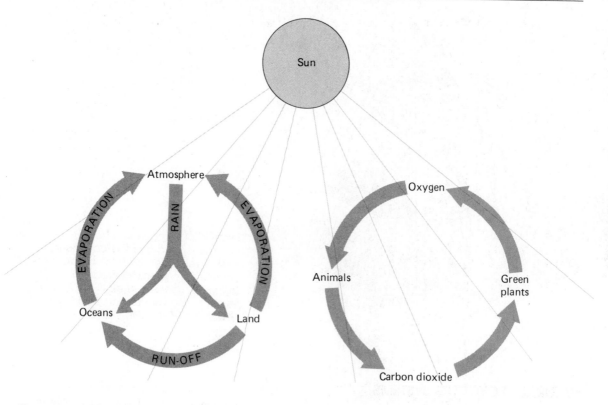

The water cycle.

The oxygen-carbon dioxide cycle.

plants take in carbon dioxide from the atmosphere and, with energy derived from sunlight, use it in the manufacture of starches, sugars, and other foods. The food-manufacturing process also results in the release of oxygen by plants. Animals consume plants and take in oxygen. The "burning" of food by animals (and also by plants themselves, which must use part of the food they make to grow and maintain their living structures) results in the release of carbon dioxide, thereby making it available again for the food-making process in green plants. A similar exchange between plants and animals takes place in ponds, in lakes, and in the oceans; however, the oxygen and carbon dioxide there are dissolved in the water.

Bacteria also participate in the carbon dioxide–oxygen cycle. When plants and animals die, bacteria of decay break down their tissues, using them as food. In releasing energy from the food, bacteria take in oxygen and release carbon dioxide.

Some bacteria that live deep in soils and in the mud of marshes and oceans have the unique capacity to live and grow in the absence of oxygen. This is fortunate for us because these microbes (called *anaerobic bacteria*) decompose organic matter and recycle valuable minerals (nitrogen, for example) that would otherwise be lost in the depths of the soils and the oceans.

There is evidence that the oxygen in the atmosphere was originally released there by early plant life. The free oxygen made possible the evolution of higher plants and animals. Today the supply of oxygen in the atmosphere is continually replenished by the process of photosynthesis, which, as we have seen, also removes carbon dioxide from the air.

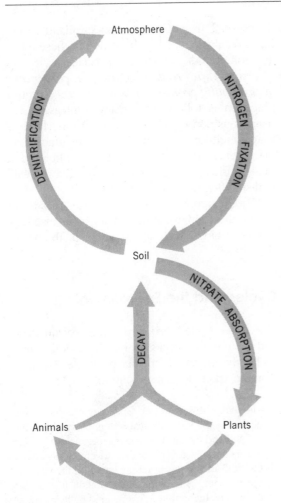

The nitrogen cycle.

The Nitrogen Cycle

Nitrogen moves in a complex cycle through the atmosphere, soil, and living things. It is an essential element for life, entering into combination with oxygen, carbon, hydrogen, and other elements in the construction of the amino acids, which are used in thousands of structures and vital processes in plants and animals. Proteins, nucleic acids, vitamins, enzymes, and hormones are all made of nitrogen-containing molecules.

Nitrogen is plentiful in the atmosphere, com-

prising about 79 percent of it, but cannot be taken in by plants in this free gaseous form. Atmospheric nitrogen becomes available to plants only when it is combined with other elements to form soluble nitrogen compounds, notably nitrates. This process of *nitrogen fixation* is the work of certain bacteria that live on the roots of clover, beans, peas, and alfalfa, and of free-living bacteria and fungi in the soil. Other soil bacteria liberate nitrates from plant and animal remains as they break down their tissues.

Plants absorb nitrates from the soil through their roots, and build the nitrogen in them into amino acids, which form the basis for the protein compounds necessary for their growth and functioning. Animals eat the plants and use the amino acids to make the kind of protein that they need. In nature, animal wastes and decomposed animal remains return nitrogen compounds to the soil and thus make them available again for the plant world. Some of the soil bacteria break down nitrates and release nitrogen to the air. So the cycle is complete.

Eutrophication

The web of life in a body of fresh water is self-sustaining. Algae provide food and oxygen for small organisms, which are eaten by frogs, fish, and other large forms. The animals return carbon dioxide to the water; algae use carbon dioxide in photosynthesis to make more food. Bacteria of decay break down animal waste and return inorganic nitrates and phosphates for the growth of fresh algae.

Under natural conditions the growth of algae in a pond or lake is limited by the amount of phosphorus available in the pond water. An excess of phosphorus may trigger an algal "bloom," a large, dense growth of algae. As the thickness of the layers of algae increases, less light reaches the lower parts of the growth. Any additional growth dies quickly. The decay bacteria that feed and multiply on the dead algae use up available oxygen for their own respiration, thereby reducing

Roots of black-eyed peas with well-developed nodules of nitrogen-fixing bacteria. The peas are grown in rotation with other crops and then plowed into the soil, adding needed nitrogen and organic matter. *(Courtesy of U.S. Dept. of Agriculture, Soil Conservation Service.)*

the oxygen supply of the pond. Then the *aerobic* (oxygen-using) *bacteria* die, since they too need and cannot get oxygen. Fish and other organisms die. The normal freshwater ecological cycle collapses and is replaced by an *anoxic* (without oxygen) *system*. This process is called *eutrophication*.

During recent years the volume of algae in many lakes has increased greatly for two reasons: (1) the increased use of phosphates, both in fertilizers in agriculture and in home and industrial use in detergents, increases the amount of this substance in rivers and lakes. (2) Farmers are using increased millions of tons of commercially manufactured nitrate fertilizer to restore soil fertility and increase agricultural productivity. The

widespread use of nitrates on farmland sometimes results in an excessive runoff of these nitrogen compounds into streams and lakes.

Thus it is just as easy to disrupt a community by promoting growth as it is by curbing it. Eutrophication is followed by many unpleasant and dangerous consequences: making formerly clear water smelly, muddy, undrinkable; the gradual replacement of desirable fish with less edible ones; massive die-offs resulting in beaches littered with foul-smelling algae and dead fish.

What happens to a lake or stream that is overburdened with too much fertilizer can also happen on a larger scale to the ocean or the whole biosphere.

Cycles and the Environment

The water cycle, carbon dioxide–oxygen cycle, and the nitrogen cycle are but three of the many cycles that make our planet habitable. To quote from an article by Barry Commoner:

> Altogether this vast web of biological interactions generates the very physical system in which we live: the soil and the air. It maintains the purity of surface waters and, by governing the movement of water in the soil and its evaporation into the air, regulates the weather. This is the environment. It is a place created by living things, maintained by living things, and through the marvelous reciprocities of biological evolution is essential to the support of living things.[4]

THE ENDURANCE OF RESOURCES

Inexhaustible Resources

The resources of the earth are of four kinds: inexhaustible, renewable, nonrenewable, and new and to-be-developed. Some resources we shall

[4]B. Commoner, "Damaged Global Fabric," in *Our World in Peril*, eds. S. Novick and D. Cottrell (Greenwich, Conn.: Fawcett, 1971).

have always. These are air, sunlight, and water. They are unique in that much as we may use them they will continue in abundance. Water is such a resource. As long as the oceans cover the earth we shall have water. Lifted (with the help of the sun's warming rays) from the ocean as vapor that eventually falls as rain, water is available for agriculture, industry, and for our personal needs. Dropping from falls, water can be used as a source of power. Limitless though it is, water presents some of our most pressing problems of conservation. These are mainly problems of its quality, distribution, and use, as we shall see later in this chapter.

Although we include air and water as inexhaustible resources, we are not excluding the grim possibility that we may diminish the quality of these resources beyond the point of no return. *Breathable* air and *drinkable* water are not necessarily inexhaustible.

Sunlight is the source of all our energy, except for nuclear energy from radioactive atoms on earth. Water power results, as we have just seen, from lifting of water with the help of the sun's energy. Nonrenewable fossil fuels, such as coal and oil, are the products of the sun's radiant energy stored by plants in past times. Solar energy can be used immediately in solar cells, which convert sunlight directly into electricity, or in solar furnaces to make steam and in solar panels for home heating and cooling (see pp. 491–495). Astronomers assure us that the sun will continue to be our powerhouse for at least a few billion years more.

Renewable Resources

Renewable resources are our soils, vegetation, animal life, and freshwater supplies. These are the resources that may be maintained indefinitely under wise management. It is to these resources that the past efforts of conservation have been mainly directed.

The renewable resources are dependent one on the other. Crops will not grow in soil without

water. Animals play an important role in the life cycle of many plants and vice versa—we need mention here only the pollinating work of the bees. Forests and grasslands store water and also prevent harmful rain runoff. Plant cover provides essential protection of the soil against erosion by water and wind. Weaken one link and the whole life-supporting chain is imperiled.

Humans are in a key position to keep this chain in working balance. The fields can continue to produce healthy crops each year if we maintain and improve the fertility of the soil. Forests can be managed to assure a perpetual yield of wood, a steady flow of water, and a constant source of pleasure. Game and other animal life can be helped to renew itself and to continue its role in the web of life.

Nonrenewable Resources

Nonrenewable resources are those that can be used up. Such materials as coal, oil, natural gas, metals, and most minerals are of this nature. When copper is mined, new copper will not "grow" in its place. When a lump of coal is burned, it is gone forever as a burnable material. All of our conventional fuels, except wood, fall into the category of resources that become unavailable once they are used.

Land as open space may be regarded as a nonrenewable resource. Once covered with concrete and steel it is "gone" as land for growing things. Wilderness once destroyed is a nonrenewable resource. The 2 million acres of the magnificent primeval redwoods of California have been reduced to $\frac{1}{16}$ of a million acres.

Government, industry, and consumer groups are tackling the problem of the conservation of our mineral and fuel resources in a number of ways: by finding new sources of material, by seeking new materials, by minimizing waste, and by learning how to use materials more effectively. Geologists are prospecting in every corner of the globe for new supplies. When deposits near the surface of the earth are depleted, men dig deeper into the earth. Wells have been drilled under the ocean to tap the petroleum and sulfur found there. Chemists have found ways to extract magnesium and bromine from ocean waters in commercial quantity and at a marketable price. Scientists are learning how to utilize low-grade ores (such as taconite, with its relatively small percentage of iron) as higher grades become scarcer. But since large amounts of energy are required to dig deeper or to concentrate dilute sources, energy itself, not the materials, limits the economic value of such procedures. Large amounts of energy are needed to extract iron and magnesium from the ocean, and this is very expensive.

Further discussion of nonrenewable resources will be found in the section "The Limits to Growth."

New and To-Be-Developed Resources

A century ago crude oil was considered a useless substance. A half century ago some scientists were saying that the atom could never be split. Yet what enormous sources of energy we have been able to release from the molecules of gasoline and from the nuclei of atoms! New resources will be added as skilled and creative scientists and engineers discover uses for materials that may be of little or no value today, and as we tap the vast supply of energy provided by the sun. Perhaps, also, we shall be able to add to our resources those of Earth's moon or the planets.

THE LIMITS TO GROWTH

How long can the world's population and industrialization continue to grow? This is the question to which a team of researchers of the Club of Rome addressed itself. The Club of Rome grew out of a 1968 meeting of 30 individuals from 10 countries—scientists, educators, economists, industrialists, and others. A research team of the club investigated five major trends of global concern: accelerating industrialization, rapid population growth, widespread malnutrition, depletion of nonrenewable resources, and the deteriorating environment. These were the conclusions of the study:

1. If the present growth trends in world population, industrialization, pollution, food production, and resource depletion continue unchanged, the limits to growth on this planet will be reached sometime within the next 100 years. The most probable results will be a rather sudden and uncontrollable decline in both population and industrial capacity.
2. It is possible to alter these growth trends and to establish a condition of ecological and economical stability that is sustainable far into the future. The state of global equilibrium could be designed so that the basic material needs of each person on earth are satisfied and each person has an equal opportunity to realize his individual potential.
3. If the world's people decide to strive for the second outcome rather than the first, the sooner they begin working to attain it, the greater will be their chances of success.[5]

In the years following the original report, the Club of Rome modified its analysis and conclusions somewhat.[6] The new approach called not for no-growth but for *selective growth* aimed at speeding up the developments of the poorer countries while slowing down that of industrialized ones.

Critics of the report[7] contend that industrial nations now face a historic change: Economic growth is no longer accompanied by increased

---

[5]D. H. Meadows, D. L. Meadows, J. Randers, and W. W. Behrnes, III, *The Limits to Growth: A Report for the Club of Rome's Project on the Predicament of Mankind* (New York: Universe Books, 1972).

[6]M. Mesarovic and E. Pestel, *Mankind at the Turning Point: The Second Report to the Club of Rome* (New York: Dutton, 1974).

[7]E. D. Larson, M. H. Ross and R. H. Williams, "Beyond the Era of Materials," *Scientific American* (June 1986).

consumption of basic materials such as cotton, wool, steel, and rubber. Causes of the change include the substitution of one material for another, design changes in products that increase efficiency of materials use, the saturation of markets, and shifting consumer preferences.

Proposals for averting the dangers to the environment implicit in the report are varied and many. Included are replacing chemically based farming (using pesticides and chemical fertilizers) with organic farming; restricting the petrochemical industry so that its processes and products are replaced with ones less dangerous to the environment; expanding the railroads and mass transportation facilities to lower the dependence on cars and trucks; and replacing nonrenewable energy sources (discussed in the next sections) with renewable solar energy systems.

Others advocate the conserving of resources; the recycling of nonrenewable materials; the use of biomass; and tapping the energy from the oceans, the wind, and the heat within the earth. These are discussed in the following sections.

The Population Explosion

A major concern is the growth of population, threatening our planet with increasing hunger and starvation, depletion of available fuels, destruction of natural resources, spreading pollution, extinction of valuable plant and animal species, and social upheaval. World population first reached 1 billion in the early 1800s. By 1930, about 100 years later, it doubled. Forty-five years later, it doubled again to reach 4 billion. By the end of this century world population will top 6 billion, by 2025, 8 billion.

Most of the projected increase will occur in the emerging nations and will be concentrated in cities already overburdened with their present populations. With shortcomings in housing, water, sewage, transportation, and employment opportunities, these urban centers are now in a crisis situation. And as the cities sprawl, industrial and residential uses and speculation are taking other valuable farmland. A number of governments in Africa, Asia, and Latin America are now sponsoring programs of family planning to slow population growth.

Can we defuse the population bomb in time?

ENERGY IN THE BIOSPHERE

The graph on page 398 shows the changes in the sources and the amounts of energy consumed annually in the United States since 1850, with projections to the year 2000. The energy unit used here is the *quad*, which is one quadrillion BTUs (British Thermal Units), equivalent to the energy contained in 8 billion gallons of gasoline, a year's supply for 10 million automobiles. It is evident that we have become more and more dependent on oil. The Arab embargo of oil exports to the United States in 1973 painfully brought our dependence on foreign oil to the attention of American consumers as they waited in long lines at gasoline pumps and watched as the price of gasoline and home heating oil escalated. Experts estimate that our own resources of conventional oil will be seriously depleted by the year 2000. This will happen despite the finding of oil in Alaska and in offshore wells. Leveling off of oil production abroad will occur in the North Sea fields, in the Soviet Union, and within a few decades, in the Arab countries.

Our supplies of coal are immense. But coal burning produces emissions that injure our lungs and contribute to acid rain. The burning of coal, and other fossil fuels, adds carbon dioxide to the earth's atmosphere that in sufficient concentration may create the dreaded greenhouse effect (see Index).

Other sources of energy (to be discussed presently) may be slow in coming and costly; some are accompanied by unpleasant and dangerous side effects.

There are no simple answers to the current energy problems. Experts agree, however, that *the*

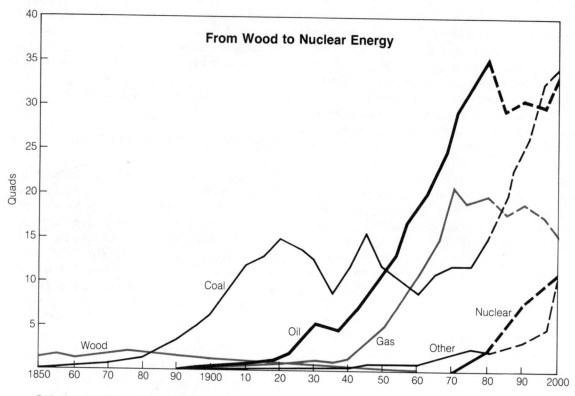

From Wood to Nuclear Energy

Quads

Coal

Wood

Oil

Gas

Nuclear

Other

1850 60 70 80 90 1900 10 20 30 40 50 60 70 80 90 2000

Projections from Energy Information Administration

quickest, least expensive, and least vulnerable energy option today is to use less by being more efficient. As Amory B. Lovins of the Friends of the Earth says,[8] "Like someone who cannot fill the bathtub because the hot water keeps running out, we need not a bigger water heater but a plug. Cost-effective plugs can double the efficiency of industrial motors, triple that of lights, quadruple that of household appliances, quintuple that of cars, and increase that of buildings tenfold or more by making them so heat tight (but well ventilated) that they need little heating or cooling."

In summary, the energy problems of earth are

1. How long will our energy resources last?
2. Can new sources of energy be developed?

[8]National Geographic Special Report, *Energy,* February 1981.

3. Can energy consumption continue to grow without an accompanying deterioration of the air, water, and land of the biosphere?
4. To what extent can limiting population growth and conserving resources meet the challenge of energy depletion?

Let's turn our attention first to the original source of energy, the sun.

Solar Energy

The sun is the ultimate source of almost all the energy now used in the earth's biosphere. Radiant energy of the sun is captured by chlorophyll in plants and stored in the food molecules manufactured there in the process of photosynthesis. Later the stored energy is released by plants and animals that eat the plants required in their life processes. When you pedal your bicycle along a country road your muscles are releasing sun energy, trapped by photosynthetic plants perhaps only weeks or months ago and incorporated into the breakfast you ate this morning: the starch recently made in a corn or wheat plant, the milk from the cow that ate grass a few days before.

When primitive people learned to use fire to keep themselves warm they took the first step toward making use of an energy resource—wood—outside their own bodies. Wood, a product of plant life, is also a sun-energized resource.

Later in history the windmill and waterwheel were invented to supply extra power. Here too, the source of energy was the sun, the driver of the "weather machine" that keeps air and water in motion.

Only in the last 125 years have we made important use of the fossil fuels—coal, oil, and natural gas. These had their origin in ancient plant and animal remains, whose molecules were first put together with the help of the sun's radiation.

It is important to note that fossilization concentrated ancient solar energy. A drop of oil is concentrated sunlight. It is no wonder we have prospered through the use of fossil fuels and would find it difficult to go on a "diet" of plain sunlight again.

In Chapter 15A we will discuss a number of devices already in operation that convert solar radiation into useful energy: solar engines, solar houses, solar collectors, and batteries of solar cells (see pp. 491–495). Advocates of one proposal for harnessing solar energy on a large scale argue that if the sunlight in 14 percent of the western desert regions of the United States were collected by special solar cells it would provide the amount of additional energy needed between now and 1990. The Alabama Power Company dedicated a solar power plant in 1987, the first large-scale facility to use the thin-film technology that now powers solar calculators and watches. Solar cells that convert sunlight directly into electrical energy are already operating on satellites.

Biomass

The devices and techniques just described make direct use of solar radiation. Another source of solar energy is *biomass,* which includes the many living or derived-from-living materials such as wood, wood wastes, agricultural products, algae, animal wastes, and municipal wastes. In contrast to the fossil fuels—coal, oil, and natural gas—biomass is infinitely renewable, since it has its origin in green plants energized by the sun in the process of photosynthesis.

Of course, the use of biomass for energy is not new. As the graph on page 398 indicates, wood accounted for almost all of the energy supply in the nineteenth-century United States. A reversion to this ancient source of energy is evidenced by the recent rush to wood stoves and fireplaces.

For many years sugarcane mills have burned the cellulose wastes (called *bagasse*), left over after sugar has been extracted from the stalks, to provide steam to run the machinery of the mills. The excess steam is also used to generate electricity. At this time the "Big Island" of Hawaii is more than halfway to energy self-sufficiency through the production of electricity obtained by burning bagasse from its sugarcane in power generators, thus decreasing markedly the island's dependency on costly imported oil.

Instead of *burning* biomass, some processes *convert* it into concentrated fuel in the form of solids, liquids, or gases. Large-scale fermentation of cane sugar into ethanol (ethyl alcohol) is practiced in Brazil. The ethanol when mixed with gasoline produces a useful fuel for autos, known as gasohol. Thousands of gasoline stations in the United States sell gasohol; here the ethanol is derived principally from the fermentation of corn, rather than sugar.

Garbage is one renewable resource that we have too much of. More than 100 cities have built or are building resource-recovery plants to use organic garbage to generate fuel and at the same time to dispose of their municipal wastes. At Freshkills, on Staten Island, a borough of New York City, bacteria are turning old buried garbage in the world's largest garbage dump into methane (natural gas). A local gas company drills down (as it might in a Texas natural gas well) and draws the gas out. The gas from this source could provide enough fuel for 16,000 homes. In St. Petersburg, Virginia, a huge plant will make ethanol from municipal garbage and from agricultural, industrial, and forest wastes. Several enzymes break down the cellulose in the waste and convert it into fermentable sugar. Yeast is then introduced, converting the sugar into ethanol. It is expected that the plant will produce 50 million gallons of ethanol a year for sale as a gasohol ingredient.

Proposed for the future are plantations of huge kelp farms in the ocean. When harvested, kelp can be converted into methane gas and other products.

Recall the law, "There is no such thing as a free lunch," and you will see that there are a number of problems associated with the use of biomass:

1. Will the securing and processing of biomass require more energy than the amount produced?
2. Should land be used for growing food or fuel?
3. Should manure and other organic wastes be used as biomass for energy or to enrich soil?
4. Will the burning of biomass, such as wood, introduce more pollutants into the environment than would other sources of energy?

Other Energy Sources

For many centuries windmills have been used to pump water for crop irrigation, to turn millstones, to grind grain into flour, and to spin saws in sawmills. In 1891, Paul LaCour began experimenting with windmills to turn generators of electricity in Askov, Denmark. His basic design supplied that town with electricity until 1960, when hydroelectric power was introduced. The increasing price of energy coupled with our growing dependence on foreign oil supplies has revived our interest in wind power. More than 16,000 wind turbines operating in California at this time generate enough electricity to supply 300,000 typical homes in the state.

Thousands of turbines, driven by winds that sweep across California's Central Valley through Tehachapi Pass and into the Mojave Desert below, feed electricity to homes as far away as Los Angeles, 110 miles southwest. Pictured here are two-bladed wind turbines in the Tehachapi Pass. *Photo by Paul Gipe. (Courtesy of American Windmill Association.)*

The world's largest solar collector is the sea, which absorbs nearly 75 percent of the sun's energy striking the earth. One way of tapping this energy, known as OTEC (Ocean Thermal Energy Conversion) is to make use of the difference in temperature between the sun-warmed surface waters and cold ocean depths. OTEC works like this: A low-boiling point fluid such as ammonia is heated by the warm surface waters. It turns into a gas at a pressure great enough to turn a turbine, which, in turn, provides the motive power of an electric generator. The spent gas is then cooled back into a liquid in a condensor by cold water pumped from the depths. The cycle is then repeated. A mini OTEC project off Hawaii has worked on a small scale. The U.S. Department of Energy estimated that by the year 2000, OTEC could replace 400,000 barrels of oil a day.

As with other proposals, there may be some environmental problems associated with OTEC: The pumping up of cold water may disturb the ecological balance of the natural life cycles of oxygen-producing algae. Also, the cold water holds a relatively large amount of carbon dioxide, which would be released on warming to the air, and which would contribute to the greenouse effect. However, it would release only about one-third as much carbon dioxide as the burning of fossil fuel for the same amount of energy.

Other energy resources of the sea include the harnessing of the rise and fall of ocean tides, wave energy, and hydrogen extracted from sea water.

Tapping the heat from molten rocks (magma) under the earth's surface has been proposed (and in several places is now used) as a source of energy. When underground water comes in contact with magma, hot water and steam are produced. Where this occurs within a few miles of the surface and in sufficient quantity, the hot water and steam can be trapped and used to turn turbines, which, in turn, power electric generators. In some areas having hot underground rocks but lacking their own natural circulating water system, cold water could be piped down, heated, and pumped to the surface. It is probable that tapping the earth's heat, known as *geothermal energy,* would be most successful in regions of volcanic activity, earthquake faults, and mountain building. Iceland, sitting astride the Mid-Atlantic Ridge (see Chapter 6A) and subject to constant volcanic eruptions, is harvesting its volcanic power crop. Thirty percent of Iceland's total energy and 70 percent of its space heating of buildings is supplied by geothermal sources. Researchers have estimated that the United States contains a largely untapped resource of geothermal energy and that by the year 2020 geothermals could add 18.5 quads annually to the national energy pool—equal to that produced presently by our consumption of natural gas.

Some problems are connected with the development of geothermal energy.

1. There may be a hazard of land sinking from the withdrawal of large amounts of water. It is thought that this can be met by limiting withdrawals to a safe rate and by reinjecting water into the wells.
2. There is concern that earthquakes may be triggered by water reinjected under pressure.
3. Large land areas are required—between 3,000 and 5,000 acres—for a typical geothermal plant.

Energy from Nuclear Fission

At the beginning of the nuclear age, in the late 1940s and early 1950s, it was hoped that, having "split the atom," science had ushered in a new era of abundant, inexpensive energy: The fissioning of one pound of uranium 235 could provide 3 million times the energy released from the burning of a pound of coal. (It is helpful at this point to read the summary of the important concepts underlying nuclear energy, and to examine the diagram of a nuclear reactor on p. 466.) In recent decades, however, four major issues have dimmed the promise of limitless energy from the atom.

1. The concern over the safety of nuclear reactors.
2. The uncertainty about the long-term disposal of radioactive wastes.
3. The rising cost of plant construction, maintenance, and eventual dismantling.
4. The worry that nuclear plants would be used to supply material for nuclear weapons.

The breakdown at the Three Mile Island reactor in 1979 alerted the United States to the potential danger in nuclear power plants; the explosion at the one in Chernobyl in the USSR in 1986 alarmed the world.

At 4 A.M. on March 28, 1979, the main feedwater pumps in the Three Mile Island Unit 2 nuclear power plant near Middletown, Pennsylvania, tripped so that the mechanism for removing heat was interrupted. This initiated a number of failures, some mechanical, some human, that caused both the core to overheat and a large amount of water, some of it radioactive, to spill and overflow. This resulted in the escape of a small amount of radioactivity into the environment.

Three Mile Island revived fears that a malfunction in the cooling system might result in a *meltdown* of the nuclear material forming the core of a reactor. The intensely heated nuclear material would then burn its way through the thick steel capsule, through the 10-foot concrete slab, and down deep into the soil beneath. Such a scenario is sometimes called the "China Syndrome," reminiscent of the childhood fantasy of digging through the earth to China. Once released into the earth the radioactive elements could contaminate the ground water or make their way to the surface. At the same time, the water and steam circulating in the reactor, freed by the meltdown, would rise as a radioactive cloud that could spread over vast areas.

The worst nuclear power plant accident of all time occurred at Chernobyl in 1986 when operator errors unleashed a power surge that blew the roof off the number 4 reactor and initiated a partial meltdown of the core's fuel. Tons of uranium fuel and fission products were flung out. The explosion and heat sent up a 3-mile (5-kilometer) plume laden with radioactive contaminants.

Clouds traveled widely, depositing contaminants over Europe, from Scandinavia to Greece. Within an 18-mile (30-kilometer) radius of the power station, 116,000 people were evacuated. All were resettled outside this zone, which will remain uninhabitable for many years.

Thirty-one died in the Chernobyl accident. Western experts estimate that 4,000 of the 116,000 evacuees received serious radiation doses and forecast that among them 100 to 200 cancer deaths

will occur. Beyond the 18-mile zone, various estimates place expected Chernobyl-caused cancer deaths from 5,000 to 75,000.

Following the Chernobyl accident the General Accounting Office (GAO) of the United States reviewed the management of the nation's nuclear power plants by the Nuclear Regulating Commission (NRC). The GAO report charged that our nuclear plants have for years been operated under inadequate safety guidelines and that existing guidelines have been applied inconsistently; that the "NRC's commissioners cannot agree on the specific types and/or degree of safety that could endanger public health and safety" enough to require the shutdown of a nuclear power plant. The report criticized the NRC's failure to resolve in a timely fashion "generic safety issues"—design, construction, or operating problems.

The present nuclear reactors obtain heat energy from the splitting of an extremely scarce form of uranium, U-235. There is danger of its depletion before the end of the century, however. To meet this danger plans were advanced for the construction of breeder reactors that "create" their own nuclear fuel, producing 14 atoms of fissionable plutonium for every 10 atoms consumed. Both the conventional reactor and the breeder reactor, however, produce radioactivity and radioactive wastes, which constitute a potential threat to life.

The breeder reactor is already operating in four foreign countries, but its development has been delayed in the United States because of the fear that a stolen quantity of plutonium the size of a grapefruit, shaped into a bomb by urban guerrillas or saboteurs, could destroy a city the size of Hiroshima. Moreover it may be impossible to recover the plutonium economically while providing adequate safety precautions.

In addition to the foregoing, the following are some of the reasons for general concern about nuclear reactors:

"Containment" structures around reactors are not the final solution to safety. They are not designed to withstand a fast-moving melt accident, and they can fail if such an accident involves a steam or hydrogen explosion.

Nuclear power plants have not been proven to be economically sound, compared to other sources of energy.

The Chernobyl accident revealed how operator errors could lead to nuclear meltdowns.

We have not solved the problem of safe storage of radioactive wastes from reactors.

Countering the concerns, advocates of the full development of nuclear power advance the following arguments:

The amount of radiation escaping from nuclear reactors is minuscule compared with naturally occurring radiation on earth. Deaths caused annually by coal-fired electricity are much larger, thus far, than those created by nuclear power plants if one includes the number of coal miners killed by accidents and "black lung" disease, and in transporting coal.

The dangers posed by nuclear wastes have been exaggerated. New storage methods and facilities can reduce the risks of contamination.

A massive commitment to coal as an alternative to nuclear expansion would increase the carbon dioxide in the atmosphere, leading to a long-term warming of the earth—the so-called greenhouse effect—with disastrous impact on the earth's climate (see Index).

Nuclear energy based on breeder reactors would make the United States safe from blackmail by the oil-producing countries.

In 1987 about 19 percent of the electricity in the United States was produced by 102 nuclear plants. Six licensed for operation were in start-up; 18 more were granted construction permits. Since the Three Mile accident orders for new plants have come to a halt.

Questioning the building of more nuclear plants and the safety of existing ones has stirred a good deal of controversy. What we have to decide is: Are the benefits from nuclear power worth the risks?

Nuclear Fusion

Recent experiments have improved the chances that energy on a vast scale may be produced not by "splitting the atom" but by joining atoms in a process known as *nuclear fusion*. This energy source is found throughout the universe: It powers the sun and the stars (see p. 150). Fusion is also the mechanism of the most powerful force for destruction created by humans—the hydrogen bomb.

For more than three decades scientists have attempted to control nuclear fusion so that its energy may be used for peaceful purposes. The "fuels" for fusion are forms of hydrogen (deuterium and tritium) available in unlimited quantity in seawater. To produce a fusion reaction it is necessary to heat the fusion fuels to temperatures as high as those in the sun's interior, so that the nuclei of the hydrogen atoms have enough energy to fuse. The fusion reaction, once started, must be self-sustaining. In fusion as in fission, there is a loss of mass and the release of tremendous energy.

The problem in the peaceful use of fusion has been to confine the hot nuclear particles; ordinary vessels—bottles, cans, and tanks—would disintegrate. Now being developed and tested is a device called the *Tokamak,* a huge electromagnet in the shape of a doughnut. The powerful magnetic field produced in the Tokamak "bottles up" the hot nuclei in the same way that a beam of electrons is controlled in a television picture tube.

Fusion offers many advantages over fission: a much smaller amount of radioactivity, no threat of a meltdown, plentiful supply of cheap fuel, amelioration of long-term large-storage waste problems, and little disruption of the environment. Fusion could provide the world with energy for millions of years, but we have yet to perfect techniques for controlling its awesome power.

Nuclear Winter

In 1983 five atmospheric and space scientists made an analysis of how the earth's climate might be severely altered by a nuclear war, even a "modest" one. In addition to the carnage, they posited that a nuclear exchange would result in a "nuclear winter," in which the blast and fire would inject great amounts of soot and dust into the atmosphere, reducing the amount of sunlight reaching the earth for many months. Widespread extinction of plants and animals might be expected, with calamitous effects on agriculture and food supplies. The impact of the war could thus extend to billions of people who live far from the blast zones.

THE DISPOSAL OF WASTES

The Recycling of Refuse

On March 22, 1987, the garbage barge Mobro, from Islip, Long Island, set out in search of a dumping ground. In its epic quest for a place to deposit its contents Mobro met with rejections in North Carolina, Alabama, Mississippi, Louisiana, Texas, Florida, Mexico, Belize, and the Bahamas. After its 155-day odyssey it returned home, docking near the Southwest Brooklyn Incinerator. There its 3,100 tons of solid waste was reduced to 400 tons of ash, later to be buried in a landfill in Islip.

Our no-return, throwaway style of living is burying us under a mountain of garbage. We are running out of open areas for dumping. What should be done?

As we have seen, in nature wastes are recycled again and again (see pp. 391–394). Carbon dioxide is used as a raw material for food manufacture by green plants. The nitrogen in plant and animal waste is reclaimed in the soil and used by plants in protein manufacture (see pp. 442–443).

We can learn from nature. Take, for example, the aluminum beverage can, which piles up at campsites, parks, and lakes, as well as in garbage dumps. Unlike the old tin-coated steel can, which eventually rusts away and disappears into the environment, aluminum cans are practically indestructible. Why don't we reuse the aluminum in them? One aluminum-producing company found that it can reduce 100 used cans into enough metal to manufacture 91 new ones. There is a

saving not only of aluminum but of electric power, since it takes 10 kilowatt hours of electricity to separate a pound of aluminum from its ore, but only about 2 kilowatt hours to melt the same amount of used aluminum. The 8 kilowatts saved means that less fuel will be consumed to generate electricity, and consequently less thermal and chemical pollution of the environment will result.

Apparently, the reclamation of a single resource, such as aluminum, initiates a chain of environmental benefits. How can we encourage and enforce an aluminum-reclamation plan? Perhaps we should consider returning to the old tin-coated steel can, or the old refillable bottles, which eventually could be ground up and used as landfill or could be remelted and used again. Or we could charge a deposit, as some states have mandated, thus encouraging users and enterprising youngsters to return them.

Turn to paper, another common material. Sixty million tons of paper and paper products are manufactured each year in this country. Recycling paper would save the cutting down of billions of oxygen-producing, soil- and wildlife-protecting trees. At the present time we recycle about 20 percent of our paper; about three times that amount could probably be recycled. To do this would require setting up a system of paper collection in which all of us would have to participate. For every ton of newsprint that is recycled, 17 pine trees are saved.

Another way of recycling paper is to convert it into food and fuel. Researchers are now raising microorganisms that can digest the cellulose in ground-up newspapers, changing it into glucose. The glucose can then be made into a sugary syrup or into ethyl alcohol, which can be used among other things as a fuel. If the cost of this process can be reduced it will constitute a new way of recycling the solar energy originally stored in the trees used to produce paper.

The disposal of solid waste is a growing problem, particularly in urban areas that are exhausting their dump space. By 1990 roughly half the cities in the United States will have run out of landfill space. One proposed solution is to compact all the garbage, made unobjectionable in terms of odor, insects, vermin, or flammability, and transport it by train to places where there are relatively few people and much land. There it could be used for beautification as landfill, reclaiming land for parks and recreation sites.

This is, however, only a stopgap measure, since population and garbage have been increasing while landfill areas are decreasing. A long-range program requires that we reduce solid waste pollution by recycling. The recycling of municipal wastes was discussed earlier. Microorganisms convert organic matter in biomass into useful products such as methane and ethanol.

Agricultural engineers at Cornell University are experimenting with a new system for treating sewage by using bacteria to break down and filter out heavy pollutants and then growing plants in the partially cleansed water. The Cornell system produces commercially useful natural gas, and unlike other systems produces no sludge or other waste matter. It is a system that has the potential for paying for itself by converting unwanted material into something useful.

Hazardous Wastes

The dumping and abandoning of hazardous chemical wastes by industry in open fields, often in rusted and leaking barrels, the discharging of toxic chemicals into our waterways, and the release of dangerous pesticides by agriculture into the environment are causing increasing concern about the safety of our air, water, soil, and food. Plastic trash is killing wildlife and threatening to choke human communities on their own waste. A few examples of recent happenings:

In a James River estuary poisoned by the long-time dumping of the carcinogenic pesticide Kepone, Virginia has forbidden the taking of fin fish because they retain the contaminant in their flesh.

Communities from New York to Oregon have reported human health problems they fear are related to ex-

posure to the deadly chemical dioxin. In laboratory experiments with animals, dioxin—an unwanted by-product of herbicides, pesticides, and other industrial products—has more harmful effects and in smaller doses than any chemical we have yet produced. About a decade ago the chemical was contained in oil sprayed along roadsides throughout eastern Missouri, where it made a ghost town of Times Beach. The immediate remedy was for the government to buy the town and relocate 2,200 people at a cost of $33 million. Dioxin was among the hazardous chemicals found in 1978 at Love Canal, New York. Federal officials are finding more and more sites where dioxin has been dumped. Humans exposed to it have suffered a variety of serious health problems, including kidney and liver ailments, birth defects, and cancer.

According to figures compiled by the Environmental Defense Fund, a nonprofit organization, nearly 1,000 of approximately 6,000 schools inspected across the country in the late 1970s were identified as containing potentially dangerous asbestos.

Urea formaldehyde foam insulation used in about one-half million American homes releases formaldehyde fumes. Various health problems have resulted from its use, including its potential carcinogenicity.

The Environmental Defense Fund estimates that more than 2 million seabirds and 100,000 marine mammals die each year by becoming entangled in or injesting discarded plastics.

One hundred solid waste incinerators for trash disposal are in use in U.S. cities and thousands more are on the drawing boards. It is feared that the toxic ash from energy-producing municipal incinerators, or resource-recovery plants, is not being disposed of in accordance with relevant hazardous waste regulations. Landfilled ash from municipal incinerators typically contains toxic metals such as lead and cadmium in concentrations considered hazardous by the EPA.

All these incidents are just symptoms of a mammoth threat to our health and safety. The enactment of new legislation and the enforcement of existing regulations for the prevention of dumping and the cleanup and safe disposal of wastes are not proceeding fast enough to contend adequately with the pollution problem. According to the EPA, the United States is generating 80 billion pounds of hazardous chemical wastes annually, but only 10 percent is being disposed of properly.

CONSERVATION OF SOIL

The Problem

Productive soil is the basis of our existence. Almost all of our food and fiber, except that derived from the sea, comes from the soil. Soil also is the source of almost all the food required by domestic and wild animal life. History records what happened to Greece, Italy, and Spain with the loss of much of their productive soil. Yet many people today in America feel that "it can't happen here." They point to the huge yields of our farms and to the improvements in agricultural technology. Our main problem seems to be to dispose of our surplus. The federal government, to support the economy, has bought up billions of dollars worth of surplus crops.

Indeed, we have increased the productivity of our land markedly: The average acre in 1970 yielded approximately twice the crops as that of 60 years before because of a combination of factors. New plant strains have been developed with increased food yield, with greater ability to withstand drought, disease, insects, wind damage, and unfavorable climatic conditions. In addition, the use of farm machinery, the placing of more acres under irrigation, and the use of fertilizers have played a role in increasing productivity.

What then is the problem? We must measure the future in terms of our new needs, created by an increased population.

While the population becomes greater, the amount of available cropland will decrease in the United States and in the world. The United States is losing valuable cropland at the alarming rate of 1 million acres a year to urban sprawl, highways, and other developments. The potato farms of Long Island, New York, are slowly being converted into housing developments. All of these factors will mean less acreage for meeting the heightened demand for crops of food, feed, and fibers.

Against this background of exploding population and diminishing land availability, the protection of valuable topsoil from erosion by wind and water and from depletion of its minerals by unwise farming methods takes on new significance.

In the United States, erosion has destroyed approximately one third of the nation's topsoil since cultivation began on this continent. More than 15 million tons of topsoil flow out of the Mississippi every minute. The damage is primarily due to our farming, grazing, and lumbering practices.

The fertile, productive land of the world is being denuded and destroyed at the rate of 14 million acres a year. Unless this process can be slowed, some scientists say, fully one third of today's arable land will be lost in the next 25 years, while the world's needs for food will nearly double.

Prevention of Erosion

Nine inches (23 centimeters) of topsoil lie between us and extinction—this is the upper layer of soil in productive farmland. In that top layer are the vital materials necessary for plant growth. Remove them, and we come to soil that can barely support vegetation.

One of the ways of preventing excessive erosion on hilly farmlands is *contour plowing* (see illustration on p. 408) in which the land is plowed around the contours of the hill instead of up and down. This prevents water from running downhill. Another way of preventing wasteful erosion is *strip farming,* in which alternate strips of grass or similar crop are left to check the downhill runoff of water. Water that begins to run downhill in the cultivated strip is stopped when it reaches the cover crop. Still another method—perhaps a better one—is not to plow steep hillsides at all but to leave them for pasture, orchard, or forest.

Terraces can also be used to prevent erosion. On ground that has been terraced, water has time

Severe gully erosion on a pasture in southwestern Iowa. *Photo by Tim McCabe.*
(Courtesy of U.S. Dept. of Agriculture, Soil Conservation Service.)

to soak into the soil during and after a rain instead of running directly down the hillside. Older nations have terraced their hilly land for centuries, but in the United States we have never had to follow such a practice to any extent because of our abundance of good land (see pp. 385, 443).

Forests are of great assistance in preventing erosion. If you have ever been in the woods during a rain you have seen that the drops of water do not hit the ground with great force. They strike leaves and branches and gradually drop to the ground or run down a tree trunk. The ground under the trees is covered with leaves. It is soft and spongy and full of roots of trees and other plants. The roots bind the soil together and hold it in place. The humus on the surface serves as a sort of sponge to hold some of the water that falls

during a period of rainfall. This water then drains very gradually into the soil during dry periods.

Soil erosion is a natural process. Ordinarily it takes place slowly, so that new soil constantly being created balances the loss. Humans, however, by their unwise practices, can speed up erosion to the point where land becomes unproductive in one generation. It takes 100 to 600 years to form an inch of topsoil. Wind and water can remove that much in a single year.

We have realized why erosion is becoming a problem, and we have learned how to slow it down. The job that remains to be done is to convince people of the importance of action and to help them see how best to work at conservation.

The Soil Conservation Service of the U.S. Department of Agriculture provides advice and

Contour plowing and strip cropping, both used to trap water and hold the soil on a New Jersey farm. Note also the farm pond for catching and holding water for livestock. (**Note:** The opening photo of this chapter shows another method of holding soil and trapping water: terracing. Every available portion of land in this rice-growing area in Indonesia is carefully cultivated.) *(Courtesy of U.S. Dept. of Agriculture, Soil Conservation Service.)*

plants to solve two big soil problems: erosion and sedimentation, the depositing of eroded soil elsewhere. Eroded soil washed into streams and lakes can reduce water quality, downgrade fish habitats, and increase flooding downstream. In addition to controlling flooding and sedimentation, the right kind of plants can provide food and cover for wildlife, beautify the landscape, and increase forage production of ranges and pastures.

Maintaining Soil Fertility

If soil is to be satisfactory for plant growth it must contain the essential mineral compounds. Compounds of nitrogen, phosphorus, potassium, calcium, sulfur, magnesium, and minute amounts of other elements are essential for plant life. Let us consider nitrogen first.

The nitrogen cycle was discussed on pages

393–394. When we harvest crops we are, in a sense, mining the soil of nitrogen. The crops will become poorer and poorer, unless we replace the lost nitrogen by adding animal manure or commercial fertilizer to the soil. We can also help replenish the soil with nitrates by growing a crop of plants such as clover and then plowing it back into the soil.

Phosphorus and potassium are essential for soil fertility, too. Lack of phosphorus not only slows growing, it also results in crops that are deficient in this substance. People depending on such crops for phosphorus required in their diet may have their health endangered by its lack. Farm animals suffer similarly from lack of this element. Potassium compounds are needed for sturdy plant growth.

CONSERVATION OF FORESTS

If only people would catch a vision of our fabulous forests, their ancient heritage, their beauty and beneficence, their meaning for our lives today ... before it is too late.

RUTHERFORD PLATT[9]

Forests not only provide wood products but they also assist greatly in preventing floods, reducing soil erosion, and in conserving water, as we have seen. Forests provide a home for birds and other wild animals, and recreation for millions of people. In consuming carbon dioxide as part of their food-making processes, forests help mitigate the major cause of the greenhouse effect.

Fire

The widespread Yellowstone National Park fires of 1988 in which about 440,000 acres, or 20 percent, of the parkland actually burned in some de-

[9]R. Platt, *The Great American Forests* (Englewood Cliffs, N.J.: Prentice-Hall, 1965).

gree stirred heated debate about the nation's policies with respect to forest protection. Some of the issues were as follows:

1. Was the general policy of the National Park Service of allowing some lightning-caused fires to burn in certain areas of the national forests (unless people, property, or endangered species were threatened) a wise one?
2. Could the September 1988 fires been averted or minimized by more aggressive fire-fighting measures against the early June and July wildfires?
3. Were the basic causes of the extensive fires the exceptionally hot, dry summer and high winds coupled with the long accumulation of tinder-dry brush in an environment where natural decay occurs slowly?
4. What weight should be given to the conclusion of Rupert Cutler, president of Defenders of Wildlife and a former assistant secretary of agriculture, that "the park will be a healthier and infinitely more interesting place because of this ecological event of 1988"?

Fires can burn diseased lumber, dead brush, and insects, allowing sunlight and moisture to nurture new growth. Following a fire, local grass flourishes, benefiting from the nutrients in the surrounding ashes and the added sunlight. This helps prevent erosion and feeds browsing wildlife. Slowly, new trees will emerge and the forest will be reestablished. Thus fire, once regarded only as a destructive agent, is now seen as a natural ecosystem process.

To control fires some of the larger forests have lookout stations and airplane patrols to locate the fires in their initial stages. Fire fighters are alerted and reach the scene before the fire has spread out of control. In addition, helicopters are used in some areas to bring "smoke jumpers" and their equipment to areas inaccessible by other means. Permanent fire lanes are cut through forests to halt the spread of fire and to facilitate the work of fire fighting.

For fighting forest fires new tools such as computers have been developed recently to forecast the possibility of lightning-caused fires in susceptible areas, to analyze such factors as the terrain where a fire has broken out for the age and size of brush and trees and the weather forecast, and to predict the rate at which the fire would spread. Infrared sensors in airplanes detect and map the fire area. A network of federal, state, and local fire-fighting agencies deploy thousands of fire fighters to the fire region.

Insects and Disease

The chief enemies of the forests are insects and disease: They destroy nearly seven times the amount of timber that fire does. Some of the insect enemies of the forest are leaf eaters; some, like certain beetles, are wood borers. The tree diseases are caused by such organisms as bacteria, fungi, and viruses; some of these disease parasites are conveyed from tree to tree by insects.

An example of the inroads of disease on trees is the case of the chestnut blight. This is a fungus disease of the American chestnut tree, which first received serious attention in 1904. Thirty years later the blight had killed off almost all of the native chestnut trees in the Northeast. Resistant strains of this valuable tree are now being developed, but it will be many decades before it is restored to its former abundance, if it ever is.

Another current concern is the destruction of the graceful elm tree by Dutch elm disease. Since its introduction into the United States in 1930, Dutch elm disease has wiped out nearly 50 million elm trees. The disease, found mainly east of the Mississippi River, is creeping farther westward. Only three states appear totally free of it— Florida, Montana, and Arizona.

The damage is caused by a fungus organism, but the fungus is spread only by tiny bark beetles. The disease can be checked by getting rid of the beetles. Communities that have carried out consistent programs have proved that the elms can be saved. Scientists have also been seeking a kind of elm that is resistant to the disease.

Many insects that are harmful to trees and other plants come here from other countries. Their im-

migration is accidental, occurring in shipments of fruits or vegetables from other shores. Even airplanes can be a source of entry. Because of this, planes arriving from other lands are sprayed with insecticides as soon as they land at American airports. Quarantine and inspection are ways of stopping the entrance of some harmful insects, but even with the most stringent care the problem will continue to exist.

The Japanese beetle is a well-known example of an insect that came from abroad and wreaked havoc upon our crops and trees. The prime reason foreign insects sometimes become a problem is that they leave their natural enemies behind when they are brought to new territory. In combating such insects we often study them in their native habitat to find their natural enemies there. Such is the case with the Japanese beetle. It was found that a particular Japanese wasp was the chief enemy. This wasp was imported and raised in quantity and then released in areas where the beetle was out of control. The wasp lays its eggs in the beetle larva. When the young wasp hatches out, it feeds on the larva and destroys it. Using a natural enemy to combat a harmful species is called *biological control.* In spite of this and other measures we have not conquered Japanese beetles, which do an immense amount of damage each year. Importation of natural enemies of insect pests must be preceded by careful study, for it is possible that the insect brought in to control one pest may itself prove to be a nuisance.

Insects can frequently be controlled on a small scale, as on a small vegetable farm, by spraying plants with chemicals that kill the insects but do not harm plants. It is obvious that the cost and difficulty of application on large areas would be prohibitive. Therefore, chemical spraying to protect our forests against harmful insects is out of the question. Moreover, widespread spraying might destroy insects and other forms of life that are essential in the chain of interrelationships described earlier in this chapter, and could lead to incalculable damage. That is why there must be unremitting study to discover natural enemies of insects.

The gypsy moth is a major killer of trees in the Northeast. A method of controlling the moth is based on the discovery that the female attracts the male with a scent known as *pheromone*. Recently chemists have succeeded in synthesizing quantities of the female moth's sex lure in a new product called Disparlure. Traps containing Disparlure attract the males; then they are sterilized (made infertile) or destroyed. Sterilized males, turned loose, displace normal males and mate with females, which then produce only infertile eggs.

Saving the Forests

More than three fourths of the original forests of the United States have been cut down. Wasteful practices in the past have been responsible for much timber loss, yet no attempts at reforestation were made. When an area had been denuded of all marketable trees the lumber companies moved on to a new area. The concept that timber should be cultivated and harvested as a crop, instead of being "mined" out of the soil like ore, is a comparatively recent one. Theodore Roosevelt created a Bureau of Forestry in the early years of this century to protect our rapidly shrinking forest reserves. Gifford Pinchot, the bureau's first chief, had the task of changing the prevailing attitude toward forests. According to Pinchot, people believed that forests were "inexhaustible and in the way." Corrective measures were initiated, including setting aside forest reserves and national parks. Forest owners slowly came to treat trees as a crop instead of as a mineral to be mined. As a result of these and other measures the forest situation has improved markedly in many respects. However, the nation's future forest requirements are still not assured.

With increasing demand for wood, economists foresee that before 1999 the projected demand for forest products will exceed the capacity of forests to meet this demand by normal growth. This means that we shall have to consume more and more of our capital of trees. Some possible solutions have already been suggested: measures

against fire, insects, and disease. These will not be enough. General improvements in forest management, further promotion of economies in the use of wood, and the utilization of wastes will help, but there are limitations to these methods. Possibilities for the substitution of other materials for forest products may include the increasing use of such construction materials as brick and concrete, aluminum, plastics, and fiberglass; the use of nonwood vegetable fibers such as sugarcane bagasse for making paper; and aluminum foil and plastics instead of paper for packing. Some of these materials, such as plastics, may introduce problems of solid waste disposal, discussed on pages 404–405 (see pp. 446–448).

In the National Forest Management Act of 1976, Congress ordered careful planning for our national forests, so that their many uses would be balanced for the benefit of all Americans, present and future. Public lands totaling 187 million acres were set aside for the national forests. Dedicated to "multiple use," the forests, by law, are supposed to fulfill six functions: recreation, watershed maintenance, wildlife preservation, timber production, grazing, and mining.

In recent years the Forest Service has been criticized on a number of grounds: Bulldozers are destroying some of the nation's last remains of pristine wilderness; instead of selective cutting the Forest Service has engaged in the clear-cutting of timber; archaic laws and regulations are allowing choice tracts of forest land to be gouged and scarred by mining operations, and nearly half of the national forage areas have been overgrazed.

In *clear-cutting,* all trees, young and old, are felled across a wide swath of forest, leaving an open strip of stumps. The timber companies argue that clear-cutting is ideal for fast regrowth and good for game. Environmental groups contend that clear-cutting both creates ideal conditions for erosion, which, in turn, clogs streams and rivers with vital topsoil and nutrients without which new stands cannot grow, and destroys wildlife habitat. In addition, clear-cutting leaves unsightly bald patches.

Moreover, it is charged, important fisheries

have been destroyed by Forest Service misman-agement of logging; unique and irreplaceable old stands that have survived for centuries have been destroyed, and our national system of hiking trails is being damaged as hundreds of miles of wood-land trails used for hiking are bulldozed into log-ging roads.

Most of the developing nations of Africa, Asia, and Latin America are experiencing a critical shrinkage of their forests. As populations have grown, and the need for food and grazing land has expanded, forests have been cut down. A utili-zation rate for fuel, higher than its growth rate, and the exporting of timber to raise money for obtaining traded products, contribute to the prob-lem. Thus the world's poor people are using up their capital to meet their immediate needs, only to intensify their poverty as their lands are eroded and as they suffer from periodic droughts and floods. Recent reforestation efforts, together with a program of education, may help the world's poorer nations preserve the potentially renewable resources that forests offer them. Also essential to a lessening of deforestation are the policies and practices of the *developed* nations. The average American consumes as much wood—a lot of it from developing countries—in the form of paper as the average resident of the Third World burns as cooking fuel.

Tropical Rain Forests

Of increasing concern is the fate of the world's tropical rain forests, which are disappearing at the rate of 25,000 square miles a year. These forests include woodlands that receive over 80 inches of rainfall per year and are close enough to the equa-tor so that their trees are evergreen throughout the year. Rain forests circle the earth from Cen-tral and South America to Africa, Malaysia, and Indonesia.

The spread of agriculture, cattle ranching, log-ging, and other commercial projects are contrib-uting to the decimation of this richest ecosystem in the world. The rain forests serve as the earth's safe deposit boxes of biological diversity, harbor-ing half of our planet's species of plants and an amazing variety of animal life.

The plants of the rain forests provide 25 per-cent of all pharmaceutical products as well as the promise of yet-to-be discovered new drugs. They are important climatic and environmental stabiliz-ers. Among their many beneficial activities is the removal of carbon dioxide from the atmosphere that might otherwise contribute to the green-house effect. They play a significant role in recy-cling fresh water through the natural Amazonian filter back into the Atlantic.

Measures to safeguard the tropical rain forests include a ban on the use of their wood products, ending the building of dams, roads, and other forest-destroying projects, and the encourage-ment of efforts to increase production of small plots of land planted with appropriate plants for each kind of soil.

CONSERVATION OF WILDLIFE

What event likely to occur in the 1980s [and 1990s] will our descendants most regret, even those living a thousand years from now?... The one process ongoing in the 1980s that will take millions of years to correct is the loss of genetic and species diversity by the destruction of natural habitats. This is the folly our descendants are least likely to forgive us.

EDWARD O. WILSON

Early American explorers told stories of animal abundance that gave them reputations as spinners of tall tales. But the tales were true: The number of animals in colonial days was prodigious. At one time 100 million bison roamed the western prai-ries. These animals were slaughtered for their hides and fur. Birds were exterminated for their decorative feathers. Enormous numbers of game and wildfowl were killed for sale as food. What saved part of our wildlife was the birth of a con-servation movement in the final quarter of the nineteenth century. For some animals this came too late: The passenger pigeon was one of those that never recovered. The last-known passenger pigeon died in captivity in 1914. Gone, too, is the great auk, the Plains grizzly, the Labrador duck, the Arizona wapiti, the Badlands big horn, and many others.

In 1970 Congress passed an Endangered Species Conservation Act providing federal protection for certain animals whose extinction was threatened. Some animals presently named in the act are the grizzly bear, the Florida panther, the whooping crane, the bald eagle, and the American alligator.

One hundred fifty-nine animals were added to the list in 1976, assuring protection to animals of the world from every continent. These species no longer can be traded in interstate commerce. Included in this recent list are the Asian elephant, the clouded leopard, the marbled cat, and all species of gibbons.

The U.N.-funded treaty organization known as CITES (Convention of International Trade in Endangered Species of Wild Fauna and Flora) has a long list that includes medicinal leeches, fruit bats, Asian elephants, giant pandas, and the gray whale. Ninety-five nations have joined CITES.

Certainly we should expect some animals to retreat from the haunts of man. Such animals as the deer, elk, wolf, bear, and lynx cannot live well in cleared sections. Muskrats, beavers, otters, minks, and other water dwellers cannot remain when swamps and lakes are drained and when streams and rivers are used for water supply and irrigation.

We must not drive these animals into extinction. We should protect them in the natural habitats that remain for them, and we should also be intelligent enough to leave desirable space for them. There is ample land that should not be cleared for agricultural or industrial purposes. In such spots the animals can live—if they are protected.

Why protect wild animals? In their natural habitat they are a pleasure to watch. They are as much a part of forests, lakes, ponds, streams, and meadows as the trees and flowers. Each wild animal, as we have seen, is part of a life chain. This chain may lead directly to the human being. The destruction of coyotes in certain areas permitted a ruinous increase in the number of rodents. The killing off of Swainson's hawk in the West was followed by grasshopper plagues that destroyed millions of dollars worth of crops.

Without birds we would certainly suffer more damage from insects to farm crops, trees, and shrubs than we do now. Many birds feed on insects and thus help to control the large numbers of them. Some of the harmful insects that birds eat are potato bugs, cutworms, chinchbugs, leaf beetles, and boll weevils.

Extinction

Currently we are deeply concerned about the increasing rate of extinction of wildlife, plants as well as animals. It has been estimated that by the year 2000, one fifth of all species on earth will have been lost.

Our civilization has been built on the products and labor of other species. Consider what just three species of grass—corn, wheat and rice—have meant to our survival. The chief ingredients of 40 percent of today's prescription drugs are compounds derived from plants. In destroying the thousands of wild plant species we are removing from our planet a vast "genetic library" of potentially useful materials that may never be replaced.

Perhaps the most important reason for teaching extinction, however, is that, whenever a population or species becomes extinct, a working part of an ecosystem is destroyed. Ecosystems provide many free "public services" without which human civilization could not survive. These services include the conversion of solar energy by plants, the maintenance of the quality of the atmosphere, amelioration of the weather, generation and conservation of soils, breakdown of wastes, recycling of nutrients essential to agriculture, provision of food from the sea, control of the vast majority of potential pests of crops and vectors of human diseases, and maintenance of the genetic library.

The degree to which most ecosystems can absorb deletions without serious interference and without interruption in the delivery of services is unknown. Two things, however, are clear. There is a critical rate of extinction that will lead to catastrophic breakdown. Secondly, satisfactory repairs will be costly, at the very least, and in most cases will be impossible.

If humanity continues its reckless assault on other species, sooner or later we will pay the price with such coins as floods and massive famine.[10]

Wildlife Sanctuaries

The need for wildlife management and protection has been recognized for a long time. As far back as the beginning of the eighteenth century practically all of the original colonies had established a closed season on deer. But it was not until after the Civil War that protective legislation was established on a wide scale. The need for wildlife sanctuaries has been recognized, and many state and national areas have been set aside where wild animals can live and breed without interference.

Nature preserves, or sanctuaries, where all wild plants and animals are protected with as little disturbance by humans as possible, are valuable as outdoor classrooms and scientific laboratories. Here the interrelationships discussed in this chapter can be studied. This is the purpose of the nature centers now being established in many communities with the guidance of the National Audubon Society and other conservation groups.

Captive Breeding

A relatively new role for zoos, aquaria, and botanical gardens is to breed individuals of threatened species in order to guarantee their survival. Zoos now exchange animals like library books on extended breeding loans. It is hoped that some forms will reestablish themselves when released

[10]Paul R. Erlich, Stanford University, California (*Science and Children*, April 1982).

in a suitable habitat—when and if this is possible. The captive or protected breeding of some threatened birds has met with success.

Critics question whether the allocation of funds for captive breeding may distract attention from more important endangered species activities such as protective regulations, law enforcement, public education, and habitat preservation. Captive-breeding scientists answer that such breeding should complement, not replace traditional endangered species conservation measures.

CONSERVATION OF WATER

Water, one of our most precious resources, is also our commonest and cheapest. Unlike copper or coal, water is indestructible; it will not wear out. Its supply is inexhaustible. The sea covers three fourths of the earth and holds 300 million cubic miles (1,250 million cubic kilometers) of water. Locked in glaciers, ice caps, and ice sheets are an additional 11 million cubic miles (45 million cubic kilometers).

In the course of the water cycle, as we have seen, water circulates from ocean to air to land to ocean. The supply of water on our planet is ample; the problem is to obtain the right amount of fresh water in the right place at the right time. Water is a resource that moves; conserving it for use means controlling its movement.

The Water Crisis

Experts warn that a water crisis of global proportions is developing because of changes both in our use of water and in our climate. As the population of the earth increases, greater demands are made on water for drinking, for agriculture, and for industry.

Water shortages affect people most acutely in two ways: in food production and in public drinking water supplies. Eighty percent of the world's people have no access to tap water. They rely on streams and wells that are often contaminated with human wastes. It is estimated that 5 million people die annually of water-borne diseases.

The irrigation of croplands takes 80 percent to 90 percent of all water used by humans, not counting rain. According to the U.N. Food and Culture Administration, to feed all people who will be alive in the year 2000 will require a doubling of the amount of water now used in irrigation.

A third growing demand for clean water comes from industry. Producing a ton of steel requires 150 tons or 40,000 gallons of water. Because industries often dump untreated waste water back into lakes or rivers, many of the natural waterways are no longer able to meet the need for clean water.

The movie *Chinatown* recreated an incident in Los Angeles that took place 75 years ago when some city water officials, in collusion with land developers and other business interests, secretly bought huge tracts of land in Owens Valley and built an aqueduct to carry the water to the city. Since then Owens Valley residents have continued to protest this piracy of its water, leaving the community so parched that it deprived them of the chance to farm the area profitably.

Recently Phoenix, Arizona, bought over 14,000 acres of farmland 100 miles to the west in order to tap the water reserves underneath it. Other fast-growing cities such as Tucson, Mesa, and Scottsdale in the arid Southwest have also been purchasing farms far from the city limits—exposing these areas to irreparable damage to their agriculture.

Watersheds

As stated previously, the problem of water conservation is one of having sufficient fresh water when and where it is needed. The watershed is of key importance in solving this problem.

Sooner or later much of the water from rain or snow appears as streams. Small at first, these upland water courses become wider and deeper as they approach valleys where they combine to form larger streams and rivers. The areas that collect the water producing a stream or river are *watersheds,* which are of many shapes and sizes. Some, such as the Columbia and Missouri river drainages, cover millions of acres (see pp. 444–446).

Under natural conditions the soil, the plants in the soil (the "cover"), and the moisture of a watershed tend to be in balance. When humans ignorantly or carelessly upset the balance by destroying much of the plant cover the soil is exposed and washes away, often resulting in dust bowls, spreading deserts and ruined valleys, water shortages, polluted rivers, mud slides, and ravaging floods.

Strip mining in large areas of the Appalachian coalfields has been held responsible for floods that have taken scores of lives and caused millions of dollars in property damage. According to testimony given to a U.S. House Subcommittee in 1977, peak flow rates in mountain streams and rivers increased five times when the adjacent watershed was strip mined. It was held that the stripping not only causes deforestation of mountain flanks, increasing the rate of rainfall runoff, but also fills the watercourses with silt, reducing their capacity to hold high water levels within their banks.

Forest land has enormous value as a regulator of water flow. Forest soils not only retain and store water but also control water movements on and beneath the surface. This control spells the difference between clear, steady streams and erratic flows of muddy water, rising rapidly after rains and shrinking as rapidly, leaving only dry riverbeds.

An old Chinese proverb says, "To rule the mountain is to rule the river." A healthy forest cover on the slopes of hills and mountains restrains floods and provides a steady flow of clear water. When the cover is removed by fire or overcultivation, an imbalance is set up that permits less and less water to be taken in and stored in the soil to the detriment of farms, towns, and cities.

Water Table

We depend not only on the surface water that we can see and measure in streams, lakes, rivers, and reservoirs but on underground water, that is, water that is some distance below the ground level. Underground water begins as rain that sinks into the ground and then soaks into porous sediment, sand, gravel, or rock. As rain continues, the bottom layers become filled or saturated with water. A formation such as this that can hold sufficient water for domestic or industrial use is termed an *aquifer*. The upper level of this underground water is called the *water table*. Above this, rock particles may be coated with a film of water, but air fills most of the pore space.

To demonstrate an aquifer and a water table, half fill a jar with gravel, and sprinkle it with water. The water percolates down to the bottom of the jar and then rises gradually as it fills the spaces between the gravel. Stop when the water level is about halfway up the gravel; this could represent the limit of rainfall in nature. The level reached represents the water table; the saturated gravel represents the aquifer.

The underground aquifers of the United States hold more water than all its surface reservoirs. The depth of the water table below the surface depends on many factors. In desert regions, for example, there may be so little rainfall that a water table never forms. Whenever the water table is high enough to reach the surface we may have a spring or swamp, or we may dig a well to tap this source. Such springs and wells are a direct source of water for millions of people in the United States, in farm areas and in many urban areas as well. A great concern in recent years has been the falling water table in many areas, caused in part by the increasing amount of water being pumped out of the ground and in part by drought.

The Ogallala aquifer is a vast underground reservoir of water that has made the Great Plains one of the richest agricultural areas in the world. This immense water system spreads over 20 million acres in Texas, New Mexico, Colorado, Oklahoma, Kansas, and Nebraska. It supports nearly half of the nation's cattle industry, a quarter of its cotton crop, and a great deal of its corn, sorghum, and wheat. Gradually built up over millions of years, the aquifer is being drained as high-capacity pumps on farms suck water from the Ogallala faster than rainfall can replenish it. It is feared that in 40 years the territory could backslide into the despair of the Dust Bowl of the 1930s—with wind-blown soil, cracked earth, and abandoned farms. In some coastal areas when the water table drops, salt water from nearby sources flows into the lowered water supply and makes it unfit for drinking.

Industrial use of underground water is a significant cause of the dropping water table. It may someday be necessary to restrict the use of water for industry to surface water from streams and rivers.

Solutions to Water Shortages and Floods

What is the answer to water shortages and floods? Of great importance is the protection and extension of watershed areas. Concurrently, storage facilities—dams and reservoirs—must be constructed so that billions of gallons of water do not flow unused into the sea or cause destructive floods. Industry can help by reusing water, and home dwellers can help by eliminating the waste caused by dripping faucets and leaking pipes, and by either installing toilets that require less water or by modifying existing toilets.

Aquifers, like the Ogallala, must be protected from depletion. Some farms are already converting from water-thirsty corn to water-thrifty crops, such as wheat, sorghum, and cotton. Evaporation of water can be slowed by *trickle irrigation,* using a network of pipes that slowly drip water at the base of each plant. Electrodes planted in the fields can measure soil wetness to determine exactly when water is needed. Also proposed are huge canal systems that would import water from South Dakota, Missouri, and Arkansas.

Before a dam is built, the question must be asked, "What effect will building this dam have on the soil, the water, the plant and animal life, the people?" Answers must be obtained not only from the engineer but also from the communities affected and from the biologist, the chemist, the economist, the sociologist, the anthropologist, and others. Pictured here is Fontana Dam, towering 480 feet, the highest dam east of the Rockies. Built by the Tennessee Valley Authority, Fontana is on the Little Tennessee River in North Carolina. The electric power installation generates 202,500 kilowatts. *(Courtesy of Tennessee Valley Authority.)*

Another series of measures to alleviate water shortages is based on nature's water cycle, also known as the *hydrologic cycle*. In this cycle, described on page 391 and in Chapter 9A, pure water vapor is evaporated into the air from the oceans and is later precipitated as rain or snow. Falling on land, it eventually runs back into the oceans. In *desalination* we are supplementing nature's hydrologic cycle by getting fresh water by removing salt from ocean water. On July 20, 1967, the largest U.S. desalination plant opened in Key West, Florida, a plant that provides up to $2\frac{1}{2}$ million gallons of fresh water daily. Seven hundred and fifty desalting plants are now providing some 300 million gallons of fresh water daily for cities and industries around the world. Since much energy is required to desalinate, this source will always be more expensive than water delivered "free" by nature's solar-powered hydrological systems.

Floods are not necessarily harmful; they can be beneficial if construction of homes and factories

District Conservationist Patrick Burke checks emitter on a drip irrigation pipe at an avocado grove near Escondido, California. Drip irrigation saves water and energy and reduces the threat of erosion. *(Courtesy of U.S. Dept. of Agriculture, Soil Conservation Service.)*

on flood plains is avoided. Where a low flow of water is a concern, developments in which flow fluctuations are no problem should be favored.

Other methods being explored to increase or conserve supplies of water are the following:

Prospecting for underground water with photographs taken by satellites.

Reshaping the land surface in arid lands into broad bowls to concentrate the rainfall into one small spot.

Irrigation with saline water of plants that tolerate brackish water.

Reducing loss of water from soils by evaporation or seepage by chemically treating the soil.

The Quality of Water

A sampling of recent news presents the problem of water quality only too vividly:

Scientists warned that new contaminants are degrading drinking water. In large amounts some of the chemicals found in drinking water could cause cancer, genetic mutations, or birth deformities.

The dumping of sewage sludge for the last 40 years in the New York Bight, an area in the ocean 12 miles (19 kilometers) off Sandy Hook, has killed off so much of the marine life in a 500-square-mile (1,300-square-kilometer) area that scientists have termed this a "dead sea."

Every day, 777 industries dump 500 million gallons of toxic wastes in the Niagara River, endangering 380,000 people in Canada and the United States who drink its waters. The chemicals include some that cause birth defects, cancer, liver ailments, and central nervous system damage (source: New York Public Interest Research Group).

Recent studies have found PCBs (polychlorinated biphenyls, a cancer-causing compound), heavy metals, hydrocarbons, and excessive nitrogen from sewage in the 4,500-mile coastline waters from Cape Cod to the Bay of Fundy. These hazardous substances are a threat to the rich fishing habitat off the coast of Maine.

A research ship from Woods Hole, Massachusetts, after towing a net to collect marine life in the Sargasso Sea, reported that after 24 hours of towing the mesh became so encrusted with oil that it was necessary to clean the net with solvents. It was estimated that there was three times as much tarlike material in the net as Sargasso weeds.

The largest oil spill in North America occurred in March 1989 when the supertanker Exxon Valdez went aground and leaked 240,000 barrels of oil into Prince William Sound, Alaska. As the oil spread over the sound it killed fish, birds and mammals and left its tarry residue on the shores of the bay. Damage to the environment and the economy was incalculable.

Of 124 major industrial and sewage treatment plants discharging into Chesapeake Bay, every one dumped more than permits allowed.

A U.S.–Canadian study found that 37 million people living around the Great Lakes generally had 20 percent higher levels of toxic chemicals in their bodies than did other North Americans.

The EPA estimated that more than one third of the 800,000 U.S. underground storage tanks were leaking motor fuels and chemical solvents into the groundwater.

Normally, nature has a remarkable ability to clean up its own water by the process of filtering it through soils and sands, by aerating it as it tosses it over falls, by settling the debris in it in quieter waters, and most important of all, by the process of recycling wastes through plant and animal food chains. But now the load of pollution is becoming too heavy. Rivers and lakes can no longer purify themselves. With nearly all our waterways befouled by sewage, silt, industrial wastes, and pesticides we are just beginning to apply solutions to the water pollution problem.

Solutions to Water Pollution

The Clean Water Act of 1972 has improved many lakes and rivers in the United States, making them "fishable-drinkable" again as sources of direct pollution have been curtailed. But in recent years a dangerous new threat to the quality of water has come to light: the contamination of the nation's groundwater supplies by hazardous industrial chemical wastes. Once groundwater becomes polluted it can stay that way for decades. Regulations to stem the flow of uncontrolled dumping either have not been enacted or have not been enforced.

On June 24, 1977, natural drinking water standards went into effect across the country. Agency regulations required that the nation's 240,000 water systems test their water on a routine basis to make sure that it was safe to drink. The regulations established limits on bacteria, chemicals, pesticides, turbidity (murkiness), and radioactivity. A novel aspect of the law was that it required utilities to notify consumers if the health standards were not met.

Earlier legislation encouraged municipalities to upgrade their sewage disposal systems by providing federal grants for that purpose and by providing for federal enforcement actions. Later a federal superfund program was enacted, charged with cleaning up toxic dump sites.

In general, measures to prevent and cure the ills of water pollution, some of which are in progress in some areas, include the following:

The treatment of industrial waste to remove toxic chemicals, detergents, algae-promoting nitrates, and phosphates.

The refining and recycling of useful waste materials of industry.

The search for methods of discharging heat from electrical power plants without disturbing life in adjacent waters.

The correction of those agricultural practices that result in the washing of insecticides, herbicides, and fertilizers into waterways.

The proper handling of wastes in animal feedlots to avoid their discharge into adjacent waters; their processing so they may be recycled in the soil as fertilizer or converted into methane gas.

The phasing out of the dumping of sludge sewage into ocean waters.

The strict regulation of ships to prevent the deliberate dumping of waste tars and oils into the ocean, and of offshore wells and oil tankers to prevent the accidental spillage of petroleum.

The setting up of standards of water purity and the enforcement of these standards by municipal, state, and federal governments, to include streams, lakes, rivers, and coastal waters.

CONSERVATION OF AIR

Air, like water, is an inexhaustible resource, but pure air—air fit to breathe, air that does not irritate our eyes, air that does not damage plant life, air that does not soil and corrode the materials that we use—is becoming scarcer.

Unpolluted air is a mixture of nitrogen, oxygen, water vapor, carbon dioxide, a few rare gases, a small scattering of dust particles from soil, pollen, and salt crystals whipped aloft by the wind from ocean spray. Normally winds and air currents distribute and dilute human-made contaminants into the ocean of air that surrounds the earth. Gradually the contaminants are eliminated by natural processes, including the cleansing action of rain. Generally these natural processes proceed at a slow rate. Wherever human activities discharge pollutants into the air faster than nature's forces are able to distribute or destroy them, a buildup in pollution concentration occurs that may be destructive to materials, to plant and animal life, and to human health (see pp. 435–436, 440).

An acutely dangerous condition may arise during a *temperature inversion,* an atmospheric phenomenon that prevents normal circulation of air (see pp. 440–441). Ordinarily, warm air rises from the earth to colder layers above it, carrying much of our pollution with it. Occasionally a layer of warm air forms above cooler air near the ground; the inversion acts as a lid, preventing the pollutants from rising and dispersing. Inversions are a major factor in the production of smog—a combination of smoke and fog.

At the beginning of December 1952 the city of London went through a four-day period of still air during which pollution accumulated in a pea soup fog. Months later a review of mortality statistics revealed that 4,000 excess deaths had occurred in the city during a seven-day period that began with the first day of the fog. The illness rate during the period, especially the cardiorespiratory illness rate, increased to more than twice the normal rate for that time of year, and did not return to normal until two to three weeks later. London went through a similar episode in 1962, and the city of New York went through much the same kind of disaster in 1953 and again in 1962 and 1966.[11]

But much more alarming than the smog disasters is the often unnoticed day-by-day erosion of the health of millions by polluted air. Among the diseases attributed in part to air pollution are the common cold, emphysema (a progressive breakdown of air sacs in the lungs), bronchial asthma, lung cancer, heart disease, and nervous system disorders.

Acid Rain

When fossil fuels such as coal and oil burn, sulfur dioxide and nitrogen oxide gases are released into the atmosphere. There they combine with water vapor molecules and are converted into sulfuric acid and nitric acid droplets respectively. Eventually the droplets are washed out of the air in rain, snow, sleet, or hail, often hundreds or thousands of miles from their original emission. Together the acid precipitations are known as *acid rain.* The dissolved pollutants can increase the acidity of rain from 100 to 1,000 times.

Sulfur dioxide, the source of 60 percent of the acid component of acid rains, is created principally from the combustion of coal and oil in power plants, smelters, steel mills, factories, and space heaters. Nitrogen oxide, which produces about 35 percent of the acid, originates in the exhausts of internal combustion engines, mostly automobiles.

An extensive study prepared for the govern-

[11]National Goals in Air Pollution Research, 1960; The Effects of Air Pollution, 1966; Air Pollution—A National Sample, 1966 (U.S. Department of Health, Education and Welfare).

Smog over a city. *(Courtesy of Environmental Protection Agency.)*

ment in 1982 by 46 scientists provided evidence that pollution from coal-burning utilities and factories in the Midwest was the major cause of acid rain falling in the northeastern United States and the southeastern corner of Canada. Natural sources of acid rain such as volcanoes, salt spray, and forest fires were found to be insignificant.

A later report by the U.S. National Acid Precipitation Assessment Program, issued in 1987, provoked considerable controversy. It asserted that the nation faced little immediate danger from acid rain. Scientists and Canadian authorities, in criticizing the report, contended that it reflected opposition to the expense of pollution controls more than it clarified scientific knowledge, and that it ignored the bulk of scientific research in acid rain that has emerged in recent years (see pp. 387 and 446).

Proposed long-range solutions to the acid rain problem include the development of solar energy; burning less fossil fuel (coal and oil) for transportation and energy generation; expanding mass transit and fuel-efficient cars; use of low-sulfur fuels and the conservation of energy. However, immediate steps should be undertaken, such as the installation of *scrubbers* on top of existing smokestacks that do not have them to reduce sulfur emissions from present coal- and oil-burning plants. All new plants should be built to conform with low sulfur-emission standards. Unfortunately, present-day scrubbers are not designed to eliminate nitrogen oxides that may constitute potentially more serious problems. New clean-coal technologies for repowering aging plants promise ultimately the greatest emission reductions—sulfur dioxide emissions by more than 80 percent and nitrogen oxide emissions by more than 50 percent.[12]

Research is continuing to determine more fully how acid rain is formed and transported, and to accurately measure the effects of this phenomenon on farmlands, forests, waterways, and freshwater and marine life.

The Pollutants

At levels frequently found in heavy traffic, *carbon monoxide* produces headache, loss of visual acuity, and decreased muscular coordination. Although the burning of any carbon material produces carbon monoxide to some extent, our primary concern is the burning of gasoline in the automobiles, and the discharge low to the ground of carbon monoxide from the automobile exhaust.

Sulfur oxides, found wherever coal and oil are the common fuels, corrode metal and stone; at concentrations frequently found in our larger cities sulfur oxides reduce visibility, injure vegetation, and contribute to the incidence of respiratory disease and to premature death. They are the principal source of acid rain.

Besides their contribution to photochemical smog (described later), *nitrogen oxides* are responsible for the whiskey-brown haze that not only destroys the view in some of our cities, but at concentrations higher than those usually experienced, can interfere with respiratory functions and, it is suspected, are a cause of respiratory

disease. They are formed in the combustion of all types of fuels and contribute to acid rain.

Hydrocarbons are a very large class of chemicals, some of which, in particle form, have produced cancer in laboratory animals, and others of which, discharged chiefly by the automobile, play a major role in the formation of photochemical smog.

Photochemical smog is a complex mixture of gases and particles manufactured by sunlight out of the raw materials—nitrogen oxides and hydrocarbons—discharged to the atmosphere chiefly by the automobile. Smog, whose effects have been observed in every region of the United States, can severely damage crops and trees, deteriorate rubber and other materials, reduce visibility, cause the eyes to smart and throats to sting, and, it is thought, reduce resistance to respiratory disease.

Particulate matter not only soils our clothes, shows up on our windowsills, and scatters light to blur the image of what we see, but also acts as a catalyst in the formation of other pollutants, contributing to the corrosion of metals. In proper particle size it can carry into our lungs irritant gases that might otherwise have been harmlessly dissipated in the upper respiratory tract. Some particulates contain poisons whose effects on humans are gradual, often the result of the accumulation of years.[13]

Chlorofluorocarbons (CFCs) from spray cans and *carbon dioxide* buildup from the burning of fuels may have an adverse impact on the earth's atmosphere and on the survival of humans.

Radon is a decay product of radium, usually associated with rocks containing slate, granite, schists, phosphate, or uranium. Emitted into the outside air, it becomes harmlessly diluted, but when it seeps into homes from cracks in the foundation, through sump pumps or porous building materials, it can collect to dangerous levels. When inhaled into the lungs, radon's decay products, principally alpha particles, pose a serious health threat, causing 5,000 to 20,000 of the 130,000 lung

---

[12]V. A. Mohnen, "The Challenge of Acid Rain," *Scientific American* (August 1988).

[13]See footnote 11.

cancer deaths in the United States each year, according to the EPA. The EPA in 1988 found that one out of three of the 11,000 homes it monitored in seven states had unsafe levels of radon.

The Ozone Hole

The breakdown of the protective ozone layer of the atmosphere by CFC propellants in spray cans was discussed in Chapter 9A (see p. 218). CFCs are also used as solvents for cleaning computer chips, in refrigerants for cars and building refrigerators, and as blowing agents used to make styrofoam egg cartons and fast-food packaging. The destruction of ozone would permit more ultraviolet radiation to penetrate the atmosphere, resulting in higher incidences of skin cancer, cataracts, and depression of the immune system. Ozone depletion would affect every nation, with possible adverse effects in climate, the growth of plants, and the food chain.

Recently a mysterious change has been detected in the atmosphere of the earth—a kind of "hole" with diminished ozone content over Antarctica. Apparently the levels of ozone there had dropped 50 percent in less than a decade. Actually the ozone hole is the shape of a wafer, about the size of the United States, its thickness equivalent to the height of Mt. Everest. Satellite instruments tell us that the *global* levels of ozone have also been decreasing over a six-year period of observation. Moreover, an international team of scientists in 1989 found surprisingly high concentrations of ozone-destroying chemicals in the stratosphere above the *Arctic.*

In 1978 the United States banned the use of CFCs in aerosol products such as deodorants and hair sprays. In September of 1987, 31 nations agreed to reduce the consumption of CFCs 50 percent by the end of the century. Later, moved by new alarming reports about threats to the earth's protective ozone, twelve European nations agreed in 1988 to halt all production and use of ozone-destroying chemicals by the end of the century.

The Greenhouse Effect

The impact of an increase of carbon dioxide in the earth's environment, impeding the radiation of heat from the earth into space, as discussed in many places in the book (see Index).

> *People often think that the greenhouse effect is something that will only affect our great-grandchildren. But actually, it's a lot closer than you think. We expect that the temperature will have increased to a level which hasn't been experienced in a hundred thousand years within the next ten to fifteen years. And, by the time we get to the year 2030 ... the temperature will be four to seven degrees Fahrenheit warmer than it is now.*
>
> **JAMES HANSON, DIRECTOR GODDARD INSTITUTE FOR SPACE STUDIES**

If the greenhouse-producing gases—and that includes not only carbon dioxide, but also CFCs, nitrous oxide, and methane—continue to increase, by the middle of the next century Denver may have 86 days of 90-degree heat instead of its present 33 days, Washington three months instead of one month, Dallas nearly half a year instead of three months (see p. 424).

The greenhouse effect will result in disruptions in agriculture and in water shortages; the Midwest may return to the days of the dust bowl; the sea level is expected to rise 3 feet within the next century, causing flooding of coastal cities and low-lying areas. The EPA estimates that rising sea levels in the next 100 years could wipe out up to 80 percent of the coastal wetlands that serve as breeding grounds for fish, birds, and other wildlife along the Atlantic and Gulf coasts.

The Attack on Air Pollution

Under the Clean Air Act of 1970, the EPA set minimum standards of air purity to curb pollution by industry and automobiles. The Clean Air Act required the U.S. Environmental Protection Agency to set limits on how much pollution is permitted

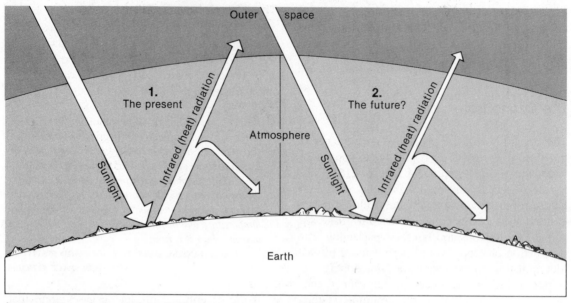

The greenhouse effect: (1) Sunlight penetrates the atmosphere warming the earth's surface. The earth radiates the heat as infrared rays. Carbon dioxide and other gasses in the earth's atmosphere trap part of the infrared radiation; the rest escapes into space. The result is a much higher average surface temperature than would be possible without the blanketing effect of the atmosphere. (2) An increase in carbon dioxide and other gases from man-made sources (which is now occurring) traps more infrared radiation, thereby heating the earth even more.

in the air you breathe. Standards to protect your health and the environment have been set for such important pollutants as sulfur dioxide, carbon monoxide, ozone, oxides of nitrogen, lead, and particulates, and requires the states and industry to meet these limits on a fixed but reasonable timetable.

The Clean Air Act expired in 1981. Presently Congress is considering reauthorizing and revitalizing the act. Key issues include both measures to reduce acid rain deposition, ozone and carbon monoxide in urban areas, the emission of toxic substances, indoor air pollution, and the development of technologies for burning coal more cleanly.

Other measures for controlling air pollution include the following:

1. Far greater use of mass transportation facilities. A busload of 50 people pollutes less than 50 auto-mobiles. A trainload of 1,000 people pollutes less than 20 buses or 1,000 autos.
2. Adoption of rigid controls on auto traffic in cities in an effort to attain acceptable air quality, including higher bridge tolls, limitations on taxi cruising, restricted parking, and restricted delivery hours. Encouragement of car pooling.
3. Substitution of electric and other nonpolluting automobiles and buses for gasoline-driven vehicles.
4. City and regional planning for the best location of industries with respect to homes, open areas, and recreation areas.
5. Prohibition of burning leaves, trash, and garbage by individuals or municipalities.
6. Production of electric power by methods other than burning fuel: solar energy, tidal energy, and natural steam and hot water sources from earth (see pp. 397–403).

The cost of pollution is so high that it cannot be estimated: the widespread exodus of people and business from big cities; the agricultural losses—including damage to livestock and crops; the deterioration of materials, structures, and machines; the blighted environment; and the damage to the health of human beings. To control air pollution government and industry must spend billions. When we consider the priceless benefits of clean air to our health alone, surely the cost of adequate control of air pollution is a bargain.

CONSERVATION OF WILDERNESS

Our National Park System, long a cherished treasure of America, is now in imminent danger. Threats to the integrity of the parks come from pressures of exploitive interests within the parks and from its borders: from real estate speculators, oil and gas explorers, unchecked air polluters, and road, airport, and tourist-resort builders.

The fight for the parks is but one chapter in the long struggle to save the remaining wilderness of America. Only $2\frac{1}{2}$ percent of our land is preserved as wilderness—in national parks and monuments, national forests, and wildlife refuges.

Wilderness was once thought of as something to be subdued and conquered, something to be fought and destroyed. There is growing recognition today that wilderness itself is a most precious heritage.

The Wilderness Act, which set up the National Wilderness Preservation System and was passed by Congress in 1964, was a clear declaration that wilderness no longer has to be fought and conquered. The act states, "wilderness, in contrast with those areas where man and his own works dominate the landscape, is ... recognized as an area where the earth and its community of life are untrammeled by man, where man himself is a visitor who does not remain." The act gave much-needed recognition and protection to wilderness areas in the national parks, national forests, and national wildlife refuges. Congress must approve any change in establishing wilderness areas and must also approve creation of new wilderness areas.

But the concept of wilderness conservation is not one of exclusive isolation for the few. Rather,

as the Wilderness Society's late Howard Zahniser (the prime mover of the Wilderness Act) put it, "We work for wilderness preservation not primarily for the right of a minority to have the kind of fun it prefers, but rather to insure for everyone the perpetuation of areas where human enjoyment and the apprehension of the interrelations of the whole community of life are possible, and to preserve for all the freedom of choosing to know the primeval if they so wish."

Wetlands

Only in recent years have we begun to understand that wetlands—swamps, bogs, and marshes—are an important natural resource. In the past, people regarded wetlands as wastelands—areas to be drained, dredged, and filled in for roads, homes, and factories.

Wetlands are generally low areas with shallow water or water-soaked soils that support aquatic or semiaquatic plants. Inland wetlands serve as natural sponges for storm and runoff water, moderating flooding and releasing water slowly to recharge underground reservoirs that serve as municipal or farmland water sources. They prevent shoreline and bank erosion. Wetlands improve water quality by trapping and breaking down toxic chemicals and organic wastes such as nitrates.

Wetlands also serve as a nursery for many species of fish: Two thirds of the fish caught commercially off the Atlantic and Gulf Coasts and one half of the Pacific Coast catch depend on wetlands and adjacent estuaries for spawning and food. The Texas wetlands are indispensable for its shrimp industry. Wetlands also provide a critical habitat for many wildlife species: birds, amphibia, small mammals.

In addition, wetlands serve as living laboratories, extending and enriching classroom learning. They provide opportunities for bird watching, wildlife photography, sketching, and fishing.

Recognizing that less than half of the nation's original 215 million acres of wetlands exist today, the U.S. Fish and Wildlife Service in 1962 began a program of acquiring wetlands to protect them

Wetlands are not wastelands. They support birdlife, are a nursery for fish, moderate flooding, and serve as reservoirs for farms and cities. (Note the pelicans above and wood ibises in the water.) *(Courtesy of the Nature Conservancy.)*

as habitats. Other wetlands have been purchased by the National Audubon Society and the Nature Conservation Agency. The federal government and a number of states have adopted wetlands protection laws. Despite these efforts, wetlands continue to be destroyed at an estimated rate of 300,000 to 450,000 acres per year.

Prairies

The prairie is much more than fields of grass. It is an intricate web of relationships among many kinds of plants and animals. A single acre of grassland may harbor as many as 300 species of plants, some of which may constitute an invaluable gene pool for plant breeders to draw on. Creatures of many kinds and sizes live there—mammals, birds, insects, and microorganisms.

Most of the open treeless beauty of this unique habitat has disappeared from the American landscape, replaced by croplands, highways, and cities. At one time 60 percent of Illinois was blanketed by grassland; today less than one hundredth of 1 percent of the state's original prairie still exists. In recent years there has been growing interest in the management of remaining prairies and the restoration or creation of new ones.

The City and the Wilderness

Most people now live in cities. It is estimated that in the next 20 years 90 percent of the people in

"There are only a few tall prairies left today, but they are worth seeking—worth going to and being in. They are the last lingering scraps of the old time, fragments of original wealth and beauty, cloaked with plants you may never have seen and may never see again." *John Madison in Where the Sky began—Land of the Tallgrass Prairie (Houghton Mifflin, 1982.)*
How many prairie chickens can you find in this photo of a prairie habitat? (Our thanks to John E. Schwegman of the Illinois Dept. of Conservation for supplying ideas about the prairie and for securing this photo.) *Photo by Marlin Roos. (Courtesy of Illinois State Museum, Springfield, Illinois.)*

the United States will live on 10 percent of the land. Not all can travel easily to the large wilderness areas—to Yellowstone, the Grand Canyon, Yosemite. Yet people long for an accessible outdoors. We must now utilize, restore, and create areas close to large cities. Many natural wild or semiwild areas are still available: marshlands, desert lands, grassland, ocean environments, geological formations, and wildlife communities. Some of these are within the boundaries of cities, many nearby. They need the same kind of protection and development for educational purposes as the large national parks.

The proximity of natural areas to urban centers makes them valuable as outdoor classrooms, where the lessons of nature can be learned *in* nature. Municipal and state parks will also serve to relieve the pressure on national parks.

To meet the needs of the millions living in urban centers, coordination in planning and in action is required of federal, state, and local authorities, as well as of conservation groups and individual citizens. Often this will require the purchase of land, or condemnation by a government agency—acquisition at a fair value without the owner's consent. This may be done if it is in the public interest. The U.S. Supreme Court, in an opinion written by Justice William O. Douglas in

1954, stated, "The concept of the public welfare is broad and inclusive. The values it represents are spiritual as well as physical, aesthetic as well as monetary. It is within the power of the legislature to determine that the community should be beautiful as well as healthy, spacious as well as clean, well balanced as well as carefully patrolled."

To provide relief from intensive urbanization it is necessary to use or create areas within the city itself, *where people are.* Cities are beginning to develop greenbelts, parks, and vest-pocket parks within their confines.

Acquisition of natural areas is not a goal for governments only; many civic groups, including watershed associations, park foundations, and wildlife and nature conservation organizations have had marked success in preserving open space. When it was proposed that 2,000 acres of the Great Swamp in Morris County, New Jersey, be drained and made into a jetport for the N.Y. Port Authority, the land was purchased by a committee of the North American Wildlife Federation, supported by civic organizations. Later the land was turned over to the federal government. Now, as the Great Swamp National Refuge, it has an observation shelter and trail for visitors who wish to study and photograph wildlife in a natural setting. The unique Sunken Forest on Fire Island, with its primeval stand of holly trees, was purchased by the Sunken Forest Preserves, Inc., to save it from a real estate developer's bulldozer. Later, when Fire Island became a national seashore, the Sunken Forest was turned over to the Department of the Interior for administration on behalf of the public. Each summer thousands of visitors under the expert guidance of park rangers explore the shaded trails of this unique forest.

Fundamental to our use of land is our attitude toward it. Aldo Leopold, in *A Sand County Almanac,* states, "We abuse land because we regard it as a commodity belonging to us. When we see it as a community to which we belong, we may begin to use it with love and respect." This attitude has come to be known as the *land ethic.*

CONSERVATION OF THE URBAN ENVIRONMENT

The rebuilding and renewing of our cities, where most of us now live, is one of the very most important of our conservation jobs. The building of new towns and communities, too, should help provide better habitats for humans. Through federal aid, numbers of new communities are now being started, some still on the drawing boards, others under construction. It is to be hoped that the new habitats will bring humans, buildings, and nature once again into proper balance (see pp. 436–438).

THE ENVIRONMENTAL AWAKENING

The most important business on earth, quite literally, [is] the business of planetary planning.
NORMAN COUSINS

In 1968 a Senate document of great potential significance stated

It is the intent of the Congress that the policies, programs and public laws of the United States be interpreted and administered in a manner protective of the total needs of man in the environment. To this end, the Congress proposes that arrangements be established to make effective the following objectives of national policy for the environment.

1. To arrest the deterioration of the environment.
2. To restore and revitalize damaged areas of our nation so that they may once again be productive of economic wealth and spiritual satisfaction.
3. To find alternatives and procedures which will minimize and prevent future hazards in the use of environment-shaping technologies, old and new.
4. To provide direction and, if necessary, new institutions and new technologies, designed to optimize man–environment relationships and to minimize future costs in the management of the environment.

The essence of this document was incorporated into the National Environmental Policy Act of 1969. The EPA was set up to implement and enforce environmental programs.

But the 1969 act was only a beginning. It is being tested as we cope with the difficult environmental problems of the United States and the world, from urban parks to agricultural pesticides, from wetlands to the disposal of industrial wastes, from automobile exhaust products to thermal pollution, from energy shortages to the blight of the inner city, from the erosion of soil to the hunger of millions on our planet.

THE STOCKHOLM CONFERENCE

A United Nations Conference on Human Environment was convened in Stockholm in July 1972. Almost a complete cross-section of the world's $3\frac{1}{2}$ billion people was represented by delegates from 114 nations. Although there were differences, the most remarkable thing was that such a conference was actually held, that it acknowledged that a worldwide environmental emergency existed, and that nations despite their sovereignty had mutual responsibilities for such common property as the atmosphere and the oceans. Approval was given to an "action program" with 200 recommendations, ranging from monitoring climatic change and oceanic pollution to the preservation of the world's vanishing plant and animal species. An administrative machinery was recommended to coordinate the worldwide environmental efforts of governments and agencies.

Margaret Mead, the noted anthropologist, summed up the thoughts of the many nongovernmental conservation groups who watched from the sidelines. In an address to the conference on behalf of these groups she said,

> This is a revolution in thought, fully comparable to the Copernican revolution by which, four centuries ago, men were compelled to revise their whole sense of the earth's place in the cosmos. Today we are challenged to recognize as a great change in our

concept of man's place in the biosphere. Our survival in a world that continues to be worth inhabiting depends upon translating this new perception into relevant principles and concrete actions.

IMPORTANT GENERALIZATIONS

In the long run, our welfare depends on the natural world. Our well-being depends on other living things, on air, on soil, on minerals, on energy resources.

Our planet is a closed system in which indefinite expansion or exploitation of its resources would be disastrous to all life, including that of humans.

Life is limited to a 13-mile-thick layer of our planet called the ecosphere or biosphere.

In the biosphere humans enjoy the benefits of a self-renewing environment.

A major goal of education is the recognition by humans of their interdependence with the environment and with life everywhere, and the development of a culture that maintains that relationship through policies and practices necessary to secure the future of an environment fit for life and fit for living.

The understanding of interrelationships of living things with each other and with their physical environment—the science of ecology—is the key to sound environmental practice.

Food chains and food webs are pathways along which materials and energy are passed along in the world of living things.

The organisms that are part of a food chain or food web act as producers (usually green plants), consumers (usually animals), or decomposers (usually bacteria and fungi).

The number of living organisms necessary to support a food chain may be represented by a pyramid with a broad base of food producers, green plants, at the bottom; with plant-eating animals on the next steps; and with carnivorous animals up to the apex.

All living things are dependent on the interwoven cycles of water, carbon dioxide, oxygen, and nitrogen.

The consequences of disturbing the web of life are often unforeseen and often unfortunate.

Pesticide chemicals and other chemicals introduced into the environment by humans must be used with caution because they may end up in plants and animals other than those for which they were intended, and because they may disturb a chain of interrelationships in such a way as to harm other forms of life.

Some resources, such as air, sunlight, and water, are inexhaustible. Air and water, however, can become unfit for living things.

Some resources, such as soil, vegetation, animal life, and fresh water, are renewable.

Some resources, such as coal, oil, natural gas, metals, land as open space, and certain kinds of wilderness, are nonrenewable. Their supply cannot be replenished.

As we use up convenient energy sources, such as the fossil fuels, we are turning more to the fission of atoms. In using both sources, however, there are serious pollution problems. We are developing new ways of using solar energy.

We must conserve resources as far as possible by recycling them and by reducing our consumption of them.

All plants and animals, including humans, are dependent directly or indirectly on the soil.

One third of the valuable topsoil in the United States has been lost since the coming of the colonists, largely because of unwise practices.

The erosion of soil can be checked by contour plowing, strip farming, and terracing.

Forests are very important in preventing soil erosion and floods.

To maintain soil fertility, it is necessary to return to the soil what the crops remove.

Rotation of crops, the planting of legumes, and the addition of fertilizers help maintain soil fertility.

Forest conservation measures include combating fire, harmful insects, and tree diseases; practicing careful lumbering methods; reforestation; the establishing of national and state forests; and the recycling of paper.

The problem of water conservation is that of having the right amount of fresh water of good quality in the right place at the right time.

A matter of concern in recent years has been the falling water table in many areas.

Water conservation involves the protection and extension of watershed areas, construction of dams and reservoirs, improved industrial practices in relation to water usage—including the reuse of water—elimination of waste, and the use of water-conserving irrigation practices on farmlands.

Acid rain has killed fish and other life in thousands of lakes, damaged forests, agricultural crops, and buildings, and poses a threat to human health.

Automobile exhausts and smokestacks produce most of the dangerous air pollutants.

Chlorofluorocarbons (CFCs) pose a threat to the protective ozone layer of the atmosphere. The breakdown of the layer would permit more ultraviolet radiation to penetrate the atmosphere, causing adverse effects on our climate, agriculture, and our health.

The dumping of toxic chemical wastes poses an awesome threat to our health and safety.

Wildlife should be protected because of its economic value—both immediate and long range—its recreational value, and its right to exist.

Whenever a species or population becomes extinct, a working part of an ecosystem is destroyed.

Wetlands prevent floods and droughts, serve as nurseries for many species of fish, provide a critical habitat for many forms of life, break down toxic chemicals, and serve as laboratories for learning.

Conservation includes the improvement of the urban environment—better housing, more neighborhood facilities, reduction of air and noise pollution, and better planning.

The preservation of open areas in and near urban centers serves many vital purposes.

Humans are a part and a partner of nature.

The new environmental challenge is not mastery by humans of their environment but mastery of their desires and judgment with respect to the use of their environment.

DISCOVERING FOR YOURSELF

1. Investigate the source of your local water supply and find out about the problems of its purification, pollution, and adequacy.

2. Investigate the arguments pro and con with respect to the further construction of nuclear energy plants, including the breeder reactor. Are nuclear power plants in operation in your area? Are any planned?

3. Find out about the Clean Air Act of 1970 and the National Environmental Policy Act of 1969. What differences have the passages of these acts made in your environment? Does your state have "clean

air" plans to comply with the standards set up by the federal government?

4. Find out about the work of the Environmental Protection Agency (EPA).

5. Investigate examples of biological control used in your community or state—for the Japanese beetle and the gypsy moth, for instance. How successful are these attempts? What hazards are involved?

6. Investigate some of the newer sources of energy that are now being tested—the sun, wind, tides, and biomass. What progress is being made? What are the difficulties? Why are these investigations important?

7. Investigate the possibilities of saving energy in your home and community.

8. Read *Silent Spring* by Rachel Carson and *Since Silent Spring* by Frank Graham, Jr. What pesticides are in common use in the area where you live? What are the results?

9. What environmental damage is created by various fuels?

10. Examine carefully a woodlot or other area that has been burned. Find out what has happened to the animal and plant life. Observe the area over a period of a month or as long as possible to see what happens.

11. Observe various hillsides after a heavy rain. Describe them and compare the results of the rain on the surface of each. Explain what happened.

12. Keep a record of the things you use in one day that come from the earth. Indicate those that are in danger of becoming depleted, those that are being replaced in sufficient quantity, and those that appear to be in plentiful supply.

13. Find out about air pollution in your state. Is smog a problem? What is being done about it?

14. Interview a county agriculture agent or some other individual who is concerned with soil, water, and wildlife conservation in your area. Find out what the most pressing conservation problems are, why they have become critical, and what is being done about them.

15. Visit an experimental farm or station and find out how research is being carried out to solve environmental problems.

16. Plan and carry out an experiment that will show the results of using or not using a commercial fertilizer in soil.

17. Get copies of the game laws of your state for the past five or ten years. Examine the laws. What changes have been made? Why have they been made?

18. Find out what the problems of forest conservation in your state are. Locate tree nurseries; visit one and report your findings. Gather seeds of various kinds of forest trees and try to germinate them. Talk with a forest ranger, forest lookout observer, or other individual who has firsthand information about forest conservation.

19. What wetlands are there in your area or state? Why is it important to protect them?

20. Investigate noise pollution in your community. Why is it a problem? What is being done about it?

21. Investigate the "let burn" policy that is being discussed and practiced by foresters and rangers in certain areas. Is it true that some forest fires are actually desirable? In what ways? Do you agree with this point of view?

22. Find out about the dolphin-killing controversy involving tuna fishermen.

23. Make a graph of world population growth, based on data given on page 397.

24. Investigate current theories about the cause of the "ozone hole" over Antarctica. (See *Scientific American,* January 1988.)

25. Prepare a list of environmental laws or amendments to existing laws that you would like enacted by your local or state legislature, or by the federal government. Present arguments to back up one of your proposals.

26. Prepare a list of organizations involved in environmental programs. Describe in detail the program of one of these.

27. Investigate air pollution inside homes and buildings. See "Controlling Indoor Air Pollution" in *Scientific American,* May 1988 by A. V. Nero, Jr.

28. Read the special issue of *Scientific American,* September 1989, on "Managing Planet Earth."

TEACHING "ECOLOGY, ENERGY, AND THE ENVIRONMENT"

Ecology, the study of living things in relation to each other and to the environment, is a natural area for the linkage of science, technology, and society. Science provides knowledge, technology provides ways of using this knowledge, and our values guide us in what to do about both to serve society (see Chapter 2, pp. 27–29).

Consider, for example, the ecological problems involved in pollution. Science investigates the extent of, and the changes in air, water, and soil pollution and its impact on our health and economy. Technology provides techniques and equipment for avoiding and reducing pollution. The needs of society—health, safety, and costs—guide us in selecting courses of action.

How can we make the study of ecology meaningful and challenging for children? Here are a few approaches:

Everything Comes from Something. Think of breakfast. The bread we eat comes, in part, from flour (bake some); flour comes from ground-up wheat seeds (grind some); wheat seeds come from wheat plants (grow some); wheat plants require soil, water, and sunlight (experiment to find out—if wheat seeds are not available, grass seeds may be used). How about orange juice, milk, butter and jelly?

What We Do Makes a Difference. Make a survey of pollution in your neighborhood—air, water, trash, noise. What can we do about it? (See p. 435.) Investigate acid precipitation in your rain, ponds and streams (see p. 446). How can your school and community area be beautified? (Start a letter-writing campaign to the proper authorities.) How can we save energy? Make a model solar energy collector (see p. 438.) Investigate electricity and water usage in your homes (see pp. 439–440).

What Food Chains Can We Discover? Investigate food chains on the lawn, in and around trees, in the soil, in a pond or lake. (See pp. 441–442).

Since ecology is based on an understanding of the interrelationships of humans with their natural and physical environment, it is sound practice to study ecology *in* the environment. Any neighborhood, city or country, can serve as a laboratory for the study of these interrelationships. The school grounds are constantly changing under the influence of the sun, rain, and wind. The trees on the street provide shade and beauty for human beings, protection for birds, food for insects. Parks, fields, streams, and rivers provide further opportunities for discovering interrelationships in nature. Bulldozers that uproot trees to provide building sites give children an opportunity to study how humans are changing the environment.

Each school can make a survey of its environment to discover changes and needs. It is effective when children, teachers, parents, and other interested individuals cooperate in making such an inventory and engage in the activities necessary to improve existing conditions. The outcome of this survey may be a campaign to clean up an area, participation in a program of recycling paper, glass bottles, and metals, or in any other project that involves children in constructive community activity. When children see that what they do makes a difference, they have learned one of the prime concepts of ecology and survival.[1]

We hope that when children become adults they will participate in and support the endeavors of local and national groups to further the improvement of our environment, that they will be able to distinguish between the selfish interests of small pressure groups and the large interests of all people, that they will not be beguiled into sacrificing our precious inheritance for momentary gains.

In addition to Chapter 13A, other chapters related to these concerns are "The Earth and Its Surface," Chapter 6A; "The Sun and the Planets," Chapter 7A; "The Air and the Weather," Chapter 9A; "The Nature and Variety of Life," Chapter 10A; and "The History of Life," Chapter 12A.

SOME BROAD CONCEPTS

We depend for our existence on living things, water, air, soil, and mineral resources.

[1] J. M. Fowler, *Energy—Environment Source Book 1980; Environmental Education in the Elementary School, 1977,* (Washington, D.C.: NSTA).

The world's population increase multiplies the problems of the care and use of its resources.

All living things are related to each other and to their environment.

Food chains are the paths followed by materials and energy in the world of living things.

Pesticides and other chemicals used by man may disturb the chain of interrelationships and must be used with caution.

Some of our resources are renewable; others are not.

We must conserve resources by recycling when possible.

All living things depend directly or indirectly on the soil.

Conservation involves the wise use of our resources in both city and rural environments.

When air, water, and soil become polluted they cannot serve their functions in the cycles of nature. Such pollution must be avoided.

Energy in various forms is used by us every day.

The fossil fuels—gas, coal, and oil—provide us with most of the energy we use today.

Additional sources of energy are wind, tides, and geothermal (earth heat) and nuclear energy.

Energy can be conserved by developing energy-saving habits.

FOR YOUNGER CHILDREN

There are many experiences for young children that will help prepare them for a better understanding of ecology. Some of these activities—for example, keeping a pet, raising a garden, observing the places where animals live, seeing how animals take care of their young—have been described in other chapters.

Here we suggest additional activities focused on the development of understandings leading to attitudes and actions essential in ecology, energy, and the environment.[2]

[2]M. McIntyre, "Human Ecology," *Science and Children* (April 1976). Describes activities for young children who are studying air pollution, living space, and noise pollution in their environment. "Some Environmental Observations for Young Children," *Science and Children* (April 1975); A. B. Bergman, "Environmental Education for Early Childhood," *Environmental Education in the Elementary School* (Washington, D.C.: NSTA, 1977).

Where Do the Things We Use Come From?[3]

As children explore their environment to see how they use plants and animals, they will also consider where these and other things they use come from. They may begin by making a list of plants and animals they use and expanding it to include additional materials, such as iron and other metals, bricks, glass, gasoline, and so on. Pictures from magazines and other sources that show things we use will be helpful. The children may then examine the list and attempt to devise a classification: from under the ground, grow in soil, come from animals, and others. Give children an opportunity to try out different classifications that they suggest.

Having made a grouping, suggest that children now try to reclassify the items according to those that we use up, those we can replace, those we can use over again, or some other classification that will help children realize that some of the materials are plentiful, some are renewable, some nonrenewable, some inexhaustible (see Chapter 13A, pp. 394–396).

In connection with the problem of "Where does milk come from?" children, if possible, should visit a dairy farm to see for themselves the feeding and milking of cows. Many children have little knowledge of where bread comes from. It will be illuminating for them to grind some wheat seeds to get an idea of how flour is produced. See also Chapter 10B, page 291, for experiences in early childhood involving the preparation of such foods as butter, orange juice, cranberry sauce, vegetable soup, and fruit cup.

This discussion of where things we use come from can lead to consideration of why we need to conserve some of the materials, how this is being done, and how children can help. Recycling may be considered. It may be possible for children to visit a plant where some kind of recycling is taking place. The practices of paper and metal

[3]J. Schwartz, *It's Fun To Know Why: Experiments with Things Around Us* (New York: McGraw-Hill, 1973).

collecting for recycling, using returnable bottles, and so on, are important to consider and engage in.

Suggestions for classroom and personal conservation should be drawn up. They may include such items as economical use of paper and other materials, use of lights and electrical appliances only when needed, and limiting the use of water. Children may add to this list and prepare their own checklist to guide them. Older children will prepare a more sophisticated list (see pp. 439–440).

What Makes the Air Polluted?

The problem of exploring air pollution is developed in detail for older children later in this chapter, but because of its importance it is also suggested here. Examine the "Air Pollution" section in the checklist that follows in the projects for older children, and select items that seem appropriate for consideration by younger children. Begin by suggesting that they observe air conditions on several different days, and see if they can notice any differences. Suggest that they consider sources of air pollution on their way to and from school (smokestacks, cars and buses, airplanes, and others) and report them. Keep a list of these sources. Help the children to discover what is being done to stop pollution. Discuss why polluted air is not healthful (See Chapter 13A, pp. 420–425).

Why Is Soil So Important to Us?

The background for the study of soil is suggested in Chapters 6A and B, and in 13A. Chapter 10B describes experiences and experiments intended to help children understand what plants need in order to live and grow.

If children have not had these experiences plan for them to

1. Examine soil to find out what it is made of.

2. Plant seeds in different kinds of soil (good and poor), and observe the effects on plant growth.
3. Use fertilizer on some plants and not on others, and note the differences.
4. Explore the schoolyard and observe plants growing in different soils, noting the difference.
5. Examine "vacant" lots to see what plants are growing there.
6. List the things they use in one day that come directly and indirectly from the soil.

Other Problems for Younger Children

1. What do we use that comes from trees?
2. How do we use plants and animals?
3. Where does our water supply come from?
4. How is water made safe for drinking?
5. What pollutes our drinking water?
6. How can we improve the appearance of our schoolyard?
7. Where do animals and plants live in our neighborhood?[4]
8. Why is the water cycle important to us?
9. What can we learn about the life of a tree?
10. What do water and wind do to soil?

FOR OLDER CHILDREN

How Can We Study a City Environment?

What is your environment like? Investigating this problem in the city involves important research skills and the gathering of data that are essential in *identifying the problems* that exist in this environment, leading to *suggestions for attempting to solve them.*

The following checklist, designed to assist students in surveying a city environment, was used

[4]See "Little Environments: In the Schoolyard, On and Under a Tree, On the Lawn, In the Soil, In the Water" in *Science, Grade 5* (Brooklyn: Board of Education of the City of New York, 1968). May be adapted for younger children; contains many suggestions for observation.

as part of an "EARTH DAY" observance.[5] The list can be altered to fit other environments and may be used at any time during the year. Use of the list involves several important processes, including *observing, collecting* and *recording data,* and *interpreting* the data.

An Environmental Checklist

EARTH DAY (now called SUN DAY), as April 22 is known, is the beginning of a long, ongoing effort to improve the environment. After collecting and interpreting the data, your class may want to consider the most effective ways in which it can participate in follow-up activities.

Names_____
PS _____ Borough _____
Address_____
Was the walk in A.M.? _____ P.M. _____
How long did the walk last? _____ hours
_____ mins.

Walk around the square block on which your school is located. Look, listen, smell, touch. Check the things you find.

Air Pollution

1. How does the sky look?_____ clear
   _____ hazy_____ darker in some parts than in others
2. Do your eyes tear or smart? _____ yes
   _____ no
3. Do you smell anything in the air?
   _____ yes _____ no
4. Do you like what you smell? _____ yes
   _____ no

5. Check any of these things you smell.
   _____ food _____ gasoline
   _____ car exhaust _____ garbage
   _____ others
6. If possible, watch a bus leave a stop. Can you see the exhaust? _____ yes
   _____ no
7. Do you see exhaust coming from automobiles or trucks? _____ yes
   _____ no If yes, from how many autos or trucks? _____
8. Do you see any airplanes? _____ yes
   _____ no If yes, (a) how many? _____
   (b) how many are leaving a trail of dark exhaust? _____
9. Do you see dark smoke coming out of chimneys? _____ yes _____ no
   If yes, are these chimneys on
   _____ apartment houses _____ private houses _____ factories
   _____ power plants
   _____ city-owned buildings
   _____ others
10. Rub a tissue against the wall of a building, a fence, a lamppost, or a mailbox. Does the tissue get dirty? _____ yes
    _____ no

Litter and Destruction[6]

1. How many litter baskets do you see on your walk? _____
2. How many are _____ empty
   _____ partly filled _____ full
   _____ overflowing
3. Is there litter? _____ along the curb
   _____ on the sidewalks
   _____ near the buildings

[5]J. Rosner, "An Environmental Checklist," in *Newsletter of the Elementary School Science Association,* Vol. 9, No. 2 (New York: spring, 1970); M. S. Griffin, "Ecological Studies in the Middle School? Yes!" *Science and Children* (October 1974).

[6]B. D. McCollum, "Litter Study: A School Research Project," *Science and Children* (April 1976). Account of a school project. R. S. Grover, "Operation Waste Watch," *Science and Children* (March 1981). A program for grades K–6 in litter control, recycling, and resources recovery.

4. How many covered garbage cans do you see?
_____

5. How many uncovered garbage cans do you see? _____

6. How many soda or beer can flip-tops do you see? _____

7. How many of the soda or beer cans are made of iron? _____ (use a magnet)

8. Is there broken glass along the curb?
_____ yes _____ no on the sidewalk?
_____ yes _____ no

9. How many times do you see evidence that people did not curb their dogs? _____

10. How many candy, gum, or ice-cream wrappers do you find on the sidewalk or along the curb? _____

11. Are there any pieces of furniture or other household articles lying on the sidewalk or in the street? _____ yes _____ no If yes, how many? _____

12. Are there any abandoned cars in the street?
_____ yes _____ no
If yes, how many? _____

13. Are there newspapers lying on the sidewalk or flying around? _____ yes _____ no

14. How many vacant lots or strips of land do you see? _____ How many are tidy and pretty? _____ How many ugly? _____

15. How many broken windows do you see?
_____

16. In how many places do you see writing on the walls, billboards, public signs, or on sidewalks? _____

Noise Pollution

1. Stand still for two minutes and listen. Check all the sounds you hear. Add others not on the list _____ fire engine _____ train
_____ horn _____ ambulance
_____ police siren _____ airplane
_____ bus engine _____ truck engine
_____ screeching brakes _____ foghorn
_____ autos or trucks moving along the street _____ shouting _____ riveting
_____ cement mixer _____ bulldozer

2. How would you rate the general noise level?
_____ very noisy _____ noisy
_____ moderate _____ quiet

Trees and Plants

1. How many trees do you see? _____

2. How many of these trees (a) are growing straight _____ bent _____
(b) have some soil around them _____
have no soil _____
(c) have broken branches _____
(d) have pictures or words carved on them _____
(e) look healthy _____ look sickly _____

3. How many of the dead or sickly trees are near bus stops? _____

4. How many places do you see where trees have been removed? _____

5. How many of the following do you see?
(a) windowboxes _____
(b) small gardens _____
(c) vest-pocket parks _____

6. Is there a park or large green area within sight?
yes _____ no

Children may make up a similar checklist for observing animals in their community. Example items:

1. How many animals did you see? _____
What kinds? _____

2. Where did you find them? _____ in the air
_____ in the trees and shrubs
_____ on the ground

3. What was the environment like where you found the animals? _____ dry _____ wet
_____ shady _____ hot

4. What do the animals eat? _____

5. How do these animals benefit us?

6. Are some of them pests? _____ yes
_____ no Why? _____

Operation New York is an example of a project designed to explore the use of a city outdoor environment, and suggest ways in which rocks, water, soil, plants, and animals may be used to provide meaningful and enjoyable experiences for children.[7] It is a guide to the study of earth forms: hills, plains, rock outcrops, lakes, rivers, harbors, and beaches. *Operation New York* also uses the locale of the school—the schoolyard, nearby buildings, excavations, sidewalks, and curbs—for an understanding of our use of earth resources. Attention is directed to the forces of nature at work: erosion of soil in a vacant lot or nearby park, formation of "flood areas" following a storm, the wearing away of stone, the decay of leaves into soil. The inter-relationships of living things—including humans—with their physical surroundings are understood as children explore the many "little environments" that are found within the city. A study of this report will provide many suggestions to other city groups for using their environments more effectively.

Children may survey a city to find out how provisions are made for water, food, and other essentials. This investigation may be followed by a survey of waste disposal, air and water pollution, and other conditions.

The scientific, technological, and social aspects of the problems of conservation are related. This is one of the places where these areas of the curriculum should certainly be considered together. Such relationships will be obvious in many of the activities in this chapter.

How Can We Use Solar Energy?

The use of the sun's energy is becoming more and more important. Suggest that children investigate their community to find examples of homes and other structures that use solar energy. If there are such structures, try to arrange for a field trip to learn about how they operate, how successful

[7]*Operation New York: Using the Natural Environment of the City as a Curriculum Resource* (Brooklyn: Board of Education of the City of New York, 1960).

The cupcake liner on this solar energy "machine" is spinning rapidly, and its vanes cannot be distinguished.

they are, and what the advantages and drawbacks are. A follow-up discussion is important. Urge children to find pictures to show different kinds of arrangements for the use of solar energy.[8]

The apparatus pictured here was made by a sixth-grade student as a summer science project and brought to his science class.[9]

[8]C. W. Knight, III and L. Wohlagen, "Solar Heated Homes: They're Here," *Science and Children* (May 1975). Contains very useful diagrams. T. Grier and J. R. Wailes, "Solar Energy: Classroom Reality," *Science and Children* (September 1979). Diagram and directions for making a solar collector. J. L. Mason and J. S. Cantrell, "Activities for Teaching Solar Energy," *Science and Children* (April 1980); R. C. King, "Solar Cookers," *Science and Children* (April 1981). Includes diagrams. H. C. Hayden, "Solar Energy: How Bright the Prospects?" *The Science Teacher* (April 1981).

[9]Adapted from J. Schwartz and M. Green, "A Summer Project Comes to School," *Science and Children* (April 1964). Based on an experience described by Rose Blaustein, the machine plans are from K. N. Swezey, *After-Dinner Science* (New York: McGraw-Hill, 1961).

He called it a solar energy machine. He used a metal can (originally a container for turpentine) painted black with the bottom removed. Three clothespins supported the can. A sewing needle was fastened by rubber bands to the neck of the can. The needle supported a fluted cupcake liner that had eight L-shaped cuts in the bottom. These flaps were folded up slightly.

When the machine was left in the sun for a while, the sun's radiation was absorbed by the can and converted into heat. In turn, the can heated air inside, setting up a convection current that caused the cupcake pinwheel to spin (see chapter 15A, p. 487)

When the children had observed the machine they asked many questions: "How fast can it go?" "How can we measure how fast it goes?" "Will it work every day?" "Will it work faster on some days than on others?" "Does the hour of the day make any difference in how fast it will work?" "What would happen if the can was painted another color?" These questions provided the motivation for the children to design their own experiments to find answers. New problems arose. There were opportunities to make up research designs, gather quantitative data, and interpret results.

The machine makes the idea of solar energy real and can lead into the exploration of other examples of the use of such energy.

The solar water heater has become common in many parts of the country. Its operation may be demonstrated by the use of a garden hose. Use a coil of hose connected to a faucet and filled with water. Close the nozzle to hold the water. Place the coil in a sunny place. Make sure that the coils are spread out to receive sunlight. From time to time feel the hose and take samples of the water to measure the temperature.

The idea of a solar air heater can be demonstrated by this easily made apparatus: Make a small hole in the lid of a large empty jar. Insert a thermometer in the hole so that only the bulb is inside the jar. Hold the thermometer in place with modeling clay. Record the temperature of the air in the jar in the shade. The place it in the sun, making sure that the bulb of thermometer is not in

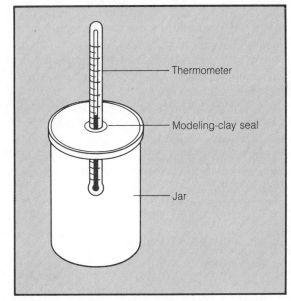

A solar air heater. How hot does the air get?

sunlight. Read the temperature every 15 minutes. How hot does the air get?

How Can We Save Energy?[10]

Since conservation and wise use of resources begins with each individual, children may wish to prepare their own checklist for saving energy, as we suggested earlier in the chapter. The more children themselves participate in preparing the list the more meaningful it will be. They might be asked first to list some of the kinds of energy they use. They should be reminded that materials they use—and waste—are produced by using energy. Consequently, conserving materials also conserves energy. Their checklist could include the

[10]H. Munson, "Energy Consumption, Calculate It!" *Science and Children* (September 1980). Practical suggestions for calculating and saving energy. T. C. Niedermeyer and E. J. Roberson, "A Checklist for Reviewing Energy Education Programs," *Science and Children* (March 1981); *Science and Children* (March 1978). An energy-education issue. *Wind, Water, Fire and Earth: Energy Lessons for the Physical Sciences* (Washington, D.C.: NSTA, 1986).

following areas (and others they may think of): (1) In the Home; (2) In the Lunchroom; (3) In the Schoolroom; (4) On Your Vacation; (5) On Your Way to and from School; (6) Outside Your Home and School; (7) At Play; (8) In the Garden and Other Outdoor Places.

Each area may be divided into items such as uses of water, electricity (including lights), and materials such as food, paper, and so on. The checklist might be duplicated and used by each child, after which a class discussion could emphasize the sources of waste as well as the action to be taken to conserve.

What Causes Air Pollution?

The section on "Air Pollution" in the checklist points up observations children can make regarding the conditions of air as well as the causes of the existing pollution. The following problems may be investigated by small groups: "What are some of the chief causes of air pollution?" "What is the meaning of thermal inversions?" "What are some of the harmful effects of air pollution?" "What is being done to stop pollution?" "What are units of the government doing?" "Why must all states cooperate?" "How do scientists study the problem?"

Children can make some relatively simple tests for air pollution by using filter paper exposed to the air in different places and examining with a magnifying glass various materials that collect after several days of exposure. The papers can be weighed before and after exposure (see next section).

Examine air filters from furnaces and air conditioners; take samples for examination.

The following procedure may be used to collect dust from the air.[11] Use cellophane tape (sticky side up) or a greased piece of paper (make a grease spot with oil or butter on white paper). Put the collecting materials in various places.

[11]Rose Blaustein, "What Kind of Dust Is in the Air?" *The Newsletter* (New York: Elementary School Science Association, 1970).

Make sure to use a control for each site where the collection will be made. (Place one piece of the collecting material in an envelope. Keep the other in the open.) Make sure to write down the date and location of each piece of collecting material.

After the dust has been collected, examine it with a magnifying glass or microscope. Note the differences in the kinds of dust collected and in the amount collected over periods of time, that is, 1 day, 3 days, 6 days. Keep records.

Date	Place	Kind of dust collected	Where do you think it came from?

Try to find out what kind of dust you have collected (for example, particles of soil, carbon, lint, hair, feathers, pollen grains).

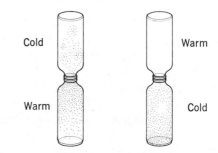

What Is Thermal Inversion?

The phenomenon of thermal inversion is increasingly evident in many areas and the principle can be demonstrated easily.

Use four milk bottles or 16-ounce (500-milliliter) laboratory bottles. Place two in the refrigerator or outdoors on a cold day. Place the other two on a radiator, stove, or in a pan of hot water.

Hold a piece of slightly moistened paper with tongs. Light the paper with a match and let its smoke rise into the mouth of one of the inverted bottles containing warm air. When the bottle is filled with smoke, stand it upright and invert the cold bottle over it. The smoke will rise from the warm air to the cold.

Repeat, placing smoke in the other cold bottle. Invert the second warm bottle over it. What happens? Smoke remains in the cold air.

Note: A smoking splinter of wood may be used instead of a burning piece of paper.

Concepts and Interpretations

1. An irregularity in the normal convection pattern is a "temperature" or thermal inversion.
2. In a thermal inversion the position of the cold and warm air layers are reversed. The cold air is close to the ground; the warmer air lies above it.
3. The cold air, being heavy, cannot rise through the layer of warm air, which serves as a lid and traps the colder air under it.

What Are Food Chains?[12]

Children comprehend the meaning of ecology and develop concern for problems in the environment as they learn more about interrelation-

[12]K. D. Smith, "Fun with Food Webs," *Science and Children* (February 1977). The energy of food webs and what happens to it.

ships of the living things around them.

The interdependence of living things with their physical environment is best understood by studying it in small samples such as food chains. A food chain might be defined simply as "Who eats whom." A school lawn is a good place to look for food chains. Grass, spiders, insects, slugs, earthworms, robins, starlings, Japanese beetles, aphids, ants, caterpillars, honeybees, and squirrels are involved in a number of food chains. Students will enjoy the detective work involved in tracking down some of these chains. For example, the students find that robins eat earthworms, which eat soil; some leaves decay to form soil while others are sucked of their juices by aphids, which, in turn, are "milked" by ants. There are countless numbers of such chains to be discovered through careful observation, with reading to verify (see chapter 13A, pp. 388–390).

In addition to school lawns, other habitats such as a forest floor, a dead tree, the area around the base of a tree, a pond, and many other environments are excellent for study. Four considerations are involved in such studies: (1) the characteristics of the environment (temperature, moisture, physical and chemical makeup, food, light), (2) the structure and characteristics of living things that

Part of the chain of life in a stream is investigated as students use a strainer to collect worms, snails, aquatic insects, and other small living forms. Samples of the stream water along with the collected forms are studied later in the classroom with hand lenses and microscopes. This activity is part of a program of environmental education. *Photo by Phyllis Marcuccio.*

Dramatization helps children understand an ecological food chain. One child represents the sun, the source of energy. The script for this "play" was worked out after several discussions and much reading. *(HRW photo)*

inhabit the environment, (3) the relationships of living things to each other and to the environment, and (4) changes that occur when human beings interfere with the relationships. What, for example, happens to the plants and animals living on a forest floor when trees are cut, and to the life in and around a pond when it is drained?

What Are Cycles?[13]

Chapter 9B describes evaporation and condensation and emphasizes the recycling of water (see also Chapter 4). These experiences and experiments may be used to introduce the concept of

cycles. The material in Chapter 10B includes material on the cycle plants make from seed to plant to flower to seed and describes the oxygen–carbon dioxide cycle as it happens in a balanced aquarium. These experiences and experiments may be added to those with the nitrogen cycle described in the preceding chapter. Children can examine soil from the woods and note the decaying bits of leaves and twigs. "Where did these materials come from?" "What will eventually happen to them?" "Then what happens to the materials?" (See Chapter 13A pp. 391–394.)

What Is Biodegradable?

Closely associated by contrast with cycles and food chains is the concept that many materials do

[13]G. O. Blough, *Cycles* (New York: McGraw-Hill, 1973); M. Brunner, "Interdependent Living Things," *Science and Children* (September 1980).

not decay or otherwise change and produce reusable materials. As an introduction to this concept, children may collect a bag or so of the usual trash that accumulates along the streets and roadsides: paper, wood, twigs, pieces of plastic, food scraps, aluminum foil, pieces of iron, cotton, leaves, wool, nylon and other synthetic materials, and so on.

"How can we find out what will happen to this material after a period of several weeks or months?" "What do you think will happen to some of the material?" "Will it all decay?" "Will some of it?" Suppose we make a list of the materials and bury each in the ground outdoors where the rain will keep the soil moist, and see what happens. At intervals of three or four weeks dig up the materials and examine them. Rebury them. Reexamine them. Use the list to record what appears to be happening to the various materials. What inferences can you draw from this experience? An indoor box of soil may be used instead of the outdoors if this is easier. Water the soil frequently (see Chapter 13A, pp. 404–406).

How Much Alive Is the Soil?[14]

Measure off an area $\frac{1}{4}$ of a square foot and collect the soil to a depth of 2 or 3 inches from each of the following places: an open pasture, under the leaves in a woodland, a badly eroded field, a lawn, a garden. (Obtain permission when necessary.) Pour out the samples on large separate sheets of white paper. Sort out the soil; count the animal life belonging to each of the following groups: worms; snails; insects; spiders, mites and ticks; others. Figure the total number of animals per acre for each group. (There are 43,650 square feet in an acre.) Of course, most of the living things in the soil such as bacteria, fungi, algae, protozoa, and nematodes require a microscope for detection.

Animals in the soil contribute to its aeration and drainage and, with microscopic plants, are responsible for converting the nutrients in undecayed organic matter into inorganic forms that growing plants can use, thus playing an important part in the food chains of life.

What Does Running Water Do to Soil?

Several of the concepts about soil and its uses may be learned from simple experiments. Students can demonstrate that soil is composed of materials of different kinds and characteristics. Refer to the experience described in "How Can We Separate Different Parts of the Soil?" in Chapter 6B. Much of the lightest material that floats or is in the top layer contains important nourishment for plants. It is carried away by water as it runs over the land that is not protected by a cover of vegetation.

After a heavy rainfall students can take samples of the water from a nearby stream and examine it to see what makes it look muddy. They can see particles of soil in the water. If the water is left standing for several hours the soil will settle to the bottom, and the water can be poured off and sediment examined so that students can see that it really is soil. The banks of the stream from which the water is taken should be examined to see the small gullies that the running water has worn away. If sections of the bank are sodded or covered with plants, these may be compared with barren parts of the bank to see how plants keep the soil from being washed away. Students may take running water samples from the stream when there has been no rain for several days and compare the two samples.

After a heavy rain, students can explore the school grounds or other nearby places to see effects of the rain. They may notice places where soil has been washed over the sidewalks and find gullies from which the soil has been removed. They can look for similar places on their way to and from school. In many schools, students have planned ways to stop such runoff erosion, and have successfully carried out their plans.

[14]A. B. Foster and A. C. Fox, *Teaching Soil and Water Conservation* (Washington, D.C.: U.S. Dept of Agriculture, 1986).

Demonstration of the importance of ground cover. Almost any schoolyard or neighborhood furnishes examples of erosion; a field trip increases the relevance of such demonstrations. *(Courtesy of U.S. Dept. of Agriculture.)*

The photograph shows an experiment planned to compare the effect of water running over bare soil with that of water running over soil covered with grass. Both slanting surfaces are covered with the same kind of garden soil; one surface is left bare, the other is covered with grass sod. Children may substitute grass, barley, or rye seed that has germinated and developed roots for the sod.

A measured amount of water is poured over each surface and caught again after it has run through the soil. The amounts and color of the two runoffs are then compared to see that the soil covered with sod takes up more water than the bare soil. Children can use these findings in their outdoor observations. In a city environment, the effect of water runoff is evident on the playground, on sidewalks, in parks, vacant lots, and similar places.

Where Does Our Water Supply Come From?[15]

The problem of an adequate water supply has become acute in many cities as well as rural areas. No matter in what region students live, they can investigate to find the answers to such problems as, "Where does our water supply come from?" "How is it made pure?" "Is there any danger that the supply may be depleted?" "Should anything

[15]T. Oznowich, "Bringing Water, Children and Streams Together" and "Water Facts," *Nature Study,* publication of Nature Study Society. E. L. Widner, "Splash Time," *Science and Children* (September 1987). Excellent activities for early childhood. R. Bock, "Water, Water . . . Everywhere?" *Science and Children* (October 1985). Many suggestions for activities. A. Goldin, "What to Do about Water," *Science Teacher* (January 1985). Discussion of natural water problems.

be done to increase it?" "Is it being polluted? By what?" "What steps are being taken to stop this pollution?" (See Chapter 13A, pp. 414–420.)

If students live where water comes from deep wells, they may be able to find a place where a well is being driven, talk to the well drillers, get samples of the soil and rock that is brought up in the drilling, and learn something about the nature of the layers through which drilling is being done.

In cities where water comes from lakes, rivers, or similar sources, students can visit the waterworks to learn what the source of the water is, whether or not it is adequate, whether there are plans for enlarging the supply, and what sources of pollution exist. While they are on the visit they will also want to see how the water supply is purified. They can see the filter beds and learn about other methods used for purifying water.

Children may not realize that rain falling directly into a reservoir produces only a small part of the supply of water. Most of the water in a reservoir flows into it from the sloping land surrounding it. This land, called a *watershed,* receives the water originally as rain. Brooks and streams from the watershed feed the reservoir.

To demonstrate how a watershed area collects water, crumple a large piece of aluminum foil, then open it, and crease it lengthwise. Place it as shown and sprinkle water on it slowly from a sprinkling can. Children will see how the water runs together from the wide area into the collecting "reservoir." Examples of such miniature "watersheds" in a city environment are rain falling on the schoolyard and running into a drain or puddle; and rain falling on sidewalks and streets and washing into gutters. Where does this water go? Is it directed into a storm system, the sewer lines, or to a reservoir? Is any of the water used in the community? What effects do you suppose paved areas, large buildings, and city drainage systems have on groundwater?

Detergents in our water supply are a continued source of pollution. Children may select several detergents, mixing them with equal amounts of water, and note how long it takes foam or bubbles to disappear. They can try to compare the results

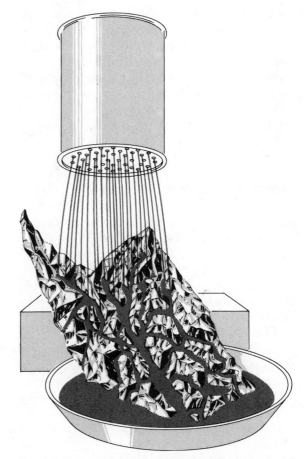

This demonstartion helps make clear the nature of a watershed. Children may be asked to compare this with a real watershed. (See text description.)

with those of mixing an equal amount of pure soap and water. Children can read accounts of contamination by various brands of detergents and help to promote the use of less polluting kinds (see Chapter 13A, pp. 419–420).

Children may be helped to develop an appreciation of the importance of water in their lives by keeping a record of the ways in which they use water over a period of three days, both at home and at school. Then they may consider if these uses wasted water and in what ways. They might observe and make a record of uses of water in the community (sprinkling, washing cars, air conditioning, and so on) for a given period of time. Can you tell if some of this water is wasted? How? They may draw up a set of rules for conserving water at home, at school, and in the community. They may discuss why some people drink bottled water, and may attempt to compare a city with a rural area with respect to the amount of water used (see p. 447).

What Is Acid Rain?[16]

Acid rain, one of our most pressing environmental problems, is discussed in Chapter 13A. The term *acid rain* is used to describe acid precipitation of many kinds—sleet, frost, dew, mist, snow as well as rain, and in addition dry particles that fall out of the atmosphere and form acids when they come in contact with moisture. More technically acid rain is called *acid deposition.*

Acid rain kills plants and animals by changing the acidity of their environment. Acidity is measured on a scale called pH, which runs from 0 to 14. Distilled water—neither acidic nor alkaline—has a pH of 7 and is neutral. Values on the pH scale below 7 are acidic and those above 7 are alkaline.

Because the pH scale is logarithmic, there is a tenfold difference between each number. If the pH drops from 7 to 6 the acidity is 10 times greater; if it drops from 7 to 5 it is 100 times greater; from 7 to 4, 1,000 times greater, and so on. For example, vinegar at pH 3 is 10,000 times more acidic than distilled water. A value of pH 1 (battery acid) is very acid and pH 13 (lye) is very alkaline.

In order to understand the meaning of pH, tests of the following common substances may be used (next to each are the expected pH levels): lemon juice (2.0), vinegar (2.2), apple juice (3.0), milk (6.6), distilled water (7.0), baking soda solution (8.2), milk of magnesia (10.5). Place small amounts of each in clean plastic containers. Dip a small piece of pH paper (available from biological supply houses) into the sample and immediately compare the color of the wet paper with the color chart that is provided with the pH paper to determine the approximate pH value. After making the measurements, students may summarize the results on a graph of the pH scale.

(You may prepare your own pH indicator by boiling red cabbage and using the colored cabbage water to test acidity, as described in "A Head for Chemistry" by William Hanschumaker in *Science and Children,* (November/December 1987.)

Following this activity students may collect samples of fresh rainwater and water from nearby ponds, lakes, and streams and test their acidity.

Current magazines and daily newspapers continue to publish accounts about acid rain. Students may collect these accounts and report their findings to the class. They may compile a list of possible sources of acid rain and find out about ways to alleviate the problems.

How Can We Study a Rural Environment?

During the study of "Ecology, Energy, and the Environment," students in rural areas can take field trips to observe some environmental factors, in contrast to the urban survey suggested earlier. Such trips will identify problems, point up their importance, and suggest solutions. These trips are

[16]The Acid Rain Foundation, Inc., 1630 Blackhawk Hills, St. Paul, MN 55122; National Wildlife Federation, 1412 16th St., NW, Washington, DC 20036. Ask for "Acid Rain: A Teachers' Guide." D. J. Klooster, "Understanding pH Through Acid Rain" and "Acid Rain Units from the Acid Rain Foundation," *Science and Children* (May 1987) with excellent poster. Department of the Interior, U.S. Fish and Wildlife Service, Natural Ecology Center, Kearneysville, WV 25430; U.S. Geological Survey, 419 National Center, Reston, VA 22092; M. Hanif, "Acid Rain," *Science and Children* (November/December 1984). Very useful teaching suggestions. National Wildlife Federation, 1412 Sixteenth Street, NW, Washington, DC 20036; A. LaBastille, "Acid Rain: How Great a Menace?" *National Geographic* (November 1981); R. Bybee, "Acid Rain: What Is the Forecast?" *The Science Teacher* (March 1984); K. Gay, *Acid Rain* (New York: Watts, 1983). Differing viewpoints with supporting evidence.

important enough to deserve some attention from the county agricultural agent or from some of his or her assistants, who are often more than willing to help plan the trip by suggesting places and persons to visit.

If extensive trips are not possible, many things can be observed by individuals and reported to the group, and some can be seen on short field trips near the school. Class discussions to interpret the observations are important.

Here are suggestions for a one-day trip. Although designed for a rural environment, many of the trips may be adapted for schools in an urban or suburban setting. Not all the things mentioned can be seen in any one place, and certainly not all can be studied on any one-day trip.

1. Observe how the highway department has taken steps to stop erosion of the roadside, especially where there are steep grades (planting, seeding, terracing, covering with straw and brush, and so on).

2. Observe fields that are idle and try to decide why the land is not being used (the county agricultural agent will help). Observe what happens to unused hilly fields if they are not covered with grass or other plants.

3. Observe the trash and debris along the roadside. How did it get there? What will happen to it? How could this accumulation be stopped?

4. Observe the difference in erosion between pasture fields and bare fields.

5. Observe how streams cut through the land; look at the banks of streams; examine the water to see whether it is muddy or clear. Is the water polluted? From what source? What can be done to avoid the pollution?

6. Go into the woods and dig down to see how the floor of the woods can absorb water more readily than hard ground can. Notice how the roots hold soil together and how the leaves decay to make soil. Bring back a sample of the soil to examine more closely in the classroom. What cycle is illustrated here? Why is it important? Notice how the trees in the woods are different from those in an open field, and see why they are better for lumber. Try to find out how many acres of land the woods cover, and if possible, find out the value of the timber.

7. Look for a place—either a forest or a roadside—that has recently been burned over. Walk over the burned area and see what has happened to plants and animals and what damage has been done. Compare it with a nearby place that has not been burned over.

8. Observe the effects of insects on the leaves of trees and other vegetation. Try to find out whether the damage is serious and whether anything can be done to stop it. Have pesticides been used? Can you find out what kinds?

9. Visit a farm where conservation practices are in operation. Try to find out how much the conservation activities cost, how they were accomplished, and why the farmer decided to invest in them. Find out whether the government gave financial assistance to the project. Ask how deep the well is, whether or not there are springs on the farm, and how the farm supplies water for its livestock. Try to determine whether there is pollution of the supply and if measures to prevent it are taking place.

10. Make and put out a campfire. If student take their lunch on the trip they may choose a location in which to build a fire, learn how to build one outdoors, and take special care in extinguishing it by using sand and water. One committee may be appointed beforehand to be responsible for making the fire, another for extinguishing it. After the latter committee has done its work, the group can evaluate the job by deciding whether the fire has actually been extinguished. Ashes should be spread out to make sure. The discussion should be held "on the spot" to make the idea real. Before leaving, students can observe the surroundings to answer the question, "What harm could this campfire have done if it had not been properly extinguished?"

11. Look for places that provide good shelter for birds, and see whether there are birds present. Try to observe the birds closely enough to see what they are eating.

12. Find places where young trees are coming up, and try to decide how they came to grow there. Were they planted? Did they perhaps grow from seeds of other trees nearby? Are they on highway property or on privately owned land? Why are they important?

13. Look for "No Hunting" and "No Fishing" signs, and

try to decide why they were put up in their particular locations.

14. Look for hawks or other preying birds, and try to decide whether they are helpful or harmful. Discuss what facts should be known before a decision is made. Are they part of a food chain? Try to describe it.

15. Take two samples of soil from a cut in the highway—one from just under the sod, the other from farther down. Measure the depth of the layer of dark soil at the top, and note how far the roots of different kinds of plants go into the soil. Take the two samples, one of topsoil and one of subsoil, back to the classroom for further examination and for use in experimenting.

16. Visit a sawmill to watch trees being sawed and see how trees are selected, cut, and trimmed for use. One group visited a sawmill and listened to an explanation of the conservation practices that were involved. Students were asked to estimate the value of one of the large trees that was about to be cut. After the students had given their estimates the mill owner told them his estimate. When the class had returned to school and was discussing the trip, each student was asked what things he or she could buy with the money the tree represented. This helped the children see the value of trees and to realize more clearly what happens when trees burn in a forest fire.

17. Select items from the checklist for urban areas and use appropriate ones for observation.

18. Find a local marsh, lake, or estuary and make it into a classroom for learning about the importance of wetlands.

Other Problems for Older Children

1. Can we start a school forest? How?
2. What plant quarantines are in effect in our area? Why?
3. What plant diseases or insect pests are dangerous in our area?
4. What living things are in danger of extinction in our environment?
5. How can we help with conservation practices in our school and home environments?
6. What is being done about the use of dangerous insect sprays in our environment?

7. How can we beautify our school and community area?
8. Who makes and enforces the laws to prevent pollution of the environment?
9. Why is the Alaskan pipeline important to us?
10. How do oil spills damage the environment?
11. What animals have become extinct in the United States in this century?[17]
12. What causes acid rain? What damage does it do? How can it be prevented?

RESOURCES TO INVESTIGATE WITH CHILDREN

1. Local air pollution and water pollution agencies, to find out about present practices, problems, and possible solutions.
2. Leaders in a 4-H Club, for information about what the young people of the state are doing to prevent pollution and to clean up the environment.
3. State soil conservation department, for information on erosion problems of local area and conservation practices in action.
4. State conservation department, for printed matter, films, and other resources useful in teaching conservation.
5. National Park Service, for regulations regarding the collection and disposal of waste materials in national forests and for similar information.
6. For information about membership and printed material available to teachers, write: The Environmental Action Magazine, 1346 Connecticut Avenue, NW, Washington, DC 20036. Friends of the Earth, 529 Commercial St., San Francisco, CA 94111. Sierra Club, 1050 Mills Tower, 220 Bush St., San Francisco, CA 94104. Keep America Beautiful, Inc., 99 Park Ave., New York, NY 10016. The Wilderness Society, 1400 Eye Street, NW, Washington, DC 20005. National Wildlife Federation, Servicing Division, 1412 Sixteenth St., NW, Washington, DC 20036. The Environmental Defense Fund, 1616 P

---

[17]P. A. Opler, "The Parade of Passing Species: A Survey of Extinction in the U.S.," *The Science Teacher* (December 1976); V. N. Rockcastle, "American Wildlife . . . Then and Now," *Environmental Education in the Elementary School* (Washington, D.C.: NSTA, 1977).

Street, NW, Washington, DC 20036. World Wildlife Fund, 1255 Twenty-Third Street, NW, Washington, DC 20037. National Audubon Society, 950 Third Ave., New York, N.Y. 10022.

7. Surrounding farm and forest areas, the school-yards, vacant lots, streets and parks, to observe good and poor conservation practices.

8. County agriculture agent and high school biology and earth science teachers, for materials, suggestions, and information on local and state conservation problems.

9. State geologist, for information about mineral deposits and other similar resources.

10. The local water purification and sewage disposal plants, to observe sources of water and to discover what pollution problems exist and what can be done about them.

11. Game warden, for information about hunting and fishing regulations. What changes have been made during recent years?

12. Local agencies, to find out what the pollution laws are, and to determine what action schools can take to assist in preventing pollution of air and water. Check the telephone number to use in reporting smoke and other kinds of pollution.

PREPARING TO TEACH

1. Prepare a large chart that diagrams the elements in a food chain and plan how you would use it in teaching some phases of ecology.

2. Make a list of practical activities you would use with children (of a particular grade) to make the material in this chapter more meaningful. Make one for use in a rural area and another for use in an urban area. Compare the lists. What does this comparison show?

3. Collect ecology and pollution newspaper items from your local newspaper and classify them for use as examples in encouraging children to make similar collections of their own (water pollution, forest fires, recycling, and so on).

4. Conduct a land-use survey in your community to determine how the area is being utilized—how much for roads, for buildings, for food production, and so on. Prepare a chart or other record that can serve as a sample to encourage children to prepare their own. Try to determine how land use has changed during the past dozen years or so. How has the population changed?

5. Prepare a poster, chart, or bulletin board to illustrate some ecological statement, such as, "Saving Energy Is Everybody's Business." "We Cannot Afford Not to Recycle." "People Start Pollution, People Can Stop It." Keep a record of how the project was done and use it to help children do a similar one.

6. Visit a recycling plant and prepare a plan that will help a group of children get the most out of such a visit (see field trip discussion in Part I).

7. Prepare a large chart that shows an important cycle that may be used to help children understand the meaning of the ideas involved. Plan ways to use the chart to help students prepare similar cycle charts (see Chapter 13A, pp. 391–394).

8. Plan a "New Town" from the beginning, taking into account the natural environment, housing, recreation, public buildings, industry, business, open space, transportation, and so on. How would you develop such a unit with your students?

9. Write to the Superintendent of Documents, U.S. Government Printing Office, Washington, DC 20402, for *Environmental Education Material*.

PART FOUR

MATTER AND ENERGY

MOLECULES
AND ATOMS

The little things are infinitely the most important.

SHERLOCK HOLMES

Matter, though divisible in an extreme degree, is nevertheless not infinitely divisible. That is, there must be some point beyond which we cannot go in the division of matter. The existence of these ultimate particles of matter can scarcely be doubted, though they are probably much too small ever to be exhibited by microscopic improvements. I have chosen the word atom to signify these ultimate particles . . .

JOHN DALTON, 1808

THE INVISIBLE BODIES

One of the most fundamental generalizations of science is that large-scale events have their causes in the behavior of minute particles. We have seen how the functioning of plants and animals is dependent on the activities of their component cells. The operations of a single cell depend on the genes within its nucleus. Let us probe more deeply for the more fundamental particles whose actions account for happenings in living and non-living things—from the turning of a plant toward the light to the formation of a universe.

Consider a small amount of a common substance—a glassful of water. What do we know about the minute makeup of the water in this glass? If we pour out half of it we still have the same substance left—water. Pour out half of the remainder and keep repeating this process. Would we ever reach a speck so small that to split it again would be to produce something other than water? Or is there no limit?

MOLECULES

There is a limit, and that limit is reached when only a single *molecule* of water is left in the glass. We can split such molecules (with the aid of an electric current or other source of energy), but,

if we do, we no longer have water; what we do have we shall discuss presently. The smallest particle of water, then, is a molecule of water (see pp. 474–475).

To our sight, touch, and taste, water appears to be a *continuous* substance; it is hard for us to imagine that it is made of separate, distinct particles. In a glass of water there are billions and billions of water molecules with a lot of empty space between them.

The theory that all substances are made of molecules is fundamental in all science. It holds true for liquids, gases, or solids. A gas such as air, for example, is made of molecules separated by wide spaces. Even an object as solid as a bar of iron is made of separate molecules, with much emptiness between the molecules.

Molecules differ from each other in a number of ways, as we shall see, but they have one thing in common: They are in constant motion. Sometimes molecules "escape" from their surroundings. A street puddle dries up because its water molecules have bounced into the air, adding to the water vapor content of the atmosphere. If the air containing these molecules is chilled somewhat, as it might be when it rises to higher altitudes, the molecules of water will lose some of their energy and merge to form the small droplets that make up a cloud.

When a lump of sugar dissolves in a cup of coffee, the molecules of sugar fly away from the lump and move in among the molecules of liquid. Soon, if you taste the coffee, you taste the sugar.

A question that may arise when we consider the molecular nature of things is this: If all matter is composed of separate particles (which means that all matter is full of holes) what holds things together? What makes an iron bar so tough, so solid, so impenetrable? The answer lies in the attractive force that exists between molecules. This force holds molecules together without any material coupling, just as a magnet exerts a force at a distance on a nail.

Thus, to our picture of molecules as separate, ever-moving entities we add one more characteristic: their mutual attraction for each other. In a solid this attraction is sufficient to prevent the object from changing shape easily. The motion of the molecules there is restricted to a small space. In a *liquid,* such as water, molecular movement is not quite as restricted as in a solid. Although the attractive forces are strong enough to keep the molecules together, and at about the same average distance from each other, they are not strong enough to fix each molecule in a specific location. The water molecules occasionally escape from their particular neighborhood and wander through the liquid. This greater molecular freedom makes it possible for liquids to assume the shape of the container into which they have been placed. In a *gas,* however, the more rapid motion of the molecules, combined with a molecular attraction reduced to practically zero, permits their rapid and free scattering. Open a bottle of ammonia in one corner of a room in which there are no drafts of air. Gradually the odor of ammonia will permeate every corner of the room as the ammonia molecules, escaping from the bottle, fly freely through the great spaces among the other molecules that comprise the air.

One more point should be stressed. The molecules of ammonia are different from the molecules of other substances. But every water molecule is identical with any other water mole-

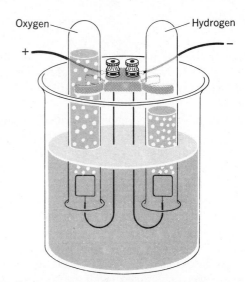

An electric current splits water into oxygen and hydrogen gases. This is possible because water molecules are composed of oxygen and hydrogen atoms.

cule, any ammonia molecule is identical with any other ammonia molecule, and so on.

To sum up, the molecular theory of matter makes four basic assumptions:

1. Matter is composed of exceedingly small particles called molecules.
2. Each different kind of matter is made up of its own particular kind of molecules.
3. Molecules are in rapid and ceaseless motion.
4. Molecules attract each other.

The molecular theory of matter is substantiated by a wealth of evidence, most of which is too detailed for presentation here. *Visual* proof is offered by the following:

1. With the electron microscope, which magnifies up to 100,000 times, scientists have recently been able actually to photograph the individual molecules of many substances, such as the very large molecules of polio virus.
2. The images of the molecules of a magnesium compound shown on page 456 reveal the molecular nature of this substance.

ATOMS

All matter, then, is made of separate, ever-moving molecules. Let us return now to the glass of water to see what would happen if we were to split its molecules.

In a common experiment performed in high school science classes, an electric current is passed through water that has been made a conductor by adding acid (or a salt or base) to it. This process, known as the *electrolysis* of water, produces two gases, which on testing prove to be hydrogen and oxygen. Careful measurements would show that the weight of water that is lost is matched exactly by the combined weight of the two new gases that have been evolved. If this experiment were continued (with appropriate apparatus) to its very end all the water would disappear and in its place there would be hydrogen and oxygen gas (see diagram on p. 455). If all the oxygen and hydrogen gas that is collected is now placed into a sturdy container and ignited with a spark there would be a powerful explosion: All the gases would disappear and all the original water would reappear.

Evidently, water can be "taken apart" to form two new substances, and these two substances can be joined again to form water. This is possible because each molecule of water is made of two kinds of smaller particles called *atoms*. Specifically, each molecule of water is made of two atoms of hydrogen and one atom of oxygen, and nothing else. The word *splitting* used in reference to molecules, however, is somewhat misleading; it conjures up a picture of breaking open a sphere and finding some new things inside. The water molecule is nothing more than a close partnership of two hydrogen atoms and one oxygen atom. The chemist's formula H_2O gives an exact name to this partnership. (The subscript $_2$ means that there are two atoms of hydrogen.)

We note also that the new substances produced bear little relationship in their properties to the original substance of which they were a part. Hydrogen is a highly burnable gas; oxygen is a gas that supports burning. The water from which they were obtained is a liquid (at room temperature) that does not burn. In other words, when hydrogen and oxygen atoms are linked in a water molecule the properties they display as unattached atoms are not in evidence. Their union results not in a compromise or a blending but in an entirely different substance. Indeed, the very essence of chemistry is to be found in such mysterious unions. Thus, an atom of a silver-colored, waxy, poisonous metal combined with an atom of a green, poisonous gas forms a molecule of ordinary table salt. The chemist would say here that

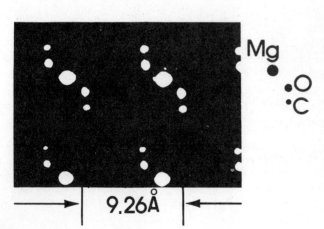

Images of atoms in a molecule obtained by a scientific team headed by Dr. George W. Stroke and including Drs. M. Halioua, V. Srinvason, and R. Sarma, using Xrays combined with holography (3-D photography) and optical computing. The images of the large atoms in each unit are magnesium atoms, the smaller pair around each magnesium atom are oxygen atoms, and the still smaller pair further away are carbon atoms. The *distance* between the atoms, as indicated by the measurement 9.26A (9.26 angstrom units), is equal to about a *millionth* that of the smallest unit in your metric ruler — the millimeter. The *size* of the atoms is proportionately small. (*Courtesy of G. W. Stroke, State University of New York.*)

an atom of sodium (Na) plus an atom of chlorine (Cl) forms a molecule of sodium chloride (NaCl).

Unions between atoms can also be broken. The salt molecule, for example, can be separated into its component sodium and chlorine atoms. These atoms, moreover, show no effects from their former association. They are pure sodium and chlorine atoms again.

Molecules are generally made of linked atoms. In some cases, as in the helium found in the atmosphere, only one atom may comprise the molecule, in which case the molecule and the atom are identical. In other substances, as in a protein, thousands of atoms may be linked together to form a giant molecule.

Let us look at some molecules to become acquainted with their atomic makeup. A molecule of carbon dioxide, the gas that makes soda water bubbly, is made of one carbon and two oxygen atoms and has the formula CO_2. The free oxygen in the air we breathe is made of molecules having two atoms in them, both of them oxygen atoms. Its formula is O_2. The kind of alcohol found in some beverages is made of molecules containing carbon, hydrogen, and oxygen atoms, with the formula C_2H_6O. The sugar in grape juice has the formula $C_6H_{12}O_6$. Thus we see that different molecules may contain the same kinds of atoms but in different quantities. This is one reason (but not the only one) for the different nature of sugar and alcohol.

That all substances, gaseous, liquid, or solid— all matter—are made of atoms is the cornerstone of modern science.

THE ELEMENTS

Humans have long been curious about the basic composition of matter. The Greek philosopher Aristotle said that all matter was made of four fundamental "elements": earth, air, fire, and water. Although we know today that not one of these four are truly basic elements, that indeed there are about 100 different ones, we are indebted to Aristotle and other Greek philosophers for their spirit of inquiry that led them to ask, "What are the fundamental particles of matter?" We are still searching for the answer to that question.

In the various substances named thus far in this chapter we have come across five different kinds of atoms: carbon, hydrogen, chlorine, oxygen, and sodium. An investigation of all substances found in nature, however, has revealed 88 different kinds of atoms up to now. In addition 19 atoms have been made by scientists, making 107 in all. These basic materials are called *elements* by the chemists. There are 107 presently known atoms, so there are 107 identified elements. Some familiar elements include the following (see p. 458):

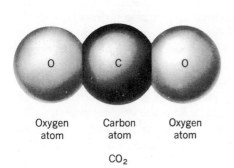

Oxygen atom   Carbon atom   Oxygen atom

CO_2

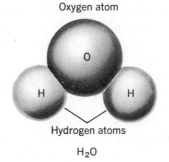

Oxygen atom

Hydrogen atoms

H_2O

The carbon dioxide molecule (*left*) is composed of one carbon atom and two oxygen atoms. The water molecule (*right*) is composed of two hydrogen atoms and one oxygen atom.

aluminum	hydrogen	nickel	silver
carbon	iodine	nitrogen	sodium
chlorine	iron	oxygen	sulfur
copper	lead	phosphorus	tungsten
gold	mercury	platinum	uranium
helium	neon	radium	zinc

These elementary substances—unlike water, salt, and sugar—cannot be broken down into other simpler substances by ordinary chemical means. The metal silver is made up only of silver atoms; the gas helium is made only of helium atoms. Water, sugar, and salt, all made of molecules built of more than one kind of atom, are examples of what the chemist designates as *compounds*. The known compounds identified thus far number more than 4 million, but all of these are composed of various combinations of less than 100 elements. The elements may be compared to the 26 letters of the alphabet; the compounds to the hundreds of thousand of words constructed from the alphabet.

Different elements are not equally abundant in nature. The most abundant element on the earth's surface is oxygen; the next is silicon. The two most abundant elements in the entire universe are hydrogen and helium. Ten common elements (oxygen, silicon, aluminum, iron, calcium, sodium, potassium, magnesium, hydrogen, and titanium) make up 99 percent of the earth (see pp. 474–476).

CHEMICAL SHORTHAND

For hundreds of years the alchemists, people who devoted their lives to the futile attempt to turn lead and other common metals into gold, used a kind of picture shorthand to represent the chemical elements that they knew. The circle, for example, was a symbol of perfection, so they used it for gold, the most perfect of all metals. Iron was represented by the lance and shield of Mars, the god of war. This colorful but cumbersome way of depicting the elements was confused by the fact

that not all alchemists agreed on the choice of symbols.

In 1814 Jöns Jakob Berzelius, a Swedish chemist, initiated the system we use today. The symbol is usually the initial letter of the name of the chemical element. C represents carbon, O oxygen, and so on. If the first letter is common to two or more elements, the initial letter and the first letter that they do not have in common is used. Thus copper is Cu (Latin *cuprum*), cobalt is Co, calcium is Ca.

To represent a compound Berzelius simply joined together the letter symbols of the atoms comprising the compound. This is its *chemical formula*. ZnS is the formula of zinc sulfide.

A symbol as used by a chemist stands not only for an element but also for *one atom* of that element. A formula stands for a *molecule*. We have already noted that the numerical subscripts refer to the element immediately preceding it. Thus the H_2S (hydrogen sulfide) molecule contains two atoms of hydrogen and one of sulfur.

CHANGES IN MOLECULES

Let us see what happens to the molecules that are involved in some of the changes that take place around us. When water evaporates from a puddle into the air no new substance is made. Water vapor is still made of water; that is, it is still made of molecules containing two hydrogen atoms and one oxygen atom. It is still H_2O but it is now in the gaseous form. The same is true when water freezes into ice. Such a change is referred to as a *physical change*. The changes described in the chapters to come on heat, machines, magnetism and electricity, sound, and light are concerned with physical changes.

Many changes, however, result in the formation of new substances that have characteristics very different from those of the original materials. The splitting of water into hydrogen and oxygen gases, previously described, is an example of this kind of change. Changes in which new substances are formed are called *chemical changes.*

vs

physical changes

Common Chemical Changes

We drop a nail outside and forget about it for a few weeks. When we pick it up we find that it has changed markedly: Instead of a smooth, shiny, hard exterior, it has a crumbly red coating. The iron in the nail has undergone a chemical change, *oxidation,* and we call the new substance that is produced rust. The chemist calls it iron oxide. Iron atoms in the nail have joined with oxygen atoms in the air to form molecules of iron oxide or rust.

Another everyday event that involves the joining of atoms is the tarnishing of silver. If a silver spoon is used for eating an egg a black layer of tarnish forms on the spoon. The silver combines with sulfur (always present in an egg) to make the black material, which is silver sulfide. The chemist describes this even in the following equation:

$$2\ Ag\ +\ S \rightarrow Ag_2S$$

In other words, two atoms of silver (2Ag) combine with one atom of sulfur (S) to form ($\rightarrow$) one molecule of silver sulfide (Ag_2S). The arrow in the equation indicates the direction in which the chemical change is proceeding; the ingredients are on the left side of the arrow and the products are on the right. This is a properly balanced equation because it has the same kind and the same number of each kind of atom on each side of the equation. *In a chemical change atoms are conserved—they are neither created nor destroyed* (see pp. 471–473).

Chemical changes also occur during the oxidation or burning of fuels. The atoms of the fuel combine with oxygen to produce a new substance. In this process energy is released in the form of heat and light. When coal burns, for ex-

ample, the carbon in it combines with oxygen to form the gas, carbon dioxide:

$$C\ +\ O_2 \rightarrow CO_2$$

The common candle has two kinds of atoms in its chemical makeup, carbon and hydrogen. When a candle burns, the carbon atoms of the candle combine with oxygen atoms of the air to form carbon dioxide, while the hydrogen atoms of the candle combine with oxygen in the air to form water:

$$C\ +\ O_2 \rightarrow CO_2 \text{ and } 2H\ +\ O \rightarrow H_2O$$

Both the carbon dioxide and the water escape invisibly into the air. The soot that is formed on the bottom of any object heated by a candle is composed of *unburned* carbon atoms, that is, carbon atoms that have not combined with oxygen atoms. If a cold glass is held in the flame the water vapor given off by the candle condenses on the glass.

The fact that the candle is finally "used up" might lead one to conclude that in burning there is destruction of matter. This is not so. *Every atom is accounted for.* Every carbon and hydrogen atom of the candle is now part of a new substance—in a different state—but not one atom has been destroyed.

The process of *digestion,* as we saw it in Chapter 11A, involves chemical changes. The large starch molecules with their many atoms, for example, are broken down into sugar molecules, which are smaller. The sugar molecules are small enough to pass through the intestinal membranes into the bloodstream.

In the making of bread, chemical changes play an important role. Yeast, a one-celled fungus, acts on the sugar in the dough to produce carbon dioxide gas and alcohol:

$$C_6H_{12}O_6 \rightarrow 2C_2H_6O\ +\ 2CO_2$$

| Dextrose sugar | ethyl alcohol | carbon dioxide |

One molecule of sugar is converted into two molecules of alcohol and two molecules of carbon dioxide. The carbon dioxide helps "blow up" the dough. This makes the bread light and spongy. The small amount of alcohol produced evaporates in the baking.

A similar change occurs in the process of wine making, except that in this case the carbon dioxide escapes, and the alcohol is retained in the final product. In both bread and wine making, the yeast cells cause a chemical change in sugar called *fermentation*. (The yeast cells also profit from this transaction: The splitting of sugar molecules liberates energy essential for their life processes.)

A chemical change that makes life possible on earth has been referred to in a number of different places in this book. It is the process of *photosynthesis*, in which green plants combine atoms from carbon dioxide and water to form sugar and oxygen (see pp. 277–278). The following equation of photosynthesis represents a summary of what is actually a series of complex steps in a living plant cell:

$$6CO_2 + 12H_2O \rightarrow C_6H_{12}O_6 + 6H_2O + 6O_2$$

Changing these symbols to words, a chemist says, 6 molecules of carbon dioxide plus 12 molecules of water yield 1 molecule of sugar plus 6 molecules of water plus 6 molecules of oxygen. In accordance with the principle of the conservation of atoms, the number and kind of atoms on the right and the left sides of this equation are equal. Count them and see. The chemical process of photosynthesis provides food and oxygen for the use of the plant and animal kingdoms and removes carbon dioxide from the earth's atmosphere.

We have seen how chemical changes are involved in rusting, tarnishing, burning, photosynthesis, digestion, and fermentation. Chemical changes are found in thousands of other everyday phenomena: the souring of milk, repairing and building of tissues of living things, and the manufacture of soap and plastics. The understanding of these chemical changes becomes increasingly important each year in agriculture, industry, and medicine.

FIRE: A CHEMICAL HAPPENING

Chemical changes involve not only the forming of new substances but also the transfer of energy. When a green plant makes sugar (see the equation on this page) it packs sun energy into each sugar molecule. When the sugar is "burned" in a living organism the energy is liberated. Similarly, when a candle burns, energy in the form of heat and light is released. Fire is one of the most dramatic of all energy-releasing chemical changes. Fire is both useful and potentially dangerous to humanity, and so merits special discussion here (see pp. 476–477).

Essentials for Burning

Three conditions are essential for any fire: First, there must be something to burn, a fuel of some kind; then this fuel must be made hot enough to burn; and last, there must be a continuous supply of oxygen to support the burning. Let us see how each of these three factors contributes to the making of a fire.

Reduced to its simplest terms, burning is the process in which a fuel unites chemically with the oxygen of the air, a process that the chemist calls *oxidation*. Carbon and hydrogen are the common atoms in the fuels we use. To emphasize the importance of the release of energy we might rewrite the equations given on page 459 in this way:

$C + O_2 \rightarrow CO_2 + e$ (Carbon plus oxygen yields carbon dioxide plus energy.)

$2H_2 + O_2 \rightarrow H_2O + e$ (Hydrogen plus oxygen yields water plus energy.)

The carbon dioxide and water pass off invisibly with any smoke, so we are not usually aware of these new products of burning. When we watch a campfire we see the smoke because it contains unburned carbon particles. We also see the ash that remains, but this is the mineral content of the wood that does not burn. We see light and feel the heat. These represent forms of energy that are released as a result of chemical union of the atoms.

We should not say that oxygen burns. Rather, it *supports* the burning of fuels. A spark applied to a bottle of oxygen will *not* set it afire; oxygen is not a fuel and it cannot burn.

The union of a fuel with oxygen requires that the fuel be heated to its *kindling temperature,* the lowest temperature at which it will catch fire. The kindling temperature varies for different fuels: for wood it is about 500°F (260°C); for phosphorus in the strike-anywhere match, it is much lower.

Extinguishing Fire

The extinguishing (also the prevention) of fires is based on the elimination of one or more of the three factors essential for burning. Thus, to put out a fire we cut off the supply of oxygen, remove the fuel, and lower the temperature of the burning material below its kindling point. The exclusion of oxygen and the lowering of the temperature are the most widely used methods of extinguishing fires. The removal of flammable material is effective for small fires, such as those in coal bins, woodpiles, or wastebaskets. Fire lanes in forests, where all trees and brush are removed, also serve to stop the spread of fire.

Among the readily available ways of excluding oxygen are covering the fire with dirt or other material that will not burn, or throwing a heavy blanket or coat over the fire. The latter is particularly effective in putting out fire on a person's clothing. If a blanket or coat is not available the flames on a person's clothing can sometimes be smothered by rolling the person on the ground. Fire extinguishers achieve their effect by cooling the fuel and by smothering, which actually means keeping the oxygen away from the fire.

DALTON AND THE ATOMIC THEORY

It is evident from the examples we have considered that atoms are involved in all chemical changes. The true character of atoms was first conceived in 1808 by John Dalton, a schoolmaster in Manchester, England. In modern form the fundamental ideas of Dalton's atomic theory might be stated as follows:

1. All matter is composed of a limited number of kinds of fundamental particles called atoms.
2. The atoms of a given element (such as carbon, oxygen, copper, zinc, and so on) are identical and cannot be broken into anything simpler by ordinary chemical means.
3. Molecules consist of definite combinations of atoms. The atomic construction of all molecules of one kind is identical. (See the images of molecules on p. 456.)
4. Chemical changes involve the making of new combinations of atoms to produce new molecules and hence new substances.

INSIDE THE ATOM

Earlier we looked into the vastness of space—at planets, stars, galaxies, and supergalaxies—trying to find some order in the universe. In this chapter we have focused thus far on the minute molecules and atoms that make up the matter of the universe. Let us now increase our magnification to "see" the architecture *within* the atom to find there the smallest specks yet discovered.

The word *atom,* first used by the Greeks about 400 B.C. to identify what they considered to be the smallest particle of matter, means *indivisible.* But the investigations of the twentieth century have taught us that atoms are *divisible,* and that they are made of smaller, more fundamental particles.

Model of an Atom

Modern science describes through modeling nature that it cannot see (and often not understand) in order to *conceptualize* the processes under study. Once the model is constructed, trials with it will allow the scientist to predict what will happen in another set of circumstances. If the prediction proves true, the use of this model is encouraged for more investigation; if the prediction provides other than perfect results, then the model must be altered to meet the new demands or discarded in favor of a totally new model.

In the sections that follow you will see how the atomic models developed by scientists were changed as experimental evidence required.

Sir Ernest Rutherford, the father of modern atomic physics, was the first to construct a model of the interior of an atom. According to this model, constructed in 1911, a single atom is a kind of miniature solar system. In the center, corresponding to the sun, is a structure called the *nucleus*. Whirling around the nucleus, like planets, are particles called *electrons*.

In 1913 Niels Bohr, a Danish chemist working in Rutherford's laboratory, proposed that the electrons of an atom revolve around the nucleus in definite circular orbits, with each orbit at a different distance from the nucleus. Later discoveries identified two particles within the atom's nucleus, *protons* and *neutrons*.

Parts Within the Atomic Model

Electrons are extremely light atomic particles possessing a quantity of electricity designated as a *negative charge*. The electron revolves at terrific speeds around the nucleus and at a relatively great distance from it. It is held in its orbit by the nucleus, just as the earth is kept from flying off into space by the attraction of the sun. In the case of the atom, however, the attraction is due to the equal but opposite *positive charge* of electricity of the proton in the nucleus. (Opposite electrical charges attract each other.) Although the electrical

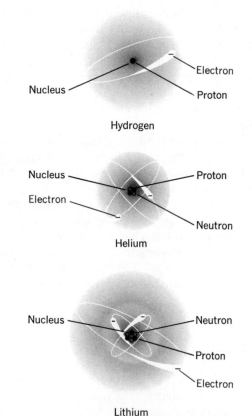

Hydrogen

Helium

Lithium

The hydrogen atom (*top*) has 1 electron whirling around a nucleus consisting of 1 proton. The helium atom (*middle*) has 2 electrons revolving around a nucleus made of 2 protons and 2 neutrons. The lithium atom (*bottom*), next in the atom ladder, has 3 electrons orbiting around a nucleus made of 3 protons and 4 neutrons. A current view is that the electrons surround the nucleus in the form of a diffuse cloud.

charges of the electron and proton are equal and opposite, their weights are markedly different, the proton being about 1,840 times as heavy as the electron. The neutron weighs about the same as a proton, but, as its name implies, it is electrically neutral—it has no electric charge.

Consider a specific atom, that of the element hydrogen, the lightest and simplest of all atoms. Its nucleus consists of a single particle, a proton. Around the proton whirls a single electron as depicted in the diagram on this page.

A hydrogen atom, then, consists of one electron and one proton. Let us turn now to the heavier atoms. After hydrogen the next heavier atom is helium. What is the architecture of a helium atom? Revolving around the nucleus are *two* electrons. As you might expect these are prevented from flying off into space by *two* protons in the nucleus. But helium (and every other kind of atom except the most common form of hydrogen) has a third kind of fundamental particle in its nucleus: the neutron.

Electrons, protons, neutrons—these seem to be the fundamental particles of atoms. (Nuclear scientists have discovered others, but we shall limit our consideration to these three.) As we examine atoms of the heavier elements we find that they contain more protons and neutrons in the nucleus and more electrons outside the nucleus. In each case the number of protons exactly equals the number of electrons. Thus, carbon has 6 protons and 6 electrons, oxygen 8 protons and 8 electrons, and radium 88 protons and 88 electrons.

Just as it is hard to visualize the immense dimensions in the astronomical universe so it is equally difficult to picture the tiny dimensions on the atomic scale. We stated before that an atom is

a sort of miniature solar system. Most of the *real* solar system, as we learned earlier, consists of empty space. The proportion of empty space in an atom, however, is 10,000 times as great as in the solar system. Assume that we want to make a giant model of an oxygen atom. If we make the nucleus of this atom 1,500 feet (460 meters) across (the length of five football fields) and place it in the center of the United States, then its outer electrons would move in an orbit that would touch New York and San Francisco.

Indeed, all matter is filled with empty space. It has been estimated that if a giant hand could squeeze all the empty space out of the earth, until the nuclei of all its atoms touched each other, then our planet could be compressed to the size of a ball only $\frac{1}{2}$ mile (800 meters) in diameter.

This model of an atom as a miniature solar system is useful, but some corrections are necessary in order to give a truer understanding of the atom:

1. The planets in the solar system move essentially in one plane—in a two-dimensional system. Electrons, on the other hand, travel in all three dimensions around the nucleus.

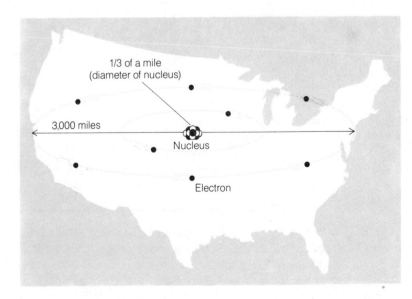

1/3 of a mile
(diameter of nucleus)

3,000 miles

Nucleus

Electron

The space within the atom is vast compared to the size of its particles. This diagram gives some notion of where the 8 electrons of an oxygen atom would be if the nucleus of the atom were enlarged so that its diameter was one third of a mile.

2. The planets are definite, discrete, round bodies. The electron is no longer thought of as a discrete particle in a well-defined orbit around the nucleus. We do not know the precise path the electron takes, nor precisely where the electron will be at a particular instant. Electrons travel so rapidly that it is assumed in our latest models that they constitute a variety of clouds of negative electricity surrounding the nucleus.

THE LADDER OF ATOMS

There is a wonderful ladder in nature, a ladder of atoms (see the chart on this page). Begin at the top rung with one electron and one proton and you have hydrogen. Descend to the second rung to where there are two electrons and two protons and you have helium. On the next rung three electrons and three protons give you lithium. Rung by rung, adding one electron and one proton each time, without a break you pass atom after atom, as shown in the table, until you reach the lowest rung. This has 110 electrons and 110 protons, the heaviest of atoms claimed *thus far* by atomic scientists. The number of neutral particles, or neutrons, increases, too, but not in this simple arithmetical way.

It is apparent that the essential difference between a substance such as lead and one such as gold lies in the *number* of electrons or protons that the atoms of these substances contain; the *kinds* of particles in each is the same. Thus, the medieval alchemists' dream of transmuting one element into another was not so farfetched after all, because all atoms are made of the same stuff. Moreover, the changing of atoms into other kinds of atoms occurs in nature as well as in the laboratories of atomic scientists.

Electrons in Orbit

The arrangement of the electrons in an atom reveals a beautiful order and symmetry in nature. The electron pattern is also the key to the chemical properties of the atom.

Examine the diagram of 6 atoms on page 465.

THE LADDER OF WELL-KNOWN ATOMS

Name of Element	Symbol	Number of Electrons Number of Protons Atomic Number
Hydrogen	H	1
Helium	He	2
Lithium	Li	3
Carbon	C	6
Nitrogen	N	7
Oxygen	O	8
Fluorine	F	9
Neon	Ne	10
Sodium	Na	11
Magnesium	Mg	12
Aluminum	Al	13
Silicon	Si	14
Phosphorus	P	15
Sulfur	S	16
Chlorine	Cl	17
Argon	Ar	18
Potassium	K	19
Calcium	Ca	20
Chromium	Cr	24
Iron	Fe	26
Nickel	Ni	28
Copper	Cu	29
Silver	Ag	47
Tin	Sn	50
Iodine	I	53
Platinum	Pt	78
Gold	Au	79
Mercury	Hg	80
Lead	Pb	82
Radon	Rn	86
Radium	Ra	88
Uranium	U	92
Neptunium	Np	93
Plutonium	Pu	94
Americum	Am	95
Curium	Cm	96
Einsteinium	Eg	99
Mendelevium	Md	101
Lawrencium	Lw	103
Rutherfordium	Rf	104
Hahnium	Ha	105
?	?	107
?	?	110

We observe that the electrons are not scattered helter skelter; they move in orbits called shells at different distances from the nucleus of the atom. In hydrogen there is but one electron revolving in its shell around the nucleus. Helium has two

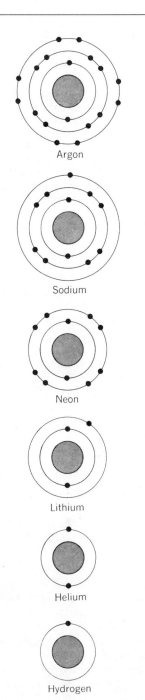

Argon

Sodium

Neon

Lithium

Helium

Hydrogen

Electrons are arranged in orbits around the nucleus of the atom. Although this diagram is useful in explaining the chemical behavior of an element, it does not show the three-dimensional structure of the atom. Moreover, the electron is no longer thought of as a discrete particle.

electrons in this first shell. Two electrons seem to be the limit for this shell. Lithium, atom number 3, has two electrons in the innermost shell and one electron in a second shell. In the next seven elements, each with one more electron, the second shell fills up, but there is a maximum of eight electrons. Consequently, in neon (the familiar gas in neon tubes), atom number 10, the first shell has its maximum of two and the second shell a maximum of eight electrons.

Continuing, sodium, atom number 11 in our ladder, has ten of its electrons arranged like neon, but the eleventh one starts the third shell.

Argon, atom number 18, fills up the first three shells with two electrons in the first shell, eight in the next, and eight in the outermost.

What happens to the electron arrangements in the other atoms found in nature as we climb down the ladder? We may summarize it in this way: (1) Seven shells or orbits in all are possible and (2) The maximum number of electrons in the different shells vary from 2 to 32.

We should not leave this consideration of atomic architecture without adding that (1) the chemical properties of an element depend on the number of its electrons and the way the electrons are arranged in the outermost shell of each atom; and (2) each of the shells represents an energy level. The energy of electrons in different shells increases with increasing distance from the nucleus; (3) the diagram and the foregoing description of electron orbits is useful but constitutes a simplification of what is known about electron arrangement. We can give an electron's location only in terms of probabilities. This location is described as a *space orbital*—a highly probable location in which an electron may be found.

We refer those of you who wish to pursue this further to recent high school and college texts in chemistry.

NUCLEAR ENERGY

In the nucleus of the atom there is a source of energy far, far greater than that which is released in such everyday chemical changes as the burning

REACTOR

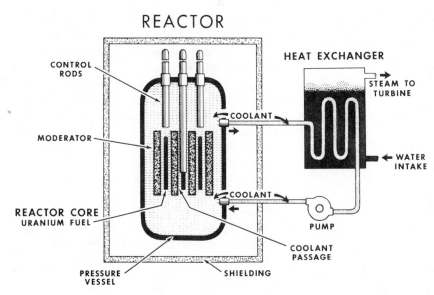

CONTROL RODS

HEAT EXCHANGER

STEAM TO TURBINE

COOLANT

WATER INTAKE

MODERATOR

COOLANT

REACTOR CORE
URANIUM FUEL

PUMP

PRESSURE VESSEL

SHIELDING

COOLANT PASSAGE

The heart of a nuclear power plant is the reactor in which the fissioning or splitting of the nuclei of atoms can be controlled and put to useful work. The coolant, heated to a high temperature by the splitting atoms, flows through a heat exchanger, where it turns water in a secondary system of pipes into steam. The steam is then piped to a turbine, which operates a generator of electricity.

of coal or even the explosion of TNT. We have space here only to summarize some of the important concepts underlying atomic energy, or more properly nuclear energy, and the use of this kind of energy in serving humanity. (Some of the environmental problems related to nuclear energy are discussed in Chapter 13A.)

Atoms are divisible. They are composed of smaller particles that include electrons, protons, and neutrons.

Some atoms, such as those of radium and uranium, are unstable and decay spontaneously into other elements through the emission of radioactive particles or rays.

Fission, the splitting of an atom, involves the bombardment of the nucleus with neutrons, which produces new kinds of atoms while releasing tremendous amounts of energy and radioactivity.

Matter can become energy; energy can become matter.

The destruction of a tiny amount of matter results in the liberation of an enormous amount of energy, as is indicated in the equation $E = mc^2$ (E = energy, m = mass, c^2 = speed of light × speed of light).

In the splitting of an atom some of its matter is converted to energy.

Neutrons are effective "bullets" for the splitting of atoms.

In a chain reaction each splitting atom releases energy, as well as neutrons for the splitting of more atoms.

The energy produced by nuclear reactors and nuclear bombs comes from a chain reaction of atoms undergoing fission, the first controlled, the second uncontrolled.

There is concern about thermal and radioactive pollution from nuclear energy plants.

All stable atoms can be made radioactive by bombardment with atomic particles in the nuclear pile or in "atom smashers."

These radioactive atoms, called *radioactive isotopes*, are useful in the fields of medicine, agriculture, and industry.

Rocks and other ancient materials may be dated by determining the percentages of certain radioactive atoms remaining in them, since unstable isotopes of these atoms decay at a known rate.

In the hydrogen bomb hydrogen atoms join to form helium atoms. This is called *fusion*, in contrast to fission that occurs in the nuclear bomb.

The energy of the stars is derived from atomic fusion.

In both fusion and fission, matter is converted into energy.

Scientists have synthesized new atoms, heavier than uranium.

The energy of atoms has a potential for good or evil for humanity.

IMPORTANT GENERALIZATIONS

All matter is made up of exceedingly small, separate particles called molecules, which are in ceaseless motion.

Molecules attract each other. In solids the attraction is greatest, in liquids less, in gases least.

Molecules are made of atoms linked together in definite combinations.

There are over 100 different kinds of atoms with different chemical properties, called elements.

Chemists have identified more than 4 million kinds of compounds.

In a physical change the composition of molecules is not changed.

In chemical changes the composition of molecules is altered. New materials are formed by assembling new combinations of atoms.

Compounds differ markedly in their properties from the elements of which they are composed.

In chemical changes atoms are conserved—they are neither created nor destroyed.

Three factors essential for burning are (1) a supply of oxygen; (2) a supply of fuel; and (3) enough heat to raise the fuel to its kindling point.

The prevention and fighting of fires is based on the elimination of one or more of the three factors essential for burning.

Chemical changes involve a transfer of energy.

Chemical changes play an important part in our lives.

Atoms are composed of smaller particles, principally electrons, protons, and neutrons.

Protons and neutrons are found in the nucleus of the atom; the rapid motion of one or more electrons creates a "cloud" of electrons around the nucleus.

The essential differences between the atoms of different elements lie in the number of protons, neutrons, and electrons that make up the atoms.

The chemical properties of an element depend on the number and arrangement of the electrons.

Energy released from the nuclei of atoms is far greater than that produced by chemical changes.

(Other generalizations about nuclear energy will be found on p. 466.)

DISCOVERING FOR YOURSELF

1. Make a list of destructive chemical changes that you observe, and indicate what is done to try to prevent each of the changes.

2. Use litmus paper to test the liquids and fruits in the kitchen to see if they are acids or bases.

3. Choose some chemical change that is important to you and learn as much as you can about it (for example, what raw materials are used, what energy is involved, what waste products there are, how the characteristics of the finished product differ from those of the raw materials used).

4. Demonstrate the difference between a chemical and a physical change by using some common materials.

5. Find out about some of the newest elements discovered by scientists. Find out where they were discovered, by whom, when, and any other information you can. Keep a list of the sources you used, and describe your method of investigation.

6. List as many as you can of the elements (in a free state, that is, not chemically combined with any other element) in your house (copper in wire and in a penny, oxygen in the air, tin on the cover of cans, and so on).

7. List some of the simple chemical compounds you encounter during a day and give their atomic makeup: water H_2O—hydrogen and oxygen; sugar $C_6H_{12}O_6$—carbon, hydrogen, and oxygen; table salt $NaCl$—sodium and chlorine; bubbles in carbonated water CO_2—carbon and oxygen; and other similar compounds.

8. Make drawings of the electron arrangements in 10 elements.

9. Investigate the Periodic Table of the elements, which can be found in any high school or college chemistry textbook. How has the table enabled chemists to predict the properties of undiscovered elements? In what sense is the Periodic Table like the calendar of a month?

10. Some famous scientists have atoms named in their honor. Find them in the list on page 464 and describe the contribution of one of them.

11. Learn how to use the fire extinguisher in your home, school, and automobile.

12. Use the Self-Inspection Blank and Fire Safety Checklist, which is available from the American Insurance Association, 85 John Street, New York, NY 10038.

13. Find out about the latest methods for fighting forest fires.

14. Find the fire alarm box nearest to your house, the telephone number of your fire department, and learn how to report a fire.

TEACHING "MOLECULES AND ATOMS"

Children's horizons are extended by introducing them to new materials and by finding new ways of investigating familiar materials. Children test the qualities and characteristics of things through tasting, feeling, lifting, listening, smelling, scratching, breaking, twisting, wetting, crushing, biting, pushing, spilling, and so on. These are tests that they themselves devise. We help this process by providing them with experiences that raise problems in their minds, and then by giving them opportunity for inquiry. In the early grades we do this when we encourage them to work with clay, sand, water, soil, and similar materials, and show what they can do by changing the materials. Their understanding of chemical and physical change may be deepened by firsthand experiences in the preparation, cooking, preserving of foods, and by observing the changes in color, shape, and texture that accompany processes such as the making of applesauce, cranberry sauce, popcorn, candy, butter, and gelatin desserts.[1]

In all these experiences the teacher emphasizes the changes as they occur. "How did it change?" "Why do you think it changed?" "Could we change it back again?" are some typical questions to give more meaning to the experiences. In later elementary school grades the phenomena of contraction and expansion of materials, burning, food manufacture in plants, and other changes are studied to see how changes in matter occur and why they are important. At this level also children may devise controlled experiments to investigate practical problems such as the effectiveness of different kinds of detergents for removing stains or of paper toweling for absorbing water.

Since direct observation of molecules and atoms is not feasible, we instead present examples of the behavior of substances that can be explained by inferring their presence: the dissolving of sugar in water, the dispersion of ammonia gas in a room, the evaporation and condensation of water, the movement of heat in a metal spoon, the rusting of iron. If these phenomena are described in terms of atoms and molecules in action, children will come to make the words *atoms* and *molecules* part of their language and their thinking.

Readings are important in this connection to provide information and insights; diagrams and models are most helpful. Children may also inspect X-ray images of molecules and atoms (see p. 456) made by scientists.

SOME BROAD CONCEPTS

All matter is composed of molecules that are made up of atoms.

Matter exists as solids, liquids, and gases.

Matter can be changed from one state to another.

There are about 100 different kinds of atoms (elements), each with different properties.

Atoms combine to make compounds. There are millions of kinds of compounds.

In a physical change the makeup of the molecules is not changed. No new material is made.

In a chemical change the makeup of the molecules is changed. New material is made.

Atoms are made of smaller particles: electrons, protons, and neutrons. The nucleus of an atom may be split to release energy.

FOR YOUNGER CHILDREN

The following activities for early grades will contribute to an understanding of what things are made of and how they change. Stress *describing* and *comparing* when these are appropriate. This is an opportunity to develop vocabulary useful in future discussion.

Refer to Piaget's experiments, Chapter 3, with conservation of matter for some methods of working, development of concepts, and descriptions of tasks for younger children.

[1]K. W. Hill, "Cooking Fun," in *Exploring the Natural World with Young Children*, (New York: Harcourt Brace Jovanovich, 1976).

What Materials Will Mix with Water?

Have on hand a lemon, some salt, commercial powder used for making cold drinks, and some sand. Ask children to *predict* what will happen in each case when the material is added to water. How can we tell what will happen? Children test their predictions. They may suggest making lemonade with the lemon, sugar, and water. Squeeze the lemon in water. Children observe and describe what they see (bits of lemon float, seeds settle, the water changes appearance). "What has happened?" Use the term *dissolve* in helping children answer. Let children taste the material. "How do you know the lemon juice has mixed with the water?" "How could we try to make the mixture taste sweet?" Add sugar. Taste. "Will sugar dissolve in water? Can you see it?" "How do you know that it's in the water?" "Will salt and the other materials dissolve?" Children may wish to try other materials, such as sand, to see if they will dissolve.

In what way could you make something dissolve faster? How about stirring? Urge children to think of a way to find out by experiment. They may recall previous experiences with the use of a control. In two glasses put together equal amounts of water, equal amounts of sugar (a lump of sugar or whatever material is to be tested). Stir one; do not stir the other. Observe and describe the results. Does heating the liquid make material dissolve faster? Would shaking? Try it.

How Can We Change Water Without Mixing Anything into It?

In order to help students understand that some materials may be in different forms—as a liquid, a solid, and a gas—suggest that they observe and attempt to describe what water is like. Use words such as wet, clear, liquid, cool, runny, and so on. "How can we change the water so that it will appear different?" Freeze it. Place the water in the freezing compartment of a refrigerator. "What do you think will happen?" "Will it still be water?"

Examine the ice. Try to describe what it is like. Take the ice cubes out and place them in a plastic container at room temperature. What happens?

Let the water stand in a glass in a warm room. Mark the height of the water in the glass. Let it stand for several days. "What happens?" "Where is the water that disappeared?" "Can you get the water out of the air?" (See Chapter 9B and Chapter 4 for evaporation and condensation experiences.)

"How are the liquid, the solid (ice), and the gas (water vapor) different from each other? How are they alike?" "Did these changes make a new material?" (Children may have different opinions about this last question, depending on what "a new material" means to them. Do not close the discussion by giving the "right" answer. Leave it open for further thought and investigation.)

Where Can We Find Air?

Young children may not think of air as being a real material. Ask them to describe their ideas about air. "What is it?" "Can you see it?" "How do you know it's there?" Encourage them to find ways to capture or collect some air—in plastic bags, paper bags, balloons, inflated toys, their mouths. Discuss what happens when such trapped air is moved about or the containers squeezed. Can the air change shape? Can they think of places without air? Try blowing some bubbles into water through a straw. "Where did the bubbles come from?" "What do you think is inside the bubbles?"

If balloons or plastic bags are used, the children can use the trapped air to blow whistles, horns, blow up other bags, and do any number of other self-initiated activities. These explorations will help them to understand that air exists even though it is not seen.

As children study materials they can make a list of places where air, a common material, is found. They may try to classify their lists: (1) Things we put air into (tires, balloons); (2) big places (the room, outdoors); and (3) little places (in an "empty" glass). "Is there air in the water we drink?" Let a glass of tap water stand for a few hours. "What do you think the bubbles are?" "Is there air in soil?" Drop some lumps of soil into a glass of water. "What do you think the bubbles are?" "Is air real?" "How can you tell?"

What's in the Bag?

The teacher assembles in paper bags a variety of materials and asks, "What do you think is in the bag?" "How can you tell without looking inside the bag?" (sense of touch). Try it, then let children describe various properties of each object—size, texture, color, rough, smooth, and so on. Children attempt to classify the materials in various ways according to their properties. Objects from the classroom, from a collecting trip, or from various other sources can be used in a similar way (see Chapter 11B, p. 346).

Other Problems for Younger Children

1. What changes in water take place outdoors?
2. How can you get salt from salt water? (Heat the salt water or allow it to evaporate slowly until crystals of salt form.)
3. How can you take the mud out of muddy water? (Pour it through a piece of cloth or paper toweling lining a kitchen strainer.)
4. What happens if you put drops of vinegar on baking soda?
5. What is soil made of?
6. How does heat change food in making applesauce, popcorn, toast, gelatin dessert; in cooking rice, cranberries, spaghetti, eggs?
7. What happens to things when they are heated and cooled?
8. How is ocean water different from water in ponds and lakes?
9. How can we make milk to drink from powdered milk?
10. How can we make dried fruit look and taste like fresh fruit? (Soak dried fruits—raisins, apricots, pears, and apples—in water for several days.)

FOR OLDER CHILDREN

How Fast Can You Melt An Ice Cube?[2]

If children have had the experiences described earlier with melting ice and evaporating water, they are ready to go further with experiences of changing materials from one form to another.

Supply each child or small group of children with an ice cube (uniform size, taken from an ice tray) and a plastic bag and ask, "How fast can you melt an ice cube?" Suggest that children use whatever methods they choose to melt the cube (heat from their hands, and so forth). Who can melt the cube fastest? How would you describe what happens? (solid to liquid). How long did it take in each case? Which method seemed to work best? Pour the water from the bag into a pan. Heat the water (or allow it to stand in the pan overnight) until it evaporates (liquid to gas). Describe what happens. Then place water in an ice cube tray and freeze (liquid to solid). "How have the characteristics changed?" "What are the distinguishing characteristics of a gas? A solid? A liquid?" "How are they alike? How different?" Note that in these examples no new material is produced. The substance has merely changed its form. Students can look for other changes from one form to another—especially in the kitchen where the refrigerator and stove are. They can read about important changes in the form of matter—for example, iron and other metals from liquid to solid, glass from liquid to solid.

How Can We Produce Some Chemical Changes?

Chemical changes function continually in the lives of children, producing many of the things they

[2]D. B. Phillips, "Chemistry for the Elementary School," *Science and Children* (October 1981); A. S. W. Sae, "Dispel Chemophobia," *Science and Children* (January 1982). Simple, safe chemistry experiments.

use and the changes they see every day. There are many simple experiments that show chemical changes. The important idea for students to understand is that as a result of chemical changes new materials are made that may have characteristics entirely different from those of the elements or compounds that went into the process. Children will be interested in the symbols for elements, the formulas of compounds, and the chemical equations that describe chemical changes. Introduce them to the simple ones, some of which are illustrated in the following examples.

The formation of rust is a common chemical change and, although children frequently observe it happening, they are unaware that it is an example of a chemical change. Get two identical, large iron nails, and paint one with any kind of house paint or nail polish that is at hand. Do not paint the other one. Place both nails on wet blotting paper in a clear plastic container and put a cover on the container. Let students predict what they think will happen and tell why they think so. Observe what happens. "Why has the unpainted nail rusted?" (Oxygen from the air has united with the iron in the unpainted nail to make the rust. Rust is a compound formed from the combining of iron and oxygen.) Scrape off some of the rust and you will see that it no longer looks like the iron. It is a brown, crumbly material. The painted nail did not rust because the paint formed a protective layer that kept oxygen from uniting with the iron. Ask children to describe the nail before it rusted. Then ask them to describe rust in the same way. Ask children to find examples in their environment of objects that are rusting and some that are not. Ask them to try to explain why. Try the experiment with nails made of copper or other metals. Children will think of other variations (see Chapter 14A, pp. 458–460).[3]

Another easily observed and demonstrated change is shown by placing some sugar in a spoon

and heating it. Ask children to use a potholder or other protection when they hold the spoon over the source of heat. Urge children to observe carefully and attempt to explain what change is taking place. Ask them to describe the sugar before it is heated and the material in the spoon after heating. Compare the two materials. After the white sugar has turned black, let it cool and taste it. It will no longer taste sweet. Why? A chemical change has taken place and a new material has been formed: When sugar is heated, its molecules break down into water and carbon. The water bubbles off leaving the black carbon in the spoon.

Still another easily demonstrated chemical change is done with baking soda. Place one tablespoon of the soda in a drinking glass and slowly pour vinegar on it. Children observe and try to explain what is happening. The bubbles that are formed are carbon dioxide. A burning match held over the bubbles will be extinguished. In this instance one kind of chemical change (production of carbon dioxide) is stopping another (burning). Again ask children to compare the materials before and after the change. "Will a match held over vinegar go out?" "Will a match held over soda go out?" "Why did it go out when these two were put together?"

Put some cooked egg yolk on a polished silver spoon and leave it for an hour or so. Ask students to observe the change in the spoon and try to explain what happened. There is silver in the spoon, sulfur in the egg yolk. The black material on the spoon is made when these two elements unite. It is a compound called silver sulfide. Again compare the characteristics before and after.

Let children thoroughly chew soda crackers before swallowing them, being especially careful to note changes in taste. The sweet taste is due to a chemical action (enzyme-caused) that changes starch to sugar.

What Chemical Changes Go on Around Us?

The foregoing experiments are examples of what happens when a chemical change takes place.

---

[3] J. Schwartz, *It's Fun to Know Why: Experiments with Things Around Us* (New York: McGraw-Hill, 1973). Gives many experiments that children can perform with iron, coal, glass, bread, paper, cement, and other materials. R. Bains, *Molecules and Atoms* (Mahwah, N.J.: Troll, 1986).

Such changes are going on all around students and even inside them. Suggest that on the basis of their experiences and observations, children attempt to make a list of chemical changes they have seen going on around them. On the basis of discussion of this list, students may be able to supply some answers to questions such as, "What happens to a bridge when it rusts, and why is it frequently repainted?" "Why do we coat cans with tin?" "What happens when a fire burns?" "Why is baking powder used in cake making?"

Suggest that students do some reading and observing to find out about other important chemical changes such as, "How is window glass made?" "What happens when silver tarnishes?" "How can sodium (an element that would burn your tongue) and chlorine (a poisonous gas) be part of the common salt that is used every day?" "What must happen to oxygen and hydrogen to make them combine to form water?" "What happens in green leaves that help to feed us?" "What must happen to the food we eat before it becomes a part of us?" "How are chemical changes used in making photographs?" "Why are chemical changes important?" Life depends on some common chemical changes: oxidation (burning) of food in the body, making of starch and sugar in plants, and many others. Others change our way of living: making plastics, making cement and paper, baking bread, and so forth (see Chapters 10A and 11A).

Obviously not all chemical changes are desirable. We go to great pains and expense to stop or retard some. Ask each student to report to the class one example of harmful chemical change and a way to stop it. Students will discover such things as painting, refrigeration, the use of dark or airtight containers, and keeping certain things dry.

How Can We Test Materials?

It is often important to find out what an unknown substance is or what a substance is made of. There are many ways to find out. Some are very com-

plicated; others are quite easy.[4] Suppose, for example, you wish to identify and distinguish among a number of white materials such as starch, baking soda, plaster of Paris, granulated sugar, and salt. Beginning activities may involve the use of the senses. Later, more sophisticated analysis with indicators and other laboratory techniques are used.

Note: A caution is in order. The sense of taste should, for obvious reasons, be discouraged as a method of identification in all cases.

Testing for the presence of starch serves to illustrate how identifying tests are useful. Suppose there are two jars of material. One has some starch in it; the other one contains a similar-looking material (chalk dust or white paint, for example) that is not starch. You cannot tell which one has starch just by looking at them, so a test is in order. Remove a sample from each jar and put a few drops of iodine on each. What happens? Whenever a substance has starch in it, it turns dark blue if it is tested with iodine. Children may test a potato, some bread, and other substances for the presence of starch by removing a small amount of it and testing it on a plate.

Suppose you want to find out if there is more carbon dioxide present in the air that is exhaled from the lungs than in the air you inhale. Limewater is used to test for the presence of carbon dioxide. Use a straw to blow air from your lungs into the limewater. What happens? Carbon dioxide makes limewater turn milky. Pump some air (use an empty rubber-bulb type of plant sprayer) into another glass of limewater. Compare the results. What does the test show?

Suppose you wanted to find out if there is acid in something. Litmus paper is used to test if things are acid or alkaline. The paper turns red in an acid medium and blue in an alkaline medium. Try vinegar, lemon juice, milk, tap water, liquid soap, and ammonia. See Chapter 13B for methods of

[4]D. B. Phillips, "The Magic Sign: Acids, Bases and Salts and Indicators," *Science and Children* (January 1986). Experiences with testing materials. S. S. Flank, "Acids, Bases and Foods," *Science Scope* (April/May 1987). Easy experiments.

determining the *degree* of acidity in water being tested for acid rain.

These examples (there are many other suggested in books in the library) introduce children to the idea that it is possible to identify what a material contains if you know how to test for it.

What Are Atoms and Molecules Like?[5]

Based on the foregoing experiences with chemical changes, children may be ready to understand that all materials are made of tiny particles and to learn something about the nature and behavior of these particles, even though we cannot support this idea with the same kinds of evidence that cause scientists to believe this. Let children crush a sugar cube into fine bits, using any method they can think of. Let them use a magnifying glass to see that the bits they produced are still tiny bits of sugar. Ask children what they think they could do to make these tiny bits disappear. If they are dissolved in water they cannot be seen. Ask children how they could find out if the sugar is still there. If the water is tasted, they know that the sugar is there. The sugar has broken up into its smallest particles—molecules. Let children use the magnifying glass to examine the water. A powerful microscope could not reveal the tiny molecules of sugar.

This activity is an example of the kind of experience that helps give clues to the idea that materials are composed of molecules. A molecule of sugar is the smallest particle of sugar possible. Can a sugar molecule be broken into anything smaller? Have children recall the experiment (p. 472) in which sugar is heated on a spoon, resulting in the formation of carbon and water. Carbon is made of one kind of atom. Water is made of two kinds of atoms: hydrogen and oxygen. The sugar molecule, therefore, contains three kinds of atoms: carbon, hydrogen, and oxygen. The scattering of sugar molecules in water is an example of a physical change: The charring of sugar in a spoon results in a chemical change (see Chapter 14A, pp. 458–460).

Pour some ammonia or perfume on a wad of cotton in a dish placed in front of the classroom. Ask children to raise their hands when they detect an odor. Why doesn't everyone smell this gas at the same time? How is it possible for the odor of a substance to be detected at a distance? (The molecules of the liquid evaporate and move through the air.) Here again is an example of a physical change. There are many other similar experiences that although they do not present the proof that convinces scientists, are examples that can be explained by the theory that all matter—solid, liquid, or gaseous—is composed of molecules.

The idea of what atoms and molecules are and how they behave is an example of science information that students can talk about quite glibly, yet understand only vaguely. One way to help them understand more clearly some of the things they learn about atoms and molecules and how they behave is to aid them in illustrating what they have read. The textbooks and encyclopedias that students use will supply ideas. Students can make some of the following, either on the chalkboard or on a large sheet of white paper: a drawing of molecules in a solid, in a liquid, and in a gas (see p. 475), a drawing to show what happens to molecules of water when the water is boiling, a drawing of a molecule of water to show the number and kinds of atoms in it, a drawing to show what happens to molecules in a piece of iron when it is heated. They will think of other ideas to illustrate.[6]

[5]R. Mebane and T. Rybolt, *Adventures with Atoms and Molecules* (Hillside, N.J.: Enslow, 1985); M. Berger, *Atoms, Molecules and Quarks* (New York: Putnam, 1986).

[6]W. H. Conrad, "Let Em Atom," *Science Scope* (May 1987). Experiments for older children. M. B. Miller, "From Plastic Blocks to Molecular Models," *Science Scope* (September 1986).

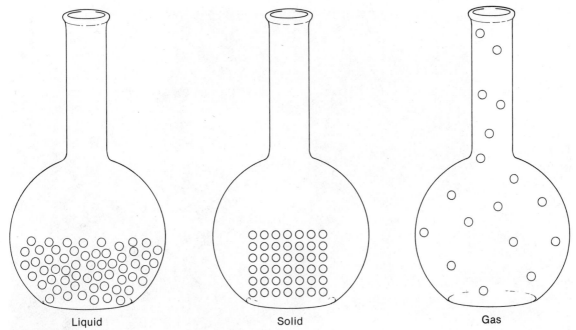

Liquid   Solid   Gas

Visualization of the molecules in a gas, a liquid, and a solid.

Where Can We Find Examples of Elements?

Students can find common objects containing such elements as iron (nails), copper (electric wiring), mercury (in some thermometers), tin (covering of cans), zinc (in galvanized iron), silver (jewelry), and many others, and display them on a table. They can find out more about some of these elements by reading in encyclopedias and elsewhere, and report their findings to the class. Before they begin reading, they may make a list of questions they wish to answer about each element such as, "Where is it found?" "For what is it used?" "Is it scarce?" The teacher can add, "What are its characteristics?" "How does it compare with other elements?" If students have questions such as these to guide their reading, they are not likely to copy from sources and tell uninteresting things that neither they nor their classmates un-

derstand. Here is an opportunity to use reading for a specific purpose.

Chlorine, iodine, mercury, neon, sulfur, lead, nickel, oxygen, phosphorus, silver, platinum, silicon, and chromium have especially interesting uses. Each student may keep track of how the information was found—people asked, books, and other sources consulted, places observed. If we believe that learning how to locate information is often as important as the information itself, we ought to make the most of activities such as this.

Discuss why water, sugar, and salt are considered to be compounds. Students can make an exhibit of such compounds and report on some of the sources and uses of common ones. This may be tied up with discovering how local industries make use of various elements and compounds in their manufacturing processes. An interesting and instructive experience in geography can result

A fusion game is an exhibit unit of the Stars Gallery in the National Air and Space Museum. The game illustrates the hydrogen fusion process (see Chapter 7A, p.150) that occurs in the central region of the sun. Visitors aim their atom-shooting gun at a field of oncoming atoms. A hit causes fusion to occur. (*Courtesy of National Air and Space Museum of the Smithsonian Institution.*)

when students attempt to discover where these elements and compounds come from and how they are transported.[7]

How Can Fires Be Prevented and Extinguished?[8]

Burning is an example of chemical change. The study of fire is of a very practical nature, for it is directly related to the safety of the home, the school, and the community. In the experiences suggested here it is essential to exercise the utmost caution. Fire safety should be practiced whenever matches or other fire is used. The activities should conform to school regulations. In some cases, with younger children, the experiments are best performed by the teacher to demonstrate safety precautions. As an outcome of this study, children should not only understand the chemical nature of burning, but also develop skills and attitudes essential for coping with fire and its prevention.

Use the material illustrated in the drawing on page 477. Suggest that children plan how this might be used to show that the chemical change of burning needs a supply of air. First they light the candle and set the lamp chimney over it on a smooth surface so that air cannot enter at the bot-

[7]J. A. Miller, "The Elements," *Science and Children* (January 1977). Subject matter about elements and activities for use in teaching about them.

[8]G. Gibbons, "Fire! Fire!" (New York: Crowell, 1984). Fire fighting.

A candle and a lamp chimney can be used to demonstrate the three essentials for burning.

tom. Observe what happens. Now they set the chimney on two flat-sided pieces of wood to permit air to enter at the bottom. Again observe what happens. Cover the top of the chimney with a piece of glass. Now what happens? Remove the glass cover from the chimney and light the candle again. If a smoking splinter is held near the bottom of the chimney, the smoke enters the chimney and moves up past the flame, showing which way the air is moving. The students will suggest that air must *enter* and *leave* if the candle flame is to continue to burn. This same principle is demonstrated to explain the cause of wind in Chapter 9B and how air carries heat in Chapter 15B. The Halloween candle in a pumpkin is another excellent opportunity for children to see the importance of providing fire with a supply of oxygen if chemical change is to continue.

After the experience with the lamp chimney,

students may be asked to tell where they have seen this same thing happen (draft through a stove or furnace, draft toward an outdoor campfire). Discuss the importance of keeping windows and doors closed when part of a house is on fire. Review with children the three essentials for burning: (1) fuel, (2) enough heat to ignite fuel, and (3) a supply of fresh air.

Having discovered what a fire needs to burn, students will be ready to discover how we keep these essentials away from a flame. There are several simple ways of showing some of the means by which we keep air away from fire in order to extinguish it. These experiments should be performed on an asbestos pad as a safety measure. Set a short candle in a bowl or a wide-mouthed jar. Light the candle and then cover the container with a piece of asbestos cloth or a plate. Observe what happens. "Why does the candle go out?" Light the candle again. This time pour sand into the container to cover the candle. Again, why does it go out? Try the same thing with water. This puts out the fire by reducing the temperature of the fuel. These simple demonstrations show why we suggest wrapping persons whose clothes are afire in a blanket, why we cover a campfire with earth, and why we use water to put out fires (see Chapter 14A, pp. 460–461).

Another method of putting out fires is by removing the fuel. Put several pieces of crumpled paper on a pie plate. Light one. We can prevent the spread of fire to the other pieces by removing them. Use a tongs to remove them. (The fire lanes in forests and the backfires started by fire fighters are examples of removing the fuel.) These experiments with fire should be performed by the teacher or under the supervision of the teacher.

Other activities that children may engage in include the following: (1) with the help of the school custodian, check the fire safety measures observed in the school (see reference in "Discovering for Yourself," p. 467); (2) check the home for fire safety; (3) visit the local fire station; (4) investigate and report on community measures for fire safety.

Other Problems for Older Children

1. What is spontaneous combustion?
2. What is the difference between the rusting of a nail and the burning of a match? How are the two changes alike?
3. Why is yeast used in bread making?
4. How can you get fresh water from salt water?
5. How can you make cottage cheese?
6. How can you grow crystals?
7. What makes popcorn pop?
8. How can you separate a mixture of sand and salt?
9. What is inside an atom?
10. How can you find out if a rock is limestone? (Drop lemon juice or vinegar on it. If it fizzes or bubbles it probably is limestone. The bubbling is caused by the carbon dioxide that is given off by limestone when in contact with an acid.)

RESOURCES TO INVESTIGATE WITH CHILDREN

1. A supermarket, to find out how food is protected from spoilage.
2. A chemistry set, to illustrate chemical change.

3. A high school chemistry teacher, for materials and an exchange of ideas about teaching the material in the unit.
4. Local industries (soap factory, plastics factory, bakery), to see and learn about the use of elements and compounds as raw materials, chemical changes, and other phases of chemistry involved in industry.
5. The school building, students' homes, and public buildings, to see how places are fireproofed and how caution should be exercised to prevent fires.
6. The school custodian, to show and demonstrate a school fire extinguisher.

PREPARING TO TEACH

1. Make a chart to use with children that shows what happens in several examples of common chemical and physical changes. Describe how you would use the chart with children and how you would help them make similar charts of their own.
2. Clip accounts of destructive fires from the local newspaper for a month. Devise a plan for helping children analyze and classify them into the causes, what might have prevented the fire, the extent of the damage, as well as other information children will think important in helping to understand the cause and prevention of fires.

HEAT AND HOW
WE USE IT

It will be convenient to begin with an instance or two of the production of heat wherein there appears not to intervene anything . . . but local motion and the natural effects of it . . . when, for example, a smith does hastily hammer a nail or suchlike piece of iron, the hammered metal will grow exceedingly hot . . . which shews the heat acquired by the piece of iron was . . . produced in it by motion.

ROBERT BOYLE, 17TH CENTURY

Heat consists in a minute vibratory motion of the particles of bodies.

ISAAC NEWTON, 1704

SOURCES OF HEAT

We rub our hands on a cold day, and they feel warmer. We burn gas under a kettle of water, the kettle gets hot, and the water boils. Electricity runs through coils of wire in a toaster, and they get red-hot. In the glare of the summer sun a sandy beach heats up.

Thus heat is produced in a number of different ways. The mechanical work done in the process of rubbing your hands, the chemical energy released in burning, the electrical energy flowing through the wire, and the radiant energy winging 93 million miles (150 million kilometers) from the sun—all these forms of energy made something warmer. How is it possible for different forms of energy to produce the same result—heat?

Before discussing the nature of heat further, we should understand the meaning of the word *energy* as the physicist uses it.

ENERGY

We live in a universe of matter and energy. We use such words as *stuff, material,* and *substance* to convey the meaning of matter. We may give countless examples of matter: steel, glass, water, sand, and air, or we may think of the fundamental particles of which all matter is composed—molecules. Matter is all around us. So, too, is energy—

the ability to do work. To a physicist *work* is done whenever a force moves an object through a distance against a resistance. Resistances against which we most frequently work are gravity, friction, and inertia. The energy of the wind supplies the force that pushes a sailboat across the water. The energy in a stream of water exerts a force that turns a water wheel. The energy stored in the molecules of gasoline, when released in the cylinders of an automobile, pushes the pistons that make the auto move. Energy released from sugar molecules in our body eventually produces the movement of our muscles.

Energy can be converted from one form to another. A light bulb is designed to convert electrical energy into light energy. A gong is a device for changing the energy of motion (mechanical energy) of a hammer into sound energy. Caruso is reputed to have shattered a glass with his great tenor voice—an example of a conversion of sound into mechanical energy. The radiant energy of sunlight striking the solar cells of a transistor radio is converted into electrical energy, which in turn is converted into sound energy. Apparently all forms of energy are interchangeable.

The energy that a moving object possesses because of its motion, such as that of a moving stream of water, is known as *kinetic energy.* Some objects possess energy because of their position. The water behind a dam may not be in motion, but it has the potentiality of moving and doing work when it falls. Energy in this form is called *potential energy*. A jack-in-the-box has potential energy stored in its squeezed spring. When the lid is opened, the energy is passed from the spring to Jack, who then has kinetic energy as he jumps up. From the two examples just given it is apparent that potential energy may result from an object's position (water held by a dam) or condition (a squeezed spring).

THE NATURE OF HEAT

What is heat? What actually happens when something gets warmer? At one time some scientists believed that heat was a real *substance,* a fluid. They thought that when something got warmer, more of this fluid, named *caloric,* flowed into it. Losing some of this caloric, it became colder. According to modern theory, heat is *energy itself,* not a substance; it is the energy of motion, not a fluid.

But how can "motion" be contained in a substance? When we finish with the rubbing of our hands, visible motion has ceased. What has happened to the energy that has been expended? The molecular theory furnishes the answer. As we learned in Chapter 14A, all matter is composed of exceedingly small separate particles called molecules. These molecules are in ceaseless motion. We have experimental evidence that when a substance is heated its molecules move with more speed or with more energy. Evidently the heat in a substance is the energy of the motion of its molecules. When you rub your hands you bump the molecules in the outermost layer of your skin and cause them to move more vigorously. These in turn bump against those just beneath them, and so on. In this way the entire thickness of your skin is heated.

In all the materials cited before—the metal of the kettle and the water in it, the wire in the toaster, the sand on the beach—molecules have been activated into more vigorous motion. This, then, is the meaning of heat: It is energy, the energy of moving molecules.

We now have an answer to the earlier question:

How is it possible for different forms of energy to produce the same result—heat? It is possible because all these forms can *make molecules move.* In the rubbing of hands, as we have seen, motion is transferred directly to the molecules of the skin. In the kettle on the stove the chemical energy released by burning produces hot gases with highly excited molecules. These make the aluminum molecules of the pot dance more vigorously, which, in turn, make the molecules of water move rapidly. The case of the kettle is particularly interesting because the agitation of the molecules is transferred from a gas to a solid to a liquid. In the toaster the activity of the electrons of the electric current causes the molecules of the nichrome coils to jiggle more vigorously. Energy from the sun comes in the form of a variety of electromagnetic waves. One range of wavelengths are called infrared rays (see Chapter 19A). When the infrared rays strike the sand on a beach they make its molecules vibrate.

When we recognize heat as moving molecules, "cold" has a new meaning. It is simply a subjective way we have of characterizing less heat, less molecular activity.

An important effect of the increased molecular activity that results from heating should be mentioned here. As the molecules of almost all substances bounce more vigorously and more freely the substance they comprise expands. The metal in the kettle, the water, the coil, the sand—all increase in size as they get warmer. Conversely, they contract as they cool. We shall discuss this more fully later and call attention to a very important exception to the rule.

TEMPERATURE

The common thermometer used to measure temperature is essentially a sealed glass tube containing a liquid such as mercury or colored alcohol. The principle involved in the functioning of a thermometer is that fluids generally expand when heated and contract when cooled. (Solids expand and contract, too, but the glass in a thermometer

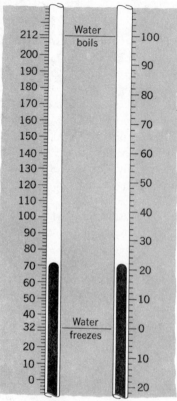

FAHRENHEIT   CELSIUS

The Fahrenheit and Celsius scales. To convert from Celsius to Fahrenheit, multiply by ⅑ and add 32. To convert from Fahrenheit to Celsius, subtract 32 then multiply by ⅝. Or simply place a straight edge across the two scales—and read!

does not expand enough to affect the reading materially.) The hollow inside the thermometer, the *bore,* is very narrow; in some thermometers it is finer than a human hair. Thus, a small change in temperature causes enough expansion or contraction in the liquid to force it a noticeable distance up or down the bore. The tube is calibrated—that is, marked in degrees—so the expansion or contraction of the fluid can be measured in exact units (see pp. 498–500).

Scales

There are two common temperatures in use, the Fahrenheit and the Celsius scale.[1] The Fahrenheit thermometer is so calibrated that it registers 32 degrees when the temperature is at the melting point of ice and 212 degrees at the boiling point of water. These measurements are written 32°F and 212°F respectively. Thus there are 180° between the melting point of ice and the boiling point of water. The scale may be extended below and above these points.

Incidentally, the zero of the Fahrenheit thermometer does not mean "no degrees." This zero point was somewhat arbitrarily selected by its originator, Fahrenheit, who, on mixing some salt and ice, achieved a low temperature that he decided to call zero. In the making of a scale two points are needed to determine the calibration, so a second point of 100 was selected, which Fahrenheit believed was the temperature of the human body. It is said that this error (body temperature averages 98.6° on this scale) was made because Fahrenheit based his figure on the temperature of a cow rather than of a human.

On the Celsius scale, zero marks the melting point of ice and 100 the boiling point of water. These measurements are written 0°C and 100°C respectively.

Absolute zero, −460°F or −273°C, represents the lowest temperature that matter can theoretically reach. Scientists have produced temperatures only one millionth of a degree above absolute zero. In terms of molecular theory, absolute zero represents the point at which molecules have the lowest possible energy, when they are very nearly at rest.

A third scale, one sometimes useful to scientists, is the Kelvin scale, also called the absolute temperature scale, which begins with absolute zero, but uses degrees that have the same size as

[1]By international agreement, the centigrade scale is now called the *Celsius* scale in honor of the man who developed it. The symbol °C refers to degrees Celsius.

	Degrees	
	Fahrenheit	Celsius
Surface of the sun	10000	5500
Electric arc light	7232	4000
Kitchen range flame	3092	1700
Iron melts	2795	1535
Mercury boils	675	357
Lead melts	620	327
Water boils	212	100
Ethyl alcohol boils	172	78
Highest official temperature record (Al'Aziziyah, Libya, Sept. 13, 1922)	136	58
Paraffin melts	128	52
Songbird's temperature	113	45
Body temperature	98.6	37
"Room temperature"	70	21
Ice melts	32	0
Mercury freezes	−40	−40
Lowest official temperature record (Vostok, Antarctica, 1960)	−129	−89
Ethyl alcohol freezes	−202	−130
Air boils (changes from liquid to gas)	−310	−190
Absolute zero	−460	−273

Celsius degrees. To convert from Celsius to Kelvin add 273° to the Celsius reading.

Some significant temperatures (approximations) are shown in the table above.

Thermometer Fluids

To be useful, a thermometer fluid must remain a liquid at the temperatures that the thermometer is intended to measure. If the fluid freezes solid it cannot flow; if it boils it will break the thermometer. The boiling point of mercury, 675°F (357°C), is high enough to permit its use in thermometers at moderately high temperatures. Its freezing point, −40°F, (−40°C), is low enough for its use in an average winter in temperate climates. Moreover, mercury expands uniformly throughout a wide temperature range, another essential in a thermometer fluid.

Alcohol boils at a much lower point (172°F or 78°C) than water; consequently, it cannot be used in thermometers that are exposed to high temperatures. Its low freezing point (−202°F or −130°C), however, makes it useful in polar and

arctic regions. Alcohol is used also because it is cheaper than mercury and because it expands six times as much for a given rise in temperature and is, therefore, more sensitive to temperature variations. Alcohol is colored with a red or blue dye for visibility.

Thermometers for Different Purposes

Thermometers come in different shapes and sizes for different purposes. The clinical thermometer has a very narrow bore, so that a difference of 1/10 degree is easily read. It is calibrated to read only from 92° to 110°F. Heat forces the mercury out of the bulb and up the bore, but a constriction in the bore keeps the mercury up in the stem when the thermometer is removed from the patient, even though the surrounding temperature is lower. In this way the thermometer registers the highest point to which the mercury goes. A quick jerk of the wrist forces the mercury back into the bulb.

Expansion and contraction is also the principle behind metal thermometers, such as those used

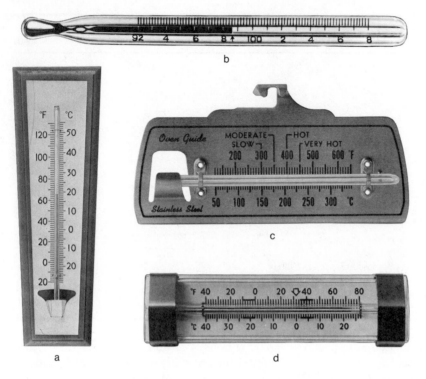

a. Wall thermometer (comfort meter); b. Clinical thermometer; c. Oven thermometer; d. Freezer thermometer. *(a, b, and d: courtesy of Taylor Instruments, Sybron Corp.; c: courtesy of Weksler Instruments Corp.*

in ovens, but here it is a solid rather than a liquid that changes size. In one common metal thermometer the basic unit is a coil made of two strips of metal welded together along their lengths. Brass is commonly used for the inside strip and steel for the outside. Brass expands more for a given rise in temperature than steel does. As a result the expansion or contraction due to heating or cooling causes the coil to loosen or tighten. This motion is conveyed to a pointer that sweeps over a scale calibrated in degrees.

MEASUREMENT OF HEAT

Which has more heat in it, a cupful of water at 100°C (its boiling point) or a potful of water at 100°C? Both have the same temperature, which, as we have learned, means that the *degree of activity* of the molecules in each is the same. But the potful of water has *more* of these active molecules, so we say that it has more heat in it. It takes

much more burning of gas to produce a potful of boiling water than a cupful; in turn, the pot has more heat to give up to something else. That is why you can warm up a baby bottle more quickly by putting it into a potful of hot water than into a cupful, other things being equal.

The unit used in measuring the *quantity* of heat is the *calorie*. The calorie is defined as the amount of heat necessary to raise 1 gram of pure water (about half a thimbleful) one degree Celsius. (This calorie is known as the small calorie; the large Calorie you use to "count the calories" in foods is equal to 1,000 of these small calories and is spelled with an uppercase "C"). Heat, then, is measured in units called calories; temperature is measured in units called degrees.

EFFECTS OF HEATING

The expansion and contraction of substances occasioned by their heating and cooling are important in everyday life. Railroad rails are laid with a small space between each section, because summer temperatures cause them to expand considerably. One mile of railroad track may be 4 feet (1.2 meters) longer on the hottest day of summer than on the coldest day of winter. The space between the sections of rail allows for expansion of steel; otherwise the expanding rails would buckle. Long metal bridges have one end of each of their sections mounted on rollers; joints between each section allow for expansion on the hottest days. Sidewalks must be laid in sections with expansion joints between them for the same reason. Otherwise the sidewalk would buckle up and break (see pp. 501–502).

Hot liquid poured into a cold glass sometimes causes it to crack because the heated inside surface expands suddenly, straining the unheated outside surface to the breaking point. Heat-resistant glass is useful because it contains substances that reduce the amount of contraction and expansion that can be induced by the loss or addition of heat.

Liquids as well as solids, as we have found in our study of thermometers, expand when they are heated and contract when they are cooled. For this reason we do not fill automobile radiators to the top with cool water.

Water, however, is unique in that at certain temperatures it reverses the rule of the association of contracting with cooling and expanding with heating: From 39°F (4°C) to 32°F (0°C), its usual freezing point, water expands slightly as it is cooled. As a result ice is lighter than water and floats on it. This peculiar behavior of water has important consequences for life on this planet. When ice forms on a lake or pond, its low density (it is only nine tenths as heavy as liquid water) keeps it on top. There it acts as an insulating blanket, preventing the rapid loss of heat from the water below it. This is why ponds and lakes do not freeze solid to the bottom but have a liquid zone under the ice for the survival of aquatic life.

The fact that water expands as it changes into ice accounts for the bursting of uninsulated water pipes and bottles in the winter. Similarly, if water is allowed to freeze in an automobile, it may break the metal block of the engine. Consequently, in cold weather we add antifreeze, a substance that has a low freezing point, to the water in our automobile cooling system. In Chapter 6A we also saw how the freezing of water is one of the forces responsible for the splitting of rocks.

Why does water behave in this unusual matter? Why does water expand almost 10 percent as it freezes? As in so many problems in science we turn to molecular theory for an answer. When water freezes into solid crystals of ice, the spaces between the molecules become larger. They cannot fit together as closely as they did in cold water in a liquid state.

We have seen how solids and liquids change in volume with temperature. Gases expand and contract even more. Air expands when heated and becomes lighter than an equal volume of cooler air. In Chapter 9A we also saw how the unequal heating of the air is one of the driving forces in the weather "machine" of our planet. We make use of this principle in the heating systems and in the ventilation of our homes.

CHANGES OF STATE

Matter can exist in a solid, liquid, or gaseous state. These states may be described in terms of shape and size.

A *solid* substance, such as a cube of ice, has a shape and size (volume) of its own.

A *liquid* substance, such as water in a pitcher, takes the shape of its container but has a size of its own.

A *gaseous* substance, such as water vapor in a pressure cooker, takes both the shape and the size of its container.

The three states of matter can also be imagined in terms of molecules. The description that follows makes two assumptions:

1. The ceaseless movement of molecules tends to make them separate from each other and to move in all directions.

2. An attractive force, *adhesion,* pulls them closer together.

In the solid state of a body, such as a bar of steel, the molecules vibrate less vigorously. The attractive forces between the molecules are strong enough to keep them vibrating in a fixed position. As a consequence, the body keeps a definite and unchanging shape.

In the liquid state of a body, such as molten iron, the molecules vibrate more vigorously than they did when the body was in the solid state. The attraction between the molecules is not strong enough to keep them in a specific location, yet it is strong enough to make the entire body hold together. This is why a liquid can flow and take the shape of its container.

In the gaseous state the molecules of a body vibrate more vigorously than in the liquid or solid forms of that body. The molecules are so far apart that the attractive force is very small. This explains why gases have no definite shape or size and why they spread to all parts of their container. The molecules in a drop of perfume pervade a room in a few seconds.

The description of these states in terms of molecules of matter also suggests why the volume or size changes when a body changes its state. In a solid the molecules are packed closely together; in a liquid they are somewhat farther apart (we noted one important exception in the preceding section); in a gas they are most scattered.

We can cause a change of state of any substance by adding or subtracting heat. Butter taken out of the refrigerator on a hot day gains heat and melts into a liquid. Water placed in the ice cube compartment solidifies as it loses heat. Gaseous water vapor in the air condenses into liquid drops as it loses heat.

When we say that a substance is a solid, liquid, or gas we really mean that it commonly exists in one of these three states at ordinary temperatures found on our planet. Thus, mercury is usually regarded as a liquid, but it will solidify into a solid at −40°F (−40°C) or boil off as a gas at 675°F

(367°C). Iron, copper, and other metals change from solids to liquids if they are heated sufficiently. Air is always thought of as gaseous, yet, with sufficient chilling, air can be converted into a liquid, known as *liquid air.* Sufficient chilling of one of the gases of the air, carbon dioxide, changes it into a solid; we know it as *dry ice* and use it when we wish to keep food at very low temperatures.

The temperature at which a substance changes from solid to liquid is known as its *melting point.* We make use of the fact that different substances have different melting points: Tungsten, the metal used for the filaments in electric lamps, can withstand temperatures of thousands of degrees without melting. On the other hand, an alloy of metals with a low melting point is useful in electric fuses, because a rise of temperature caused by a short circuit or an overloading of the electric line will cause it to melt and break the circuit (see pp. 542–543). Automatic sprinkling systems also use such metals for plugs; the heat produced in a fire causes the plugs to melt, thereby releasing water from the pipes.

We also make use of the fact that different substances have different *freezing points.* Alcohol, for example, freezes only when it has been chilled to −202°F (−130°C), but mercury, as we have seen, freezes at −40°F (−40°C). For this reason alcohol is used in thermometers in cold regions; mercury frozen into a solid would be useless there. Saltwater mixtures freeze only at temperatures lower than the freezing point of water. The practice of scattering salt on icy sidewalks results in a mixture that has a freezing point lower than the temperature of the air; hence, the ice melts.

HEAT MOVES

An iron poker is left in a campfire. In a few minutes its handle gets hot. In a tree branch 40 feet above the fire a bird feels the fire's warmth. Campers sitting around the fire feel a warm glow on their faces.

In each of these instances heat was transferred—from the fire to the poker, bird, and campers, respectively. But the principal *method* of heat transfer involved in each was different. Let us consider each of these ways—called *conduction, convection,* and *radiation*—to see how objects gain or lose heat (see pp. 503–504).

Conduction

Heat traveled from the end of the poker in the fire to the handle by conduction. It is simple to understand conduction when we recall that the poker, like all other substances, is made of molecules, in this case mostly iron molecules, and that the heat in the poker is due to the vibrations of its molecules. The molecules in the end of the poker in the fire vibrate more vigorously. These, in turn, strike adjacent molecules in the cooler part just outside of the flames, and cause them to vibrate more vigorously. This activity continues inch after inch up the poker until the handle becomes hot.

(The excellent heat conductivity of metals is due to the fact that the electrons of its atoms can flow along through the metal very rapidly and transfer energy to the atoms in cooler regions. In nonmetals, electron movement is restricted and heat energy is passed stepwise from atom to atom, but the process is much slower than in metals.)

Conduction, then, is a method of heat movement in which energy is transferred from molecule to molecule by collision or bombardment. You burn your fingers on the handle of a hot skillet because the heat from the flame has started molecular activity that reaches your skin by conduction. Even the molecules in your skin vibrate vigorously as they are heated. Sense organs in your skin detect this vibration and send a special nerve message (*not* by heat conduction) to your brain. You thus become aware of the heat.

Not all objects conduct heat equally well. Because wood is a poor conductor of heat we use it for the handles of pots and pans. In general,

metals are better conductors than nonmetals. Liquids, gases such as air, and nonmetal solids, all poor conductors of heat, are designated as heat *insulators* and are used to shield our bodies or objects from heat or to prevent the loss of heat. When we use a potholder to pick up hot pans and kettles we are making use of the insulating qualities of both the material and the air that is trapped in it to protect our hands from the heat.

Convection

How was the bird high in the tree warmed by the campfire? A layer of air directly over the fire was heated. The heat caused it to expand and thus made it lighter than the surrounding colder air. The heavier, colder air around the base of the fire swept into the fire and pushed the warmer, lighter air up to the bird. We saw in Chapter 9A how convection currents like these, caused by the unequal heating of the earth, are responsible for the large-scale movement of air and, therefore, of weather around the earth.

Convection currents are responsible for the heating of a room by a radiator. (A better name for this type of heater would be "convector.") Warm air heated by the radiator is pushed up and sweeps across to cooler parts of the room. Cold air falls and moves toward the radiator, where it is heated. Fireplaces are poor room heaters because most of the heat is convected up the chimney rather than out into the room.

Radiation

In conduction, heat is transferred as molecules bounce against adjacent molecules. In convection a whole volume of heated material—gaseous or liquid—circulates. The transfer of heat by radiation is quite different from both of these. The transfer of heat from campfire to face is effected not by vibrating molecules or circulating air but by a form of energy transfer called *radiation*.

Radiation is a most important method, because it accounts for the heating of the earth by the sun. Obviously, conduction and convection could not carry heat from the sun to the earth because most of the 93 million miles between them is empty space, almost devoid of molecules.

Radiant energy from the sun is transmitted in the form of waves (see pp. 595–596). Most apparent are the waves that produce visible light. In addition there are ultraviolet waves, sometimes called "black light" because one cannot see them. Ultraviolet light causes sunburn and tanning. And there are infrared rays, sometimes called heat rays. Visible light and infrared rays, primarily the latter, are responsible for most of the heating of the earth by the sun.

Infrared rays themselves should not be thought of as heat. The space between the sun and the earth is not heated by these waves, because there is practically nothing there to be heated. The rays might be compared to television waves emanating from a broadcasting station. These waves must be picked up by your TV set and converted into light for you to see a picture. Similarly, the infrared rays broadcast by the sun produce heat only when they strike and excite the molecules of substances.

Infrared rays are invisible to the human eye, lying just beyond the visible red rays in the spectrum of the sun's colors. All substances give off infrared radiation. If you hold your hand *under* an electric iron (to avoid heat by air convection) it is heated by radiation. You can detect the radiations of your own body by holding your open hand very close to the side of your face without touching it.

INSULATION

Stated simply, the purpose of insulation is to prevent heat from going where we do not want it to go. This is true whether we are considering our bodies or our homes. In all instances the flow of heat is regulated by controlling conduction, convection, and radiation, because these are the three methods by which heat travels (see pp. 502–503).

Clothing

The purpose of clothing is to keep the wearer comfortable in surroundings that are warm or cold, dry or moist. Our bodies are heat machines, maintaining an average temperature of 98.6°F (37°C). In cold weather clothing prevents the rapid loss of heat from the body. It does this by providing layers of air pockets, that is, still air trapped in the fine meshes of the fabric. As we saw earlier, air is a poor heat conductor. Moreover, when air is trapped in this way it cannot transmit heat by convection; it prevents your body from losing heat. Birds protect themselves from cold by fluffing their feathers, thereby trapping more air. Woolen clothing is generally warmer than other materials because it can hold more pockets of trapped air, called "dead air." Thicker fabrics are generally warmer than thinner ones because they hold more dead air.

In designing clothing for warmth, provision must also be made for the evaporation of perspiration. If the moisture is permitted to accumulate in the inner layers of the cloth it will fill some of the tiny air spaces that would otherwise provide insulation. Thus heat would be conducted away from the body more rapidly. To provide for the evaporation of perspiration several layers of fabric are generally better than a single layer.

Wind is also a source of danger and discomfort in cold weather, because the currents of air carry heat away from the clothing. That is why it is wise to have tightly woven cloth in the outermost layer of clothing to serve as a windbreaker.

In warm weather the problem is still insulation—insulation against the blistering heat of the sun. Clothing must be thick enough to prevent the sun's rays from penetrating and yet porous enough to permit evaporation, which, as we recall, is the body's natural cooling process.

Dark-colored materials absorb more radiant heat than light-colored materials. Place a piece of dark fabric and a piece of light-colored fabric of the same size and material in the sunlight. Feel each after a few minutes and you will find that the dark cloth is much warmer. For this reason light-colored clothing is cooler than dark clothing of similar material when worn in sunlight and is recommended for summer wear.

Homes

The prevention of heat loss from homes makes them healthier and more comfortable to live in, conserves energy, and lowers fuel bills. The principles involved are similar to those employed in clothing. Buildings are insulated in a number of ways. One method is to fill the spaces between the inner and outer walls with poor conductors, such as spun glass. Insulation is thus improved, because these materials prevent air currents from

convecting heat away; they also provide a way of trapping air, which, as we know, is a poor heat conductor (see figure on this page).

Wood, brick, cement, and cinder block are used in building construction partially because they, too, are poor conductors of heat, and hence will retard the flow of heat out of the building. Inside the building, hot-air pipes and steam pipes are often covered with spun glass or other material to prevent loss of heat from the pipes in the cellar or in other parts of the building where warmth is not needed. Refrigerators have a thick, fibrous packing between the inner and outer walls to prevent the heat of the room from getting inside them. Weather stripping around windows and storm doors also prevents considerable loss of warm air through these openings.

If a house is not insulated (*left*), the heat provided by the heating system is lost rapidly through the walls. Heat is transferred by conduction through walls and by convection currents in the air spaces between walls. In the insulated house, (*right*), the heat is retained within the living space. Because insulation material is a poor conductor, heat is lost slowly by conduction, and because insulation fills the air spaces it prevents convection currents from being set up.

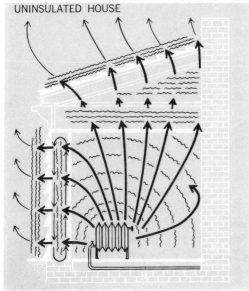

UNINSULATED HOUSE

INSULATED HOUSE

HEATING OF HOMES

At one time fireplaces were the only means of heating homes. But the fireplace was never a very effective heating device. Pioneers often had to spend winter evenings in bed to keep warm. Even if they came close to a roaring fire to receive heat by radiation, cold air chilled their backs. Commonly our ancestors heated a soapstone on the fire and then hurried off with it to warm an icy bed. No wonder they used feather beds and thick comforters!

In today's homes the fire or other source of heat has been moved into the basement or into a special utility room. The heat that is generated is conveyed to the rest of the house by means of circulating air or water.

This oil-burning hot-water heating system illustrates the ways in which heat is transferred from one place to another. The flame from the oil burner heats the water by conduction through the walls of the boiler. The hot water flows upward by convection, being pushed up by the cool water returning from the radiator for reheating. The radiator warms the air of the room partly by radiation, but mostly by the convection currents of air indicated by arrows.

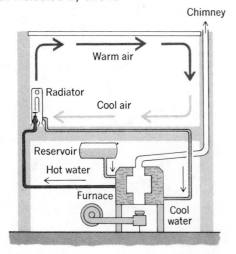

EVAPORATION COOLS

Dip your finger into water that is at about body temperature and hold it up to the air. It feels cool as the water evaporates. Evaporation is a cooling process, or to put it in other words, a heat-removing process. Why? The molecular theory comes to our help again. We have found that the heat of a substance is due to the energy of all its moving molecules. But not all the molecules have the same speed. Some of the faster-moving (higher-temperature) molecules escape from the surface of the water on your skin, leaving the slower-moving (lower-temperature) ones behind. Consequently, the moment that evaporation begins, heat leaves the water that remains on your finger. The water, on being chilled, removes heat from your skin, making it feel cool. We hasten cooling of a feverish patient by sponging the body with alcohol, which evaporates quickly and thus cools more effectively than water.

The evaporation of perspiration from your skin serves to regulate body temperature. Our bodies are heat machines: The skin serves as a cooling system, with perspiration the cooling fluid whose evaporation provides the means by which excess heat is disposed of.

REFRIGERATION

A discussion of refrigeration belongs in a chapter on heat because to cool something means to subtract heat from it. A refrigerator is a heat subtractor, at least as far as the food stored in it is concerned.

Mechanical (iceless) refrigerators have revolutionized the care of food. Such refrigeration is not confined to homes: Refrigerated railroad cars, trucks, and planes bring fruit, dairy products, fresh vegetables, meat, and fish hundreds and thousands of miles to our tables. We are able to keep food from a few months up to a year in deep-freeze units that make out-of-season foods much more available. Let us see how refrigerators work.

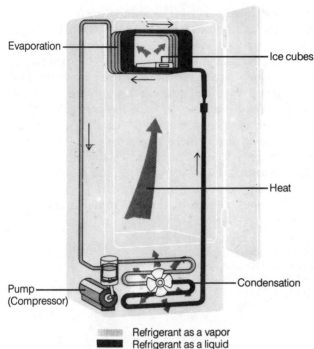

Evaporation

Ice cubes

Heat

Pump
(Compressor)

Condensation

▒ Refrigerant as a vapor
█ Refrigerant as a liquid
▒ Heat flow

Basically refrigeration depends on the principle that evaporation is a cooling or heat-removing process. Dab some alcohol on your wrist. It will feel cool as the alcohol evaporates. The evaporating alcohol carries heat away from your hand; the alcohol vapor then disperses in the air of your room. If you had a way of collecting the alcohol vapor and could compress it back into a liquid you could repeat the original operation and thus keep your wrist cool. This kind of a cycle is possible in a refrigerator, as shown above.

Instead of alcohol, *refrigerants* such as ammonia, methyl chloride, or Freon are used as evaporating fluids.[2] The refrigerant travels through pipes in a closed system. As the refrigerant (in a liquid state) passes through the coils

---

[2]Certain refrigerants, such as Freon and others in a class called chlorofluorocarbons (CFCs), are now being replaced, because it is believed that CFCs attack atmospheric ozone which shields life on earth from harmful ultraviolet radiation (see Chapter 13A).

The mechanical refrigerator keeps its contents cold by transferring heat from the cooling compartment to the outside air.

around the freezing compartment it evaporates into a gas, thereby removing heat from the interior of the refrigerator. (Recall that evaporation is a cooling or heat-removing process.) The gas then moves to the electricity-driven pump and is forced into a condenser. Here it loses heat through the walls of this coiled-tube structure to the air of the room and is compressed to a liquid again. The cycle is repeated as long as cooling is required in the refrigerator. In this way the heat of the foods, the air, and surfaces inside the refrigerator is conveyed to the air of the room. Thus refrigeration transfers heat from where it is undesirable to where it is unobjectionable.

SOLAR ENERGY

The sun lavishes energy on the earth. Not only does the sun warm the earth, but energy from sunlight makes it possible for plants to synthesize the food that provides fuel for their own needs and for the animals that eat them. The heat of the sun causes water to be evaporated from oceans into clouds. Falling as rain on the mountains the water from the clouds rushes down to the sea in streams and rivers. In the path of falling water engineers place turbines hitched to generators that convert its wild energy into useful electricity. The common fuels we use—whether gas, oil, coal, or wood—are the remains of products of organisms that derived their original energy from the sun (see pp. 398–400).

Coal, natural gas, and oil—the so-called fossil fuels—are limited in their supply. In the long run

these fuels will be exhausted: natural gas first, then oil, and finally coal. That is why all over the world there is an intense search for new sources of heat energy (see Chapter 13A). Perhaps the solution to the problem is staring us in the face when we look up at the sky—in the sun itself, which for millions of years has poured its essentially perpetual energy on us. The energy the United States receives from the sun in about two hours is equivalent to the energy produced for our present fuel consumption in a whole year.

Why don't we use some of this vast supply? Various attempts have been made to utilize the

Artist's rendering of a projected "Solar Dome" power plant. Each dome, called a heliostat, would track the sun across the sky and bounce its rays onto a central receiving tower. The heliostat consists of an aluminum-coated plastic mirror enclosed in a transparent plastic dome for environmental protection. (*Courtesy of Boeing Engineering and Construction, A Division of the Boeing Co.*)

This solar oven uses a reflecting surface that concentrates the sun's rays on the centrally placed plate. India is among the countries experimenting with devices such as this to develop new sources of energy. (*Courtesy of the United Nations.*)

heat of the sun directly. Many generations of children have had the experience of using a magnifying lens as a "burning glass" by focusing the sun's rays on a scrap of paper, making it smolder, scorch, and burn. So-called sun machines, which concentrate the sun's rays on a small area by means of a number of mirrors or lenses, have been able to change water into steam and thus furnish power. Some of these devices have been used experimentally to melt metals; temperatures up to 7000°F (3900°C) have been obtained in this way. Experimentation and testing are now going on in a number of countries to develop solar power plants. All use a large field of mirrors to focus sunlight on a tank mounted on a tower. Although the fluid used in the tank differs in the plants, all provide the heat needed to convert water into the steam that turns an electric generator (see Chapter 17A).

The sun's rays have been used in another way

in subtropical and even temperate climates to furnish part or all of the heat needed in homes. You may be familiar with the fact that the inside of an automobile becomes quite warm, even in cool weather, if the sun is shining and if the windows are closed. Glass admits much of the radiant energy from the sun. This radiant energy is changed to heat energy when it strikes the upholstery in the interior of the car. The heat accumulates and the car warms up.

The underlying principle is often called the greenhouse effect, because it accounts for the warmth that builds up in a gardener's hothouse in the winter. Here, again, the large expanse of glass permits the sun's rays to penetrate and to warm the soil and other materials in the greenhouse. These heated substances also broadcast heat waves, but these are different from the original solar waves, so that instead of passing out through the glass roofs and walls they bounce back. Ordinary window glass, then, has the unique property of being transparent to 90 percent of the sun's radiant heat energy but opaque to the heat waves reradiated by objects under the glass. A greenhouse is thus an energy trap.

The greenhouse effect has been used in solar houses, which have been developed by engineers. In these houses much of the wall area consists of glass. Such houses require little artificial heat even on winter days in as cold a climate as that of Chicago—provided the sun is shining. Fuel bills have been materially reduced as a result. Overhanging

eaves prevent the summer sun's rays from entering the house.

The sun's radiation may also be used to heat water. (You may have observed that the water first coming out of a length of garden hose that has been exposed to the sun for some time is surprisingly warm.) Solar water heaters have been used for many years in California and Florida and in Israel. One type, the flat-plate solar collector, has blackened coils of pipe under a glass cover in a flat box that is placed on the roofs of houses and tilted in a southerly direction to receive as much radiation as possible. When the sun is shining the water becomes warm, circulates to a tank, and is distributed as needed for hot-water use or for heating a swimming pool.

Some experimental homes are now heated all year round by solar heat. The sun's heat is absorbed by water in a number of flat-plate solar collectors. The warmed water is stored in an insulated tank, and the heat from it is transferred to the various rooms as needed. This system works for extended periods when the sun is obscured by clouds. Such homes also make use of the greenhouse effect when the sun is shining.

Solar energy is now being converted directly into electrical energy by *solar cells*. In such cells, sunlight provides the energy to dislodge electrons and to produce a current in a circuit. (See Chapter 17A for a fuller discussion of electrical circuits.) The principle is not new; the photoelectric meter used in photography and the "seeing eye" for

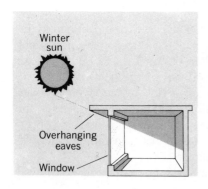

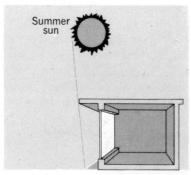

This schematic diagram shows how a solar house is warmed by the sun in winter and yet not overheated during the summer. Remember that the sun is much lower in the sky in winter than it is in summer.

In this test facility, panels of solar cells convert sun energy directly into electricity. Photons, particles of light energy, knock electrons loose from each cell; the electrons are collected, run through wires, and returned to the cells after being put to work.

A solar cell recently developed at Sandia National Laboratories in Albuquerque, New Mexico, demonstrated a 31 percent sunlight-to-electricity conversion efficiency—the highest ever recorded. (*Courtesy of Florida Solar Energy Center.*)

door openers convert light into electricity. The knowledge that light could knock electrons out of their orbits around the nuclei of atoms to form an electric current was explained by Einstein in 1921, when he won the Nobel Prize for his work on the "photoelectric effect." (Photons, "bullets" of sunlight striking the surface of semiconductor materials such as silicon, liberate electrons from its atoms. A path is provided for the freed electrons, thus creating an electrical circuit.)

Solar cells are now used to supply electrical energy for equipment in many kinds of earth-orbiting satellites: weather, communication, navi-gation, earth resources, and others. Solar cells also power unattended lighthouses and meteorological observation stations in remote places, such as the one at 11,000 feet (3,300 meters) on Mammoth Mountain, California. (See Chapter 13A for a discussion of solar cells as a source of energy.)

Looking to the future, power modules with 100-foot-long panels of solar cells may be deposited into earth orbit by the space shuttle and left there as a kind of electrical outlet. Laboratories, satellites, and factories in space could plug into such modules for their power needs.

IMPORTANT GENERALIZATIONS

Energy is the ability to do work.

Heat is a form of energy: It can do work.

Energy can be converted from one form to another.

The energy of a body may be due to its motion (kinetic energy) or its position or condition (potential energy).

As a substance gets warmer its molecules move more vigorously; as it cools, the molecules move less vigorously.

Cooling is the loss of heat.

Substances generally expand when heated and contract when cooled.

Water is unique in that it expands just before it freezes; this explains why ice is lighter than water.

The temperature or heat intensity of a body is measured in degrees; the total quantity of heat in a body is measured in calories.

Substances exist in three states: solid, liquid, and gaseous.

A solid has a shape and size of its own.

A liquid takes the shape of its container, but has a size of its own.

A gas takes the shape of its container and spreads to all parts of it.

The addition or removal of heat from a substance may cause it to change from one state into another.

Heat is transferred by conduction, convection, and radiation.

Different materials vary in their ability to conduct heat; those that conduct heat slowly are called insulators.

Clothing keeps us warm because it prevents the body from losing its heat too rapidly.

Clothing, blankets, and some house-insulating materials are effective in preventing the loss of heat because they contain trapped air, which is a poor heat conductor.

Dark-colored materials absorb more radiant heat than light-colored materials.

Heating systems make use of all three methods of heat transfer.

Modern refrigerators utilize the cooling effects of evaporation in their operation.

Scientists and engineers are trying to find economical ways of using the abundant energy of the sun.

DISCOVERING FOR YOURSELF

1. What heat problems must be solved in space travel?
2. Locate the different kinds of thermometers in your home and school. Compare their construction, purpose, and operation.
3. Identify the ways in which heat insulation is used in your kitchen.
4. Observe the sources of heat in your environment. List three sources.
5. Observe examples of heat that cause materials (solids, liquids, gases) to expand. Record them.
6. Find examples of heat traveling by conduction, convection, and radiation.
7. Find examples of the use of insulation (against conduction, convection, and radiation) in your home and school.
8. Examine a refrigerator and a furnace to see how they use the principles of conduction, convection, and radiation.
9. Find out about current projects on solar energy, as reported in newspapers and magazines.
10. If possible, visit a home, school, or factory employing some form of solar heating. With the help of a diagram, describe how it operates.

TEACHING "HEAT AND HOW WE USE IT"

Because heat is involved in many phenomena it is included in the chapters on astronomy, weather, living things, ecology, molecules and atoms, and space.

The study of heat provides an opportunity for helping children move from subjective feelings: "It feels cold," "It feels warm," "It feels hot today," to objective measurements: "The temperature is 70°F (about 21°C) today," "The water is 38°F (about 3°C)," "The thermometer shows that today is warmer than yesterday."

Concepts about heat—its sources, its methods of travel, its effects on solids, liquids, and gases—are important in our modern world and relate to the warming and insulation of homes; the refrigeration of foods; the construction of sidewalks, railroad tracks, and iron bridges; the building of greenhouses; and the use of solar panels.

SOME BROAD CONCEPTS

Heating and cooling change the size and shape of substances.

Substances exist in three states: solids, liquids, and gases.

Substances may be heated by conduction, convection, and radiation.

Heating systems make use of all three methods of heat transfer.

Heat is a form of energy, the energy of moving particles.

Energy may be converted from one form to another.

Materials that conduct heat slowly are called insulators.

Dark-colored materials absorb more radiant heat than do light-colored materials.

FOR YOUNGER CHILDREN

How Do We Use Heat?

Suggest that children observe different uses of heat at home and elsewhere, or take them on a "heat trip" around the school building to see what is heated and how it is done. The children will keep track of such examples as boiling water, making popcorn, baking cookies, drying wet things, melting butter, heating the building, and so forth. Children can collect a list of such activities and prepare a record of their findings by using drawings, magazine pictures, and sentences. Summarize their experiences in a three-column chart: Where observation was made, what was being heated, and the source of heat.

What Does the Sun Warm?

Refer to "What Makes the Earth Warm?" and "How Much Does Temperature Change in a Day?" in Chapter 7B. These activities emphasize the idea that heat comes from the sun. "Where can you feel the heat of the sun?" (on the sidewalk, grass, windowsill, and so on). Put a pan of water in the sun and a similar one in the shade. Measure the temperatures. "What does this show?" Try this on both a cloudy and a sunny day. Introduce the term *solar energy* so that children will begin to understand what the term means. Ask, What is solar energy used for? Do you know places where it is used? Why do you suppose it is important for us to use more solar energy? (See Chapter 15A.)

How Hot Is It?

Ask such questions as, "Is it hot or cold today?" "Is the water in this cup hot or cold?" Then, "How can we be more exact about what is hot or cold?"

Even young children have had experiences with thermometers and will make suggestions about their use. The use of this measuring instrument is one way to introduce children to objective measurement. Use thermometers marked with both Fahrenheit and Celsius degrees or thermometers just with Celsius. *Emphasize Celsius so that children associate it directly with their own sensory experience and not with a conversion problem.* Children hear Celsius temperatures used in weather reports and are fast becoming accustomed to it. Give them an opportunity to examine a thermometer carefully, reporting what they can discover through *observation*. Let them *describe* what they see and then try to *explain* how a thermometer can show temperature. Check to see that they are reading the thermometer correctly. A large thermometer available from supply houses is useful. Discuss what they have discovered about the markings. "What do you observe about the numbers?" "What is the red (or silver) line?" "Can you make it change? How? Let's try it." Children may suggest, Put it in the sun; put it in cold water; put your finger around the bulb; breathe on it; and so on. Suggest that students select one or more of these ideas and try them, keeping a record of "before and after" temperatures. They may classify their ideas about the temperature line: "gets longer," "gets shorter," "stays the same." Students can then examine their records and try to decide, "What makes the line on the thermometer change?" "How does it change if something is warmed? Cooled?" Students can explore problems such as, "How are thermometers used?" "What things around us change temperature?" They can keep a chart of temperature changes from day to day. They can look for places where thermometers are used and try to decide why it is important to know the temperatures in those places.

How Can We Keep Ice from Melting?

Discuss what makes ice melt (heat changes ice from solid to liquid). Where does the heat come from (from warmer surroundings)? Conduct an experiment to see how well the children can prevent ice cubes from melting. Children's suggestions, such as wrapping ice cubes in paper toweling, aluminum foil, or wax paper, placing them in plastic containers, and so on, should be accepted and tested. Each group should be given the same number of similar ice cubes. Except for the kind of cover used, the ice cubes should be treated in a similar way and placed in separate open bowls. Compare the sizes of the ice cubes after 15 minutes, 30 minutes, and so on. In cases of doubt about the effectiveness of each method, pour the water from each of the trials into a measuring cup. (Children may need help in understanding that the cups with the least amount of water came from the cubes that melted the least.) Conduct a similar experiment to see how *fast* ice cubes can be melted. How long does it take to change the ice cubes into water?

Other Problems for Younger Children

1. How does heat change things?
2. Do some things heat faster than others?
3. How can we keep things warm?
4. How can we keep things cool?
5. How does the temperature change at night?
6. How does the sun heat homes?

FOR OLDER CHILDREN

Where Does Heat Come From?[1]

Students can make a list of many different sources of heat—for example, friction, electricity, fires, nuclear energy—and tell some of the uses for heat from each source. Then they can try to trace each of the sources back to the sun. This activity may raise several questions about heat, and is, therefore, useful in introducing the study of how we use heat. The questions can also form the beginning of a list of problems to solve, to which more will be added both by students and teacher as the study continues.

How Does a Thermometer Work?

Children will already have some ideas about how thermometers work that may be listed, discussed, and defended. Individuals may suggest various methods for testing their ideas.

Depending on the responses and backgrounds of the children the teacher can, if necessary, provide some assistance by assembling the apparatus pictured on page 500.

[1]L. Santrey, *Heat* (Mahwah, N.J.: Troll, 1985).

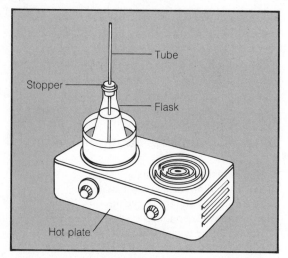

The flask filled with colored water can be used to show how heat causes a liquid to expand. A string may be tied around the glass tube to mark the level of water before heating.

Use a heat-resistant flask, a one-holed rubber stopper to fit, and a $1\frac{1}{2}$-foot (45-centimeter) piece of glass tubing that will fit into the hole of the stopper. Wet the tube and stopper with soapy water or glycerine to make the tube slip in easier. Nearly fill the flask with water that has been colored with a few drops of red ink or vegetable coloring to make it easier to watch. Fit the glass tubing into the stopper so that a little of the tubing extends through the stopper (see drawing above). In inserting glass tubing into a stopper precautions are necessary to avoid breaking the tube and cutting oneself: (1) Make sure that the hole is large enough to admit the tubing, (2) wet the tube and the stopper, (3) hold the part of the tube *near* the stopper and twist the stopper around the tube. Fit the stopper into the flask firmly. A little of the water should extend up into the tube. Tie a piece of thread around the tube at the level of the water. When the apparatus is assembled, the teacher may ask, "Can we use this material to test some of the hypotheses that were made about how thermometers are made?" "How is it like a real thermometer?" "How is it different?" Children may suggest

putting it in hot and cold places and using the thread as a marker (see pp. 481–484).

The flask can be placed on an electric hot plate or into a container of hot water. Urge the children to watch the water level in the tube. (It rises as heat expands the water.) Hopefully they will suggest marking the new level with another piece of thread. Now cool the water by setting the flask in a pan of ice cubes. Watch the level of the water fall. (Cooling contracts the water.) Ask the children to try to explain what they have seen: "How hot was the water? How cold?" Obviously the children cannot tell because there are no degree markings. How could we improve on this apparatus to make it function more nearly like a thermometer? An adaptation of the following ideas may be worked out with the children.

Fasten an index card to the tube with cellophane tape. Place the flask up to its neck in a jar of hot water. Let it stand until the water stops rising in the tube. Then with a commercial thermometer take the temperature of the water in the jar. Mark the card at the level of the water in the tube, and next to it write the temperature just read. Now place the flask in a jar of cold water and let it stay there until the water stops falling in the tube. Again take the water temperature and mark it on the card.

With these two points you have a basis for making a *scale* of degrees. Mark off the degrees between the two points and then below and above them.

To use this crude thermometer over a period of time it will be necessary to place a drop of oil on top of the water in the tube to prevent evaporation. Also, if it is to be used outdoors in cold weather it will have to be remade, using about three parts water and one part alcohol to prevent freezing.

The foregoing procedure presents the children with a partially completed instrument; they propose methods of testing it and offer hypotheses to explain how it works. They have invented a method of making it into a measuring device. This is an example of how a piece of apparatus can be used creatively with children. How much student participation takes place depends on the teacher's intentions and on the background and experiences of the children.

What Does Heating Do to Solids?

Why do you suppose that running hot water over the metal lid of a glass jar makes it easier to unscrew? Ask children to recall any other experiences related to the effect of heat on solids. Ask children if they can formulate a general statement that they believe will be an answer to the problem. Ask them if they can demonstrate or suggest observations that bear out their statements (see Chapter 2, pp. 19–20).

The screw and screw eye pictured (see below) is a substitute for the commercially available ball and ring, which is often used to show that solids expand when they are heated and contract when they are cooled. The handles are made of $1\frac{1}{2}$-inch dowels about 1 foot long. With a nail first make a hole in one end of each stick. The large screw eye is then screwed into the end of one stick and the large screw head (just a little too large to go into the eye) is screwed into the other. When the screw eye is heated, it expands so that the screw head will go through it.

The homemade apparatus and the commer- cially manufactured ball and ring and bimetallic bar may also be used to observe the effects of heat on metals.

These experiments do not show that *all* solids expand when they are heated and contract when they are cooled, so students should experiment with other materials. They will find suggestions in books and elsewhere, and devise some themselves. They may also need to read to substantiate their ideas. Students should be urged to find other solids in their environment that are expanded by heat and contracted by cold. Examples are telephone and telegraph wires suspended from poles, pavements, sections of railroad tracks, and iron bridges. In some cases students can also observe how allowance is made for this expansion and contraction—for example, by leaving spaces between sections of concrete sidewalks.

What Does Heating Do to Water?

Use the same apparatus and approach that demonstrated the principle of the thermometer. Applications of the principle that heat expands water are evident in automobile radiators, in our hotwater heaters, and other places where liquids are heated. (The unusual behavior of water between 39° and 32°F, discussed in Chapter 15A, is not characteristic of other liquids.) The thermometer itself is an example of the principle that heat

The screw and screw eye may be used to show that a solid expands when heated and contracts when cooled.

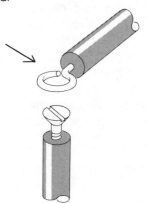

This improvised scale helps experimenters determine how much expansion takes place as the wire is heated.

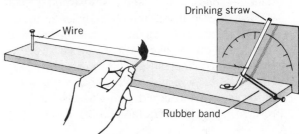

causes liquids to expand; in thermometers the liquid is either alcohol or mercury.

What Does Heating Do to Air?

Using the ideas previously suggested, and drawing on the experiences and suggestions of the children, you may use the following, with adaptations.

Fasten a toy rubber balloon over the opening of a heat-resistant flask or a soda bottle. Set the glass container into a pan of very hot water. The balloon begins to fill up as the gas expands. Now put the bottle in a pan of ice water. What happens? The idea of air expanding on being heated has been used in the study of the cause of winds (see Chapter 9B).

The flask, stopper, and tube used previously to show the expansion and contraction of liquids may also be used to show the expansion of air. Empty the flask and replace the stopper and the tube. Invert it so that the end of the tube is in a glass of water. Warming the flask, even by holding both hands around it, will be sufficient to cause air bubbles to escape from the tube into the water because the heat causes the air to expand. When the air cools, it contracts, and water will be forced up the tube into the flask by outside air pressure.

Does it really work? Children feel water heated by sun energy in a solar water heater. (*Courtesy of Roger Wall.*)

How Do Heating and Cooling Change the Size and Form of Matter?

Introduce the idea that the expansion of substances—solids, liquids, and gases—when heated is due to the fact that its minute particles, its molecules, bounce more vigorously and move away from each other (like popcorn when heated). How does cooling cause substances to contract? How does heating and cooling change the *form* of matter (solid to liquid, liquid to gas—and the reverse)? (See Chapters 14A and B.)

How Does Sunlight Affect Dark and Light Objects?

Children may recall having had experiences with heat on light and dark objects. Build on such experiences, and give children an opportunity to express their ideas about them. Then give children pieces of black and white paper, and ask them how they might use these to find out more about the effects of heat on them. Put the papers over the thermometers and place them in bright sunlight. Measure the differences and compare results.

There are many other ways to show that dark objects absorb heat more readily than light ones.

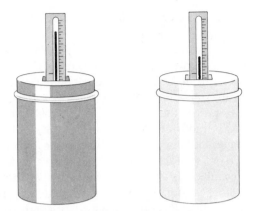

Two cans, one painted black and the other white, may be set in sunlight to show its effect on dark and light objects. The two thermometers fit through slits made in the can covers, which may be plastic.

The "tin" cans shown in the drawing (see above) have lids that fit tightly. One can is painted black, the other is painted white, or it may be left with its tin surface unpainted. Each can top has a hole in it just a little larger than the thermometer that extends through to the inside. After inserting the thermometers, seal the openings around them with modeling clay. Ask children how they might use these cans to find out more about the effects of sunlight on temperatures under these conditions. Urge them to predict what will happen when their suggestions are followed (see Chapter 15A, pp. 488–489).[2]

After the two cans are set in bright sunlight, the children keep a record of the thermometer readings every minute for a period of about 15 minutes or until there are no further changes in the thermometers. Have them enter the observations on a graph, connect the points, and try to draw conclusions. After this experience urge children to apply their observations to their own environmental experiences. They should be able to apply the findings to explain why dark and light clothing is worn at different seasons or in different parts

[2]M. Yates, *Sun Power: The Story of Solar Energy* (Nashville: Abington, 1983); I. Asimov, *How Did We Find Out about Solar Power* (New York: Walker, 1983).

of the world, and why solar collectors on the roofs of houses are usually painted black.

Light and dark pieces of cloth spread on snow show similar results when the sun shines. The snow under the dark piece of cloth melts more rapidly. One application of the principle involved here is in the design of spaceships, where dark outside surfaces may be utilized to absorb energy from the sun's rays and white surfaces may reflect the energy. By the proper use of such surfaces satisfactory temperatures for human beings can be maintained within the ships.

How Does Fanning Cool You?

Have some children wet both hands with water at room temperature, and ask some classmates to fan one hand briskly with a cardboard. Compare this with the hand that has not been fanned. What difference is felt? "How do you account for this?" "What happens to the water?" Evidently, fanning makes water evaporate more rapidly. Why should this make a difference? When a liquid evaporates it carries off heat. In this case water gets its heat from the surface of the skin, leaving the skin cooler. The more quickly the water evaporates, the more heat is removed, and the cooler the skin becomes.

An easy way to tell the direction of the wind is to go outdoors, wet the index finger, and hold it up as high as possible. The side of the finger that faces the wind feels cool. Students may recall having been sponged with alcohol when ill. Alcohol evaporates rapidly, and the cooling is rapid.

How Does Heat Travel?

An understanding of how heat is transferred from one place to another is important if students are to understand how their homes are heated and how temperature is controlled in other ways. It is not very important for them to be able to define the terms convection, radiation, and conduction, but they may be able to use these terms as they understand the processes. They should understand that heat travels in different ways, then come to the realization of how we make use of this knowledge. Each of the experiments and demonstrations that follow requires students to observe carefully and attempt to draw conclusions from their observations. The conclusions may then be applied to solve problems in their environment.

How Does Air Carry Heat? Use a lamp chimney and a candle. Refer to "What Makes the Wind?" in Chapter 9B. Light the candle and set the chimney over it on two blocks to raise it above the table surface. Ask children to observe what happens when they hold a smoking paste stick at the bottom of the chimney. (The smoke will show that air is moving into the bottom of the chimney and is traveling up past the flame to the top of the chimney.) Carefully feel the warmth at the top of the chimney. It is this moving air that carries the heat. Hold a thermometer 1 foot above the top of the chimney and note changes as the air is warmed. Hot-air heating systems operate on the principle of cold air pushing the warm air into rooms that are heated by the furnace (convection). (See diagram on p. 477.)

How Does Water Carry Heat? Fill a flask or heat-resistant baby bottle or a beaker nearly full of water and heat it at the bottom. Hold a thermometer in the water at the top. Ask a child to read the thermometer when it is first inserted and again at intervals. "What does the temperature show?" "How did the heat get to the top of the water?" The warm water at the bottom expands and is lighter than the water at the top, so it rises, carrying heat with it. The heat is carried by what is called convection currents. Some grains of sand or pieces of sawdust placed in the water will show how the currents are traveling. In hot-water heating systems heat is carried to the rooms by circulating water.

How Is Heat Carried by Radiation? There are many common examples of heat being carried by radiation. Light a candle and suggest that children read a thermometer held about 8 inches above it. The higher temperature *above* the candle is caused by convection currents. Remove the thermometer from the candle and wait until it returns to room temperature. Now hold the thermometer at the *side* of the burning candle. The heat is caused by radiation. Read the thermometer before and after holding it at the side of the burning candle. Most of the heat from an open fireplace is transmitted by radiation. Hold an open hand very close to, but not touching, one side of your face. The heat felt on your face is carried from your hand by radiation. The sun's heat reaches the earth by radiation.

How Do Solids Carry Heat? Place the bottom of a metal spoon in a glass of hot water or other hot liquid. Let a child feel the handle from time to time to note what is happening. How do you think the handle gets warm? The heat has traveled along the spoon by conduction (see Chapter 15A). Hot pans on the kitchen stove and fireplace tools conduct heat in this way. Ask, "Will all kinds of spoons carry heat equally well?" Try a wooden one, then a plastic one. "Which one carried the heat better?" Try other materials.

After these experiences students should be asked to look for places in their environment where heat travels from one place to another—at home, at school, in restaurants, and elsewhere. Kitchens, fireplaces, furnaces, and so on, all depend on heat transfer. This investigating will probably lead to questions about other phases of the problem of heat control—insulation and home heating.

Other Problems for Older Children

1. What is the range of degrees of different thermometers (room, thermostat, oven, freezer, clinical, meat, and so on)? What is expanding and contracting in each case?[3]

[3]G. W. Nahrstedt, "An Energy Lesson: Building a Working Thermostat," *Science and Children* (October 1981). Clear directions; for fifth grade and up.

2. Make a solar energy machine (see Chapter 13B).
3. How can you prove that water expands when it is frozen?
4. How does a bimetallic (two-metal) thermometer work?
5. Fill two cans or plastic containers, one painted black and one white, with water. Cover, place in sunlight, and measure temperatures at half-hour intervals. Make a graph of your results.

RESOURCES TO INVESTIGATE WITH CHILDREN

1. Local builders, to see how homes are equipped for good heating and how they are insulated. Children's homes, to see how they are heated and insulated.
2. The kitchen at home (or at school) to see how heat is controlled in utensils, stoves, refrigerators, and other equipment.
3. A bakery, to find out about sources and control of heat and about utensils that are used.
4. Home economics departments, for literature concerning cooking utensils and preservation of foods.
5. State university extension service, for materials describing the heating of farm buildings, greenhouses, hotbeds, and other places.

6. The school building and the school custodian, to learn how the school heating plant works and what science principles are involved in its operation.
7. Buildings or homes equipped with air conditioning.
8. Buildings that use solar energy.
9. Places that use geothermal energy.[4]

PREPARING TO TEACH

1. Plan some original experiments to show the advantage of wearing light-colored clothing in warm weather and dark clothes in cold weather. Plan how you would use the experiments to help children understand this concept.
2. Build and test the wire-expansion indicator, or the screw and screw eye on page 501. Prepare questions that might be helpful in encouraging the creative use by children of these devices for experimentation and for application of the concepts involved to everyday constructions.

[4]M. Yates, *Earth Power: The Story of Geothermal Energy* (Nashville: Abington, 1981).

MACHINES AND
HOW THEY WORK

It appears contrary to reason that a large weight should be set in motion by a small force; yet a weight that cannot be moved without the aid of a lever can be moved easily with it.

ARISTOTLE, 3RD CENTURY B.C.

Give me a fulcrum on which to rest and I will move the earth.

ARCHIMEDES, 2ND CENTURY B.C.

EARLY MACHINES

We do not know what machine was first used by humans, but it may well have been a club. Primitive people in many places must have discovered the club's effectiveness as a weapon against wild animals. Even the simple club is a machine, because it made work easier by permitting one to apply a force to one's advantage.

When humans attached a pointed stone to a club to make it into a spear, or an edged stone to make it into an ax, they became more effective in coping with their environment and raising their standard of living. When they used a stout branch of a tree to pry up a heavy rock they invented a *lever,* a machine destined to find thousands of uses. From our study of the remains of Stone Age people, we know that they used wood, bone, stone, or ivory to fashion tools such as axes, hammers, knives, spear points, scrapers, drills, <u>awls</u>, pins, and needles.

By the time of the Common Era (the era beginning with the year 1), the pulley, screw, and windlass had been invented. The wheel, which revolutionized transportation and without which our modern machinery would be impossible, had long been in use. We have evidence of the wheel's use from pictures and remains that show that chariots existed in Egypt and Babylonia several thousand years before the Common Era. (Although the wheel was a great mechanical invention it is not considered a machine when it turns around the axle of a wagon or chariot. We shall see later how the wheel can be part of a machine, in the sense that physicists define the word.)

SIMPLE MACHINES

The intricate mechanism of a watch, the complex construction of an automobile, and the elaborate machinery of a factory are all combinations of simple machines such as the lever, pulley, wheel and axle (including the gear wheel), inclined plane, wedge, and screw. These basic machines serve any of the three following purposes:

1. They increase speed. Examples: egg beater, drive wheel of a bicycle.
2. They increase force. Examples: car jack, <u>crowbar</u>, screwdriver.
3. They change the direction of a force. Example: a single fixed pulley.

Some machines serve two of the three purposes at the same time: While they are changing the direction of a force they either increase the speed or increase the force.

As you survey the many machines you encounter every day, try to determine which of the three purposes they are accomplishing. Remember, however, that these *machines do not produce energy but make use of the energy supplied to them.*

The Lever

Children are amused when they are told that they can lift their teacher. The only material needed for a teacher-lifting machine is a block of wood and a plank about 6 feet long. The block is placed under the plank and near one of its ends. The

Here levers are being used in two different ways to do work. How they are used depends partly on the amount of force required and partly on convenience.

teacher stands on the short end of the plank. The child is delighted to find out that it is possible to lift the teacher by pushing down on the other end. In using this device, which is a lever, the child is realizing one of the purposes of a machine, that of increasing force (see pp. 24, 520–522).

If the block is placed 1 foot away from the end where the teacher is standing, the child (who will be 5 feet from the block) need exert a downward push of only 25 pounds to lift his or her 125-pound teacher. The effectiveness of the child's muscles is thus multiplied fivefold. The supporting block furnishes the pivot point, or *fulcrum,* for the lever. The child's part of the lever is five times as long as the teacher's, and the force exerted is five times as effective.

Is this magic? It looks as if we are getting something for nothing—a 125-pound return for an investment of 25 pounds. This is true, but it is not the whole truth. If you watch the lever as it works you will notice that to lift the teacher 1 inch the child must push down on the other end of the plank for a distance of 5 inches. In other words, the child's force must be exerted five times the

distance that the *resistance* to this force (the teacher) moves.

In this illustration force is gained and distance is lost, but one thing is the same—work. The term *work,* as used by the physicist, means the use of *force through a distance.* The amount of work put in by the child is the mathematical product of the force (25 pounds) and the distance (5 inches). Compare this with the work put out in lifting the teacher (125 pounds × 1 inch), and you will see the result is the same.

The physicist sums this up by saying that the work put out equals the work put in. This ideal situation is true, however, only if losses due to friction are disregarded. (In the other machines discussed in this chapter frictional losses are similarly disregarded.) In the teacher-lifting machine the work put out is slightly less than the work put in due to the friction of the plank on the block as the plank moves.

Levers are in common use. In lifting a boulder a worker uses the same principle as the child does in the teacher-lifting machine. Also, when a hammer is used to pull a nail its long handle makes

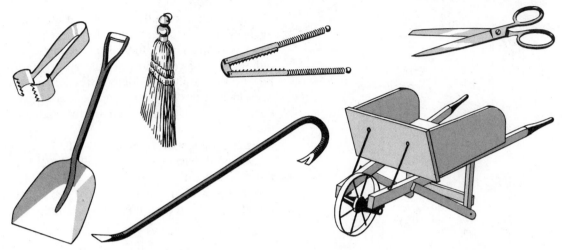

Can you explain how each of these machines helps make the job easier?

it possible for the user to exert a strong pull. The hammer is a bent lever; the nail offers the resistance; the point of contact of hammer with wood is the fulcrum; and the pull of the hand holding the hammer serves as the force.

In other uses of the lever the fulcrum, or balancing point, is not always between the force exerted and the weight moved. In lifting a stump the fulcrum is near the end of the lever, where the lever is resting on the log. Here again, the advantage depends on the distance of the worker's hand from the fulcrum as compared to the distance of the stump from the fulcrum. By using the lever the force is increased, but the worker must also exert his or her force through a greater distance.

In some cases we deliberately use a lever that gives us *less* force than we expend. One example is the use of a fishing pole. Here the fulcrum is the butt end of the pole pressed against the body. The force exerted is greater than the weight of the fish. However, in this case the gain is one of *speed*. The fish is jerked out of the water; it does not have a chance to escape from the fast-penetrating hook.

The Pulley

All of us have seen a flag raised to the top of a flagpole by the use of a pulley and a rope. This arrangement makes it possible to raise the flag without climbing the pole. A pulley used in this way is called a *fixed* or *stationary pulley*. Fixed pulleys have many uses. They help to raise hay into barns, sails to the top of masts, and objects from the holds of ships to the wharves. They have many uses around factories, stores, and garages. Many windows are raised with the aid of fixed pulleys and sash weights. The weight is arranged so that it will almost lift the window by itself. If you grasp the cord and lift up you can feel the pull of the sash weight. One has to exert only a little force to lift a window that has been properly fitted with pulleys and weights (see pp. 522–524).

A fixed pulley does not increase the force but makes it more convenient to apply. With a fixed pulley, as much force is required to pull down on the rope as to lift the weight without the use of the pulley. In fact, a little more force is needed, because we must overcome the friction between

This single pulley does not multiply either force or speed but provides a convenient means of raising loads, flags, sails, and other items.

the rope and the pulley wheel. It is usually easier, however, to pull down than to lift up. One reason for this is that the *weight* of the person's body helps pull the rope. Note also that with a fixed pulley the distance moved by the rope being pulled is equal to the distance moved by the rope supporting the weight.

A combination of several pulleys, in which one or more actually move, is called a *compound pulley*. These magnify force. Using the pulley shown, a person can lift a 100-pound weight with a 50-pound pull if the loss due to friction is disregarded. You will recall that to gain force in the lever it was necessary to increase the distance through which the smaller force moved. The same is true here: One must pull the rope down 2 feet to hoist the weight up 1 foot, as we have seen, with a force only one half that of the weight (see illustration opposite).

Combinations of pulleys are often used in moving heavy objects. The more pulleys there are, the less force is required. Increasing the number of pulleys is, however, effective only up to a point. Beyond this point the additional friction and the resistance of the rope to being bent are greater than the advantage provided by the additional pulleys.

Each combination of pulleys is called a *pulley block*, and the arrangement of pulley blocks and their ropes is called a *block and tackle*. The block and tackle are in common use. Lifeboats are raised and lowered by them. Riggers hoist safes

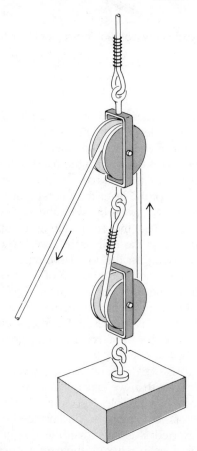

By use of this arrangement of pulleys, force is gained at a sacrifice of distance. A man must pull the rope 2 feet to raise the weight 1 foot, but he can raise a weight with half the effort needed with a single pulley.

All these machines make use of the wheel and axle. In all, force is multiplied by an investment of distance. (See pp. 511–512.)

to the upper stories of buildings, and painters move their scaffolding with the block and tackle.

The Wheel and Axle

Every time you turn a doorknob you are using a *wheel and axle* (see above). You will appreciate the value of this machine if you unscrew the knob and try to turn the axle with your fingers. Restored to its normal place on the axle the knob becomes a force-multiplying device. A little force applied on the rim of the wheel will cause a larger force to be transmitted to the axle. The axle, in turn, turns the mechanism of the door lock. The steering wheel of an automobile is another example of a wheel and axle (see pp. 523–526).

A screwdriver, when it is used for turning a screw, is a wheel and axle with the part gripped by the hand serving as the wheel and the steel shaft as the axle. Other devices employing the wheel and axle are the fishing reel and pencil sharpener, except that here the "wheel" has been reduced to one "spoke" or handle to which the force of the user is applied. A wrench, a brace and bit, a meat grinder, pepper mill, wall can opener—all illustrate the wheel and axle in use. In all, force is multiplied by applying it at a distance from the turning axis or axle to overcome the great resistance at this point.

In the wheel and axle, as in the lever and in the pulley, force is gained but at the expense of distance. Consider the windlass shown above, used for hoisting water from a well. Each time the handle (the wheel) makes one full turn the rope is wound one full turn around the axle. It is apparent that the distance traveled by the handle is greater than the distance traveled by the rope. Let us say that in this case it is five times as great. Then the effort needed to lift a 25-pound bucket of water will be only 5 pounds. The effort required is only one fifth that of the weight but it must be applied for five times the distance.

Two sets of wheels and axles connected by a belt can also be used to *transmit power*. You may have seen such an arrangement in a shoe-repair shop. Here a continuous belt runs on two wheels. The lower wheel is turned by an electric motor. A belt transmits the motion to a wheel above, thereby turning the shaft to which the various buffing and sanding wheels are attached.

Gears

Power can also be transmitted from one wheel to another by equipping the wheels with intermeshing teeth. Such wheels are called *gears,* or *gear wheels* (which, together with their mounting, are variants of the wheel and axle). The purpose of gears, like other machines, is to increase speed, increase force, or change the direction of a force.

A close look at an egg beater will help you understand gear wheels. An egg beater has a big wheel with a handle attached. Notice this large gear wheel and the two small gear wheels. Turn the handle and watch the wheels. You will see that the small ones turn faster. Watch carefully and you will see why. The teeth of the big wheel fit into the teeth of the much smaller wheels that turn the beater. Thus, the smaller wheels make many turns while the larger wheel makes one. You can check the effectiveness of your egg beater by marking a spot on the little wheel with a crayon and then counting the number of turns it makes for one turn of the large one. In one common type of egg beater the little wheel turns five times while the big wheel turns only once. Gears make it possible to operate the egg beater rapidly. The gears in this device also serve to change the *di-*

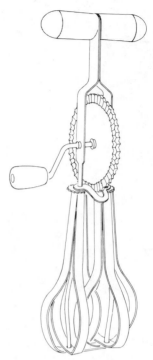

The gears in this egg beater increase speed and also change the direction of the force.

rection of the force. Your hand revolves conveniently in a vertical plane; the egg beater blades swirl effectively in a horizontal plane.

Sometimes, as in a bicycle, the two gear wheels are connected by a chain. Notice that the front gear wheel, the one where the force is applied, is larger than the one on the rear wheel. If you turn a bicycle upside down and turn the front gear wheel one complete turn you will find that the rear wheel makes several turns. Thus, one turn of your foot on the pedals gives you several turns of the bicycle wheel. Here again *speed* is gained by an investment of force (see p. 513).

The Inclined Plane

If someone wants to raise a heavy object onto a truck, he or she may use a board, resting one end against the truck floor and the other end on the

How many simple machines are involved in transmitting force from your foot to the wheel of your bicycle?

it up into the truck. Less force is used, but it has to be exerted for a longer distance. Essentially the job is easier, because at any one moment more of the weight is being supported by the plank and less by the individual's muscles. The inclined plane of the plank thus serves to make the job a more gradual one.

Consider a specific example of this principle. Assume that the truck floor is 5 feet above the ground and that the plank is 15 feet long. Then the mover must move the barrel three times farther than if lifting it straight up, but the effort required is only one third as much. It is believed that the huge blocks of stone used in the construction of the Egyptian pyramids were placed in position by being rolled up long sloping hills of earth constructed for that purpose.

We encounter inclined planes frequently. Highways are carefully graded so that when we drive over them, very steep hills are not encountered. Access to buildings is made easier through the use of ramps for the handicapped. Walt Disney World was designed with ramps instead of stairways (see pp. 526–527).

ground. The mover then rolls the barrel up this ramp, thereby using a machine called an *inclined plane,* which is simply a sloping surface. Why is the job easier this way? Is the mover doing less work? Recalling the definition given before of work as a force exerted through a distance, we would find that the same amount of work is needed to roll the barrel up the incline as to lift

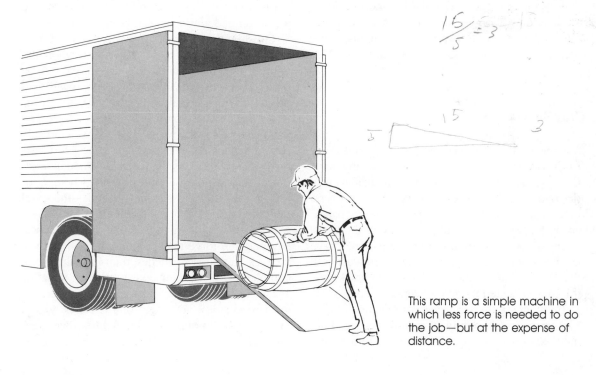

This ramp is a simple machine in which less force is needed to do the job—but at the expense of distance.

The Wedge

The *wedge* is a kind of inclined plane, but it is used in the opposite way a ramp or hill is. (A wedge is actually two inclined planes, fastened back to back.) On a ramp or hill objects are raised by rolling or sliding them up the incline. A wedge, on the other hand, moves objects by being forced under them or between them. A most common use of the wedge is in separating or splitting an object. An example of this is seen when the woodcutter splits logs by driving an iron wedge into the wood with heavy blows of a sledgehammer. An ax is also a wedge, as is the chisel, knife, and even the common tack. With all of these, as with the inclined plane, less force is needed because it is applied over a longer distance (see p. 527).

Consider, for example, the steel wedge that the woodcutter drives into a log to split it. Assume that it is 1 inch thick at its outer end and 6 inches long. When the wedge has been driven in 6 inches, the end of the log is split open 1 inch. The ratio 6:1 gives the theoretical advantage (the *mechanical advantage*) of this machine. For 600 pounds of force exerted on the log the woodcutter must invest only 100 pounds of force. (The actual advantage will be much less than this, however, because of the loss due to friction.)

The Screw

A *screw* is essentially a coiled inclined plane. You can prove this to yourself in the following way: Cut a rectangular piece of paper in half with a diagonal cut. The new edge made by the cut represents an inclined plane. Now roll the paper around a pencil, beginning with one of the arms of the right triangle and continuing down to a corner. The inclined plane is now a spiral around the pencil in the shape of a screw. On any screw this plane is called the screw's *thread* (see p. 527).

In actual use the screw is a combination of two simple machines: both a wheel and axle and an inclined plane. An example of such a combination

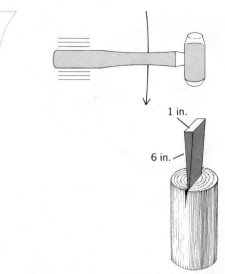

A wedge is a simple machine. Here a 100-pound force is multiplied into a 600-pound force.

is a wrench turning a bolt. The wrench and the body of the bolt are the wheel and axle; the thread on the bolt is the inclined plane. The advantage of one machine is multiplied by the other, hence the combined advantage can be tremendous.

Consider the jackscrew that is used to lift buildings when they are to be moved or when the timbers that rest on the foundations are to be repaired. It is essentially a *bolt* with a screw thread on it (to which a handle is attached), which fits into a *nut,* the base on which the jack stands. The handle serves as the wheel in the wheel-and-axle part of this machine. The weight to be lifted rests on the screw head. As the screw is turned, it *twists* out of the base and elevates the load resting on it. In a sense the load is riding up a hill—the spiral hill of the thread. One complete turn of the screw may lift the weight only $\frac{1}{4}$ inch, but the mechanical advantage in force may be great. If the length of the jack handle is 21 inches, then in making one complete turn its outer end travels $2\pi \times 21$, or 132 inches—a circle of 11 feet. This confers an ideal mechanical advantage of 132 : $\frac{1}{4}$ or 528! A force of only 2 pounds could lift $\frac{1}{2}$ ton. The great multiplication of effort is paid for by having to

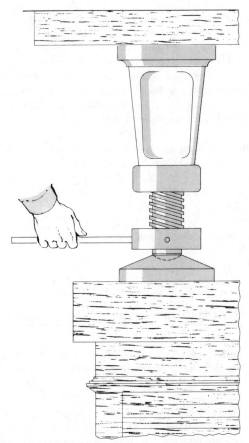

The jackscrew increases force by multiplying the mechanical advantage of two machines, the screw and the wheel and axle.

turn the handle of the screw through a long distance to raise the weight only a little. Again, the actual mechanical advantage is much less than the ideal mechanical advantage because of loss due to friction.

The great mechanical advantage of the screw makes it useful when a very heavy object is to be moved or lifted and only a small force is available. Some automobile jacks use a screw. Derailed locomotives are moved by jackscrews. Some common devices around the house employ screws: a twist drill or power drill, wood screws, food grinders, jar covers, and corkscrews.

FRICTION: LIABILITY OR NECESSITY?

Friction occurs whenever two surfaces move against each other. The work against friction generates heat, which you can detect if you rub the palms of your hands together. In most machines this heat represents wasted energy. In addition to being wasteful, the heat that results from friction may cause serious damage. When the *bearings* or rolling parts of machines are not lubricated properly they may melt or "burn out."

What causes friction? A magnified view of the surface of an apparently smooth material would show that it possesses many irregularities, many jagged hills and valleys. According to classic theory, friction is caused by the bumping and tearing of irregular surfaces as they slide over each other. More recent studies indicate that friction arises in part from the *attraction* of the molecules of the contacting surfaces. This is the same kind of attraction that makes water stick to your hands after washing; it is called *adhesion*.

Friction is reduced in machines by the use of wheels, bearings, and rollers, and by the application of lubricants. The ordinary wheels used on vehicles reduce friction, because they permit the surfaces involved to roll rather than to slide over each other. The friction of a wheel against its axle may be reduced by putting steel balls, called *bearings,* between the two. In this way the sliding friction of the hub of the wheel against the axle is replaced by rolling friction. You can see ball bearings if you take apart the wheel of a roller skate. When we put rollers under a heavy box or ball casters under furniture we are also substituting rolling for sliding.

Lubrication reduces friction in part because it fills in some of the irregularities of the surfaces and thus prevents their interlocking. When lubricants are used, the solid surfaces easily slide on the lubricant rather than on each other. It is believed also that the rolling motion of the molecules of the lubricant over one another reduces friction. Recent research in connection with the adhesion theory of friction that we mentioned previously, indicates that the lubricant is effective because it increases the distances between the surfaces and, therefore, decreases the strength of the adhesive force.

A variety of lubricants—including oil, grease, soap, wax, and graphite—are used in gears and wheels. It is important to select the right lubricant for each particular use. Lubrication not only saves energy, it also prevents unnecessary wear. This is well illustrated in the automobile. The entire mechanism must be constructed so that a sufficient amount of the lubricant will reach every moving part at all times (see pp. 527–528).

Friction is not always a hindrance. We would not be able to walk without friction between our shoes and the ground, because our feet would slip backward. That is why walking on ice is difficult. Automobiles and trains would not be able to start without friction between the wheels and the surface beneath. Without friction the brakes in automobiles would be useless. Everyday activities would be impossible without friction. Doorknobs would slip through our hands without turning. Chalk would not write on chalkboards. The violinist's bow would slip silently across the strings.

We often increase friction intentionally. The baseball pitcher rubs rosin on his hands to get a better grip on the ball, while the opposing batter rubs his hands in the dirt to get a better hold on the bat. When roads are icy we scatter sand over them and put chains on our tires.

IMPORTANT GENERALIZATIONS

Machines help in different ways. Some produce a gain in force, some in speed; some change the direction of a force.

Work is done when a force is exerted through a distance.

Disregarding the losses due to friction, the work put into a machine equals the work put out.

A gain in force in a machine is at the expense of speed; a gain in speed requires an investment of force.

Six simple types of machines include the lever, pulley, wheel and axle, inclined plane, wedge, and screw.

Friction occurs when any two substances rub together.

All machines lose some of their efficiency because of friction.

Wheels, rollers, and ball bearings reduce friction by substituting rolling for sliding friction.

Lubrication reduces friction by filling in the irregularities of the contacting surfaces and by decreasing the attraction between them.

Friction can be an asset: It prevents slipping and makes possible thousands of everyday activities.

DISCOVERING FOR YOURSELF

1. Observe the results of friction in your environment; indicate which examples are helpful, which harmful. What lubricants are used in your home or school building?
2. Visit a playground to identify examples of machines (levers, inclined planes, pulleys, and so on) in the play equipment and in the vehicles and toys children use. How do these machines help children enjoy and profit from their outdoor experiences?
3. Examine the machines in a kitchen. Classify them according to which of the simple machines they are.
4. Observe an egg beater and a bicycle, and compare their operations.
5. Watch a carpenter or a garage mechanic at work, and describe and explain how simple machines help him or her to do work that could not be done as easily without them.
6. Observe a building under construction. Describe the machinery being used.

TEACHING "MACHINES AND HOW THEY WORK"

The study of machines lends itself to the development of the concept of *interaction*, the relationships among objects that do something to one another, thereby bringing about a change. For example, study the photograph on page 525. What happens when the child turns the large pulley wheel? It turns the small pulley wheel to which it is connected, but the smaller pulley wheel turns faster. Other illustrations in the chapter show similar interactions. The concept of interaction is important in science because it stresses that (1) changes occur because objects interact rather than because some mysterious "spirit" moves them, (2) these changes are measurable, (3) these changes can be reproduced by others, if the conditions are the same, and, therefore, (4) these changes are predictable.

Using and studying the simple machines in this chapter provide valuable inquiry experiences. They encourage *exploration, improvisation,* and *experimentation* that can result in *discoveries* and lead to *applications* of science principles to everyday life. Careful measuring is important in order to compare results. Look at the photograph on page 519. Since experience is said to be the best teacher, get a tennis ball and a baseball and place them on an incline. "How are the balls alike?" "How are they different from each other?" Roll the balls down the incline and see what happens. Do this several times and observe carefully just as you would encourage children to do. What questions come out of this? If the two balls start at the same time from the top of the incline, try to predict which one will reach the bottom first. Which ball will roll the farthest before stopping? (It may be necessary to shift the experiment to the classroom floor or the schoolyard to determine this.) What would happen if you used a Ping-Pong ball? A marble? If you let each ball hit a small box what would happen? If you wanted to roll the ball *up* the incline, which object would require a harder push? How could you make the balls roll more *slowly* down the incline? Faster? What does all of this have to do with skating or cycling on a hill, skiing on a slope, or carrying a load up a hill? Thus, in experimenting with small "hills," the children, like scientists, are setting up a working model of a part of the real world. (See Chapter 3, "Investigating and Experimenting.")

The approaches suggested here in studying one machine—the inclined plane—can also be used for the others discussed in this chapter. If you have this experience yourself you see how important it is to begin by doing something, observing, raising questions, and then going on to further exploration.

SOME BROAD CONCEPTS

Machines help make work easier.
A push or pull that makes something move is called a force.
Some machines produce a gain in force; some increase speed; some change the direction of a force.
Machines must have a source of energy to do work.
Machines are devices that transfer force.
Force may come from muscles, electric current, fuel, wind, springs, or falling water.
Work is done whenever an effort overcomes a resistance and moves something.
The amount of work put into a machine equals the amount of work put out, disregarding friction.
The lever, pulley, wheel and axle, inclined plane, wedge, and screw are types of simple machines.
All machines are made up of one or more simple machines.
All machines lose some of their efficiency due to friction.
There are several ways to reduce friction in machines.
Friction is useful to us in several ways.

FOR YOUNGER CHILDREN[1]

Even very young children are interested in answers to "What makes it go?" and "How does it work?" Before they enter school their toys and the tools they use have introduced them to the world of wheels and gears. The following activities emphasize observations and hands-on expe-

[1]K. Hill, "Moving Things," in *Exploring the Natural World with Young Children* (New York: Harcourt Brace Jovanovich, 1976).

(Courtesy of Florida Dept. of Education.)

riences that have been carried on successfully with young children.

What Things Move on Wheels?[2]

Suggest that children watch at home, on the streets, at school, and elsewhere to find things that move on wheels. Ask them to observe how many wheels there are, to look at them as they move, and to try to tell what makes them move. Suggest that they make a short record of their observations using drawings or magazine pictures to illustrate

[2]J. Schwartz, *Go on Wheels* (New York: McGraw-Hill, 1966); A. Rockwell, *Things That Go* (New York: Dutton, 1986). For very young children.

their ideas. After each picture place a number that tells how many wheels are used and, if possible, what made the wheels move (muscle, gasoline, and others). They may make use of toys with wheels in their observations and demonstrations by noticing how the wheels turn, how many there are, and so on.

How Do Things Move on Hills?

Refer to the inclined plane discussion in the introduction to this chapter. Help children recall their observations and experiences with hills—sliding downhill, riding roller coasters, and so on. Suggest that they try to build a hill using boards, blocks, and other materials. Groups of children can each make such a hill and then have the experience of rolling various sizes and shapes of balls, toy trucks, and other things down the hills they have made. For obvious reasons this is a good outdoor activity. Help the children compare the results of using steep hills and gently sloping hills and of using different-sized balls and other materials. They will use measuring to compare differences in results. They will observe that things roll downhill without a push, that round things roll more easily than square or flat things, and what happens when the objects reach a level surface. They may try rolling a round object *up* the hill and observe what happens.

What Kinds of Work Do Machines Do?

As children observe machines at home, at school, on a farm, in garages and gas stations, and elsewhere, ask them to try to see what kinds of work machines do. A record of the observations may consist of (1) name of the machine, (2) picture of the machine, (3) where it was observed, and (4) kind of work it was doing (lifting, digging, and so on). The pictures may be children's drawings or from magazines. The record can then be used for discussion, and additions to it can be made from time to time. Children will become more observant of their surroundings and better able to describe and report their observations as a result of this experience.

How Can You Balance Your Seesaw Partner?

The experience with a seesaw constitutes a background for a later, more detailed study of levers and gives young children an opportunity to get the "feel" of the interaction of objects. Let them try out different combinations of children (both heavy and light), children of equal and unequal weights, and see what happens as children shift positions nearer to and farther from the fulcrum. Suggest that they use the seesaw to try to tell

which child is the heavier. They may choose partners to see which ones will balance. The activity begins with free play: "Let's see what happens if ..." Then the group can discuss what they think they have observed. Finally they can gather around one seesaw to try out and demonstrate their ideas. They may be able to demonstrate how a heavier child can balance a lighter one, how two people can balance one, and so on (see Chapter 16A, pp. 507–509).

After these experiences they can use blocks and other materials to make seesaws indoors to review the ideas they have learned. Use a variety of sizes and shapes of blocks, some equal, some unequal in weight. Suggest the use of other materials such as toys, stones, and pails of soil. Some children will get the idea of using the seesaw as a scale to determine relative weight. Others may suggest using a series of blocks of approximately the same weight as units of measure and draw such conclusions as; "The eraser weighs 2 blocks," or "The toy truck weighs 6 blocks."

Other Problems for Younger Children

1. What makes machines move?
2. How is friction helpful and harmful?
3. Where do we use gears?
4. Where do we use levers?
5. Where do we use pulleys?
6. Why do we have to be careful when we run or ride down a steep hill?
7. How are machines used in the city? On a farm?
8. How do toys work?

FOR OLDER CHILDREN

How Do Levers Make Work Easier?[3]

Direct hands-on experiences from which to make observations, hypotheses, inferences, predictions,

---

[3]A. Rockwell and H. Rockwell, *Machines* (New York: Harper, 1972). Easy exercises. *Wind, Water, Fire and Earth* (Energy Lessons for the Physical Sciences) (Washington, D.C.: NSTA, 1986).

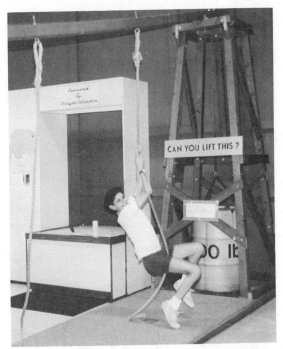 

This device in the South Florida Science Museum challenges visitors to lift 500 pounds. Why is it easier on the far rope? *Photo by Michael B. Schwartz.*

and possible discoveries are important. Children may use a board and brick as a lever arrangement to lift the teacher (see pp. 507–508). A three-sided (triangular in cross-section) length of wood, which can easily be made in a shop, may also be used as a fulcrum. This kind of large lever that students can work with is useful because they get the "feel" that the machine actually makes it easier to do the work. Let children try to lift one another. Let students work in groups, and in the beginning do not give them any suggestions. After they have explored various possibilities urge them to exchange any ideas they may have observed. Which group has found the easiest way to lift a weight? Describe the way. Does it make any difference where you place the fulcrum? Why do you think these conditions make lifting the weight easier?

Let a group demonstrate how placing the fulcrum at various distances from the person being lifted shows that there is a relationship beween

the distance that the "push" moves and the ease with which the work is done. Urge students to try to determine whether there is a mathematical ratio between the "push" and the work done. Note that students may use the words *force, fulcrum,* and *resistance* as they discuss the lever, for they will soon come to realize what each is. It is important that such science vocabulary be introduced but not stressed to the point of getting in the way of interest, appreciation, and understanding. At the beginning the children may substitute descriptive words such as teetering point, weight, pull, push, and so on for the technical ones (see Chapter 16A, pp. 507–509).

The lever provides opportunity for the use of measurement to see the relationship between the distance that the force moves (downward) to the distance the resistance moves (upward)—an example of interaction as mentioned in the introduction. If the force moves four times as far as the resistance does, is it easier to move the resistance than it is if the force moves only twice as far? The relationship will be obvious if students actually measure the two distances. Try the experiment with the fulcrum placed so that the force moves 2 feet (about 60 centimeters) to raise the resistance 1 foot (about 30 centimeters). Then move the fulcrum so that the relationship is 3:1, and so on. (The fulcrum should be placed so that the distance from it to the point where the force is applied is three times the distance from the fulcrum to where the resistance is located.) Students will soon feel the difference even though they may not have exact measurements.

After using this lever, students can go out and use a seesaw on the playground to see that if the force is far from the fulcrum (the teetering point) more weight can be lifted without increasing the force. They can try various positions and various numbers of students to check out the relationships between the force and the resistance.

After experimenting the students should try to bring useful levers to school and demonstrate how they work. For each lever they should try to measure to see how the force and the fulcrum position are related. Suggest that students answer such questions as, "Does the machine increase speed?" "Does it increase force?" "Does it change the direction of the force?" "What other advantages does it have?" They will see that not all levers gain force. Examples are (1) *A claw hammer.* Drive a nail into a board, and then try to pull it out with your fingers. Then use the claw hammer. Observe how easily the nail comes out. Why? (2) *A nutcracker* (two levers). Crack a nut with it. Observe the arrangement and see how far the force moves. (3) *A can opener* (lever type). Make the observations suggested for other levers. (4) *A pair of scissors* (also two levers).

How Do Pulleys Make Work Easier?[4]

Direct experience using the flagpole is a convenient device to show students the principle of a

[4]R. H. Tennies, "Up, Up, and Away," *Science and Children* (January 1981). Experiences with pulleys.

fixed pulley. Urge observation and description of just what happens. "In what way does the pulley help?" "How many pulleys are there?" "Is the pulley like the lever in any way?" They may observe the way in which the rope is placed through the pulley and see the advantage of a fixed pulley in getting the flag to the top of the pole. Help them to discover the relationship between the distance that the force (hand pulling rope) moves down and the distance that the resistance (the flag) moves up. Fixed pulleys do not save force, they are just convenient. They are found on clotheslines, some curtain rods, venetian blinds, and classroom window shades (see Chapter 16A, pp. 509–511).

Pulleys can be purchased in many stores where toys are sold, in hardware stores, in marine-supply stores, in variety stores, or they can be ordered from scientific supply houses. Pulley systems that actually help in lifting heavy things are a great asset in helping students understand how pulleys operate.

First let students "mess around" with pulleys to make any observations possible. Then help them arrange pulleys as shown on page 524. Let them operate the pulley systems to note the interactions and try to explain their observations. It is important for them to see that in these pulley arrangements, force is exchanged for distance; that is, much rope is pulled through the pulleys (distance) to make the weight easier to lift. Again they can observe to see the relationship between the distance that the force moves down and the distance that the resistance (the weight) moves up.

Suggest to children, "You remember that in the case of the lever we measured with a ruler to see the relationship of force and resistance. Can you suggest some possible measurement we could make with pulley arrangements?" They can use a spring scale to show how the use of pulleys reduces the amount of force necessary to lift a weight. Again let them work in groups to use pulleys and the spring scale and try to make some inferences from their observations (see p. 523). If possible, use pulleys that can hold a heavy weight, such as a pail of sand or several books tied to-

Encourage children to work with pulleys, cords, spring scales, and weights to make their own weight-lifting devices.

gether. First use the spring scale to lift the weight directly. Note the reading of the scale. Now use a block of two pulleys at the top and two at the bottom, and attach the spring scale to the rope that will be pulled. Lift the weight. Again read the scale. Use different weights. If possible, increase the number of pulleys on the blocks to three or four, and repeat in each case. Note the reading of the scale.

Students may observe pulley systems in garages, where one person easily lifts the whole front end of an automobile. In some classrooms fixed pulleys are used to raise the windows and window curtains. A weight concealed in the window frame helps to lift the window, and in some window frames the pulley can be observed at the top. Clotheslines often operate by means of pulleys. A bird-feeding station may be hauled away from the window on a pulley and line.

How Does a Wheel and Axle Make Work Easier?[5]

It is easy to make a simple windlass that students can use in the classroom to lift things. The school custodian, a parent, or the shop teacher may be willing to work with a committee of students in constructing it. It may be made of wood of any desired dimensions and operated from the side or corner of a desk. The one illustrated on page 525 is 18 inches (46 centimeters) long; the supports at the ends are 12 inches (30 centimeters) high. A broomstick serves as the axle and the handle is made of wood and nailed to the end of the broomstick. Strong twine is used as the "rope" to lift the weights.

Suggest that students use the apparatus to lift a pail of sand or some other heavy object and observe what happens. "Is it easier with the windlass?" "Why do you suppose this is true?" "Where is the force?" "The resistance?" "What relationship exists between them?" "Is it like any other simple machine?" (See Chapter 16A, pp. 511–512.)

It may be necessary to explain how this is like the wheels they are accustomed to seeing (the handle is one spoke of the wheel). Students should see first that the handle is fastened to the axle and turns it. As they use the windlass they will see the relationship between the number of turns the handle makes (the distance the force travels) and the short distance the weight travels. Again, this experience will be more meaningful if students can arrive at figures they can compare. The students will discover how to measure the distance that the force travels (the circumference of the circle made by the end of the handle) and compare it with the distance that the weight travels. They will then see that here, as in the case of other simple machines, force may be gained at a sacrifice of distance. Students should compare the

[5]B. Zubrowski, *Wheels at Work* (New York: Morrow, 1984).

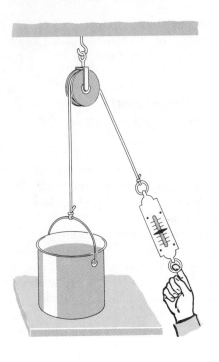

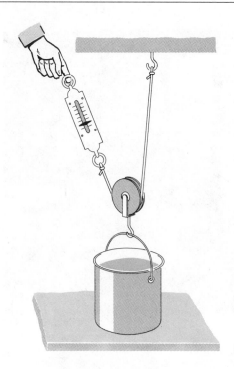

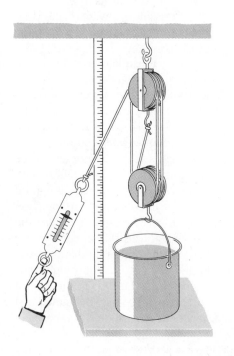

Using pulleys under different conditions and in various combinations along with the spring scale helps to make the scientific principles more easily understood. (*Upper left*): A fixed pulley does not increase the force, but makes it more convenient to apply. With a fixed pulley as much force is required to pull down on the rope as to lift the weight without a pulley. The distance moved by the rope being pulled is equal to the distance moved by the rope supporting the weight. (*Upper right*): A movable pulley magnifies force. Using the pulley shown, a 10-pound pail can be lifted by a 5-pound pull—but you have to pull the rope twice as far. (*Lower left*): A combination of fixed pulleys and movable ones in this block and tackle makes it possible to lift very heavy loads.

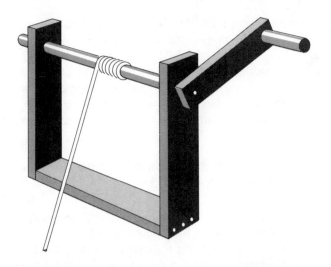

A handmade windlass helps pupils see the relationship between the distances traveled by the force and the weight.

handle of the windlass to the driving wheel of a car; they will see that it may be thought of as one spoke of an imaginary wheel that turns the axle. On this handmade piece of equipment the relationship is easy to see. Other examples are pepper mills, meat grinders, and mechanical can openers.

The pencil sharpener is another illustration of the wheel and axle. So is the doorknob of the classroom. A fifth-grade teacher once unscrewed the knob of her classroom door and asked some of her students to try to open the door. They tried turning the wheel bar with their fingers but they couldn't do it. Then she put the knob on again, and students saw how easy it was to open the door. To make clear that the knob was a wheel and the steel bar which it turned was the axle of the wheel-and-axle machine, the students pushed a large nail through one of the screw holes in the

What will happen to the small wheel when she turns the large one? What will happen to the large wheel if she turns the small one? This student is observing evidence of interaction as she manipulates this simple apparatus. Many other examples of this principle of interaction are available in children's experiences: in the attraction and repulsion of magnets, in the sandpapering of wood, and so forth. (*Courtesy of the Science Curriculum Improvement Study.*)

bar and used it to open the door. They could see that the nail constituted a spoke of a wheel. Students remembered this experience because they could see how the wheel and axle, a simple machine, made it easy for them to open the door.

How Do Gears Work?

The egg beater is an example of the wheel and axle that students can bring to school for observation. Students can use the egg beater to observe the operation of the gears, and try to describe what they see. "What turns the big wheel?" "The small wheel?" "What relationship does one have to the other?"

The observations will introduce the idea of gear wheels and make clear the relationship between the large gear wheel and the small one. Students can thus see an example of one wheel used to turn another. "How many times does the small wheel turn while the big wheel is turning only once?" Several egg beaters may be examined to compare the relationships of the turning of the large and small gears. Make a mark on one of the teeth of the small wheel so that you can tell when it has made one complete turn. Count the number of turns the small gear makes as the large one turns once. Ask the children to count the number of teeth of each of the gear wheels and see if they can figure out the relationship between the speeds with which the two wheels turn. If the large wheel, for example, has six times as many teeth as the small gear, the small gear will make six turns for every turn of the large one. The different egg beaters may be compared by this count. This is a case where force is sacrificed to increase speed. In the egg beater students will see that gears also change the direction of the force (see Chapter 16A, pp. 512–513).

Bicycles also illustrate gear wheels, as well as the use of belts or chains to drive the wheels. They are easy to examine and should be brought into the classroom and demonstrated. If the bicycle is turned upside down, it is easy to see how the pedal turns a wheel and how this motion is even-

tually transmitted to the rear wheel. Students can count the number of turns of the rear wheel for one turn of the pedals.

Students should be urged to find other machines in which belts of various kinds are used to make one wheel turn another. Shoe-repair shops, garages, and farms are good sources for examples.

How Does the Inclined Plane Make Work Easier?

Students can make a simple inclined plane with a board and use a toy wagon to pull up a load. If they attach a spring scale to the wagon they can tell how much pull is needed (see p. 528). A rubber band may be substituted for a spring scale in this and in other experiences. The greater the stretch the more the pull. To determine the pull more accurately, use a ruler to measure the stretched rubber band. This can be compared with how much force it takes to lift the load up the same distance without the use of the incline. The same procedure described in the section on pulleys can be used here to compare the distance that the force travels with the distance that the weight is lifted. When the inclined plane is used, the distance is greater but not as much force is needed. Suggest that students work out ways to change the slope of the plane and try to predict what difference the changes will make. If the slope is not very steep the distance is great, and the force may be less. If the slope is very steep the distance is less, but more force will be needed. Estimating, measuring, and computing will help students understand the "why" of various inclined planes (see Chapter 16A, pp. 512–513).

An ideal situation for teaching the inclined plane results if the school custodian can help students make one with boards somewhere in the building or on the school grounds. Use an empty barrel as the object to be lifted. In all probability students would have considerable difficulty lifting the barrel 2 feet (60 centimeters) vertically, but with the boards utilized as an inclined plane they can easily lift it by rolling it up the gentle slope. Experiences such as this not only help bring about a real comprehension of the science principles involved but are also enjoyed by children.

Students can often find examples of inclined planes in the neighborhood. If bicycles are kept in the basement of the school, for example, an inclined plane is probably used to move them in and out. School supplies are often unloaded by the use of an inclined plane. Stores, factories, and many other places use them, too.[6] Students can observe the unloading of new automobiles at a nearby sales office and see how inclined planes are used.

How Does a Wedge Make Work Easier?

Again, the actual experience of using a simple machine and observing the effect is a reasonable way to begin. A small wedge can be driven into a piece of pine wood so that the wood will split. Suggest that children try different sizes and shapes of wedges to see how they push things apart. The wedge also changes the direction of the force. Short, thick wedges require more force to drive them than long, thin ones. Chisels, ice picks, axes, and knives are examples of wedges. If these tools are examined, students can see that they are actually inclined planes that wedge between things and push them apart (see Chapter 16A, p. 514).

How Does the Screw Make Work Easier?

Again the actual experience of using a simple machine and observing the effect is a reasonable way to begin. It is worth the trouble to bring an au-

---

[6]M. R. Malone, "Investigating Ramps and Sliders," *Science and Children* (February 1986). Using simple materials, children roll marbles down a ramp (a grooved ruler) to discover how energy is transferred as the marbles strike a slider (a paper cup). Many variables are tested—the steepness of the ramp, the number of the marbles, and the mass of the slider.

tomobile or house jack (screw-type) to school to see how it enables one person to lift an automobile. Jacks are made of more than one simple machine: A lever operates the screw. Students can observe what happens as the screw makes many turns to lift only a short distance (see Chapter 16A, pp. 514–515).

Students will find many examples of screws. Some desk chairs, for example, use a screw. Some pepper grinders, jar covers, and nutcrackers also use a large screw. The screw is an incline that winds around a spiral. If they examine a large screw, students can trace the spiral path of the grooves. Screws, like wedges and inclined planes, help us to gain force, but we sacrifice distance.

How Does Friction Help and Hinder Us?

Use several sets of wooden blocks with flat surfaces. Suggest that children rub the surfaces together and report what happens. Rub them together briskly. Feel the surfaces. "How could you make the blocks move more easily?" Put drops of oil between them. Try it. "What happens?" Try soap, wax, petroleum jelly, and other materials that the children suggest (see Chapter 16A, pp. 515–516).

A simple device for measuring smoothness and roughness of surfaces can be made by using a flat block of wood with a rubber band fastened to one end of it with a screw eye. The stretch of the band shows how hard or easy it is to pull the block across a surface. With a ruler, measure the stretch of the band as the block is pulled across the classroom floor, a cement sidewalk, a polished floor, a piece of glass, sandpaper, and other surfaces that children will want to try. Make a chart to show the stretches on different surfaces, so that it will be easy to compare them.

Urge students to observe the effects of friction on flat surfaces—their shoes on the floor, and so on. Suggest that children lay blocks on a roller skate and pull them with the rubber band. What conclusions can they draw now?

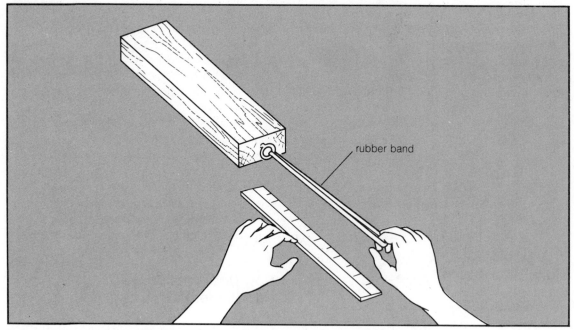

The stretch of a rubber band tells us how easily the block slides. *(From* Science, Grades 3–4, *New York City Board of Education.)*

Reducing friction by the use of bearings is also easy to demonstrate. Roller skates, both those with bearings and those without, can be brought to school and compared. A wastebasket can be used to demonstrate how effective bearings are in reducing friction. Fill it with books and try to push it along the floor. Then set it on some marbles and try to push it along. Individual students can do this with piles of books to note the difference when marbles are used to reduce friction.

The stretch of the rubber band tells us which is easiest. *(From* Science, Grades 3–4, *New York City Board of Education.)*

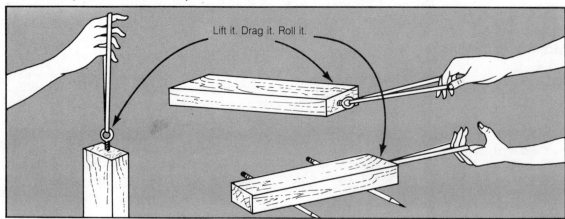

Lift it. Drag it. Roll it.

Other Problems for Older Children[7]

1. How is friction reduced in an automobile?
2. How do garden tools help us?
3. What machines are used in our neighborhood?
4. What safety rules are important to use with machines?
5. What machines are used in house construction?
6. What machines are moved by wind, water, steam, and electricity?
7. What would the world be like without friction?

RESOURCES TO INVESTIGATE WITH CHILDREN

1. The kitchen at home (or at school), to observe how pulleys, levers, wheels, wedges, screws, and inclined planes are used.
2. Local buildings under construction, to watch the use of machines.
3. Hardware store, to observe kinds of machines for use in tool shops, garages, farms, buildings, and so on.
4. A garage, to observe the use of pulleys for lifting motors, the use of inclined planes, and many other machines at work.
5. A carpenter, to explain proper use of tools and to show different kinds for different uses.

[7]H. S. Cramer, "Simple Machines," *Science and Children* (February 1976). Activities and constructions for children. R. Baines, *Simple Machines* (Mahwah, N.J.: Troll, 1985). Useful reference.

6. General merchandise catalogues, for pictures of many different kinds of machines. Pictures show how complex machines are made from simple ones for the purpose of doing different types of work.
7. Toy stores, to see machines used in various toys.
8. Dealers in agricultural implements, to get a better understanding of machines used on the farm.
9. A manufacturing plant, to see machines in operation.

PREPARING TO TEACH

1. Prepare a bulletin board that might be used as a summary of the study of simple machines. Also plan how to use it.
2. Investigate machines available for observation in your school, in the playground, and in the neighborhood.
3. Make a list of materials you would need to teach a unit on machines. Classify the list according to source: (1) supply house, (2) the environment, or (3) to be furnished by the children.
4. Prepare an evaluation instrument that can be used to determine the extent to which students have attained objectives that you think are important in this unit.
5. Make a plan that might be utilized in order to help students answer the following: "How are machines used in our community?" or "How would our way of living be different if we had no modern machines at our disposal?"

MAGNETISM AND ELECTRICITY

When I sailed from Spain to the West Indies, I found that as soon as I had passed 100 leagues [roughly 300 miles, or 500 kilometers] west of the Azores . . . the needle of the compass, which hitherto had turned to the northeast, turned a full quarter . . . to the northwest . . .

COLUMBUS, 1492, IN A LETTER TO THE KING AND QUEEN OF SPAIN

The electrical matter consists of particles extremely subtile, since it can permeate common matter, even the densest metals, with such ease and freedom as not to receive any perceptible resistance.

BENJAMIN FRANKLIN, 1747

NIGHT WITHOUT LIGHT

We used to take electricity for granted, but the brownouts and blackouts of recent years have alerted us to the vulnerability of this source of energy. The following excerpt from *Newsweek* recounts the events that followed a power failure on the evening of November 9, 1965:

The Longest Night

The northeastern U.S. is the megalopolis—a vast intermeshing of cities, towns, suburbs, and exurbs. It is urban America of the mid-twentieth century brought to its fullest flower—and its fullest fragility. It is utterly dependent on turbine technology—a world that runs on electricity and on the faith that one has only to push a button, flick a switch or throw a lever to make electricity work. Electricity is its pulse, its power, its élan vital. And then one night last week the electricity stopped.

At 5:17 P.M. in Buffalo, 5:17 P.M. in Rochester, 5:18 in Boston, 5:28 in Albany, 5:24 to 5:28 in New York City, the clocks in the megalopolis sputtered to a standstill. Lights blinked and dimmed and went out. Skyscrapers towered black against a cold November sky, mere artifacts lit only by the moon. Elevators hung immobile in their shafts. Subways ground dead in their tunnels. Streetcars froze in their tracks. Streetlights and traffic signals went out—and with them the best-laid plans of the traffic engineers. Airports shut down. Mail stacked up in blacked-out post offices. Computers lost their memories. TV pictures darkened and died. Business stopped. Food started souring in refrigerators. Telephones functioned but dial tones turned to shrill whines under a record overload. Nothing else seemed to work except transistor radios. . . .

At its peak, the power failure was simply beyond human scale; it engulfed 80,000 square miles across parts of eight U.S. states and Canada's Ontario province—and left 30 million people in the dark.

MAGNETISM

Historically, our knowledge of magnetism and our knowledge of electricity form two separate streams, originating in antiquity and merging near the beginning of the last century. In nature, magnetism and electricity are, in fact, intimately related, each one capable of producing the other. Almost all the devices referred to in the foregoing news story are indicative of how humans, through their inventions, have made good use of this two-way relationship. Let us consider magnetism first. Later, we shall investigate electricity and see how it is linked to magnetism.

The Magnet as Iron Attractor and as Compass

The phenomenon of magnetism has been known for centuries. The fact that certain kinds of iron or iron ore had the power to attract other bits of material containing iron must have been known in ancient Greece (see pp. 555–558).

A second discovery made the magnet an important instrument in navigation. It was found that if a magnet were suspended so that it could turn freely it would swing into a north–south position.

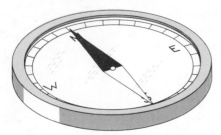

The essential part of a compass is a magnet that that can swing freely.

1. It attracted and held bits of iron.
2. When freely suspended, it took a north–south position.
3. When pieces of steel were rubbed against it, the steel acquired the lodestone's power.

For centuries the practical uses of magnetism extended no further than the compass.

Natural Magnets

Natural magnets, or lodestones, are a kind of iron ore called magnetite (Fe_3O_4). Lodestones are usually irregular in shape, that is, they look like ordinary stones you might pick up anywhere. Like the artificial magnets with which you are probably more familiar, they attract iron. Small pieces of lodestone are inexpensive and are easily obtained from scientific supply companies. Small bits of iron (iron filings) or small carpet tacks will respond to the attraction of these stones. Like other magnets, lodestones have north and south poles (sometimes several sets of these), but it is necessary to do some experimenting to find them.

Artificial Magnets

The common artificial magnets found in schools are generally made in two shapes. Their shapes give them their names: horseshoe and bar magnets. Except for their shapes they are the same, for horseshoe magnets are essentially bent bar magnets.

Artificial magnets are usually made of steel. In recent years more powerful magnets made of an alloy of aluminum, nickel, copper, and cobalt, patented under the name Alnico, have found many practical uses. Magnets help close cabinet and refrigerator doors; they help us pick up pins and needles; they hold the lids of cans after the can opener has removed them; they keep papers on bulletin boards; they make cloth potholders stick to the sides of ovens; they hold kitchen knives on the wall; they are found in many toys. In all these gadgets either two magnets attract each other or a magnet attracts iron or steel.

Thus the magnet became a compass. Some legends ascribe this knowledge to the ancient Chinese; presumably they used magnets as compasses more than 1,000 years ago. In the writings of Hebrews, Greeks, and Romans the magnet is often referred to as a "lodestone," meaning "leading stone" or "directing stone." Eventually a magnetized bit of iron was used in making a crude magnetic compass, but it is thought that this valuable instrument was not used much until the Middle Ages.

You can make a compass much like those used by early mariners by repeatedly stroking the length of a steel darning needle in one direction only with one end of a magnet and then laying the needle on a cork floating in water. The container for the water should not be made of iron. This kind of compass is essentially the kind used by Columbus in his voyage to America. Needles in Columbus's time were made of poor steel and did not retain magnetism very long. It was, therefore, necessary to remagnetize the needle every few days by rubbing it on a lodestone.

The discovery of the magnetic compass marked an important milestone in the struggle to explore our planet. No longer did mariners have to steer by the North Star or by landmarks along a coast. With the compass, directions could be determined accurately when clouds or storms hid the stars from view. This new invention made it possible for human beings to venture out into the great unknown—the oceans of the world.

In summary, the ancients knew three important facts about the lodestone.

Several forms of magnets: horseshoe, bar, natural lodestone, and U. Magnetism has been induced artificially in all but the lodestone.

Magnetic Attraction

If a magnet is laid flat in a dish of iron filings or small tacks and then lifted out, masses of filings or tacks cling to the ends of the magnet but very few near the middle. These ends, where the strength appears to be greatest, are called *poles.* All magnets, no matter what their shape, have poles. (In flat magnets, both rectangular and circular, used in many household devices and toys, each of the two flat surfaces is a pole.) Horseshoe magnets are given their particular shape in order that both poles (where the magnetism is strongest) may be used together.

Most commonly we observe that magnets attract objects that contain iron; however, cobalt and nickel also respond well to a magnet's pull. Other substances respond to a magnet's influence, but it requires sensitive instruments to detect this.

Permanent and Temporary Magnets

Common magnets are often called *permanent magnets;* if kept properly they will retain their magnetism for a long time. To increase the life of bar magnets they should be stored in pairs, side by side, north pole next to south pole. Horseshoe and U magnets should have a "keeper," a piece if iron placed across their ends.

Some magnets are temporary in nature. Pick up an iron carpet tack with a magnet. To the end of this tack, bring another tack. You will find that the first tack picks up and holds the second. The second tack will hold a third. The length of the string of tacks you can make in this way will depend on the strength of the magnet, the weight of each tack, and the extent of your patience. If you now remove the magnet from tack number one, the others drop off rather quickly. Each tack was magnetized only temporarily. A steel sewing needle, on the other hand, will retain its magnetism for a much longer time, particularly if it is given its initial magnetism by stroking it with a magnet. (Why steel retains its magnetism better is explained on pp. 536–537.) Another kind of temporary magnet, and a very important one, is the *electromagnet,* which will be considered later in the chapter.

Magnetic Penetration Through Materials

Children soon discover for themselves, if they are allowed to experiment, that magnetism acts through many substances. If a magnet is brought toward tacks covered by a sheet of paper the tacks will cling to the underside of the paper. If tacks are placed in a drinking glass they can be manipulated from the outside by a magnet. Paper, glass, and wood—as well as air, water, copper, and many other substances—are "transparent" to magnetism. On the other hand, a magnet's ability to pick up and hold tacks is reduced if an iron object is interposed between the magnet and the tacks, because the iron retains some of the magnetic influence.

Attraction and Repulsion Between Magnets

If a bar magnet or a magnetized steel needle is suspended in a horizontal position by a thread it will come to rest pointing north and south. The end of the magnet that points to the north is called the north pole of the magnet; the end pointing to

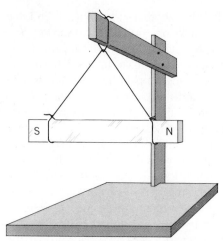

A bar magnet suspended in the manner shown here comes to rest in a north–south line. To avoid deflecting the magnet the support should be made of wood or some other nonmagnetic material.

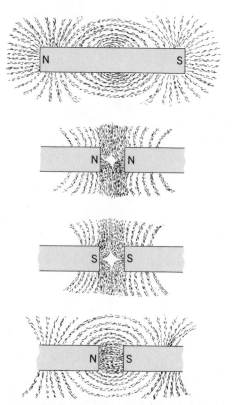

The magnetic field around a magnet can be explored with iron filings. The repulsion between similar magnetic poles and the attraction between opposite poles is revealed by these bits of iron.

the south, the south pole. A magnet thus suspended, as indicated previously, is essentially a compass.

If the north pole of another magnet is now brought close to the north pole of the suspended one, the latter will swing sharply away. If the north pole is brought close to the *south* pole the attraction will pull the suspended magnet to the other one. In short, *like poles repel and unlike poles attract*. This is known as the *law of magnets*.

Magnetic Fields

What is the nature of magnetic attraction? We do not know the full answer to this question, but we can trace the shape and direction and strength of the invisible *magnetic field* that exists around a magnet. This field can be explored with small bits of iron—iron filings. A bar magnet is placed on a table and covered with a sheet of paper. Iron filings are then sprinkled on the paper. A very interesting pattern develops as the iron filings come under the influence of the magnetic field. Each bit becomes a tiny temporary magnet and takes a position following the so-called *lines of force* that extend from the magnet. Together, the filings

form a map of the field. They reveal the presence of the invisible lines of force (see figure above).

If like poles of two bar magnets are brought near each other under the paper and sprinkled with iron filings, the repulsion of their lines of force is shown. Between two unlike poles the lines of force indicate mutual attraction.

The Earth as a Magnet[1]

Why does a freely swinging magnet point in a north–south direction? The experiments in mag-

[1]C. R. Carringan and David Gubbons, "The Source of the Earth's Magnetic Field," *Scientific American*, February 1979; A. Cox, G. B. Dalrymple, and R. R. Doe, "Reversals of the Earth's Magnetic Field," *Scientific American*, February 1967.

netic attraction and repulsion just described suggest the answer: The earth itself acts like a magnet. The earth's magnetic field exerts an influence on all compasses, causing them to line up in the direction of the field—in a generally north–south direction.

Practical mariners found that the compass needle does not point exactly toward the geo-graphic north and south poles that mark the ends of the imaginary axis of the earth. Rather, it is attracted to the *magnetic* pole in each hemisphere. The magnetic pole of the Northern Hemisphere (the North Magnetic Pole) is located above Boothia Peninsula, nearly 1,200 miles from the geographic North Pole. Similarly, the magnetic pole in the Southern Hemisphere (the South Mag-

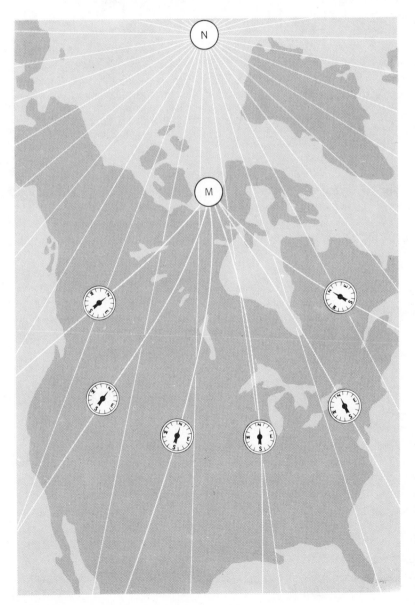

The north magnetic pole (M) is located at a distance from the true North Pole (N). As a result, compass needles at most parts of the earth point somewhat east or west of true north. Navigators must compensate for this difference when they use the compass.

(handwritten:) magnetic declination

(handwritten: ATOMS)

netic Pole) is located in Antarctica, some distance from the geographic pole. As a result, compass needles at most points of the earth point somewhat east or west of true north, as shown in the illustration on page 535. This was observed but not understood by Columbus (see p. 531). Navigators of ships and airplanes carry charts showing the angle difference (called *declination*) of a magnetic needle from true north for each point on the earth's globe. These charts are revised every few years because the earth's magnetic poles shift slowly all the time, and there is evidence that the earth's magnetic poles have reversed every million years or so, north becoming south, south becoming north.

What is the source of the earth's magnetism? Down through the ages a favorite theory was that there were mountains of lodestone that attracted compass needles. William Gilbert, often called the "father of magnetism," came closer to the truth when he proposed in 1660 that the entire earth was a huge spherical magnet. But he believed, incorrectly, that the great bulk of the earth was composed of lodestone-like matter.

Current theory of the earth's magnetism is based on the following:

1. The earth's core consists of a giant iron-nickel sphere (see Chapter 6A).
2. The flow of matter in the liquid outer part of the core generates an electric current.
3. The electric current generates a magnetic field (see pp. 546–548).

The Wrong Name

Two facts presented in the preceding material may appear to be contradictory: *Fact 1*. Opposite poles of magnets attract each other; like poles repel. *Fact 2*. The north pole of a magnet or compass is attracted to and points toward the north magnetic pole of the earth.

Indeed, there is a contradiction here—made by history, not science. It is a contradiction in name only, not in principle. It occurred because the poles of compasses were named before the laws

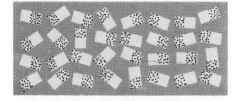

(Top) In an unmagnetized bar of iron the particles show no orderly arrangement, but lie with their poles pointing in all directions. *(Bottom)* When the bar is magnetized, the particles are arranged so that almost all like poles point in the same direction.

of attraction and repulsion were fully understood. If we could alter the course of history we might want to call the end of the magnet that points to the north its south pole, and the one that points to the south its north pole. Then the principle of opposites attracting and the terminology used would agree. To change now, however, might cause endless confusion. Some texts clarify the issue by calling the north pole of the magnet the north-seeking pole and the south pole the south-seeking pole.

THE NATURE OF MAGNETISM

Magnetism, like many other everyday phenomena, presents many perplexing problems to scientists, And, as with many other phenomena, the atomic theory gives a plausible explanation (see pp. 456–457). What, for example, is it that makes a substance magnetic? Scientists offer a tentative answer to this question. They point out that if you break a magnet in half, each half becomes a perfect magnet with new poles forming at the break. If you continue breaking these halves into quarters and so on, each new piece becomes a magnet with a north and south pole. This led to the theory that magnetism resides in the smallest particles of the magnet, in its atoms. Indeed, there is ample evidence that *each atom of a magnetic substance is a tiny magnet—an atom magnet* (see p. 557).

If magnetism is a characteristic that resides in atoms, what is the difference between an unmagnetized bar of iron and a magnetized one? In an unmagnetized bar the atoms are arranged like a group of children who, after play, have flopped on the ground to rest. They face in all directions. In a magnetized bar the atoms are arranged like children seated in straight rows. In unmagnetized iron the atom magnets neutralize each other; in the magnetized iron the atom magnets add to each other to make the whole bar a magnet. Why does rubbing a steel needle with a magnet cause the needle to be magnetized? Under the close influence of the magnet a majority of the atom magnets in the steel needle are pulled into line (see figure on p. 536).

Let us apply the atom-magnet theory to other everyday experiences with magnetism.

Why, for example, does frequent dropping (or hammering) of a magnet cause it to lose its magnetism? The answer: Shaking up the atoms causes them to lose their common orientation and throws them into a random one.

Why does heating a magnet make it lose its magnetism? The answer: Heating makes the magnetic atoms move more vigorously, enough to disrupt their common alignment.

Why does an iron nail become a magnet if a magnet is brought near it without touching it? (This is called *magnetizing by induction*.) The answer: If, for example, the south pole of the magnet is brought near the nail, most of the atoms in the nail are forced to line up according to the law of magnets with their north poles toward the south pole of the magnet—as long as the magnet is near the nail.

How does this theory explain why relatively pure iron (sometimes called soft iron) is a temporary magnet, whereas magnets made of steel do not lose their magnetism readily? The answer:

Steel is essentially iron with a small carbon content, usually about 1 percent, and sometimes small amounts of other metals such as tungsten and vanadium added to give it special physical and chemical properties. The carbon atoms seem to fit into the spaces between the iron atoms and limit their freedom to rotate or move. Thus steel is difficult to magnetize, but once the magnetic atoms are aligned they resist being disarranged because the carbon atoms tucked into the spaces between them do not permit them to move about readily. On the other hand, magnetizing a piece of soft iron does not require much energy, but once magnetized, the iron atoms can be easily disarranged.

You may ask *why* are some substances, such as those of iron, more easily magnetized than others? The answer is also found in the atom (see Chapter 14A). As we saw, electrons revolve around the nucleus of the atom. It can also be shown that each electron *rotates* on its own axis. (In this dual motion the electrons resemble the planets of the solar system.) The phenomenon of rotation, known as *electron spin,* causes each electron to behave like a small permanent magnet. It has also been found that each electron spins in one of two directions, which we might call clockwise or counterclockwise. In the atoms of most elements there are about as many electrons spinning in one direction as the other; this neutralizes their magnetic effect. In certain elements, however, such as iron, nickel, and cobalt, there is a significant surplus of electrons spinning in one direction over that of the opposite. The unbalanced surplus (four in the case of iron) is responsible for the magnetic behavior of the atom as a whole.

STATIC ELECTRICITY

Electricity that accumulates and stays on the surface of a substance is customarily called *static electricity*. But we notice static electricity more when it is not static, when it jumps. Have you observed flashes of lightning in a thunderstorm? Have you heard a crackling sound when you stroked the fur of a cat? Have you felt a tiny shock after scuffing your feet on a rug and then touching a doorknob? In all these phenomena two things happened: (1) *electricity accumulated* and (2) *electricity jumped*. But this was not always known (see pp. 558–559).

Thales, a Greek philosopher who lived about 600 B.C., experimented with static electricity. He discovered that when he rubbed a piece of amber with a woolen cloth it would pick up light objects, such as bits of straw, dried leaves, and cork. At the beginning of the seventeenth century William Gilbert, the discoverer of terrestrial magnetism, repeated some of Thales's experiments. He found that glass and sealing wax, as well as amber, would attract light objects when they were rubbed. Gilbert named this mysterious force electricity, after the word "electron," which means amber in Greek. You can perform experiments similar to Gilbert's by rubbing a hard-rubber comb briskly on a woolen sweater or coat. Bits of paper will jump up to the comb and cling to it.

The study of static electricity was continued by many other scientists and led to many important discoveries. However, its fundamental cause was not determined until the nature and structure of the atom were known. As we learned in Chapter 14A, the atoms of all matter are made of negatively charged electrons whirling around nuclei containing positively charged protons (as well as other particles). You recall that there are an equal number of electrons and protons in each atom; as a result, atoms are ordinarily electrically neutral.

Now consider what happens when a comb is rubbed on a piece of cloth. The rubbing of the two materials causes some electrons to be torn away from the cloth and to adhere to the comb. The atoms making up the comb seem to be "hungrier" for electrons than those of the cloth. They grab some electrons from the cloth. We say that the comb has acquired a *negative charge* of electricity. It now has more electrons than protons.

But what of the cloth? Some of its atoms are left with an electron deficit or, what amounts to the same thing, a proton surplus. We say that the

cloth has acquired a *positive charge* of electricity. It now has more protons than electrons.

Electricity, then, is a phenomenon that stems from the electrical particles of which atoms are composed. Fundamentally, *matter itself is electrical.*

When we say that an electron has a negative charge of electricity and a proton a positive charge we are simply saying that there are two kinds of electric charges. We find that electrons repel each other and that protons repel each other, but that electrons and protons are attracted to each other.

Why does the charged comb with its surplus of electrons attract bits of paper that are electrically neutral? When the comb is brought *near* the paper two things happen.

1. The electrons in each of the atoms in the paper are repelled to the side away from the comb (because similar charges repel each other).
2. The surface layer near the comb now contains the atoms with a proton surplus, which causes it to be attracted to the negatively charged comb.

The comb acquires a negative charge when rubbed on wool. When, however, a glass rod is rubbed on a piece of silk the silken cloth picks up electrons, acquiring a negative charge, and leaves the glass rod with a positive charge.

Have you ever charged your hair by combing it? The comb removed electrons from your hair and thus left it with a positive charge. Being similarly charged, each strand of hair repels its neighbor, and so the hair tends to stand on end.

Scuffing your shoes on a rug causes you to pick up electrons from it. These accumulate on the surface of your skin. You are a charged body! When you bring your finger to an object such as a doorknob or a light switch, the electrons jump from you to that object. You are discharged!

Materials, then, become charged by grabbing or shedding electrons. Why not by grabbing or shedding protons? In atoms, as we have seen, electrons move in orbits around the nucleus. They are not held too tightly to the nucleus and may be removed by the application of energy, the out-

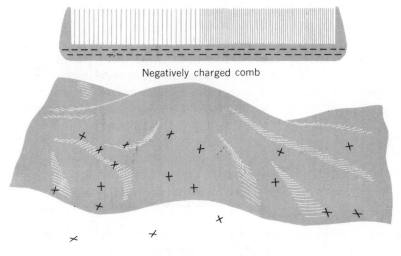

Negatively charged comb

Positively charged cloth

When a comb is rubbed on cloth the cloth loses electrons and the comb gains them. The comb acquires a negative charge of electricity, and the cloth acquires a positive charge.

ermost ones most easily. Protons, on the other hand, are held by powerful forces within the nucleus. To move the positively charged protons it would be necessary to move the entire atom along with them. In the previously mentioned solids— the comb, glass, or silk—atoms are held in place and are not easily displaced by rubbing.

Lightning was discussed in Chapter 9A as a weather phenomenon. Further details are in order now, because lightning is a form of static electricity. In a cumulonimbus (thunderstorm) cloud, the upper part becomes positively charged, while the lower part usually becomes negatively charged. (The reverse happens much less frequently.) As the cloud passes over the land it repels electrons near the ground (recall the comb–paper experiment) and causes the ground to become positively charged. A series of streams of negatively charged particles called *leaders* lash out from the cloud toward the ground but do not touch it. When a leader finally comes close enough to the ground the positively charged particles there jump the gap and travel upward toward the cloud on the path taken by the leader. This upward jump of charged particles, or *return*

stroke, is the main lightning stroke. It may be succeeded by further downward and upward surges in the same path. All of this takes place in less than one second.

When a negatively charged comb is brought near a neutral piece of paper, the electrons on the surface of the paper are repelled, leaving the surface with a positive charge.

Negatively charged comb

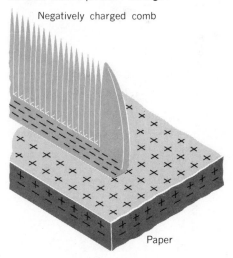

Paper

CURRENT ELECTRICITY

Electron Traffic

Flick a wall switch—the room is flooded with light. Push the toaster handle down—its coils heat to a red glow. Move the starting switch of a vacuum cleaner—its motor starts spinning. Light, heat, and motion are all at your fingertips through the magic of electric current. You are the engineer. You control the flow of electricity in these and dozens of other devices that serve you daily. More precisely, you are a kind of traffic engineer; when you throw the switch you are completing a pathway over which electrons will flow from

where they are in excess to where they are lacking.

Current electricity, as its name implies, is a flow—a flow of electrons, the particles that are part of the atoms of all matter. All matter contains electrons, so it is not necessary (or possible) to "make" electricity; all that is needed is something to push the electrons along. We shall see later how this is done with batteries and with generators.

The Electric Circuit

In understanding electron traffic it is helpful to know that *current electricity travels in a continuous path*—in an electric circuit. Every time you throw a switch to light a lamp or make a motor turn, you are completing an electrical circuit; you are setting in place a bridge for electrons. Every time you snap a switch to "off" you are lifting the bridge out of the circuit (see pp. 559–562).

The electric cord that connects your table lamp to the wall socket contains *two* wires to make a circuit possible. At any one moment electrons are flowing into the lamp through one of these wires and out through the other. To complete your "view" of the circuit it would be necessary to go all the way back from the wall socket to the electric generator in your locality. When you flick the switch of your lamp you are starting a movement of electrons in a continuous circuit all the way from the generating station to your lamp and back to the generating station.

Highways for Electricity

The electron flow of an electric circuit takes place along a highway made of metal. Strip a lamp cord (disconnected, of course) of its coverings and you find part of that highway in the twisted strands of copper wire. Examine the inside of an electric bulb and you will see the coiled filament made of the metal tungsten. From the powerhouse to the appliances in your home, electrons are mov-

There is a continuous electric circuit between the lamp and the power station when the switch is turned on.

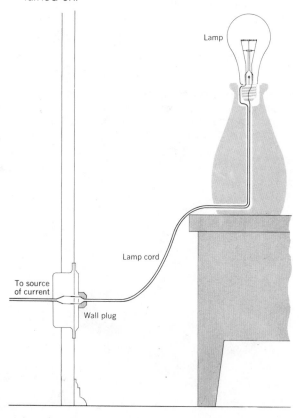

Lamp

Lamp cord

To source of current

Wall plug

ing along metal paths. Materials that permit easy flow of electrons through them are called *conductors.* Silver, copper, gold, iron, aluminum, platinum, and lead are examples of metals that are good conductors of electricity. Carbon, although not a metal, is also a conductor of electricity.

Most nonmetals are poor conductors of electricity. Rubber is one of the poorest conductors. Cloth, leather, glass, porcelain, and many of the new plastics are also poor conductors of electricity. All of these are termed *insulators,* which are used to keep electricity from going where it is *not* wanted. In a lamp circuit, for example, the plug is covered with rubber or some other nonmetallic material. The copper wires in the cord are covered with fabric and rubber or a plastic coating.

Electricians use rubber gloves so that they will not be shocked. Telephone and electric wires supported by poles are separated from the wooden crossarms by glass or porcelain insulators. The wood of the poles does not carry electricity when dry, but when wet can conduct electricity quite readily. Wires supported by steel towers require large insulators.

Pure water itself is not a good conductor of electricity, but almost any object will become a good conductor when wet. Bathrooms become electrocution chambers if individuals coming out of a tub or standing on a wet floor touch lamps or plug in radios with poor insulation.

Resistance on the Electrical Highway

There is a considerable difference in the ease with which electrons can travel through various conductors. Another way of putting this is to say that conductors vary in their opposition to the flow of electrons. The property of a substance that limits the flow of electrons through it is called its *resistance.* The resistance of any part of a circuit depends on the following factors:

1. *The nature of the material of which it is composed.* Copper offers about one sixth the resistance that iron does. (Think of auto traffic on a smooth high-

The electric meter, which is located in the basement or in the kitchen or on the outside wall of almost every house, is easy to read. The present reading on this one is 15,023 kilowatt hours. The amount used for any period is computed by subtracting the previous reading from this one. (*Courtesy of General Electric Co.*)

way in comparison to that on a bumpy country road.)

2. *Its length.* A long wire offers more resistance than a short one. (Think of a long trip versus a short one.)
3. *Its thickness.* A thin wire offers more resistance than a fat one. (Compare a one-lane road with a three-lane highway.)
4. *Its temperature.* For most materials the higher the temperature, the more the resistance. (Heat makes some of the electrons speed up and causes "crashes" with other electrons, increasing resistance and slowing down the movement of electron traffic.)

MEASURING ELECTRICITY

Certain units have been devised by scientists to measure electricity. We see these marked on many of the electrical appliances we use: Ampere, volt, ohm, watt, and watt-hour are some of the common units we encounter.

An *ampere* is a measure of the rate of flow of electrons through a wire. A common 60-watt lamp requires about $\frac{1}{2}$ ampere. An electric iron takes about 4 or 5 amperes.

A *volt* can be thought of as a unit of electrical push behind each electron. A new dry cell has a push of about $1\frac{1}{2}$ volts; a storage battery in an auto, 12 volts; house circuits, 110 to 120 volts; long-distance electric circuits, 200,000 volts or more.

An *ohm* is a unit of electrical resistance. It measures the resistance offered by any conductor to the flow of electrons. Copper is used in electrical circuits because a wire made of this metal offers less resistance to the flow of electrons than a similar wire made of any other metal except silver.

The *watt* is a measure of electric *power*, which, in turn, is a product of the number of amperes (rate of flow) and the number of volts (push). Thus, a lamp in your 120-volt house circuit through which $\frac{1}{2}$ ampere is flowing has a wattage equal to $\frac{1}{2} \times 120$, or 60 watts. Because the watt is a small unit, the *kilowatt,* equal to 1,000 watts, is often used.

The *kilowatt-hour* is the unit that measures the amount of electrical energy supplied to do work. The power company uses this unit in calculating your bill. Thus, in a 100-watt lamp used for 10 hours the work done is 1,000 watt-hours or one kilowatt-hour. If the cost of electricity is 10 cents per kilowatt-hour the cost of this will be 10 cents. Examine an electric bill and you will learn how many kilowatt-hours were used to determine your bill.

The names of all the units given here (and a number of others not mentioned) are derived from the names of scientists who made significant contributions to our understanding of electricity.

FUSES: THE WEAKEST LINK

When electrons flow through any conductor they cause the conductor to become heated. The

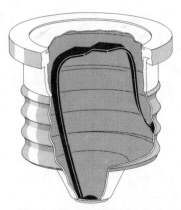

The fuse is the weakest link in the electric circuit. The heart of the fuse is a metal strip with a low melting point, shown here in black.

amount of heat produced depends largely on the strength of the current and the resistance offered by the conductor. The heating effect of an electric current is due to the electrons jostling the atoms of the conductor, causing them to vibrate more vigorously. This vibration we identified as heat (see pp. 561–562).

If an electric wire is carrying too much current for its size (thickness) it will heat up considerably. If this happens in the wiring of a building it may set fire to some combustible material near it. To prevent this, electric fuses are included in the wiring systems of buildings.

Examine an electric fuse of the screw-socket type. When this fuse is in place in a fuse box, electricity flows through it; it is part of the electric circuit. The essential part of the fuse is a flat strip of metal with a low melting point. You can see this strip if you look through the window of the fuse. If you can manage to break the metal seal or the plastic window on a fuse and take it apart, you will be able to inspect the fuse metal more carefully. Take it out of the container and apply a lighted match to its midpoint. The strip melts easily and falls apart. This is what is meant by the "blowing" of a fuse. Instead of a match the heat is provided by the surging of too many electrons through the fuse metal. The blowing of a fuse, then, is really the heating, melting, and breaking of the fuse metal (see p. 564).

Fuses are described as the "weakest link in the electrical chain." They are made that way so that if there is any overloading of the circuit this link will break and thus cut off the flow of electricity. The heating that occurs when a fuse blows takes place within the safe confines of the fuse, so no damage is done. Excessive heating along the rest of the line and the danger of fire are averted. The destiny of a fuse is its destruction.

Fuses may blow for two reasons: overloading or short-circuiting. An electric iron plugged into a circuit already sustaining an electric broiler causes a large number of electrons to flow into that circuit from the supply that is always available from your electric company. The load may be too great for your electric wires to sustain, but before they can heat up sufficiently to cause damage the fuse metal will melt and break the circuit. What should you do? The first thing to do it to unplug the appliance you plugged in just before the fuse blew. Then go to the fuse box, equipped with a new fuse. You will probably see that one of the fuses looks different because of the break in the metal strip inside it. There may also be a deposit of vaporized fuse metal on its window. Unscrew this fuse and then screw in the new one.

A short circuit may also cause a fuse to blow. If, for example, you have a long electric cord connecting your table lamp to a wall socket, and this cord is stepped on or frequently bruised by moving furniture over it, the insulation may be worn off at some point. The two bare wires then touch. A tremendous amount of current goes racing around this new and easy path. The electrons begin to heat up the wires in the circuit, but the fuse metal responds immediately by melting and breaking the circuit. What should be done? Locate the offending appliance (or extension cord) and check for fire. Unplug it carefully and install a new fuse. The worn cord should be replaced; further short circuits should be avoided by having an electrician install sufficient outlets so that long cords become unnecessary. Sometimes shorts develop inside electrical appliances. These should be repaired.

Extra fuse plugs should always be kept on hand. Some individuals bothered by fuses blowing frequently resort to dangerous alternatives. Instead of looking for the cause of the trouble they replace a burned-out 15-ampere fuse with a 30-ampere fuse. They are thus substituting a less effective fuse for this particular circuit; the wires in the circuit, which are designed to carry only 15 amperes safely, may overheat dangerously before this fuse melts. These people are forgetting that a fuse is built not for strength but for weakness.

Another practice, even more dangerous, is the replacing of a burned-out fuse with a penny or slug. The penny, being made of metal, is a good conductor of electricity, in fact, too good. If the line is overloaded, or if there is a short circuit, the electric wiring system of the house is converted into a huge toaster, with the house getting the toasting.

In many homes circuit breakers have replaced fuses. As you might suspect from its name, a circuit breaker is a kind of switch. In one common type, an extra surge of electricity causes an electromagnet (see pp. 546–548) to attract an iron bar. The bar trips a latch that breaks the circuit. After the source of the trouble is eliminated, the circuit breaker is restored to its original position by hand. In another kind of circuit breaker a bimetallic (two-metal) strip breaks the circuit when it is heated by the extra current.

GENERATING CURRENT ELECTRICITY

We found earlier in this chapter that we really do not manufacture electricity, that all matter has electrical particles in its atoms. Then why do we use a dry cell to ring a bell or a storage battery to start a car? Why do we plug a lamp into an outlet? Just what are we getting when we pay our electric bills?

We pay for the energy that is used to cause electrons to move steadily through the wires of the electric circuit. It is true that each atom in the copper wires of your lamp cord has a great many electrons in it. But it is only when some of these electrons are jarred loose from one atom and hop to the next one that we have an electric current. The process of electron passing may be initiated by the chemical action in a dry cell or battery. It may be the result of electromagnetic action in a generator. We shall study each of these sources presently. Both supply the energy for electron traffic. This is what we pay for.

How fast does electric current travel? Imagine a powerful generator of electricity in Chicago connected in a circuit to an electric lamp in San Francisco, which is about 1,860 miles (about 3,000 kilometers) away. Within 1/100 second after closing the switch the lamp would flash on, because electricity travels at about the speed of light, which is 186,000 miles (about 300,000 kilometers) per second. However, a *particular electron* in such a circuit would take years to drift along the Chicago-San Francisco wire. To understand this seeming paradox, think of a mile-long freight train starting up, with the engine in the rear pushing the whole train. Within a few seconds the first car is moving. But it might take 15 minutes for the engine car to cover the mile. This analogy suggests how the electric current can travel rapidly, although the individual electrons move very slowly.

Volta's Discovery

The chemical way of making electricity in cells and batteries is the older of the two methods used in making current electricity. An Italian scientist, Volta, discovered about 150 years ago that a chemical reaction could product a continuous flow of electricity. He found when he placed a strip of copper and a strip of zinc (not touching each other) in an acid solution, and then connected the dry end of each of these metals with a wire, that electricity began to flow in the wire. He hazarded the brilliant guess that these metals were undergoing a chemical change in the solution, which produced an electrical force. Chemical sources of electricity dominated the field for 100 years after Volta's discovery. It was found that any two unlike metals in a solution of an acid, base, or salt can produce an electric current. Our mod-

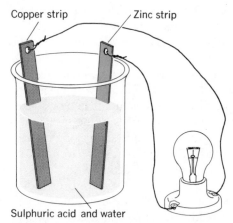

Copper strip   Zinc strip

Sulphuric acid and water

Chemical action in this simple wet cell produces a flow of electricity strong enough to light the small lamp.

ern dry cells and batteries are based on Volta's work.

A full understanding of how the cell worked was only possible when the inner structure of the atom was known. We shall not describe the entire process involved, but will summarize the effects of the chemical activity in a zinc-copper cell.

1. Extra electrons pile up on the zinc strip, making it rich in electrons, or negative.
2. Electrons are lost from the copper strip, making it "electron-hungry," or positive.
3. If a path, such as a wire, is provided outside the cell from the zinc to the copper plate, electrons will travel through the wire from the zinc to the copper.

Thus the chemical action in the cell is a kind of electron pump that produces an electric current.

The demonstration cell just described is called a "wet cell." The common "dry" cells used in flashlights and for portable radios are not really dry, for they would not work if they were. If you compare the dry cell with Volta's cell, you will find that it has comparable but not identical parts. Zinc is still one of the metals used; in the dry cell it also serves as a container. Instead of copper a carbon rod is used; it stands vertically in the center of the cell. Instead of sulfuric acid in water a moist chemical paste of ammonium chloride fills

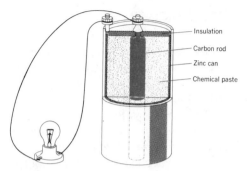

In a "dry" cell chemical changes produce an electrical current.

most of the cell. As in the wet cell, chemical action produces an electrical charge. The zinc container accumulates electrons and becomes negative, while the carbon rod becomes positive. In the dry cell shown, two posts on top serve as a convenient place for attaching wires. This dry cell is commonly used to supply current for a bell or buzzer, and also for classroom experiments. It produces $1\frac{1}{2}$ volts, as do the small cells used in flashlights. (The size of the cell does not determine its voltage but does indicate the quantity of charge available.) The dry cell is convenient to carry about because it is compact and because there is no liquid to spill.

Storage batteries (a battery contains two or more cells) have found an important use in automobiles. Contrary to popular opinion, storage batteries do not store electricity in the sense that a can stores fruit. When a battery is being charged by the generator of the car, the electrical energy going into it produces a *chemical* change. Chemical energy is what is "stored." When the battery is used to turn the starter, operate the lights and heater, spark the gasoline-air mixture, or run the radio, it operates on the same principle as cells described previously. Chemical energy is converted into electrical energy.

The storage battery commonly used in automobiles has six cells arranged in series. Each cell produces 2 volts; the combined voltage is 12 volts.

Storage batteries are often installed in hospitals

and other institutions as an auxiliary source of electricity, ready to supplant the regular supply in an emergency. They are also used in lighting buildings in country places not connected by electric lines to a central power station. These batteries are charged by a generator (to be discussed next) driven by a gasoline engine.

Generators

The English scientist Sir Humphrey Davy once said, "My greatest discovery was Michael Faraday." Michael Faraday began his scientific career as a bottle washer in Davy's laboratory, but soon took his place in the world of science. In his 50 years of research Faraday performed 16,000 experiments, which he faithfully recorded in his scientific notebooks. One, a very simple one, was destined to make possible our modern electrical world, for Faraday discovered a new and simple way of making an electric current without using messy chemicals or clumsy batteries. In 1831, he found that under certain conditions *magnetism could produce electricity*. He discovered that when he moved a magnet near a coil of wire, electricity flowed in the wire—although the wire was not connected to a battery. When he thrust the magnet into the coil, electricity flowed one

Faraday's discovery: A magnet moved near a coil of wire causes an electric current to flow in the wire.

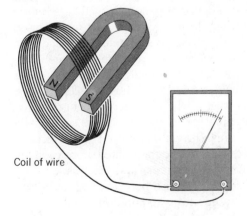

Coil of wire

way through the wire. When the magnet stopped moving, the electricity stopped. When he pulled the magnet out, electricity again flowed in the wire, but in the opposite direction. When he kept moving the magnet in and out, a regular, but pulsating, current was produced. Faraday also found that moving the coil back and forth over the magnet had the same effect as moving the magnet in the coil.

Moving a magnet near a coil of wire or a coil near a magnet caused a movement of electrons in the coil. Note that only three things were needed: a magnet, a coil of wire, and motion. In the years that followed Faraday's classic discovery, scientists found how to use the rush of falling water and the pressure of steam to provide the motion needed to turn huge coils of wire near huge magnets. Today, from hundreds of stations all over the country, power from water turbines is converted into electricity, which, a split second later, is turning a lathe in a nearby factory, cooking a dinner in a home, pumping water, and running a machine on a far-off farm.

AC and DC

The electron flow in a circuit connected to a dry cell or battery is always in one direction. This kind of current is called *direct current* (DC). A generator can produce this kind, too; however, 95 percent of the homes and factories in the United States are supplied by generators with *alternating current* (AC). In this type the electrons flow in one direction, come to a complete halt, and then go in the opposite direction. This change of direction occurs very rapidly, usually 120 times every second (60 cycles are thus completed in one second). That is why your electric light does not seem to blink.

Alternating current is preferred over direct current because it can be transmitted more economically from power stations to distant places. Alternating current can also be converted into direct current, where this is required for local use.

THE ELECTROMAGNET

Faraday and the American scientist Joseph Henry laid the basis for the making of enormous quantities of electricity by showing that *magnetism could be converted into electricity*. A few years before this, Hans Christian Oersted, a Danish professor of physics, found that *electricity could be converted into magnetism*. While lecturing before a class Oersted accidentally pushed a compass under a wire connected to a battery. He noticed that instead of pointing north the magnet needle swung at right angles to the wire. This happened only when the current was on. Oersted was thus led to suspect that electricity had a magnetic influence, that a wire carrying electricity had a magnetic field around it. Such a wire might be regarded as an "electricity magnet" or, as we call it, an *electromagnet* (see pp. 562–563).

It took another scientist, an Englishman named William Sturgeon, to show how to take advantage of Oersted's "magnetic" wire. He reasoned that if the magnetic field spread over a long wire could be concentrated, a very powerful magnet could be made. Care had to be taken, however, in the way in which the wire was gathered together. If in two adjacent parts of the wire the currents were flowing in opposite directions their fields would be neutralized. The only way in which one could wind a wire and have neighboring parts of the wire carry the current in the same direction would be to wind the wire into a coil or helix. Such a wire is called a *solenoid*.

You can demonstrate the principle of the electromagnet with a piece of insulated bell wire and a dry cell. Twist the wire into a coil by winding it around a cylindrical object, such as a pencil, for 40 or 50 turns. Remove the pencil, scrape both ends of the wire free of insulation and connect them to a dry cell. The coil will then attract and hold small bits of iron (iron filings). It will also cause a compass needle to be deflected from its original position. The coil behaves like a magnet as long as current is flowing through it. To make a much stronger electromagnet, wind the insulated wire around a large iron nail. This electro-

Faraday's discovery that magnetism can produce electricity led to the electric generator. In the Dallas Dam, Oregon, the rush of falling water spins turbines that turn huge coils of wire near giant magnets. (*Courtesy of General Electric Co.*)

magnet will pick up heavy objects, such as steel scissors and knives.

The electromagnet has many advantages over permanent magnets. First, it can be made very strong. Its strength can be augmented by increasing the number of turns of wire in the coil or by increasing the amount of current. Perhaps you have seen huge electromagnets attached to cranes in junkyards picking up a load of scrap iron and dropping it into a truck.

A second advantage of the electromagnet is that it is a temporary magnet. That is why, in the lift

Oersted's discovery: An electric current flowing through a wire makes that wire behave like a magnet.

magnet just described, it can pick up a load of metal and then drop it. When the current is on it is a magnet; when the current is off it is not.

THE TELEGRAPH

The fact that an electromagnet is a temporary magnet is the essential principle underlying the functioning of a telegraph. Think of an electric circuit a number of miles long with a switch at one end and an electromagnet and an iron bar at the other. A person sending a message at one end of the line completes the circuit by closing the switch (see pp. 562–563). A person at the other end, miles away, finds that an electromagnet connected to this circuit attracts an iron bar. When the sender breaks the circuit the iron bar is no longer attracted, and returns to its original position. A quick on-off movement of the sending switch makes a quick click-clack of the receiving electromagnet and bar, a "dot." A slow on-off switch action makes a slow click-clack in the receiver, a "dash." A code of letters based on dots and dashes makes it possible to send messages instantaneously to individuals miles away.

With the help of other inventors, Samuel Morse succeeded in making a practicable telegraph. In 1844 the famous message "What hath God wrought!" flashed over the wires from Washington, D.C., to Baltimore.

THE TELEPHONE

In the telegraph a spurt of electricity causes an electromagnet to attract an iron bar and make a click. In the telephone a spurt of electricity causes an electromagnet to attract an iron disk, which then emits speech. How is this accomplished?

The telephone is the product of two branches of science: sound and electricity. Sound will be considered in detail in Chapter 18A. For the moment it will help to know that anything that makes sound—a drum, for example—does so by shaking rapidly, by vibrating. This vibration is transferred to the air and thence to our eardrums.

The telephone, invented in 1875 by Alexander Graham Bell, consists of two parts: a transmitter and a receiver. The transmitter into which you talk is part of an electric circuit that extends all the way to the receiver of the person at the other end of the line. The telephone company, besides connecting you to the person you are calling, provides the electricity needed for the circuit.

Inside the transmitter there is a little box filled with thousands of grains of black carbon. These grains are part of the electric circuit; electrons have to flow through them to complete the connection. When you speak, the vibration produced by your vocal chords causes the sides of the carbon box to move in and out. Each time the sides move in, the carbon grains are squeezed together. Each time the sides move out, the grains spread farther apart. This squeezing and unsqueezing does something to control the flow of electricity (see figure on p. 549).

When the carbon particles are squeezed together they come in close contact, making a broad solid path for electricity. Electricity flows easily through them. When the pressure is released, the carbon particles spring apart and touch each other more lightly. Now the electrical path is thin and

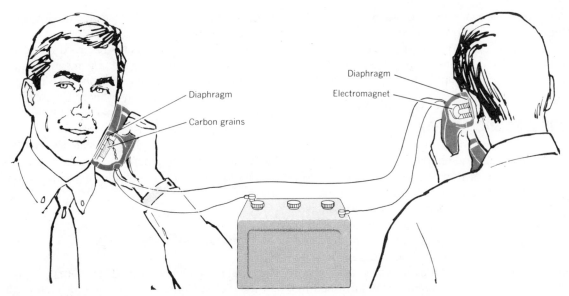

When you speak into the mouthpiece of a telephone you make the diaphragm there vibrate. This affects the electric current, which in turn causes the diaphragm in the receiver to vibrate and to duplicate the original sound.

broken—resistance is increased—and the electricity flows weakly.

The effect of speaking into the transmitter, then, is to cause electricity to travel in irregular "spurts," now strongly, now weakly, through the circuit that connects the speaker to the listener. Note that the *sound vibration does not travel through the wires.* Instead, it causes electrons to move in varying amounts instead of their usual steady stream. The sound vibration has been converted into a kind of fluctuating electrical impulse that is transmitted with lightning speed from speaker to listener.

The telephone receiver converts the electrical impulses back into sound vibrations. The essential parts of the receiver are an electromagnet and an iron disk. Let us see what the effect of a current varying in strength has on these essential parts. A strong flow of electricity makes the electromagnet stronger. It pulls harder on the disk. When the flow is weaker the disk moves back. In this way the fluctuating electrical circuit causes the disk, or

diaphragm, to vibrate. The vibrating disk causes the air nearby to vibrate. The air vibrations strike the eardrum of the listener, and he or she hears a sound that is a duplication of the speaker's voice.

To summarize:

1. Sound vibrations cause fluctuations in an electric circuit in the transmitter of the telephone.
2. The fluctuating electrical impulses are transmitted along the line to the receiver.
3. In the receiver the electrical impulses acting on the electromagnet set the diaphragm in motion in a sequence of vibrations similar to those made on the diaphragm of the transmitter.

Recently, light-wave, or fiber-optic, systems have been used in telephone networks to convert the electrical pulses of your telephone call into light pulses that travel as laser beams over hair-thin glass fibers. A single fiber-optic cable, which contains numerous fibers and is about the size of your finger, is capable of carrying 1.75 million simultaneous phone conversations. By comparison a conventional copper cable, which is about the size of your arm, can generally carry only about 11,000 calls. Fiber-optic cable is also less subject to electrical interference and provides better transmission quality.

THE ELECTRIC MOTOR

In the telegraph and telephone an electromagnet attracts a piece of iron. In a motor there are two electromagnets, one of which drives the other.

One of the electromagnets in a motor is fixed in position. It is attached to the outer frame of the motor and is known as the *field magnet*. The other electromagnet is on the rotating shaft of the motor and is known as the *armature*. When the motor is plugged in, current is furnished to the field magnets, producing north and south poles in them. Current is also furnished to the armature magnet, giving it north and south poles, too. The opposite poles of the two electromagnets, like those of permanent magnets, attract each other. The armature magnet, being free to move, turns so that its north pole nears the south pole of the field magnet and its south pole nears the north pole. If nothing else happened, the motor

In a motor the poles of the field magnet attract the opposite poles of the armature, causing it to turn. The small arrows show the electron path.

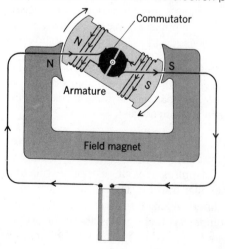

would come to a complete standstill. However, just before the unlike poles get near each other the direction of the current is reversed in the armature of the electromagnet by means of the *commutator*, shown in the diagram on this page, thus reversing the position of its poles. North is now near north, south near south. These repel each other, so the motor keeps turning.

The electric motor is the reverse of the electric generator. In the generator motion produces electricity; in the motor electricity produces motion.

SUPERCONDUCTORS

In 1908, H. K. Onnes, at the University of Leiden in the Netherlands, produced liquid helium for the first time, by lowering the temperature close to absolute zero. You will recall (see Chapter 15A) that at this temperature of $-460°F$ ($-273°C$ or $0°K$) all molecular motion is presumed to come to a standstill. Three years later, while experimenting with mercury frozen into a solid block after immersion in a liquid helium bath, Dr. Onnes observed to his surprise that the mercury had suddenly become a perfect conductor of electricity, totally without resistance. It had become a *superconductor*, even though it was several degrees above absolute zero. Since 1911 dozens of metals and hundreds of metal alloys have exhibited superconductivity, losing all their electrical resistance as they approached absolute zero.

This characteristic enabled the superconductors to carry currents without the loss of energy and to generate powerful magnetic fields. However, reaching and maintaining the low temperatures necessary for superconductivity in these metals was difficult and prohibitively expensive: difficult because they would have to be bathed constantly in liquid helium, and expensive because of the cost of producing this fluid.

Recently researchers have fabricated a different class of materials—ceramics—that become superconductive at significantly higher temperatures, as warm as $120°K$ ($-243°F$). At this temperature liquid nitrogen can be used to cool the material instead of liquid helium. (Nitrogen constitutes 79 percent of the air and is obviously abundant; helium constitutes only five parts per million of air and only 2 percent of gas in certain natural gas wells. It is much more difficult and expensive to liquify than nitrogen.)

It is expected that superconductors will have many practical uses: levitated trains that speed at hundreds of miles per hour on a cushion of magnetism; fusion reactors using superconductivity safer than nuclear fission to initiate operation; the transmission of electricity on high tension lines, with savings of as much as 20 percent of the energy; smaller, less expensive, and more powerful medical diagnostic imaging machines.

In a classroom demonstration of superconductivity (now available from scientific supply companies) one of the new ceramic materials is immersed in a dish of liquid nitrogen, and a magnet is placed above it. Since superconductors repel magnetic fields, the magnet remains suspended in midair.

This characteristic of superconductors is used in the "super-train" now being tested in Japan. Powerful superconducting electromagnets, built into the sides of each train car, suspend the train 4 inches above hundreds of oppositely charged metal coils set in the base of a U-shaped guideway. Other electromagnets propel the train forward as it "flies" along the guideway. West Germany and Britain also are developing trains employing superconductivity.

ELECTRICITY FOR HEAT AND LIGHT

Two significant changes occur when electricity flows through a wire: (1) a magnetic field appears around the wire and (2) the wire becomes warm. We have already discussed the first of these two effects. Let us now turn our attention to the heating effect of an electric current.

Many household appliances, such as electric toasters, percolators, irons, ranges, and heaters,

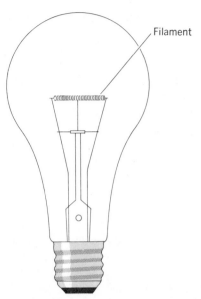

Filament

The electric bulb uses a very thin filament, which, because of its high resistance, becomes hot enough to glow brilliantly.

change electrical energy into heat energy. Some of the energy of the moving electrons is turned into heat as the electrons are forced to move against the resistance offered by the molecules of the wires of the appliance. This resistance is increased by making the wires thin or by using wires of some highly resistant material such as iron or nichrome (an alloy of nickel, chromium, and steel).

The common electric bulb uses a very thin filament, which because of its high resistance becomes hot enough to glow brilliantly, but because it has a high melting point, does not melt. The phenomenon of glowing when hot is called *incandescence*. Thomas Edison began his experiments leading to the invention of the electric lamp in 1877. Many scientists prior to this date had searched for a practical way of using electrical energy to produce light. It remained for Edison to show that a successful incandescent lamp has to have a hairlike filament to provide the necessary high resistance. The filament was enclosed in a sealed space devoid of oxygen so that it would not burn up. This was achieved by removing the air from the bulb and sealing it, thus creating a vacuum.

The first filament was a charred or carbonized piece of cotton thread. Later, after a long search, certain kinds of bamboo fibers when charred were found to produce a stronger filament. Carbon filaments were used in lamps for about 25 years. Eventually they were replaced by the more economical tungsten filament, which not only uses less electricity but also can be heated to higher temperatures without melting, thus yielding a whiter light. Another change, one that increased the life of bulbs, was the filling of the lamp with inactive gases, such as argon, that do not support burning. In these new lamps the evaporation of the filament was reduced; consequently, the lamps lasted longer.

IMPORTANT GENERALIZATIONS

Objects made of iron (and several other metals) are attracted by magnets.

When freely suspended, a magnet aligns itself in a north–south position. It becomes a compass.

Magnets are strongest at their poles.

Like poles of magnets repel, unlike poles attract each other.

The earth acts like a magnet.

The magnetism of a substance is due essentially to the magnetic properties of its atoms and to the arrangement of its atoms.

The magnetic behavior of an atom depends on the spin of its electrons.

A steel needle or rod can be magnetized by stroking it with a magnet.

Electricity, whether static or current, stems from the loosely bound electrons of atoms.

Matter is essentially electrical in nature.

When two different surfaces are rubbed together and then separated, electrons may be torn away from one and deposited on the other. Both surfaces acquire a charge of static electricity.

The object that loses electrons acquires a positive charge; the one that gains electrons, a negative charge.

Like electrical charges repel; unlike electrical charges attract.

Lightning is an abrupt discharge of electricity through the air.

Current electricity is the flow of electrons in a circuit.

Electrical current travels at about the speed of light, while individual electrons move slowly through a conductor.

A fuse is the weakest link in the electric circuit.

In cells and batteries chemical action starts electrons moving in one direction to make a current.

Moving a coil of wire near a magnet or a magnet near a coil of wire causes electrons to flow in the coil. This is the principle of the generator.

When electricity flows through a wire the wire becomes a magnet. This is the principle of the electromagnet, which is fundamental in the electric motor, the telegraph, the telephone, and many other devices.

Electrical energy can be converted into other forms of energy—into heat, light, sound, and mechanical energy.

DISCOVERING FOR YOURSELF

1. Read an electric meter and make a record of it; read it again 24 hours later. How much work, in kilowatts, was performed for you?

2. Survey your environment to find permanent magnets in use.

3. Make a list of places in a house where accidents with electricity might occur, and suggest precautions that should be taken.

4. Find examples of static electricity in your environment. Keep a list of the places where you observed the phenomena and explain what conditions caused the charges to be generated.

5. Find out what uses are made of the electricity that is generated in the storage battery of a car.

6. Make a survey of electrical appliances in a house. Find out which ones use an electric motor and which ones use wires of high resistance.

7. Objects containing iron, such as radiators, railings, and others, often acquire magnetism from the earth's magnetic field. Use a compass to determine the north and south poles of these objects.

8. Plastic wrap is very good for demonstrating static electricity. Crease a piece 2 inches by 10 inches (5

centimeters by 25 centimeters) over a pencil, so that it forms an inverted V. Place your hand between the two "wings" thus formed. What happens? Why? Try placing various objects between the wings such as a pen rubbed on cloth, a piece of glass rubbed on silk, and so on. Are the wings attracted or repelled?

9. Buy an unassembled electric motor kit. Assemble the motor and explain how it works.

10. Take a flashlight apart and see if you can explain how it works. What is the path of the current? How does the switch make and break the circuit? Take out one of the dry cells and unscrew the bulb. Can you make the bulb light by using the cell? Look at the bulb with a magnifying glass. What is the path of electricity through the bulb?

11. "All matter is essentially electrical in nature." Find evidence for this statement in readings.

12. Repeat Faraday's discovery, illustrated on page 545, using a "battery tester" sold in many radio supply stores.

13. Read in newspapers and magazines of progress in the use of superconductivity.

TEACHING "MAGNETISM AND ELECTRICITY"

The study of magnetism and electricity provides many opportunities for the exploration of ideas and the manipulation of materials: What will my magnet pick up? How can a compass help me find my way? How can I make my bulb light up? The materials used—magnets, wires, bulbs and dry cells—furnish the answers. They also may raise perplexing problems when the experiment "doesn't work": When the compass needle points the "wrong way"; when the bulb doesn't light, when the magnet fails to pick up paper clips. Here children experience real challenges that bring them close to the true nature of science as they make original (for them) hypotheses, test them, and draw conclusions.

There are many "open-ended" possibilities in the study of magnetism and electricity: What happens if we use more coils of wire in our electromagnet? If we connect more batteries in a circuit? If we make static electricity by rubbing different materials? If we use a compass as an iron "detector"?

This study has direct application to understanding the role of magnetism and electricity in everyday appliances and in our electrical civilization. Also important are the safety rules and conservation measures in using electricity in the home.

SOME BROAD CONCEPTS

Materials made of iron and a few other metals will be attracted by magnets.
Unlike poles of magnets attract, like poles repel.
A freely suspended bar magnet acts like a compass.
A steel needle can be magnetized by stroking it with a magnet.
An electric current will flow only through a closed circuit.
An electric circuit commonly consists of a source of electron "push," a conductor, and an appliance that uses the current.
Electrical energy may be transformed into other energy forms.
Electricity can produce magnetism; magnetism can produce electricity.
Electric current is controlled by switches, fuses, and insulating materials.

FOR YOUNGER CHILDREN

What Can a Magnet Do?

Free play with magnets results in questions, some information, some speculation, some discussion, and some unsubstantiated conclusions. In many classes children bring magnets of assorted shapes and sizes from home to add to the school supply. The more opportunity children have to work individually and independently with magnets and materials the better. Supply a box of assorted heavy and light things—some iron, some other metals, chalk, rubber, pieces of cardboard, wood, cloth, glass—that children can test to see if magnets will pull them.

Provide the opportunity for children to discuss and report their observations. A list of these observations may be made. List correct as well as incorrect conclusions and then plan ways of testing with the children. Children will, as a result of these and other related activities, be able to state and demonstrate such ideas as: magnets attract some things and not others; some magnets are stronger than others; magnets are stronger at the ends; and magnetism can travel through some materials.

How Strong Is Your Magnet?

Testing to find out who has the strongest magnet helps children become more exact in their observations and reporting. Supply each child or each small group of children with a magnet. How can we be sure whose magnet is strongest? Children may suggest using paper clips or some other iron objects as units of measure (see p. 21). They may count the number of such units as a basis for comparison. Many children think that the largest magnets are strongest. Test this idea. Children will discover that most of the paper clips cluster at the ends of the magnets and conclude that magnets are "strongest" at their ends. They may measure the distance through which the magnetism of various magnets operates by approaching a paper clip slowly with a magnet and then measuring with a ruler the distance the clip "leaps" to the magnet.

How Do Magnets Affect Other Magnets?

As children manipulate magnets, they are almost sure to demonstrate that some poles of magnets pull each other, some push each other away. If the poles are marked "N" and "S" they will find that similar poles repel each other, unlike poles attract. This is the "law of magnets." Cylindrical magnets demonstrate this law graphically: One rolls the other away when like poles are adjacent. They roll toward each other when opposite poles face each other.

What Does Electricity Do?

Encourage children to observe various things that electricity does over a period of several days at home, on the streets, in stores, at school, and elsewhere. Make a list of these things and use the list to develop vocabulary, as well as to help children develop an appreciation for the many uses of electricity. Encourage children to examine the list to see if they can work out a classification. There are several possibilities. One meaningful one is according to usage: (1) heat giving; (2) light giving; and (3) making movement. The children may search in magazines and elsewhere for pictures that illustrate the list, and perhaps prepare charts according to their classification.

Suggest that children report on "power outages" in their neighborhood. What happened? What was the cause? How long was the outage? How was it repaired?

How Can We Connect a Dry Cell to a Bulb to Make It Light?

See the discussion suggested for older children later in this chapter and adapt it for use with younger children. Present them with a bulb, a dry cell, and some wires, and let them try individually or in small groups to light the bulb. A project of installing a small light in a playhouse in the classroom is an interesting motivation. As a result of having learned to light the bulb in the small circuit, children may be able to use what they have learned to make the more extensive hookups, perhaps with the help of older children and the teacher.

Other Problems for Younger Children

1. How do we use magnets at home?
2. What can a natural magnet or lodestone do?
3. How do magnetic games work?
4. What toys use electricity? What does the electricity do in the toys?
5. How can we make electricity by rubbing?
6. Where does our electricity come from?
7. How does a flashlight work?
8. How can we save electricity at home and in school?
9. What safety rules should be followed in using electricity?

FOR OLDER CHILDREN[1]

What Can We Discover by Experimenting with Permanent Magnets?

Children should be encouraged to manipulate magnets and make their own observations. Class experience with magnets may begin by letting students show the class any observations they have made. They should be encouraged to comment on their observations, to compare their experiences, and to raise questions, which should be

---

[1] L. J. Garigliano, "Something Missing in Magnetism," *Science and Children* (January 1981); M. Iona, "Teaching Electricity," *Science and Children* (February 1982). Excellent suggestions. S. Fields, "The Measure of the Magnet," *Science and Children* (November/December 1987). Measuring, recording and making conclusions with magnets. D. Adler, *Amazing Magnets* Mahwah, N.J.: Troll, 1983).

recorded for future investigation. Encourage students to devise their own experiments to try to solve the problem; to propose hypotheses that they can try to test; to formulate tentative answers; and to use several sizes, shapes, and kinds of magnets (see Chapter 3, "Using Learning Centers").

The following are examples of problems:

What kind of materials will a magnet attract?

How can we find out if some magnets are stronger than others? (By seeing how many paper clips the magnet can hold and by determining the number of pieces of paper through which the magnets can hold a paper clip.)

How can we tell where the strongest parts of the magnets are? (By observing how many paper clips or other iron objects are attracted at various places on a magnet.)

Through what kinds of things will magnetism travel?

How can we make a steel needle into a magnet?

How can we make a simple compass with a bar magnet?

How can we tell whether a lodestone has poles? (Use a compass.)

How do the poles of magnets act toward each other?

These problems, and others children may pose, provide opportunities for them to work as individuals or in small groups, and to share their observations and findings. If possible, the activities should be unhurried and thus provide opportunities for children to progress at their own rates of speed. They should be encouraged to predict what may happen under different circumstances and to test these predictions.

Guide children not to generalize from one instance. For example, an experience with the use of *one* pin or nail is not sufficient evidence from which to conclude that "Magnets attract all nails and pins." Children can discover that it is the material that an object is made of that is important, not the kind of object itself. Lifting a "tin" can with a magnet is no basis for saying that magnets attract "tin." Tin cans are usually made of steel and are merely covered with a very thin coating of tin; the magnetism travels *through* the tin and attracts the steel inside it, just as it travels *through* paper and attracts iron filings or tacks placed on it.

Another kind of error is the failure to use an adequate control before making a judgment. At a science fair one student concluded that wood "blocks" magnetism more than other substances that he tested: paper, glass, plastic, aluminum foil, and a piece of steel from a can. What he failed to take into account was that he was using a *thick* piece of wood between the magnet and the steel paper clip. The other substances he selected were thin sheets. He did not control distance.

How Can We "See" Magnetism?

After children have experienced the push and pull of magnets under various circumstances they are curious about this invisible force. "Can you see it?" "Can you feel it?" Some children have seen "pictures" of magnetic fields like those on page 534. If possible, give each child or each small group of children a magnet, a small shaker of iron filings, and a piece of cardboard. Have them shake the filings onto the cardboard that is resting on a magnet. Let them compare their results. What can you discover by examining the results? (The force gets weaker as the distance from the magnet increases. You can see in what directions the force extends, and so on.) (See Chapter 17A, pp. 533–537.)

Note: As we mentioned in the section on safety in Chapter 5, children should be cautioned against rubbing their eyes when handling iron filings.

The activity is more meaningful when children understand that this is a way of "seeing" the invisible force of magnetism. In effect the filings form a map of the invisible field of force surrounding the magnet. A piece of glass can also be substituted for the cardboard.

How Can We Make and Use a Compass?

Give several bar magnets, some string, and some wooden supports to individuals or small groups

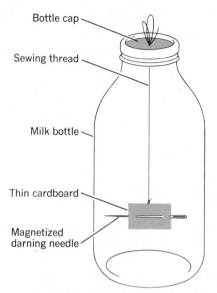

Bottle cap

Sewing thread

Milk bottle

Thin cardboard

Magnetized
darning needle

If a milk bottle is not available a jar may be substituted in making this simple compass. Two needles, magnetized in the same direction, may be used to make the compass work more effectively.

of children and suggest that they try to use the materials to find out which way is north (see pp. 531–532). They will compare results and try to account for what happens. Refer to the lesson plan on pp. 51–54 for suggestions on helping children make a compass using a flat cork, a magnet, a needle, and a saucer of water. The needle is magnetized by rubbing it (in one direction, not back and forth) on one of the poles of the magnet, and is then laid on the cork that is floating on the water. The needle will soon point north and south. Although the floating-needle compass is interesting historically (originally a lodestone, a natural magnet, was used in this manner) it is helpful to have a commercially made compass for examination. As is the case of many of the other experiments in this chapter there are many opportunities to make this experiment more open-ended: "Is the pointed end of the needle always the north pole?" "Can you magnetize only one end of a needle?" "Can you demagnetize the

needles?" "Can you use an unmagnetized needle as a compass?" (See Chapter 17A, pp. 531–532.)

Compass study may include some additional problems: "What are some of the different kinds of compasses in common use?" "How can we use a compass to tell the direction of the sun at different times of the day?" "How can you use a compass to tell where your house is from school, what direction your school faces, which way the wind blows, or to put directions on a map of the neighborhood?"

How Can We Make an Electric Charge?

Students can demonstrate a form of electricity by activities such as combing their hair, rubbing a rubber comb on a woolen sleeve, or holding tissue paper against the chalkboard and rubbing the paper rapidly with a silk cloth. Suggest that groups of children choose one of these demonstrations or similar ones to show their classmates; then observe the results and try to explain what they see. They may also do the demonstration illustrated on page 559 by using a piece of glass, two books, some tiny scraps of paper, and a piece of silk cloth. Lay the two books on the table about 4 inches (10 centimeters) apart. Sprinkle the scraps of paper on the table between the books. Lay the piece of glass over the books so that it covers the paper scraps. Rub the glass vigorously with the silk cloth. The paper will jump up from the table to the glass. Experiment with books of various thicknesses to see how far the pieces will jump. Children will suggest other variations.

Some experiences with static electricity are more effective if they occur in the dark, so that students can observe sparks. Children are then more likely to see the connection between the static electricity and lightning.

Students will wonder about the connection between rubbing and static electricity. In the upper grades discuss (or review) the structure of atoms. Every atom has electrons that whirl around a nu-

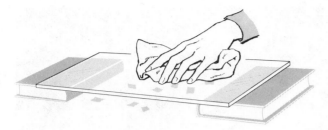

Rubbing a glass with a silk cloth is one way to demonstrate static electricity.

cleus. When you run your comb through your hair you scrape electrons away from the hair and onto the comb, thereby building up a greater charge of electrons. This charge is static electricity, although it is not static in the usual sense of the word. It can and does jump as observed in the sparks in some of the experiences and in the case of lightning (see Chapter 17A, pp. 537–539).

Static electricity, then, results from the building up on a surface of particles from atoms. Looked at from another viewpoint static electricity reveals the electrical nature of matter.

Static electricity experiments work better on dry days than on humid ones. Students will be interested in experimenting on different days to see that this is true. Some kinds of material, such as plastic wrap, show the effects of static electricity in almost any kind of weather.

How Can We Measure Static Electricity?

A rough way of demonstrating and measuring static electricity is to suspend a puffed wheat kernel by a thread from some support. Decide on a fixed distance from the kernel that you will use in measuring and comparing the strength of a static electric charge. For example, rub an inflated balloon with a wool cloth and bring it to the agreed-upon distance from the kernel. How far does the kernel swing out from its original position? Vary the experiment by rubbing the balloon a different number of times or by rubbing other materials.

How Can We Make an Electric Circuit?

Electrical circuits constitute an example of a system in which interaction of the parts is obvious; through experimentation and manipulation children can demonstrate these interactions and see for themselves that change results from interaction of the members of a system (for example, battery, conductor, light bulb). When the members of the system are properly arranged, the bulb glows, indicating interaction.[2]

Firsthand experiences by individual children, or at least in small groups, is essential. We suggest that each child or small group be given a dry cell, some wire, and a light bulb, with the suggestion that students attempt to light the bulb using the equipment. (It is perhaps better to furnish the students initially with wire having a few inches of insulation stripped from both ends of the wires.) A few students will probably be successful in a short time. Others will take longer. Do not hurry the manipulation; it may result in children "copying" from their neighbors instead of discovering for themselves (see Chapter 17A, pp. 540–543).

Children may be urged to make simple line drawings to show what they did, classifying them into "It works" and "It doesn't work." Examination of the drawings and the material itself will form the basis for making inferences and for ver-

[2]K. Brandt, *Electricity* (Mahwah, N.J.: Troll, 1985); K. Whyman, *Electricity and Magnetism* (New York: Watts, 1986); G. Vogt, *Generating Electricity* (New York: Watts, 1986). General references with experiments.

Individual investigations using prepared materials in shoe boxes provide opportunities for communicating and checking ideas. New problems are raised and new methods of investigating are proposed. (*Courtesy of Phyllis Marcuccio.*)

ification by comparing. From the simple circuit experience children will proceed to constructing other circuits; using various switches; using more than one dry cell; lighting more than one bulb in the circuit; and connecting bulbs in a series and in parallel arrangements (see later demonstrations).

As children continue their experiences with circuits, vocabulary develops—closed circuit, open circuit, conductors, and so on. Children may make a list of "science words or terms" and use them for reference. Questions also arise that lead to further experiences. For example, "Is copper wire the only material that will carry a current?" "How is a switch built to break a circuit?" "What happens when bare wires touch each other in a complete circuit?"

Children may be able to devise a circuit like the one pictured and to test other materials to see if they, like copper, will conduct a current. They

A knife switch is used between the dry cells and the lamp to make and break the circuit.

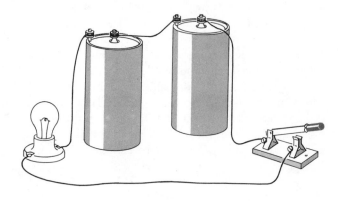

can test many materials—such as rubber, aluminum, iron, glass, cloth, and so on—by placing them in the circuit. They can then classify materials as conductors and insulators, and examine various circuits they have used to identify the conductors and insulators.

The students may discover what happens when bare wires touch by the following activities. Connect a dry cell to an electric bulb using copper wires that have had their insulation removed in several places. Ask students if they can put out the light without using the switch. Touch a bare spot on the wire to a bare spot on another. Touch (carefully) the wire in the circuit. It may be hot. When students use the short circuit they will note that when bare wires touch in a completed circuit, heat results. An application of this idea is incorporated in the construction of fuses. Students will devise variations of this experiment to show other ways of making short circuits. This experiment has applications to learning the causes of fire in buildings and to the dangers in the use of worn extension cords. Ask students to look for these applications.

The drawing illustrates a simple demonstration showing how a fuse protects a house. Use a block of soft wood, two thumbtacks, a dry cell, some copper wire, and a narrow piece of metal foil or fuse wire (available from a supply house). Press

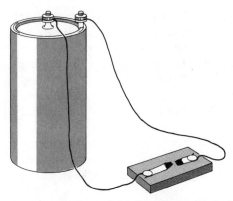

A piece of thin metal foil is used to illustrate how a fuse works. Double V-shaped notches are cut near the center of the strips, leaving a very narrow path for the current.

the thumbtacks into the wood, and connect them with the narrow strip of foil, making sure that the foil makes a good connection with the tacks; then connect the wires to the cell. It is helpful to cut a notch on either side of the metal foil near the center to make a very narrow place in the foil. The foil melts. (If the demonstration does not work at first let students decide why. It may be because the foil strip is too wide, because the connections are not properly made, or because

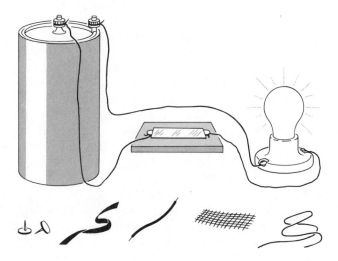

A simple way of finding out if materials are conductors or nonconductors of electricity. Materials to be tested are laid across the two thumbtacks. The pupils will think of many materials to test.

the dry cell is weak or dead. The problem solving involved in trying to decide why the demonstration does not work may be as important as understanding the demonstration itself.) Encourage children to try a circuit with two dry cells and a "fuse" of similar size. What happens? Students should examine burned-out fuses to look at the fuse wire and note what has happened to it. In many homes circuit breakers are used to replace such fuses. Suggest that children investigate at home, with an adult (see pp. 542–543, Chapter 17A).

How Can We Make an Electromagnet?

Before beginning this activity, students might review what they know about permanent magnets: They attract iron, have poles, are strongest at poles, their like poles repel, their unlike poles attract. These ideas will be used in comparing the permanent magnets they have used with the temporary magnet they will make.

Each child or small group of children should, if possible, be supplied with two dry cells, 2 or 3 feet (60 to 90 centimeters) of insulated wire, a large nail, a switch, and some steel thumbtacks. Show the children a diagram of an electromagnet and ask them to try to make one. The purpose here is to develop skills for making a construction from a diagram (see p. 563).

This would be a good time to suggest that in

Making and testing a simple homemade switch teaches science skills.

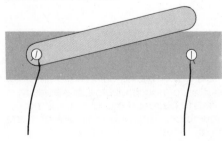

order to conserve the source of energy they not leave the circuit closed for very long and not ever connect a nail directly across the terminals of the dry cell (see Chapter 17A, pp. 546–548).

When several electromagnets have been made ask, "Who do you think has the strongest electromagnet?" "How can we tell?" Test with the thumbtacks or paper clips by counting how many are held by the electromagnet. When the strongest magnet is discovered, ask if they can tell why this electromagnet is strongest (more coils of wire, fresher dry cells, care in winding coil, and so on). "How can all the magnets be made stronger?" Children are encouraged to test their ideas.

Here is an opportunity for students to use mathematics in helping to discover relationships. Have them discover how many tacks (or paper clips) are picked up with 6 turns of wire, 12 turns, and so on, with one dry cell. They may make a simple graph of the results.

"What other way can you think of to make the electromagnet stronger?" (Use two cells.) Again test.

Does an electromagnet have poles? How can we find out? Children suggest bringing a permanent magnet, marked "N" and "S" for its poles, close to each end of the electromagnet, or using a compass. "What can you discover?" (The magnet has poles.) "Can you tell by using the compass which pole is N and which is S?" "How?" "How do you suppose you could change the poles of the magnet?" (Switch the connections to the dry cell.) Most children will need help here.

As children continue to use the electromagnets, such questions as the following may arise: "Can an electromagnet be made with uninsulated wire?" "Will a pencil work instead of a nail?" "Will a coil of wire work without any nail in it?" Children's questions will suggest other ideas to try.

Students can compare the electromagnets with the permanent magnets they have used. "How are they alike?" "How are they different from each other?"

After the electromagnet has been made and used, students can be asked to hunt for places where electromagnets are utilized at home, at

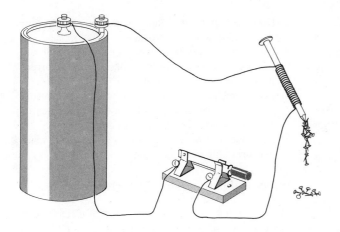

When electricity flows through the electromagnet it can pick up objects of iron. When the circuit is broken it drops them. An electromagnet is a temporary magnet; its strength can be changed and its poles reversed.

school, and elsewhere. After the investigations the class can make a list. (It will include doorbells, electric motors, telegraph sets, and so on.)

How Can We Make Electricity?[3]

Children can make a simple device that illustrates Faraday's discovery that magnetism can be converted into electricity. A bar magnet is thrust vigorously in and out of a coil of insulated wire. Start with 20 or 30 turns of wire. If the two ends of the coil are connected, electricity will flow in the

[3]C. W. Boltz, *How Electricity is Made* (New York: Facts on File, 1986). General information and demonstrations. M. S. Gutnik, *Simple Electrical Devices* (New York: Watts, 1986). How they work and are used.

wire. But how can you make sure? A simple meter (galvanometer) can be constructed as shown on this page by wrapping a coil of wire around a compass. (Instead of an improvised meter, you may use the inexpensive battery tester sold in radio or electronic stores.) Connect the two ends of this coil to the two ends of the other coil (see diagram). Now use the magnet as directed, and observe the compass needle. Here we have an example of electricity being converted into magnetism (Oersted's discovery). In summary: (1) In the "generator" the movement of the magnet in and out of the coil causes electricity to flow in the wire: magnetism → electricity; (2) in the "meter" (coil of wire around a compass) electricity in the wire produces magnetism that deflects the needle: electricity → magnetism (see Chapter 17A, pp. 545–546).

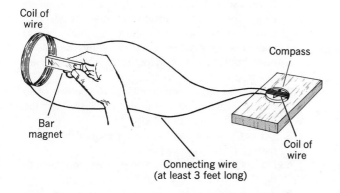

Coil of wire

Compass

Bar magnet

Coil of wire

Connecting wire (at least 3 feet long)

A magnet in motion produces electricity in a coil of wire. The deflection of a compass needle shows that an electric current is flowing.

Note: In huge generators the mechanical energy—motion—produced by flowing water or steam turns the magnets—electromagnets—near coils of wire and generates electricity in the same way.

This is another example of open-ended possibilities: (1) "What happens if there are more vigorous thrusts?" (2) "More turns of wire in the generator?" (3) "More turns of wire around the compass?"

What Are Some Safety Rules for Using Electricity?[4]

As children study electricity they may make some of their own safety rules from the knowledge they have gained. These rules can be checked against those given here, and any important ones that have been omitted can be added. Children should be encouraged to take this list home and talk it over with their parents to decide which rules apply especially to their homes.

The safe use of electricity is important to all of us; these general rules are stated simply and organized according to their applications. Rules such as these should not be merely memorized by children. As children study electricity they come to understand the reason for precautions, and consequently they see the sense of observing them. The rules apply to home, school, and any other place where electricity is used.

Note: *It is important to stress that children should not work with house current or replace fuses.*

Safety Rules for Using Electric Appliances

1. Disconnect electrical appliances when they are not being used.
2. If there is a switch on an electrical appliance turn it off before you disconnect the appliance. Also be sure that the switch is turned off before you connect the appliance.

[4]W. L. Beauchamp, G. O. Blough, and M. Williams, *Discovering Our World, Book 3* (Glenview, Il.: Scott, Foresman, 1967).

3. Never use an electrical appliance or an electric cord that you know is out of order.
4. Never try to experiment with an electrical appliance or an electric cord that is connected to the current in your home or at school.
5. Never touch an electrical appliance, cord, or switch with wet hands. Also be sure not to touch them if any part of your body is touching a water pipe.
6. Read and follow the precautions given by the manufacturer with each appliance.

Safety Rules for Using Electric Wires

1. Never touch electric wires or use an electric cord on which the covering is worn.
2. Keep electric wires and cords from rubbing against things or becoming kinked. Rubbing may wear off the covering, and kinking may break it.
3. Stay away from broken wires that hang from poles or buildings.
4. Never climb a pole that supports electric wires.

Safety Rules for Using Fuses and Switches

1. Never try to repair a "burned-out" fuse. Ask an adult to replace it with a new one.
2. When a fuse "burns out," always put in a new fuse that carries the same current. If the old fuse is labeled 15A the new fuse should be labeled 15A.
3. Never try to use a penny instead of a new fuse. The penny is made of copper. It will not melt until the copper wires do, too.
4. Have a switch repaired at once if you get a shock when you use it to turn current on or off.

Safety Rules for Using Electric Heaters

1. Never use a knife, fork, spoon, or any metal object to get bread out of an electric toaster while it is turned on. You may get a shock or a burn, or you may cause a short circuit. Wooden tongs are sold in household sections of department stores. They are safe to use.
2. Do not use a damp cloth to clean the outside of an electric heater while it is turned on. Disconnect the heater and wait until it cools.
3. Do not go away and leave an electric iron connected. It may cause a fire.
4. Do not hang wet clothes on an electric heater to dry. You may cause a short circuit or a fire.
5. Never touch an electric heater or any other electrical

device while you are in a bathtub or shower or while any part of your body is touching a water pipe, a faucet, or a radiator.

6. If you use an electric heating pad be sure that it has a waterproof cover. You may get a shock if perspiration soaks into it.

Other Problems for Older Children

1. What are the common sources of electricity?
2. How are houses wired for using electricity?
3. How does an electric motor work?
4. How can we make an electrical questioner?
5. How can we make a telegraph set?[5]
6. How does a telephone work?
7. How do electrical appliances produce heat and light?
8. How do thermostats work?
9. How can you hook up some lights in parallel? In series?
10. What is a superconductor?

RESOURCES TO INVESTIGATE WITH CHILDREN

1. An electrical shop, for odds and ends of wire, insulating materials, magnets, and other materials, as well as for information about electricity.
2. Variety store, for purchase of inexpensive electrical materials for use in experiments.
3. Junk shop, for metals to test as conductors, for magnets, and for other odds and ends.
4. The local power company, for information about the source of electricity, its costs, and so on.
5. The local telephone company, for a visit to see how electricity is used in communication.
6. The school custodian, to show students where electricity enters the school; fuse box or circuit breaker; the electric meter, the switches; how insulating materials are used for safety; to provide burned-out fuses; to read the electric meter; and for other similar purposes.
7. Children's homes, for illustrations on ways in which electricity is used to do various kinds of work in the home.
8. The community, for examples of the many kinds

of work done by electricity in factories, homes, stores, in public buildings, on the streets, and so on.

9. Local hardware store or department store, to see how many tools and appliances use magnetism and electricity.
10. Local radio or television station, to see how programs are put on the air.
11. Local electricity-generating plants, for information and possible class visits to find out how electricity is produced and distributed.
12. Local electrical contractors, for regulations related to electrical installations and uses of electricity.
13. Toy store, for toys that use magnetism or electricity.
14. A local doctor, for information on the uses of magnetism and electricity in the instruments that he or she has.
15. A street excavation, to see how electric cables are connected to buildings.

PREPARING TO TEACH

1. Discover the following things about a specific house: Where does electricity enter? How many fuses are there or is there a circuit breaker? Which appliances use the most electricity? What is the source of the electrical supply? Prepare plans for a trip with an elementary school group to make similar observations. Draw up a list of the observations you would plan for them to make.
2. Examine the activities, experiences, and experiments suggested in this chapter and plan how you would increase their "open-endedness."
3. Make plans for an exhibit by the children of the various experiments and experiences in this chapter. Devise uses for this exhibit: (1) to share the findings with another group that has not studied the material; (2) to review the findings; (3) as an exhibit in a display case in the school corridor. Suggest ways to help children improve their communication skills through this activity.
4. Survey sources of films and filmstrips that are available to supplement the materials in this chapter. Preview them and plan how they can be used with children.
5. Assemble the materials and perform the experiments in this chapter if you have not had previous experiences with them.

[5]G. V. Bruce, "Morse's Miracle Revisited," *Science and Children* (May 1985). How to make a simple telegraphic device.

SOUND AND
HOW WE USE IT

The location of the ear is most fittingly adapted to all positions in space. Sounds are made and heard by us when the air . . . is ruffled by a rapid tremor into very minute waves and moves certain cartilages of a tympanum in our ear. External means capable of thus ruffling the air are very numerous, but for the most part they may be reduced to the trembling of some body which pushes the air and disturbs it. Waves are propagated very rapidly in this way, and high tones are produced by frequent waves and low tones by sparse ones.

GALILEO IN THE ASSAYER, 1623

A WORLD OF SOUND

Our language reflects our keen awareness of sound. In the country we mark the *hum* of mosquitoes, the *rustle* of leaves, the *lowing* of a cow, the *flutter* of wings, the *roar* of a waterfall. In the city we note the *blare* of automobile horns, the *rumbling* of trains, the *blast* of factory whistles, the *patter* of children's feet, the *cries* of street vendors. Each season, each mood of nature is announced by its own special sounds. Humans also make their contributions in the complex sound combinations they evoke from musical instruments—from violin strings, organ pipes, drumheads, and from their own vocal cords.

This chapter is the story of sounds. It is the story of how sounds are made, how sounds differ, how they travel, how they are detected, and how they may be controlled.

WHAT CAUSES SOUND?

Pluck a stretched rubber band and listen to its sound. Look at it and observe the rapid back-and-forth motion—its vibrations. When the vibrations stop, the sound stops.

Put your fingers on your throat and say "ah." Something inside is vibrating, something very much like the rubber bands. These vibrations are your vocal cords.

Place a thin plastic ruler across the edge of a table so that about half of it protrudes. Hold it down firmly, with one hand placed just inside the edge of the table. Slap it lightly with the other hand. Hear, feel, and see the vibrations.

Whenever a sound is produced, something is quivering, trembling, shaking back and forth—vibrating. That something may be a string, a membrane, a reed, a column of air. It may originate in an insect's wings, a ticking clock, an animal's throat, a tuba's horn, or a thunderbolt.

HOW IS SOUND CARRIED?

A tree crashes in a far-off forest. No human, no animal is present to hear the crash. Was a sound produced? The answer depends on our definition of sound. If sound is defined only as that which is heard, then no sound was produced. If sound is defined as a certain kind of vibration, then sound was produced, whether it reached the ears of a living thing or not (see pp. 579–581).

Sounds from crashing trees or vibrating violins or people's throats usually reach our ears through the air. Just how do sounds travel?

Consider a bell ringing from the impact of its clapper. As the bell vibrates, it imparts its trembling motion to the air particles—molecules—immediately around it. These molecules, in turn, pass the vibratory motion to the air molecules adjacent to them, and so on. In this way the vibration travels outward in all directions from its source. A small part of the air wave strikes a little membrane in your ear, your eardrum, and starts it trembling in the same way that the bell was trembling. A vibration originating in a bell has

A tinkling bell starts a sound wave of condensation (air particles jammed together) and rarefaction (air particles spread apart). The wave moves away from the bell in all directions.

been transferred to the air molecules and from air molecules to your eardrum. Later we shall see how we become aware of the sound.

Sound Waves

A *sound wave* set in motion by a bell has reached our ears. The only thing that has traveled is a vibratory motion; the sensation the sound evokes within us is quite another thing. A sound wave is often compared to what happens when a pebble is dropped into a quiet pond. A wave spreads outward until it strikes the edge of the pond.

So, when we say that sound is traveling through the air we really mean that a certain kind of wave is proceeding through the air. This may be compared to what happens when a police officer tries to hold back a curious crowd. As the officer pushes against nearby individuals they are forced back. In turn, they force those behind them back, and so on over an ever-widening area. Each individual may have taken only one step backward, but the wave of "compression" has traveled many feet through the crowd.

In a sound wave the particles of air between the sounding object and your eardrum move back and forth only a tiny distance. Each impulse started by a vibrating object, such as a violin string,

begins a wave in which air particles are successfully jammed together and then spread apart. The part of the wave in which the particles are compressed together is called a *condensation;* the part in which they are farthest apart is called a *rarefaction.*

A Medium for Sound

Astronauts on the moon had to communicate with each other by radio, for there is no air there. In a classic demonstration in physics, the air is pumped out of a jar in which a ringing alarm clock is suspended. As the air is gradually exhausted from the jar, the sound gets fainter and fainter until it cannot be heard, although the clapper of the bell is seen moving. As air is admitted into the jar, the alarm is heard again.

Gases such as air are not the only medium for the transmission of sound. When two stones are clapped together under water, divers many feet away can hear the sound through the water. American Indians put their ears to the ground to hear the sound of far-off hoofbeats. The rumbling of a train many miles away can be detected by placing one's ear against the train rail. These illustrations show that sound travels well through liquids and solids.

THE SPEED OF SOUND

A flash of lightning is seen several seconds before the crash of thunder is heard, although both occur at the same time. The sound of a woodcutter's ax reaches a distant observer's ears after the ax is seen striking the wood (see p. 581). These and many other observations and experiments make it apparent that it takes time for sound to travel from the sounding object to our ears, certainly much more time than light takes to reach our eyes.

The speed of sound through air was determined by the Dutch scientists Moll and Van Beek in 1832. Two high hills 11 miles (18 kilometers) apart were used for this experiment. A cannon on one of the hills was fired. An observer on the other hill noted the flash of fire (the experiment was done at night to make it more visible) and then counted the number of seconds until he heard the report. The experiment was repeated a number of times. It was also checked by firing a cannon on the opposite hill, to cancel any error that might have been caused by the wind. From this experiment the average speed of sound was calculated to be about 1,100 feet (335 meters) per second. (In the experiments, it was assumed that light travels instantaneously. Actually, light travels at the rate of about 186,000 *miles*—300,000 *kilometers*—per second; this obviously would not affect the interpretation of the results of the experiment appreciably.)

Careful observations have shown that speed of sound through the air is 1,090 feet (332 meters) per second when the temperature is 32°F (0°C). At temperatures higher than 32°F (0°C) sound travels faster; and at lower temperatures it travels more slowly. An easy way of remembering the speed of sound is to consider that it takes sound about five seconds to travel 1 mile (or three seconds to travel a kilometer). In Chapter 9A this fact is used to provide a method for determining the distance of a lightning flash from an observer.

Sound travels more quickly through liquids and solids than through air; it travels about 4 times as fast through water, about 10 times as fast through pine wood, and about 17 times as fast through steel.

SOUND BOUNCES

Echoes

Have you ever heard your voice come back to you as an echo from a cliff, a building, or a hill? An echo is heard because sound bounces off these structures, just as a ball bounces off a wall. An echo also resembles the reflection of light from a mirror. An echo is a sound reflection.

Echoes are heard as separate sounds only if they reach the listener 1/10 second or more after the original sound. It takes at least that time for the human ear to separate one sound from another. If you want to hear your echo you must stand at least 55 feet (16.75 meters) away from the reflecting wall. If you shout against a cliff 55 feet (16.75 meters) away the sound will travel 55 feet (16.75 meters) to the cliff and bounce 55 feet (16.75 meters) back to you, a total distance of 110 feet (33.5 meters). Sound travels about 1,100 feet (335 meters) per second, so it can make this trip in 1/10 second. The echo will reach your ear 1/10 second after you hear your original voice. You will, therefore *just* be able to distinguish it as an echo.

If, on the other hand, the reflecting wall is only 11 feet (3.35 meters) away, as it might be in your living room, the sound bounces back too fast, taking only 1/50 second for the trip. In this case the sound reflection, known as *reverberation,* only prolongs the original sound; it is not detected as an echo.

An echo may interfere seriously with hearing, particularly in a large gymnasium or in an auditorium. The echoes overlap the words of the speaker in such a way as to cause confusion. This difficulty may be overcome by using sound-deadening materials for the walls, ceilings, and floors. Soft materials, such as canvas, curtains, soft wallboards, and rugs, absorb sound waves and reflect little sound. Auditoriums often have softwood walls for this reason. Restaurants, broadcasting and television studios, and rooms in schools and homes are also soundproofed to eliminate echoes and excessive reverberations of sound waves.

Concentrating Sound

Sound waves may be reflected from curved surfaces and concentrated in such a way as to increase audibility. Large auditoriums often have stages that are curved at the back like the reflector in an automobile headlight. Sound waves strike the curved surface and are reflected out into the auditorium.

Cheerleaders often use megaphones to shout directions to their "rooters." Megaphones, like band shells, permit sound to go out in only one direction. The energy is thus concentrated rather than dissipated over a wide space.

Before electronic hearing aids were common, partially deaf people used ear trumpets, which are essentially megaphones used in reverse. The large end gathers more sound waves than the ear alone could catch. Your outer ear is a sound catcher, although you could hear very well without it. If you cup your ears you collect more sound waves and thus convey their energy to your eardrums.

The stethoscope is used by physicians to detect heart and other internal sounds that furnish clues to the condition of the body. The end of this instrument, which is placed against the patient, contains a diaphragm that is much larger than the human eardrum and consequently collects more sound energy. The tubing of the stethoscope channels the sound to the doctor's ears without much loss.

CHARACTERISTICS OF SOUND

How do we distinguish among the many sounds that we hear when, for example, we listen to a full orchestra playing a symphony? There are three characteristics by which we identify sounds: loudness, pitch, and quality. All of these have to do with the nature of the vibrations that are producing the sound waves.

We have compared a sound wave to a water wave. Let us identify some of the general characteristics of all regular waves. The distance between two adjacent wave crests is known as the *wavelength*. The number of waves that pass any point in a given period of time is known as the *frequency*. The height of a wave over the original undisturbed surface of the body of water is the *amplitude*. (When oceanographers refer to wave height, however, they measure the distance from trough, the lowest point, to crest, the highest point.)

Wavelength and frequency are related phenomena. If you drop one pebble in the middle of the pond every 10 seconds, you will start a series of waves that will reach the shore 10 seconds apart. The frequency is 6 waves per minute. Let us assume that in this case the distance between every wave crest, the wavelength, is 12 feet. If you now drop a pebble in every 5 seconds, one wave will reach the shore every 5 seconds. The frequency then is 12 waves per minute. However, the distance between the wave crests, the wavelength, is shorter—only 6 feet in length. In other words, the greater the frequency, the shorter the wavelength. Or, in simple beachcomber language, the more waves, the less distance between them. These characteristics of water waves apply to all regular waves, such as radio waves, light waves, and sound waves.

Loudness

It is obvious that when the tympanist strikes the drum hard, a louder sound is produced than when it is tapped gently. A powerful stroke causes the drumhead, and consequently the particles of air next to it, to move back and forth for a greater distance than does the gentle stroke. In terms of the sound wave the amplitude is greater. A powerful wave travels from the drum to you, making your eardrums vibrate back and forth vigorously. The loudness of the sound you hear depends, then, on how far the sound waves make your ear-

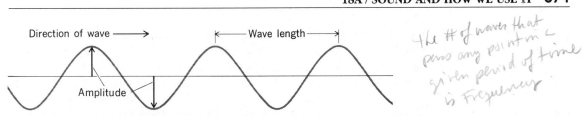

Direction of wave ⟶ |← Wave length →|

[handwritten: the # of waves that pass any point in a given period of time is Frequency]

Amplitude

Representation of a sound wave. The amplitude, or height of the crests above or below the baseline, determines the loudness of the sound. The wavelength determines the pitch of the sound: the longer the wave length, the lower the pitch.

drums move in and out. In a literal sense the tympanist "has your ear."

Loudness depends also on the distance of the listener from the source of the sound. If sound waves were visible, a sounding drum would be seen to be in the center of a series of concentric spheres, each sphere representing a compression of air particles. We recall that sound is a form of energy. The energy in this instance is first imparted to the drumhead by the tympanist, and then by the drumhead to the surrounding air. As the sound wave advances from sphere to sphere the energy is "spent" in setting more and more air particles in motion. The loudness or volume decreases with distance. In an auditorium this loss is partially compensated for by the reflection and concentration of sound by the sides, back, and top of the hall.

The crashing of cymbals starts a large wave moving across a concert hall. The strings of a piano, on the other hand, are not large enough to cause very much of a "splash" in the air. To make their sounds louder, the strings are connected to a sounding board, which is set vibrating by the strings connected to it. Its broad area permits it to set a large amount of air into motion at any given moment. The same principle applies to the violin, cello, and all other stringed instruments.

To demonstrate this principle, rap the prongs of a tuning fork against the heel of your shoe and listen for the sound. Do this again, but this time press the end of the handle against a wooden table. The sound is louder because the fork's vibration is transmitted to the table, which, in turn,

causes a large amount of air surrounding it to begin vibrating.

The loudness of a sound may be measured by means of a sound-level meter. The unit for measuring sound is the *decibel* ("bel" from Alexander Graham Bell). The rustling leaves in a light breeze have a rating of about 10 decibels; sound within the average home about 20 decibels; traffic at a busy intersection about 55 decibels; a machine shop 100 decibels; a plane taking off 110 decibels; and very loud thunder 120 decibels. At 120 decibels sounds become physically painful. Continuous noise above 150 decibels is thought to be harmful to a person's emotional well-being. The problem of "noise pollution" in modern life is one that is compelling more and more attention.

Loud sounds are not universally disliked. Most young people eagerly attend a pop music concert that produces sound intensity levels in excess of 110 decibels. The audience is not immune from the risk of hearing impairment, but the band members are almost certain to sustain permanent hearing loss due to greater exposure time and closeness to the speakers.

Pitch *[handwritten: = Frequency]*

If sound is compared to an ocean wave, then loudness, as we have seen, is associated with the *height,* or amplitude, of the wave. Pitch, by the same analogy, is a characteristic determined by the frequency, the *number* of waves that pass a point in a given period of time. In the science of sound we say that pitch depends on the number of vibrations per second made by the vibrating body. By definition one vibration, sometimes called a *cycle,* includes both the backward and forward motion of the vibrating body. (The international unit for frequency is the Hertz (H_z), defined as one cycle per second.)

If you draw your fingernail over the back of a linen-covered book the nail will produce a sound because it is being vibrated by the many little ridges in the cloth. As you increase the speed with which you move your finger the pitch increases to higher and higher tones. The pitch of the note depends on the rapidity with which your nail is quivering, that is, the frequency of its vibrations. Few vibrations per second produce a low tone; many vibrations per second a high tone.

The ear of a human being is able to pick up vibrations ranging from 16 to 20,000 vibrations per second (children exceed this upper limit), with the greatest sensitivity around 1,000 to 5,000 vibrations per second. It is no accident that sirens and emergency vehicles' horns are pitched near these frequencies. Insects and other animals may detect sounds that humans cannot. Special dog whistles produce a high-pitched *ultrasonic* sound that is audible to dogs but not to human beings.

There is quite a range of pitch represented in an orchestra. *A* above middle *C* of a piano should vibrate 440 times per second, if the piano is in tune. The scales used by musicians are based on this frequency. Some of the high piano strings vibrate 3,500 times per second. An organ can produce a frequency as low as 16 vibrations per second (see pp. 580–581).

How are sounds of different pitch produced in string instruments? If you look inside a piano you will see that three factors are responsible for the difference in pitch of the various strings: length, weight per unit of length (which depends on the thickness and the material used), and tightness. Low notes are produced by long, heavy, loose strings; high notes by short, light, more tightly stretched strings. In general, a long string (or a heavy or loose one) vibrates slowly; consequently a low-pitched note is produced. A short string (or a light or more tightly stretched one) vibrates rapidly, producing a high-pitched sound.

In wind instruments the air in the instrument is made to vibrate by a player either with pursed lips, or by blowing along a reed that periodically interrupts the flow of air. Here the pitch is determined principally by the length of the column of air producing the sound. Different pitches are obtained by changing the length of the air column. Shorter air columns produce higher-pitched sounds; longer columns, lower-pitched sounds.

Quality

As we listen to a symphony orchestra we are aware not only of pitch and loudness but also of the quality of the sound of different instruments. The oboe sounds different from the clarinet; the bassoon different from the violin. How are the differences in quality produced?

We recall that loudness depends on the strength and that pitch depends on the frequency of the sound wave. Quality depends on the "shape" imposed on the sound waves by the *overtones.* The production of overtones can be demonstrated by a simple experiment.

If you stretch a guitar string between two screws that are firmly set in a board, and pluck the string, it will vibrate throughout its entire length, producing a musical tone. This, the lowest tone that the string is capable of producing, is called its *fundamental.* If you now press down the middle of the string tightly with one finger and pluck either half string, that part will vibrate to produce a tone one octave higher than when the whole string vibrates. This note is called the *first overtone.* Now, if you remove your finger quickly while half of the string is vibrating, the string will vibrate not only in half its length but also as a whole—*at the same time.* You then should hear two sounds—the note made by the string vibrating as a whole and the note made by the string vibrating in half its length.

If you now place your finger one third of the

way from the end of the string (at either end) and hold it down, plucking this third of the string will produce a note higher than the first overtone. This is the *second overtone*. Many other overtones are possible.

In the playing of musical instruments a large number of overtones are produced simultaneously with the fundamental tone. The number and intensity of the overtones are different in different instruments. Thus, *A flat* on a clarinet sounds different from *A flat* on a violin. In singing or speaking, some individuals are able to produce more overtones than others. They can do this in part because they are skilled in controlling their voices. The number of overtones given off by a violin and by other musical instruments depends on their construction, as well as on the skill of the musician (see pp. 581–582).

The difference in character of two tones of the same pitch and loudness is due, then, to the difference in the relative prominence of the fundamental and the various overtones.

SYMPATHETIC VIBRATIONS

It is possible for one vibrating object to make another object vibrate without touching it. If you open a piano, press down on the damper pedal to remove the damper from the strings, and sing into the strings you will hear some of the strings sing back faintly. Which strings? Those in tune with the pitch of your voice, with its fundamental tone and overtones. We call this a *sympathetic vibration*. If you sing at a different pitch, different strings will be set into sympathetic vibration. By feeling the strings you can find the ones that are vibrating.

Each sounding object has a natural frequency of vibration. If sound waves of that note strike it, it will respond sympathetically. Some singers are reputed to be able to shatter fine crystal glass by singing loudly into it at its natural pitch.

Why does a seashell held to the ear seem to have the "sound of the sea" in it? The air in the seashell reinforces the slight sounds that are present in the environment by vibrating sympathetically with those in tune with it. The sound waves are bounced back and forth in such a manner that the reflections from the wall of the seashell add up and strengthen the sound. These sounds are not the sounds of the sea unless you are listening to the seashell on the seashore. This quality of responding sympathetically to certain sounds and reinforcing those sounds is called *resonance*.

The human voice, produced by the tiny vibrations of the vocal cords, is reinforced by the sympathetic vibration of air in the throat, mouth, and nose, and is thus given its resonant quality, allowing people to hear us speak and sing. You can note the effect of the nasal cavity on this resonance by singing a single note while alternately squeezing and releasing your nose.

HOW WE SPEAK

Like all other sounds, speech is produced by vibrations. Stretched across the inside of the voice box, or *larynx*, are two folds of tissue called the vocal cords. It is the vocal cords that vibrate when we speak. The cords are elastic fibers that can be stretched and relaxed by the action of muscles in the voice box. You can illustrate the way that sound is produced by blowing upon the edges of a wide rubber band, stretched around two separated pencils so that the band's two segments are close together.

All the air that is breathed in and out passes through the voice box. Ordinarily, the vocal cords are relaxed on the two sides of the voice box. The air passes in and out between the vocal cords without producing sound. When you talk or sing, your brain sends messages along the nerves to the muscles controlling the vocal cords. The muscles pull the vocal cords together so that there is only a narrow slit between the cords, like that between the edges of the wide rubber band that you stretched. As the diaphragm and chest muscles force air out of the lungs, the air makes the vocal cords vibrate. The pitch of the sound is controlled by making the vocal cords tighter or looser.

The natural range of pitch of the voice is determined by the length of the vocal cords. Women have higher-pitched voices than men because their vocal cords are shorter. Children's voices are higher than those of adults for the same reason.

The voice box is not the only part assisting in the making of speech. The lips, tongue, teeth, palate, and mouth help in the formation of spoken sounds. When we whisper, the sounds are produced by placing the mouth and tongue in the required positions without vibrating the vocal cords.

The quality of the human voice depends on the many spaces that resonate sympathetically with the vocal cords. These include the sinuses, the nasal cavities, the mouth, throat, windpipe, and lungs, as well as the voice box itself. Scientists have analyzed voice quality electronically and have determined that individual voice "prints" are every bit as personal to you as your fingerprints. We now are developing door locks and robots that will respond only to your voice!

HOW WE HEAR

The ear is essentially a mechanism for the reception of sound waves and for the conversion of sound waves into nerve impulses. The ear consists of three parts: the outer ear, the middle ear, and the inner ear. The outer ear collects air vibrations; the middle ear amplifies them and passes them along to the inner ear; the inner ear changes the vibrations into nerve messages. The explanation that follows will be easier to understand if frequent reference is made to the illustration on this page.

Outer Ear

The outer ear is composed of a shell of flexible cartilage and skin attached to the side of the head, leading to a canal that funnels inward. The outer ear acts on the principle of a hearing tube; that is, it collects and concentrates sound waves and conducts them, so that they strike against the eardrum. In humans the value of this is slight; we can hear almost as well without the outer ear. In many animals, however, the external ear can be turned toward the source of the sound and can play an important function in collecting sound waves.

The *eardrum* is set obliquely across the auditory canal, thereby providing a greater surface for receiving vibrations than if it were stretched squarely across it. It is a wonderfully designed membrane, with many delicate fibers running in

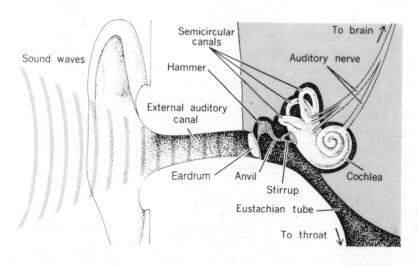

The delicate mechanism of the ear is shown here. Can you describe how the parts function in the process of hearing?

concentric circles around it to make it elastic and springy, and with coarse fibers arranged like the ribs of an umbrella to give it strength.

Middle Ear

Within the middle ear is a chain of three little bones. The outer one, called the *hammer,* is attached to the eardrum. The hammer is connected by means of a joint to the bone called the *anvil.* This, in turn, is jointed to the *stirrup.* The footplate of the stirrup rests against the *oval window* of the inner ear.

The three bones act as levers, magnifying about twenty-two-fold the strength of the initial vibration received by the eardrum. This strengthened impulse is conveyed to the membrane covering the oval window.

Before ending our discussion of the middle ear we should mention the *Eustachian tube,* which connects the middle ear to the throat. The purpose of this tube is to permit the equalization of pressure on both sides of the eardrum. If, for example, you ascend in an elevator the pressure on the outside of the eardrum decreases with altitude. The air inside the middle ear tends to push the eardrum outward. However, some of the air escapes through the Eustachian tube into the throat, thereby equalizing the pressure on the eardrum. Chewing or swallowing helps clear the air pressure because it opens the end of the Eustachian tube near the throat. (This is why flight attendants sometimes distribute gum when the pressure is being changed in the plane cabin.) When you descend in an elevator the pressure increases; the Eustachian tube permits air to flow from the throat *into* the middle ear.

Inner Ear

The inner ear is composed of the *cochlea* and the *semicircular canals.* Only the cochlea will be discussed here, because it is the auditory sense organ. (The canal apparatus is concerned with balance and with the sense of position. It is discussed

in Chapter 11A). The cochlea is a small snail-shaped structure with $2\frac{1}{2}$ turns in it. It is filled with lymph, a fluid resembling blood except that it has no red blood cells in it. The sound waves from the eardrum are transmitted by the three bones in the middle ear to the fluid in the cochlea. Running through the cochlea is the important *basilar membrane,* upon which is a structure containing 24,000 *hair cells.* These cells are thought to be the true receptors of hearing.

Thousands of sensory nerve fibers are connected to the hair cells. These fibers join to form the auditory nerve, which leads from the cochlea to the brain. By a number of complex mechanisms not fully understood, sound waves in the fluid of the cochlea are converted into electrical energy that triggers nerve impulses in the nerve fibers. These impulses travel along the auditory nerve to the brain, where they are perceived as sounds of varying pitch, loudness, and quality.

To sum up our discussion of how we hear: Sound waves pass from the eardrum to the three bones, then to the cochlea where they initiate nerve impulses, which are then transmitted to the brain.

IMPORTANT GENERALIZATIONS

Sounds arise from vibrations.

Sound vibrations travel in a wave motion in all directions from their source.

Sound vibrations travel through gases, liquids, and solids.

Sound travels through the air at the rate of about 1,100 feet (335 meters) per second.

An echo is a reflected sound.

Porous, soft materials are good sound absorbers.

Waves, such as those of sound, are characterized by their wavelength, frequency, and amplitude.

Sounds are characterized by their loudness, pitch, and quality.

Loudness depends on the amplitude of the sound wave.

Pitch depends on the frequency, the number of vibrations per second.

Sounds cause our eardrums to vibrate.

The inner ear converts sound vibrations into nerve impulses.

DISCOVERING FOR YOURSELF

1. Listen for sounds in your environment. Make a list of the things that make the sound. Explain what causes each sound to change in loudness and pitch.

2. Observe the inside of a piano to discover how sounds are made, how pitch is determined, how loudness is controlled, what the sounding board does, how the piano is tuned.

3. Devise some original experiments to show that some substances carry sound better than others.

4. Perform a demonstration to show that sound travels more slowly than light.

5. Examine a variety of musical instruments to see how they make sounds and how pitch and loudness are controlled.

6. Examine a hearing aid to see how it works.

7. Find out what a decibel is, and what the terms *ultrasonic* and *supersonic* mean.

8. Find out what some cities and institutions do to reduce noise.

9. Try to obtain a model of the human ear and explain how it works.

10. Examine an old phonograph record (78 rpm) with a 10-power magnifying glass. See if you can find the waves in the grooves that produce sound. Do the waves differ in length and height? How would such variations affect the sound?

11. Find out how fathometers and sonar are used to measure the depth of water.

12. Try to demonstrate and explain echoes.

13. Make and use a megaphone. How does the megaphone affect sound? How can you prove this?

14. Make a survey of your community for sound pollution and try to find out what, if anything, is being done to reduce the noise level.

TEACHING "SOUND AND HOW WE USE IT"

Children are stimulated, mystified, informed, and delighted by many sounds. Capitalize on their fascination and experiences to teach them some of the important principles of sound—its production and nature, and its control. Children can make and experiment with toy xylophones, for example, and discover the relationship between high and low tones (pitch) and the length of the bars. They can make a string "telephone" from two paper cups and a length of string to find out how sound travels. There are many opportunities to use the senses for discovering that sound is associated with vibration.

Children's interest in the musical instruments that they or their classmates play and in the recordings they listen to can be extended to the understanding of the science of sound. "The study of sound offers an opportunity to emphasize an interdisciplinary approach between science and music."[1]

SOME BROAD CONCEPTS

Sounds are caused by vibrations.
Sounds travel in all directions from their source.
Sounds travel in waves.
Sounds travel through gases, liquids, and solids.
Some materials (soft, rough) absorb sounds.
Some materials (hard, smooth) reflect sound.
Sounds have loudness, pitch, and quality.
Sounds cause the eardrum to vibrate.

FOR YOUNGER CHILDREN[2]

What Sounds Are Around Us?

Listening is an obvious way to interest children in the sounds around them and to make them aware of the number and variety of sounds in their en-

vironment. Start by sitting quietly and listening in the classroom. List the sounds heard and then take a walk through the school and outdoors to add to the list. Encourage children to add sounds they hear at home in various places indoors and out.

Encourage them to listen to animal sounds—insects, birds, and others. They may devise a game centered around listening to sounds made by the teacher or other children behind a screen and trying to guess what made the sound.

Let children try to describe the sounds they hear and tell how they are alike and different from each other. Classify the sounds as (1) high and low, (2) loud and soft, (3) pleasant and unpleasant. They may also classify sounds according to (1) those that warn us of danger (auto horns), (2) those that give us pleasure (musical instruments), (3) night sounds, (4) those that give us signals, and so on. Tap different objects in the classroom and listen to the sound. Listen to various toys that make sound (drums, whistles, and others). Try to feel the vibrations.

Our main objective in the activities just described is to make children aware of the many sounds around them, and to help them identify differences in these sounds and to discover what made the sounds.

How Do Musical Instruments Make Sounds?[3]

Assemble several instruments that children can bring and those available in school such as triangle, drum, piano, bells, cymbals. Studying them involves using the senses of touch and sight as well as hearing. Feel the various instruments as they make sounds. Use a magnifying glass to try to see strings that are making sounds. Use the result to direct children's attention to "What makes the sound?" "Can you describe what happens?" "How can you stop the sound?"

[1]K. Williams, A. Williams, and W. Stacey, "Physical and Musical Vibrating Systems," *Science and Children* (January 1981).

[2]M. McIntyre, "The Sound of Music," *Science and Children* (February 1981). Musical instruments for young children. D. Janke, "The Sounds of Music in the Science Classroom," *Science and Children* (May 1982).

[3]K. Lind, "The Beat of the Band," *Science and Children* (November/December 1985) and "The Beat Goes On" (April 1986). Making and using musical instruments. D. Knight, *All About Sound,* (Mahwah, N.J.: Troll, 1983).

What happens when you cover the openings? Through experiences with various musical instruments, children are introduced to many of the concepts of making and controlling sound. (*Courtesy of Abby Bergman.*)

How Are Sounds Different from Each Other?

From the experience children have had in listening to sounds, describing them, and learning what causes them they should come to realize that sounds differ in pitch, intensity, and quality. Let them try to make and identify high and low sounds, loud and soft sounds, and pleasant and unpleasant ones. Ask, "Can you tell why these sounds differ from each other?" Use the wooden chalk box described on page 580, some stringed instruments, or any other easily observed sound-maker that will demonstrate sound characteristics. Let the children use these things to make different sounds, and try to observe what happens when sounds are made. Not all young children will be able to associate the characteristics of sound with the vibrations that produce them.

Other Problems for Younger Children

1. What sounds do toys make and how are these sounds different from each other?
2. How does the wind make different sounds?
3. How can we use bottles to make different sounds?
4. Will a meter (or yard) stick carry sound?
5. How can we make a string telephone? (See p. 581.)
6. How do bells and horns make sounds?

FOR OLDER CHILDREN

What Causes Sound?

Many experiences will help students to understand that sound is caused by vibration. One involves the use of a triangle, which may be obtained from a kindergarten. Strike the triangle to make it vibrate. Listen to the sound. Touch the triangle. What happens? Thrust the triangle into water after it has been struck. Describe what happens. The waves are caused by the vibrations. (Tuning forks may be used for this experience if they are available. They may be ordered from scientific supply houses. Some music teachers have small tuning forks.) Touch the vibrating triangle or tuning fork with the fingertips. "What do you feel?"

Ask students to suggest other ways of showing that vibrations cause sound. Ask them to *compare* what they hear, to *predict* what will happen under different circumstances, and try to *make interpretations* of their experiences. Here are some possibilities: Stretch a rubber band; pluck it; listen to it; stop it from vibrating; listen again. This may also be done with a violin string. Touch a piano or radio while it is playing to feel the vibration; then stop the sound. Hold the fingers against the throat while making a sound; stop the sound and feel the throat.

After several such experiences students may *tentatively* conclude that "all sound is caused by vibration." This conclusion can then be checked by reading and investigating further.

After they have tried to decide in each case what vibrates to produce the sounds, several students may, one at a time, make the sounds again, and the class can be asked to tell how these sounds differ from each other. Students will discover that sounds differ in loudness, pitch, and quality, although they will not necessarily state their observations in these terms. This will lead to the problem of why sounds differ from one another.

How Can We Make High and Low Sounds?[4]

An empty wooden chalk box or cigar box and some rubber bands can be used to make high and low sounds and to demonstrate how these are made (see Chapter 18A, p. 572). Stretch a rubber

[4]C. R. Coble and D. R. Rice, "Bottle Music," *Science and Children* (January 1981). K. Brand, *Sound* (Mahwah, N.J.: Troll, 1985).

band across the opening of the box and pluck it. (Thumbtacks can be placed at different distances down the sides of the box to hold the bands as they are stretched tighter.) Listen to the sound; keep on tightening the rubber band and plucking it. Ask students to try to interpret. Now stretch a wide and a narrow rubber band across the box about equally tight; pluck each and listen to the sound. Increase the tension of both and listen to each. Again urge students to interpret and try to classify the sounds that are made (high, medium, low).

From these experiences students begin to realize that the more tightly the bands are stretched, the higher the pitch, and that thin bands produce a higher pitch than thick ones. If they watch the bands carefully they may be able to see that this difference is due to the speed of vibration. The use of a flexible ruler, as suggested on page 567, will also serve to show students the relationship between speed of vibration and pitch. Urge students to find other examples showing these ideas. The thick bands and the loosely stretched ones vibrate so slowly that they can be seen moving back and forth, whereas in the thin and tightly stretched bands the vibrations are too fast to be seen. (See also the later section on musical instruments.)

An index card makes a sound if it is drawn across the teeth of a comb. The faster the card is moved, the higher the pitch. Why?

Principles of sound can also be observed on a guitar. In many classes one or more of the students take music lessons, or at least have an instrument available. Let students predict (on the basis of what they have learned) how they think the instrument is built to (1) make sounds, (2) make sounds of different pitch. Students notice the effect of stretching and loosening the strings, and they hear the difference between the sounds of thick strings and those of thin ones. They can also see the effect of the length of the string on pitch. Pressing down on the string keeps part of it from vibrating. Consequently, they can see that the shorter the string the higher its pitch, and that long strings make sounds of lower pitch. Students can examine other stringed instruments (violin, cello, and others), and describe how they make sounds, predict from their observations what the differences in pitch will be among strings of different lengths and thicknesses, and interpret what they have observed.

How Does Sound Travel?

If there is a place in the school where metal pipes go from one floor to the next students can learn how sound travels through metal by noting that sound (made by tapping the pipe) will travel along the pipe from one floor to another.

There are many experiences that help children see that some things carry sound better than others. For example, if one child strikes a tuning fork at one end of a table and holds it in the air, children at the other end of the table may not hear it. Ask, "Could we do something to make it possible to hear the sound at this distance?" If the child sets the stem of the vibrating tuning fork on the table and the other children put their ears down to the table they can easily hear the sound. They can experiment to see which carries the sound of a tuning fork better, a yardstick or a necktie or another long piece of cloth. A long window pole may be used to demonstrate how solids carry sound by striking a tuning fork and then touching its base to one end of the pole while a student places his or her ear at the other. This can also be done by scratching one end of the pole with a fingernail and listening at the other. Many children may have had the experience of hearing sounds under water, when a friend claps two stones together under the surface (see Chapter 18A, p. 568).

An interesting way to learn more about how sound travels is through a paper cup telephone. This does not operate on the same principle as a real telephone, but it serves to show how vibrations from the human voice can be transmitted along a wire or string from one place to another.

To make the telephone, assemble two sturdy paper cups, two buttons, and 15 or 20 feet of string. Punch a small hole in the center of the bottom of each cup. Thread one end of the string through this hole to the inside of each cup and tie it to the button. The telephone is used by two students standing far enough from each other to pull the string taut. One speaks into the cup, holding it close around his or her mouth. The other holds the cup to his or her ear. In answering, the process is reversed. Children may try different materials and variations of the cups to see if any of the variations make a difference (large or small cups, wire or string, and so on).

In summary, various experiences and experiments should develop the concept that sound travels through air (you hear voices); through solids (tuning fork and table; string and paper cup telephone); and through liquids (under water in a swimming pool).

Does It Take Time for Sound To Travel?

Let a student carry a large drum or something else that will make a sound a block or so away from the rest of the class. When he or she strikes the drum with a broad gesture that can be seen at a distance, students will observe that they do not hear the sound until the drummer's arm is ready to strike the drum another time. They see the drummer because light travels from the student to them. They hear the drum because sound travels from the drum to them. But the sound travels very slowly compared with the light. Students may recall that they have watched a man hammering on a roof in the distance and heard the sound when the hammer was already in the air ready to hit the nail again, or that they see lightning before they hear the thunder even though both occur simultaneously.

Interested students may wish to find out about and report on how the speed of sound was determined by the Dutch scientists (see p. 569).

How Do Musical Instruments Make Sound?

Many students take music lessons. It is appropriate to apply the facts and principles they have learned in science to the instruments they play. Students who have had instructions from their music teachers about how the instrument produces sounds can demonstrate for the class (see Chapter 18A, pp. 570–573).

As the musical instruments are demonstrated, students can observe and listen to discover what vibrates to make the sound, how the sounds are varied in pitch and loudness, and what influences the quality of the sound produced. For demonstration purposes students can play a scale.

Many students have never seen the inside of a piano. The piano boards are not difficult to remove and the strings and hammers are easy to observe. The three observations suggested in the preceding paragraph are as appropriate for learning about the piano as they are for the saxophone, cornet, violin, or any other instrument students are likely to bring in. A mouth organ is especially interesting to examine. If there is one available that is no longer usable the cover can be removed. Students can see the differences in the reeds.

If there is a music teacher in the school or in the community he or she will be able to contribute information that will not only help students to understand the instruments but will enrich their study of sound.

Other Problems for Older Children

1. How are rooms made more soundproof?
2. How does a megaphone direct sound?
3. What are sympathetic vibrations?
4. How can flowerpot chimes, a xylophone, and a drinking glass scale be made?
5. How do we make sounds with our voice box?
6. How do we hear sounds?
7. How are echoes made?
8. How does a phonograph record produce sound?
9. How does sonar work?
10. How do insects make sound?

11. What can we find out about noise pollution?
12. How does a dog whistle work?
13. How does a stethoscope work?
14. How are sounds recorded on magnetic tape?
15. How are bats able to fly in total darkness without striking objects?

RESOURCES TO INVESTIGATE WITH CHILDREN

1. The local movie theater and other public buildings, to see how soundproofing and other sound controls are accomplished.
2. The school custodian, to learn about soundproofing in the school auditorium and elsewhere in the building.
3. Music teachers, to show various musical instruments and explain how they produce and control sounds.
4. A music store, to see and examine instruments and hear about how they produce and control sound.
5. A speech teacher, to explain how we produce and control sound and how voices can be improved.
6. A builders' supply company, to obtain samples of soundproofing materials.

PREPARING TO TEACH

1. Assemble and test materials that children can use to help them learn how sounds can be changed in pitch, loudness, and quality. Work out a plan for using these.
2. Try some of the activities suggested in "Discovering for Yourself" at the end of Chapter 18A.
3. Obtain or make a tape recording of sounds produced by different musical instruments. Plan how you would use them to introduce the topic of sound.
4. Obtain a recording of different bird sounds and plan how you would use these to stimulate an interest in bird identification.
5. Prepare a list of individual investigations that interested children might carry out and report on for their classmates, or use in a science fair.

LIGHT AND
HOW WE USE IT

Colours in the Object are nothing more but a Disposition to reflect this or that sort of Rays more copiously than the rest.

SIR ISAAC NEWTON, 1704

The light in the world comes principally from two sources—the sun, and the student's lamp.

BOVEE, 1842

What would the world look like if I rode on a beam of light?

ALBERT EINSTEIN IN HIS TEENS

1:30 seconds

A WORLD OF LIGHT

A beam of light originating in the excited atoms of the sun starts on its way to the earth. Eight minutes and 93 million miles (150 million kilometers) later it reaches the sidewalk outside your home. A child races through the steady stream of light, interrupts it momentarily, and causes a shadow to fall on the walk. Some of the light is reflected from the sunlight-bathed objects to your eyes, making it possible for you to see the scene outside your window.

Light is a messenger bringing us news of the universe. Light excites the most important sense, that of sight, initiating nerve impulses that our brain interprets as a distant star, a glorious sunset, a familiar face.

Light rules life. Plants and animals are governed by the rhythm of day and night. Sunlight provides the energy for the food-making process in green plants and consequently is essential for all life on our planet. The fossil fuels—coal, gas, and oil—have stored within them the energy that winged down from the sun millions of years ago. The cycle is complete when the fuels are burned: The sun energy locked in their molecules is liberated as heat and light.

LIGHT TRAVELS

One of the most important discoveries made concerning light is that it travels, racing through space at the rate of about 186,000 miles (300,000 kilo-

meters) per second. Nothing in our everyday experiences conveys this concept. When we pull up the shade of a darkened room light seems to fill it instantaneously. Distances on earth are too short for the travel time of light to make much difference. It does have significance, however, for the viewing of heavenly bodies: If the sun were suddenly to stop shining we would continue to see it for about eight minutes, for it takes that time for light to travel from the sun to the earth. Moonlight (which is really reflected sunlight) takes about $1\frac{1}{3}$ seconds to travel the 238,000 miles (383,000 kilometers) from the moon to the earth. Other interesting implications of the traveling of light through space are discussed in Chapter 8A: We learned there that the distance covered by the light in a year furnishes us with a yardstick, the light year, for measuring the universe.

WHAT IS LIGHT?

The nature of light has been the subject of controversy for many centuries. Plato and other ancient philosophers believed that light was a kind of emanation *from* the eye that made objects visible. Sir Isaac Newton proposed the corpuscular theory of light in 1700. He believed that light was a stream of particles or corpuscles shot off by a luminous body. At about the same time Christiaan Huygens, a Dutchman, countered with the theory that light was a vibration, a wave that rippled through space. Each of these theories, those of Newton and Huygens, explains some phenomena satisfactorily but not others. Einstein theorized that a beam of light is a shower of small packets of energy, which he called *photons*. At present we can at least agree to define light as the kind of energy that causes us to see.

SHADOWS

Perhaps the simplest picture that nature paints of an object is its shadow. We notice shadows most in the early morning or late afternoon, when opaque objects, such as trees or people, cast elongated silhouettes. A moment's consideration will show that the object is not really "casting" anything, instead it is blocking the sunlight, which, streaming past its edges, traces the form of the object on sidewalk or lawn (see pp. 600–601).

The earth, too, casts a shadow—into space. When the moon enters this cone-shaped shadow we have a lunar eclipse. When, on the other hand, the moon comes between the sun and the earth, its smaller shadow sweeps across the earth, and we have a solar eclipse.

Not all substances are *opaque* to light. Glass and some plastics are *transparent*: They both permit light to pass through and objects to be clearly seen. Our ancestors used oiled paper in their windows to permit light to enter their houses. Substances such as oiled paper or frosted glass, which allow some light to go through but through which objects cannot be clearly seen, are called *translucent*. In lighting our homes and schools we make use of various materials that transmit light differently.

SEEING THE THINGS AROUND US

A red rose in a glass vase is set on a white doily on a dark table—in a totally dark room. Your eyes are wide open, but you do not see any of these objects. Light a candle and they become visible. Why? (See diagram on p. 586.)

Light travels from the candle source to the petals and stem. Some of it is *absorbed* by the atoms of these plant structures, and some is *reflected* in various directions from the surface of the flower. Part of the reflected light enters your eye and causes an image to be formed in the back of the eye. This stimulates the nerve endings there to carry impulses to your brain, which interprets the impulses as a flower.

Although the flower reflects the candle *light* to your eye, you do not see the candle *flame* reflected as you would by a mirror. This is because the petals reflect light irregularly, in such a way as to reveal their own texture and shape rather than that of the candle. In other words, it is the *effect* of the surface texture on light that makes the object visible. A perfectly smooth reflecting surface would not be visible; the source of light rather than the surface would be seen. It would be a mirror.

Even if you put an opaque screen between the candle and the flower you would still see the flower, because some of the candlelight would be reflected from the walls and the ceiling to the vase. Light from the candle travels in all directions and is reflected in all directions.

The table appears darker to your eyes than the flower, the flower darker than the doily. Why? The atoms of the table surface *absorb* a good deal of the light (photons or waves) that strike them, and convert it into heat, emitted as infrared radiation which we cannot see (see pp. 595–596). Very little visible light is reflected to your eyes. The red flower absorbs some light but reflects more than the dark table does. The while doily reflects the most light, absorbing very little. Thus, the variation in brightness of different surfaces under equal illumination is due to the different amounts of light energy soaked up and "bounced off" by their constituent atoms.

Why do rose petals look red, the stem green? What makes an object have a color? To understand color we must know a little more about the nature of light itself. If a narrow beam of white light from the sun or from a lamp passes through a triangular glass prism a rainbow of colors appears on a screen or wall on the opposite side (see p. 587). The white light fans out to form a spectrum of red, orange, yellow, green, blue, and violet, in that

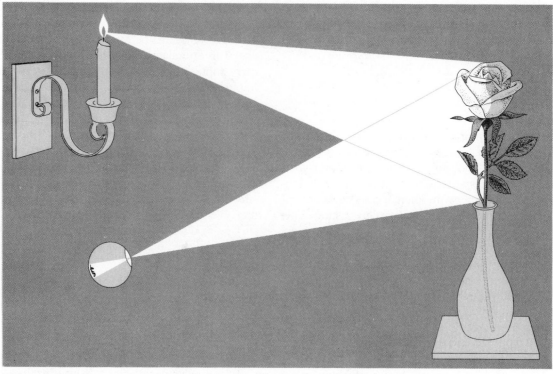

We see a rose because light travels to it and is reflected to our eyes.

order, each color merging imperceptibly into the next. White light, then, consists of a mixture of many colors. Sir Isaac Newton showed this in a simple but ingenious experiment using two prisms. A beam of white light was directed at the first prism and emerged on the opposite side as a spectrum of colors. Newton then placed the second prism, upside down with respect to the first, in the path of these colored rays. The rays joined in the second prism to form a spot of white light on a screen (see later discussion). White light can be separated into colors; these colors can combine to make white light. If, on the other hand, a narrow beam of green light was allowed to pass through a prism, it would emerge as green light.

The reason that we are discussing white light is that we live in a world that is bathed in it. The colors we see "in" objects (except for those that make their own light) are influenced by the fact that these objects are "painted" by a white light that is a combination of red, orange, yellow, green, blue, and violet.

To come back to the original question, why do the rose's petals appear red and the stem green? Bathed in white light the petals are receiving red, orange, yellow, green, blue, and violet rays. All of these are absorbed as energy into the atoms of the pigment of the petals *except the red ones*. This color is reflected; in your eye it stimulates certain nerve endings resulting in the sensation of red. In other words, the color of an opaque object is determined by the kind of light it does *not* absorb, by the kind that bounces off it. *The red you see "in" the rose is the red originally in the white light bathing the rose and then reflected from it*. The green stem appears green because it absorbs most colors except those near the green part of the spectrum; it reflects green (see p. 588).

A white flower reflects a large percentage of *all* the different colors in white light and so ap-

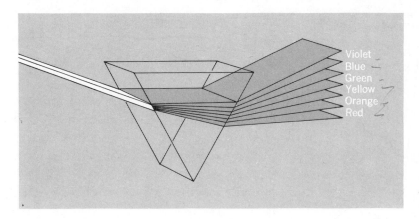

Violet
Blue
Green
Yellow
Orange
Red

When a beam of white light is passed through one side of a triangular glass prism, a rainbow of colors emerges from the other. White light is a mixture of many colors.

pears white. In nature there are very few objects that are pure red or blue or green. A red apple, for example, reflects more red than the other colors, but it also reflects a little blue and green.

RAINBOWS

White light, as we have learned, is a mixture of many colors. When white light, traveling through the air, passes obliquely (at some angle other than

90°) through a substance of different density, like a glass prism or a container of water, the various colors separate to produce a spectrum. We see this in a classroom sometimes when sunlight passes through an aquarium.

Spectrum making on a large scale occurs when nature displays a rainbow in the sky. Here nature's "prisms" are thousands of water droplets left slowly settling in the sky after a shower. Each droplet fans out the white sunlight into a tiny spectrum, but the angle of vision of the viewer on the ground permits him or her to see only one

White light fans out to form a spectrum of colors; the colors rejoin to form white light.

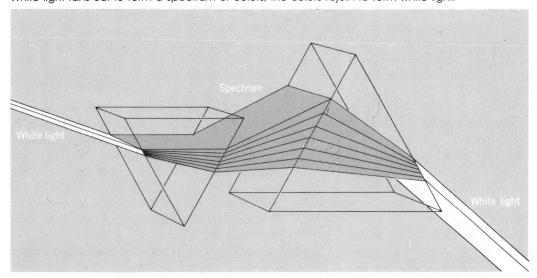

Spectrum

White light

White light

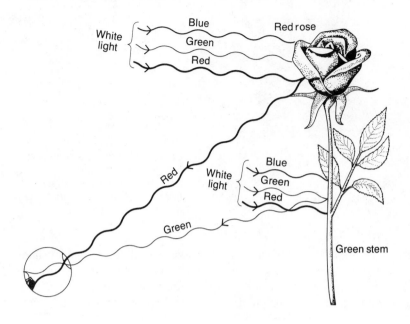

Roses are red because they absorb all the colors in white light except red. This color is reflected to your eye. Why is this stem green?

of these colors in each of the bands that characterize a rainbow. From the highest part of the arch red is bent to the eye; then, in descending order, we can see the bands of orange, yellow, green, blue, and violet.

You can make a small but real rainbow by spraying a shower of droplets from a garden hose. Standing with your back to the sun, adjust the nozzle to the finest spray and direct it at a rather high angle. The rainbow will be more beautiful if the spray is directed toward a shaded or dark background. This homemade rainbow is produced in the same way as nature's larger ones.

WHY IS THE SKY BLUE?

The sky may also be red, orange, other colors, or even gray or black. Before answering the question why the sky is blue it must be understood that the color we ascribe to the "sky" is an effect produced only in the lower part of the atmosphere—in the air up to 20 or 30 miles (32 or 48 kilometers) above the surface of the earth. This lower atmosphere, which is dense with air molecules and dust, has an interesting effect on sunlight.

Light coming from the sun is white, which, as we have seen, is a mixture of all colors. When small particles in the atmosphere interfere with the direct passage of white sunlight, the individual colors are scattered at different angles. However, the blue light in the sunlight is scattered more than the red light. This blue light reaches our eyes from all parts of the sky, so that the sky appears blue. The sun itself appears yellow, which is a combination of the remaining colors in the sunlight; that is, those left after the blue has been subtracted.

A simple way of demonstrating atmospheric scattering of light is to stir a few drops of milk into a bottle of water. (The milk represents the air molecules and dust particles in the atmosphere.) Shine a flashlight against the side of the bottle. (The flashlight represents the sun.) The mixture will appear blue because the blue light has been scattered sideways (to your eyes) out of the flashlight beam by the milk particles. Now move the flashlight around to the back of the bot-

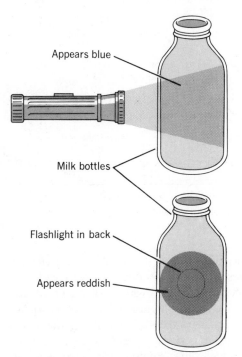

Appears blue

Milk bottles

Flashlight in back

Appears reddish

Demonstrating why the sky has color (see text for details).

tle so that you view its beams head on. (This is like looking at the sun directly.) The blue disappears, and the light from the flashlight appears to be redder than normal. The blue has been scattered out of the beam and you are now viewing what is left—the reds and yellows that combine to give the effect of orange.

Sky color, then, is a characteristic of our atmosphere. As flights into space take us out of the lower atmosphere the sky around appears black at all times, because there are no atmospheric particles to scatter the sunlight. On the moon, which has no atmosphere at all, the sky is always black, even when the sun is shining.

MIRRORS

We noted previously that a perfectly smooth reflecting surface would not be visible, that the source of the light rather than the surface would be seen, that this kind of surface would be a mirror. How is an object seen "in" a mirror? (See pp. 601–602.)

Light, like a ball, bounces away from the objects it strikes. Consider a rose again, but this time see it "in" a mirror. How is this possible? Again we begin with light traveling from a source, such as a candle or perhaps the sun and striking the flower. The light reflected from it on this occasion travels from its surface in many directions. Part of it strikes the walls of the room, part a mirror. In turn, the walls and the mirror reflect the light from the rose in all directions—part of it toward your eyes. Why, then, do you "see" a rose in the mirror and not on the wall?

A mirror produces an image because it bounces light in a way called *regular reflection*. Each individual ray from the flower is reflected from the flat, smooth, shiny surface of the mirror so that each point of the rose results in a corresponding point in its image. As a consequence a perfect image of the object is carried to the viewer's eye. When, however, rays of light are reflected from a relatively rough surface, such as the walls of the room, they bounce off in many directions. The light is scattered and so is the image. This is called *diffuse reflection*. This kind of reflection is useful; otherwise, you would see your image on this page instead of the print (see figure on p. 590).

Let us examine the bouncing of light more carefully. Any billiard player knows that the angle at which a ball strikes the side of the table influences the angle at which it will rebound. In the absence of other factors (an irregularity in the table or a sidespin imparted to the ball), the angle of strike with the table equals the angle of bounce. This is also true of a ray of light striking the surface of a mirror. However, the physicist erects an imaginary perpendicular to this surface (called the *normal*) at the point of contact and measures the angle between that perpendicular and the path of the incoming and departing light ray. The angle made with the incoming ray is called the

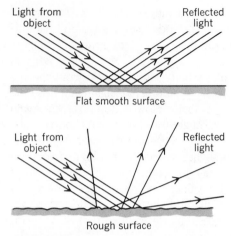

Flat smooth surface

Rough surface

(*Top*) Regular reflection of light—as from a mirror.
(*Bottom*) Diffuse reflection of light—as from a wall.

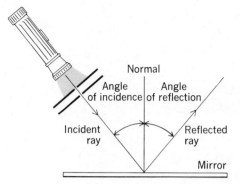

The law of reflection: The angle of incidence equals the angle of reflection.

angle of incidence and with the departing ray the *angle of reflection*. The angle of incidence equals the angle of reflection. This phenomenon is known as the *law of reflection*. This law explains the faithful point-by-point reproduction by a mirror of the original rose in the eyes of the viewer.

We commonly speak of looking *into* a mirror to see our reflection. Obviously, nothing occurs behind the mirror. It is true, however, that light coming from any point in front of a mirror, such as the light of a candle flame, appears to come from a point an equal distance behind the mirror. Although we speak of "mirror images" the image is actually formed in your eye from the light that the mirror has reflected to it.

Most mirrors are made of glass, the back being coated with a substance such as silver, which will reflect light readily. Unbreakable mirrors are made of highly polished steel, although such mirrors do not reflect light as well as glass ones, because the glass is smoother than the steel.

Convex mirrors, the kind that bulge out in front, produce small images of a large area. Because of this they are commonly used as rearview mirrors on autos.

Concave mirrors are used in reflecting telescopes to gather light from a distant object, such

as a star, and focus it so that it may be viewed. The telescope at Mt. Palomar, as we have seen, has a concave mirror with a diameter of 200 inches (5 meters)—an area of about 200 square feet (20 square meters). Every bit of this enormous reflecting surface receives the essentially parallel rays from a single object, such as a star, and then reflects all of them so that they converge and meet in a single point in the tube of the telescope. Here it is reflected by a small plane mirror into an eyepiece, where it is viewed conveniently. Because stars are at great distances from the earth their images, even in the most powerful telescopes, are points of light—no details of the star itself can be seen. The significant advantage is that the light-gathering capacity of the huge concave mirror can make the stars appear a million times as bright. Very faint stars, which cannot be detected by the unaided eye, are thereby revealed. The sun, the moon, and the planets, however, *are* close enough to be magnified in such a telescope so that their details are revealed. (Caution! Never look directly at the sun, especially with a telescope or binoculars. Instead project its image on a paper or board as shown in Chapter 19B.)

Concave mirrors also are used in headlight reflectors of cars, in searchlight reflectors, and as magnifying mirrors. The solar furnace, which can produce temperatures as high as 7000°F (3900°C), is a large concave mirror that brings the rays of the sun to focus.

LIGHT BENDS

If you have ever tried to catch a goldfish in your hands you know that the fish is not where it appears to be. Why is this so?

Light travels in straight lines, but its direction may be changed when it passes from a medium of one density to another. The fish fooled you because the rays of light reflected from it were bent as they passed from the water to the air. For the same reason a pencil or a spoon partially submerged in the water looks crooked—so does the handle of a fishnet or the oar of a rowboat. Anyone spearing fish must aim below the spot where the fish appears or they will miss it. In all these examples we do not see light being bent; we see the effects of this bending.

The bending of light as it passes obliquely from one medium to another is known as *refraction*. The apparent "twinkling" of stars (stars actually do not twinkle) is due to the bending of starlight as it passes through the various shifting layers of hot and cold air in the atmosphere.

The refraction of light by the earth's atmos-

Light is bent as it passes obliquely from one medium to another if the mediums differ in density. To the man on the bank the fish appears to be in the position of the unshaded fish. Actually, it is in the position of the shaded one. We see an object in the last direction in which light from that object enters our eyes. We see in straight lines.

phere makes it possible for us to see the sun when it is actually below the horizon. At sunrise and sunset the rays of the sun pass obliquely through the dense air of the lower atmosphere and are bent toward the earth. They no longer come in a straight line from the sun to the viewer. Thus, the rays are bent to our eyes, even though the sun is below the horizon. The effect of all this is to make the day longer than it would if the earth had no atmosphere. The moon, the sun, and the planets also "twinkle," but because of their relatively large image sizes this is not obvious, and they appear to shine with a constant light.

LENSES

The first lenses used by humans were the ones that they have in their own eyes. We have extended the use of this lens with the aid of many others. Lenses in eyeglasses correct the deficiencies in our eyes. Clouded lenses or cataracts can now be replaced surgically by artificial ones implanted directly into the eyes. Lenses in telescopes extend our view into space; lenses in microscopes permit us to penetrate into the mysteries of the minute; lenses in cameras help us make a record of the present for the future (see pp. 599, 602–603).

Lenses are useful because they are effective light benders: They are designed to refract light according to the purpose of the optical device they are used in.

There are two principal types of simple lenses. Those thicker in the middle than at the edges are called *convex lenses* or *converging lenses*. Those thinner in the middle than at the edges are called *concave lenses* or *diverging lenses*. As their names imply, a converging lens makes light passing through it converge or come together, whereas a diverging lens bends rays passing through it so that they diverge or spread apart.

Pictures from Lenses

A magnifying glass is a common example of a convex lens. A simple experiment that you can

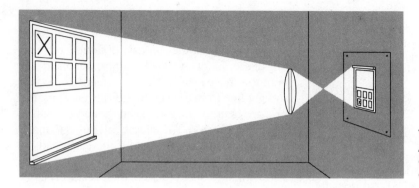

Your room can be a camera. All you need is a magnifying glass. How does the image compare with the original?

perform with such a lens will reveal what it does to light. First, go to a room with a window brightly illuminated by light from the sky. Draw the blinds or shades on the *other* windows to darken them. Tack a sheet of white paper to a wall on the side of the room opposite the illuminated window. Hold the magnifying lens near the paper. Move the lens back and forth until you see a sharp image of the window on the paper. (At night you can get the same effect by using a bright lamp instead of a bright window.) Look at the image carefully and you will notice that it is upside down (see above). The convex lens bends the light and causes it to form a small inverted image of the window.

The Camera

If you could now place a piece of unexposed photographic film on the wall instead of paper, and then develop it in the usual manner, you would find that you had made a negative of the image in the same way that a camera does. You have stripped the camera down to its two most basic essentials—lens and film. A *pinhole camera* even disposes of the lens, using instead a tiny hole to admit the light. A study of the diagram of this camera will show why cameras produce inverted images (see adjacent figure). (See p. 603.)

A camera is essentially a light-tight box with a

lens in front, an opening for light, a shutter for allowing light to enter the opening for a fraction of a second, film, and a device in back for holding and advancing the film. When the shutter is snapped open, light is admitted and passes through the lens, which focuses it on the film. There it produces a change in the silver salt that is embedded in a gelatin layer on the film. This change is made visible by the developing, which also serves to preserve the image on film. Since *light* actually causes *dark* grains of silver to be deposited on the film the developed film is a negative. White teeth are black in a negative; black hair is almost colorless because it reflects little light. In making a print, light is made to shine through the negative to the photographic paper, which is also coated with a sensitive silver compound. Thus, a reversal of the image is effected, and a positive is produced.

In the previously described experiment with

The camera in its simplest form is a light-tight box with a tiny pinhole at one end. This diagram shows how an inverted image is produced.

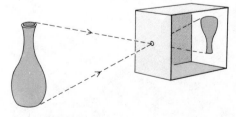

the magnifying glass, focusing was done by moving the lens back and forth. In all kinds of fixed-focus cameras, the only focusing that is done is accomplished by moving the entire camera; the lens is not moved in relation to the camera. Because of this the fixed-focus camera is somewhat limited in its use; however, it can take satisfactory pictures of subjects that are from 6 feet (2 meters) away to as far as the eye can see. Cameras with focusing devices permit the lens to be moved back and forth to secure sharp focuses for each picture for varying distances. In cameras other than the simplest, the amount of light admitted can be controlled in two ways: by varying the length of *time* the shutter is open and by regulating the *size* of the opening with a device called a diaphragm.

Motion Pictures

The process by which pictures are made to produce the illusion of motion may seem complicated but actually is quite simple. The principle is illustrated by a certain kind of picture book in which the pictures are printed close to the edge of the page. One holds the book's edges with the thumb, bends the pages, and then releases them rapidly one by one. If the pages slip by rapidly enough, the illusion of motion is created.

Motion pictures are simply a series of still pictures projected on a screen in rapid succession. Each picture is motionless while it is being shown and is only slightly different from the one before it. Our eye receives each of these pictures and focuses it on its own "screen," the *retina*, in the back of the eyeball. The movie projector is constructed to make each image persist for ¹/₂₄ second on the screen. The retina retains a picture for as long as ¹/₁₅ second after it has disappeared. This phenomenon is known as *persistence of vision*. Because of the rapidity with which pictures appear, the eye blends each image with the following one so that we get the impression of continuous, lifelike motion.

THE EYE

The eye is often compared to the camera. The eye is a light-tight box, with dark pigment on the inside to prevent the bouncing around of light. It has a lens to focus light and a light-sensitive screen in the back on which an image is actually formed. It has an opening in front comparable to the opening of a camera; the size of this opening can be varied, as in a camera, to admit more or less light. The eye has a kind of shutter, the eyelid, which can exclude light as well as serve as a kind of windshield wiper to keep the eyes clean. The resemblance of eye and camera is even more detailed and striking than indicated by these terms. We shall note other similarities as we go along.

The Outer Eye

Observe your own eye in a mirror to find some of its external structures. It will be helpful if you refer to the diagram on page 594 as you make this study. You are looking at a portion of an almost spherical ball about 1 inch (2.4 centimeters) in diameter. You are looking right through a thin transparent membrane that guards the front of the eye, called the *conjunctiva*. This membrane is continuous with the inner surface of the eyelids. The conjunctiva is kept free of dust and is lubricated by the tears that are spread in a thin film every time you blink. After flowing over the surface of the eye, the tears are drained into the nose cavity by two tiny tubes, one in the inner corner of each eye. The continual washing and lubrication of the eyeball by tears prevents the delicate conjunctiva from becoming dry and inflamed. The tears also contain the substance *lysozyme*, which destroys bacteria.

Under the conjunctiva is the "white of the eye," the *sclera*, which is made of tough, fibrous tissue that extends around the entire eye to make up the "box" of this instrument. The sclera becomes transparent over the *iris* and *pupil*, forming the somewhat bulging *cornea*. The pupil is a hole in

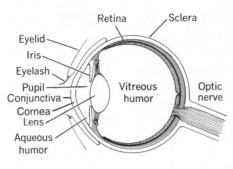

(*Left*) Front view of eye. (*Right*) Vertical section of eye. Which of the eye's structures can be seen in the front view? (See the text for a description of how the eye functions.)

the iris through which light is admitted into the eye. It appears black because the small opening of the pupil allows very little light to reflect out. The pupil is surrounded by the doughnut-shaped iris, which is the pigmented or colored portion of the eye. The iris is a muscle that controls the size of the pupil. You can see it at work if you sit for a few minutes in a dimly lit room, with just enough light to see your iris and pupil in a mirror. When you switch on a nearby light the iris gets bigger and the pupil smaller. This reflex action of the iris automatically regulates the amount of light entering the eye. The need for such control becomes apparent when one realizes that the light from a sunny beach is thousands of times as strong as the light in a dim theater. In dim light the pupil opening is large to admit as much light as possible; in bright light it becomes small to reduce the amount of light. In a camera, too, a diaphragm is adjusted by the photographer to permit more or less light to enter the opening at its center.

The eyeball lies in a bony socket of the skull and is manipulated by the muscles that are attached to it. These muscles tilt the eyeball up and down, left and right, and in a rotary motion.

Inside the Eye

The internal structure of the eye can be understood with the aid of the diagram on this page, which represents a vertical section of the eyeball from front to back. In this section we recognize

some structures previously seen in the external view: the eyelids, cornea, iris, pupil, and sclera. In addition, we note two important structures—the *lens* and the *retina*—and two fluids—the *aqueous humor* and the *vitreous humor*. The aqueous humor is a watery fluid in front of the lens; the vitreous humor is a denser fluid behind the lens that fills most of the eyeball.

The Eye Makes a Picture

The lens of the eye acts like the lens of a camera: It gathers light, bends it, and forms a picture. The light rays are focused to make a sharp image on the light-sensitive retina in the back of the eye. As in the camera the image is an inverted one.

The lens of the human eye is not focused by moving it back and forth. Instead, focusing is accomplished by *changing the shape of the lens*. The eye lens is a transparent disk, convex on both sides and about $\frac{1}{3}$ inch (almost a centimeter) in diameter. It is within the globe of the eye just behind the iris, and is made up of a material whose shape can be altered by the action of muscles attached to it. When the lens is thin and flat it is adapted for focusing faraway objects. When it is fatter and rounder it is adapted for close vision.

The ability to adjust the lens shape is called *accommodation*. This works well in most young people. In older individuals the lens loses some of its elasticity, and eyeglasses are sometimes required to compensate for this loss.

The Screen of the Eye

The parallel between eye and camera holds for the light-sensitive retina, which is analogous to photographic film. In the retina there are two kinds of sensitive cells, the rods and cones. *Cones* are sensitive to light of different colors and are also used in bright light. *Rods* are sensitive to dim light; when stimulated, they produce sensations only of light intensity—of varying shades of gray. As you might expect, the retinas of some night animals contain only rods.

In intermediate-strength light both the rods and cones respond. As brightness increases, the cones take over entirely. This change corresponds to the photographer's use of "fast" or "slow" film in the camera.

The cones, then, are used in bright light and respond to varying colors in that light. How does the eye see color? It is thought that human color vision is dependent on the responses of three different kinds of cones, each with a different light-sensitive pigment. One type is sensitive to red light, one to green light, and one to blue-violet light. Color sensation is the sum of responses to impulses from all three types of cones. Thus, the human retina resembles not only black and white film but color film, which also contains three different chemicals sensitive to different colors. Color-blind individuals, apparently, lack either one or two sets of these cones.

Seeing with Our Brains

Impulses initiated by the 130 million light-sensitive cells in each retina are sent over nerve fibers to the brain. These are nerve impulses, not light waves. The brain interprets them according to the type of cell over which the impulse comes and the particular spot in the brain where the impulse is received. The brain produces some kind of a learned response (not a picture) to the image on the retina.

What happens in the brain is fantastically complex; what one "sees" depends on many factors.

An ink blot means different things to different people. Seeing is not simply a matter of the physics of light; it depends on the operation of the mind. The complex nature of vision was expressed well by Adelbert Ames, an expert in the field of visual perception: "What the eye sees is the mind's best guess as to what is out in front."

THE KEYBOARD OF LIGHT

Light is similar to sound in a number of ways. Both are messengers carrying information of the world about us to our senses. Both travel, although light travels almost one million times as fast as sound. Both apparently are wave phenomena; a wavelike disturbance proceeds in all directions from a source. In both sound and light, the length of the wave (from "crest" to "crest") varies.

Each color has its particular wavelength. The deepest red visible to the eye as a color has a wavelength of about 1/30,000 inch (8/10,000 millimeter); the deepest violet at the other end of the spectrum has a wavelength of 1/60,000 inch (4/10,000 millimeter).

We recall that some sound waves (the ultrasonic ones) cannot be detected by the human ear. This has its parallel in "invisible" light waves. Just beyond the violet is the invisible *ultraviolet*, with a shorter wavelength than violet. Ultraviolet radiation, found in sunlight, is important to life because it stimulates the production of vitamin D in organisms exposed to it. Ultraviolet radiation is also responsible for the sunburning and suntanning effects of exposure to sunlight. The harmful effects of excessive ultraviolet radiation, which might be accelerated by the destruction of the ozone layer of the atmosphere, was discussed in Chapters 9A and 13A. Although not detected by the eye, ultraviolet does affect photographic film, and therefore the appearance of the developed image.

At the other end of the visible spectrum, just beyond the longest wavelength of deep red, is *infrared*. These waves, also occurring in sunlight, are extremely important, for they are the radiant

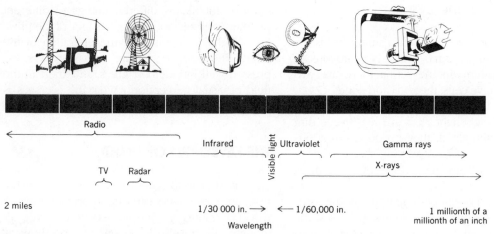

Radio

TV   Radar

Infrared   Visible light   Ultraviolet   Gamma rays

X-rays

2 miles   1/30 000 in. →   ← 1/60,000 in.   1 millionth of a
                      Wavelength   millionth of an inch

Visible light is a small part of the electromagnetic spectrum.

heat waves that help warm the earth. All warm bodies radiate infrared light. Infrared radiation affects special photographic film that is sensitive to this invisible color.

BEYOND THE REDS AND BLUES

Beyond the reds and blues of visible light there exists a larger spectrum of waves known as the *electromagnetic spectrum*. We can compare this spectrum to a supergrand piano containing not seven octaves but seventy. On the keyboard of this imagined piano, which is ten times as long as the conventional grand piano, visible light occupies only one octave, near the center.

As you run your eye over the keyboard you discover that this piano is capable of many effects: radio, television, radar, visible light, X rays, and gamma rays. Note that as you move from radio waves at one end to gamma rays at the other, the wavelength decreases progressively from about 2 *miles* to 1 millionth of 1 millionth of an *inch*.

In Chapter 14A we found that all matter consists of the same fundamental particles: electrons, protons, neutrons, and others. Electromagnetic waves, first described in 1865 by James Maxwell, are another example of basic unity in nature. The electromagnetic spectrum demonstrates that many forms of radiation consist of waves of the same fundamental nature, which travel at the same speed of 186,000 miles (300,000 kilometers) per second. Radio waves, light, and X rays differ only in the lengths of their waves and in the frequency of their vibrations.

IMPORTANT GENERALIZATIONS

We are able to see objects because they reflect or emit light to our eyes.

A mirror image is produced by the regular reflection of light by the reflecting surface to the viewer.

The angle at which a ray of light strikes a mirror equals the angle at which it is reflected from it.

The light that is not absorbed by an opaque object is reflected by it. This reflection may be regular or diffused.

Light is bent or refracted when it passes obliquely from a medium of one density to another.

Lenses are light benders.

The eye resembles the camera in many ways.

The color of light is determined by its wavelength.

Sunlight is a mixture of many colors.

The color of an opaque object viewed in sunlight is determined by the portion of the sun's colors that it reflects.

When white light passes through a triangular prism it fans out into a spectrum of colors.

Rainbows are formed when sunlight is separated into its colors by water droplets in the air, much like a prism.

Light behaves in some respects like waves and in others like a shower of energy packets.

Light travels through space at the rate of about 186,000 miles (300,000 kilometers) per second.

Visible light resembles other forms of radiation, such as radio waves, X rays, and cosmic rays, in that all are electromagnetic waves and all travel at the same speed in the same medium. Only the wavelength is different.

DISCOVERING FOR YOURSELF

1. Examine and use various kinds and shapes of lenses to see how they differ.

2. Experiment with a prism to break sunlight into its component colors.

3. Find examples of reflection and refraction in your environment.

4. Identify and describe the mirrors in your home, auto, school, and local stores. How are they different? What is their function?

5. Examine and use a light meter. Find out why it is useful.

6. Use light to make a blueprint and explain what happens.

7. Examine a camera and a projector to see how they control and use light.

8. Make a pinhole camera and explain how it forms an image.

9. Experiment with production of shadows to see changes in size and sharpness.

10. Make a color wheel and attach it to a motor, or find some other way to spin it. Experiment with various combinations of colors. Can you make white?

11. Examine a model of the eye and explain how the model might be used with children.

12. Some local astronomical societies help their members make telescopes. Investigate the possibilities of one of the members visiting your class and demonstrating the use of lenses.

13. Find out about those powerful sources of light called lasers.

14. Find out how fiber optics, the transmission of messages by light waves along light-conducting fibers, may replace electrical waves for communication in telephone circuitry.

TEACHING "LIGHT AND HOW WE USE IT"

Children see reflections, rainbows, colors, shadows, sunsets, and moonlight. They use cameras, magnifying glasses, and mirrors. They play shadow games; they mix colored paints. Problems for investigation come from observations and experiences such as these.

The study of light provides a simple direct consideration of *cause and effect.* We turn a mirror and the light reflected from it moves. We move an object nearer a screen and its shadow changes in size. We move a lens closer to an object and its magnification changes. The sun moves lower in the sky; shadows lengthen. A lamp is switched on and there is light.

SOME BROAD CONCEPTS

Shadows are made when light is blocked by some
    opaque object.
We see objects when they reflect light or are themselves
    luminous.
Light is a form of energy.
Light travels from its source in all directions at about
    186,000 miles (300,000 kilometers) per second.
Materials differ in the amounts of light they reflect, ab-
    sorb, or allow to pass through them.
Lenses bend light rays.
White light is composed of the colors of the rainbow.
The color of an opaque object in sunlight is determined
    by the portion of the sun's colors it reflects.
The sun is our main source of light.
Shadows can help us tell time.

FOR YOUNGER CHILDREN

What Can We Do with a Magnifying Glass?

Frequent references have been made to the use of the magnifying glass, because children enjoy using this important tool to explore and learn.[1]

[1]See J. Schwartz, *Through the Magnifying Glass* (1954) and *Magnify and Find Out Why* (1972) (New York: McGraw-Hill).

Note: A magnifying glass should not be left where sunlight may strike it—this could cause a fire.

They have many ideas of their own about where and when to use it, and they enjoy sharing their observations with each other. "Let's see what it looks like through the magnifying glass" can often be the first suggestion when gathering data by observations is indicated. If there is a science table, an aquarium, or a terrarium, a magnifying glass will help to develop appreciations, as well as to explain and provide information. (See also Chapter 10B for other suggestions.)

Have the children look at such objects as a pinch of sand, a spoon full of soil, a flower, snail eggs on an aquarium plant, different kinds of seeds, the scales on a turtle, a fingerprint. They will conclude that a magnifying glass "makes things look bigger," "helps us see things more clearly," "helps us see tiny things," and "sometimes helps us to see what is happening."

What Can A Mirror Do?

In the primary grades the day-to-day experiences of children often provide exciting opportunities for learning and enjoying scientific happenings. The following experience is such an example. It arose accidentally. The teacher recognized the interest of the children, and she acted as a guide in helping them explore and develop the situation; she helped them formulate and solve problems that involved sensing the problem, making observations, attempting to see relationships, gathering data, applying these data, and eventually explaining the mystery. The experience is presented here as it was related by the teacher.[2] It illustrates what can happen when a teacher is interested, alert, and creative.

In our kindergarten we had a problem of "What makes the light on the ceiling of our room?" These lights were seen over a period of several months in

[2]Anne W. Anderson, kindergarten teacher, Louisville Public Schools, Louisville, Kentucky.

a room where there is much sunlight. The following account describes briefly what took place.

One day, hearing the children laugh, I looked up to see Donna making a reflection on the ceiling with the bottom of her tin lunch box. I asked Donna why she didn't use the top of her lunch box (which was painted dark red). She said it wouldn't work. I asked her to let me try it. I was sitting on the shady side of the room and it wouldn't work. I suggested to the children that they try to make a light on the ceiling with any kind of object. They tried paper, cardboard, a piece of wood, a towel, a pair of scissors, pocketbooks, and an aluminum pitcher.

As we discussed our observations we agreed that to make a light on the ceiling two things were necessary—something *shiny* and *sunshine*. One child said one day, "I know what you call it. It is a reflection." After we got this far I produced small mirrors and let all the children make bright reflections.

On another day there was a bright reflection in the shape of a ring on the ceiling. We called it the "doughnut" light. What made it? It must be something shiny in the sun. Children took turns trying to decide what it was. They examined everything on the sunny side of the room. One child decided that it was a 4-inch aluminum cap on the radiator. We covered the cap with cardboard and the reflection disappeared. When the cap was uncovered, the reflection reappeared. Many children covered it to see—so we were sure.

On another day there were 6 to 8 pale balls of light on the ceiling. What made them? Here was the toughest problem we had struck. Again everything on the sunny side of the room was examined. All the vases and flowerpots were moved off the plant table. The problem remained unsolved for several weeks—just coming up now and then to pester us. On cloudy days, there was no light of any kind. On sunny days the pale balls were there. Upstairs in the hall, too, there were beautiful balls of light on the ceiling.

Finally, one boy thought of climbing up on a chair and looking out in the yard. He discovered some pieces of broken glass outside and thought they might make the pale reflections. So he went out with a box and picked up the broken glass. Our pale balls of light were gone. But we made him go out and put the glass back! Upstairs, we climbed on chairs, and sure enough the lower roof was covered with many pieces of broken glass.

On another day a large pale reflection danced all over the ceiling and then settled down to a small bright spot. After the same trial-and-error method of examination we found that it came from a cup of water on the plant table. When the water shook, the light danced; when the water was still, the light was still. One day, after a rain, we had pale dancing reflections and found clear puddles outside. The wind was ruffling the puddles.

These experiences were responsible for other questions children raised as they reacted to and discussed the exciting class happenings. It helped us realize how close we are to science problems.

Where Can We Find Colors?[3]

As young children learn to identify and name colors, they are often interested in finding colors in different places. Using a prism is fascinating to children. Encourage them to name the colors in the prism spectrum and note their sequence. An aquarium in the sunlight sometimes acts as a prism to produce a spectrum. Children may try to compare these colors with those of the prism. Lawn sprays may be used in the sunlight to produce a spectrum of colors, as described on pages 587–588. If the occasion arises, observing a rainbow is an exciting experience not to be missed.

How Do Shadows Change?[4]

In addition to the experience with shadows noted in Chapter 7B, which describes observing shadows out-of-doors, children can use a strong light, such as the bulb from a filmstrip projector, to

[3]F. M. Branley, *Color From Rainbows to Lasers* (New York: Crowell, 1978).

[4]G. F. Consuegra, "Science with Shadows," *Science and Children* (February 1982). Activities. M. McIntyre, "Light and Shadows," *Science and Children* (January 1978); S. Simon, *Shadow Magic* (New York: Lothrop, 1985); E. Feher and K. Rice, "Shadow Shapes," *Science and Children* (October 1986). Clarifies children's understanding of the nature of shadows.

make observations and discoveries about the nature of light and shadows. First, direct the light on a translucent screen or a white cotton sheet. Have children sit on the side of the screen opposite the light in a darkened room. Hold various objects between the light and the screen. Observe to see (1) "What happens when the object is moved closer to the screen?" (Shadow is smaller.) "Away from the screen?" (Shadow is larger.) (2) "What happens when the object is turned?" (A ball looks the same; an object such as a book changes shape.) Children will predict what will happen if the screen is moved or if the light is moved. Then try it. Have them try to identify "mystery" objects by their shadows on the screen.

Other Problems for Younger Children

1. What casts a shadow?
2. What shadows move?
3. How can we make a picture of our shadow? (Draw it on a large sheet of paper, or on the ground.)
4. How do shadows change during the day?
5. How can shadows help us tell time?
6. What different things give us light?
7. How should we take care of our eyes?
8. How do you use your eyes to make discoveries?
9. What can you do with lenses?
10. What can you do with mirrors?
11. How is light used on your street?
12. How many colors can you see with a prism?

FOR OLDER CHILDREN

How Well Does Light Pass Through Different Objects?[5]

Use flashlights or some similar sources of light and supply each group of children with materials, such as pieces of clear glass, a mirror, frosted glass, paper, pieces of leather or rubber, aluminum foil, waxed paper. Begin by suggesting that

[5]R. Baines, *Light* (Mahwah, N.J.: Troll, 1985).

children try to predict what will happen when the light is shined on each piece of material. Then test the hypothesis, letting each group work independently. (This activity will be more effective if conducted in a darkened room.) Finally, let them attempt a classification of materials according to objects: (1) through which all or almost all the light striking it can pass (transparent); (2) through which only part of the light travels (translucent); and (3) through which no light travels (opaque). (See Chapter 19A, p. 585.)

Follow this experience with a hunt to identify ways in which materials in the classification are used in their environment—lampshades, package wrappers, medicine containers, and so on.

What Do Mirrors Do to Light?[6]

Try to provide each child or small group of children with a small mirror, suggesting that they use the mirrors in any way they wish to collect ideas about how mirrors work (move the mirror in different positions—up, down, sideways, closer, farther away). Discuss their findings. Urge them to use the terms *object* for things they observe, and *image* for what they see in the mirror. Suggest that they use a mirror in the sunlight or in the path of a lighted flashlight. Caution them about reflecting strong sunlight into each other's eyes (see Chapter 19A, pp. 589–590).

"What can you discover about the way a mirror reflects light?" With a flashlight and mirror children may be able to discover that the angle at which light strikes a mirror determines the angle at which it is reflected. Another way of illustrating this idea is to place a large mirror in front of the classroom and ask selected students to tell which of their classmates they can see in the mirror and which ones they cannot see. Urge them to try to formulate a statement that will explain this idea. After some classroom experiences children can

[6]R. J. Whitaker, "Reflecting in a Cylindrical Mirror," *Science and Children* (March 1985).

observe the uses of mirrors in stores and store windows, in automobiles, in elevators, in barbershops, and in dentists' offices, and discuss why the mirrors are shaped as they are and why they are placed as they are.

Suggest that children dust chalk from an eraser on half of the mirrors they are using. "Observe what happens. Try to explain it." (Smooth surfaces reflect more light than rough surfaces. The clean mirror reflects light in regular reflection. The dusty mirror scatters the light in diffuse reflection.) The same idea may be illustrated by shining one shoe to make it a smooth surface and dusting chalk on the other one. Urge children to find other examples.

Students may experiment with other materials (tin surfaces, glass, smooth paper, cloth, and so on) to see if they will reflect light, and try to explain what they observe. "What characteristic must a reflecting surface have?" "Do all materials reflect light equally well?"

From the activities children learn that an object is reversed in a mirror left to right, that tilting a mirror helps us see different objects, that a mirror "works" because it reflects light, and that we see an object "in" a mirror because light travels from the object to the mirror to our eyes.

How Are Lenses Used?[7]

The lens from a flashlight, a magnifying glass, lenses from a projector, from old discarded optical instruments, as well as an assortment of lenses purchased from a supply house, and the eyeglasses of students in the class are all useful in the study of lenses.

---

[7]V. Bar and A. Terkel, "Teaching Optics in a Classroom," *Science and Children* (October 1979). Experiments and experiences. M. L. Beaney, "Microbiology For First Graders," "How to Use the Microscope" and C. Herman, "Through the Magnifying Glass," *Science and Children* (September 1987); J. Frank, "Learning to Use the Compound Microscope," *Science and Children* (February 1987).

Supply individuals or small groups of children with lenses of various shapes and sizes (convex, concave, and so on). Suggest that children describe the shapes of the lenses and compare them with each other. Then ask the children to see what they can discover by using the lenses to look at print, at distant objects, and so forth. In a short time they may "invent" such devices as a magnifying glass (one lens), a more powerful magnifying glass (two lenses next to each other), a telescope (one lens held at a distance from another). (See Chapter 19A, p. 591.)

Following the students' free experimentation and the reports of their findings, problems such as the following may be investigated: "How can you make an image with a lens?" Hold a large magnifying glass near a wall opposite a window. Move the glass nearer and farther from the wall. Watch until there is a sharp image of something near the window. This is called focusing. "How large is the image compared to the object?" "What position is it in?" (Upside down.) (See Chapter 19A, pp. 591–592.)

Children may discuss, "What happens if we use two lenses?" They may attempt to demonstrate using the lenses they have on hand. (Convex lenses magnify. Concave lenses reduce.) Two convex lenses properly used together increase magnification as in a telescope. Students certainly should not be encouraged to wear one another's glasses, but looking through the various lenses to see how objects appear through them will help them to see how lenses differ.

A magnifying glass may be used in bright sunlight to focus light strong enough to burn paper. Be sure that the fire is out at the end of activity. Exercise caution, for it is possible for students to burn themselves or one another by careless use of the glass. It is easy for students to see how moving the lens back and forth focuses the light and to see how the lens acts as a light "gatherer." It is interesting to note that the intense spot produced is an image of the sun.

From the activities children learn that a convex lens is a magnifier, a concave lens a reducer, and that optical instruments use lenses to help us see objects that are small or far away.

Note: Children should realize that it is dangerous to look at the sun directly or with any kind of lenses and that light from the sun should never be reflected into anyone's eyes.

How Does a Camera Work?[8]

A general idea of how a camera operates may be demonstrated by darkening the classroom and asking the children to turn their backs to a window that does not have its shade drawn. Suggest that they hold a sheet of white paper vertically with one hand and a convex lens in the other. Let them experiment to try to make a "picture" of the window on the paper by moving the lens back and forth. Ask them to describe the "picture." "Is it smaller or larger than the window?" "How else is it different from the window?" (Smaller, upside down.) (See Chapter 19A, pp. 592–593.)

In almost any upper-elementary class there are students who have cameras. Urge children to bring their cameras, explain their operation in its simplest form, and then insert film and take pictures of the class. Students can demonstrate loading the film, holding the camera, getting proper light, using the finder, and so on. They can also describe various cautions in the use of the camera to ensure good results. In some instances it is even possible for them to explain how the film is developed. Students should understand where light enters the camera, where the lens is, what the shutter does, and how the picture is focused on the film. The demonstrator may also introduce

students to the light meter and show how it behaves under various light intensities. The use of the camera can demonstrate many of the scientific principles involved in the study of light. If old cameras that are no longer used are available students can open them to see how a camera is constructed. Students may like to make a pinhole camera. Directions are given in many books.

Children should be encouraged to use their cameras to illustrate a project, a trip, a study of the school environment, the progress of an experiment, or to prepare a photographic "essay."

Other Problems for Older Children

1. How can we make a periscope?
2. How do artificial lamps give light?
3. How is a kaleidoscope built?[9]
4. How do we see?
5. What are good lighting conditions for study?
6. What does a prism do to light?[10]
7. How are motion pictures produced?

RESOURCES TO INVESTIGATE WITH CHILDREN

1. Local photographers, camera shops, camera clubs, and camera manufacturers, for information about photography.
2. An optician, for discarded lenses that may be used in performing simple experiments with light.

---

[8]S. I. Granderson, "The Pinhole Camera Revisited," *Science and Children* (February 1987). Constructing and using a pinhole camera to teach that light travels in straight lines, and how an image is formed. M. Luke, "Trying Your Hand at a Handmade Camera," *Science and Children* (February 1987). Instructions for using a pinhole camera to take photographs.

[9]G. Wiener, "Kaleidoscope Capers," *Science and Children* (September 1987). How to build and use a kaleidoscope.

[10]H. Simon, *Sight and Seeing: A World of Light and Color* (New York: Philomel, 1978); C. J. Engels, "Chasing Rainbows," *Science and Children* (March 1985).

3. The power company or electrical institute, to learn about the measurement of light, types of lighting, and the amount of light necessary for various activities.
4. Hardware and electrical supply stores, to observe the various types of light fixtures and to learn how science principles are utilized in their construction and use.
5. The school building and the school custodian, to learn how the school is lighted and, with the help of a light meter, to see how light is used for various purposes in school.
6. Children's homes, to observe the different kinds of lighting fixtures and how they are related to light needs.
7. The National Society for the Prevention of Blindness, Inc., 79 Madison Ave., New York, NY 10016, for catalog of publications and films.

PREPARING TO TEACH

1. Assemble magazine pictures, photographs, and other illustrative material that may be used in teaching the unit. Plan how these may be used by children.
2. Examine books for children that are appropriate supplementary books, and annotate the list. Plan how you would use them to teach a unit on light.
3. Select one or more items from the "Other Problems" and make a lesson plan to introduce questions and outline activities you would use with children (see Chapter 4).
4. List activities you would consider useful in stimulating interest in the topic of light.
5. Set up a learning station (see Chapter 3) with different kinds of magnifiers and mirrors for informal investigation by students.

FLIGHT AND
SPACE TRAVEL

> *The greater the velocity . . . with which a stone is projected, the farther it goes before it falls to earth. We may therefore suppose the velocity to be so increased, that it would describe an arc of 1, 2, 5, 10, 100, 1000 miles before it arrived on the earth, till at last, exceeding the limits of the earth, it should pass into space without touching it.*
>
> SIR ISAAC NEWTON (1642–1727)
>
> *Space is the new ocean. And we must sail on it.*
>
> JOHN F. KENNEDY, 1961

THE SPACE ERA

In less than one average lifetime, we have progressed from the first powered flight of 120 feet (37 meters) into the air to a landing on the moon.

Orville and Wilbur Wright achieved sustained flight with a powered aircraft for 12 seconds on December 17, 1903. Sixty-six years later, on July 20, 1969, Neil Armstrong stepped onto the surface of the moon—after a journey of 230,000 miles (370,150 kilometers) in less than four days—while about 500 million people around the world watched the event on television or listened to it on radio.

Then on April 14, 1981, astronauts John Young and Robert Crippen (after circling the earth 36 times), guided the space shuttle *Columbia* to a safe landing on the desert at Edwards Air Force Base in California, concluding the first demonstration of a new approach to extraterrestial travel, the reusable spacecraft.

The spectacular views of the planets provided by space probes (described in Chapter 7A) will be followed by other science-oriented NASA projects: the launching of the Hubble Space Telescope, which will see almost to the edge of the universe; the Galileo orbiter-and-probe of Jupiter and its four giant moons; the Magellan Venus-orbiting radar mapper; the Earth-orbiting Astro-l ultraviolet observatory; and the Cosmic Background Explorer designed to map the pattern of emissions remaining as evidence of the big bang at the birth of the universe.

Still undetermined is a return to Mars to learn more about this most Earthlike planet—to investigate traces of its widespread floods, channels of dried riverbeds, and violent volcanic eruptions—first by placing robots and later men on the Martian landscape. Also in the future is the building of a permanent space station, the forerunner of a possible colony in space.

WHAT MAKES AN AIRPLANE FLY?

Almost 100 years before the historic feat of the Wright brothers, Sir George Cayley, an English scientist, made a remarkably astute statement on the problem of flight. He said that flight would be possible if we could make a *surface* support a weight by the application of *power* to the *resistance of the air*. In this Cayley was giving proper recognition to

1. *The supporting surface* (the wings of the modern plane).
2. *Power* (the motor and propeller—later the jet—that would pull or push the wings through the air).
3. *The air itself* (the "resistance of the air," as we shall see, provides the "lift" on the wing needed to overcome gravity).

Air is a real substance, just as real as liquid water or solid earth. A parachute falling through air descends slowly because its inside surface encounters and pushes against many air molecules. The crowded molecules, in turn, push back

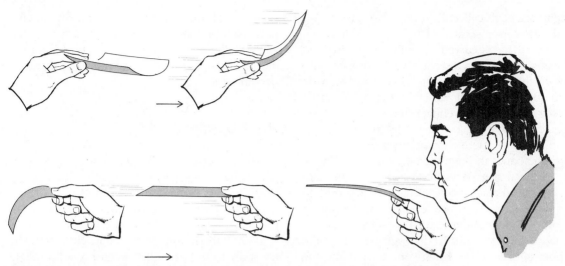

(Upper) When a surface is pushed against the air, the air pushes back. The text tells how this gives an airplane part of its lift. (Lower) The pressure on the upper surface is decreased. How does this help to lift an airplane?

against the parachute, retarding its downward drop. If the chute fails to open, however, it plummets to earth rapidly.

The Resistance of the Air

Because air is a substance it offers resistance to the movement of objects through it. At first this might seem to be only an obstacle to horizontal flight. But a simple demonstration will reveal that this resistance can serve a helpful purpose, too: Hold one end of a lettersize sheet of paper, forefinger on top, supported by the thumb and second finger underneath it. Hold it in a horizontal position, curved slightly so that it does not droop. Now tilt it at a slight angle, so that the opposite end of the paper is slightly higher than the end you are holding. Push the paper directly forward, but hold on to it. You find that the free leading edge tilts up. Why? (See figure above.)

As the surface of the paper is pushed against the molecules that make up the air, it crowds them together. The crowded molecules, in turn, spring back and push against the paper. Part of

this air resistance impedes the forward progress of the paper, but because the crowded molecules beat against the paper in all directions, *part of the resistance serves to lift the paper*, tilting its free end up. With a little practice you can flick the paper or a piece of cardboard so that on leaving your hand the upward push serves to lift the entire sheet against the pull of gravity.

The sheet of paper that you have experimented with has some of the characteristics of an airplane wing. You have used it in a way that fulfills Cayley's requirements for heavier-than-air flight. You have applied power (the push of your hand) to the resistance of the air, and in that way you have achieved a small amount of "lift." You have found that when a tilted surface is pushed against the air the air pushes back, partially slowing it down, partially lifting it up.

The Pressure Difference

Now take a look at a real airplane to find the flat tilted surface that presses against the air. You discover it in the wings, set at an angle so that their front edge, called the *leading edge*, is higher than their back edge, called the *trailing edge*. However, only the lower surface of the wings is flat; the upper surface is curved or arched. Why? To find the answer perform a second demonstration with paper, this time with a strip about 2 inches wide and about 6 inches long. Hold it at one end between thumb and forefinger, thumb on top (see figure on p. 607), so that it falls in a curve not unlike that of the top of an airplane wing. Now *pull* the paper through the air. Its free end rises, as in the first experiment. You may argue with good reason that the lower edge is being pushed up, as in the previous experiment, by the impact of the air from underneath. This is true, but it is only part of the truth. To discover the role of the upper surface alone, bring your fingers and the paper under your lips and blow over the top of it only (see figure). The paper rises again. Why? (See pp. 632–633.)

We recall that air is a real substance made of bouncing molecules. We should also recall that because of the never-ceasing bouncing of these molecules, air, even when it is not moving as a mass (wind), exerts a push in all directions—up, down, sideways. At sea levels this pressure amounts to about 15 pounds on every square inch of surface on which the air presses. When an airplane is at rest on the ground on a windless day the pressure on top of the wing is counterbalanced by an equal pressure from the bottom. The net effect is zero. But when the wing begins to move forward through the air an interesting thing happens. The air flowing over the curved upper surface is forced to travel a greater distance and at a greater speed than the air on the lower surface. Rushing over the upper surface of the wing, the air expends some of its energy in motion and consequently loses some of its pressure. Thus, the pressure on the upper surface becomes less (forming a partial vacuum) than the pressure on the lower surface. The relatively higher pressure on the lower surface lifts the wing and, therefore, the plane against the pull of gravity.

To summarize, two factors operate to give a moving wing its lift: (1) the impact of the air against the lower surface of the wing and (2) the decreased pressure on the upper surface of the wing. Of the two, the second contributes more to the total lift of a plane, accounting for about 80 percent of it.

The Propeller's Job

In your experiments, the power to move the paper "wing" was supplied by your muscles. In the propeller plane, the power is supplied by the engine. This power is conveyed by a shaft to the propeller.

Both of the factors operating to give a wing its lift apply to the propeller. Each propeller blade resembles a wing in its construction. As it is rotated, the action of its surfaces on the air gives it useful "lift," but in the direction in which the plane is moving. This propeller lift produces the forward thrust that drives the aircraft through the air at a speed necessary to give the wings their lift. As an airplane races down the runway the propeller pulls it along the ground faster and faster until the impact of the air and the excess pressure on the under surface of the wings is sufficient to lift the plane into the air.

In jet planes no propellers are required; jet action, which will be explained later, thrusts the plane through the air.

HOW AN AIRPLANE IS CONTROLLED

The Control Surfaces

Airplanes move in three-dimensional space. Reference to the diagram on page 609 will show three kinds of changes in position relative to this space. It might be helpful in understanding these to think of *yourself* as a plane, arms outstretched, flying through space like Superman. You might want to change your *pitch* so that the length of

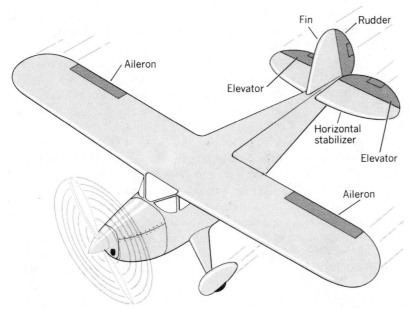

The control surfaces of a plane permit it to change its position in three ways. The text explains how the elevator, rudder, and ailerons are manipulated to control pitching, yawing, and rolling.

your body is tilted with respect to the earth, pointing up or pointing down. The word pitch is also applied to a similar motion of a ship at sea. You might want to *yaw,* that is, alter the direction in which you are heading toward the left or toward the right. You might want to *roll* (or bank), so that one of your arms is higher than the other. Rolling is also a nautical term, well known to those who have suffered from seasickness.

The pilot is able to cause these changes in position by manipulating adjustable control surfaces that are hinged to the plane and can be turned like a door. When these surfaces are turned to "catch the breeze," they alter the position of the plane in the air (see p. 634).

Pitching is effected by moving the *elevator,* part of the tail of the plane. When the elevator is tilted up, the plane's tail goes down and its nose up. When the elevator is down, the opposite movement occurs.

Yawing to the left or right is effected by moving the rudder, also part of the tail of the plane.

Rolling (banking) requires the operation of the two *ailerons,* which are hinged strips attached to

the trailing edge of the plane's wings. The ailerons work in opposition to each other, so that when one is turned up the other automatically moves down.

One other control should be mentioned here—the engine *throttle,* which regulates the amount of forward *thrust* supplied by the propellers.

Having given the functions of the *movable* controls of a plane we must hasten to correct an impression that some may have about the function of the rudder. It is natural to assume that it serves exactly as a rudder does on a ship, that is, it is used in a similar way by a pilot to execute right and left turns in the air. The rudder does help, as we shall see, but it is the ailerons and the wings that are the chief factors in turning. We quote from the *Flight Instruction Manual* of the U.S. Civil Air Authority in this regard:

Turns are *not* made with the rudder. Turns are made in an airplane by tipping, or canting, the direction of the lift of the wings from vertical to one side or the other, causing this "lift" to pull the airplane in that direction as well as to overcome gravity. This is done by using the ailerons to roll the airplane toward the side to which it is desired to turn.[1]

The manual goes on to say that the rudder is used while banking in a turn to correct the tendency of the plane to yaw toward the outside of the turn. In other words turning is done by tilting the plane so that part of the lift on the wings is used to pull the plane to the left or right. To try to turn by using the rudder alone is like trying to make a sharp turn in an auto while traveling rapidly on an icy road. The car may point in a new direction, but it continues skidding off in the original one.

In addition to the three angular motions of the plane—pitching, yawing, and rolling—there are the more obvious movements of the plane in space: its forward motion, which gets you where you want to go; its sideways motion, caused by a wind across the direction of flight or by certain deliberate maneuvers; and the up-and-down movement in bumpy air, which sometimes makes you wish you had taken a train.

JETS

The propeller, as we have seen, is a device that makes use of the air to pull the plane forward. Jet planes, however, generally have no propellers. How do jets work? (See p. 633.)

A simple demonstration with a toy balloon illustrates the jet principle. If a balloon is inflated and then released, it zips around as the air escapes. We note that the balloon zips in the opposite direction from that of the escaping air. Why does the balloon behave in this way?

Jet action is an example of *Newton's third law of motion,* which states that for every action there is an equal and opposite reaction.

In the balloon demonstration the force of the escaping air is the action and the balloon's motion

forward is the reaction. The force of the air streaming out of the opening produces an action backward and a *thrust* on the *inside* of the balloon in the opposite direction. Thrust, however, does not depend on the presence of air *outside* the balloon, for, as we shall see, jet action is possible, in fact more effective, in the vacuum of airless space.

Another way of looking at jet action is to think of the molecules bouncing around in an inflated balloon, with its neck tied. The air molecules inside the balloon are striking the surface with equal force everywhere. All forces are balanced, so nothing moves. When the neck of the balloon is opened, the molecules that were striking against the neck surface from the inside now find no surface to strike against. They rush out and are no longer part of the "team": The whole system (the balloon and its contained air) moves in the direction of the stronger force, which is now toward the end opposite the neck. The same is true in a jet engine: Burning fuel and an *air compressor* together produce a highly compressed exhaust gas inside the engine chamber. The compressed air pushes equally in all directions, but can escape only backward, out of the *tail pipe*. The greater force in the opposite direction pushes the engine and the plane attached to it forward.

There are a number of kinds of jet planes, but all work on the same principle. In all, a large quantity of gas is produced by the rapid burning of fuel in a combustion chamber; the gas is blasted out of an opening in the rear end; and the reaction thrusts the plane forward—from the inside.

The powerful jet engine made possible the construction of the "jumbo jets," a new generation of transports nearly double the size and capacity of their predecessors. In 1969 the Boeing 747, the world's first commercial jumbo jet, made its maiden flight, carrying 375 passengers.

SUPERSONIC FLIGHT

As planes traveled faster and faster, new obstacles to flight developed. When a plane moved at a

[1] U.S. Civil Air Authority, *Flight Instruction Manual,* Technical Manual 100 (April 1951), p. 43.

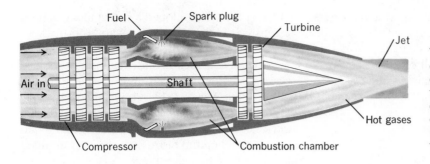

This turbojet illustrates some of the features common to all jets. The rapid burning of fuel in a combustion chamber causes a blast out of a rear opening. The reaction to the blast thrusts the plane forward.

speed of 750 miles (1,200 kilometers) per hour, approaching the speed of sound, a curious thing happened. The plane began to shake and bounce. Going still faster, at the very speed of sound, the shaking increased, becoming so violent that the wings were sometimes wrenched off the plane. At still greater speed the plane had smooth sailing again.

The plane had passed through an invisible wall in the air—the *sound barrier*. Just what is this barrier?

You can recall from Chapter 18A that sound moves in a wave of compression; molecules of air are pushed closer together as the wave proceeds. This wave of compression advances at about 1,100 feet (330 meters) per second or about 760 miles (1,200 kilometers) per hour at sea level.

When a plane moves slower than the speed of sound (roughly 660 miles or 1,000 kilometers) per hour at an altitude of 35,000 feet (10,500 meters), the sound made by the plane speeds away from it. But when the speed of sound is reached, the plane keeps pace with its own sound waves. The compression waves cannot speed away from the plane. They pile up in front of the wings and body of the plane, forming a veritable wall called a *shock wave*. Shock waves interfere with the smooth flow of air around the plane and cause irregularities in the forces that act on the plane. When a plane succeeds in breaking through and flying at *supersonic speed*—that is, faster than the speed of sound—the sound waves no longer bother it, for they are left behind the plane.

Planes have been designed to move through

the sound barrier without damage. A long needle-like nose and thin swept-back wings enable the plane to slip through the sound barrier smoothly. The *delta*, or triangular wing, is common in military craft designed for efficient flight at supersonic speeds.

Work on the development of a commercial supersonic transport (SST) began in 1959 in the United States, and shortly thereafter in the U.S.S.R. and in a joint project of Britain and France. The U.S. SST was planned to have about two thirds the passenger capacity of the 747, but three times its speed. Traveling at about 1,750 miles (2,800 kilometers) per hour it would be able to fly from New York to Europe in only about $2\frac{1}{2}$ hours.

However, in 1970 the SST program in the United States came under fire in Congress. Ecologists contended that the SST constituted a danger to the earth's environment because it produced a sonic boom that is heard on the ground as an explosive sound; because of the increased noise in the immediate area of the plane on takeoff; and because it pollutes the upper atmosphere, thereby threatening the ozone blanket that shields the earth from ultraviolet radiation (see pp. 218, 423). These arguments were contested by the proponents of the SST, but the ecologists won—at least for the time being. As a consequence, the SST program was dropped, but it continued in England and France resulting in the Concorde, now flown in regular transatlantic passenger service.

In 1976 limited operation of the Concorde from Europe to Washington, D.C., began on a trial basis. After considerable controversy and protests by ecologists and by residents affected by the flight, trial runs of the Concorde to New York City began in October of 1977. All commercial supersonic flights *over* the continental United States are prohibited at present.

THE ROCKET PLANE

Perhaps the ultimate stage in the flying machine is the rocket, which does not rely in any way on the air to sustain its motion. With the development of more and more powerful propulsion systems, the thrust provided by the rocket is sufficient to overcome the pull of gravity even without the "lift" provided by the wings of the conventional plane. When rocket planes leave the lower atmosphere and fly at heights of hundreds of miles or more the air is too "thin" for wings to be of any use anyway.

The rocket engine, unlike any of the others discussed so far, carries its own oxygen supply (or other chemicals to serve as oxidizers) for the burning of fuel and is, therefore, not limited to flight within the atmosphere. This, plus its enormous engine-power-to-vehicle ratio, makes it the only known engine that can drive manned or unmanned vehicles into space.

Rockets and Space Flight

The history of rockets is closely related to the history of space travel, because only with the rocket principle is space travel possible. The first recorded use of rockets occurred in 1232 A.D., when the Chinese repelled Mongols with "arrows of flying fire," which were actually incendiary firecrackers. Rockets were brought to Europe shortly after. In 1379 a crude rocket powered with gunpowder scored a lucky hit that destroyed a defending tower in the battle for the Isle of Chiozza during the Venetian-Genovese War.

In the nineteenth century Sir William Congreve of Great Britain developed a rocket that was used extensively in the Napoleonic Wars. The "rocket's red glare" in *The Star-Spangled Banner* refers to the Congreve rocket missiles that the British fired against Fort McHenry during the battle for Baltimore in the War of 1812. A humanitarian use for the Congreve rocket was first patented in 1838: a device that carried a line from shore to a stranded vessel, enabling the distressed crew to be pulled to shore on a breeches buoy.

All rockets up to the twentieth century employed a solid fuel, such as gunpowder. In 1903 a Russian schoolteacher, Konstantin Ziolkovsky, proposed an interplanetary rocket in an article entitled "Investigating Space with Rocket Devices." He urged that a spaceship be powered by a liquid-propelled engine supplied with liquid hydrogen and liquid oxygen. It is interesting to note Ziolkovsky's statement that "probably the first seeds of the idea were sown by that great fantastic author, Jules Verne." Ziolkovsky's ideas remained unknown outside of Russia, and at that time the Russians themselves gave them little attention.

Working separately, Herman Oberth, a Rumanian-German, and Robert H. Goddard, an American, laid the basis for modern rocketry. Oberth stimulated experimental rocket work in Germany with his book *The Rocket into Interplanetary Space,* published in 1923.

In 1919 Dr. Goddard, a professor at Clark University in Massachusetts, sent to the Smithsonian Institution in Washington, D.C., a copy of a 69-page manuscript entitled "A Method of Reaching Extreme Altitudes." This paper attracted the attention of the press because of a brief comment on the possibility of shooting a rocket to the moon and exploding a load of powder on the surface. Shortly thereafter, Goddard hypothesized that a liquid fuel would be superior to the powder pellets that he had been using to power his rockets. Between 1919 and 1926 Goddard worked to perfect his ideas. On March 16, 1926, a momentous day for rocket flight, the world's first liquid-fuel rocket was launched. Although it covered a distance of only 184 feet (55 meters) it proved that

This is an illustration from Jules Verne's science fiction novel, *From the Earth to the Moon,* published in 1865. The passengers in Verne's spacecraft are enjoying their first feeling of weightlessness. (*Courtesy of NASA.*)

this kind of a rocket would work. Goddard continued his research in the more open spaces of the southwestern United States. In 1935 his rockets achieved altitudes of 7,500 feet (2,250 meters) and speeds of over 700 miles (1,100 kilometers) per hour.

On October 4, 1957, the first man-made satellite, *Sputnik I,* was rocketed into orbit by the Soviet Union. The Space Age opened. Less than four

months later, on January 31, 1958, the United States launched its first satellite, *Explorer I.*

UP, UP, AND AWAY

Circling the earth today are over 1,000 satellites that, unlike the moon, were placed there by humans. Included in the new array of heavenly bodies are satellites for watching the weather picture; surveying the earth's resources; monitoring the earth's environment; relaying telephone and television messages around the earth; assisting aircraft and seacraft in navigation; and for serving as astronomical observatories far above the dust and fog of our atmosphere-blanketed earth.

Spaceships have left the earth and visited the moon, Venus, and Mars. Some space vehicles have passed close to Mercury, Jupiter, Saturn, Uranus and Neptune and then are moving out into interstellar space beyond the solar system.

To place a satellite into orbit around the earth or to send a spaceship to a planet requires an understanding of gravity. At this point it might be well to reread the section "Gravity and the Solar System" in Chapter 7A. Briefly, it was stated there that the strength of the gravitational force between two bodies depends (1) on the amount of material in them (their masses) and (2) on the distance between them.

One significant implication of the laws of gravity for space travel is that the attraction between two bodies—between the earth and an apple, for example—is a definite, measurable force. This fact removes gravity from the realm of the inexorable, the unconquerable. Gravity is something that can be contended with and can be opposed, although not yet abolished—science fiction claims notwithstanding.

The same apple that Newton is reputed to have observed falling from a tree can be made to travel away from the earth—if we engage a powerful "apple hurler" to pitch it outward with sufficient force. Later we shall examine the amount of force necessary to escape from the earth. For the moment let us consider one unique characteristic of gravity.

Assume that the imaginary earthbound "apple hurler" is allowed only one chance—one mighty heave—to send the apple on its way. Earth's gravity, however, tugs at the apple with unseen fingers every moment of its outward flight, slowing it down more and more. It looks like a losing battle, but that is not necessarily so, because the strength of gravity diminishes with distance. Although the apple is slowing down, the pull on it by the earth is getting weaker. What will happen to the apple? Will it be pulled back to Earth? Will it land on the moon, Venus, or Mars, or go into orbit around one of these bodies? Will it become an "apple planet" of the sun? The sections that follow discuss the factors that control the destiny of objects hurled into space.

Getting into Orbit

What is necessary to make a satellite go into orbit around the earth? Conduct the following "thought experiment." (Incidentally, this is similar to one that Newton described; see p. 606.) Picture a cannon mounted on a huge tower that extends 200 miles (320 kilometers) above the surface of the earth. If a cannonball is allowed to roll out of the end of the barrel it will fall directly to the earth, landing somewhere near the base of the tower. If, however, the ball is fired with a small amount of powder in a direction parallel to the surface of the earth it will fall in an arc, striking the earth at some distance from the cannon tower. A larger charge will make it land at a point still farther away. As the launching speed of the cannonball is increased, its path carries it farther and farther around the earth. Finally a speed is reached that is sufficient to give it a circular path around the earth. The ball is in orbit.

Has gravity ceased to exert its influence on the cannonball? An observer stationed in the cannon tower, watching the ball leaving the cannon, would see it falling constantly, but never striking the ground. At the speed with which it is traveling, the curved surface of the earth "tips out" from under it. The ball remains the same distance from the ground and "falls around" the earth in a complete circle.

Let us carry the implications of this thought experiment to the launching into orbit of a satellite from the surface of the earth. First, there is no tower, so the satellite must be boosted up to the desired height by rockets with thrust sufficient to overcome the pull of gravity and the frictional resistance of air. Second, at the point at which the satellite is placed into orbit, it must be traveling at the right speed for that altitude (slightly less than 5 miles or 8 kilometers per second at a height of 200 miles or 320 kilometers) to counteract the force of gravity. Third, it must be traveling in a direction parallel to the earth's surface when the rockets burn out. An error of only 1°— upward or downward—may spell the difference between a successful orbit and one which brings the satellite so close to the earth that the resistance of the air will make it lose speed rapidly. Under such conditions it may not be able to complete a single orbit (see pp. 635–637).

The earth itself is an example of a body moving rapidly enough (about 18 miles or 29 kilometers a second) in its orbit not to fall into the sun, but not so rapidly that it tears out of the solar system to wander in the Milky Way galaxy. Man-made satellites become less mysterious when we realize that they obey the same laws that govern all the planets in their orbits around the sun.

The Shape of an Orbit

Generally the path of most satellites resembles that of all the planets around the sun: They are ellipses. It is virtually impossible to put a satellite into a perfectly circular orbit around the earth; the orbit is usually elliptical. The elliptical path of the *Gemini IV*, for example, brought this spaceship as far away as 179 miles (288 kilometers) from the earth and as near as 101 miles (163) kilometers). When a satellite is at its greatest distance from the earth it is at its *apogee* (from the Greek, *apo,* away from, + *ge,* earth); when it is closest it is at its *perigee* (*peri,* around, + *ge,* earth).

Staying in Motion

When people realize that once in orbit satellites generally have no engines for propulsion (except for adjustments of position or special maneuvers), they ask, "What keeps a satellite moving?" This is a perfectly natural question, because our experiences on Earth teach us that moving vehicles— cars, trains, boats—stop moving unless continuously propelled by some kind of engine. However, what is not always understood is that these moving objects are constantly opposing the force of friction that results from their contact with the ground, water, air, and so on. Without friction a moving car could coast along forever with the motor turned off. Newton expressed this idea in one of his laws when he stated that a body continues in uniform motion (unchanging speed and direction) unless compelled by some applied force to do otherwise.

At altitudes of 100 or more miles (160 kilometers) above the earth, the effect of the atmosphere is negligible, so that there is practically nothing to slow down the speed of satellites. Some satellites have had a short life because they were launched into orbits that cut across the lower, denser portion of the earth's atmosphere. This may have occurred by design or error. In either case friction with the air in these lower layers robs the satellite of the speed necessary to maintain it in orbit.

Speed and Orbital Distance

What speed is required to maintain satellites in orbit at various distances from the earth? Gravity decreases with distance, so the speed required decreases with distance from the earth. The table shows the relationship of distance to velocity in orbit. At a distance of 22,300 miles (35,882 kilometers) from the earth the orbital period is one day. Since the earth is spinning at the rate of one turn per day such a satellite would appear to stand still, provided it was placed in a circular orbit in the plane of the earth's equator, moving in the same west-to-east direction as the earth. (A satellite's orbital plane may be imagined as a flat plate passing through the center of the earth. The plate's rim is the satellite's orbit.) Because both the satellite's revolution and the earth's rotation are completed once every 24 hours, the satellite will remain in the same spot over the earth's equator at all times. The satellite is in a *geostationary orbit* (see p. 617).

In July 1963 the communications satellite Syncom II was the first operational satellite to be placed in such a stationary position. A few months later Syncom III achieved fame in the early days of communications satellite demonstrations because it transmitted live broadcasts of the 1964 Olympics from Japan over the Pacific to California. From here the telecast was sent over land lines throughout the United States. Three such stationary-type satellites, called *synchronous satellites*, are required to provide a global communication network with uninterrupted 24-hour-a-day television and telephone service, because each satellite can "see" only a little less than half the earth. Similarly, the Synchronous Meteorological Satellite program, initiated in 1974, provides full-time coverage of the world's weather (see pp. 229–230).

At a distance of 230,000 miles (370,000 kilometers) from the earth the period for one revolution is 27 days. Such a satellite already exists—the moon itself.

Multistage Launching

Multistage rockets with two, three, four, or more stages mounted on top of each other piggyback fashion are often used for orbital or space flight. In succession each part of the vehicle separates from the space vehicle after it has burned its fuel, ultimately leaving only the *payload*—which may be a satellite or space shuttle orbiting the earth or a spaceship on its way to the moon, Venus, Mars, or the outer planets. What are the advantages of a multistage vehicle?

1. All the stages after the first stage have the speed of the prior stage imparted to them.
2. Dropping the stage after it has burned its fuel gives the succeeding stages less "dead weight" to carry as they push the vehicle into higher and higher speeds.

Thrust

The force produced by the huge rocket engines is measured in pounds of *thrust*. To boost a spacecraft into orbit from the ground requires a thrust greater than the total weight of the launch vehicle. Two factors determine the amount of thrust that a rocket can deliver: the rate at which the fuel is burned and the speed at which the resulting gases are exhausted from the jet.

To place an object in orbit around the earth requires that enough energy be imparted (1) to lift the object against the force of gravity to the desired height, and then (2) to give it enough speed in its orbital path to counteract the force of gravity.

The atmosphere must also be taken into consideration in planning the trip from the moment of launch on the surface of the earth until the space vehicle is above the air. The vehicle must be streamlined so that air resistance is kept to a minimum. Speed in the lower atmosphere must not be too great, because friction increases with speed. Moreover, frictional heating results in temperatures that may adversely affect the material of the spacecraft.

A rocket rises slowly from its launching pad and gradually gains speed as it climbs. Thus it passes through the dense lower layers of the atmosphere with speeds at which friction heating does not constitute a serious problem. The rocket reaches full speed at heights where the air is too thin to cause any important resistance to flight.

Escaping from the Earth

A spacecraft sent to another planet or the moon must achieve *escape velocity;* that is, it must be able to coast away from the earth indefinitely with its engines turned off. This is done by accelerating the vehicle to a certain speed (see pp. 633–635).

At or near the earth's surface, escape velocity is slightly more than 7 miles (11 kilometers) per second, or about 25,000 miles (40,000) kilome-

SPEED AND ORBITAL DISTANCE

Height above Earth (miles)	(kilometers)	Velocity (feet per second)	(meters per second)	Time for One Orbit
0	0	26,113	7,913	84.32 min.*
100	160	25,793	7,816	87.5 min.
1,000	1,600	23,348	7,075	97.3 min.
# 22,300	35,882	10,141	3,073	1,440 min = 1 day
23,000	37,000	10,000	3,033	1,497 min = 1 day +
230,000	370,000	3,399	1,030	26.6 days
d 234,800	378,028	3,361	1,019	27.3 days

*Neglecting slowing caused by the earth's atmosphere
actual geostationary orbit
d actual mean distance to the moon (Earth's surface to center of the moon.)

ters) per hour. If a space vehicle attains that speed, even if all its fuel is burned up it can escape from the earth.

The attainment of escape velocity does not mean that the spacecraft is free of the earth's gravitational influence, which extends to infinity. As it races into space the spacecraft is slowed by earth's gravity, but it will continue outward until it becomes subject to the gravity of the moon or a planet or the sun. The classical saying "What goes up must come down" is no longer true.

At present multistage rockets are used to launch spacecraft into escape flights. Each rocket stage is fired in sequence at different altitudes until the escape velocity is achieved.

Escape velocity from any astronomical body depends on the strength of gravity on its *surface*. On Venus, whose mass and size are close to those of Earth, the escape velocity is 6.3 miles per second (10 kilometers per second). On smaller Mars the escape velocity is only 3.1 miles (5 kilometers) per second. On the moon escape velocity is about 1.5 miles (2.5 kilometers) per second.

An Earth–Moon Trip

In a trip to the moon and back a spaceship is under the constant gravitational influence of both the earth and the moon. Consider some of the

implications of this dual attraction (see p. 635):

1. As the ship coasts from the earth to the moon, earth's gravity slows it down from its initial speed of about 25,000 miles (40,000 kilometers) per hour to about only 2,000 miles (3,000 kilometers) per hour.
2. It reaches this slowest speed at a point about nine tenths of the way to the moon. Here the gravitational pull of the earth and the moon are equal.
3. Entering the moon's sphere of greater gravitational influence the spaceship speeds up, reaching a speed of over 5,000 miles (8,000 kilometers) per hour.
4. Escaping from the moon requires approximately the same speed achieved in the closest approach of the coasting spaceship before braking by rocket action—over 5,000 miles (8,000 kilometers) per hour.
5. On the return trip the spaceship is first slowed down by the moon's pull. Reaching the sphere of earth's gravitational influence it speeds up, finally reaching 25,000 miles (40,000 kilometers) per hour.

LIFE SUPPORT IN SPACE

When we place a human being into a spaceship, we are adding a complex and delicate structure to it. We can alter the nonliving mechanisms in a space vehicle to fit the conditions of space. But we have to take humans more or less as they are— and alter the conditions to fit their needs.

How do we protect and support astronauts in space? Although the precise methods will vary with the nature of the vehicle and the duration of the trip certain guiding principles can be stated.

Pressure

We must encase astronauts in an airtight vehicle or space suits that protect them from the vacuum of outer space. Without such protection, an astronaut's blood and other body fluids would boil and turn to gas, rupturing body structures. In the space shuttle, described on pages 623–624, and in future spacecraft, pressure inside the cabin will be maintained at about 15 pounds per square inch, the same as sea-level pressure on earth, thus making a "shirtsleeve" environment possible.

Astronauts also don space suits when it is necessary for them to leave the cabin for a "space walk," or for the exploration of the surface of the airless moon. Under these circumstances either the cabin is completely depressurized—emptied of all air and reduced to zero pressure—or the astronauts may exit through the airlock.

Oxygen

Oxygen must be carried along and delivered to the astronaut in regular and uniform concentration at the rate of 150 gallons (570 liters) per day. There are several methods of supplying oxygen. One is to carry the total supply in containers either in gaseous or liquid state. A second method is to obtain oxygen from certain oxygen compounds. A third is to have green plants along to produce oxygen. A fourth method would be to split the oxygen away from the carbon dioxide breathed out by the astronaut and thereby reclaim it for use.

Wastes

Waste gases, such as carbon dioxide and water vapor, must be removed from the cabin's atmos-phere. Lithium hydroxide is a chemical that can remove carbon dioxide. Other gaseous contaminants are removed by activated charcoal.

Water vapor exhaled into the atmosphere can be removed by condensation on a cold surface. The condensed water can then be reused as drinking water.

In addition to human wastes, one must remove contaminants resulting from the operation of batteries, motors, and waste-removal systems, and from other parts of the total system.

Temperature

Research has been conducted in simulators and in Skylab space stations to determine the best methods for maintaining cabin air temperature and humidity for the comfort of the crew and for the proper functioning of equipment.

Optimum operating temperatures can be maintained by both passive and active means. The spacecraft exterior surface generally is white to reflect radiation. Excess heat generated by the crew, as well as the electrical equipment, and so on, is absorbed and transmitted by heat pipes to thermal radiators contained in the cargo bay doors of the shuttle orbiter.

Radiation

On Earth the potentially harmful radiation, particularly ultraviolet and X rays from the sun, is absorbed by the atmosphere. In space, however, the crew equipment must be shielded from the solar and cosmic radiation, as well as from high-energy particles. The spacecraft cabin or the space suit contains sufficient material to absorb an adequate amount. (The amount of radiation received by an Apollo astronaut on the moon was equivalent to an ordinary individual living in Denver for a year.) For spaceflights of several months duration or less, the amount of radiation received by the crew members is not a serious problem. However, for long-term space flight, whether going to Mars or working on a space station, we need to do more research.

Acceleration

As a rocket ship picks up speed on its way up, the astronaut feels heavier and heavier. This is similar to the experience we have momentarily when we are in an elevator that suddenly shoots upward. We feel ourselves pushed hard against the floor of the elevator. When a rocket ship accelerates, the astronaut also feels the extra push. The strength of this push is measured in "g's" (the "g" represents gravity's pull). The astronaut's weight on earth is, as we know, just the amount that the earth's gravity pulls on him. This amount is called 1 g.

Shortly after a rocket leaves the launch pad it may have an upward·thrust of about twice that of gravity's pull. The astronaut would then feel a 2-g push. A spring scale placed under a 150-pound astronaut at this time would indicate that he weighs 300 pounds. As the rocket picks up speed a space shuttle astronaut experiences as much as 3 g's. A person will experience 3.5 g's while riding on a modern roller coaster. Next time you ride a roller coaster just think that you are getting a rougher ride than a space shuttle astronaut!

Extra g's are also experienced when a spaceship slows down. This can be compared to the pressure against one's legs experienced when a downward moving elevator slows suddenly for a stop.

It is important to note that increased g's result not from speed but from a *change* in speed. When we travel in jet airliners across the country at speeds of 400 miles (about 650 kilometers) per hour we often feel that we are motionless, unless we look at clouds and the landscape we pass.

As a spaceship leaves its launching pad and picks up speed, the blood in an astronaut's body would tend to pool in the lower part of the body—if he sat upright. The heart could not supply the force needed to carry the blood to the brain, causing loss of consciousness. If, on the other hand, the astronaut lies on his back with his legs elevated the blood will not collect in the lower part of his body. In this position, also, the astronaut does not have to support the full weight of head, arms, and torso. The extra g's are distributed over the astronaut's back area.

Weightlessness

An astronaut in orbit around the earth is said to be in a state of weightlessness. For an understanding of weightlessness, again enter the elevator in which you were a passenger in the discussion on acceleration. Imagine that you are standing on a weighing scale on the floor of the elevator. When the elevator is at rest the earth pulls you down with a force equal to your weight—say 130 pounds. The scale reacts by pushing you upward with an equal force. The dial consequently shows a reading of 130 pounds. It is the upward-supporting force of the scale (or any other supporting platform) that gives you the sensation of having weight.

Assume now that the elevator is hoisted to the very top of the shaft and that someone cuts its cable. The scale is no longer supporting you because it is falling away from you as fast as you are falling toward it. Your *apparent* weight as shown on the scale is zero. If you release a book from your hand it appears to hover in the air. You and the objects in the elevator are weightless, not because gravity has been "turned off" but because you and all these objects are unsupported and are falling freely.

Objects inside an orbiting satellite are also weightless because they are falling freely. You will recall from the discussion on pages 614–615 of the launching of the cannonball into orbit that it, too, falls freely. When a satellite is in circular orbit its orbital speed takes it away from the earth during each second just as far as gravity pulls it toward the earth. Although it stays the same distance from the earth it is constantly falling. The satellite, the astronauts, and all other objects in it are apparently weightless.

Thus, it is evident that weightlessness is not produced by lack of gravity but by a particular

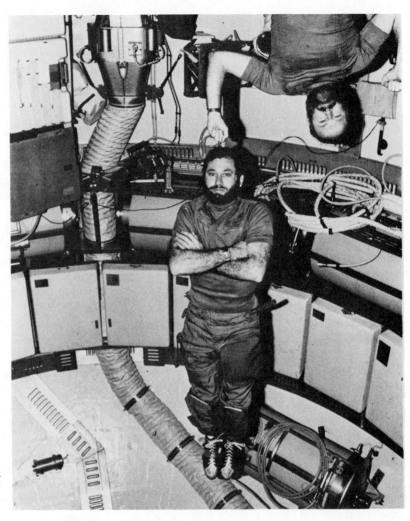

Astronauts demonstrate weightlessness on Skylab 4. Three Skylab crewmen lived in this weightless environment for a total of 84 days. (*Courtesy of NASA.*)

kind of motion, which we might call *free motion.* (Usually this is called *free fall,* but this term suggests falling down whereas in space a person or object can fall in any direction.) In traveling through space to the moon, or beyond, weightlessness occurs only when the spacecraft is coasting, that is, when the rocket engines are shut off and the spacecraft is subject only to the force of gravity.

John Glenn, weightless for 4 hours and 40 minutes in his history-making orbital flight of the Mercury, reported the following observations:

Objects within the cockpit can be parked in midair. For example, at one time during the flight, I was using a hand-held camera. Another system needed attention; so it seemed quite natural to let go of the camera, take care of the other chore in the spacecraft, then reach out, grasp the camera and go back about my business.... I had one tube of food that was squeezed into my mouth out of the tube. This presented no problem swallowing or getting it down at all.

I think the only restrictions of food would be that it not be particularly crumbly, like cookies, with a lot of little particles that might break off, because you wouldn't be able to get all these back unless you had a butterfly net of some kind.

The astronauts all reported that the sensation of weightlessness is a pleasant one. There is no disorientation. Weightlessness has not been a serious problem for astronauts thus far for periods up to seven months, but it has resulted in loss of muscle tone and loss of calcium from bones, and in other effects on the cardiovascular system, body fluids, and endocrine and nervous systems. A major lesson learned from extended stays in weightlessness on manned space stations is that the human body may be the most delicate machine of all in the space vehicle. To counteract perilous body atrophy, tough physical fitness exercise regimens have been designed. In addition to exercise it is hoped that certain drugs will help astronauts maintain their health in zero gravity.

Food

From what we have just quoted, it is apparent that it would not be comfortable for a weightless individual to eat in the same way as he does on Earth. Dry foods on a spoon lifted to an astronaut's mouth would keep on traveling after the spoon had stopped and would land on the roof of the spacecraft. Moist solid foods that stick to the spoon by surface tension may be eaten in conventional ways. Liquids, such as water, cannot be poured into one's mouth because there is no gravity to cause them to leave the glass. Consequently, water must be packaged in squeeze tubes.

During later missions, space cuisine improved; heated food was available; selections could include prime rib, lobster Newburg, and filet mignon. Single-serving portions packed in stackable containers were designed to be snapped into the oven for heating and then attached to trays.

For long space trips of the future the total food required cannot be stowed and lifted from the earth. Some method of growing food must be provided.

Water must be produced or reclaimed during flight. Water from the astronaut's urine, feces, breath, and sweat is one source. The wastes will be processed to reclaim water and chemicals that may be utilized to promote the growth of plants. Another possible source is the water formed by fuel cells when hydrogen and oxygen are used to produce electric energy. The by-product is water—H_2 plus 0 yields H_2O.

THREE STEPS TO THE MOON

A major goal of the U.S manned spaceflight program was to put human beings on the moon and to bring them back safely to Earth. Step one was Project Mercury, in which the astronauts first ventured into space and completed six flights ranging in length from 15 minutes to 34 hours. Step two was Project Gemini, which was concerned with further development of spacecraft and launch vehicles and preparation of astronauts for operations of ever-increasing complexity. Step three was reserved for Apollo; its climax was the lunar landing.

Mercury, Gemini, and Apollo were the three steps to the moon. More importantly, however, they were steps in our ability to operate in and use space. They have made it possible to explore another body of the solar system and to do important scientific research there. Our experience with these programs has led to our present understanding of the importance of having a flexible, economic space transportation system for our future work in space.

Project Mercury

Project Mercury paved the way for the moon goal by using one-person vehicles and proving that human beings could be sent into space and then returned safely to earth. A milestone in Project Mercury was the three orbital flights of astronaut John H. Glenn, Jr., in 1962.

Space Shuttle Mission Profile

LAUNCH | SOLID ROCKET BOOSTER SEPARATION | EXTERNAL TANK SEPARATION | ORBITAL INSERTION

ORBITAL OPERATIONS | ATMOSPHERIC ENTRY | LANDING | SERVICING FOR RELAUNCH

The stages of a space shuttle mission from the liftoff through the landing on a runway. (*Courtesy of NASA.*)

Originally Project Mercury was assigned only two broad missions: (1) to investigate man's ability to survive and perform in the space environment and (2) to develop the basic space technology and hardware for manned space flights to come. Beyond succeeding in these basic goals Mercury accomplished the following:

Explored the fundamentals of spacecraft reentry—the return to Earth.

Started a family of launch vehicles from existing rockets that led to new booster designs.

Set up an earth-girding tracking system continuously reporting the location of spacecraft.

Trained a pool of astronauts for future space exploration.

Made scientific observations, including earth photography.

Project Gemini

Because it was flown by a crew of two astronauts, the second project was named Gemini for the twin stars Castor and Pollux in the constellation Gemini. The 1965–1966 Gemini missions into space demonstrated that an astronaut can do the following:

Maneuver the craft in space, changing its flight path and changing its orbital distance from the earth.

Leave the craft and do useful work in space.

Rendezvous, by finding and moving closer to another object or craft in space.

Dock, by joining and locking with another craft in space.

Function effectively during prolonged space flights of at least two weeks and return to earth in good physical condition.

Control the spacecraft during its descent from orbit and land it in a selected area on earth.

Perform scientific experiments in space.

Observe and photograph the earth from space.

Use earth photography for earth resource surveys.

Project Apollo

Apollo was the third step to the moon. Its goal was to land explorers from the United States on the moon and bring them safely back to earth.

Three astronauts served as the crew for Apollo, but only two landed on the lunar surface. The third kept the mother craft in orbit around the moon in readiness for the return of the two astronauts and for the journey back to Earth.

On July 20, 1969, with the whole world waiting breathlessly, Neil Armstrong, Apollo 11 Commander, became the first human to set foot on the moon, uttering, "That's one small step for a man, one giant leap for mankind." Edward Aldrin joined him 19 minutes later. Michael Collins remained on the orbiting mother ship.

In their brief $2\frac{1}{2}$-hour moon walk the astronauts explored the moon's surface near the landing site; planted a U.S. flag; took photographs; collected samples of moon rock; and walked, ran, and exercised in the moon's low-gravity environment. In addition they set up a group of experiments that would continue to radio information to earth on solar wind, meteoroid impacts, moonquakes, earth–moon distances, and moon size. The astronauts then blasted off to rejoin the mother ship, and started on their journey back to Earth.

From Earth launch to Earth splashdown the total moon trip took 195 hours, 19 minutes—or about eight days.

SPACE SHUTTLE[2]

The space shuttle markedly expands our ability to do things in space—more often and more effectively than ever before. Like conventional earth-bound carriers of today—trucks, trains, ships, and planes—which move freight and passengers routinely between cities and nations, the shuttle will offer the same workhorse capabilities to space, lifting payloads and people to do work not possible on Earth.

The space shuttle is a vehicle that takes off like a rocket, orbits like a satellite, and returns like an aircraft. The shuttle is composed of three parts: the *orbiter,* the planelike element that carries the crew and the payloads; an *external tank* that contains the propellants used by the orbiter's three main engines; and the two *solid rocket boosters.*

At liftoff the boosters and the orbiter's three main engines fire together. The two boosters are jettisoned after burnout—about 2 minutes and 12 seconds into the flight and at a height of 27.5 miles (44 kilometers)—and are recovered by a parachute system and prepared for another shuttle flight.

The orbiter's main engines continue to burn until the vehicle is just short of orbital velocity, at which time the engines are shut down and the external tank is jettisoned. During its plunge through the atmosphere, the tank breaks up and falls into a safe predetermined ocean area.

The shuttle's small orbital maneuvering system engines are then used to attain the desired orbit and to make any subsequent maneuvers that may be needed during the mission. The crew begins their payload operations in orbit by performing a multitude of assigned tasks, depending on the purpose of the mission. On some missions they might be setting out satellites in orbit, or retrieving satellites for return to Earth. Or they might be servicing currently orbiting satellites, conducting experiments in weightless space that cannot be

[2]Adapted from *Space Shuttle,* NASA.

duplicated on Earth, or studying the earth from their unique vantage point high above the atmosphere.

After orbital operations are completed, the orbiter begins to enter the earth's atmosphere. It levels into horizontal flight at low altitude for an unpowered aircraft-type approach and landing at a speed of 208 miles (335 kilometers) per hour. The thermal materials on the orbiter protect it from the extreme heat of reentry into the atmosphere.

Already planned for the shuttle are payloads that will help to further improve weather forecasting and communications, and earth-observation satellites that will permit a continuous inventory of the world's natural resources and permit them to be applied more effectively to meeting human needs. Other shuttle payloads will continue to obtain information on the chemistry and physics of the sun, stars, planets, and the space through which the earth is traveling. Still others will extend into space our earthbound research in such areas as medicine, biology, chemistry, physics, and material-manufacturing processes.

Spacelab, a fully equipped space laboratory, was developed by eleven European nations under the guidance of the European Space Agency and supported by NASA, with the Marshall Space Flight Center performing as the lead center. Carried into space by the orbiter, Spacelab is adaptable for many types of space operations over long periods of time. (See "Space Station" section that follows. See also the illustration at the beginning of this chapter showing an artist's concept of the International Space Center complex that will house research laboratories for fundamental research and for the development of new technologies.)

Another significant payload planned for the early 1990s is the Hubble Space Telescope, which many astronomers feel may virtually revolutionize their field. The shuttle will place the unmanned telescope into orbit and later serve as a base from which astronauts may make repairs and modifications (see Chapter 8A).

AEROSPACE PLANE

The future of both high speed long-distance air travel and travelling into space may be accomplished with the same craft, the National Aerospace Plane. The research is promising for an aircraft/spacecraft. A craft capable of flying upward of 7,000 miles per hour would provide efficient intercontinental travel or the ability to fly into space and return! It would take off from a runway with a jet engine, and after reaching supersonic speeds would switch over to a supersonic combustion ramjet (SCRAMJET) engine burning hydrogen, which is carried aboard the craft, with oxygen, taken in during the flight and stored for use. The SCRAMJET engine would propel the craft from Mach 5 to Mach 25 (or from 5 to 25 times the speed of sound). At this point it could switch over to a hydrogen/oxygen rocket engine for entry into Earth orbit. Taking in oxygen from the atmosphere during the flight phase would overcome the problem of having to carry all of the propellants at takeoff. Upon return, the plane would have the ability to maneuver in the upper reaches of the atmosphere, which would allow it to land on any commercial runway.

SPACE STATION

A station in permanent orbit around the earth, long a favorite idea of science fiction writers, now promises to become a reality. In 1971 the Soviets launched the first space station, Salyut, which was occupied briefly by three cosmonauts.

Skylab, the first space station of the United States, was launched on May 14, 1973, orbiting the earth at a distance of some 270 miles (430 kilometers). On May 25 three astronauts, flying an Apollo spacecraft, rendezvoused and docked with the workshop. They spent the next 28 days in this 100-ton vehicle.

The astronauts on Skylab were able to function well in space, working 12 or more hours a day, and taking long unplanned space walks to make

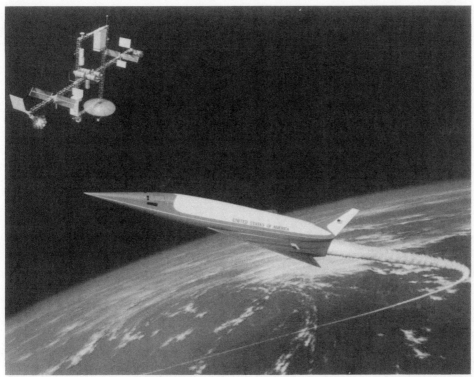

The aerospace plane would have the capability to routinely cruise and maneuver into and out of the atmosphere. Flying upwards of 7,000 miles an hour, it could reach the Orient in two hours, or could go directly into orbit to work in space—taking off and returning on a conventional airport runway. (*Courtesy of NASA.*)

spaceship repairs. They took 30,000 photographs of the sun with Skylab's eight solar telescopes and 14,000 photographs of the earth. These photographs demonstrated that an orbiting spacecraft could be used as a platform for scientists "in residence" to study geology, agriculture, forestry, oceanography, and land use of the earth.

A second crew of three astronauts began a 59-day mission on July 28, 1973, followed by a third crew on November 16 of the same year, who remained in space for 84 days. This was the last visit to our mobile home in the sky. Skylab ended its six years in space when it predictably tumbled and broke up in the atmosphere in 1979.

In the decade following Skylab, the Soviets launched a series of space stations. Salyut 6, the most long-lived of this series, was orbited in 1977. It was visited by 16 crews of cosmonauts on individual missions lasting up to six months, thus doubling the record of Skylab's crews. In addition, unmanned capsules were coupled automatically with the station, bearing fuel and supplies, as were a number of other robot vehicles. One of these, Cosmos 1267, was a huge "building block" module that doubled the station's size when it docked with Salyut in 1981.

Salyut 6 carried myriad pieces of scientific and observational gear, and conducted studies to compensate for the stresses of a zero-gravity environment on humans. Salyut 6 reentered the earth's

The Viking lander spacecraft on the surface of Mars searches for evidence of life; it samples the soil and the atmosphere and photographs the surrounding area. See Chapter 7A for details. (*Courtesy of NASA.*)

atmosphere and burned up after half a decade in orbit.

Salyut 7 was launched in 1982 and one crew of two cosmonauts lived and worked in it for 211 days. The Soviet station MIR was placed in orbit in 1986, with improved control and operation systems, expanded crew space, and a docking adapter with five ports for visiting spacecraft.

Although the United States is concerned about the advances the Soviets have made in orbiting stations, proposals for a new-generation manned space station remain unresolved.

SPACE, SCIENCE, AND TECHNOLOGY

Science principles developed over the centuries have guided the course of space explorations. Conversely, space techniques and structures developed in the space program have provided new tools for science and new processes, methods, and products for everyday living.

Space techniques have provided a new window on the stars and planets. Eight of the nine planets (including Earth) and their many moons have been viewed by spacecraft that have yielded a tremendous amount of information about these bodies. Photographs taken by Tiros, Nimbus, ESSA, Application Technology Satellites, Gemini, and Skylab show what information can be obtained with observation of the earth from space. A familiar example are the weather satellite photographs of the earth and its cloud cover, seen daily on millions of television screens.

A new era of earth study began on July 23, 1972, with the launching into earth orbit of the first of the earth resources technology satellites, now known as Landsats. These earth-watching packages of sensors, electronic scanners, and thematic mappers can perform such functions as gathering data that can be used to determine the potential yield of a wheat or coffee crop; detecting the spread of water pollution; mapping the movement of glaciers; and monitoring dozens of other phenomena on a scale never before possible. Information gathered will yield better understanding in such areas as agriculture, forestry, oceanography, geology, geography, ecology, and meteorology. A truly global inventory of the storehouses and life-supporting systems of spaceship Earth is developing from this program.

Over 80 countries have now become involved in the space program, some of them quite extensively. Many countries carry out their own sounding rocket launchings. Dozens of countries use U.S. weather satellites for their own operational purposes. Tracking networks span the globe. A global satellite communication system provides telephone, television, telegraph, and data-transmission services to six continents.

The exploration of outer space is no longer a fantasy. Artificial satellites orbit around the earth performing myriad functions. Astronauts have orbited around the earth, "walked" in space, flown around and landed on the moon, and conducted scientific investigations in space laboratories and space shuttles. Later may come permanent space stations, factories, power plants, and possibly colonies in space. Manned flights to the planets and missions beyond the solar system, perhaps to other worlds whirling around other stars, may be in our future.

IMPORTANT GENERALIZATIONS

The movement of the wings of a plane through the air provides the lift needed to offset the pull of gravity.

The lift on a wing moving through the air arises from (1) the impact of air on its lower surface and (2) the decrease in pressure on its upper surface.

The propeller's or the jet's function is to provide the forward thrust necessary to move the plane through the air.

The position of a plane in the air may be altered by the movement of hinged surfaces—the elevator, rudder, and ailerons.

In jets, fuel is burned rapidly in a large chamber producing a large volume of gas. The force of gas streaming out of the opening of the jet produces a backward kick or thrust that moves the vehicle.

Jet action is an example of Newton's third law of motion, which states that for every action there is an equal and opposite reaction.

Rockets work on the jet principle; unlike jets, however, they carry their own oxygen supply and consequently can operate in airless space.

Rockets have made space travel possible.

To place a satellite into orbit it is necessary to contend with the resistance offered by the earth's atmosphere and with the pull of gravity.

If an object reaches a speed of about 5 miles (8 kilometers) per second or 18,000 miles (29,000 kilometers) per hour it can orbit the earth at an altitude of several hundred miles (kilometers).

To stay in orbit a satellite must move fast enough to counterbalance the gravitational attraction of the earth.

Satellites maintain their speed in orbits high above the earth because there is no air to slow them down.

The earth itself is a body in orbit around the sun, moving at a rate of about 18 miles (29 kilometers) per second.

The speed required to maintain a satellite in orbit decreases with distance from the earth.

Spaceships and man-made satellites in orbit around the earth move in elliptical paths. In this respect they resemble the moon's orbit around the earth and also the orbits of the planets around the sun.

If a space vehicle reaches the speed of about 7 miles (11 kilometers) per second or about 25,000 miles (40,000 kilometers) per hour, it can escape from the earth.

The speed needed to escape from the earth does not depend on the mass of the escaping body: It is about 7 miles (11 kilometers) per second for all.

The velocity needed to escape from the moon is about 1.5 miles (2.5 kilometers) per second.

On its way to the moon a spaceship is slowed down by the pull of Earth's gravity to about 2,000 miles (3,200 kilometers) per hour.

When a spaceship is about nine tenths of the way from the earth to the moon the gravitational pull of the earth and the moon on it is equal.

To support the life of humans in space we must cope with such factors as pressure, food and oxygen supply, suitable temperature, disposal of wastes, acceleration, radiation, and weightlessness.

When astronauts are accelerated away from the earth or decelerated on reentry, they experience extra weight or extra g's.

Weightlessness is experienced by astronauts in spaceships orbiting the earth or "coasting" through space. During weightlessness the apparent weight of an object is zero.

DISCOVERING FOR YOURSELF

1. Find out more about how progress in weather prediction has influenced aviation and how space launchings depend on weather forecasts.

2. Examine an airplane to see how the principles you have learned in this chapter are put into operation. Examine the wings, fuselage, tail, and other parts. Examine the instrument panel and find out what the pilot can tell by looking at the various indicators.

3. Visit a museum, if possible, to see various historic and modern aircraft.

4. Visit an airport for help in understanding the material in this chapter. Find out how weather forecasts relate to flight.

5. Assemble and try to fly a simple model airplane and use the experience to learn the parts of the aircraft.

6. Watch the takeoff and flight of a helicopter and an airplane and list the similarities and differences.

7. Search the various newspapers and magazines for materials with which to make a chronological list of space activities.

8. Compare the source of thrust of a jet, an airplane, a helicopter, and a rocket.

9. Examine models of various rockets, satellites, or other space vehicles to see how they are shaped and constructed to perform their specific functions.

10. Swing a ball on a string on a vertical plane. Find out whether the length of the string, the weight of the ball, neither, or both affects the speed necessary to keep the ball in "orbit."

11. Various satellites are in orbit at different altitudes from the earth. Find out their purposes.

12. Why is Cape Canaveral on the Atlantic coast a good site for spaceship launchings?

13. Has the investment in the space program been worthwhile? Give arguments to back your stand.

14. Make a graph relating the distance from the earth of an earth satellite with the velocity needed to keep it in orbit (data on p. 617).

TEACHING "FLIGHT AND SPACE TRAVEL"

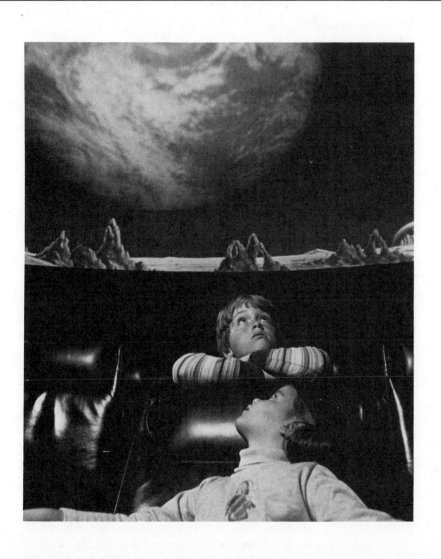

In an interview with Dick Scobee[1] conducted a few weeks before he and the members of his crew perished in the explosion of the space shuttle Challenger on January 28, 1986, he answered the following questions. They are the kind that children continue to ask about space flight.

What does a launch feel like in the space shuttle?
How do you feel in the last few seconds of a countdown?
How do astronauts move around in the orbiter?
How do astronauts eat in space?
What is it like to sleep in space? What are the sleeping arrangements for the crew members?
How do you go to the bathroom and keep clean in space?
If you could take a pet dog or a cat into space, which one would you take and why?
What are the routine jobs that astronauts have to do each day?

In your spaceflight experience, were there any experiments that you particularly liked or were interested in? How do you think these can help the world's growth in knowledge and technology?
If students wanted to create an experiment to be performed in space, what might you suggest to help them get some ideas?
What do astronauts do for entertainment in space?
Do the stars, moon, and sun look different from the way they do on Earth?
What does the earth look like from orbit?
What were your thoughts about Earth as you drifted above its continents?
Do you think human beings can benefit from spaceflight?
Some people say of their favorite vacation spot that it's a nice place to visit, but they wouldn't like to live there. Is that how you feel about space?
After a space mission is complete, what preparations do the astronauts make in order to deorbit and return to Earth?
What do you recall as your happiest moments in your flight?
What education does a person need to become an astronaut, and what education has proven most helpful to you in your career as an astronaut?

[1]June and Dick Scobee, "An Astronaut Speaks," *Science and Children* (March 1986).

A good place to begin a unit in flight and space is to ask the students what questions *they* have. Their questions and concerns can lead to problems that follow here, and others, culminating perhaps in a class or school space show where experiments, constructions, imaginative writings, and artwork may be featured.

A knowledge of the material in Chapter 20A is important for guiding learning. Chapters 7A, 8A, and 9A contain related content, and the corresponding B chapters present related activities.

SOME BROAD CONCEPTS

The movement of the wings of a plane through the air gives the lift needed to overcome the pull of gravity.
Propellers provide the thrust for some types of planes.
Jet engines propel some planes.
Some vehicles are propelled with rocket engines.
An object must reach a speed of 5 miles (8 kilometers) per second to orbit the earth.
To remain in orbit a satellite must move fast enough to counterbalance the earth's gravitational attraction.
Satellites maintain their speed high above the earth because there is no air to slow them down.
The speed required to keep a satellite in orbit decreases with the distance from the earth.
To escape from the earth a spaceship must go 7 miles (11 kilometers) a second.
On its way to the moon a spaceship is first slowed down by the pull of the earth's gravity. When it is about nine tenths of the way to the moon it is speeded up by the pull of the moon's gravity.

FOR YOUNGER CHILDREN

What Happens at an Airport?

Though today's children are space-minded a visit to an airport is a memorable experience, especially if there is someone on hand to answer questions. Even if they are experienced travelers, and today many children are, they may not have had opportunities to observe and ask. Today, security at airports is becoming very strict but it is still possible to arrange visits to a large transport plane, see the instrument panel, talk with the pilot and a flight attendant, find out about the cargoes carried by planes, observe the control tower, see different sizes and types of planes and observe the general "goings on." Such a trip produces the best results if children go with questions to ask and have enough background to appreciate what they are seeing and hearing. For young children the trip should be relatively short and uncomplicated, for older children more detailed and comprehensive. In any event don't show them more than they care to see.

How Can We Make and Use a Glider?

By making paper gliders, children can learn how the shape of a folded piece of paper can assist it to fly through the air. Use a letter-size piece of paper.

1. Fold it in half the long way and make a crease.
2. Open the paper; fold and crease both corners at the end of the paper to the original crease.
3. Now fold and crease again the slanted ends to the original crease.
4. Fold and crease again the slanted ends to the original crease.
5. Fold *back* along the center fold and pinch together to form a glider. A paper clip may be used to keep it together.

Outdoors or large rooms are good places to try the gliders and observe their flights; try to improve the flights by making changes in the size, shape, and other factors in the gliders. Let children measure and compare the distances and duration of various glider flights. Compare how the

Making a paper glider.

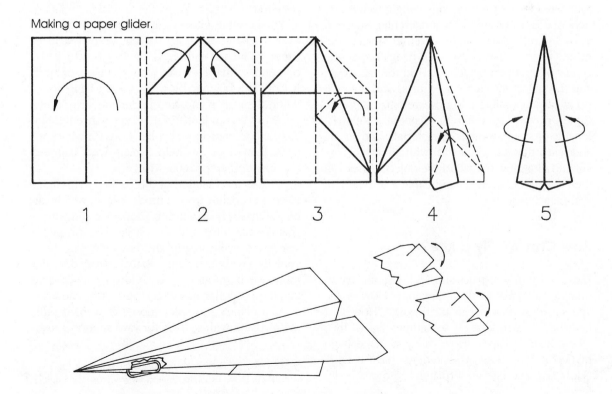

gliders operate indoors with how they behave outdoors on a windy day.

Try to make elevators by making two cuts in the rear of each wing, and then folding the flaps up or down.

How Can We Make a Parachute?

In studying how things fall to the earth children may watch pieces of paper (letter-size) fall to the floor when they are dropped. They may try dropping the papers in different positions and from different heights and observe the falling time. They may then make a crumpled wad of paper and compare the falling time, and discuss reasons for what they observe. Their discussion will begin to develop the idea that a flat piece of paper falls more slowly then a crumpled-up one because of the push of air. This activity may lead into the construction and use of small parachutes. Children will suggest various ways to make them. Tie four threads or strings of equal length to the corners of a facial tissue or a handkerchief. Suspend a toy figure, a small stone, or other object connected to the threads so that it hangs below the center of the open parachute. Fold the parachute and the object into a compact mass and throw it up as far as possible and observe what happens. Children will try different materials, different lengths of string, weights of materials, and so on, and learn that parachutes fill with air when they fall and thus slow the fall of the objects. They can then attempt to apply this principle to the uses of real parachutes.

How Can We Fly a Kite?

Have children construct and fly kites, and try to find out answers to the following: "How is the kite made so that it can be flown?" "How is it launched?" "Why does it sometimes fail to fly?" "What keeps it up?" "How can you make it go higher?" "Why does it sometimes have a tail?" "How is a kite like an airplane?" "How is it different?"

Other Problems for Younger Children

1. What makes a rocket blast off?
2. How is the earth like a spaceship?[2]
3. What kinds of things do airplanes carry?
4. How is a ride on a roller coaster like blasting off into space or returning to Earth?

(For other problems see introduction to this chapter.)

FOR OLDER CHILDREN

What Keeps an Airplane Up?

Students may need to review some of their experiments with air pressure, especially those that show that air pressure is exerted in an upward as well as downward direction. Holding a cardboard over a full glass of water and inverting the glass, for example, will help children see that air can press up.

To show the effect of an air current's passing over a surface let each student hold a strip of paper (2 inches wide by 4 or 5 inches long) by one end so that they can blow a stream of air at it. Until they begin to blow, the papers hang down. When their air is directed under the strip, it lifts up. Why? Let students try this experience individually and then propose explanations for what happens. How does this help explain what happens to a plane? (See pp. 606–610.)

What is the function of the propeller in flight? Place a propeller from a model plane, which can be purchased from a hobby shop, on a stiff wire—coat-hanger wire will do. Strike the propeller sharply to make it spin and hold the wire horizontally—without a slant—so that gravity does not influence its motion. The children will observe that the propeller moves forward along the wire.

As a plane's propeller moves forward it pulls the airplane with it. This forward motion causes

[2]J. Schwartz, *The Earth Is Your Spaceship* (New York: McGraw-Hill, 1963); D. Housel, "Up, Up and Away: Aerospace Studies," *Science Scope* (September 1986).

A sheet of paper attached to a strip of cardboard serves as a "wing." When air is blown under the paper it lifts up. Why? When air is directed *over* the paper it also lifts up. Why? (*Courtesy of John King.*)

air to sweep over the wings and gives lift to the plane. (A common error is to think that the wind from the propellers washing backward across the wings is responsible for lift. This is not true: Airplanes fly just as well when propellers are located behind the wings.)

How Does Jet Action Push a Plane?

As a preparation to an understanding of jet action let children blow up balloons and release them. What happens? How can you make the balloon move farther? In which direction (compared to the escaping air) do the balloons move? Why? How is this like a jet engine?

The jet-propelled balloon pictured on page 634 will help students understand the principle of jet propulsion. The "track" is made of wire stretched from one side of a room to the other. The balloon is held to the track by strings attached to paper clips. As the air escapes from the inflated balloon it "jets" along the wire. Speed may be controlled by inserting a plug in the open end of the balloon, which will regulate the amount of air that escapes.

Make the plug of paper. Students can experiment with the size of the plug and get varying results.

How Does Gravity Affect Space Flight[3]

In preparation for solving the problem review the concepts of gravity in Chapter 7B. Children need to understand that the concept of gravity applies not only to the attraction that the earth has for bodies on it but also the attraction between heavenly bodies. All bodies in the universe attract each other. Their attraction depends on (1) the amount of material in them and (2) the distance between them (the attraction decreases as the distance increases).

The demonstration on page 635 serves to help students understand how spaceships escape from

[3]W. T. Spade, "The Heritage Hill Space Center," *Science and Children* (May 1976). Children learn about space by building a space center in their classroom. K. O'Connor, *Sally Ride and the New Astronauts in Space* (New York: Watts, 1983); F. M. Branley, *From Sputnik to Space Shuttle: Into the New Space Age* (New York: Crowell, 1986).

A "rudder" may be made with folded file cards balanced with a pin on a cork. It is tested by blowing air at it through a straw. (*Courtesy of John King.*)

earth. Keep in mind that this is only a representation. The long trough represents the earth's gravity. The short trough represents the moon's gravity. The marble represents the spaceship.

If a marble is propelled with the right force up the long ramp, it will coast just past the dividing line and fall into the "moon." If too much force is used, the marble will skip over and beyond the "moon." If too little force is used, it will fall back to "earth."

Will it take as much force to launch a ball from the moon to earth? (Try it!) No. Why? (Less of a hill, less gravity to overcome.)

Note: This demonstration should not lead students to think that the earth's gravity *ends* and the moon's gravity *begins* at a given point. Both are present everywhere. The troughs merely show where the gravity of one is stronger than that of the other.)

Jet propulsion demonstrated. (See text for explanation.)

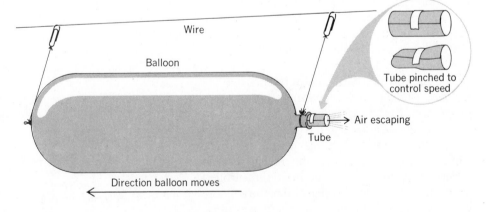

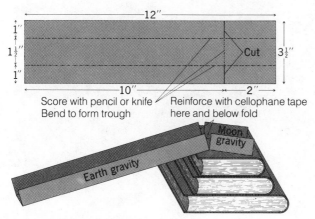

Making an Earth–Moon launching ramp:
1. Cut out a piece of cardboard 12 inches by 3½ inches.
2. Rule two parallel lines down its length, each 1 inch from edge. Score each of the lines with a sharp knife or razor blade.
3. Rule a line across, 2 inches from one end. Score it and cut part of it as shown.
4. Fold on each long scored line to make a ramp with sides.
5. Bend the ramp on the short scored line to form a long and short "hill." Strengthen with cellophane tape under the peak of the "hill" and across the V-shaped opening formed by the bending.
6. Place the ramp on a flat surface. Elevate the short end by resting it on books.

What Happens to the Speed of a Spaceship on an Earth–Moon Trip?

This is a good opportunity for students to read about any of the Apollo spaceship missions to the moon and to organize their reading to answer specific questions. It will also provide a good occasion to use library skills in locating appropriate specific information. Ask the students to imagine that *they* are on an earth–moon trip. Discuss the following:

1. How fast would the spaceship have to go to escape from the earth? (25,000 miles an hour.)
2. What happens to the speed of the ship as it travels away from the earth? (It slows down to 3,000 miles an hour.) Why? (The pull of earth's gravity continues.)
3. What happens when the spaceship gets closer to the moon? (It speeds up to 5,000 miles per hour.) Why? (The pull of the moon's gravity increases.)

4. How fast must the spaceship travel to escape from the moon? (About 5,000 miles an hour.)
5. Why only 5,000 miles an hour? (Because the moon's gravitational pull is much less than the earth's.)
6. What happens when the spaceship travels toward the earth? (It speeds up to 25,000 miles an hour.) Why? (The pull of the earth's gravity increases.)

How Do Satellites Get Into Orbit Around the Earth?

In addition to hoisting a spaceship away from the earth at faster and faster speeds, rocket engines used for earth-circling spaceships or satellites perform one other job: They direct the spacecraft into a *path* that makes it possible for it to orbit the earth. How is this done?

The following demonstration requires only a string, a small object (such as a wooden bead) attached to one end of the string with a paper clip

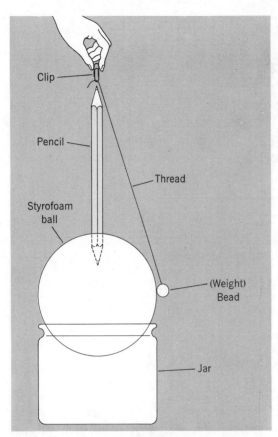

Prepare to launch a "satellite" into orbit around a styrofoam "Earth." (*Adapted from* Science: *Grade 6, by permission of the N.Y.C. Board of Education.*)

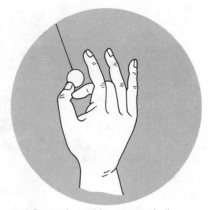

(fingers in position to snap ball)

Holding the fingers in position to snap the bead. (*Adapted from* Science: Grade 6, *by permission of the N.Y.C. Board of Education.*)

attached to the other end, a pencil sharpened at both ends, and a Styrofoam ball—as shown in the illustration above.[4]

The bead represents the satellite and the ball represents the earth. Hold the clip in one hand directly over the center of the ball so that the weight rests against the "equator" of the ball. The pencil is pushed partway into the ball and toward its center. The ball is positioned so that the pencil is vertical and points directly over the center of the ball. Ask students to try to launch the "satel-

lite" into orbit around the earth by tapping it with a finger to move it from its resting position. They may tap it in any direction, but they must start from the resting position against the "earth." They are not allowed to maneuver it with the clip, which is held directly over the point of the pencil. They find that no matter what they do, the bead does not make a complete orbit. It always returns to the "earth." The best that it can do is return to the place from which it was launched (see Chapter 20A, pp. 613–615).[5]

Then how can it be launched into orbit? What must be done differently? Again no maneuvering with the clip is permitted; it must be held over the center of the ball and not moved. But students are allowed to *start* the satellite from wherever they please. They find that if they hold it away from the ball and push it parallel to its surface they can effect a successful launching of two, three, or more orbits. The hand position shown in the diagram above is an effective one.

How hard do the students have to push the

---

[4]Adapted by permission from *Science—Grade 6* (Brooklyn: Board of Education of the City of New York, 1972).

[5]Write for materials to NASA, Community and Education Services Branch L.F. G-11, Washington, DC 20546; J. Moxon, *How Jet Engines Are Made* (New York: Facts on File, 1985).

bead to get it into orbit? If they give it a slight push it will not complete the orbit; it will fall back to "earth." If they snap it too hard it will go far out, but hit the "earth" again. A moderate push is most successful.

Other Problems for Older Children

1. What weather information is important to pilots?
2. How are satellites important to us?[6]
3. What fuels are used in rockets?
4. What are some of the most difficult problems yet to be solved in space travel?[7]
5. Why are rocket engines used in space travel?
6. What keeps a satellite in orbit?
7. What is a space station?[8]
8. What is a space shuttle?[9]
9. What is gravity like on the moon?
10. What is weightlessness? Plan an experiment that you would like to conduct in a weightless environment.
11. How do space shuttles overcome the heat barrier?
12. Plan a manned trip to Mars.
13. Construct a wind tunnel to test model planes and gliders.
14. How is the supersonic plane different from other planes?
15. How does a helicopter fly?

[6]J. R. White, *Satellites of Today and Tomorrow* (New York: Dodd, 1985); F. M. Branley, *Mysteries of the Satellites* (New York: Dutton, 1986).

[7]D. Baker, *History of Manned Space Flight* (New York: Crown, 1982).

[8]*Working in Space*, PS 11 NSTA, Washington, DC 20009; R. McPhee, *Your Future in Space: The U.S. Space Camp Training Programs* (New York: Crown, 1987).

[9]Write to NASA (see footnote 5). Also contact the U.S. Government Printing Office, Washington, DC 20402, for lists of space materials.

16. What vocational opportunities are available in aviation and space travel?

RESOURCES TO INVESTIGATE WITH CHILDREN

1. Local airport, to learn how airplanes fly and how they are controlled; to see types of aircraft, landing fields, and hangars; and to gain other information.
2. Local airline ticket offices, for maps, pamphlets, charts, and other printed matter, and films about air transportation.
3. Pilots, to explain aviation matters and to answer questions about flying.
4. Radio, for reports on "flying weather."
5. Manufacturers of airplanes or airplane parts, for materials and information about airplanes, parts, and instruments.

PREPARING TO TEACH

1. Keep a file of current news reports (clippings, pictures, and so on) that will help keep your background up-to-date. Plan ways to use this material in your classes.
2. Write to NASA (see footnote 5) for very helpful materials to read and assemble for use with children. Also write for *Space*, a free list; *America in Space*; and *Rockets and Satellites* from the Superintendent of Documents, U.S. Government Printing Office, Washington, DC 20402, for complete information about government publications about space.
3. Watch the newspapers for announcements of the time and location of visible satellites. Try to observe these satellites for a number of evenings. Plan how you would use this activity with children.
4. Find out how the Jet Age is affecting your environment with respect to air pollution, noise, city traffic. What problems may arise from supersonic jet flight? How may they be solved?
5. Find out what spin-offs from the space program have been important for everyone, such as the development of new materials, communication systems, computer uses, medicine, and health studies.

COMPUTER SOFTWARE
IN SCIENCE EDUCATION[1]

The following guide was prepared by Stephen Wulfson, assistant principal of Eugene T. Maleska Intermediate School (I.S. 174) in the Bronx, New York. Mr. Wulfson is the column editor of "Software Reviews" for *Science and Children.*

It is suggested that you write to the companies listed for detailed descriptions of their products, borrow (if possible) the software programs appropriate for your grade and subject matter, and then evaluate them before final purchase. The National Science Teachers Association (NSTA) has an extensive library of computer software packages for various computers that were contributed by many software publishers. These packages can be used at the Pocono Environmental Education Center, Dingmans Ferry, PA 18328.

As the computer becomes commonplace in our daily lives, it also becomes important in the daily activities of the science classroom. A perusal of the hundreds of computer software packages available to teachers show that these materials can be used in different educational modes and can serve many needs and purposes. The selection of programs is presented here in a number of important subsections; space does not permit others such as games and adventures. Wherever a company has many useful programs, they are noted as part of a series.

[1]See material on computers in Chapter 3. See also "Software Evaluation Form" by K. E. Reynolds, E. Walton, and T. Logue and "How to Use the Software Evaluation Form" by K. E. Reynolds in *Science and Children*, September 1985.

TUTORIAL

A tutorial program introduces new concepts to students and then tests their comprehension of the material presented. The best programs use state-of-the-art graphics and provide for a reteaching of material that is not learned.

The *Explore A Science* series, Collamore Educational Publishing, D.C. Heath and Co., 125 Spring Street, Lexington, MA 02173, gives the students scientific facts while allowing the student to become a scientist and to interact with the environment. Includes *Tyrannosaurus Rex, Desert Habitat.*

Heath Science Software (see previous address) presents background material in a textbook format that allows the student to solve problems that are presented to him or her. Includes *Life in The Oceans, Classifying Animals Without Backbones, Heat Energy.*

The Human Body, Educational Activities, P.O. Box 392, Freeport, NY 11520, is an interactive tutorial that contains an instant glossary for those who need it. The teacher management system is an additional plus.

Prentice Hall Courseware Series, Prentice Hall, School Division, Sylvan Ave., Englewood Cliffs, NJ 07632, uses an interactive mode to present concepts with extensive use of graphic material. Students can ask for help within the program, and can call up a glossary as needed. Includes biology, earth science and physical science disks.

Introduction to Biochemistry, Educational Activities (see previous address) reviews and reinforces concepts pertaining to atoms, compounds, and carbohydrates, proteins, and fats. The management system allows the teacher to further enhance a student's weak area.

DRILL AND PRACTICE

A software package that utilizes the drill and practice mode will take the place of a workbook and tailor instructions to the needs of an individual, while often adding a management section to show the teacher how well a child is doing. The best programs will not only tell a child that the answer is incorrect, but will also offer a short remedial lesson.

The Human Systems Series, Focus Media, Inc., 839 Steward Avenue, Garden City, NY 11530, helps the student learn about the various organs in the human body and the importance of the major component in the organ. Includes three programs that cover all of the major body systems.

M–ss–ng L–nks, Sunburst Communications, 39 Washington Ave., Pleasantville, NY 10570, presents science paragraphs with various letters or words missing. Students practice finding word patterns, and are drilled in the vocabulary of science.

PROBLEM SOLVING

Given a set of data, the student is taught how to organize it, come up with a scientific rule, and solve the problem presented. Programs that rate high should have a wide range of problems, from simple to complex, along with a method of showing the solution to the problem.

Discovery, Milliken Software, Milliken Publishing Co., 1100 Research Blvd., P.O. Box 21579, St. Louis, MO 63132, allows the student to use scientific methods to plan, hypothesize, do an experiment and collect data, and study the results.

Safari Search, Sunburst Communications (see previous address) uses various strategies and logical thinking modes to challenge the student to solve problems after collecting and analyzing his or her data.

The Pond, Sunburst Communications (see previous address) shows students how to think logically, evaluate the data, and formulate rules that will solve a set of problems.

Creative Contraptions, Bantam Books, 666 Fifth Avenue, New York, NY 10019, is an unusual program that

uses Rube Goldberg-like devices to get students to organize and predict various outcomes.

SIMULATIONS

A simulation presents the students with an activity from the real world in a mode that compresses time from days and years to minutes and seconds. This genre of programs contains by and far the largest number of programs.

Oh, Deer! MECC, 3490 Lexington Avenue N., St. Paul, MN 55126, clearly demonstrates how humans interact with a deer population. Ecologists versus urbanists are involved in managing a deer herd in this real-life simulation that deals with the problems of cities encroaching on wildlife.

Geo World, Tom Snyder Productions, 123 Auburn St., Cambridge, MA 02138, takes a student on a geological trip to permit him or her to use a wide variety of geological tools to explore and search for 15 mineral resources.

Microgardener, Educational Activities (see previous address) condenses 18 weeks of plant growth into less than 20 minutes as students note results of varying amounts of light, water, and heat on the seeds they planted in different environments.

Simulator Series, Focus Media, Inc. (see previous address) provides the student with the tools and environments needed to either conduct an experiment or to see how the earth behaves under a set of conditions. The use of animation and graphics enhance the various programs. Includes *The Earthquake Simulator, Earth and Moon Simulator, Plant Growth Simulator, The Microscope Simulator.*

The Observatory, CBS, One Fawcett Place, Greenwich, CT 06836, allows the class to "see" the stars in the daytime. Using graphics that appear rapidly on the screen, the students are able to input their coordinates, time of day, date, and which way they are facing, and to see the position of the stars and constellations.

MICROCOMPUTER-BASED LABS

One of the best uses for a computer is that it gathers the data for you and presents it in logical order. These programs use probes and other pieces of equipment to gather measurements, put them in table or chart format, and allow you to interpret the data. You don't even have to be present as long as the data is being gathered, for example, 24-hour temperature measurements.

Science Toolkit Series, Broderbund Software, 17 Paul Drive, San Rafael, CA 94903, contains a master module into which you plug in temperature, heat and light probes, or a seismograph or spirometer to take measurements over a period of time. These data are presented in table format or via a graph. Includes *Master Module; Module 1: Speed and Motion; Module 2: Earthquake Lab; Module 3: Body Lab.*

Playing With Science: Temperature; Sunburst Communications (see previous address) is similar to the preceding but has a very extensive set of teacher lesson plans to assist the new teacher.

Forecast, CBS (see previous address) is another laboratory-type tool that relies on the student inputting information collected from various weather instruments. Using this data, the computer then comes up with a weather forecast. This program contains weather information for every region of the country for the past 10 years.

DATABASE

When it is impossible to schedule your class for the library to do science research, you might be able to rely upon a collection of data that is stored in computer format. The various disks, however, rely upon other computer programs to access the data.

Bank Street Filer Database, Sunburst Communications (see previous address) contains up-to-the-minute databases to enhance any class report or research. Glossaries and booklists are included in these programs. Topics include astronomy, the United States and North America, animals and space. The student or teacher may add to the included information.

Easy Search Series, Focus Media, Inc. (see previous address) is an information-filled database that contains files on foods (water content, protein, fat, carbohydrates, fibre, etc.), or chemicals (household and comon materials).

INTERACTIVE LASER DISK

This new form of technology integrates a database that is stored on a laser disk and whose information can be called up by the computer. A laser disk can hold over 100,000 images either in the form of still pictures or movies. Many disks come with bilingual audio channels.

Knowledge Disc, Grolier, Sherman Turnpike, Danbury, CT 06816, contains 30,000 articles from the Academic American Encyclopedia. Includes science, technology, geography, biography, and history.

Windows on Science, Optical Data Corporation, 66 Hanover Rd., Florham Park, NJ 07932, is a multidisk series that covers most of the sciences. Though rather costly at this time, this series replaces most overhead transparencies, filmstrips, and film loops. The clear pictures and diagrams, along with the glossary in English and in Spanish should satisfy the needs of most schools.

BIBLIOGRAPHY

PROFESSIONAL PUBLICATIONS FOR TEACHERS

Abruscato, Joseph. *Teaching Children Science* (Englewood Cliffs, N.J.: Prentice Hall, 1988), 432 pp. General methods.

Anderson, Ronald, et al. *Developing Children's Thinking Through Science* (Englewood Cliffs, N.J.: Prentice-Hall, 1970), 370 pp. A methods book.

Baez, Albert V. *Innovations in Science Education—World-wide* (New York: UNESCO, 1984), 249 pp. Comprehensive review.

Barman, Charles R., et al. *Science and Societal Issues: A Guide for Science Teachers* (Ames: Iowa State University Press, 1981), 154 pp.

Butts, David P., and Faith Brown, eds. *Science Teaching: A Profession Speaks* (Washington, D.C.: National Science Teachers Association 1983 Yearbook, 1742 Connecticut Ave. NW, Washington, D.C. 20009), 112 pp.

Bybee, Roger, ed. *Science/Technology/Society* (Washington, D.C.: National Science Teachers Association 1985 Yearbook), 268 pp.

———, et al. *Redesigning Science and Technology Education* (Washington, D.C.: National Science Teachers Association 1984 Yearbook, 1742 Connecticut Ave. NW, Washington, D.C. 20009), 248 pp.

Carin, Arthur A., and Robert B. Sund. *Teaching Modern Science* (Columbus, Ohio: Merrill, 1985), 336 pp. Methods of using the discovery approach.

———. *Teaching Science Through Discovery* (Columbus, Ohio: Merrill, 1985), 502 pp.

Champagne, Audrey, and Leslie Hornig. *Science Teaching* (Washington, D.C.: American Association for the Advancement of Science, 1986), 238 pp.

DeVito, Alfred, and Gerald H. Krockover. *Creative Sciencing: Ideas and Activities for Teachers and Children* (Boston: Little, Brown, 1980), 388 pp. Techniques for teaching.

Esler, William K., and Mary K. Esler. *Teaching Elementary Science* (Belmont, Calif.: Wadsworth, 1984), 584 pp. Concepts, models, and techniques.

Friedl, Alfred E. *Teaching Science to Children: An Integrated Approach* (New York: Random House, 1986), 301 pp. Features discrepant (surprising, curious) events for teaching science.

Gega, Peter C. *Science in Elementary Education* (New York: Wiley, 1986), 610 pp. Methods and their applications in teaching science.

Harlan, J. *Science Experiences for the Early Childhood Years* (Columbus, Ohio: Merrill, 1988), 288 pp.

Henson, Kenneth T., and Delmar Janke. *Elementary Science Methods* (New York: McGraw-Hill, 1984), 496 pp. Activities in elementary science.

Hill, Katherine E. *Exploring the Natural World with Young Children* (New York: Harcourt, 1976), 154 pp. An excellent, practical sourcebook.

Hofman, Helenmarie, and Kenneth S. Ricker, eds. *Science Education and the Physically Handicapped* (Washington, D.C.: NSTA, 1979), 284 pp. Comprehensive and practical.

Holt, Bess-Gene. *Science with Young Children* (Washington, D.C.: National Association for the Education of Young Children, 1977), 142 pp. Practical suggestions.

Jacobson, Willard J., and Abby B. Bergman. *Science Activities for Children* (Englewood Cliffs, N.J.: Prentice Hall, 1987), 198 pp. Methods and science background for teachers.

———. *Science for Children: A Book for Teachers* (Englewood Cliffs, N.J.: Prentice Hall, 1987), 448 pp. A methods book.

Kauchak, Donald, and Paul Eggen. *Exploring Science in the Elementary School* (Chicago: Rand McNally, 1980), 351 pp. Themes, teaching models, and anecdotes.

Lansdown, Brenda, Paul E. Blackwood, and Paul F.

Brandwein. *Teaching Elementary Science Through Investigation and Colloquium* (New York: Harcourt, 1971), 433 pp. A methods book.

Levenson, Elaine. *Teaching Children about Science* (Englewood Cliffs, N.J.: Prentice-Hall, 1985), 211 pp. Teaching units, with emphasis on earth and physical science.

McIntire, Margaret. *Early Childhood and Science* (Washington, D.C.: NSTA, 1984), 136 pp.

Nelson, L. W., and G. L. Lorbeer. *Science Activities for Elementary Children* (Dubuque, Iowa: W. C. Brown, 1984), 416 pp.

New UNESCO Source Book for Science Teaching (New York: UNESCO, 1975), 270 pp. Experiments and science teaching methods.

———. *Handbook for Science Teachers* (New York: Unipub, 1980), 199 pp. A companion to the sourcebook.

Ochs, V. Daniel, ed. *Improving Practices in Middle School Science* (Columbus, Ohio: Clearinghouse for Science, Mathematics and Environmental Education, Ohio State University, 1981), 277 pp. The AETS yearbook.

Padilla, M. *Science and the Early Adolescent* (Washington, D.C.: NSTA, 1983), 127 pp.

Penick, John E., ed. *Focus on Excellence: Elementary Science Revisited* (Washington, D.C.: NSTA, 1988), 60 pp. Takes a look at 13 of the nation's elementary science programs.

———, and Richard Meinbard-Pellens. *Science/Technology/Society* (Washington, D.C.: NSTA, 1984), 104 pp.

———. *Elementary Science* (Washington, D.C.: NSTA, 1983), 140 pp. Describes a variety of programs.

Petreshene, Susan S. *A Complete Guide to Learning Centers* (Palo Alto, Calif: Pendragon House, 1977), 324 pp. Detailed guide.

Renner, John W. *The Learning Cycle and Elementary School Science Teaching* (Portsmouth, N.H.: Heinemann, 1988), 214 pp. (paper)

———, et al. *Teaching Science in the Elementary School* (New York: Harper & Row, 1988), 408 pp. Methods and approaches.

Roche, Euth L. *The Child and Science* (Washington, D.C.: Association for Childhood Education International, 1977), 42 pp. Practical suggestions for teaching science to young children.

Rowe, Mary Budd. *Teaching Science as Continuous Inquiry* (New York: McGraw-Hill, 1978), 590 pp. Methods and philosophy of science teaching.

Schmidt, Victor E., and Verne N. Rockcastle. *Teaching Science with Everyday Things* (New York: McGraw-Hill, 1982), 224 pp. Use of readily available materials for science experiences.

Trojcak, Doris A. *Science with Children* (New York: McGraw-Hill, 1979), 312 pp. Skills of science investigation.

U.S. Department of Education. *Science Education Programs That Work.* (U.S. Government Printing Office, Washington, D.C. 20402, stock number 065-000-00299-0; $1.50, 1988), 20 pp. A collection of 13 science programs that have been tested in schools across the United States, from preschool through high school.

Victor, Edward. *Science for the Elementary School* (New York: Macmillan, 1985), 789 pp. Methods and subject matter.

———, and Marjorie S. Lerner. *Readings in Science Education for the Elementary School* (New York: Macmillan, 1975), 465 pp. An organized collection of readings from many sources.

Wadsworth, Barry J. *Piaget for the Classroom Teacher* (New York: Longman, 1979), 303 pp. A comprehensive readable treatment.

———. *Piaget's Theory of Cognitive Development* (New York: Longman, 1984), 189 pp.

Wall, Janet. *Compendium of Standardized Science Tests* (Washington, D.C.: NSTA, 1981), 66 pp.

What Research Says to the Science Teacher, Vols. 1–5 (Washington, D.C.: NSTA, 1980–1987), 107 pp. Indispensable material.

GENERAL SUBJECT MATTER BACKGROUND BOOKS FOR TEACHERS

Abell, George O., David Morrison, and Sidney C. Wolff. *Exploration of the Universe* (New York: Saunders, 1987), 748 pp. A popular college text in astronomy, providing also a glimpse of the history and character of science and scientific thinking.

Attenborough, David. *Life on Earth* (Boston: Little, Brown, 1979), 319 pp. Based on BBC television series.

Ballard, Robert D. *Exploring Our Living Planet* (Washington, D.C.: National Geographic Society, 1983), 366 pp. The dynamic earth described with the help of magnificent paintings, diagrams, and maps.

Barnard, Christian, and John Illman, eds. *The Body Ma-*

chine (New York: Crown, 1981), 256 pp. The body as a machine.

Beatty, J. Kelly, et al., eds. *The New Solar System* (Cambridge: Sky, 1982), 192 pp. Twenty authors collaborate.

Boyle, Robert H., and R. Alexander Boyle. *Acid Rain* (New York: Schocken Books, 1983), 146 pp. Scope of problem, damage, and solutions. See text for further references.

BSCS. *Biological Science: An Inquiry into Life* (New York: Harcourt, 1979), 700 pp. The "yellow version" of high school biology prepared by the Biological Science Curriculum Study.

_____. *Biological Science: A Molecular Approach* (Lexington, Mass.: D.C. Heath, 1985), 785 pp. The "blue version" of high school biology prepared by the Biological Science Curriculum Study.

_____. *Biological Science: An Ecological Approach* (Dubuque, Iowa: Kendall/Hunt, 1987), 1048 pp. The "green version" of high school biology prepared by the Biological Science Curriculum Study.

Brown, Lester et al. *State of the World, 1989: A Worldwatch Report on Progress Toward a Sustainable Society* (New York: W. W. Norton and Co., 1989), 256 pp. The latest edition of a series begun in 1984; a complete guide to the world's resources.

Curtis, Helene, and N. Sue Barnes. *Invitation to Biology* (New York: Worth, 1985), 696 pp. Lives up to its title.

Ehrlich, Paul R. *The Machinery of Nature* (New York: Simon & Schuster, 1986), 320 pp. How plants and animals—including man—interact with each other and their environments. Outlines the scientific framework that can help us understand the environmental crisis that confront us and formulates policies to deal with them.

Hoskings, Wayne. *Introduction to Aerodynamics* (Washington, D.C.: NSTA, 1987), 56 pp.

Laycock, George. *The Bird Watcher's Bible* (Garden City, N.Y.: Doubleday, 1976), 207 pp. A fine introduction.

Levin, Harold L. *Contemporary Physical Geology* (Philadelphia: Saunders, 1981), 579 pp. Earth materials, causes and results of crustal movements, how water, ice, and wind modify planetary surfaces.

_____. *The Earth Through Time* (Philadelphia: Saunders, 1983), 513 pp. The history of the earth, revealed by decoding the rock record.

Lutgens, Frederick F., and Edward J. Tarbuck. *The Atmosphere: An Introduction to Meteorology* (Englewood Cliffs, N.J.: Prentice-Hall, 1986), 576 pp.

Morrison, Philip, and Phylis Morrison. *The Ring of*

Truth: An Inquiry into How We Know What We Know (New York: Random House, 1987), 307 pp. Lives up to its title with a blend of vivid illustrations and exciting text by a pair of master teachers.

Nebel, Bernard J. *Environmental Science: The Way the World Works* (Englewood Cliffs, N.J.: Prentice-Hall, 1986), 768 pp.

New York Times Almanac (New York: New York Times Company). A useful book of facts published annually.

Nilsson, Greta. *The Endangered Species Handbook* (Washington, D.C.: Animal Welfare Institute, 1983), 245 pp.

Palmer, E. Lawrence, and H. Seymour Fowler. *Fieldbook of Natural History* (New York: McGraw-Hill, 1975), 779 pp. For identification and information.

Planet Earth (Alexandria, Va.: Time-Life Books, 1983). A series of 17 books that examine the workings of planet Earth from the geological wonders of its continents to the marvels of its atmosphere and its ocean depths. Beautifully illustrated; written by experts in the various fields together with the editors.

Ramsey, William L., et al. *Modern Earth Science* (New York: Holt, 1987), 503 pp. A high school text.

Sagan, Carl. *Cosmos* (New York: Random House, 1980), 365 pp. Based on television series; an original treatment of astronomy.

Schiefelbein, Susan, et al. *The Incredible Machine* (Washington, D.C.: National Geographic Society, 1986), 384 pp. The wonders of the human body, revealed by incredible photographs and paintings, and with text by a number of talented writers.

Schneider, Herman, and Leo Schneider. *The Harper Dictionary of Science in Everyday Language* (New York: Harper & Row, 1988), 352 pp. A thousand scientific terms explained in non-technical language. Conveys the spirit of adventure that propels the discoveries that we read about in the news. With 168 line drawings. A valuable resource for teachers.

Tanzer, Charles. *Biology and Human Progress* (Englewood Cliffs, N.J.: Prentice-Hall, 1986), 544 pp. Text for nonacademic high school students, but useful in elementary biology education.

Teter, et al. *Living Things* (New York: Holt, 1985), A general biology text.

U.S. Department of Agriculture Yearbooks: *Soils and Man* (1938), *Climate and Man* (1941), *Grass* (1948), *Trees* (1949), *Insects* (1952), *Plant Diseases* (1953), *Water* (1955), *Soil* (1957), *Land* (1958), *Food* (1959), *A Place to Live* (1964), *Outdoors U. S. A.* (1967), *Food for Us*

All (1969), *A Good Life for More People: Landscape for Living* (1972), *That We May Eat* (1975) (Washington, D.C.: U.S. Government Printing Office).

World Almanac (New York: Newspaper Enterprises Association). A useful book of facts published annually.

Zeilik, Michael. *Astronomy: The Evolving Universe* (New York: Harper & Row, 1985), 494 pp. For nonscience majors.

MAGAZINES FOR SCIENCE TEACHING

Air Space (Washington, D.C.: National Air and Space Museum, Smithsonian Institution.) Six issues. Also *NASA Facts,* available from Superintendent of Documents, U.S. Government Printing Office, Washington, D.C. 20402.

American Biology Teacher (National Association of Biology Teachers, 11250 Roger Bacon Drive #19, Reston, VA 22090.) Nine issues a year.

American Forests (Washington, D.C.: American Forestry Association.) Bimonthly.

Appraisal: Science Books for Young People (Boston University, Department of Science and Mathematics Education, Boston, MA.)

Audubon (National Audubon Society, New York, NY 10028.) Bimonthly.

The Curious Naturalist (Massachusetts Audubon Society, South Lincoln, MA.) For children; nine issues a year.

Current Science (Zerox Education Publications, Columbus, OH.)

Discover (Family Media Inc., 3 Park Ave., New York, NY 10016.) Monthly.

Earth in Space (Earth in Space, 2000 Florida Ave. NW, Washington, D.C. 20009.) Nine issues a year.

Environmental Education (Dembar Educational Research Services, Madison, WI.) Quarterly.

International Wildlife (National Wildlife Federation, 1412 16th St. NW, Washington, D.C. 20036.) Bimonthly.

Journal of Research in Science Teaching (New York: Wiley.) National Association for Research in Science Teaching). Quarterly.

National Parks Magazine (Washington, D.C.: National Parks Association.)

National Wildlife and *International Wildlife* (Washington, D.C.: National Wildlife Federation.) Bimonthly.

National Geographic (Washington, D.C.: National Geographic Society.) Monthly.

Natural History (American Museum of Natural History, New York, NY 10024.) Monthly.

Nature Conservancy Magazine (The Nature Conservancy, Arlington, VA 22209.) Committed to the global preservation of natural diversity.

Nature Study (Journal of the American Nature Study Society, Homer, NY 13077.) Quarterly.

Odyssey (Astromedia Corporation, 625 E. St. Paul Ave., Milwaukee, WI 53202.) Monthly magazine of astronomy and outer space for young people.

Ranger Rick's Nature Magazine (Washington, D.C.: National Wildlife Federation). Eight issues a year.

School Science and Mathematics (Bowling Green State University, Bowling Green, OH 43403.) Monthly (except July, August, and September).

Science Activities (Washington, D.C.: Heldref Publications.) Quarterly.

Science and Children (Washington, D.C.: National Science Teachers Association.) Eight issues a year.

Science Books and Films (Washington, D.C.: American Association for the Advancement of Science.) Five issues a year.

Science Education (New York: Wiley). Published in February, March, April, October, and December.

Science News (Science Service, Washington, D.C. 20036.) Weekly.

Science Scope (Washington, D.C.: National Science Teachers Association). For middle/junior high level. Eight issues a year.

The Science Teacher (Washington, D.C.: National Science Teachers Association.) Monthly, September through May.

Science World (Scholastic) (Englewood Cliffs, N.J.: Scholastic Magazine.) For high school science students; good teacher background.

Scientific American (Scientific American Publishers, New York, NY 10017.) Monthly. The advancing front of science, written by scientists.

Sky and Telescope (Sky Publishing Corp., Cambridge, MA 02238.) Monthly.

The Planetary Report (The Planetary Society, Pasadena, CA 91106.) Six issues a year. Devoted to the exploration of the solar system.

The Young Scientist (New York: Fusion Energy Foundation.) Monthly.

Wilderness (The Wilderness Society, Washington, D.C. 20005.) Quarterly. The society is devoted to preserving wilderness and wildlife and fostering an American land ethic.

World Magazine (National Geographic, Washington, D.C. 20077.) Monthly.

PHOTO CREDITS

INDEX